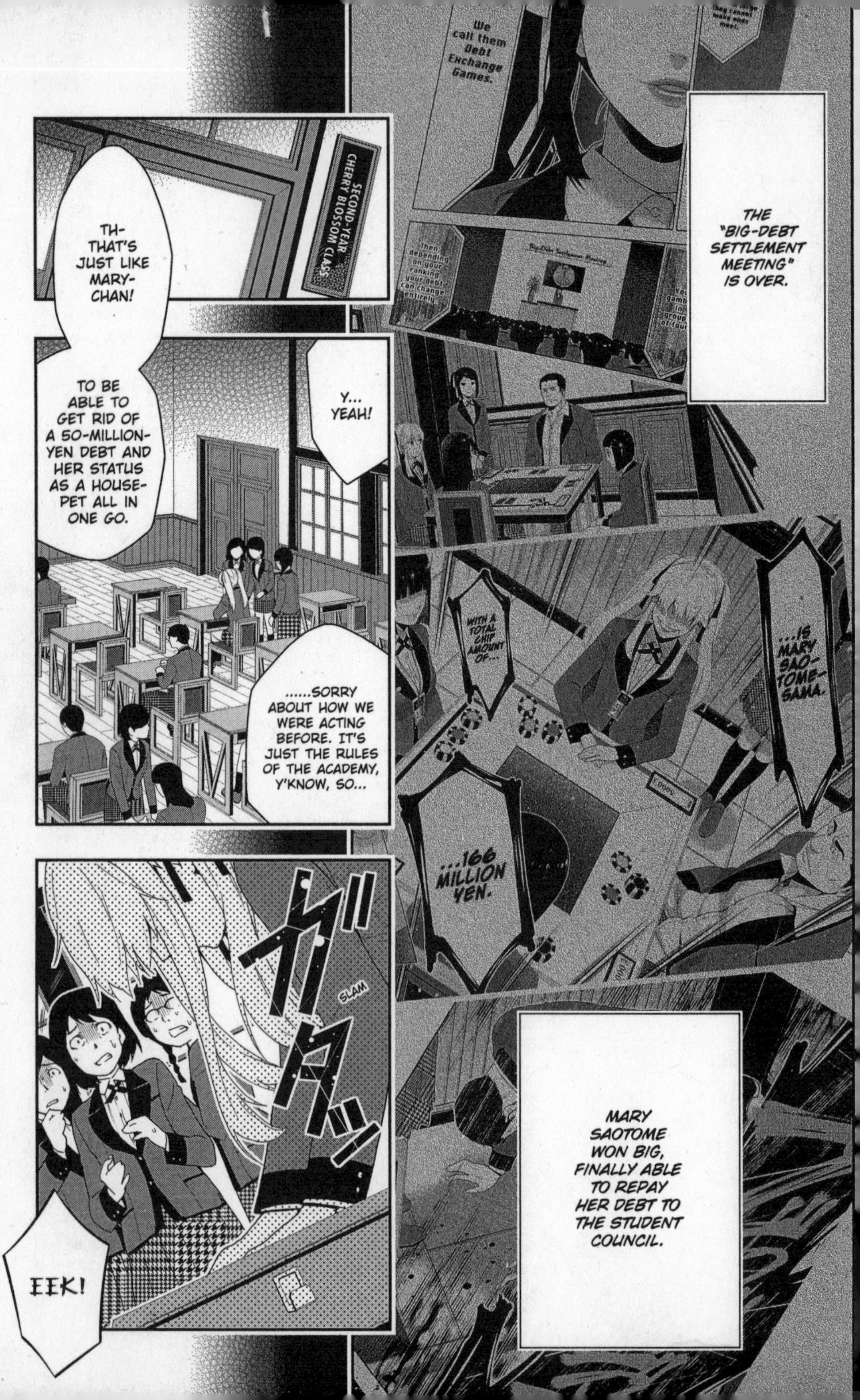
THE "BIG-DEBT SETTLEMENT MEETING" IS OVER.
We call them Debt Exchange Games.
Then, depending on your ranking, your debt can change entirely.
...IS MARY SAOTOME-SAMA.
WITH A TOTAL CHIP AMOUNT OF...
...166 MILLION YEN.
MARY SAOTOME WON BIG, FINALLY ABLE TO REPAY HER DEBT TO THE STUDENT COUNCIL.
SECOND-YEAR CHERRY BLOSSOM CLASS
TH-THAT'S JUST LIKE MARY-CHAN!
Y... YEAH!
TO BE ABLE TO GET RID OF A 50-MILLION-YEN DEBT AND HER STATUS AS A HOUSE-PET ALL IN ONE GO.
......SORRY ABOUT HOW WE WERE ACTING BEFORE. IT'S JUST THE RULES OF THE ACADEMY, Y'KNOW, SO...
SLAM
EEK!

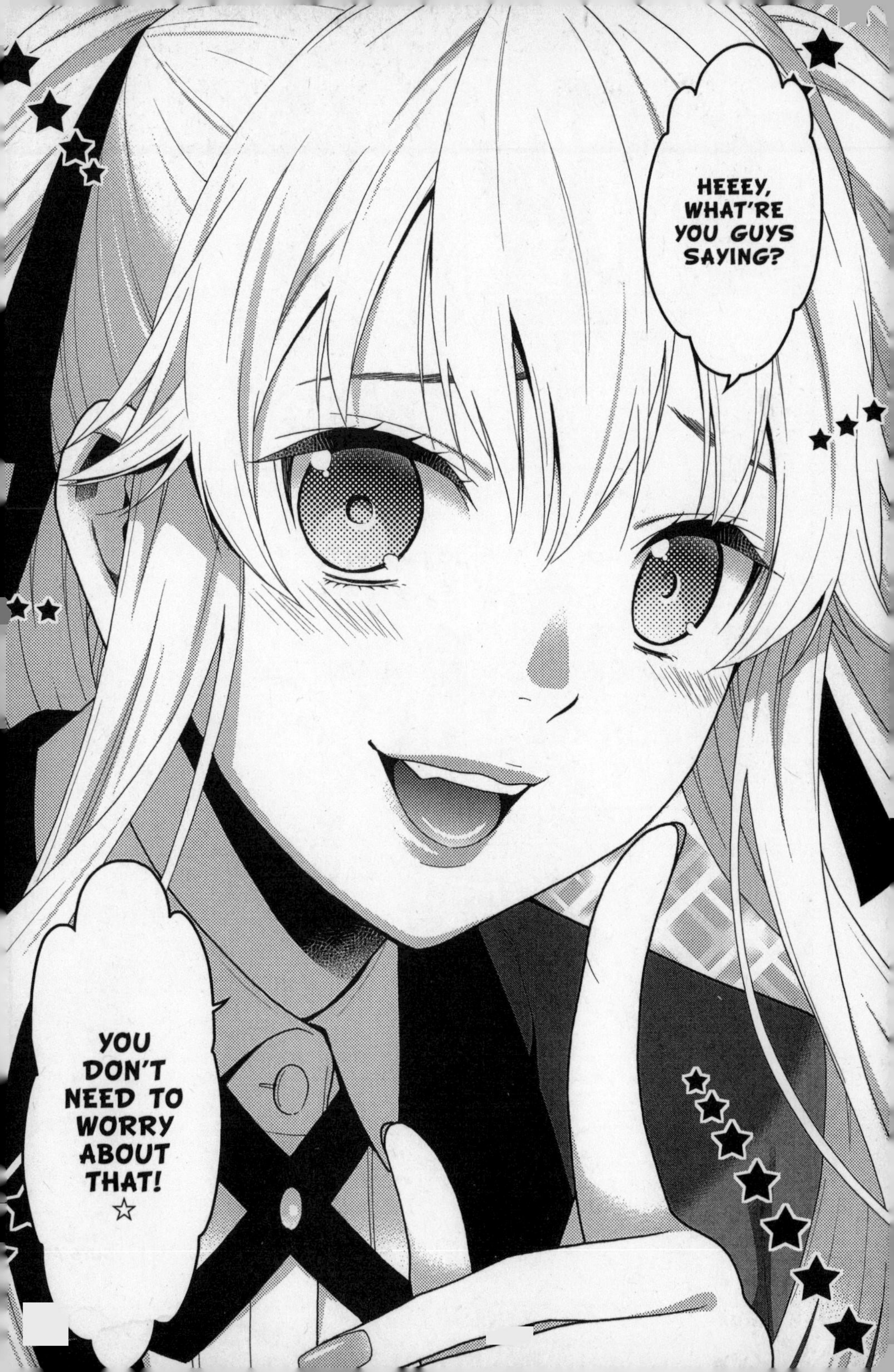
HEEEY, WHAT'RE YOU GUYS SAYING?
YOU DON'T NEED TO WORRY ABOUT THAT! ☆

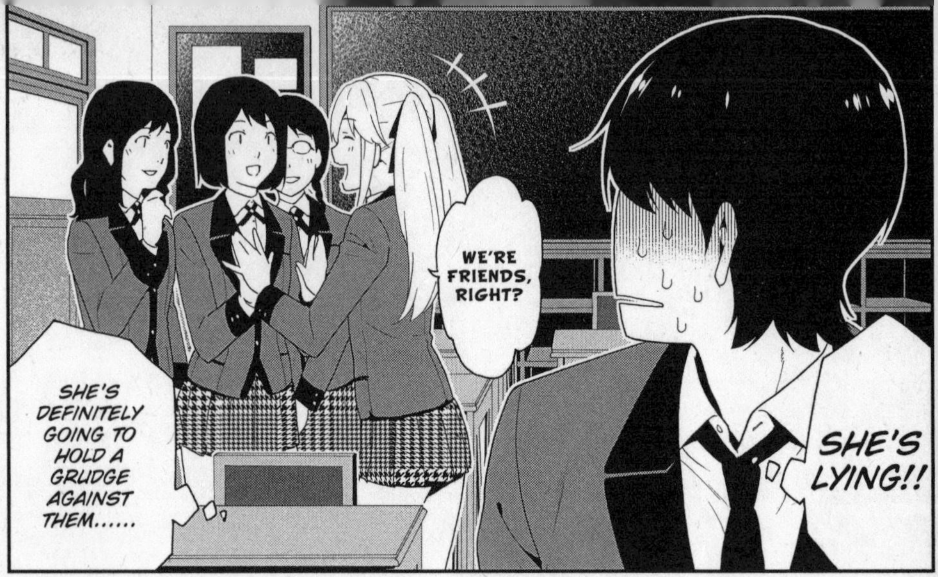
WE'RE FRIENDS, RIGHT?
SHE'S LYING!!
SHE'S DEFINITELY GOING TO HOLD A GRUDGE AGAINST THEM......

CHAPTER TEN
INVITING GIRL

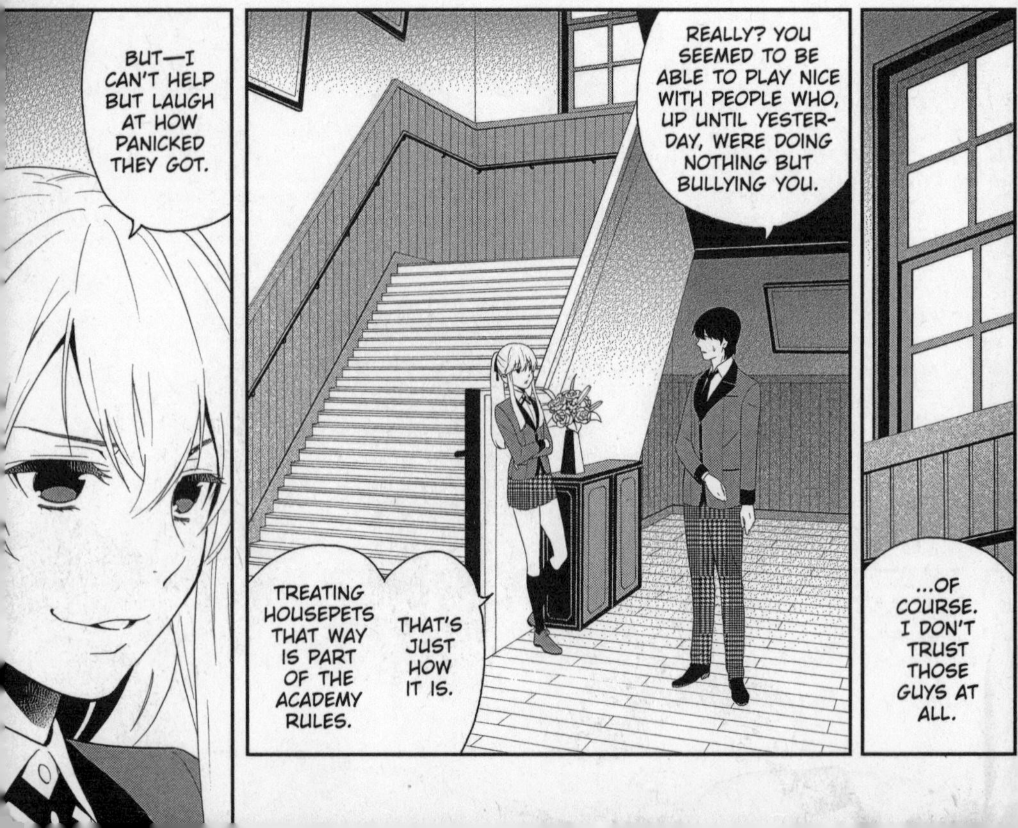
...OF COURSE. I DON'T TRUST THOSE GUYS AT ALL.
REALLY? YOU SEEMED TO BE ABLE TO PLAY NICE WITH PEOPLE WHO, UP UNTIL YESTER-DAY, WERE DOING NOTHING BUT BULLYING YOU.
TREATING HOUSEPETS THAT WAY IS PART OF THE ACADEMY RULES.
THAT'S JUST HOW IT IS.
BUT—I CAN'T HELP BUT LAUGH AT HOW PANICKED THEY GOT.

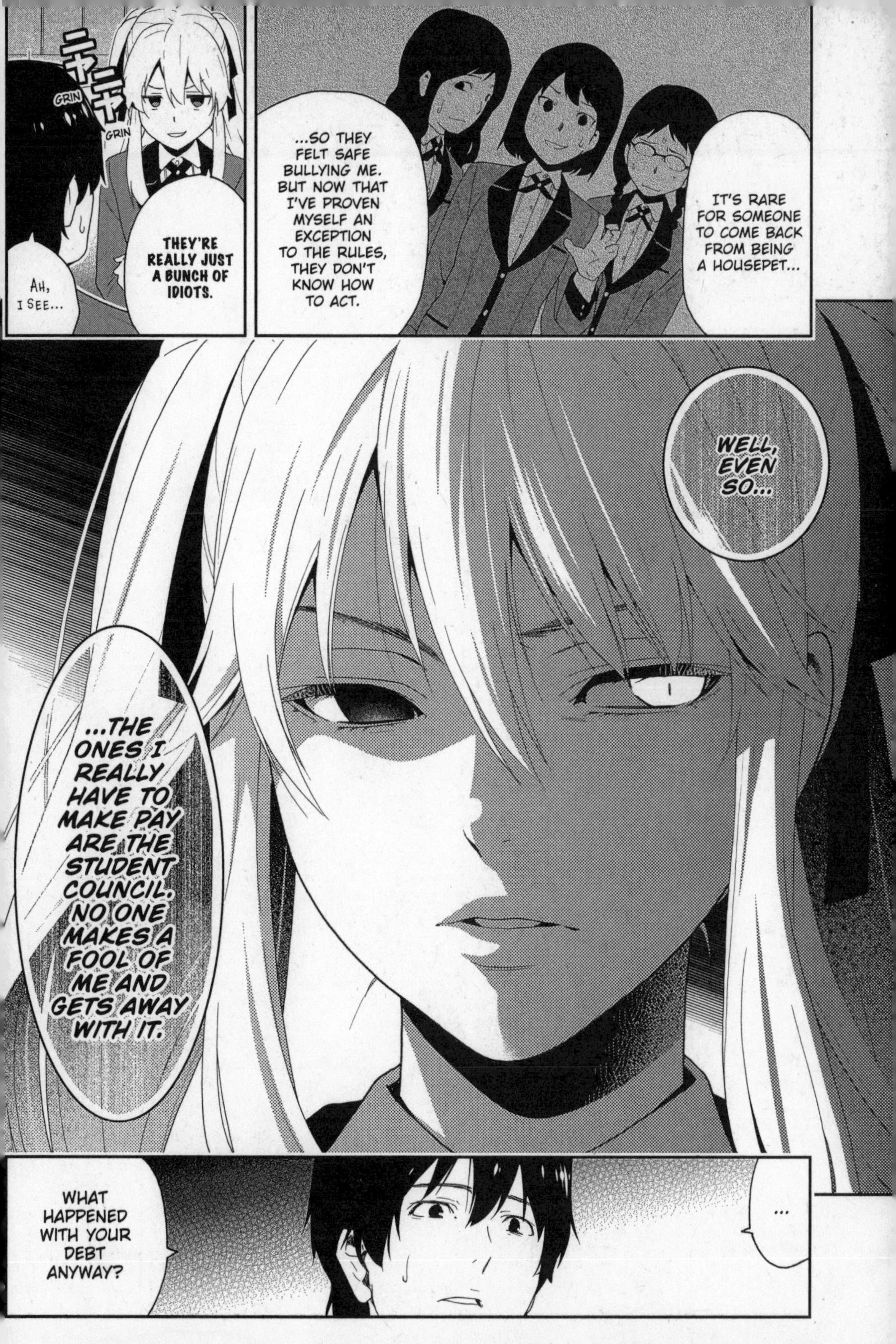

IT'S RARE FOR SOMEONE TO COME BACK FROM BEING A HOUSEPET...
...SO THEY FELT SAFE BULLYING ME. BUT NOW THAT I'VE PROVEN MYSELF AN EXCEPTION TO THE RULES, THEY DON'T KNOW HOW TO ACT.
ニヤニヤ
GRIN
GRIN
THEY'RE REALLY JUST A BUNCH OF IDIOTS.
AH, I SEE...
WELL, EVEN SO...
...THE ONES I REALLY HAVE TO MAKE PAY ARE THE STUDENT COUNCIL. NO ONE MAKES A FOOL OF ME AND GETS AWAY WITH IT.
...
WHAT HAPPENED WITH YOUR DEBT ANYWAY?

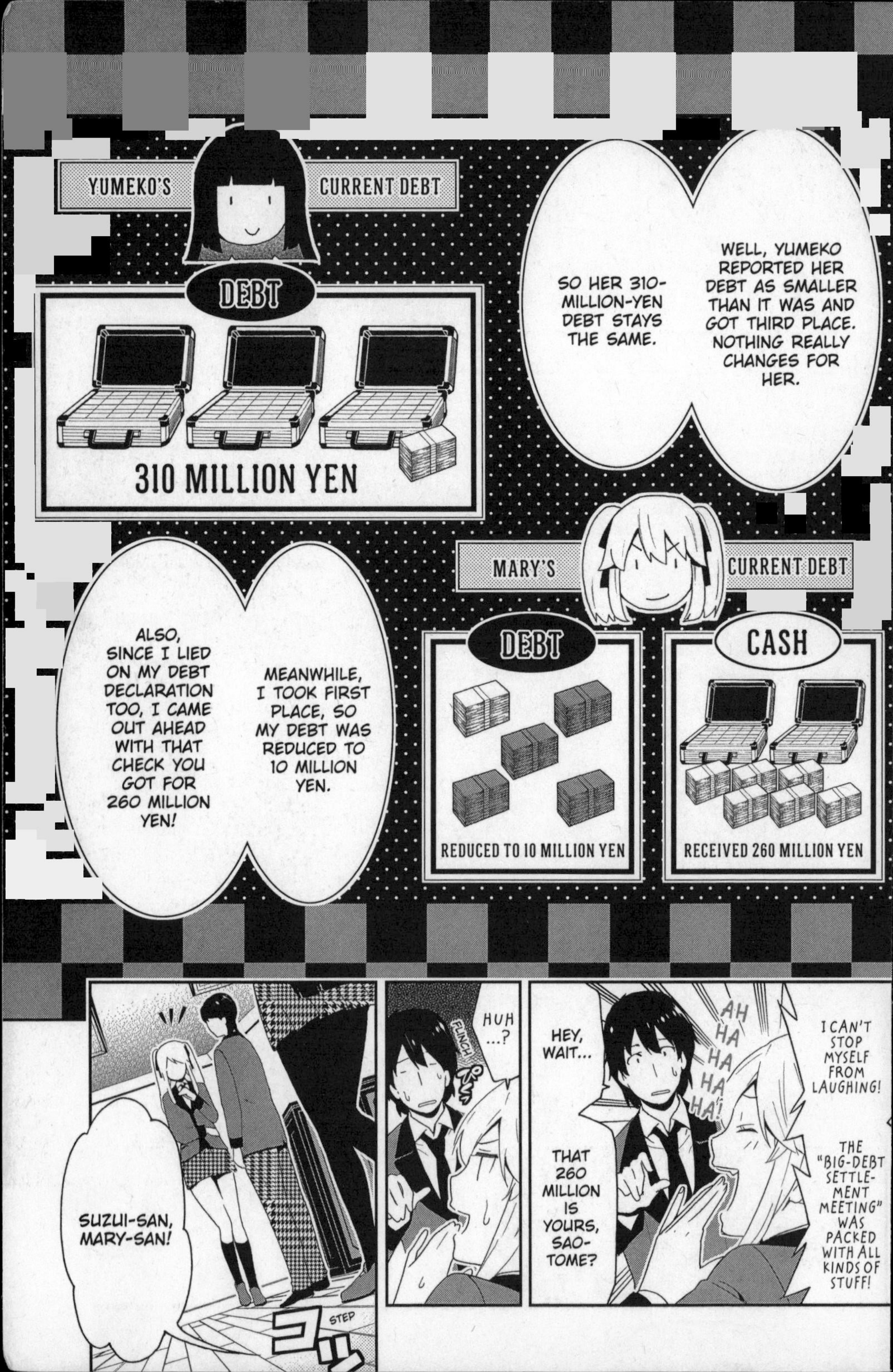
WELL, YUMEKO REPORTED HER DEBT AS SMALLER THAN IT WAS AND GOT THIRD PLACE. NOTHING REALLY CHANGES FOR HER.
SO HER 310-MILLION-YEN DEBT STAYS THE SAME.
YUMEKO'S CURRENT DEBT
DEBT
310 MILLION YEN
MARY'S CURRENT DEBT
CASH
RECEIVED 260 MILLION YEN
DEBT
REDUCED TO 10 MILLION YEN
MEANWHILE, I TOOK FIRST PLACE, SO MY DEBT WAS REDUCED TO 10 MILLION YEN.
ALSO, SINCE I LIED ON MY DEBT DECLARATION TOO, I CAME OUT AHEAD WITH THAT CHECK YOU GOT FOR 260 MILLION YEN!
I CAN'T STOP MYSELF FROM LAUGHING!
AH HA HA HA HA HA!
HEY, WAIT...
THAT 260 MILLION IS YOURS, SAOTOME?
THE "BIG-DEBT SETTLEMENT MEETING" WAS PACKED WITH ALL KINDS OF STUFF!
HUH ...?
FLINCH
SUZUI-SAN, MARY-SAN!
STEP

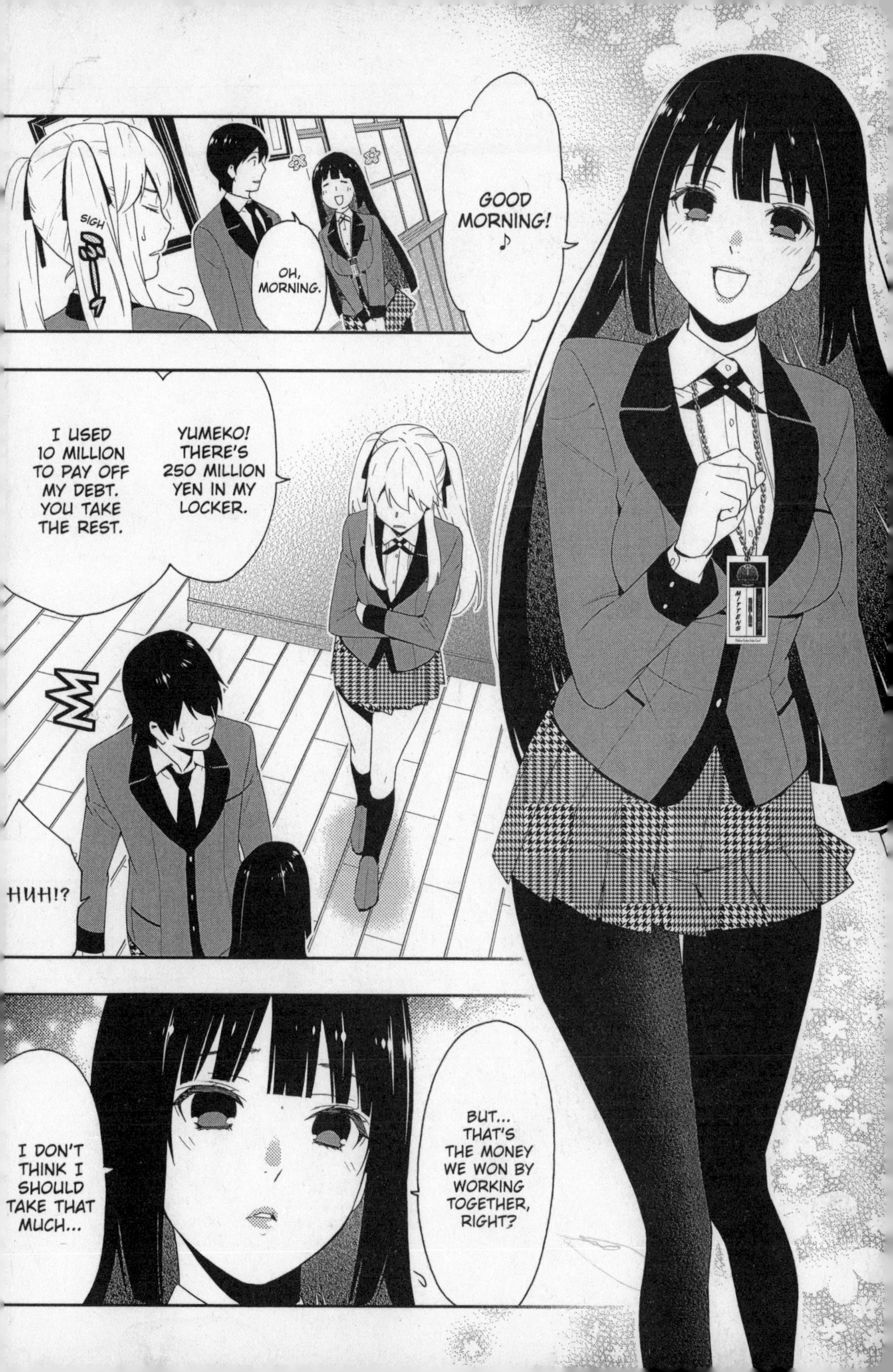
GOOD MORNING! ♪
SIGH
OH, MORNING.
YUMEKO! THERE'S 250 MILLION YEN IN MY LOCKER.
I USED 10 MILLION TO PAY OFF MY DEBT. YOU TAKE THE REST.
HUH!?
BUT... THAT'S THE MONEY WE WON BY WORKING TOGETHER, RIGHT?
I DON'T THINK I SHOULD TAKE THAT MUCH...

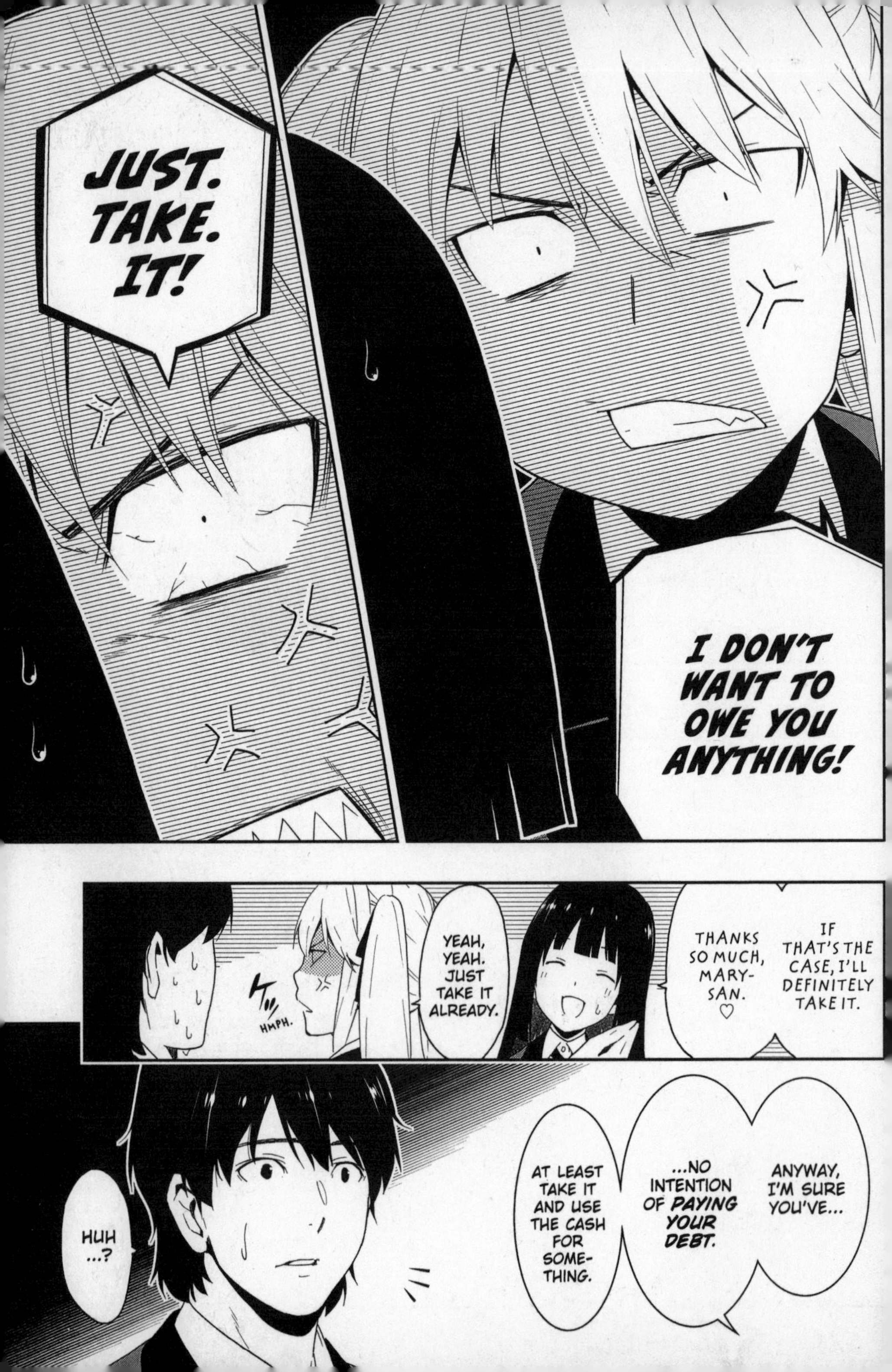
I DON'T WANT TO OWE YOU ANYTHING!
JUST. TAKE. IT!
IF THAT'S THE CASE, I'LL DEFINITELY TAKE IT.
THANKS SO MUCH, MARY-SAN. ♡
YEAH, YEAH. JUST TAKE IT ALREADY.
HMPH.
ANYWAY, I'M SURE YOU'VE...
...NO INTENTION OF PAYING YOUR DEBT.
AT LEAST TAKE IT AND USE THE CASH FOR SOMETHING.
HUH ...?

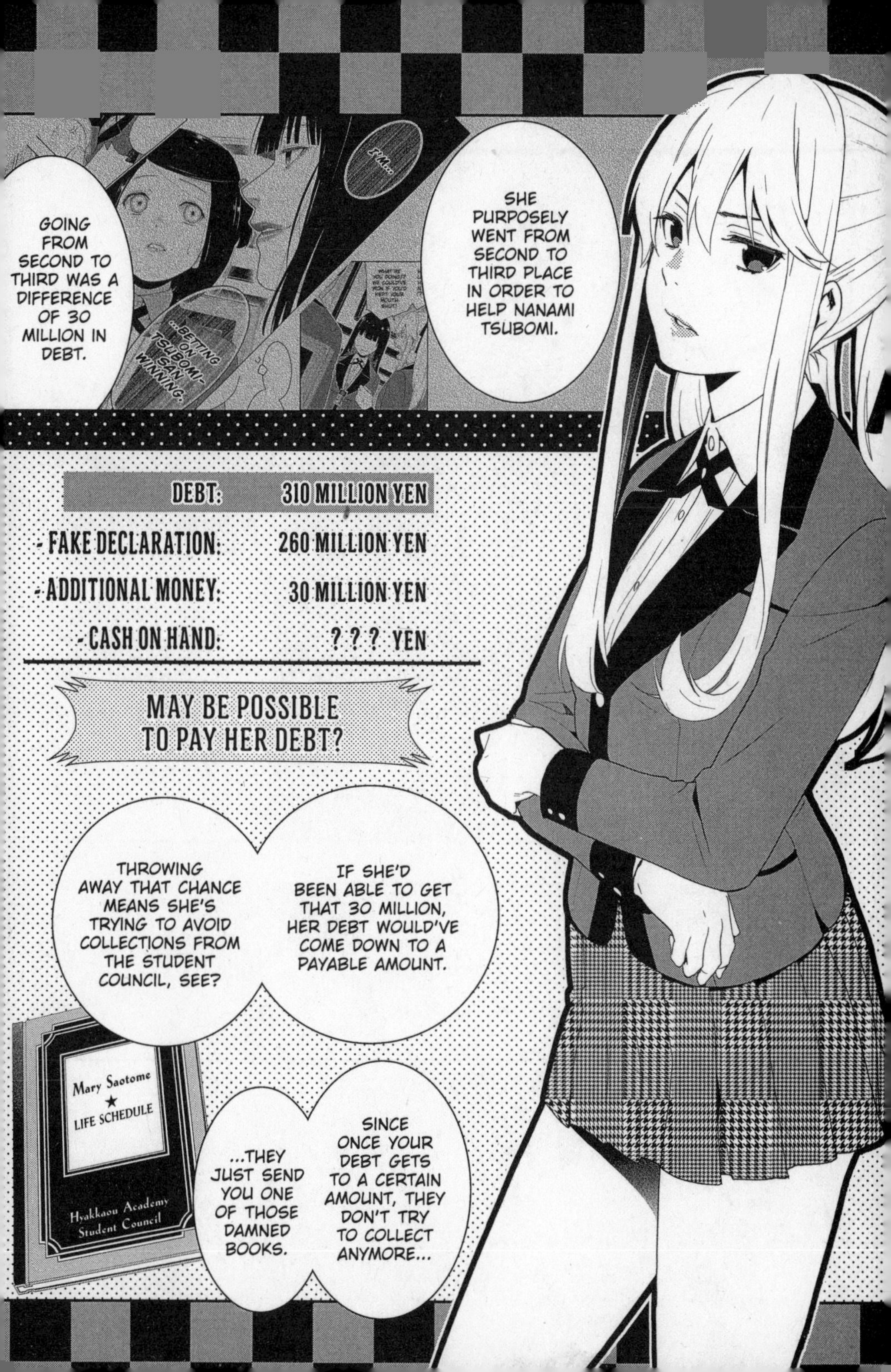
SHE PURPOSELY WENT FROM SECOND TO THIRD PLACE IN ORDER TO HELP NANAMI TSUBOMI.
I'M...
...BETTING ON TSUBOMI-SAN WINNING.
GOING FROM SECOND TO THIRD WAS A DIFFERENCE OF 30 MILLION IN DEBT.
DEBT: 310 MILLION YEN
- FAKE DECLARATION: 260 MILLION YEN
- ADDITIONAL MONEY: 30 MILLION YEN
- CASH ON HAND: ??? YEN
MAY BE POSSIBLE TO PAY HER DEBT?
IF SHE'D BEEN ABLE TO GET THAT 30 MILLION, HER DEBT WOULD'VE COME DOWN TO A PAYABLE AMOUNT.
THROWING AWAY THAT CHANCE MEANS SHE'S TRYING TO AVOID COLLECTIONS FROM THE STUDENT COUNCIL, SEE?
Mary Saotome ★ LIFE SCHEDULE
Hyakkaou Academy Student Council
SINCE ONCE YOUR DEBT GETS TO A CERTAIN AMOUNT, THEY DON'T TRY TO COLLECT ANYMORE...
...THEY JUST SEND YOU ONE OF THOSE DAMNED BOOKS.

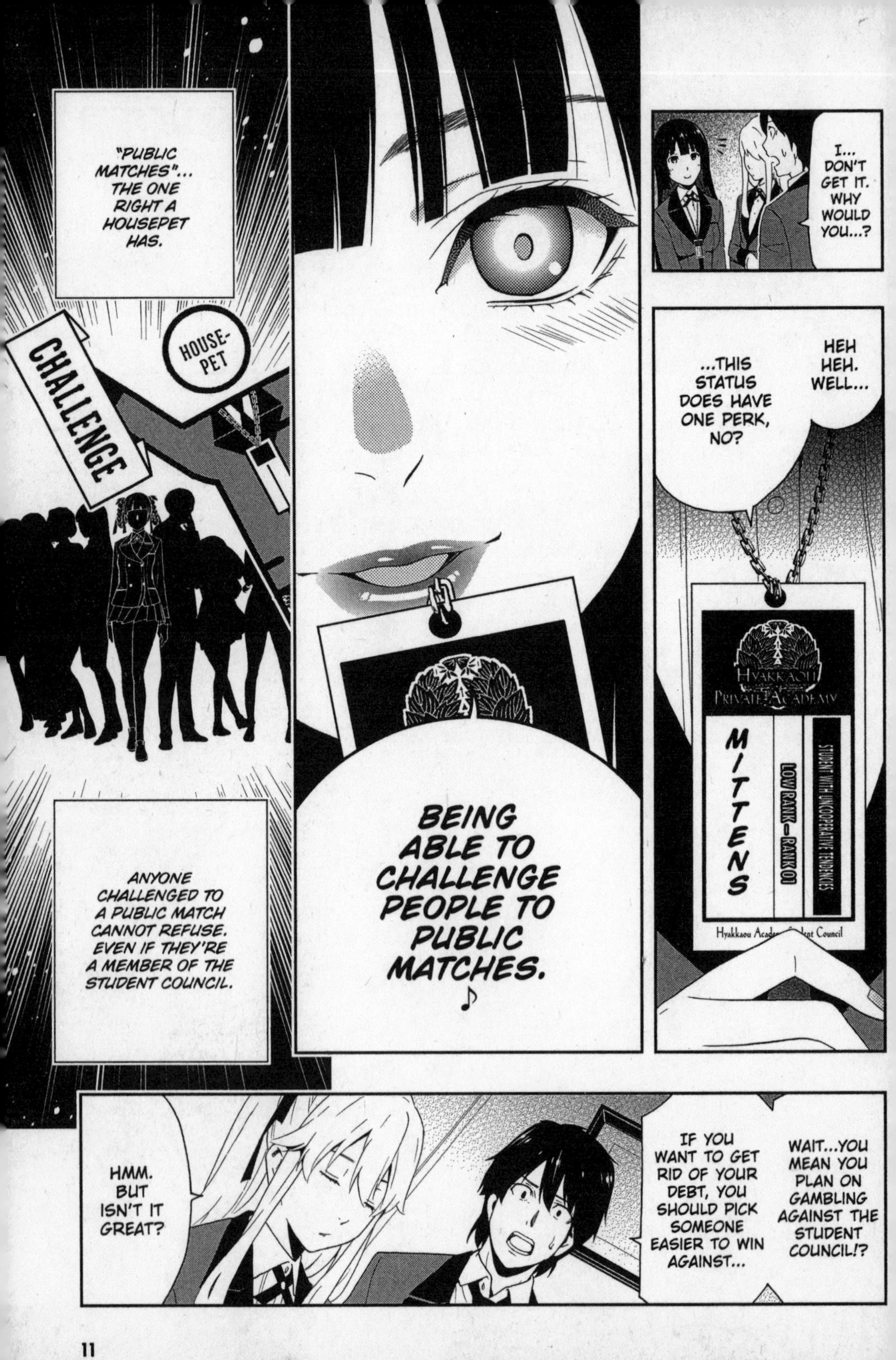
I... DON'T GET IT. WHY WOULD YOU...?
HEH HEH. WELL...
...THIS STATUS DOES HAVE ONE PERK, NO?
HYAKKAOU PRIVATE ACADEMY
STUDENT WITH UNCOOPERATIVE TENDENCIES
LOW RANK—RANK 01
MITTENS
BEING ABLE TO CHALLENGE PEOPLE TO PUBLIC MATCHES. ♪
"PUBLIC MATCHES"... THE ONE RIGHT A HOUSEPET HAS.
HOUSE-PET
CHALLENGE
ANYONE CHALLENGED TO A PUBLIC MATCH CANNOT REFUSE. EVEN IF THEY'RE A MEMBER OF THE STUDENT COUNCIL.
WAIT...YOU MEAN YOU PLAN ON GAMBLING AGAINST THE STUDENT COUNCIL!?
IF YOU WANT TO GET RID OF YOUR DEBT, YOU SHOULD PICK SOMEONE EASIER TO WIN AGAINST...
HMM. BUT ISN'T IT GREAT?

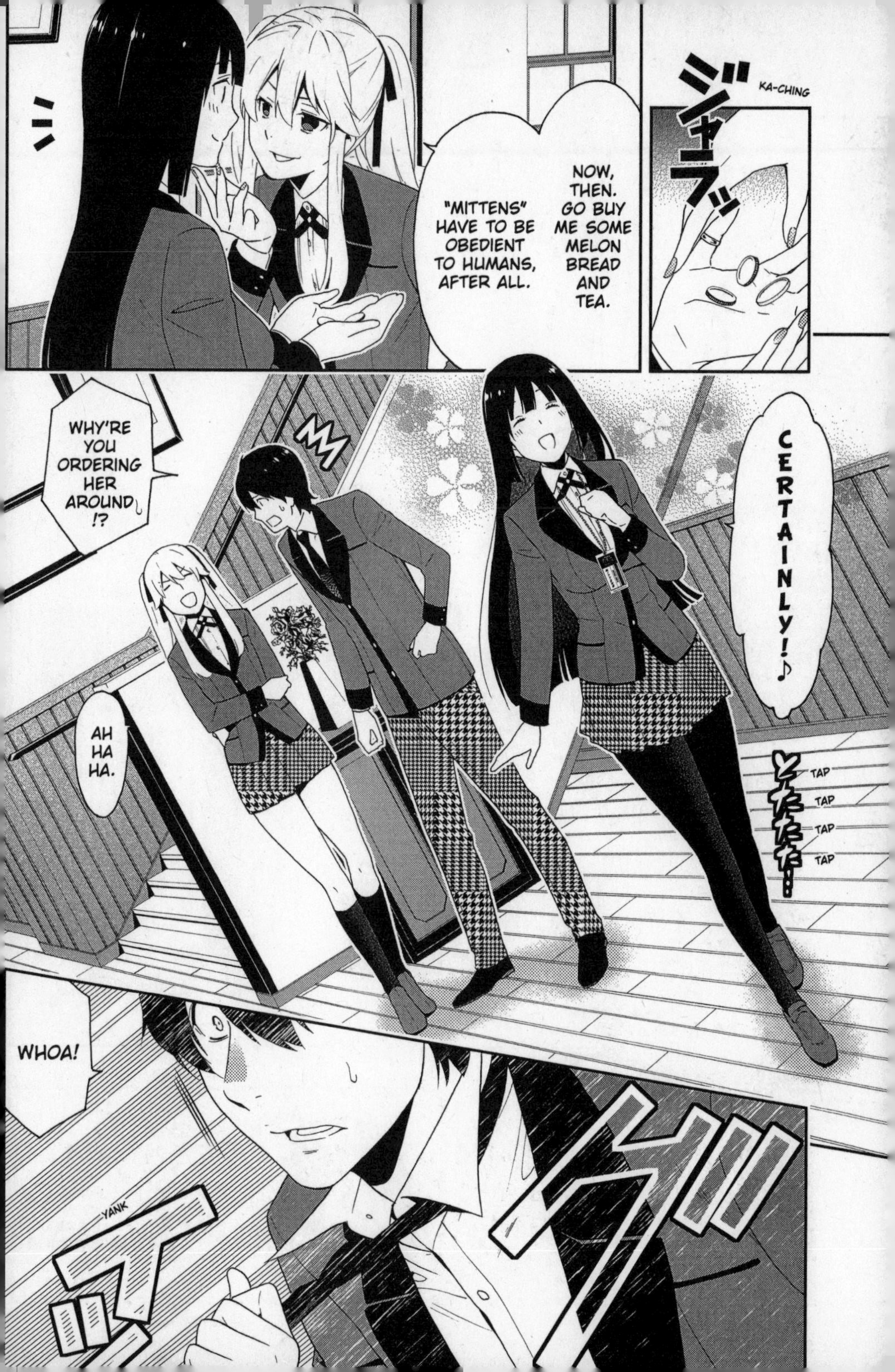

KA-CHING
NOW, THEN. GO BUY ME SOME MELON BREAD AND TEA.
"MITTENS" HAVE TO BE OBEDIENT TO HUMANS, AFTER ALL.
CERTAINLY!♪
TAP TAP TAP TAP
WHY'RE YOU ORDERING HER AROUND!?
AH HA HA.
WHOA!
YANK

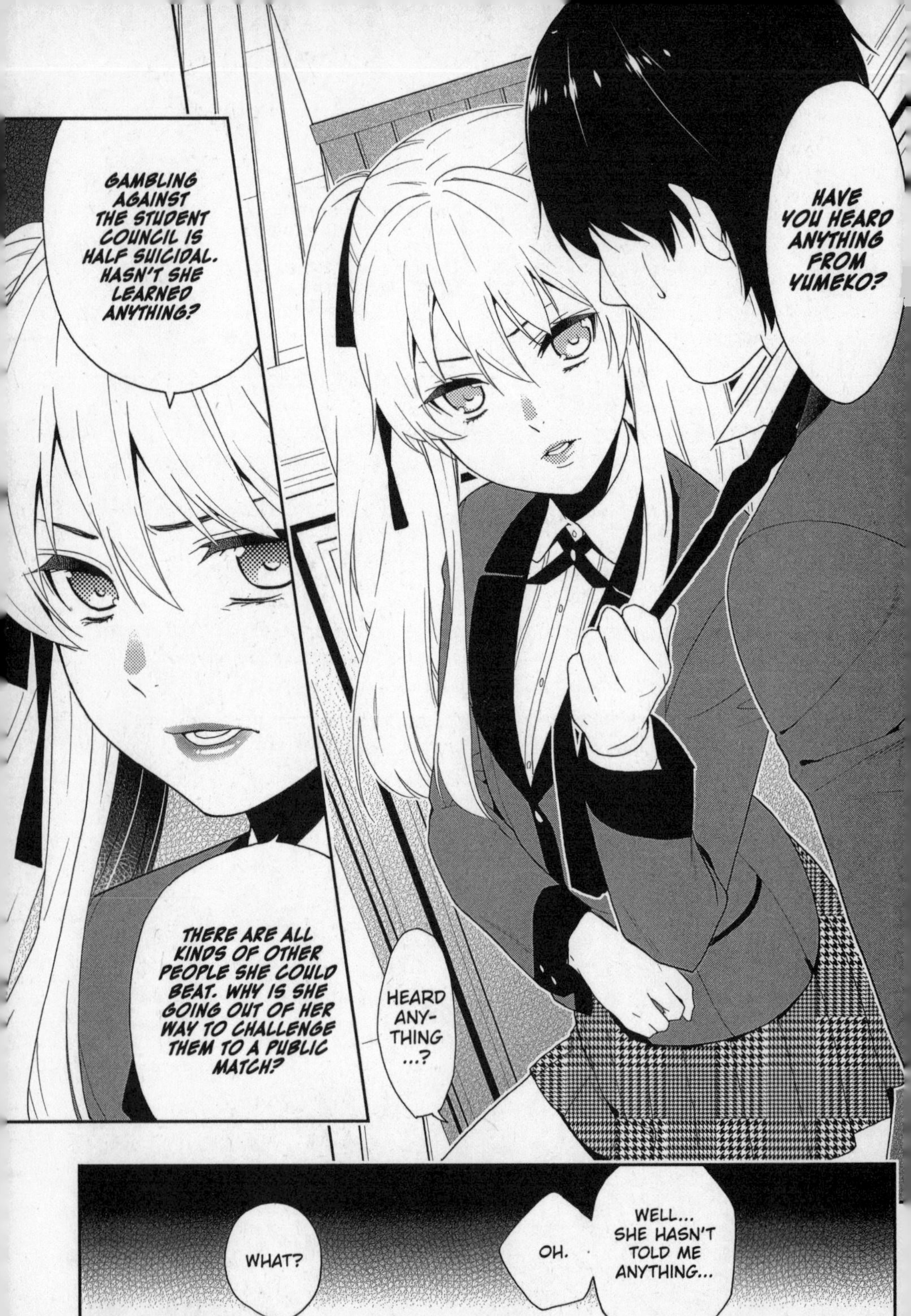
HAVE YOU HEARD ANYTHING FROM YUMEKO?
HEARD ANYTHING...?
GAMBLING AGAINST THE STUDENT COUNCIL IS HALF SUICIDAL. HASN'T SHE LEARNED ANYTHING?
THERE ARE ALL KINDS OF OTHER PEOPLE SHE COULD BEAT. WHY IS SHE GOING OUT OF HER WAY TO CHALLENGE THEM TO A PUBLIC MATCH?
WELL... SHE HASN'T TOLD ME ANYTHING...
OH.
WHAT?

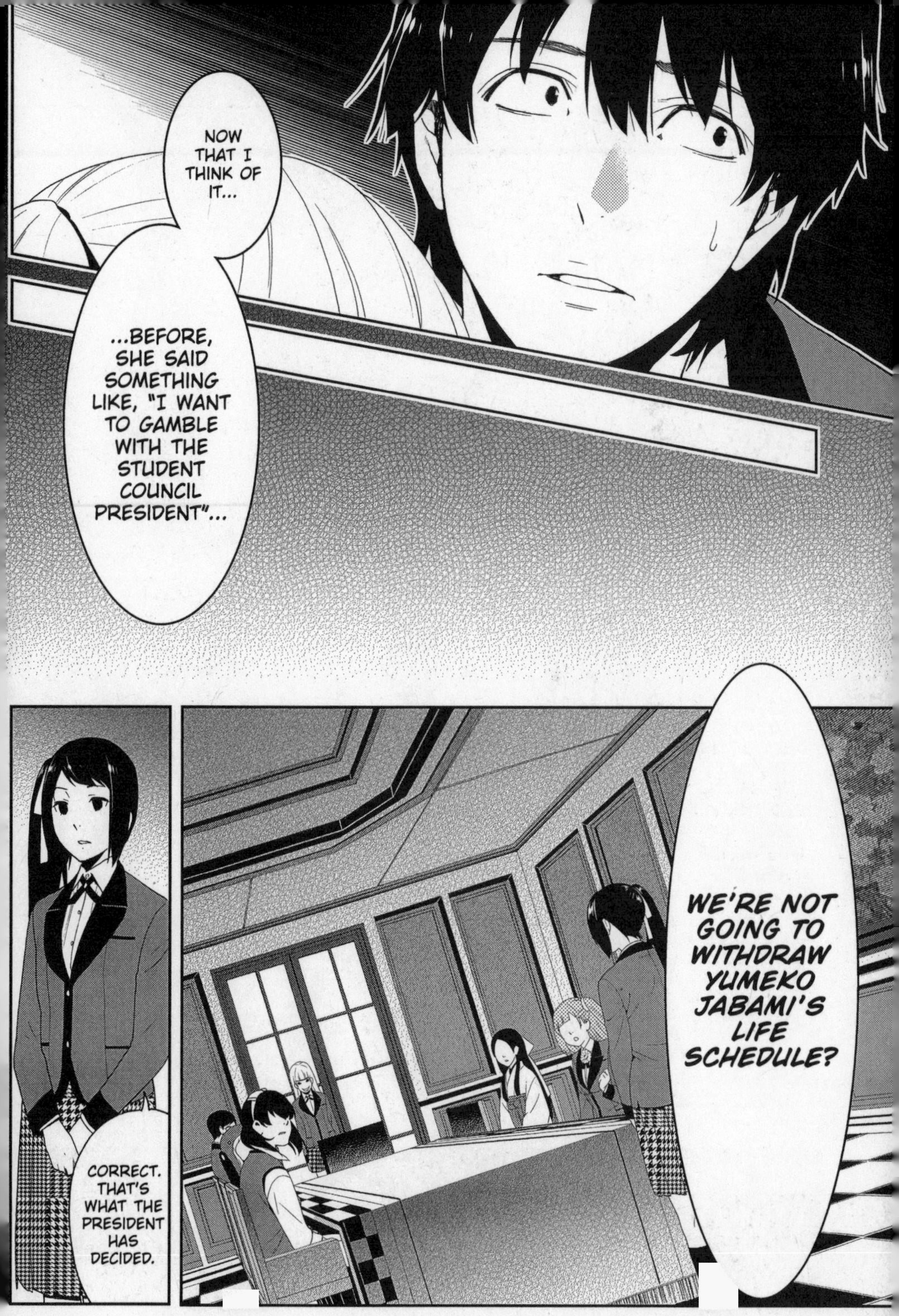
NOW THAT I THINK OF IT...
...BEFORE, SHE SAID SOMETHING LIKE, "I WANT TO GAMBLE WITH THE STUDENT COUNCIL PRESIDENT"...
WE'RE NOT GOING TO WITHDRAW YUMEKO JABAMI'S LIFE SCHEDULE?
CORRECT. THAT'S WHAT THE PRESIDENT HAS DECIDED.

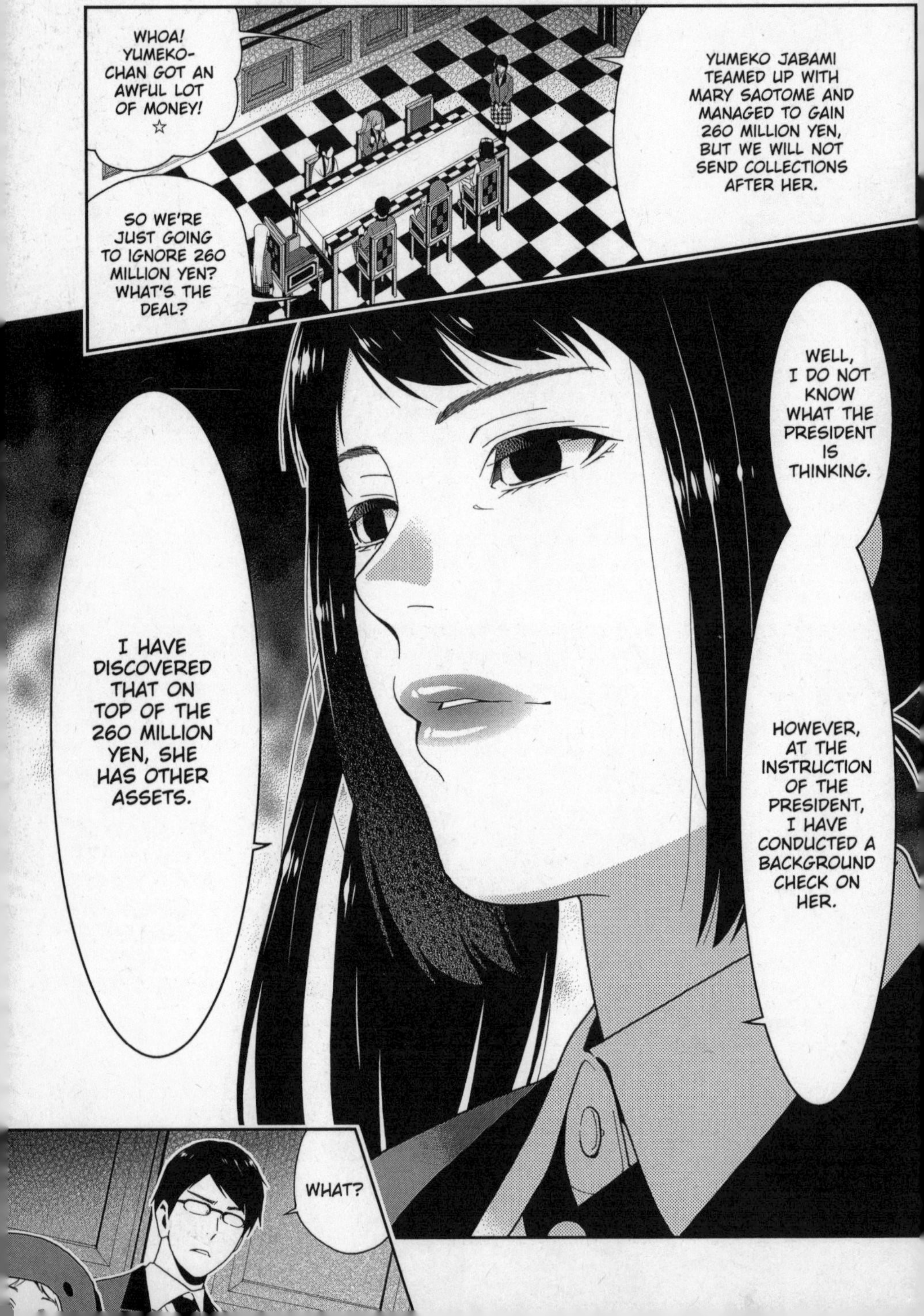
YUMEKO JABAMI TEAMED UP WITH MARY SAOTOME AND MANAGED TO GAIN 260 MILLION YEN, BUT WE WILL NOT SEND COLLECTIONS AFTER HER.
WHOA! YUMEKO-CHAN GOT AN AWFUL LOT OF MONEY! ☆
SO WE'RE JUST GOING TO IGNORE 260 MILLION YEN? WHAT'S THE DEAL?
WELL, I DO NOT KNOW WHAT THE PRESIDENT IS THINKING.
HOWEVER, AT THE INSTRUCTION OF THE PRESIDENT, I HAVE CONDUCTED A BACKGROUND CHECK ON HER.
I HAVE DISCOVERED THAT ON TOP OF THE 260 MILLION YEN, SHE HAS OTHER ASSETS.
WHAT?

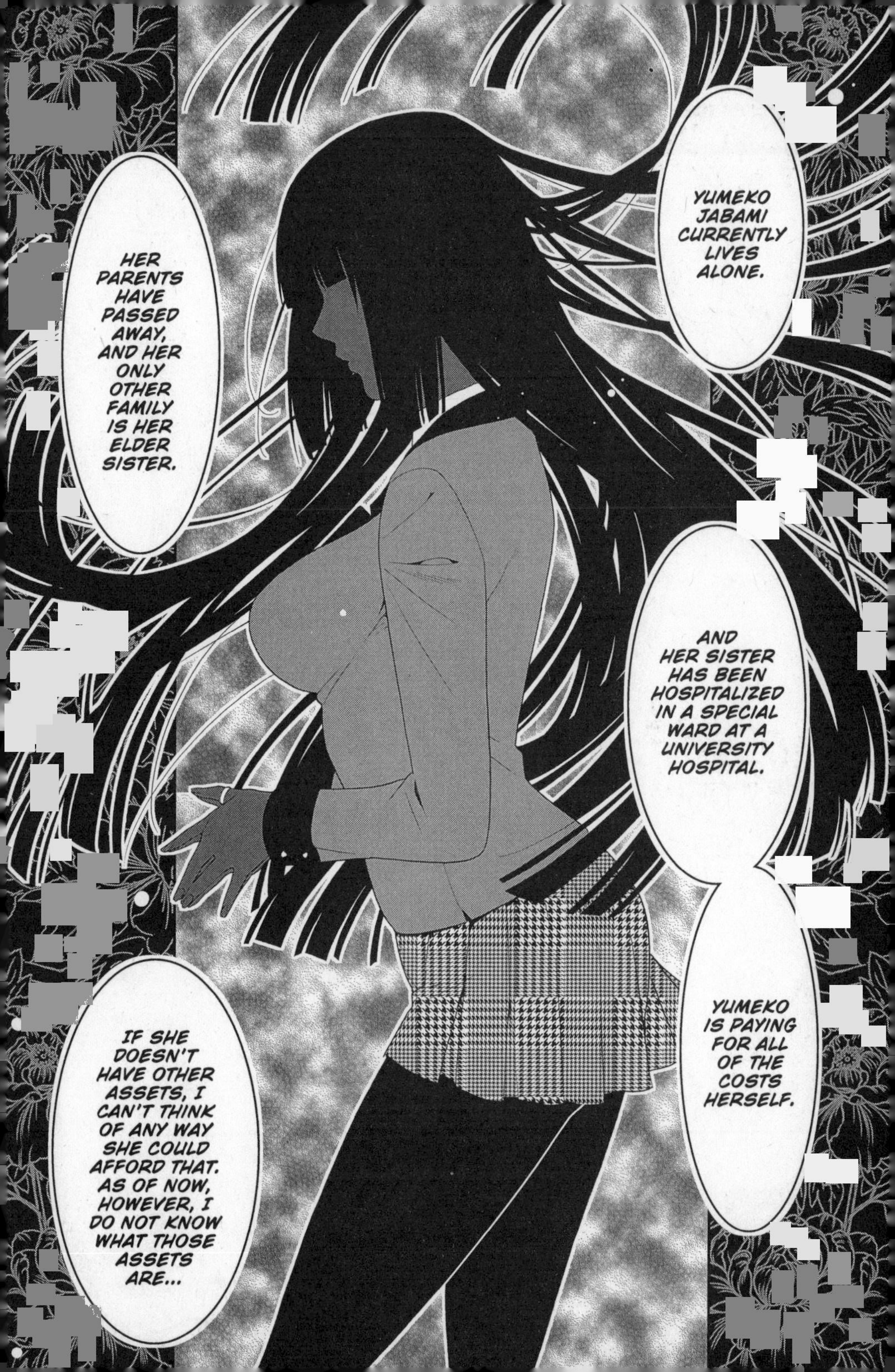
YUMEKO JABAMI CURRENTLY LIVES ALONE.
HER PARENTS HAVE PASSED AWAY, AND HER ONLY OTHER FAMILY IS HER ELDER SISTER.
AND HER SISTER HAS BEEN HOSPITALIZED IN A SPECIAL WARD AT A UNIVERSITY HOSPITAL.
YUMEKO IS PAYING FOR ALL OF THE COSTS HERSELF.
IF SHE DOESN'T HAVE OTHER ASSETS, I CAN'T THINK OF ANY WAY SHE COULD AFFORD THAT. AS OF NOW, HOWEVER, I DO NOT KNOW WHAT THOSE ASSETS ARE...

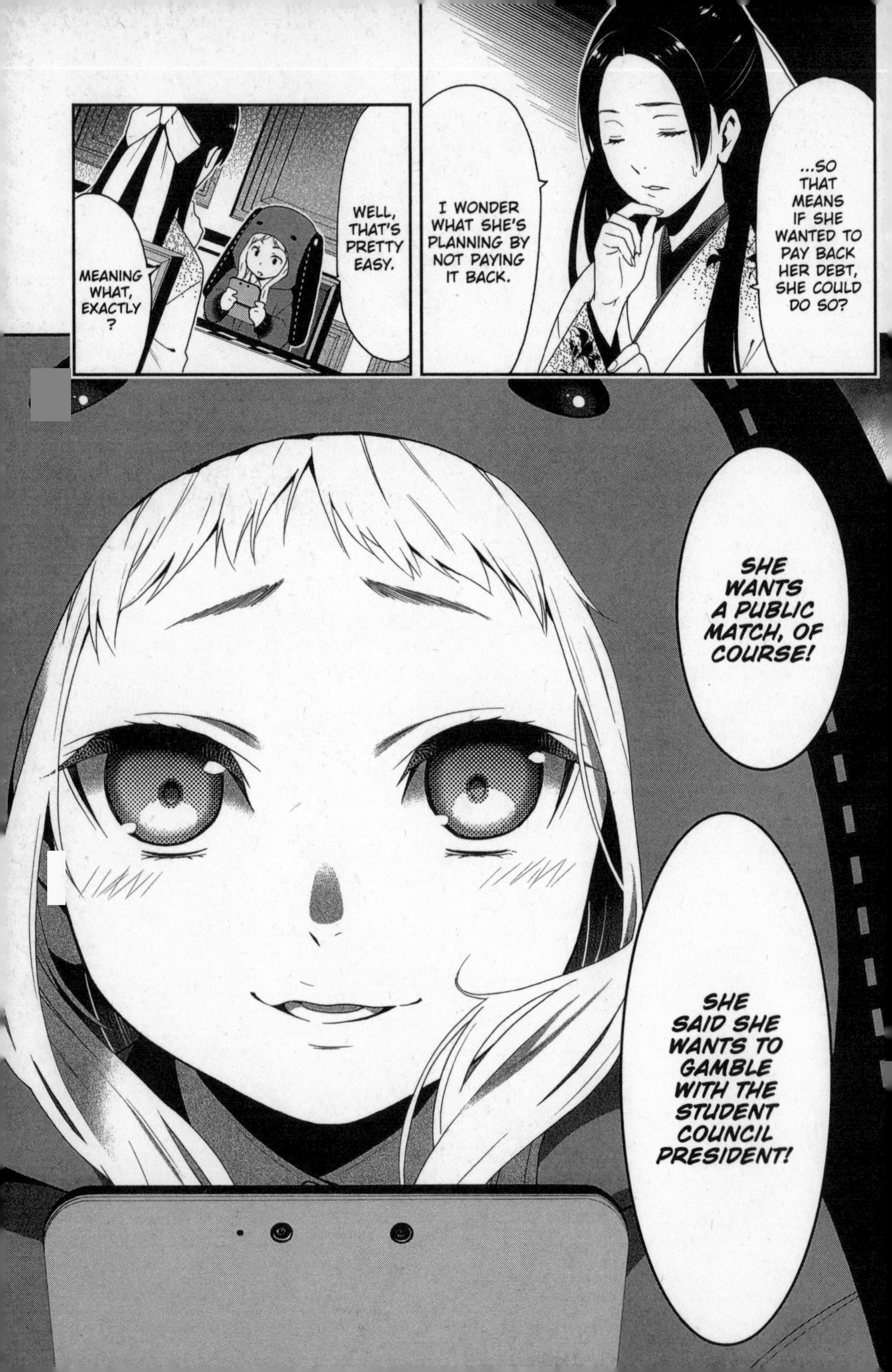
...SO THAT MEANS IF SHE WANTED TO PAY BACK HER DEBT, SHE COULD DO SO?
I WONDER WHAT SHE'S PLANNING BY NOT PAYING IT BACK.
WELL, THAT'S PRETTY EASY.
MEANING WHAT, EXACTLY?
SHE WANTS A PUBLIC MATCH, OF COURSE!
SHE SAID SHE WANTS TO GAMBLE WITH THE STUDENT COUNCIL PRESIDENT!

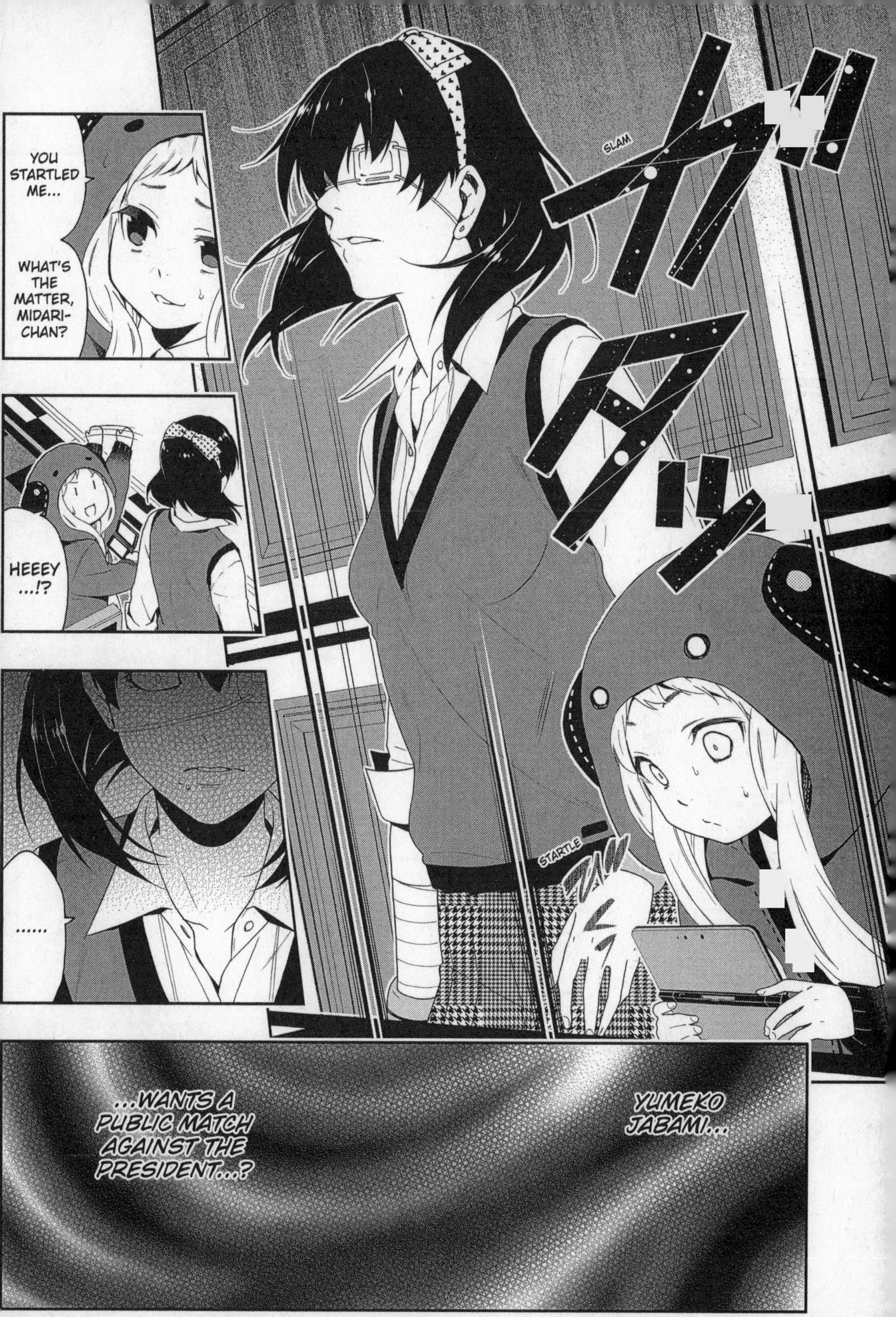
SLAM
STARTLE
YOU STARTLED ME...
WHAT'S THE MATTER, MIDARI-CHAN?
HEEEY ...!?
......
YUMEKO JABAMI...
...WANTS A PUBLIC MATCH AGAINST THE PRESIDENT...?

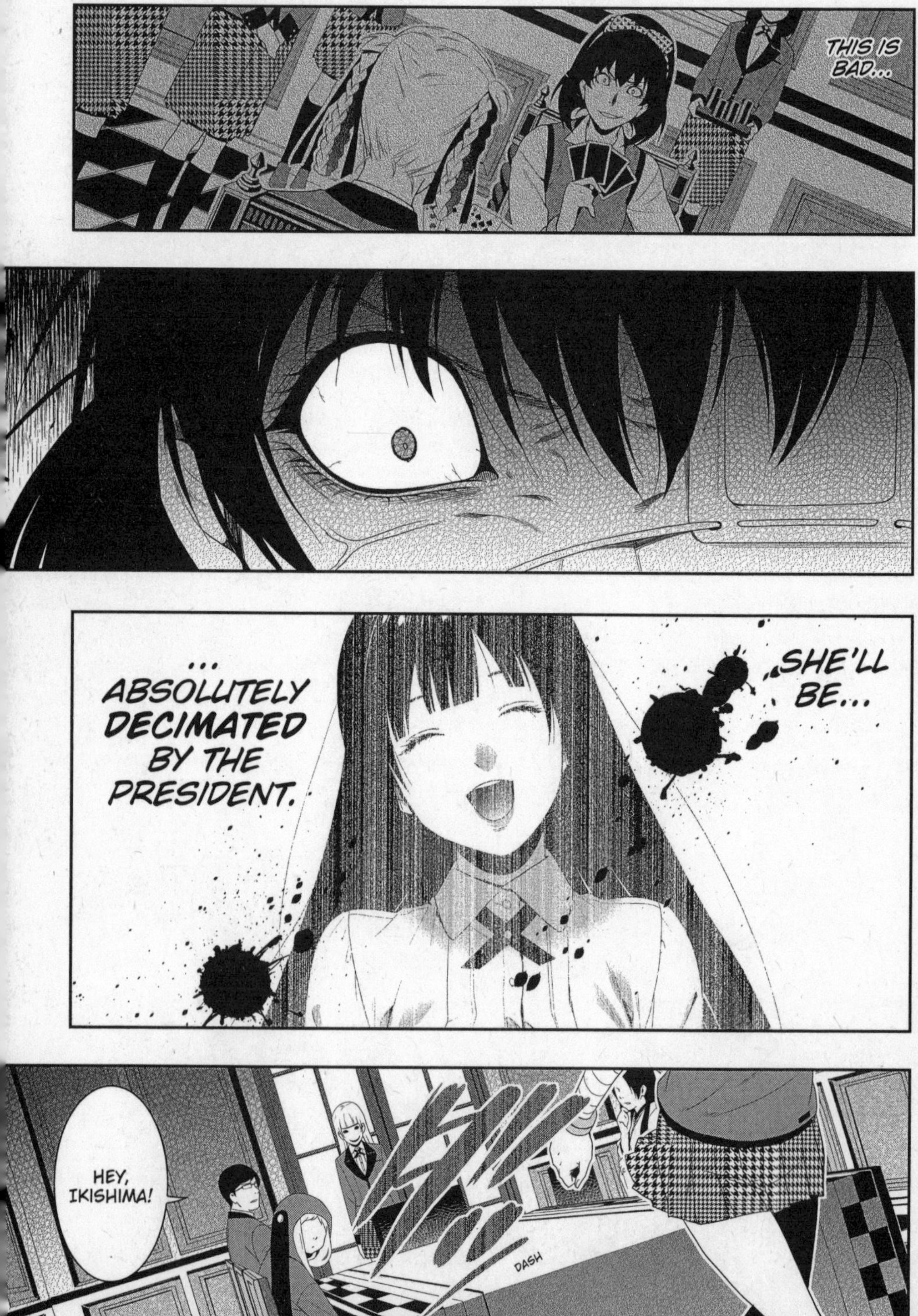
THIS IS BAD...
...SHE'LL BE...
...ABSOLUTELY DECIMATED BY THE PRESIDENT.
HEY, IKISHIMA!
DASH

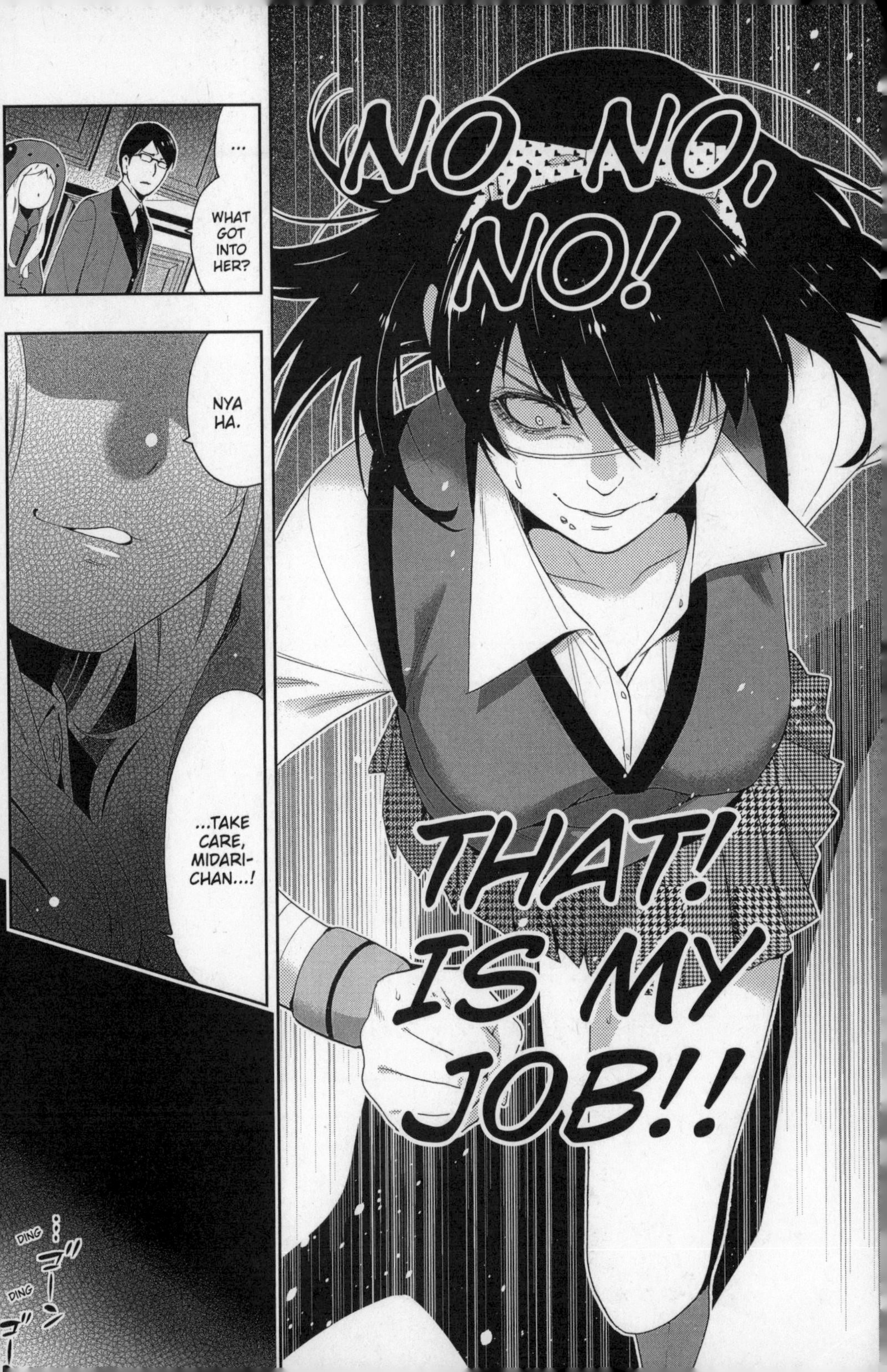

NO, NO, NO!
THAT! IS MY JOB!!
...
WHAT GOT INTO HER?
NYA HA.
...TAKE CARE, MIDARI-CHAN...!
DING
DING

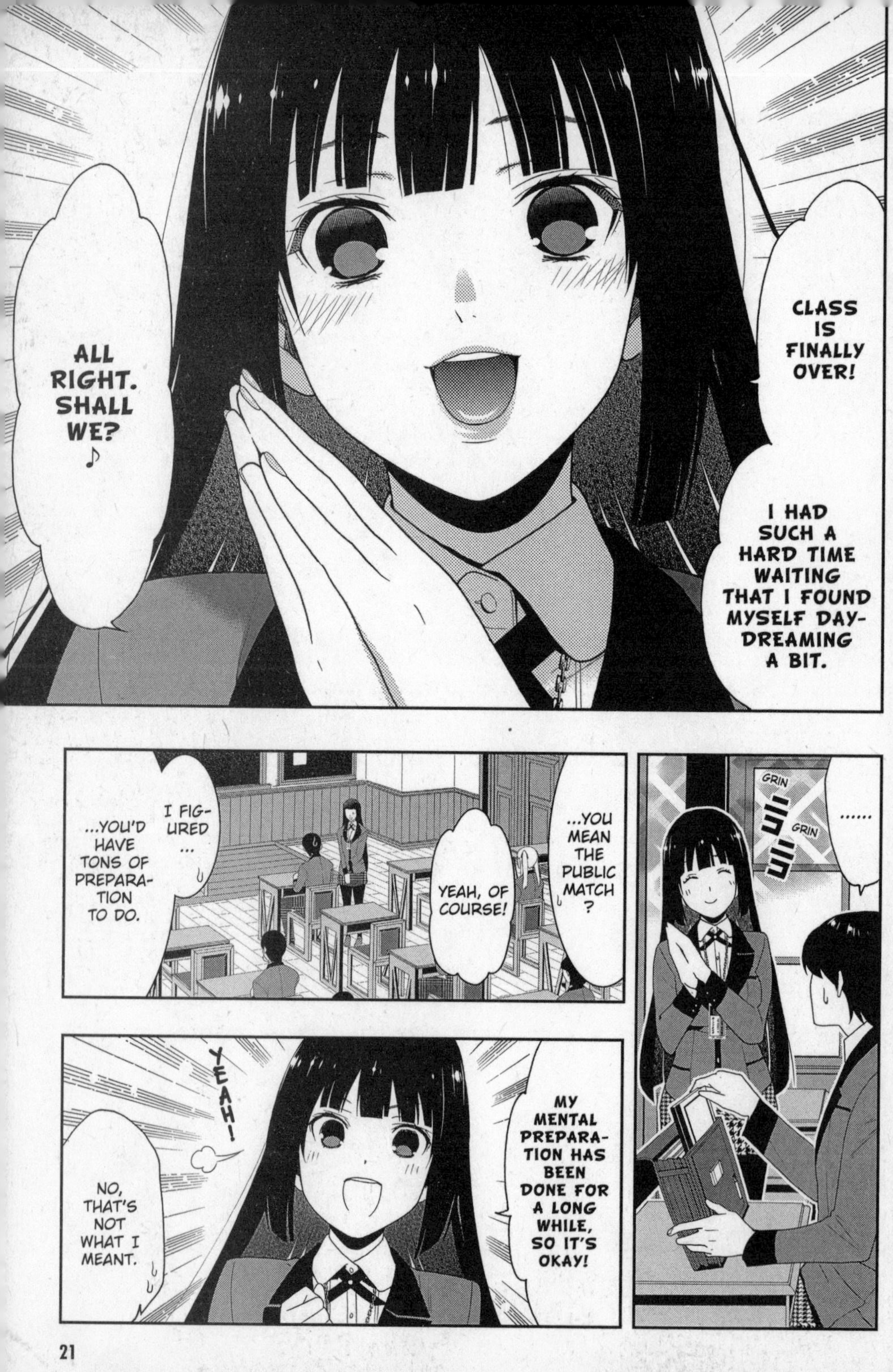
CLASS IS FINALLY OVER!
I HAD SUCH A HARD TIME WAITING THAT I FOUND MYSELF DAY-DREAMING A BIT.
ALL RIGHT. SHALL WE? ♪
GRIN
GRIN
......
...YOU MEAN THE PUBLIC MATCH?
YEAH, OF COURSE!
I FIG-URED ...
...YOU'D HAVE TONS OF PREPARA-TION TO DO.
YEAH!
MY MENTAL PREPARA-TION HAS BEEN DONE FOR A LONG WHILE, SO IT'S OKAY!
NO, THAT'S NOT WHAT I MEANT.

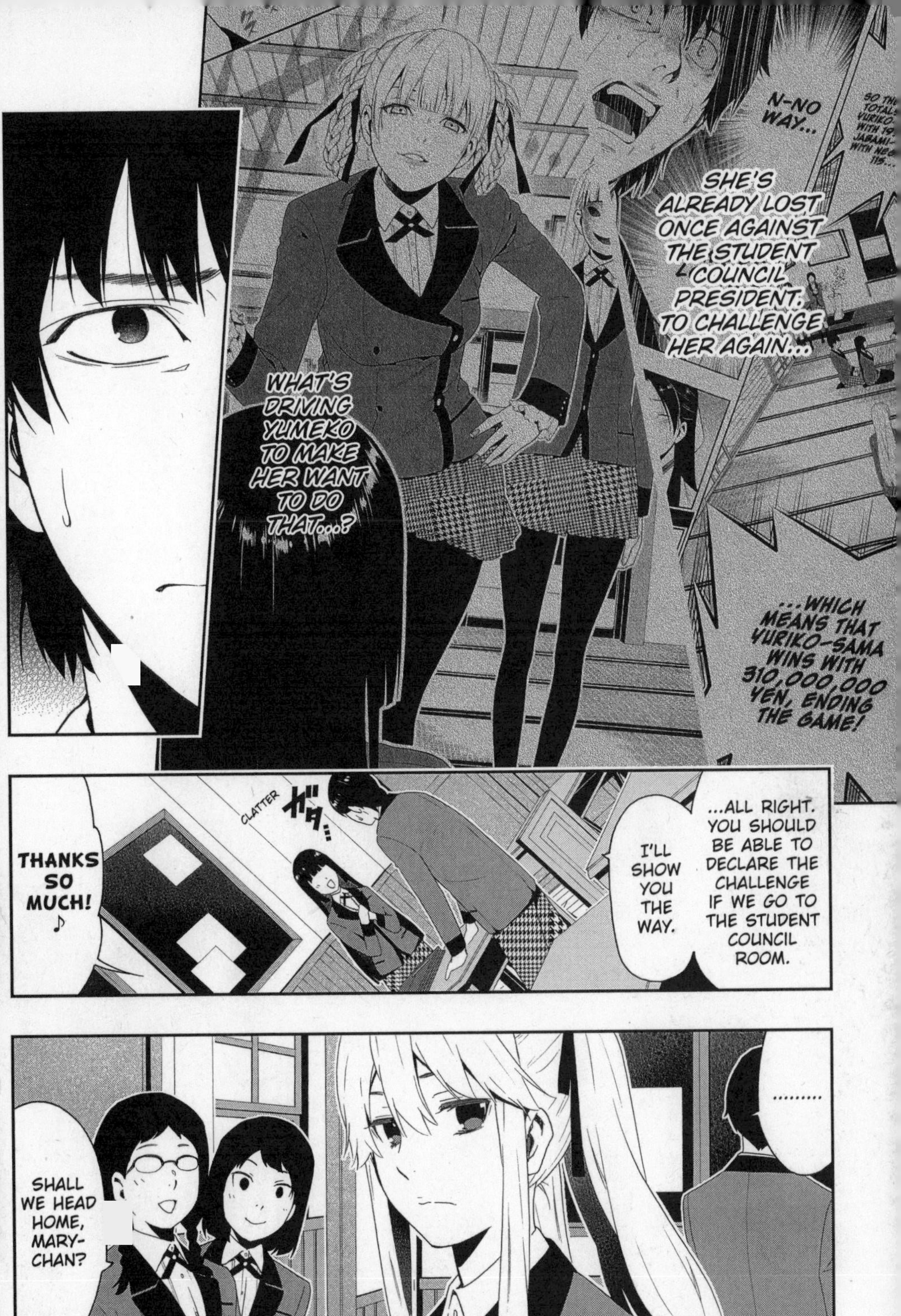
N-NO WAY...
SHE'S ALREADY LOST ONCE AGAINST THE STUDENT COUNCIL PRESIDENT. TO CHALLENGE HER AGAIN...
...WHICH MEANS THAT YURIKO-SAMA WINS WITH 310,000,000 YEN, ENDING THE GAME!
WHAT'S DRIVING YUMEKO TO MAKE HER WANT TO DO THAT...?
...ALL RIGHT. YOU SHOULD BE ABLE TO DECLARE THE CHALLENGE IF WE GO TO THE STUDENT COUNCIL ROOM.
I'LL SHOW YOU THE WAY.
CLATTER
THANKS SO MUCH! ♪
....
SHALL WE HEAD HOME, MARY-CHAN?

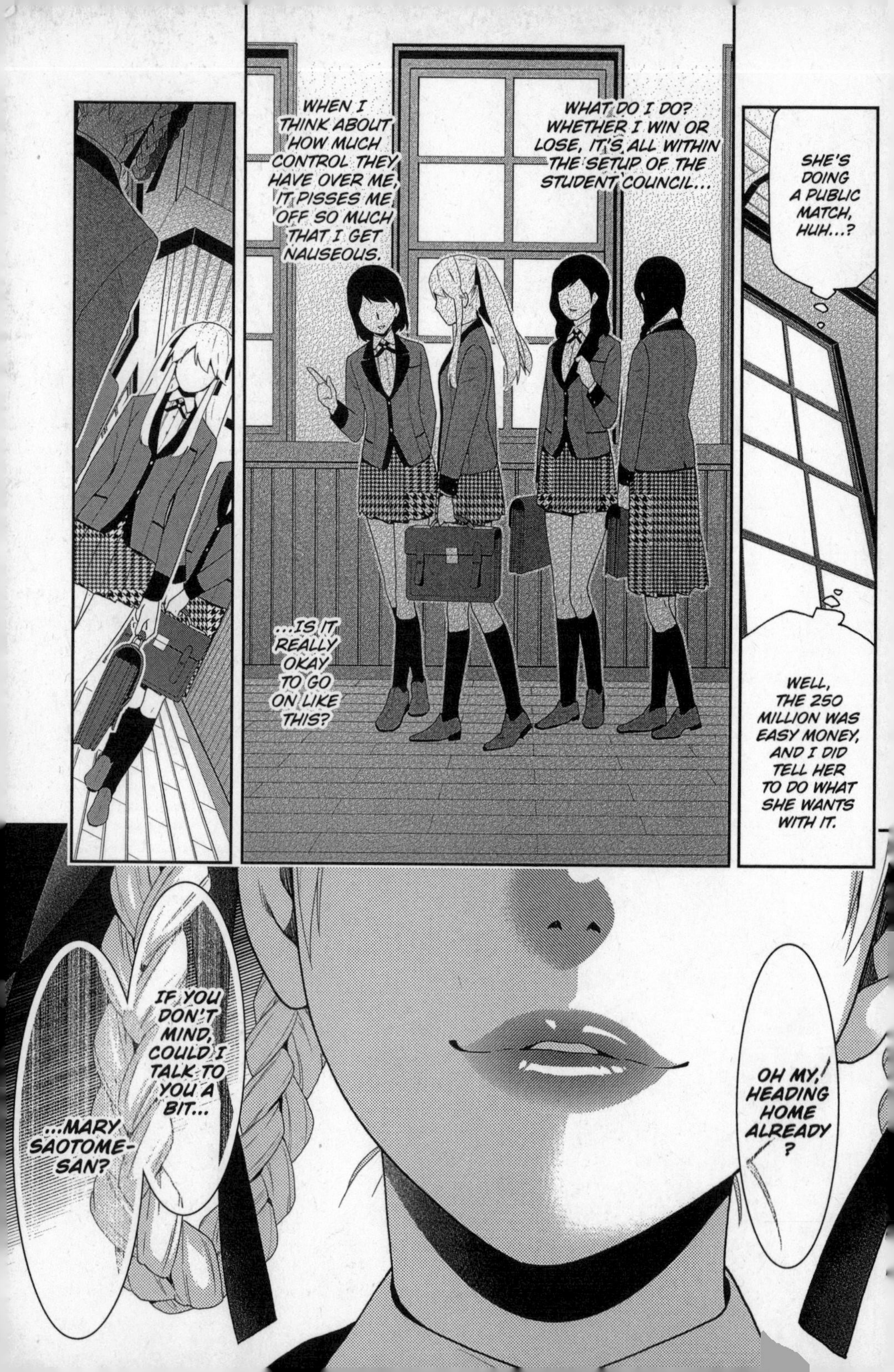
SHE'S DOING A PUBLIC MATCH, HUH...?
WELL, THE 250 MILLION WAS EASY MONEY, AND I DID TELL HER TO DO WHAT SHE WANTS WITH IT.
WHAT DO I DO? WHETHER I WIN OR LOSE, IT'S ALL WITHIN THE SETUP OF THE STUDENT COUNCIL...
WHEN I THINK ABOUT HOW MUCH CONTROL THEY HAVE OVER ME, IT PISSES ME OFF SO MUCH THAT I GET NAUSEOUS.
...IS IT REALLY OKAY TO GO ON LIKE THIS?
OH MY, HEADING HOME ALREADY?
IF YOU DON'T MIND, COULD I TALK TO YOU A BIT...
...MARY SAOTOME-SAN?

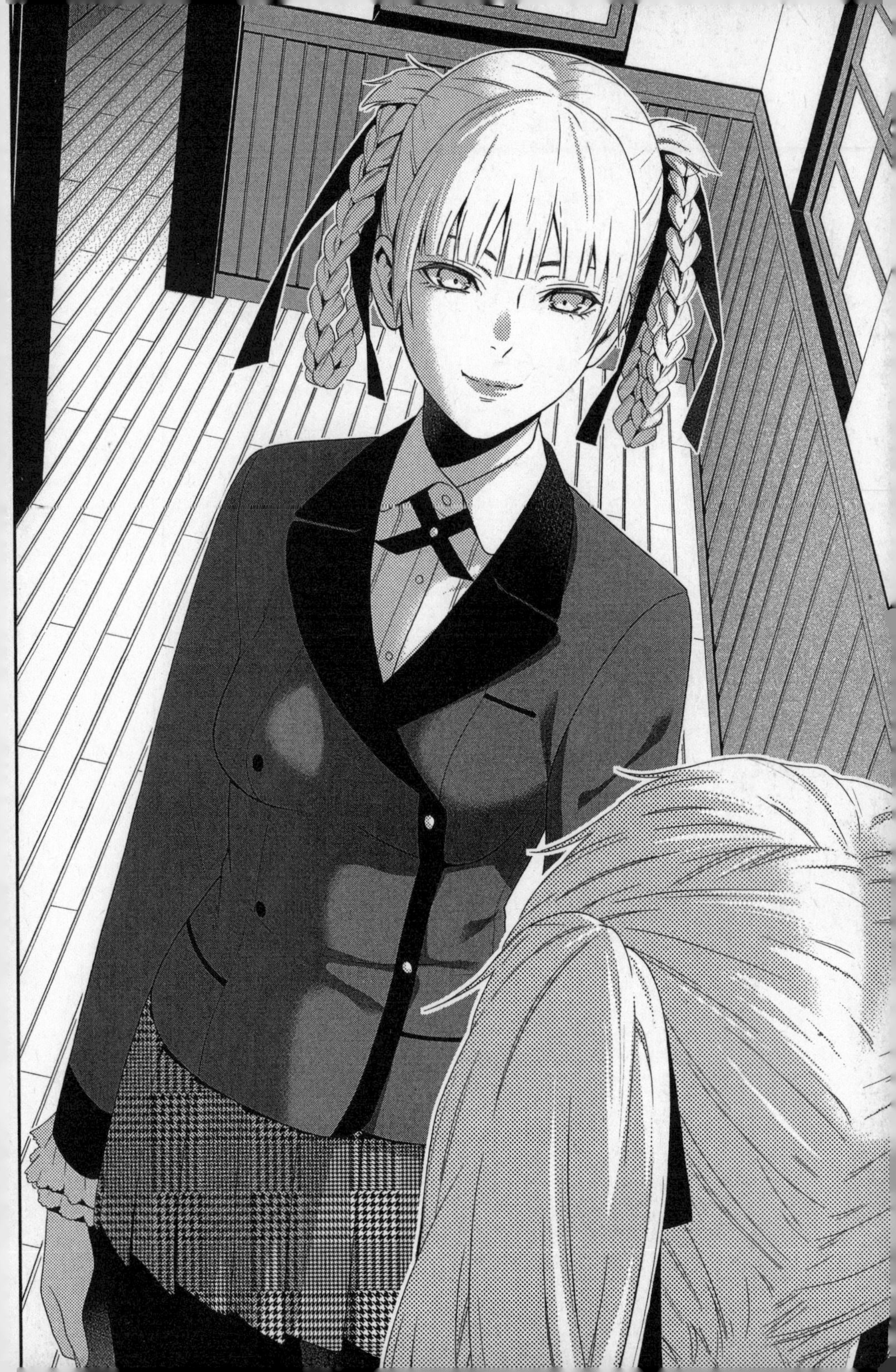

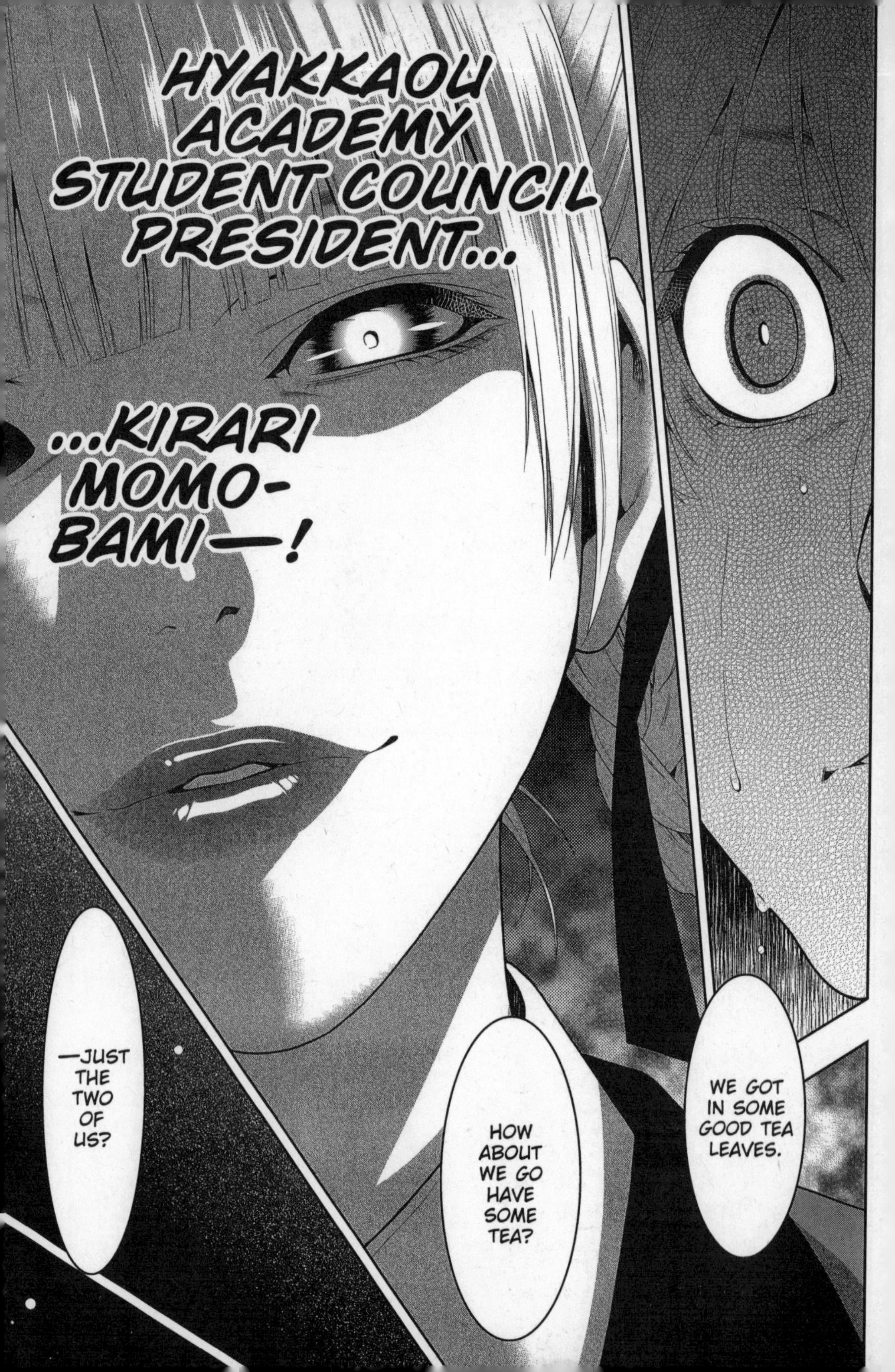
HYAKKAOU ACADEMY STUDENT COUNCIL PRESIDENT...
...KIRARI MOMO-BAMI—!
WE GOT IN SOME GOOD TEA LEAVES.
HOW ABOUT WE GO HAVE SOME TEA?
—JUST THE TWO OF US?

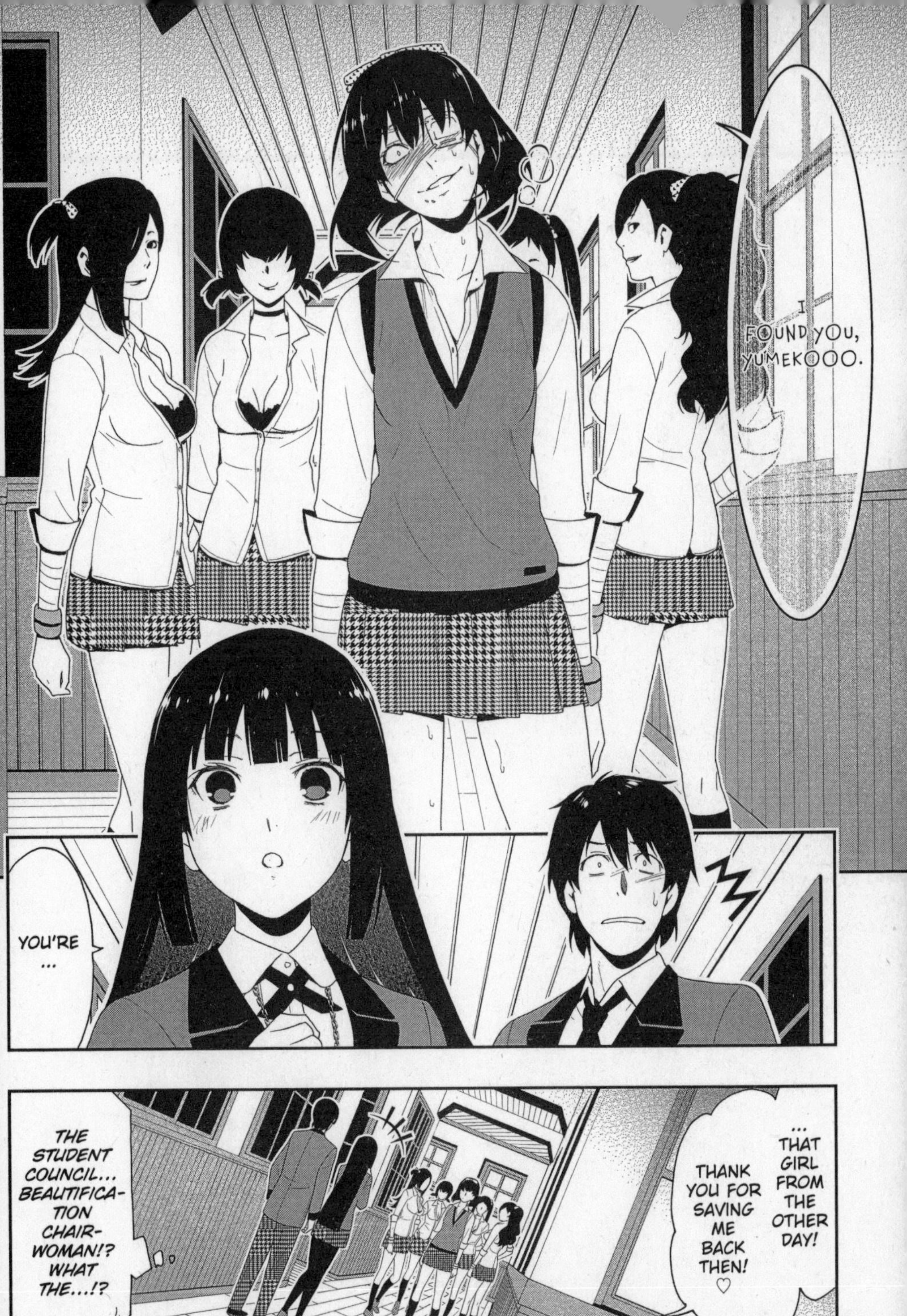
I FOUND YOU, YUMEKOOO.
YOU'RE ...
... THAT GIRL FROM THE OTHER DAY!
THANK YOU FOR SAVING ME BACK THEN! ♡
THE STUDENT COUNCIL... BEAUTIFICATION CHAIRWOMAN!? WHAT THE...!?

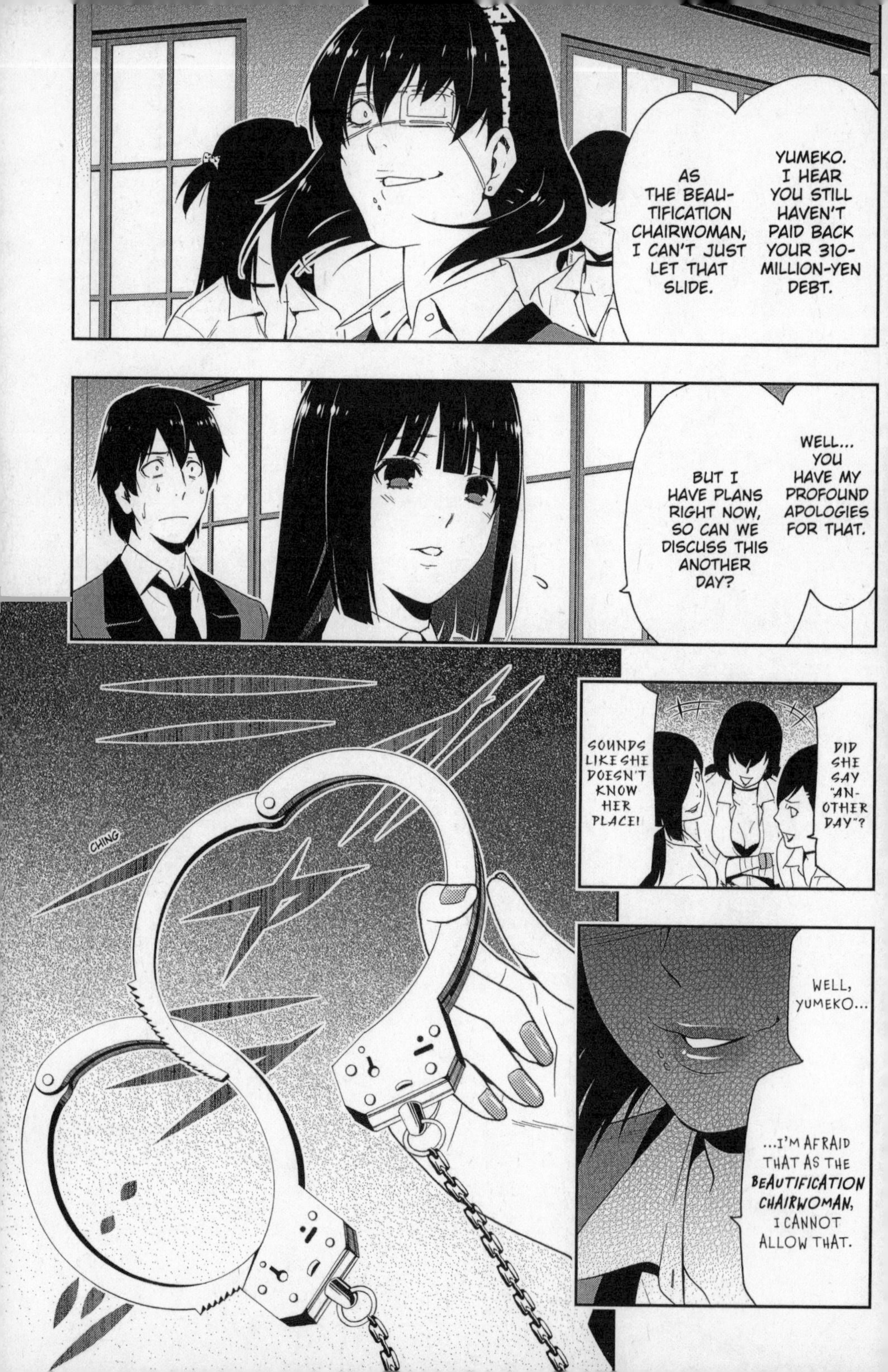
YUMEKO. I HEAR YOU STILL HAVEN'T PAID BACK YOUR 310-MILLION-YEN DEBT.
AS THE BEAU-TIFICATION CHAIRWOMAN, I CAN'T JUST LET THAT SLIDE.
WELL... YOU HAVE MY PROFOUND APOLOGIES FOR THAT.
BUT I HAVE PLANS RIGHT NOW, SO CAN WE DISCUSS THIS ANOTHER DAY?
DID SHE SAY "AN-OTHER DAY"?
SOUNDS LIKE SHE DOESN'T KNOW HER PLACE!
WELL, YUMEKO...
...I'M AFRAID THAT AS THE BEAUTIFICATION CHAIRWOMAN, I CANNOT ALLOW THAT.
CHING

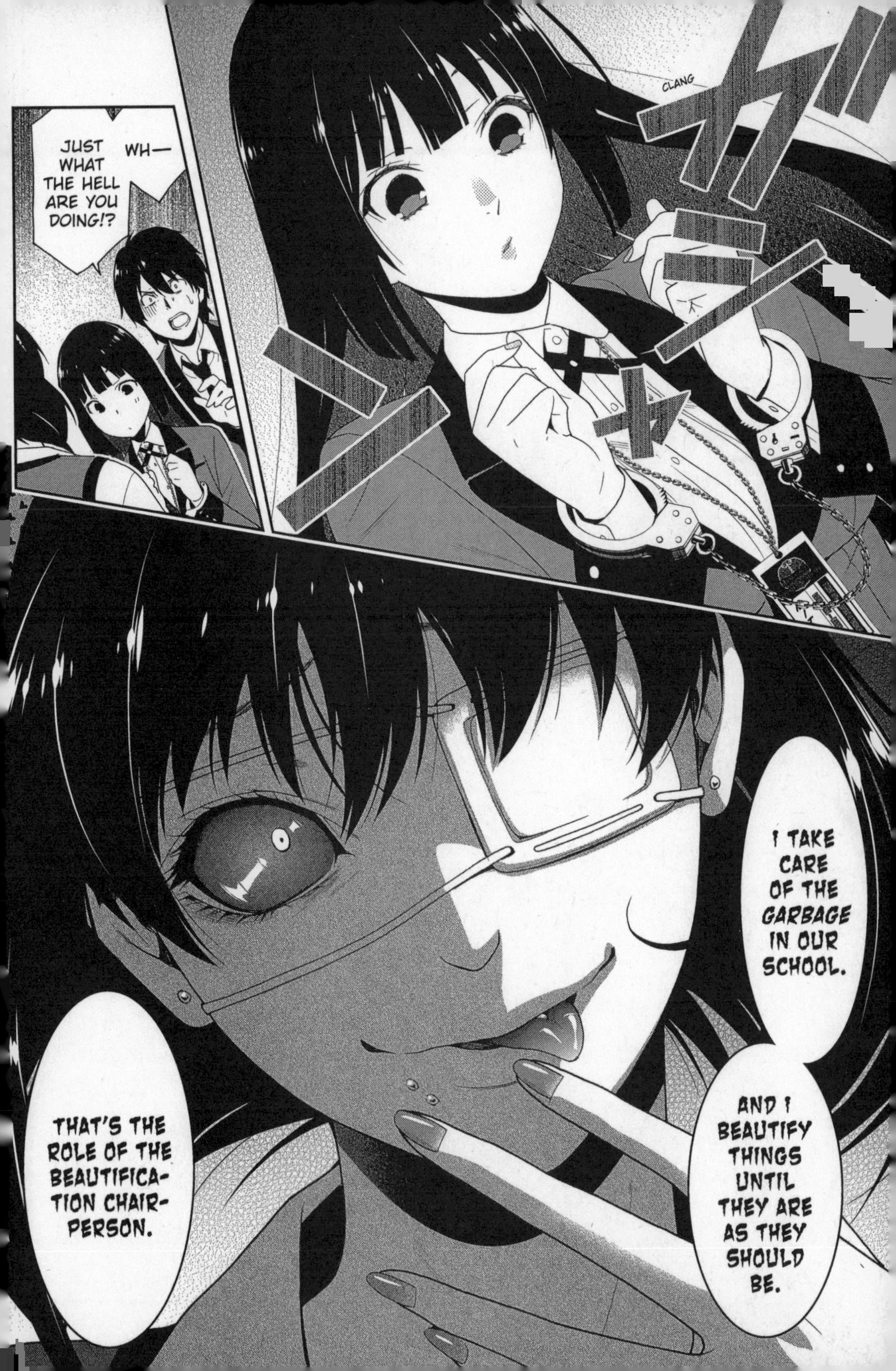

CLANG
WH—
JUST WHAT THE HELL ARE YOU DOING!?
I TAKE CARE OF THE GARBAGE IN OUR SCHOOL.
AND I BEAUTIFY THINGS UNTIL THEY ARE AS THEY SHOULD BE.
THAT'S THE ROLE OF THE BEAUTIFICATION CHAIRPERSON.

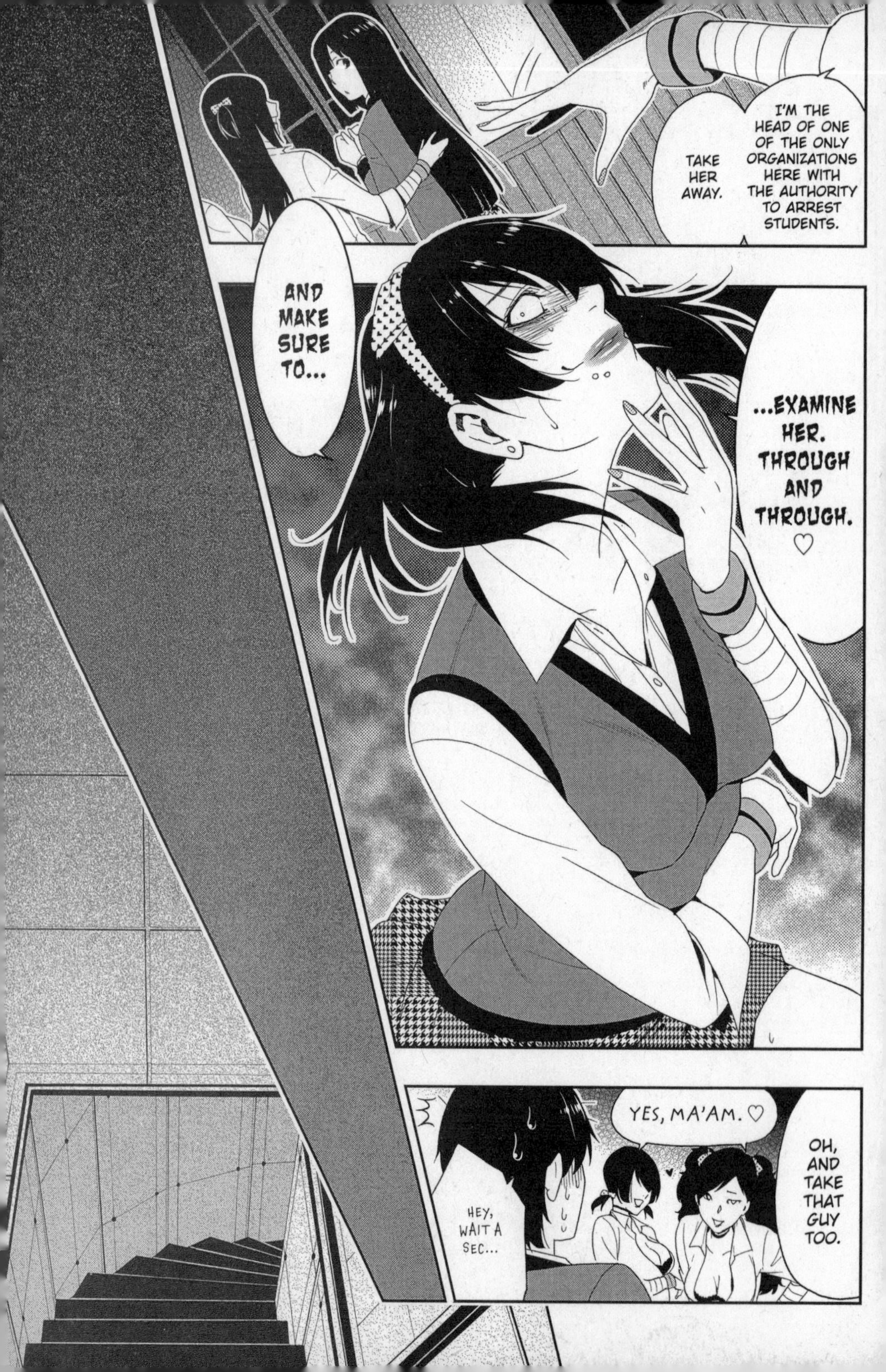
I'M THE HEAD OF ONE OF THE ONLY ORGANIZATIONS HERE WITH THE AUTHORITY TO ARREST STUDENTS.
TAKE HER AWAY.
AND MAKE SURE TO...
...EXAMINE HER. THROUGH AND THROUGH. ♡
OH, AND TAKE THAT GUY TOO.
YES, MA'AM. ♡
HEY, WAIT A SEC...

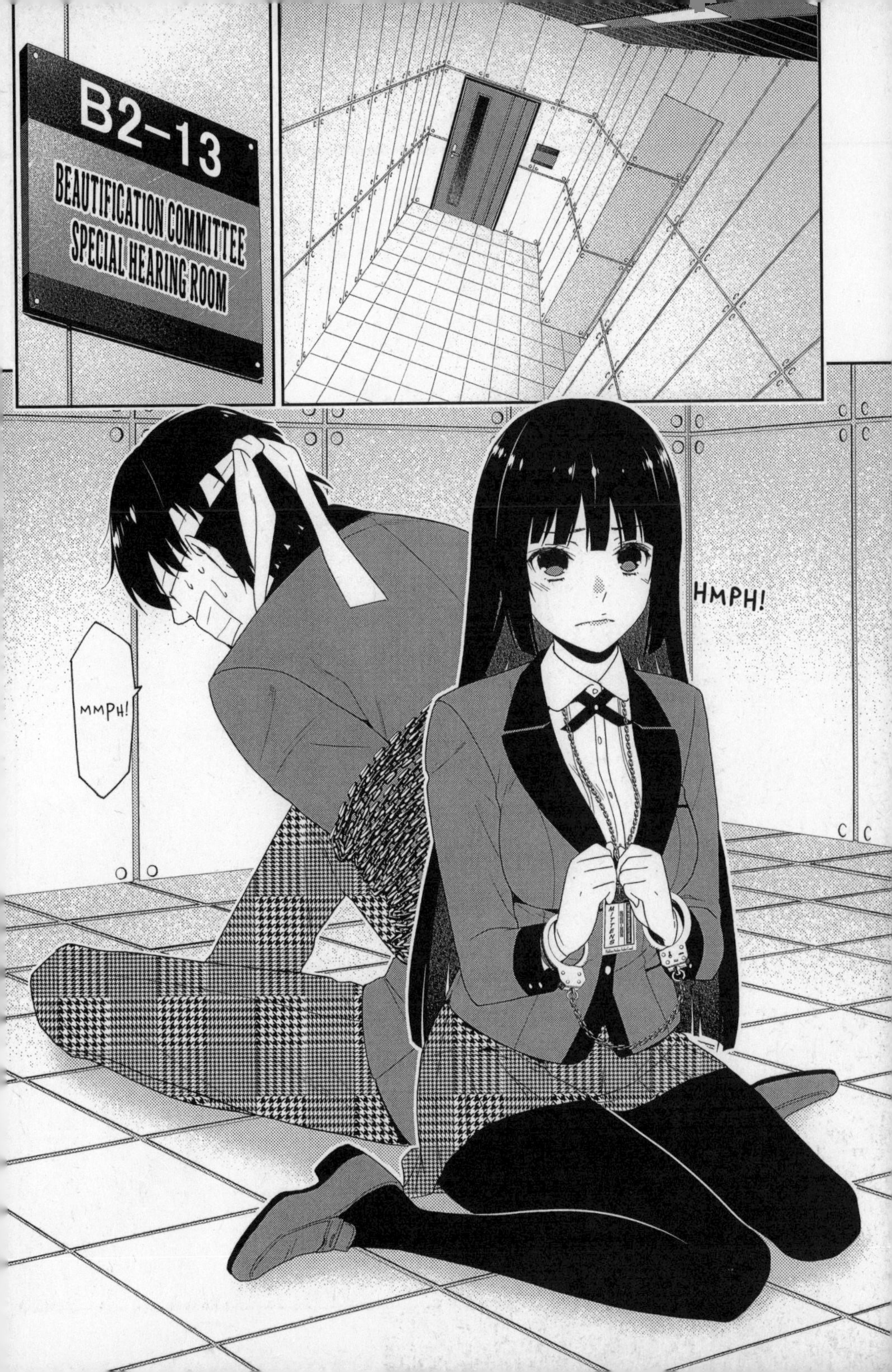
B2-13
BEAUTIFICATION COMMITTEE
SPECIAL HEARING ROOM
HMPH!
MMPH!

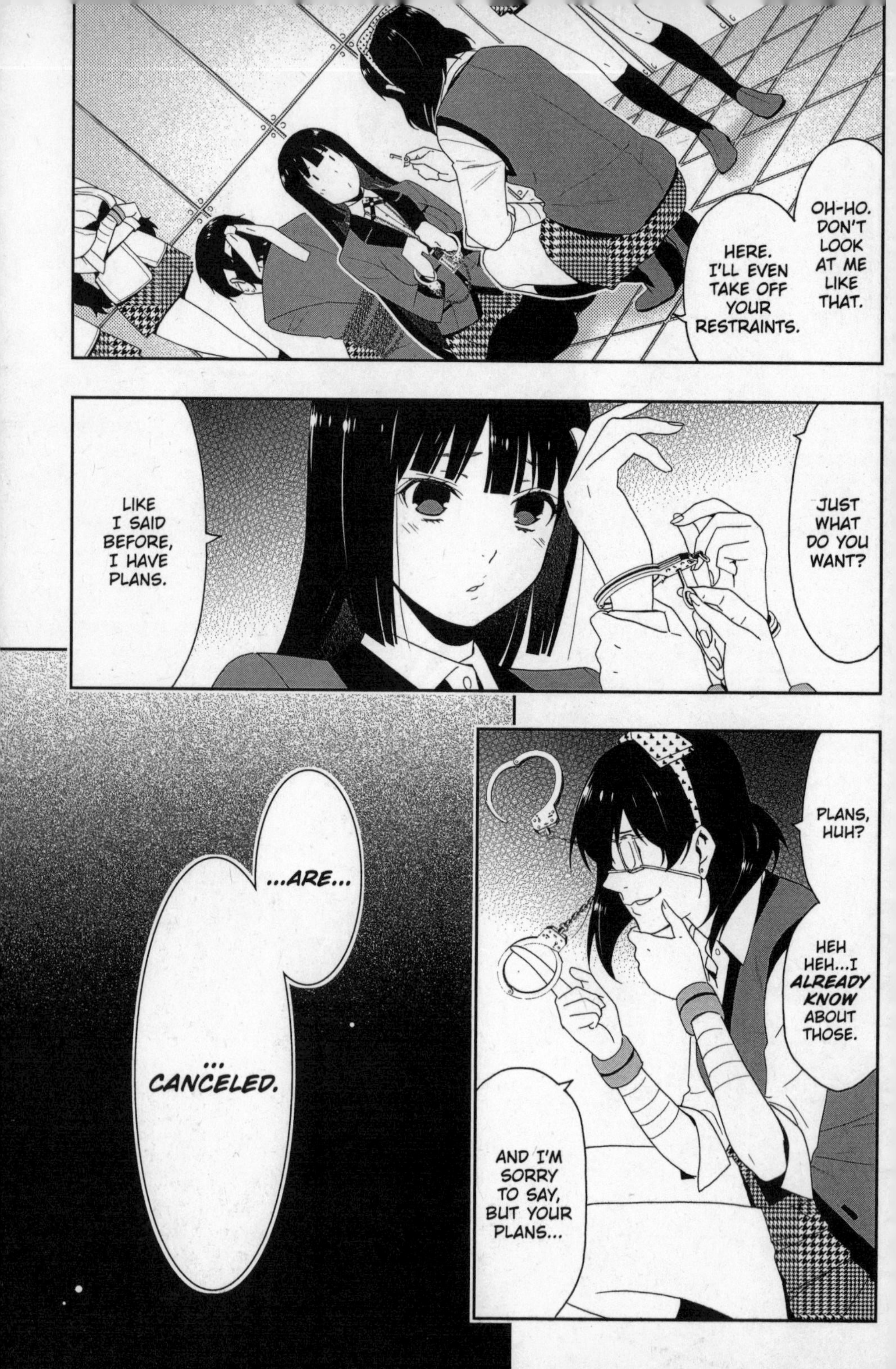
OH-HO. DON'T LOOK AT ME LIKE THAT.
HERE. I'LL EVEN TAKE OFF YOUR RESTRAINTS.
JUST WHAT DO YOU WANT?
LIKE I SAID BEFORE, I HAVE PLANS.
PLANS, HUH?
HEH HEH...I *ALREADY KNOW* ABOUT THOSE.
AND I'M SORRY TO SAY, BUT YOUR PLANS...
...ARE...
... CANCELED.

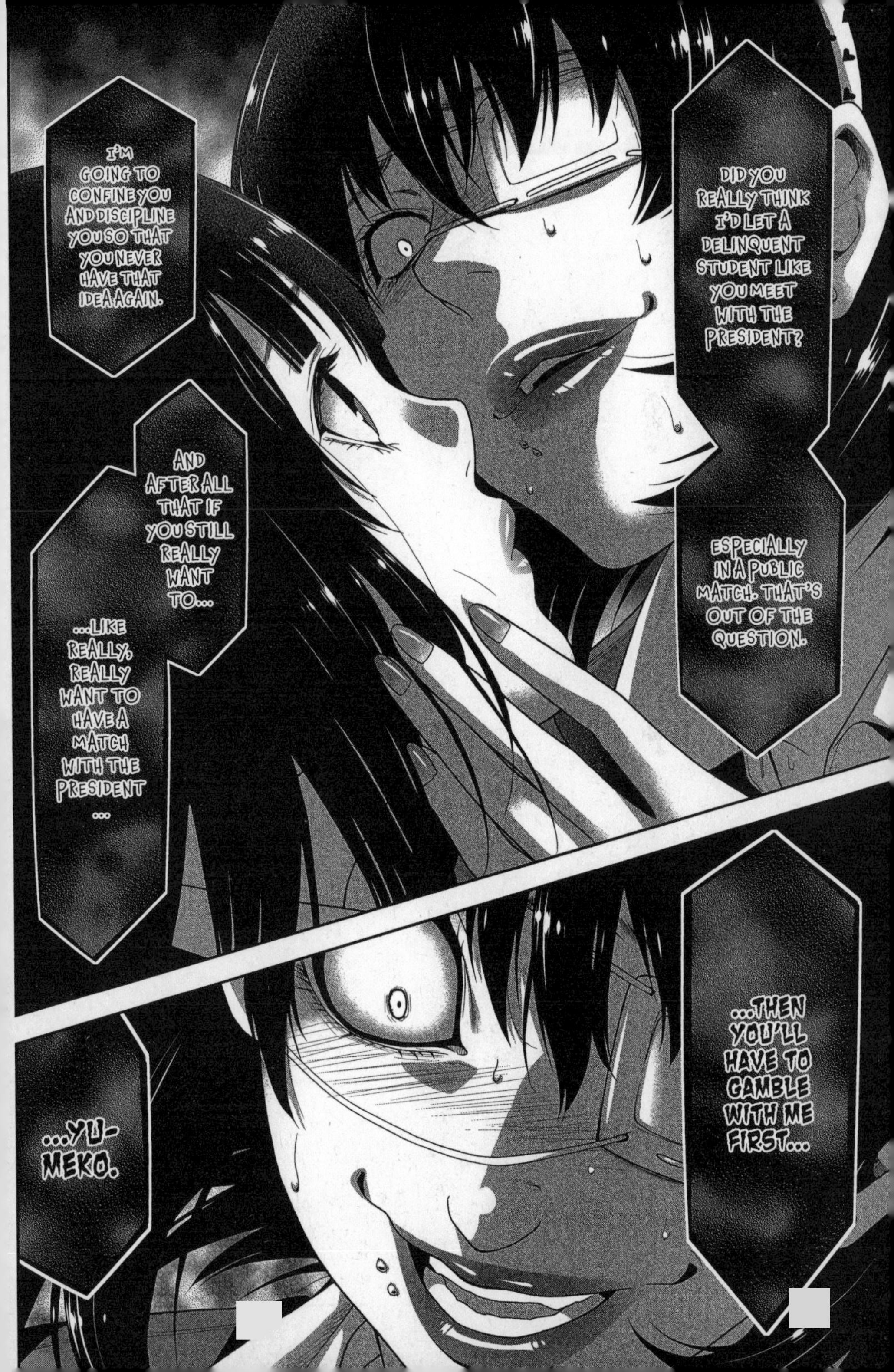
DID YOU REALLY THINK I'D LET A DELINQUENT STUDENT LIKE YOU MEET WITH THE PRESIDENT?
ESPECIALLY IN A PUBLIC MATCH. THAT'S OUT OF THE QUESTION.
I'M GOING TO CONFINE YOU AND DISCIPLINE YOU SO THAT YOU NEVER HAVE THAT IDEA AGAIN.
AND AFTER ALL THAT IF YOU STILL REALLY WANT TO...
...LIKE REALLY, REALLY WANT TO HAVE A MATCH WITH THE PRESIDENT...
...THEN YOU'LL HAVE TO GAMBLE WITH ME FIRST...
...YU-MEKO.

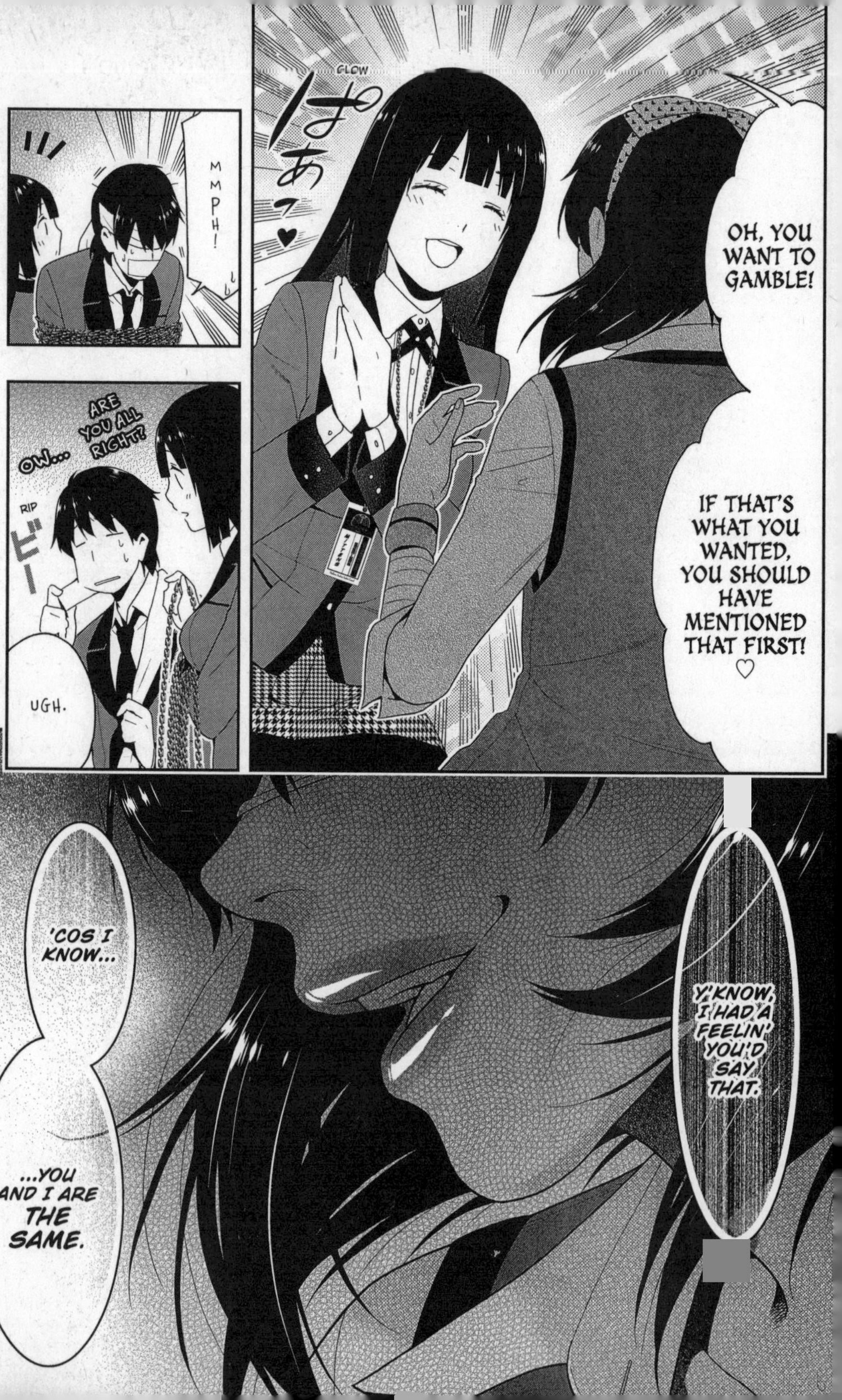
GLOW
ぱあっ♥
OH, YOU WANT TO GAMBLE!
IF THAT'S WHAT YOU WANTED, YOU SHOULD HAVE MENTIONED THAT FIRST! ♡
MMPH!
ARE YOU ALL RIGHT?
OW...
RIP
ビー
UGH.
Y'KNOW, I HAD A FEELIN' YOU'D SAY THAT.
'COS I KNOW...
...YOU AND I ARE THE SAME.

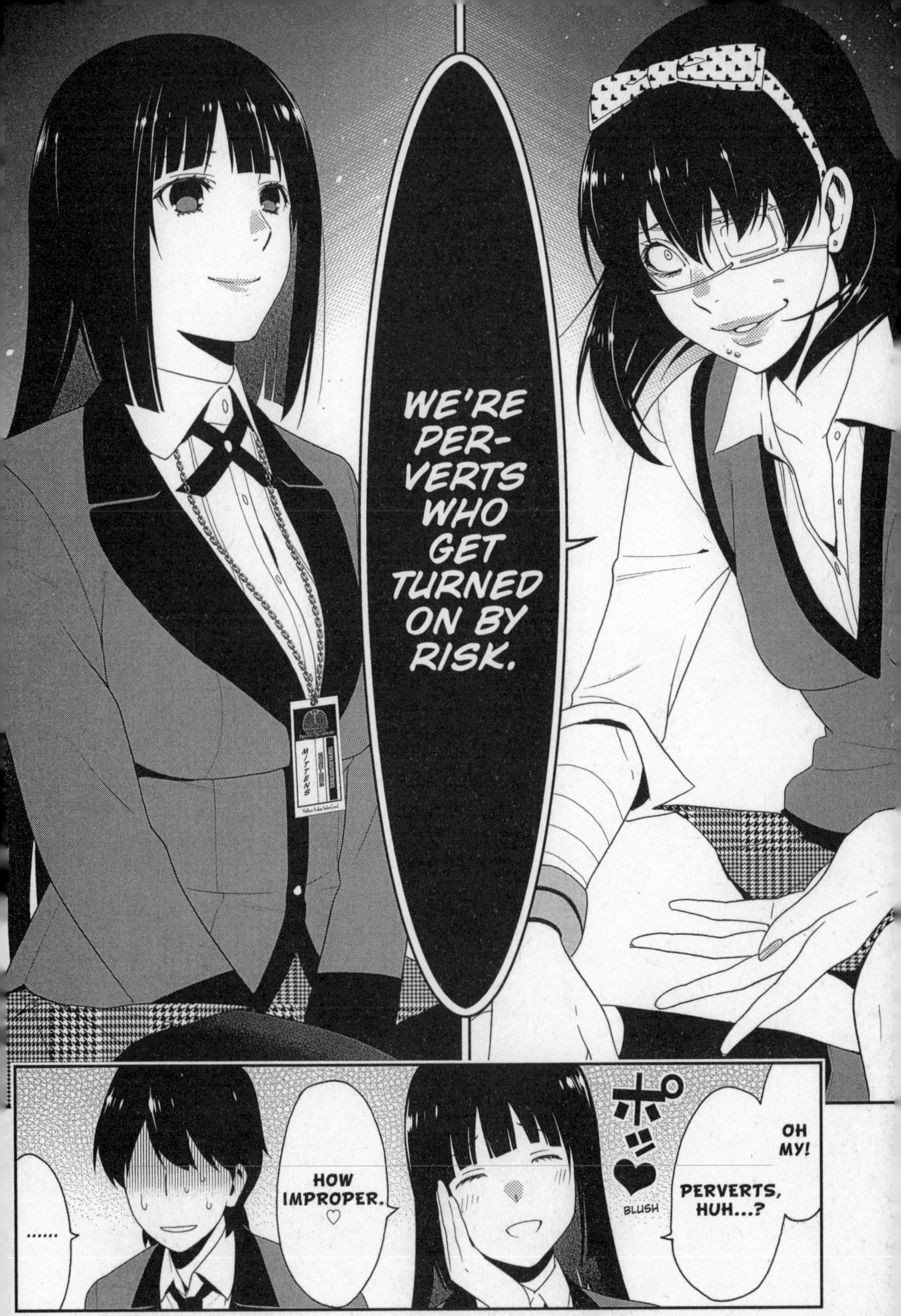
WE'RE PERVERTS WHO GET TURNED ON BY RISK.
OH MY!
PERVERTS, HUH...?
BLUSH
HOW IMPROPER. ♡
......

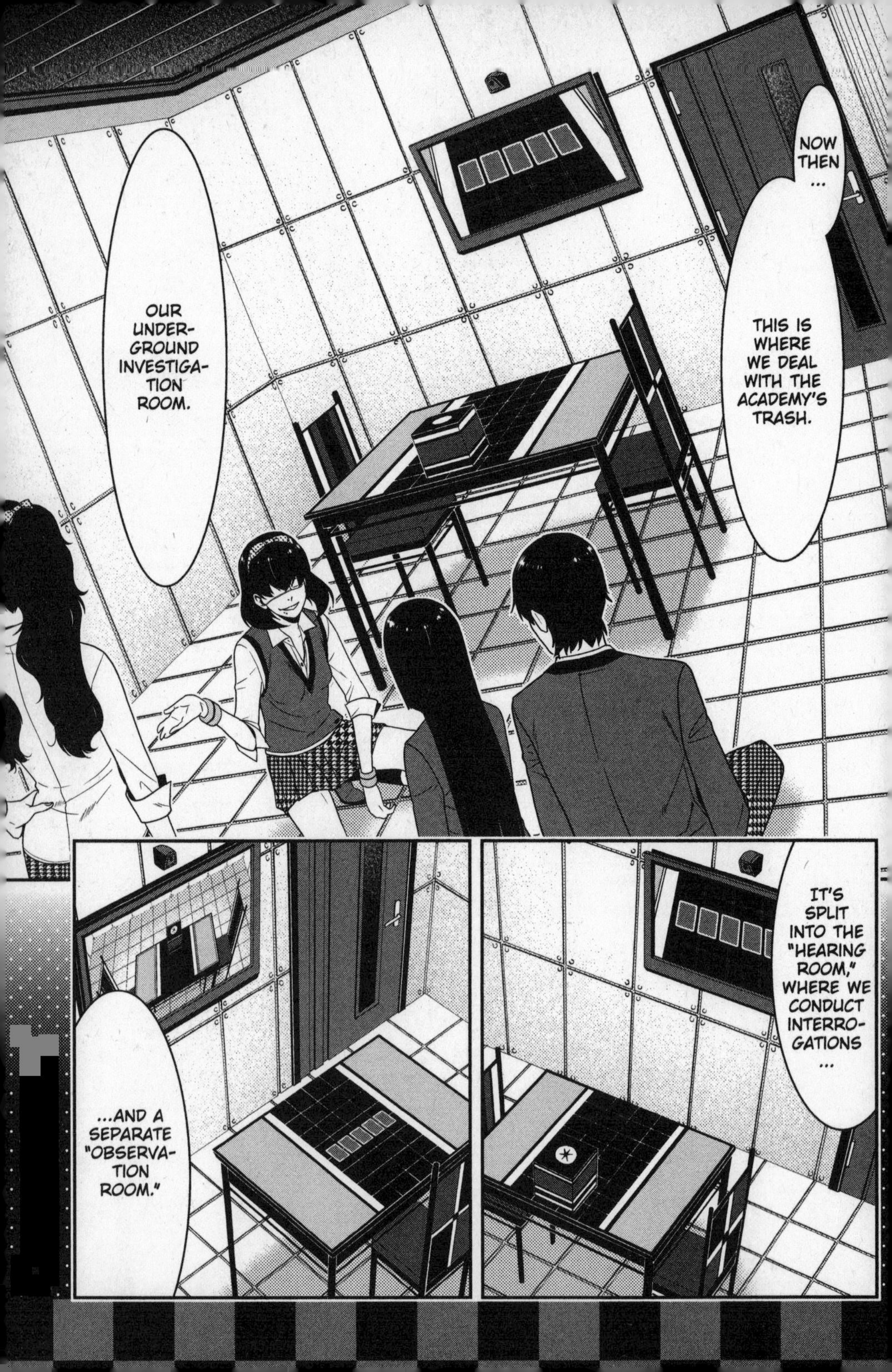
NOW THEN ...
THIS IS WHERE WE DEAL WITH THE ACADEMY'S TRASH.
OUR UNDER-GROUND INVESTIGA-TION ROOM.
IT'S SPLIT INTO THE "HEARING ROOM," WHERE WE CONDUCT INTERRO-GATIONS ...
...AND A SEPARATE "OBSERVA-TION ROOM."

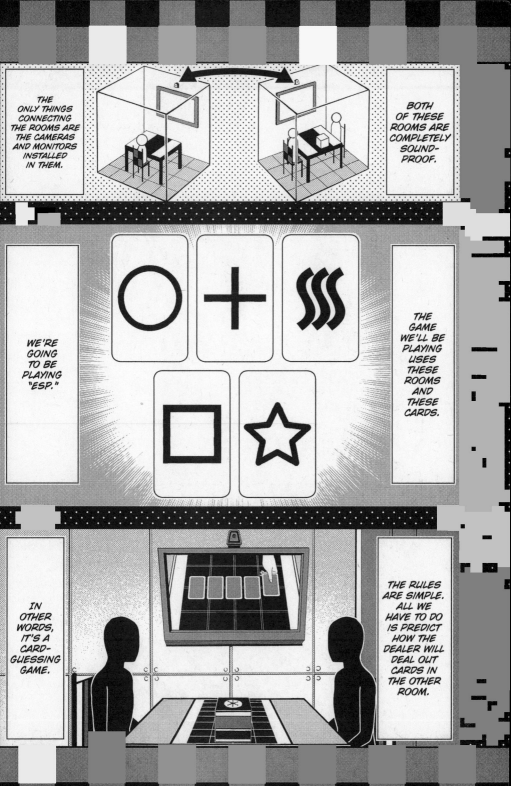

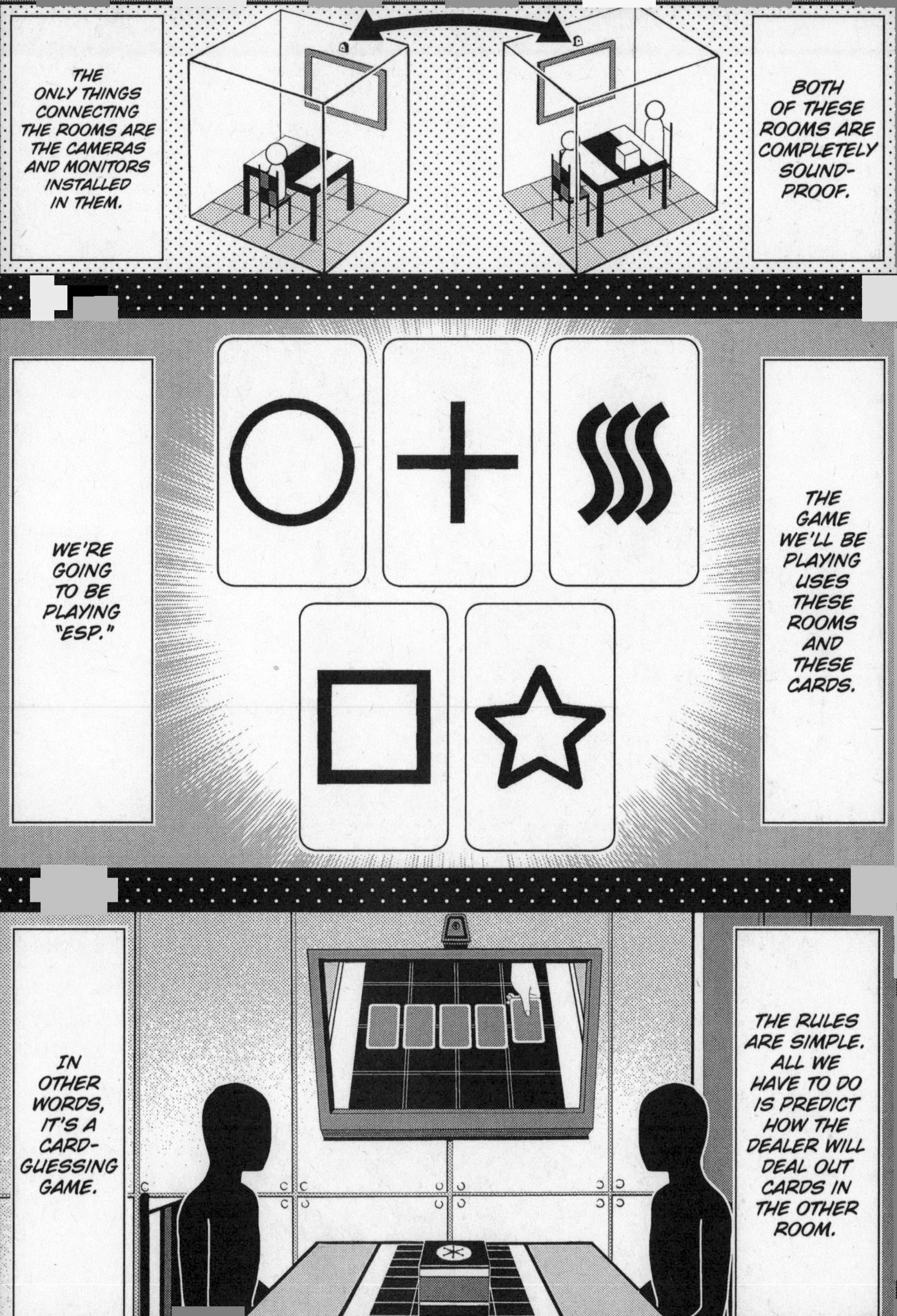
BOTH OF THESE ROOMS ARE COMPLETELY SOUND-PROOF.
THE ONLY THINGS CONNECTING THE ROOMS ARE THE CAMERAS AND MONITORS INSTALLED IN THEM.
THE GAME WE'LL BE PLAYING USES THESE ROOMS AND THESE CARDS.
WE'RE GOING TO BE PLAYING "ESP."
THE RULES ARE SIMPLE. ALL WE HAVE TO DO IS PREDICT HOW THE DEALER WILL DEAL OUT CARDS IN THE OTHER ROOM.
IN OTHER WORDS, IT'S A CARD-GUESSING GAME.

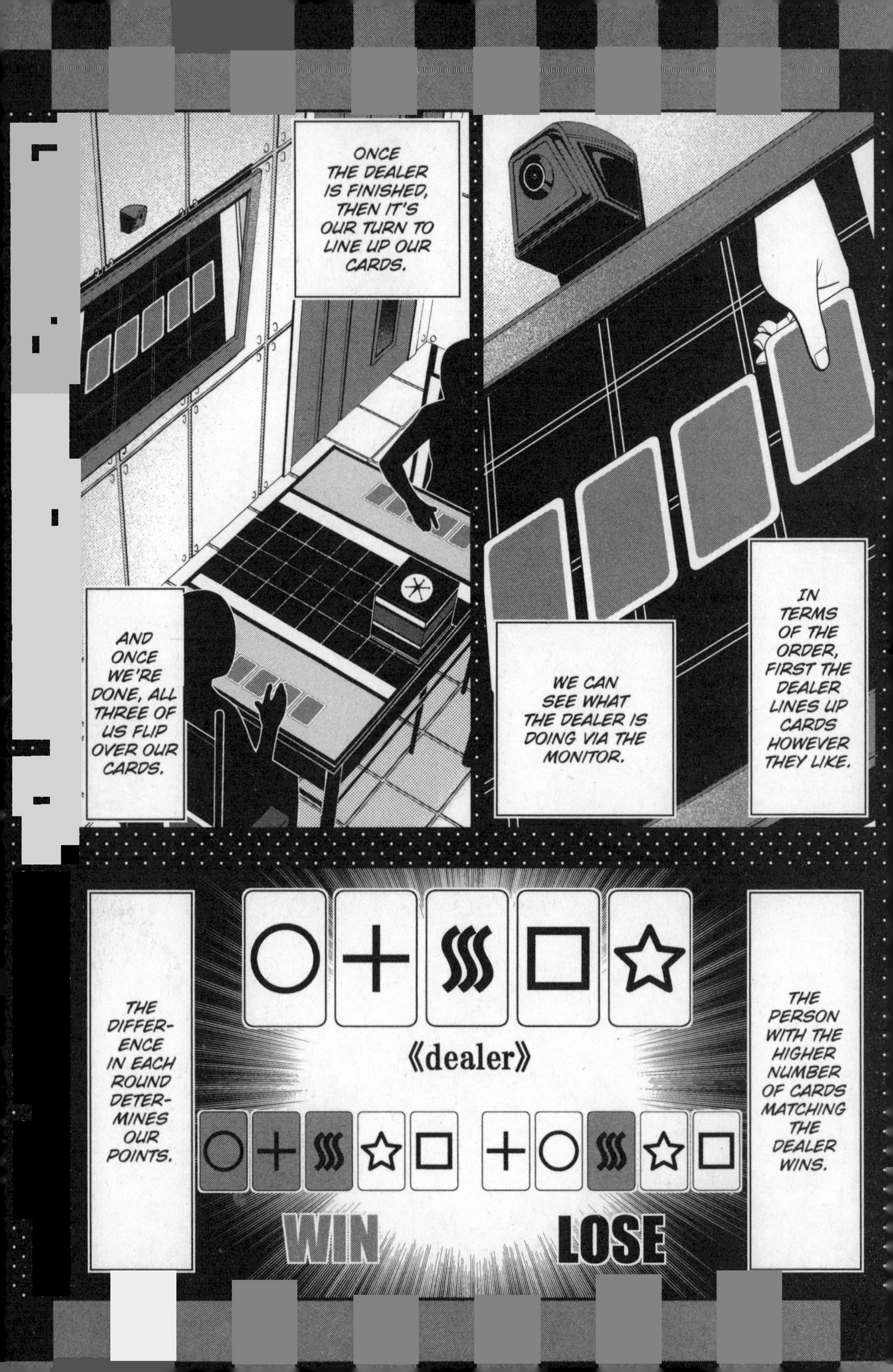
IN TERMS OF THE ORDER, FIRST THE DEALER LINES UP CARDS HOWEVER THEY LIKE.
WE CAN SEE WHAT THE DEALER IS DOING VIA THE MONITOR.
ONCE THE DEALER IS FINISHED, THEN IT'S OUR TURN TO LINE UP OUR CARDS.
AND ONCE WE'RE DONE, ALL THREE OF US FLIP OVER OUR CARDS.
THE PERSON WITH THE HIGHER NUMBER OF CARDS MATCHING THE DEALER WINS.
《dealer》
LOSE
WIN
THE DIFFERENCE IN EACH ROUND DETERMINES OUR POINTS.

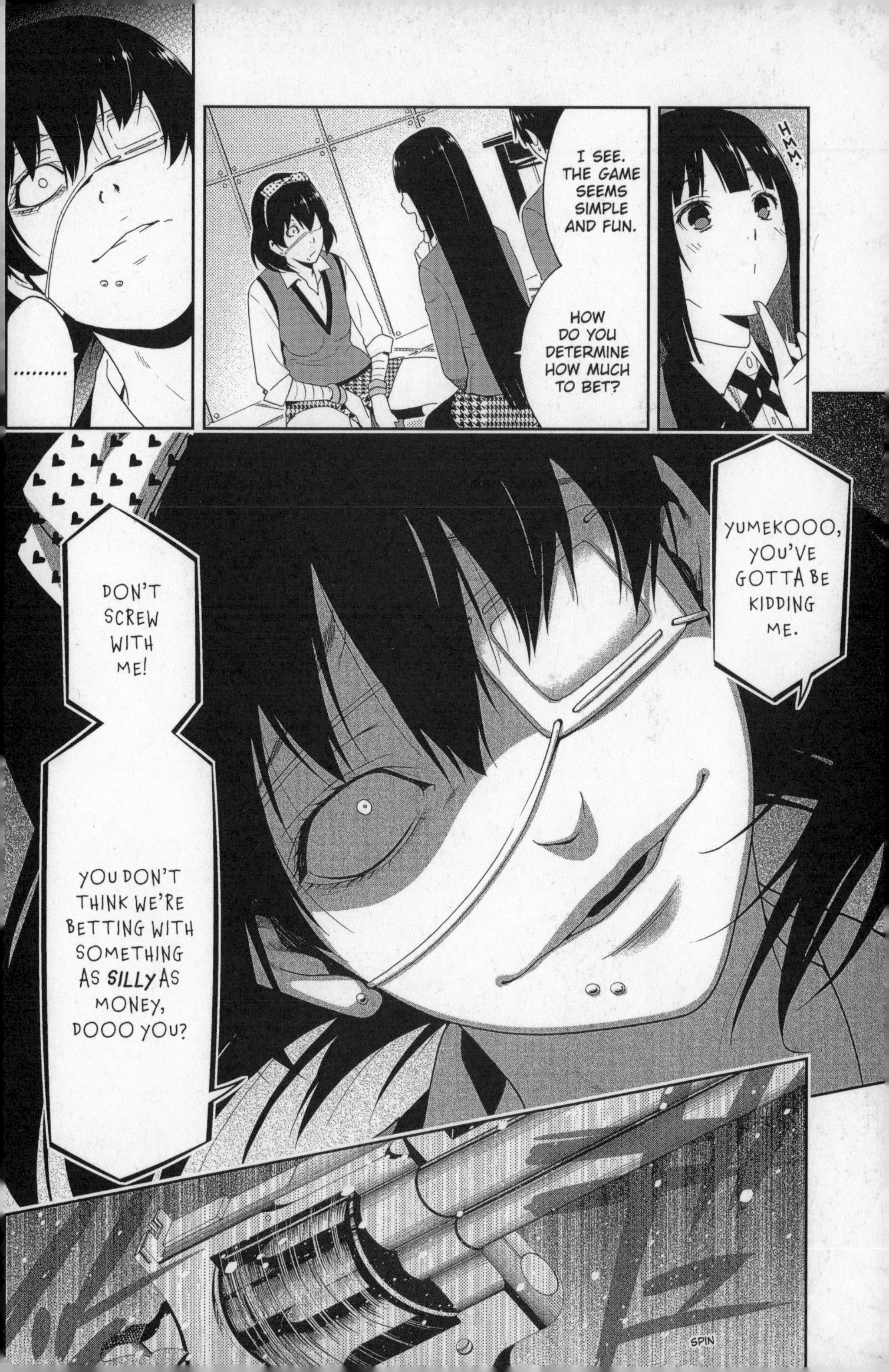
HMM.
I SEE. THE GAME SEEMS SIMPLE AND FUN.
HOW DO YOU DETERMINE HOW MUCH TO BET?
....
YUMEKOOO, YOU'VE GOTTA BE KIDDING ME.
DON'T SCREW WITH ME!
YOU DON'T THINK WE'RE BETTING WITH SOMETHING AS SILLY AS MONEY, DOOO YOU?
SPIN

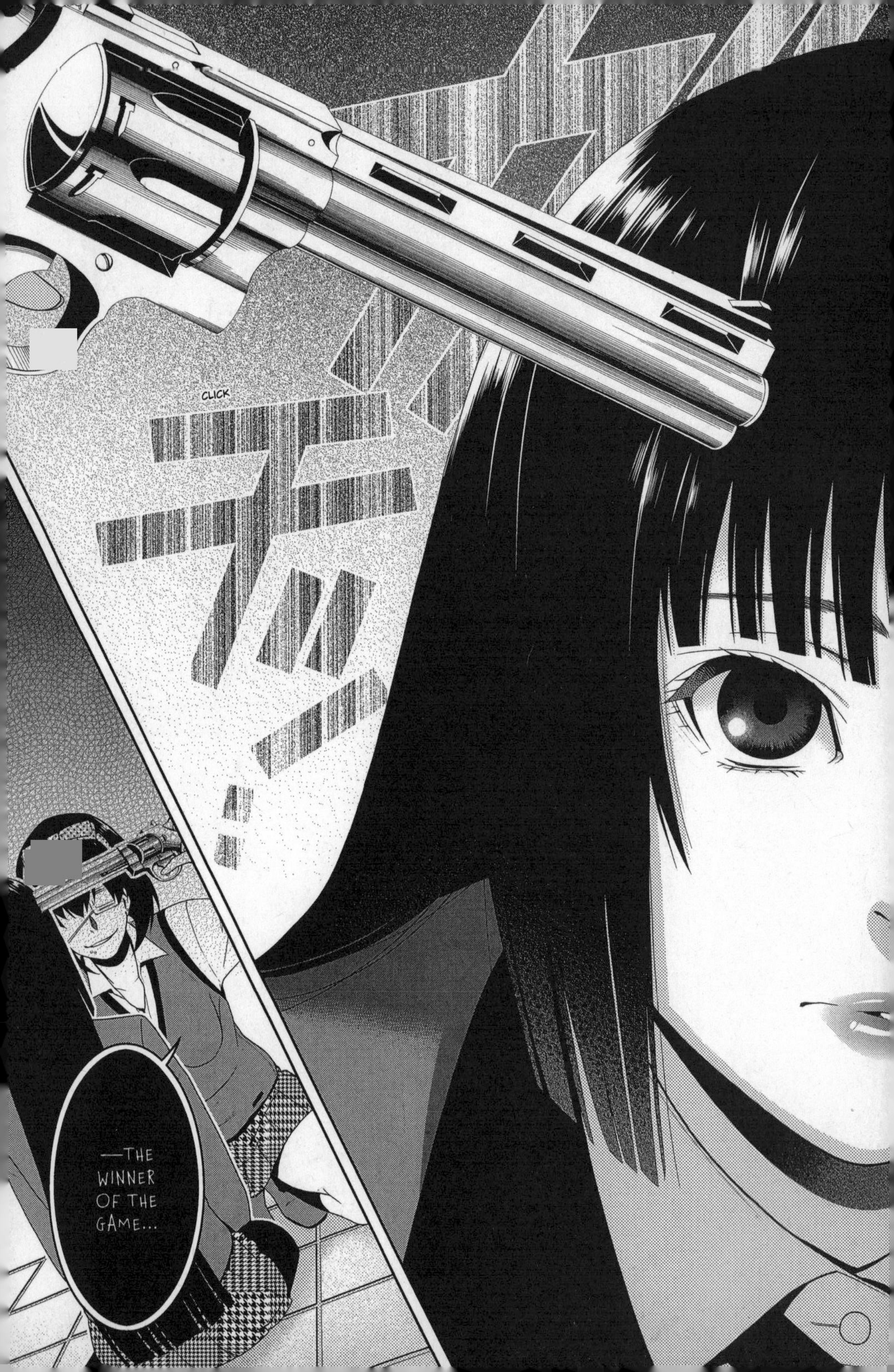
CLICK
—THE WINNER OF THE GAME...

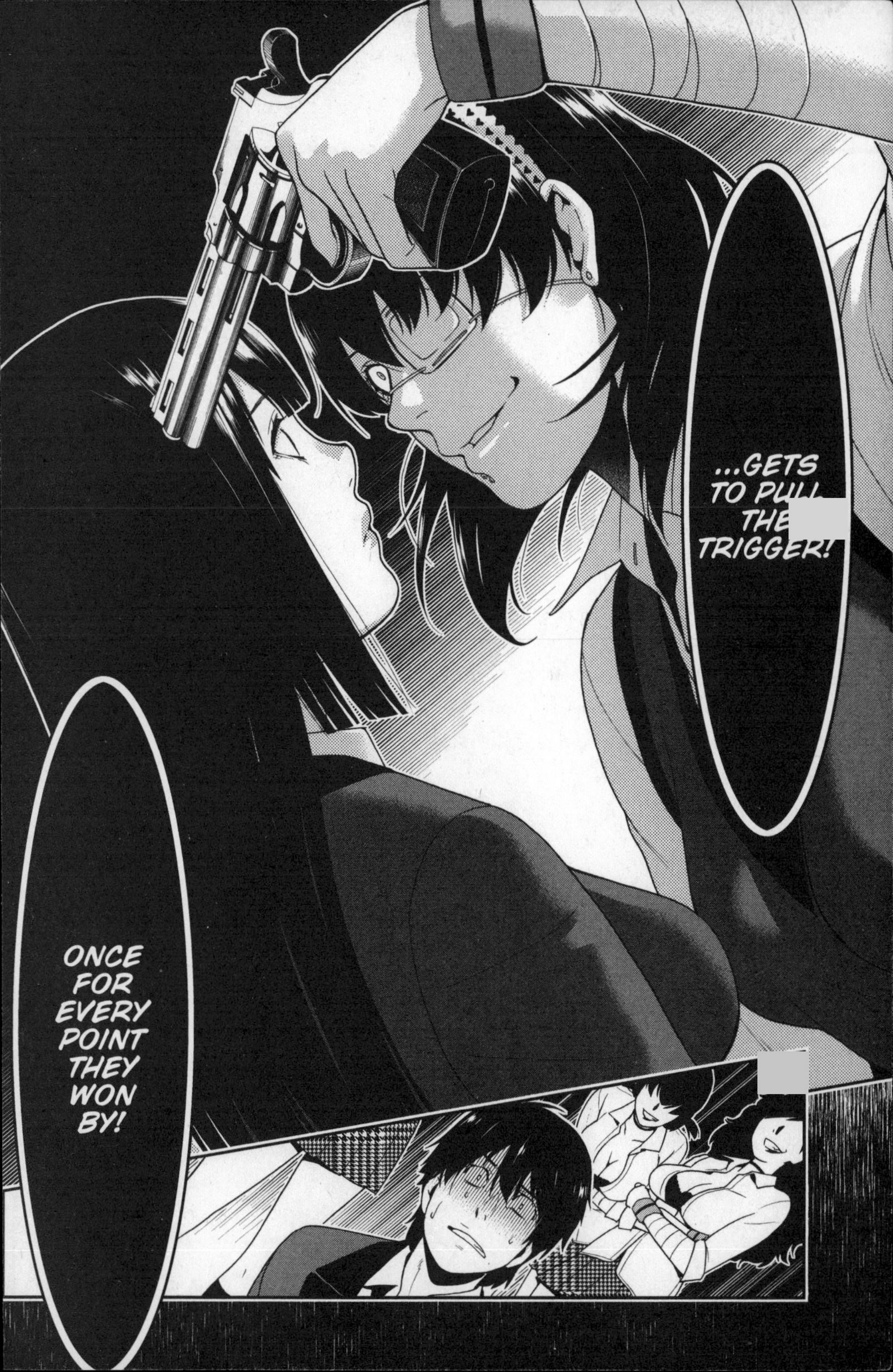
...GETS TO PULL THE TRIGGER!
ONCE FOR EVERY POINT THEY WON BY!

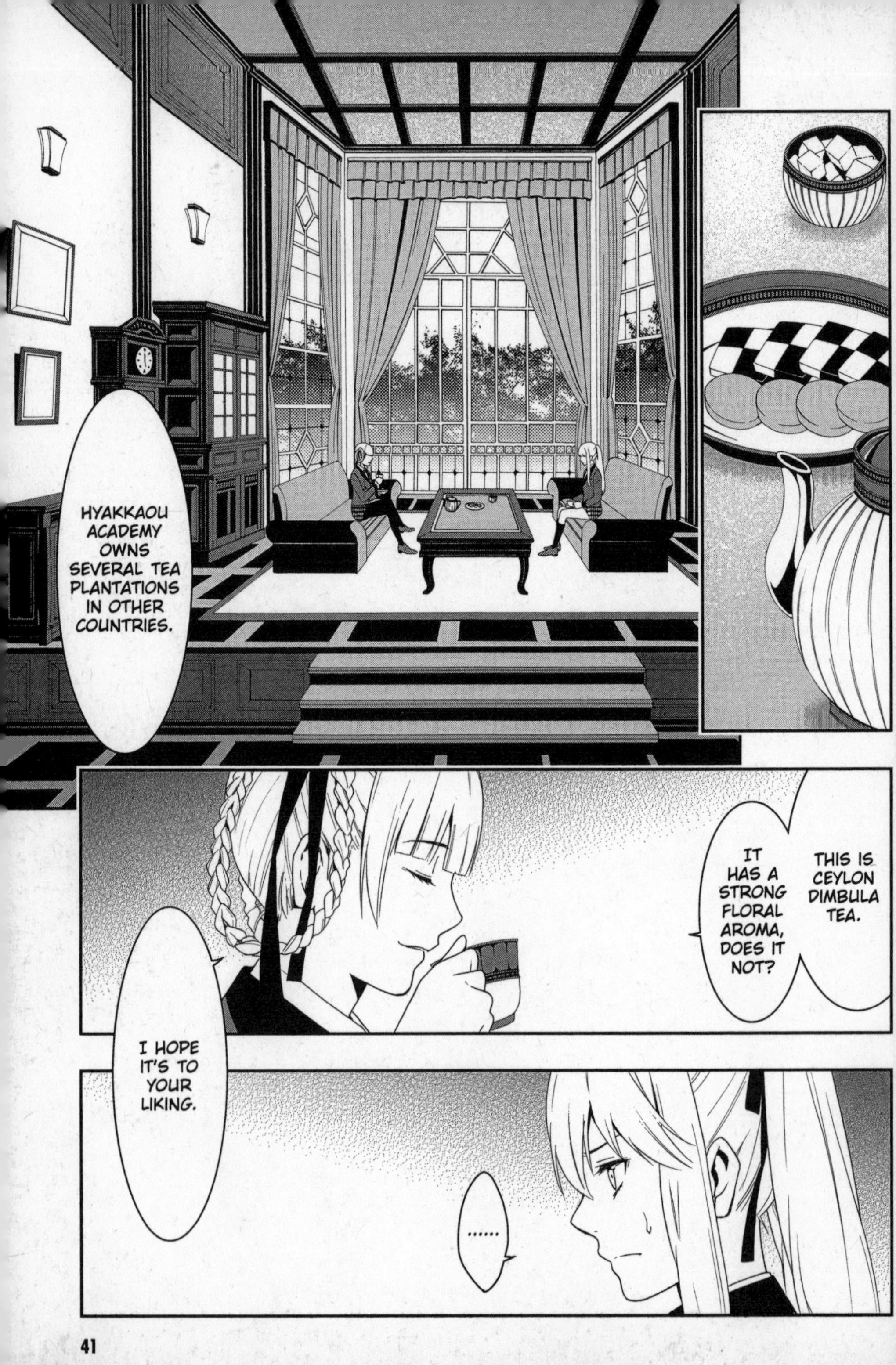
HYAKKAOU ACADEMY OWNS SEVERAL TEA PLANTATIONS IN OTHER COUNTRIES.
THIS IS CEYLON DIMBULA TEA.
IT HAS A STRONG FLORAL AROMA, DOES IT NOT?
I HOPE IT'S TO YOUR LIKING.
......

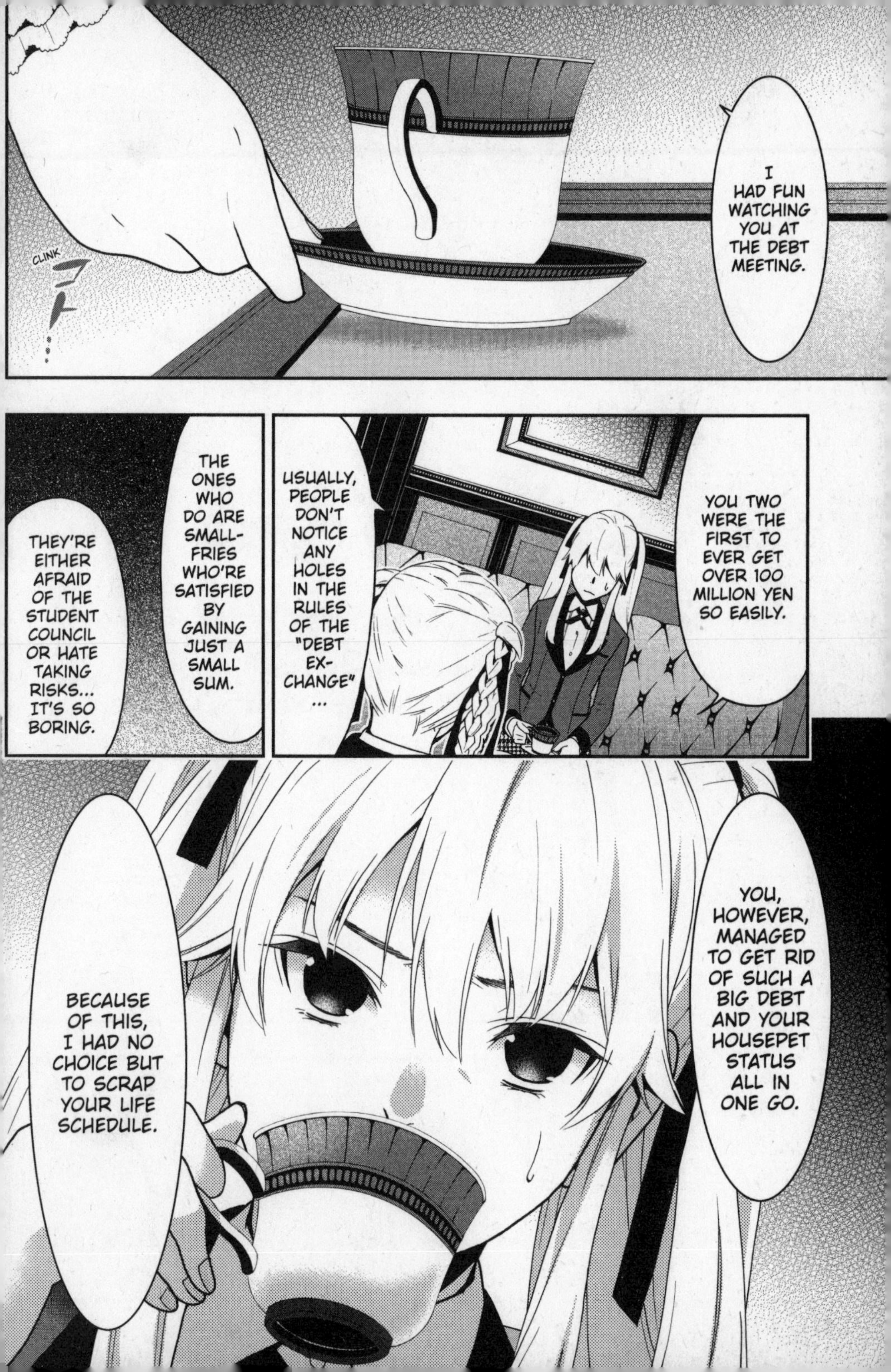
I HAD FUN WATCHING YOU AT THE DEBT MEETING.
CLINK
YOU TWO WERE THE FIRST TO EVER GET OVER 100 MILLION YEN SO EASILY.
USUALLY, PEOPLE DON'T NOTICE ANY HOLES IN THE RULES OF THE "DEBT EX-CHANGE"...
THE ONES WHO DO ARE SMALL-FRIES WHO'RE SATISFIED BY GAINING JUST A SMALL SUM.
THEY'RE EITHER AFRAID OF THE STUDENT COUNCIL OR HATE TAKING RISKS... IT'S SO BORING.
YOU, HOWEVER, MANAGED TO GET RID OF SUCH A BIG DEBT AND YOUR HOUSEPET STATUS ALL IN ONE GO.
BECAUSE OF THIS, I HAD NO CHOICE BUT TO SCRAP YOUR LIFE SCHEDULE.

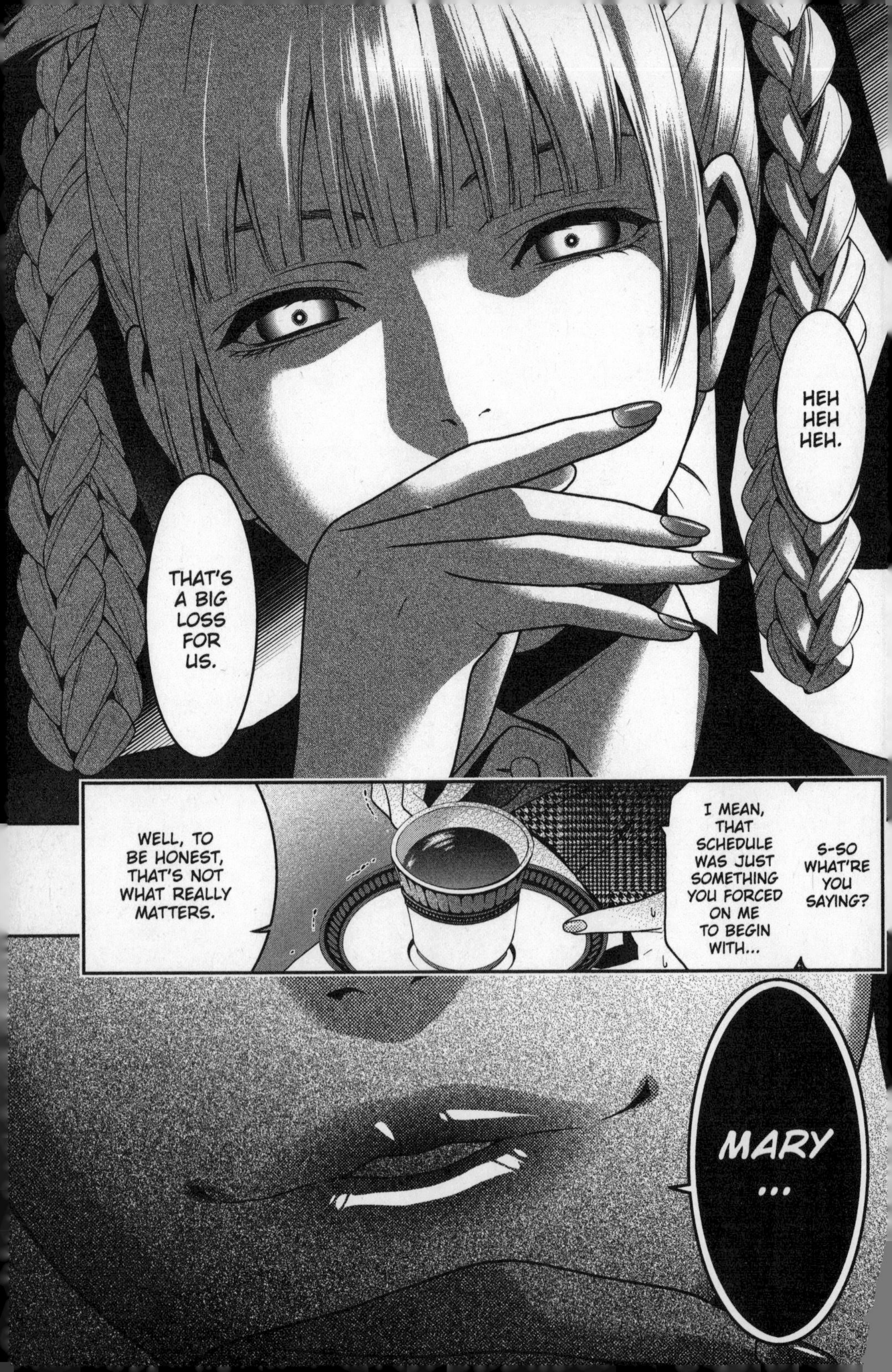
HEH HEH HEH.
THAT'S A BIG LOSS FOR US.
S-SO WHAT'RE YOU SAYING?
I MEAN, THAT SCHEDULE WAS JUST SOMETHING YOU FORCED ON ME TO BEGIN WITH...
WELL, TO BE HONEST, THAT'S NOT WHAT REALLY MATTERS.
MARY ...

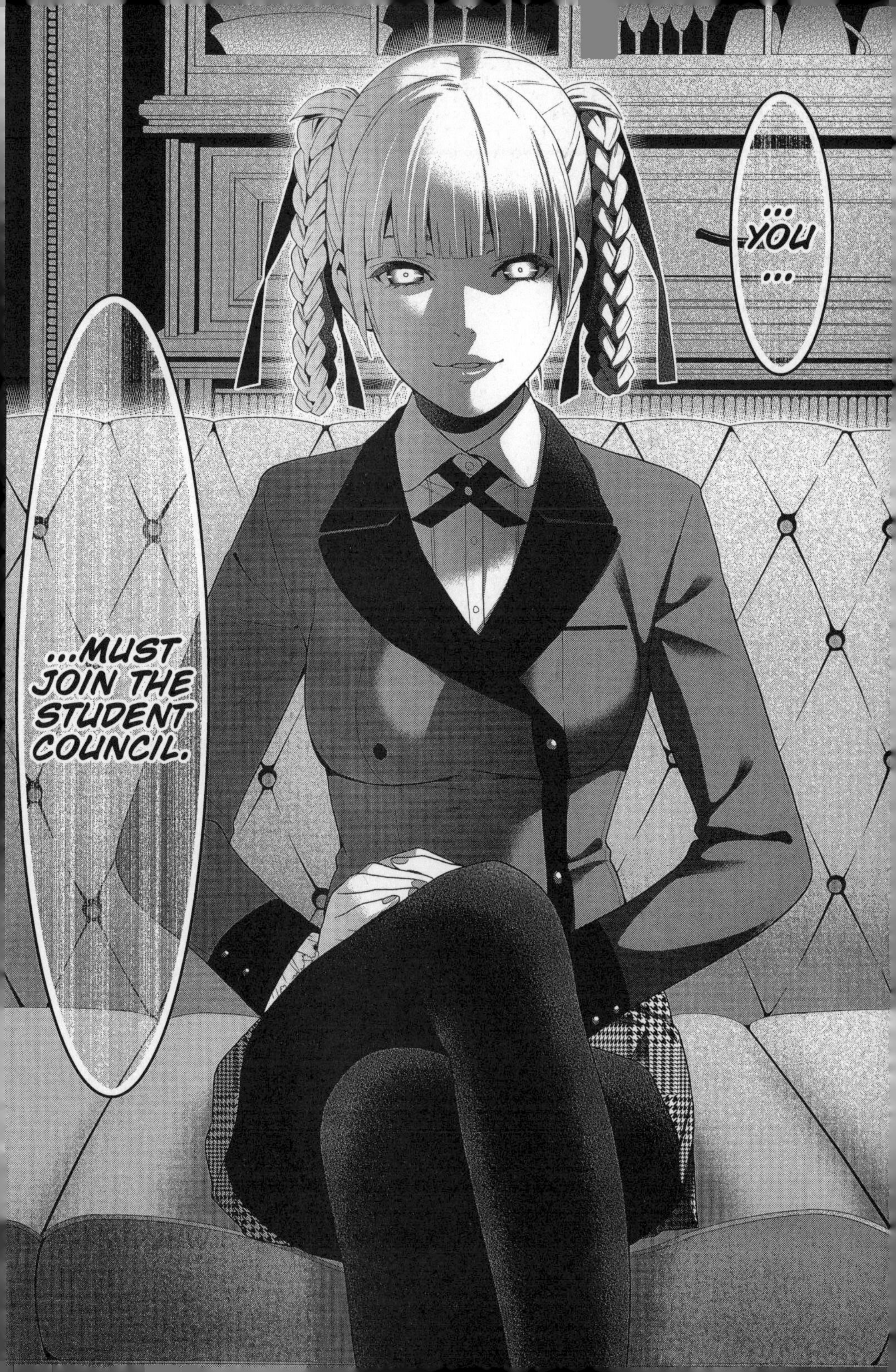
...YOU...
...MUST JOIN THE STUDENT COUNCIL.

CHAPTER ELEVEN
EXCITED GIRL

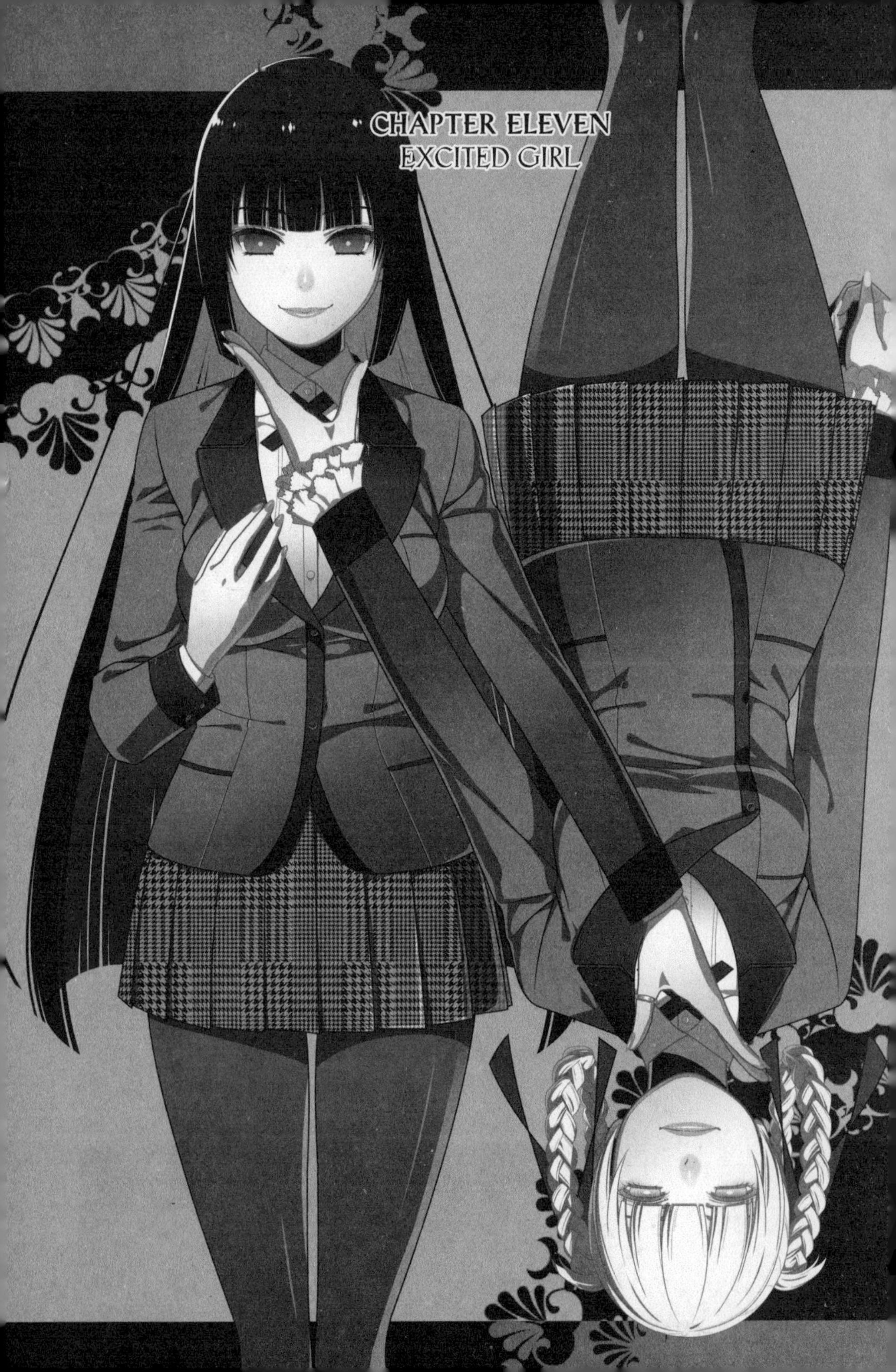

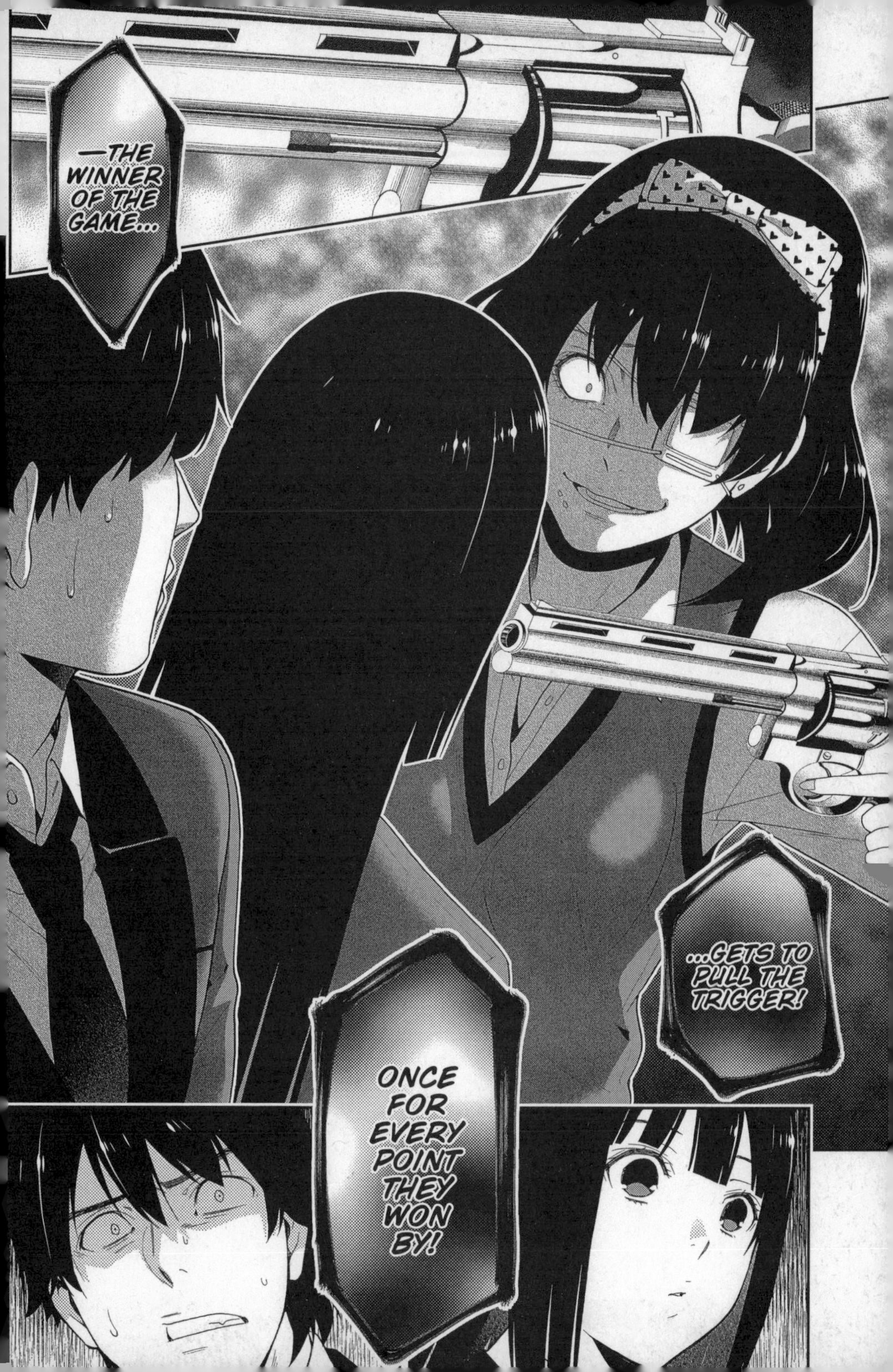
—THE WINNER OF THE GAME...
...GETS TO PULL THE TRIGGER!
ONCE FOR EVERY POINT THEY WON BY!

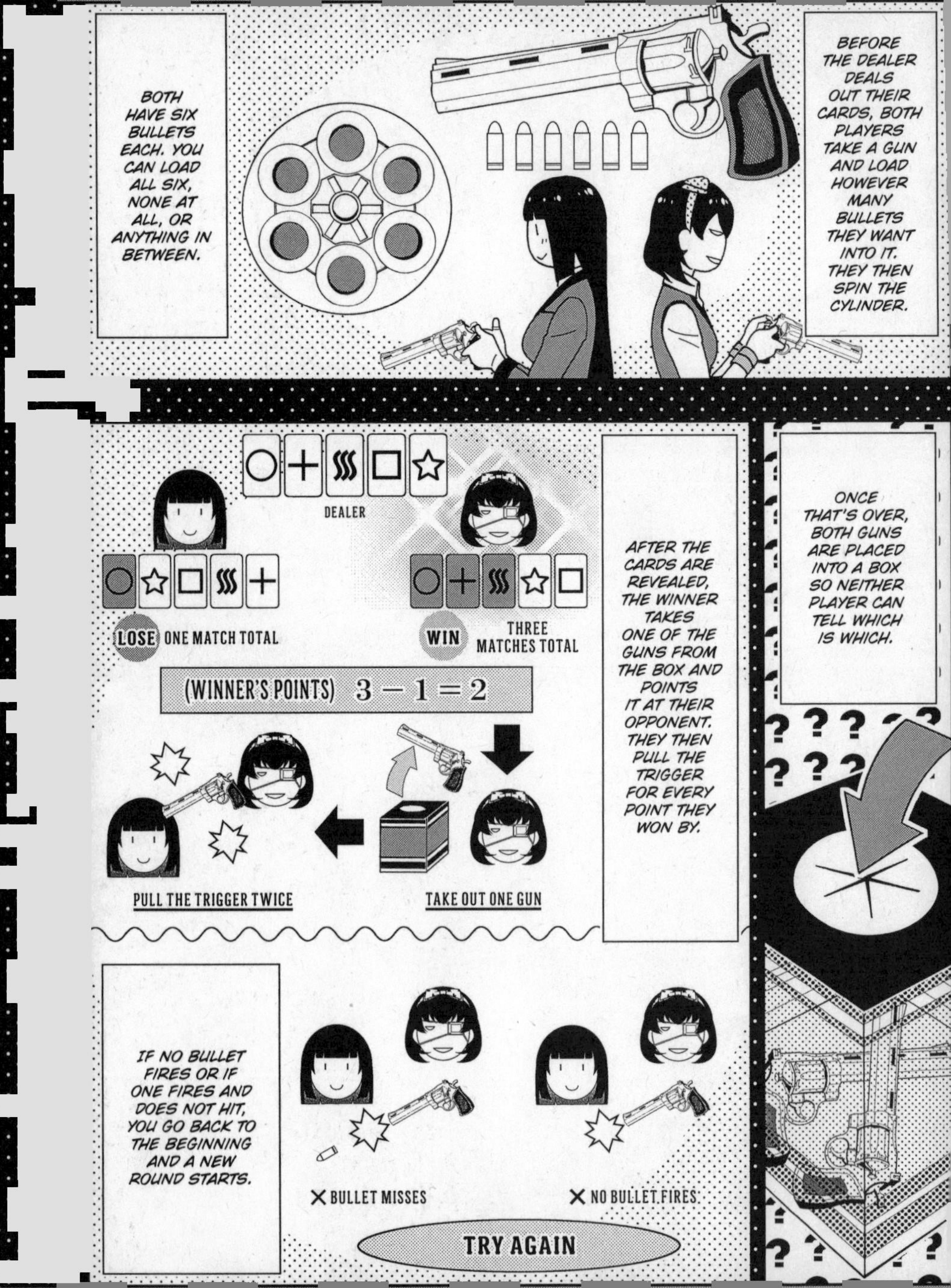

BEFORE THE DEALER DEALS OUT THEIR CARDS, BOTH PLAYERS TAKE A GUN AND LOAD HOWEVER MANY BULLETS THEY WANT INTO IT. THEY THEN SPIN THE CYLINDER.
BOTH HAVE SIX BULLETS EACH. YOU CAN LOAD ALL SIX, NONE AT ALL, OR ANYTHING IN BETWEEN.
ONCE THAT'S OVER, BOTH GUNS ARE PLACED INTO A BOX SO NEITHER PLAYER CAN TELL WHICH IS WHICH.
? ? ?
? ? ?
AFTER THE CARDS ARE REVEALED, THE WINNER TAKES ONE OF THE GUNS FROM THE BOX AND POINTS IT AT THEIR OPPONENT. THEY THEN PULL THE TRIGGER FOR EVERY POINT THEY WON BY.
DEALER
WIN THREE MATCHES TOTAL
LOSE ONE MATCH TOTAL
(WINNER'S POINTS) 3 − 1 = 2
TAKE OUT ONE GUN
PULL THE TRIGGER TWICE
IF NO BULLET FIRES OR IF ONE FIRES AND DOES NOT HIT, YOU GO BACK TO THE BEGINNING AND A NEW ROUND STARTS.
✕ NO BULLET FIRES
✕ BULLET MISSES
TRY AGAIN

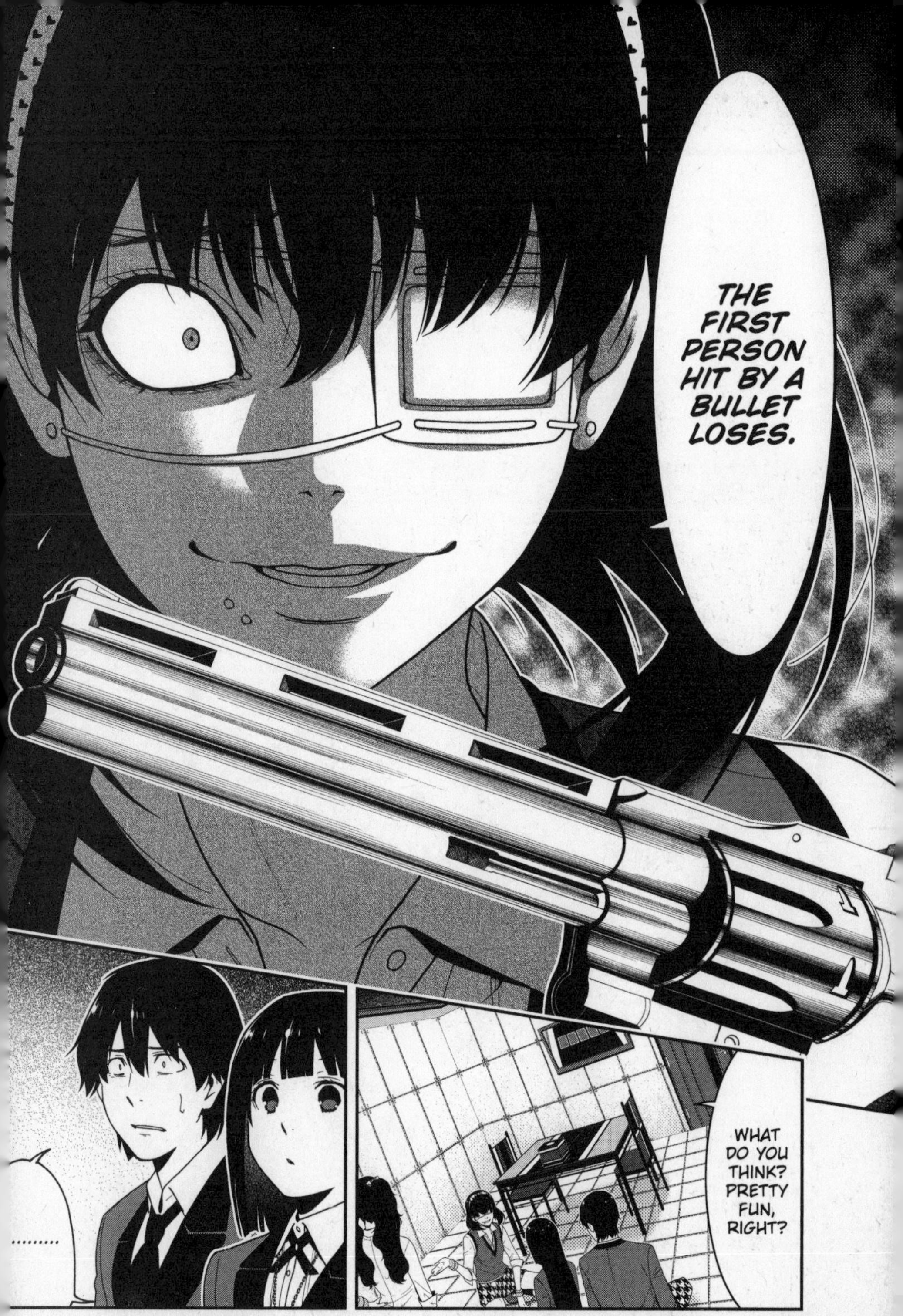
THE FIRST PERSON HIT BY A BULLET LOSES.
WHAT DO YOU THINK? PRETTY FUN, RIGHT?
....

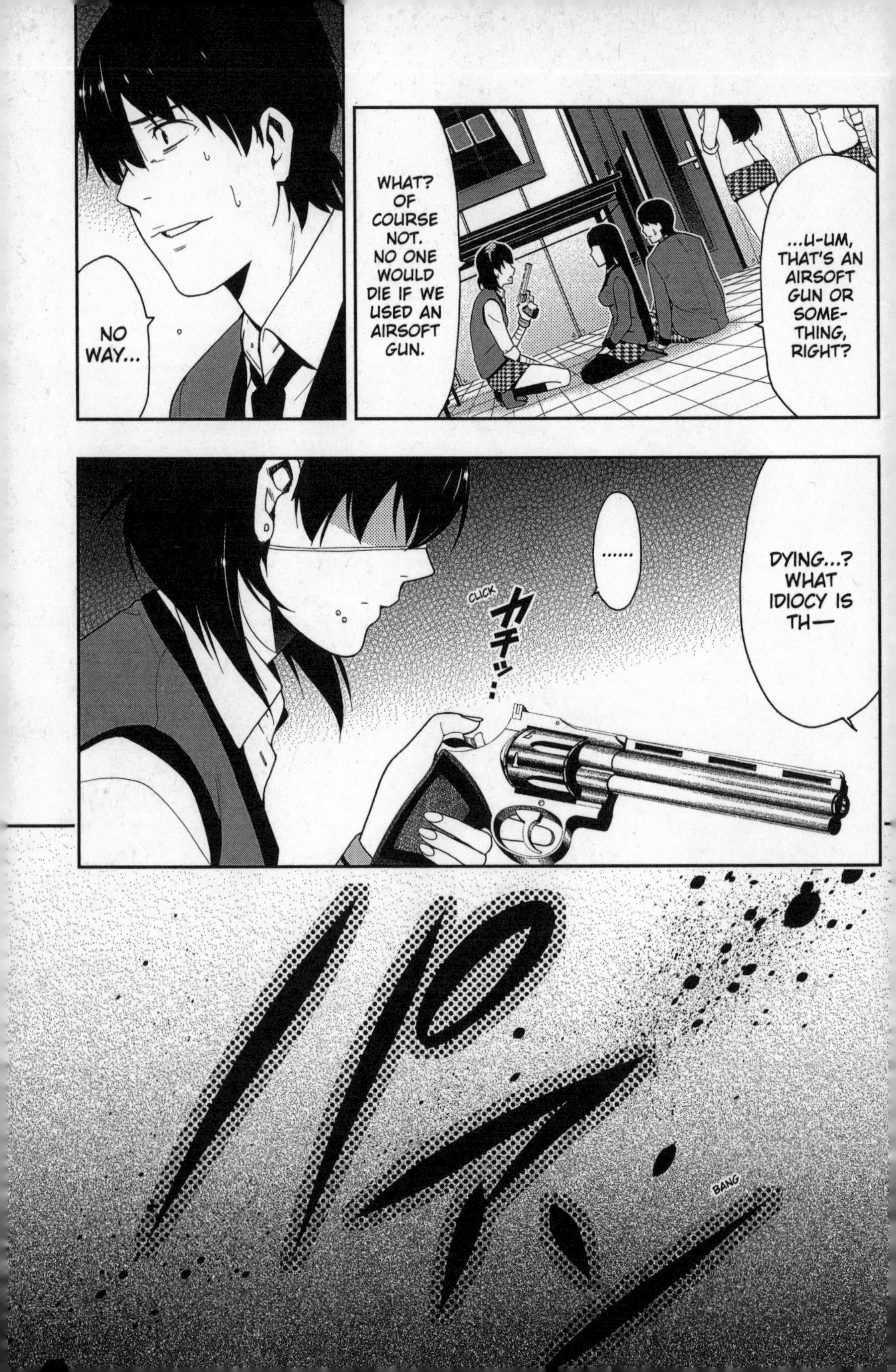
...U-UM, THAT'S AN AIRSOFT GUN OR SOME-THING, RIGHT?
WHAT? OF COURSE NOT. NO ONE WOULD DIE IF WE USED AN AIRSOFT GUN.
NO WAY...
DYING...? WHAT IDIOCY IS TH—
......
CLICK
カチッ
BANG

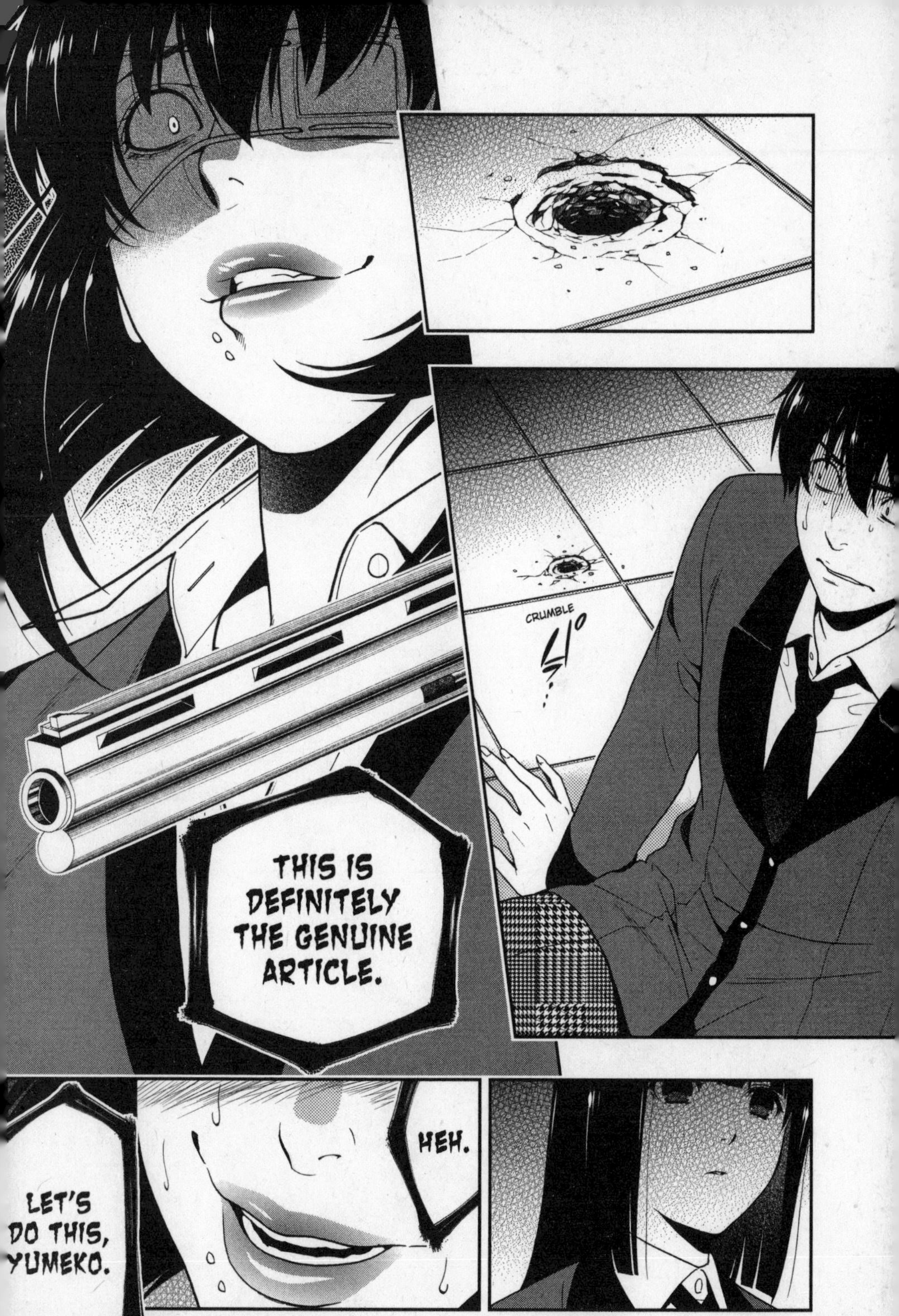
CRUMBLE
THIS IS DEFINITELY THE GENUINE ARTICLE.
HEH.
LET'S DO THIS, YUMEKO.

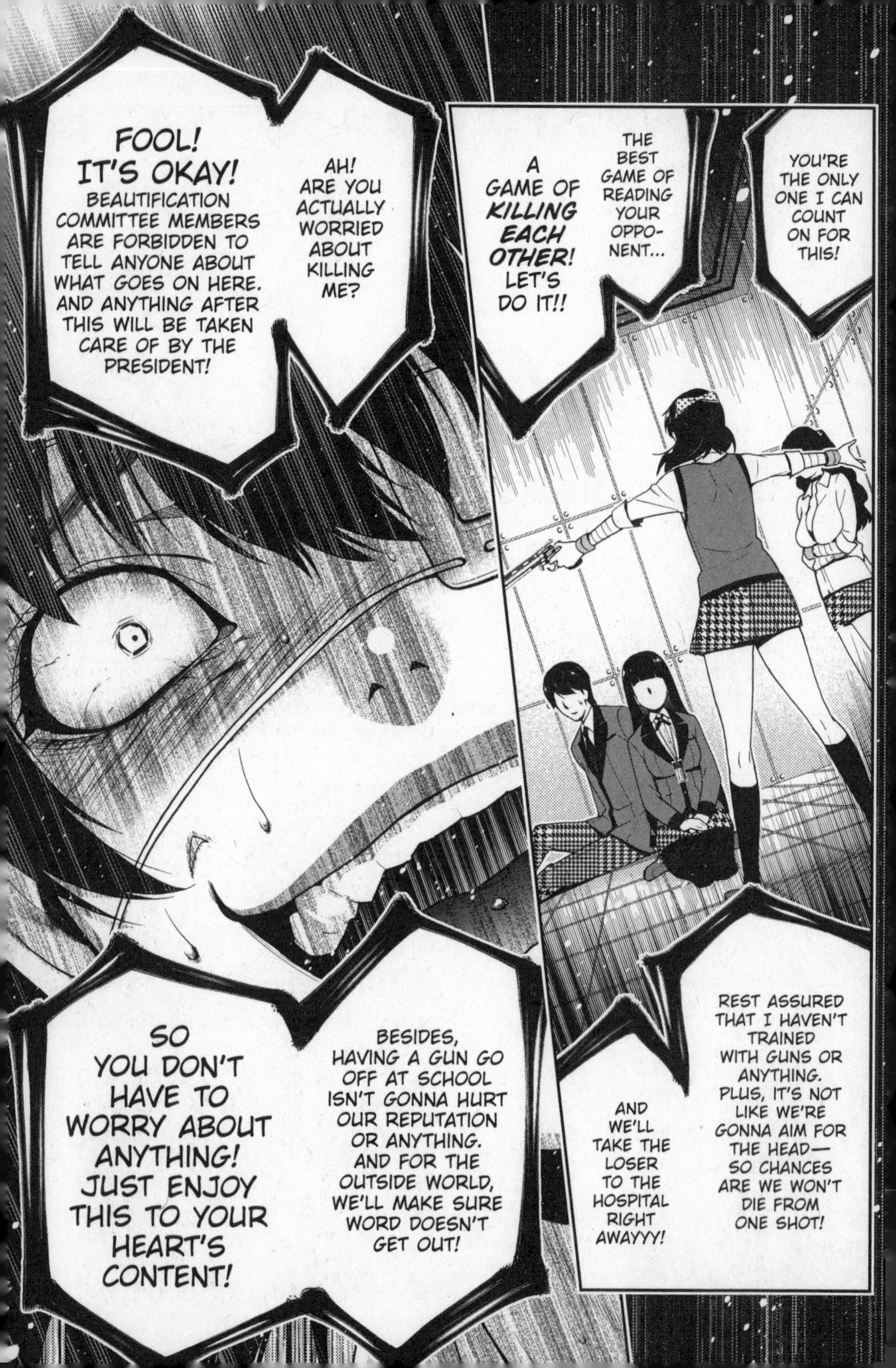
YOU'RE THE ONLY ONE I CAN COUNT ON FOR THIS!
THE BEST GAME OF READING YOUR OPPO-NENT...
A GAME OF *KILLING EACH OTHER*! LET'S DO IT!!
REST ASSURED THAT I HAVEN'T TRAINED WITH GUNS OR ANYTHING. PLUS, IT'S NOT LIKE WE'RE GONNA AIM FOR THE HEAD— SO CHANCES ARE WE WON'T DIE FROM ONE SHOT!
AND WE'LL TAKE THE LOSER TO THE HOSPITAL RIGHT AWAYYY!
AH! ARE YOU ACTUALLY WORRIED ABOUT KILLING ME?
FOOL! IT'S OKAY! BEAUTIFICATION COMMITTEE MEMBERS ARE FORBIDDEN TO TELL ANYONE ABOUT WHAT GOES ON HERE. AND ANYTHING AFTER THIS WILL BE TAKEN CARE OF BY THE PRESIDENT!
BESIDES, HAVING A GUN GO OFF AT SCHOOL ISN'T GONNA HURT OUR REPUTATION OR ANYTHING. AND FOR THE OUTSIDE WORLD, WE'LL MAKE SURE WORD DOESN'T GET OUT!
SO YOU DON'T HAVE TO WORRY ABOUT ANYTHING! JUST ENJOY THIS TO YOUR HEART'S CONTENT!

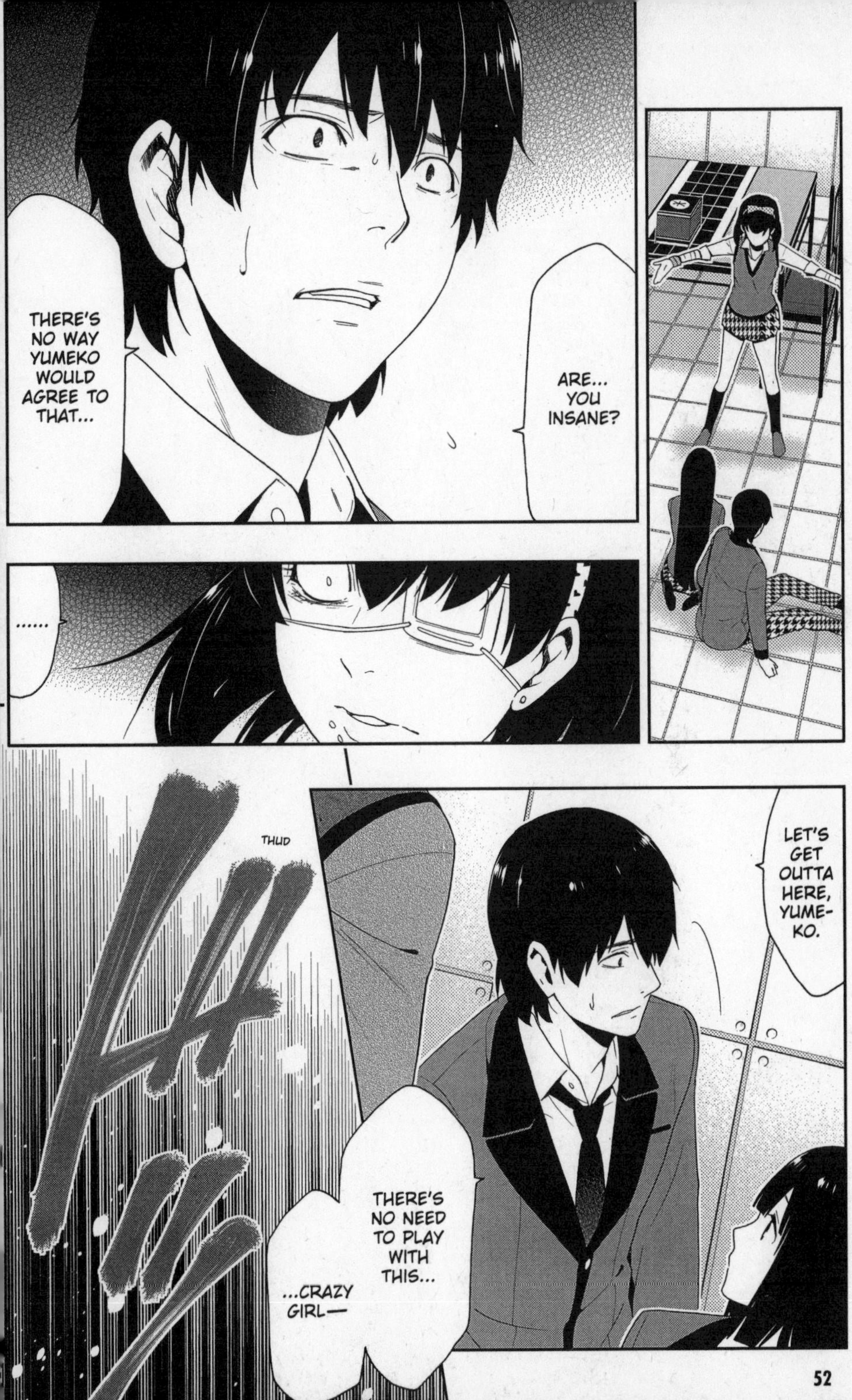
ARE... YOU INSANE?
THERE'S NO WAY YUMEKO WOULD AGREE TO THAT...
......
LET'S GET OUTTA HERE, YUME-KO.
THUD
THERE'S NO NEED TO PLAY WITH THIS...
...CRAZY GIRL—

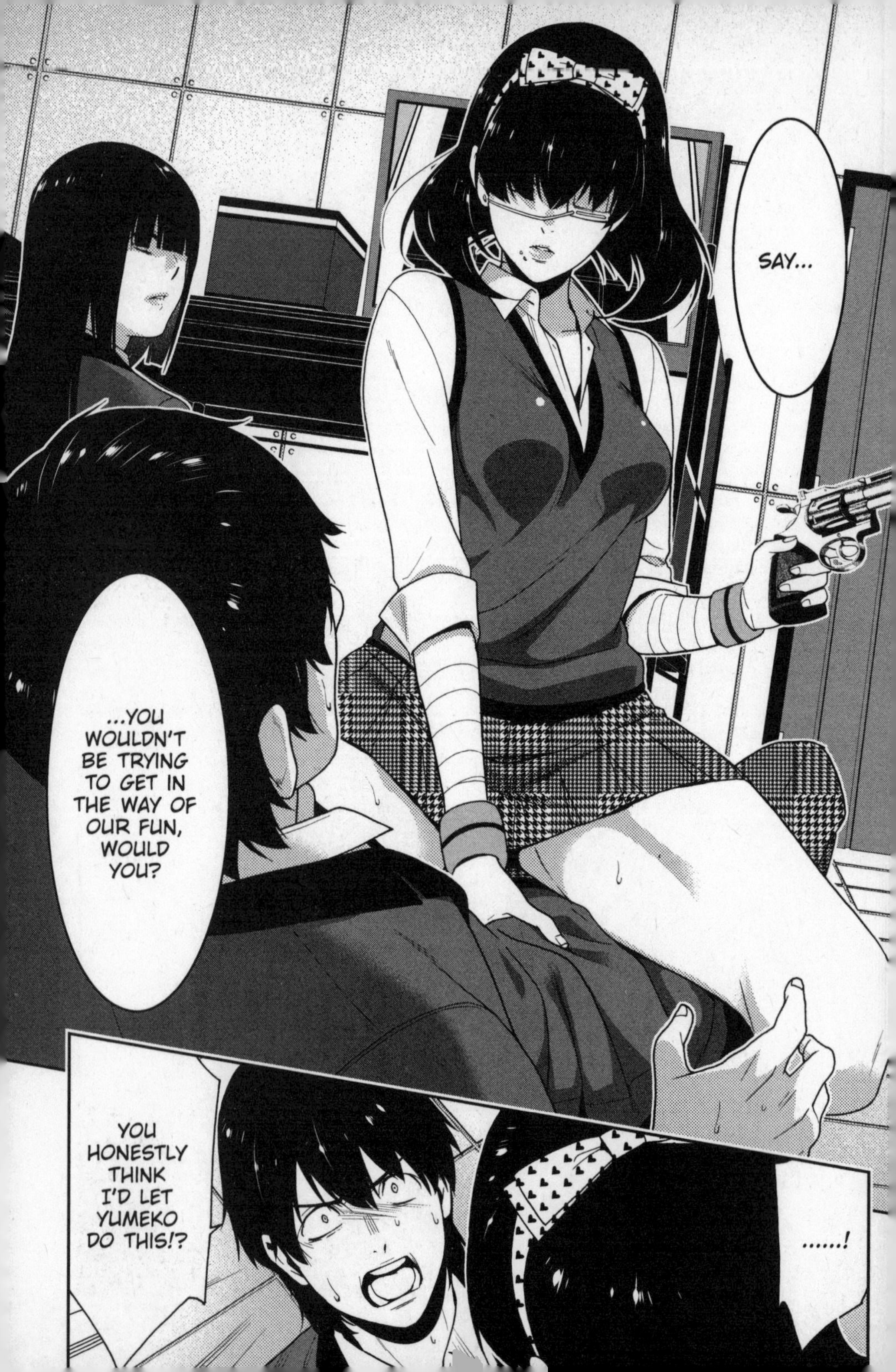
SAY...
...YOU WOULDN'T BE TRYING TO GET IN THE WAY OF OUR FUN, WOULD YOU?
......!
YOU HONESTLY THINK I'D LET YUMEKO DO THIS!?

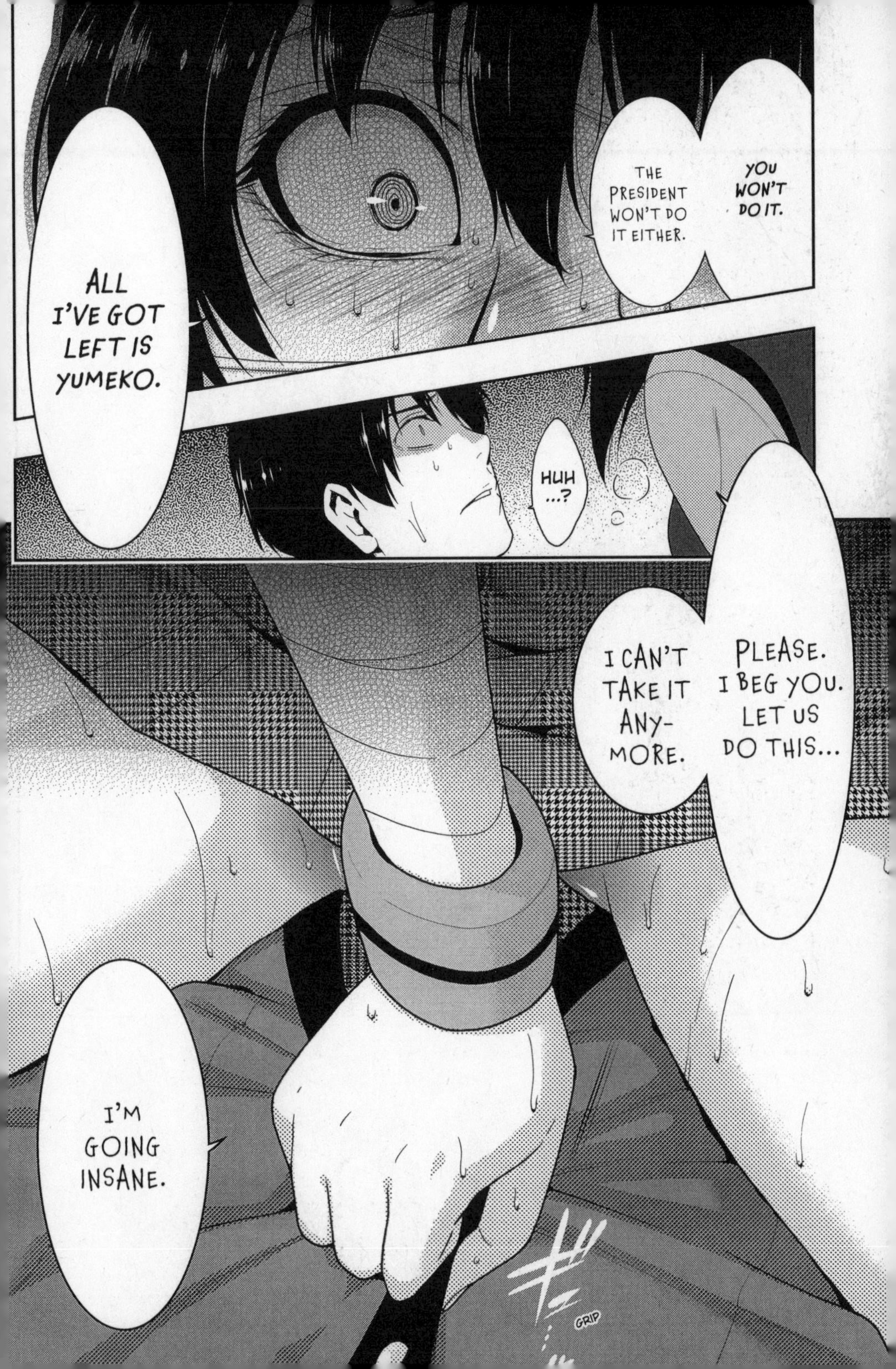
YOU WON'T DO IT.
THE PRESIDENT WON'T DO IT EITHER.
ALL I'VE GOT LEFT IS YUMEKO.
HUH ...?
PLEASE. I BEG YOU. LET US DO THIS...
I CAN'T TAKE IT ANYMORE.
I'M GOING INSANE.
GRIP

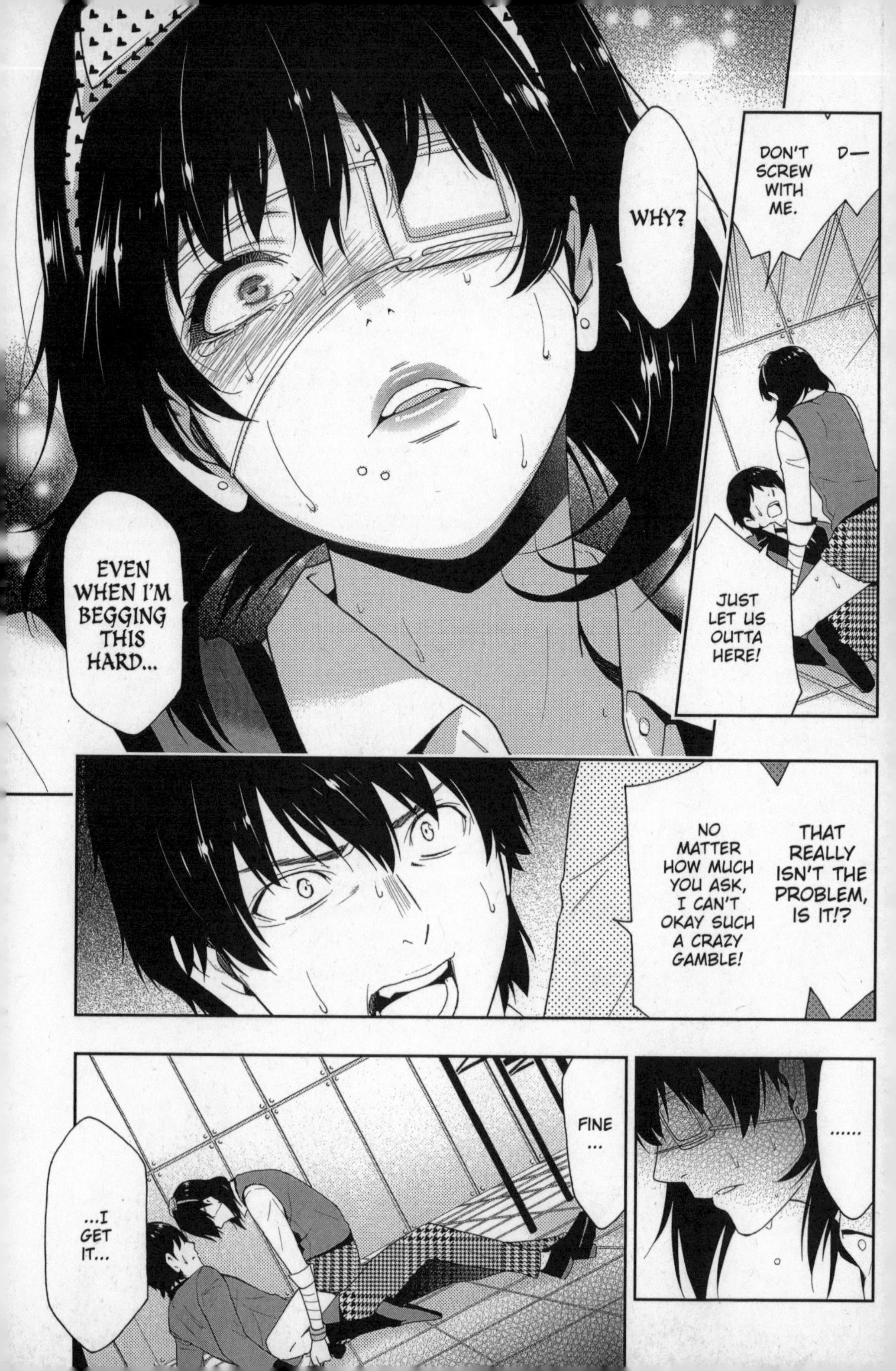
D— DON'T SCREW WITH ME.
JUST LET US OUTTA HERE!
WHY?
EVEN WHEN I'M BEGGING THIS HARD...
THAT REALLY ISN'T THE PROBLEM, IS IT!?
NO MATTER HOW MUCH YOU ASK, I CAN'T OKAY SUCH A CRAZY GAMBLE!
......
FINE ...
...I GET IT...

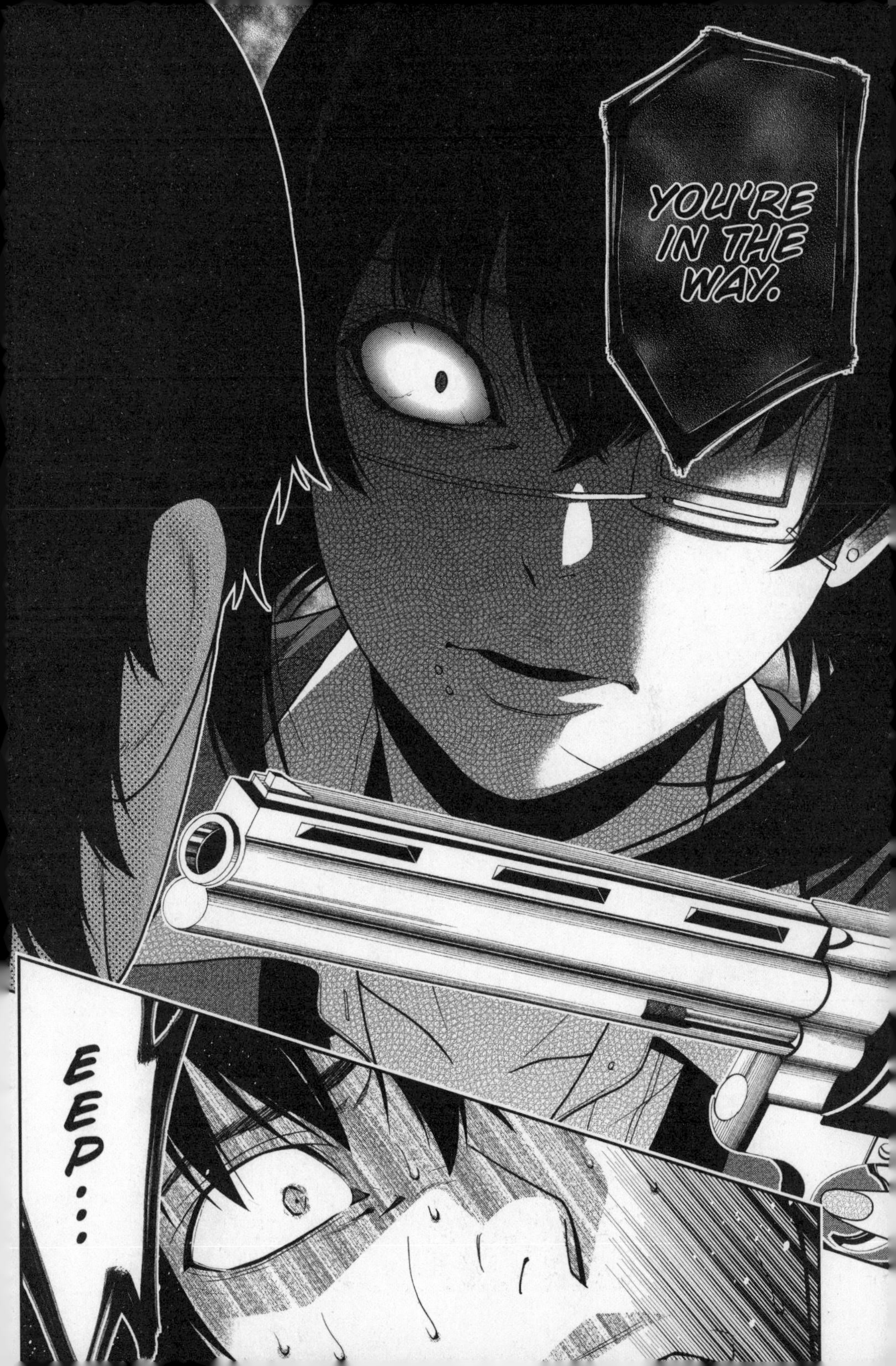
YOU'RE IN THE WAY.
EEP...

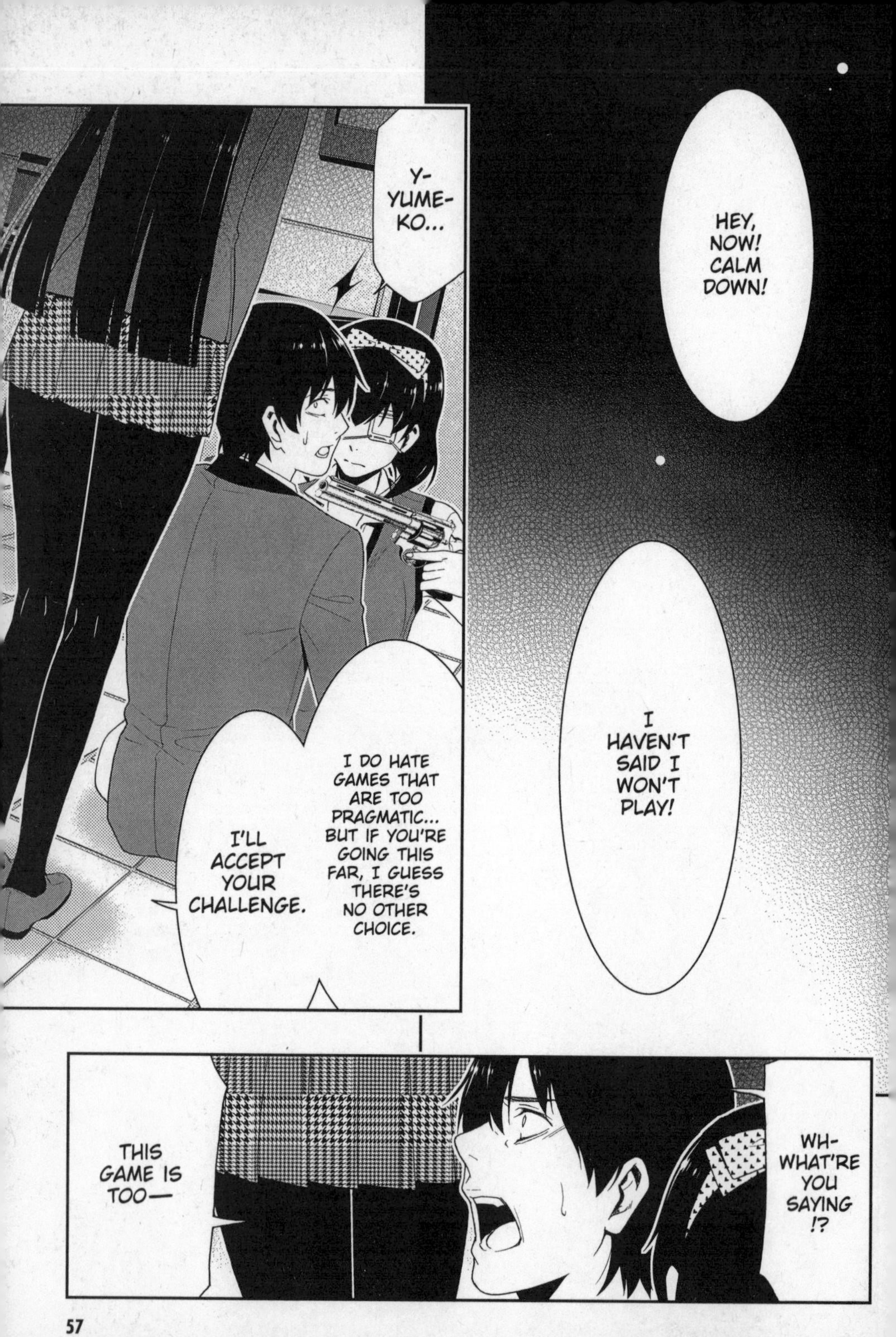
HEY, NOW! CALM DOWN!
I HAVEN'T SAID I WON'T PLAY!
Y-YUMEKO...
I DO HATE GAMES THAT ARE TOO PRAGMATIC... BUT IF YOU'RE GOING THIS FAR, I GUESS THERE'S NO OTHER CHOICE.
I'LL ACCEPT YOUR CHALLENGE.
WH-WHAT'RE YOU SAYING!?
THIS GAME IS TOO—

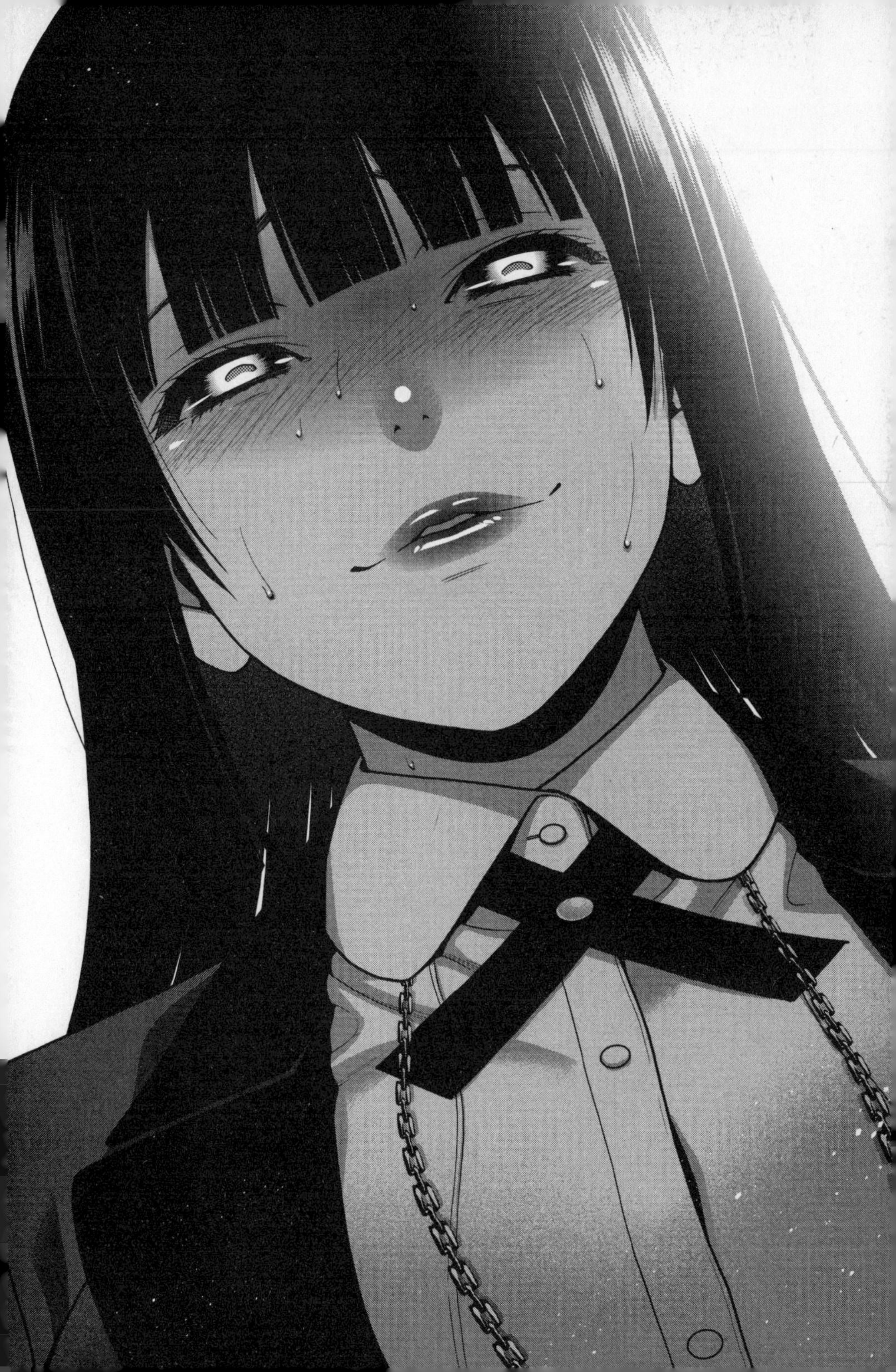

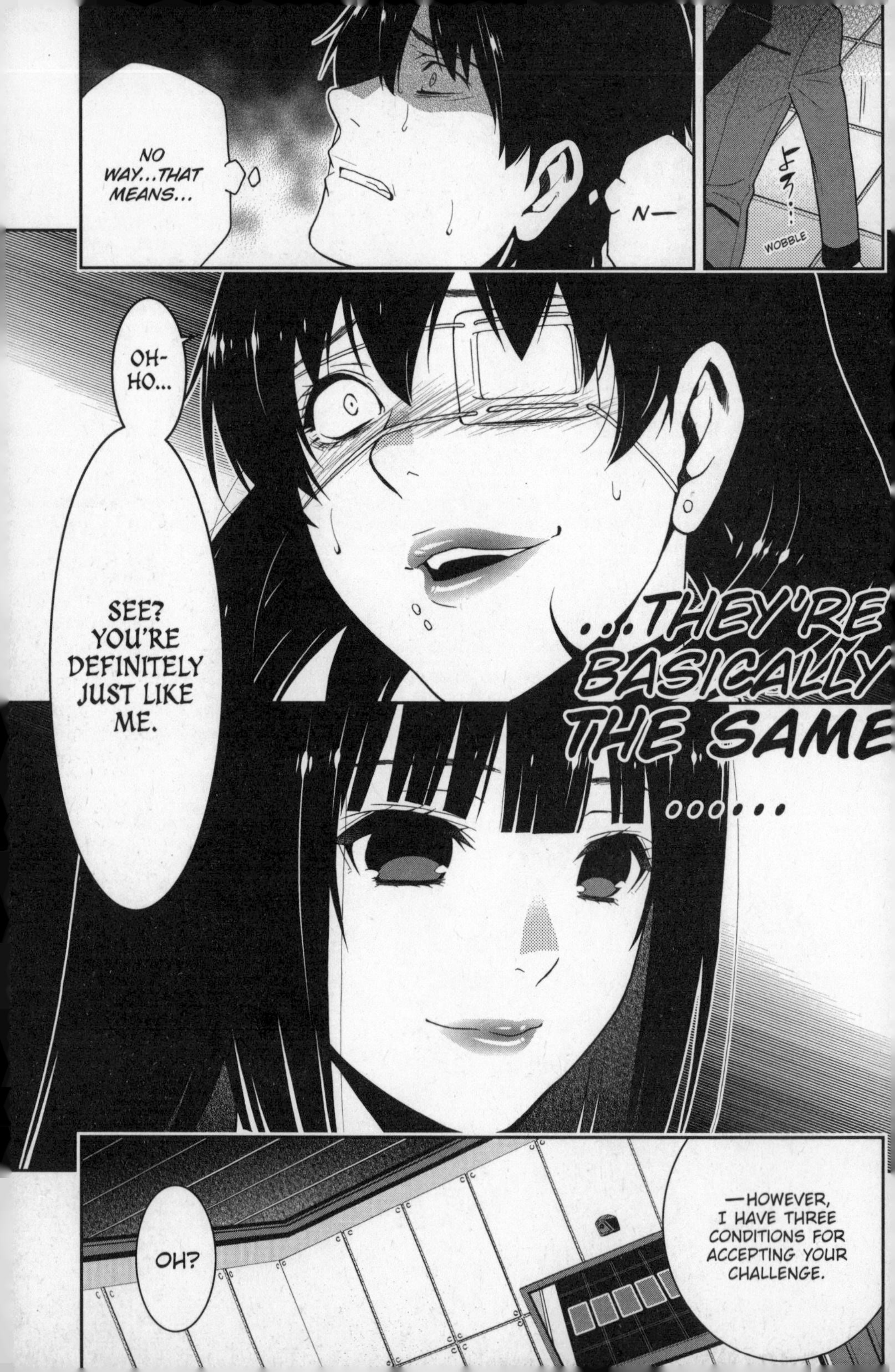
WOBBLE
N—
NO WAY...THAT MEANS...
...THEY'RE BASICALLY THE SAME ooo...
OH-HO...
SEE? YOU'RE DEFINITELY JUST LIKE ME.
—HOWEVER, I HAVE THREE CONDITIONS FOR ACCEPTING YOUR CHALLENGE.
OH?

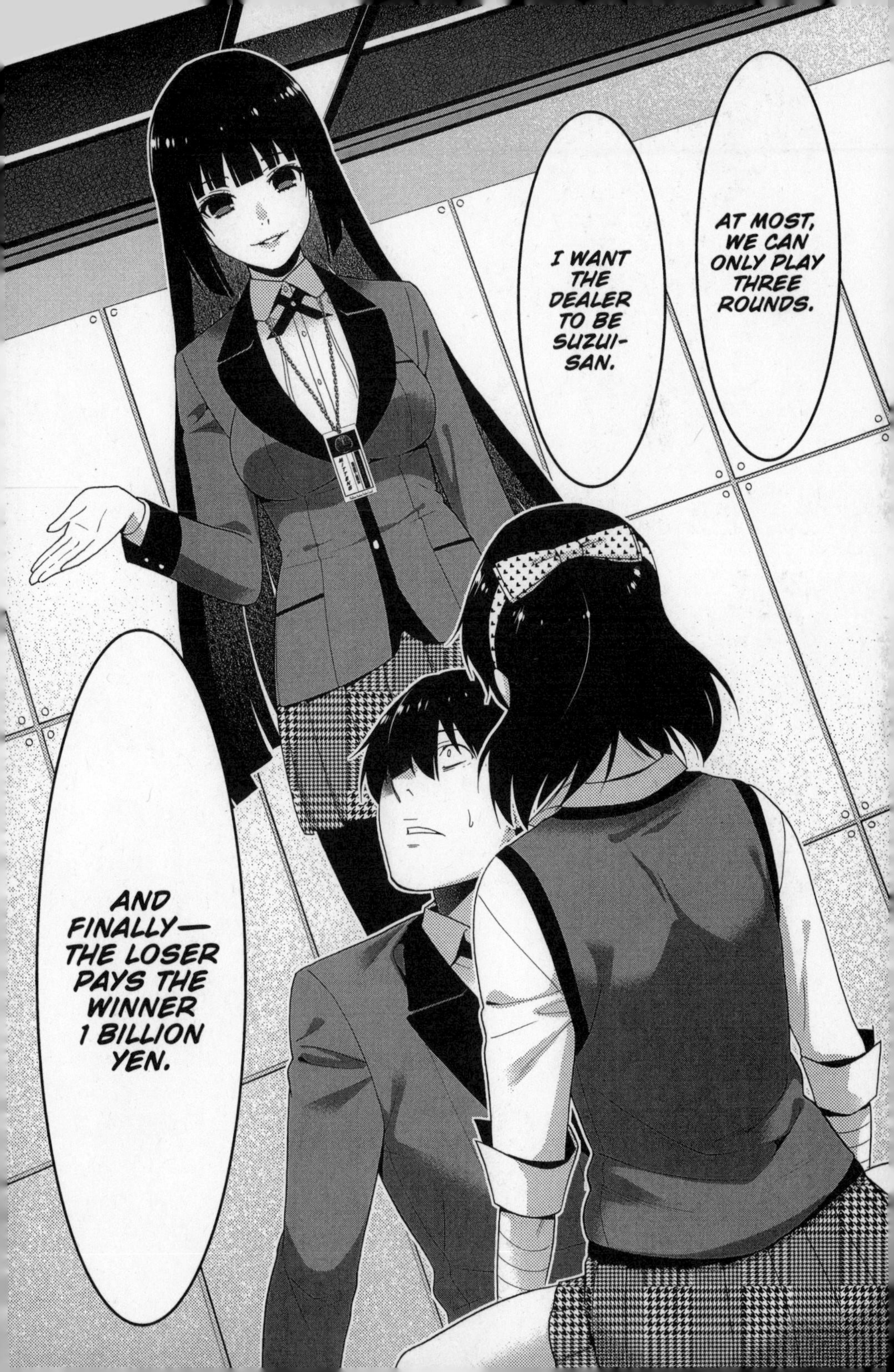
AT MOST, WE CAN ONLY PLAY THREE ROUNDS.
I WANT THE DEALER TO BE SUZUI-SAN.
AND FINALLY— THE LOSER PAYS THE WINNER 1 BILLION YEN.

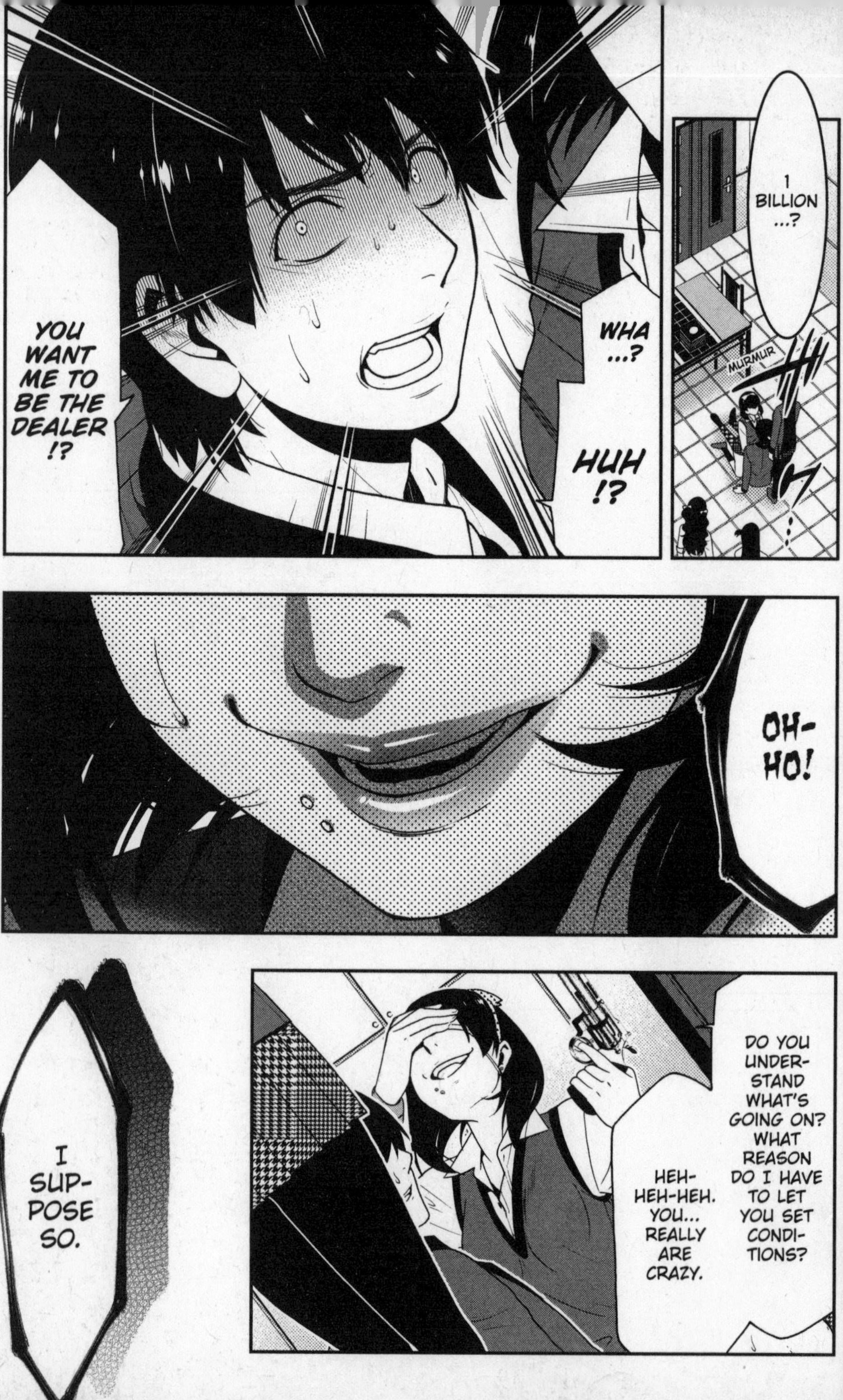
1 BILLION ...?
MURMUR
WHA ...?
HUH !?
YOU WANT ME TO BE THE DEALER !?
OH-HO!
DO YOU UNDER-STAND WHAT'S GOING ON? WHAT REASON DO I HAVE TO LET YOU SET CONDI-TIONS?
HEH-HEH-HEH. YOU... REALLY ARE CRAZY.
I SUP-POSE SO.

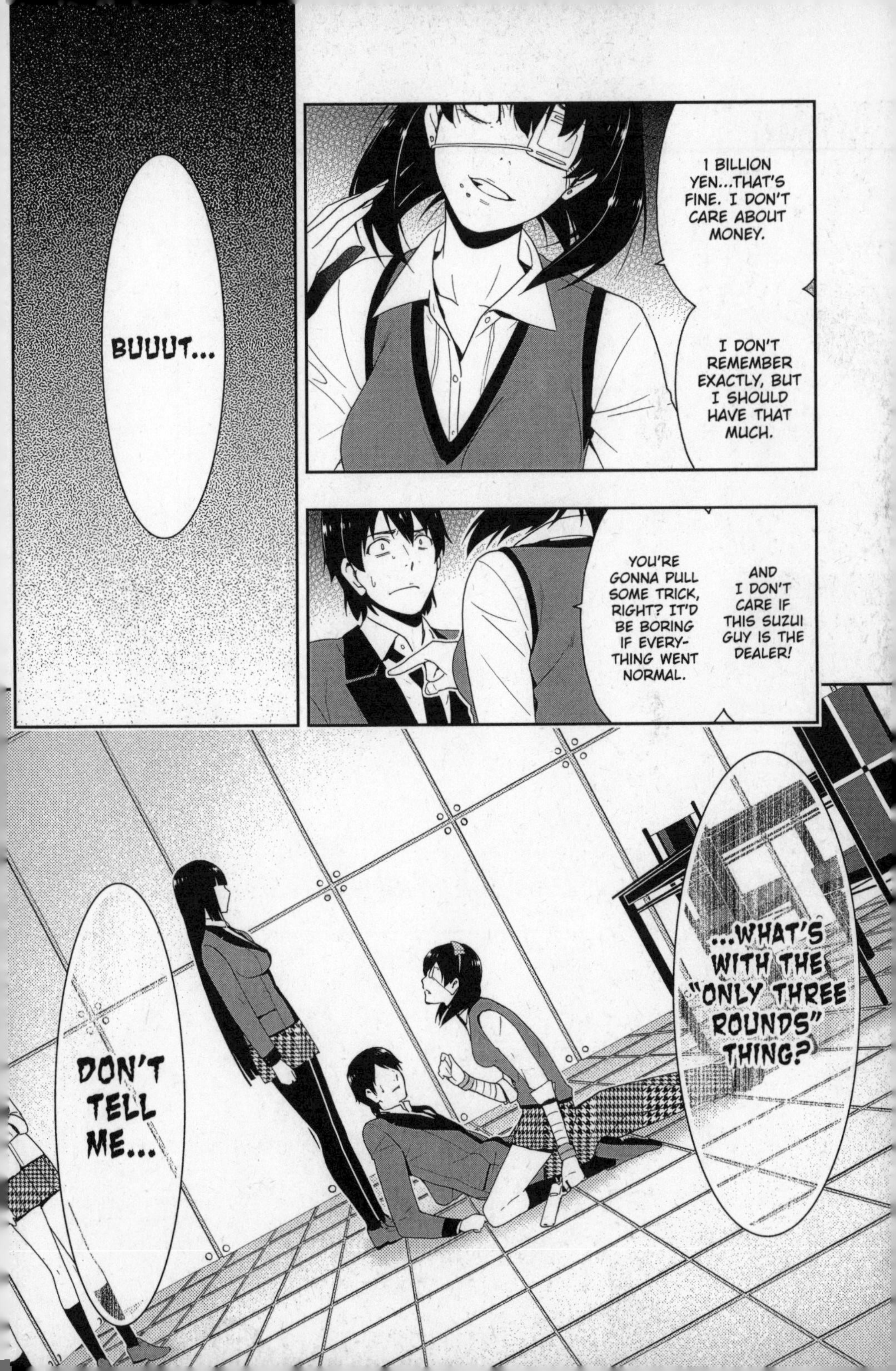
1 BILLION YEN...THAT'S FINE. I DON'T CARE ABOUT MONEY.
I DON'T REMEMBER EXACTLY, BUT I SHOULD HAVE THAT MUCH.
AND I DON'T CARE IF THIS SUZUI GUY IS THE DEALER!
YOU'RE GONNA PULL SOME TRICK, RIGHT? IT'D BE BORING IF EVERY-THING WENT NORMAL.
BUUUT...
...WHAT'S WITH THE "ONLY THREE ROUNDS" THING?
DON'T TELL ME...

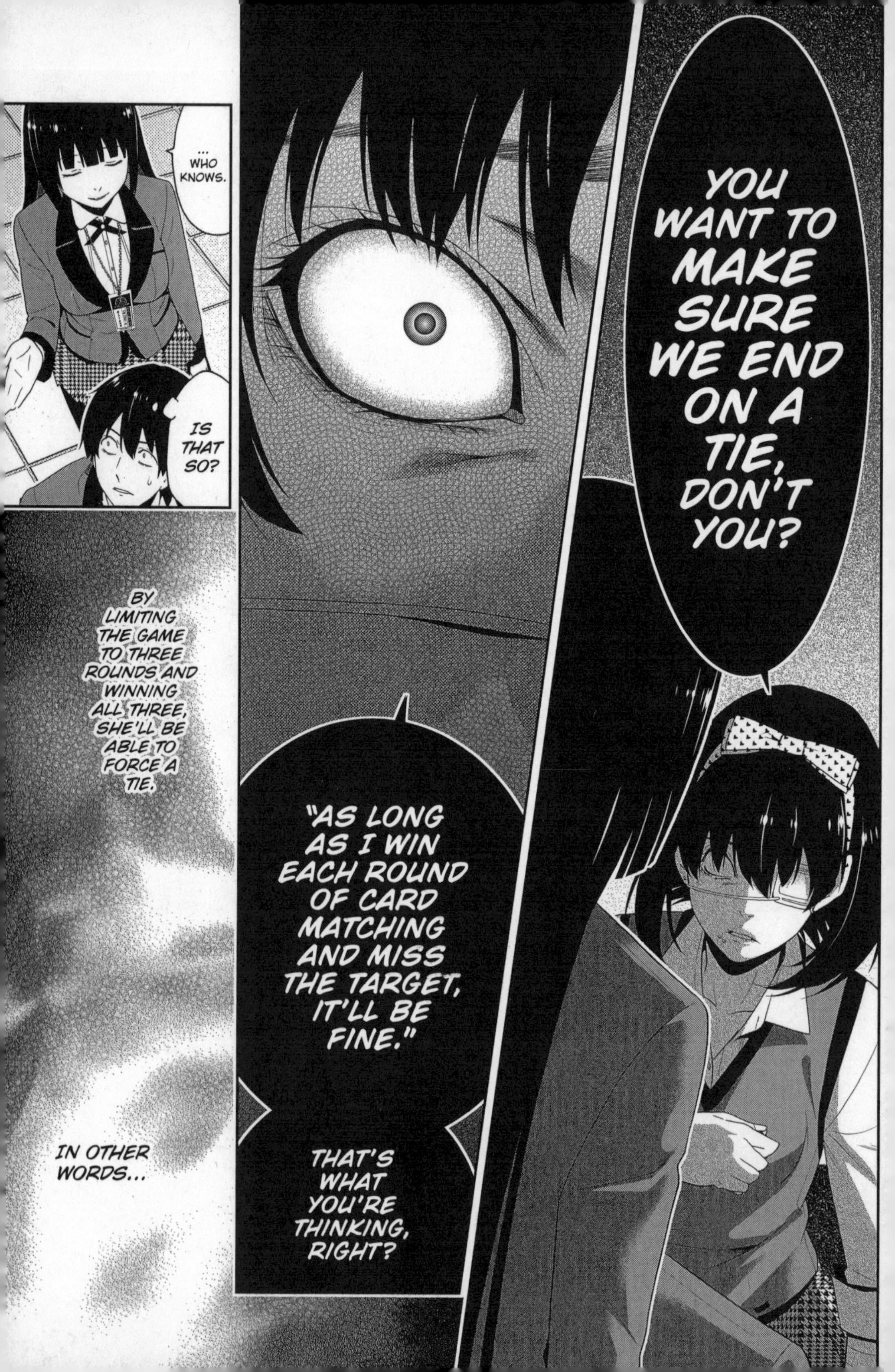
YOU WANT TO MAKE SURE WE END ON A TIE, DON'T YOU?
"AS LONG AS I WIN EACH ROUND OF CARD MATCHING AND MISS THE TARGET, IT'LL BE FINE."
THAT'S WHAT YOU'RE THINKING, RIGHT?
... WHO KNOWS.
IS THAT SO?
BY LIMITING THE GAME TO THREE ROUNDS AND WINNING ALL THREE, SHE'LL BE ABLE TO FORCE A TIE.
IN OTHER WORDS...

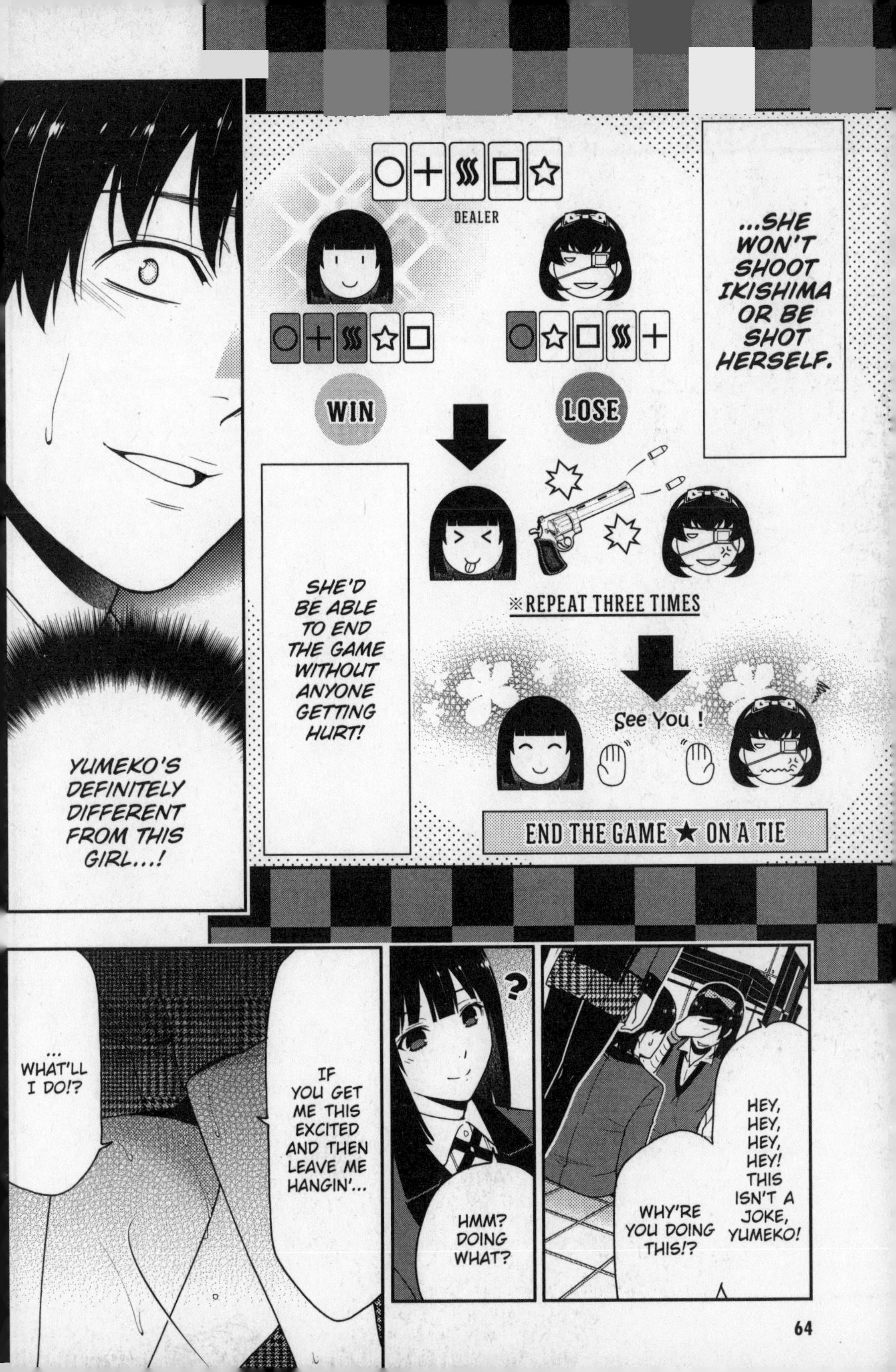

...SHE WON'T SHOOT IKISHIMA OR BE SHOT HERSELF.
DEALER
WIN
LOSE
※REPEAT THREE TIMES
See You !
END THE GAME ★ ON A TIE
SHE'D BE ABLE TO END THE GAME WITHOUT ANYONE GETTING HURT!
YUMEKO'S DEFINITELY DIFFERENT FROM THIS GIRL...!
HEY, HEY, HEY, HEY! THIS ISN'T A JOKE, YUMEKO!
WHY'RE YOU DOING THIS!?
?
HMM? DOING WHAT?
IF YOU GET ME THIS EXCITED AND THEN LEAVE ME HANGIN'...
... WHAT'LL I DO!?

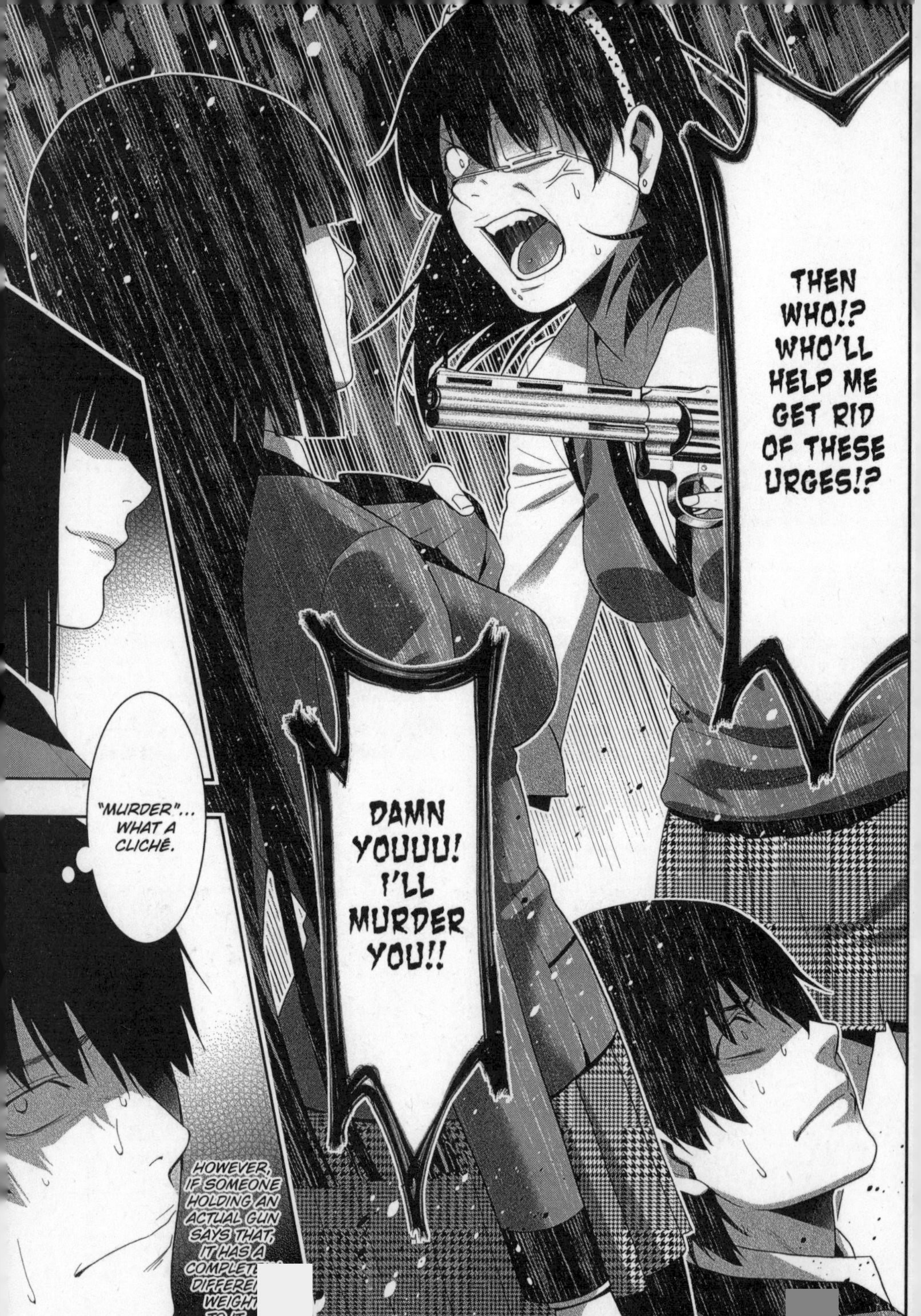
THEN WHO!? WHO'LL HELP ME GET RID OF THESE URGES!?
DAMN YOUUU! I'LL MURDER YOU!!
"MURDER"... WHAT A CLICHÉ.
HOWEVER, IF SOMEONE HOLDING AN ACTUAL GUN SAYS THAT, IT HAS A COMPLET DIFFERE WEIGHT TO IT...

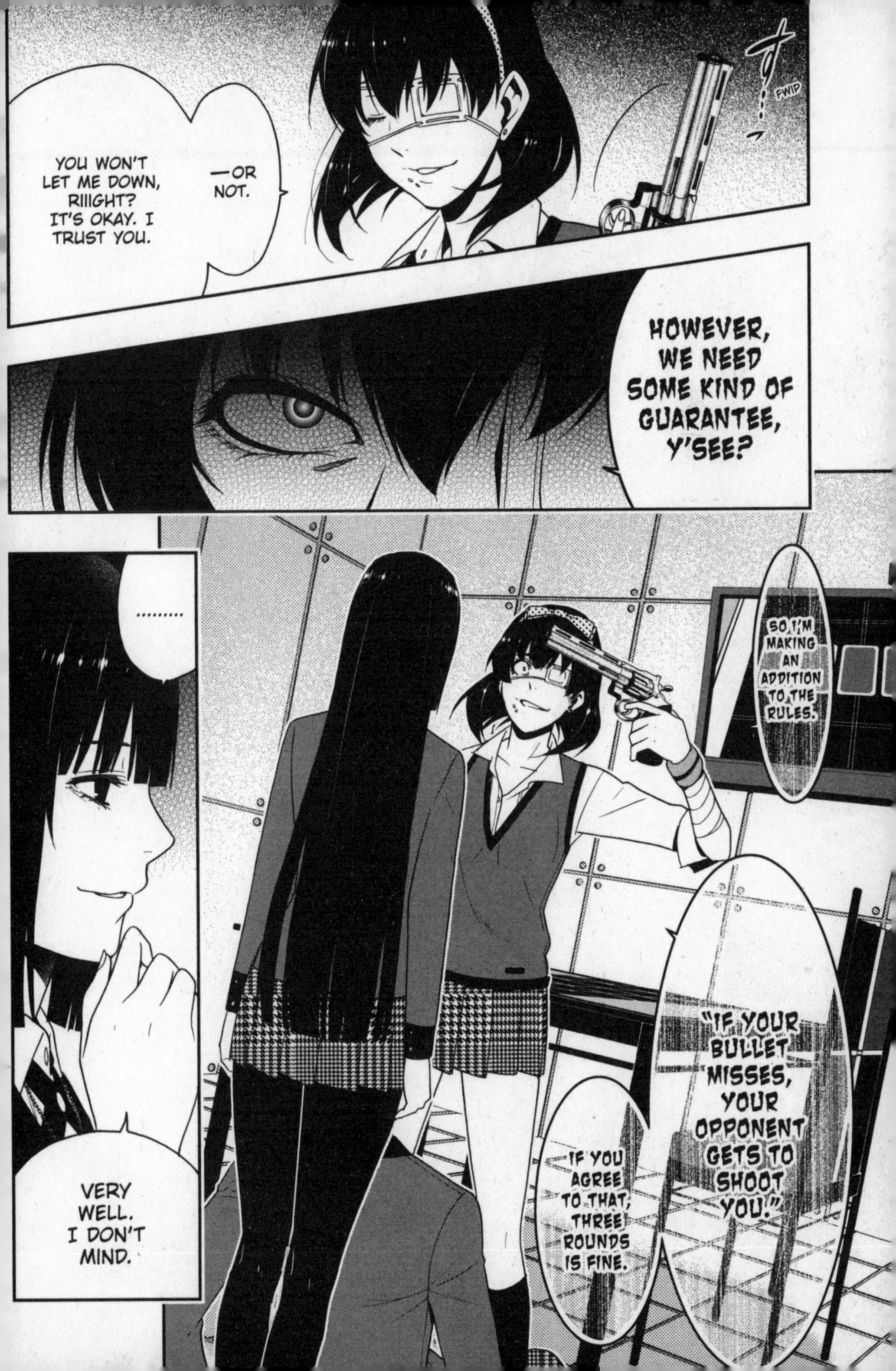
す…っ
FWIP
YOU WON'T LET ME DOWN, RIIIGHT? IT'S OKAY. I TRUST YOU.
—OR NOT.
HOWEVER, WE NEED SOME KIND OF GUARANTEE, Y'SEE?
SO I'M MAKING AN ADDITION TO THE RULES.
"IF YOUR BULLET MISSES, YOUR OPPONENT GETS TO SHOOT YOU."
IF YOU AGREE TO THAT, THREE ROUNDS IS FINE.
....
VERY WELL. I DON'T MIND.

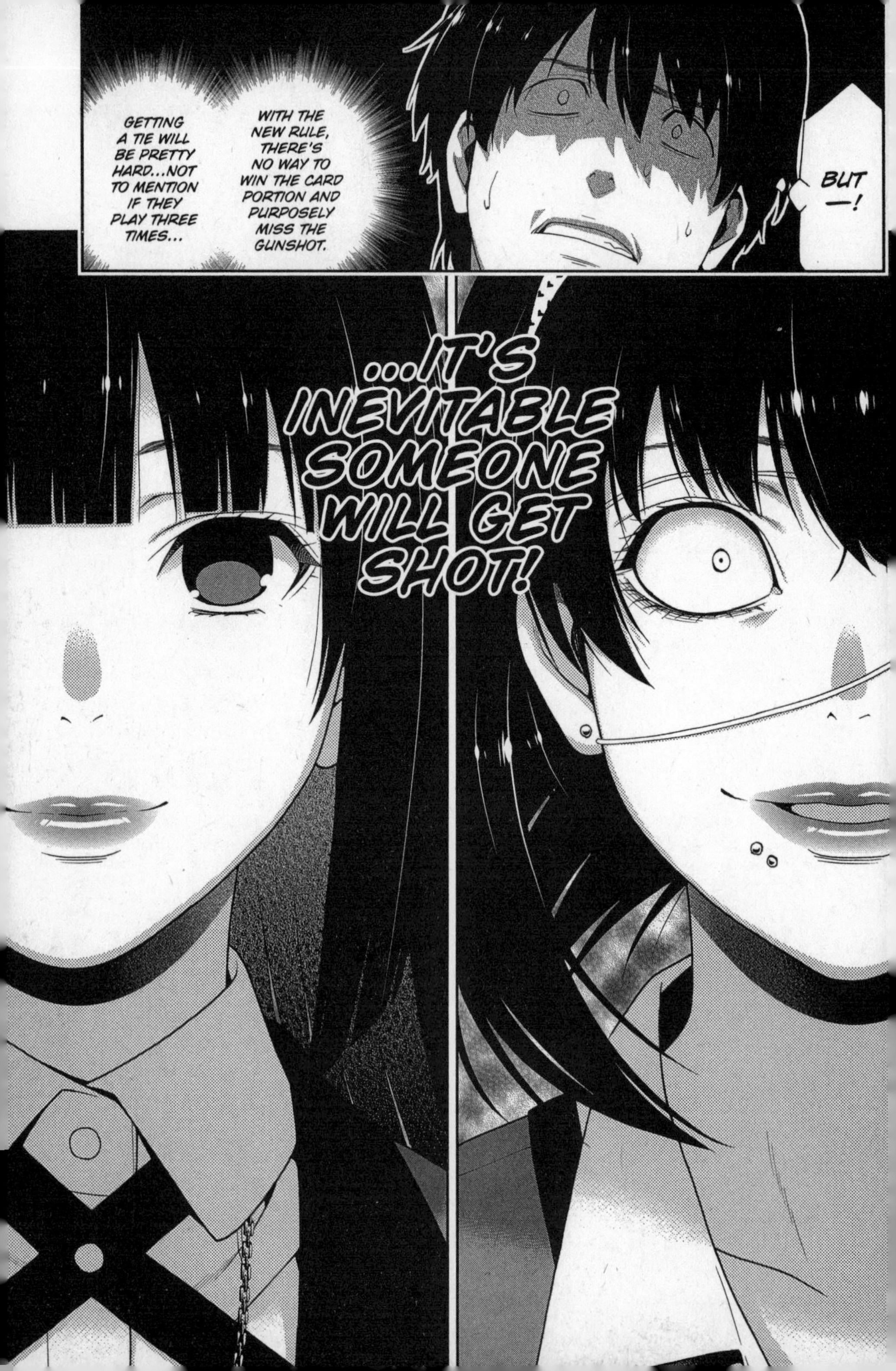

BUT—!
WITH THE NEW RULE, THERE'S NO WAY TO WIN THE CARD PORTION AND PURPOSELY MISS THE GUNSHOT.
GETTING A TIE WILL BE PRETTY HARD...NOT TO MENTION IF THEY PLAY THREE TIMES...
...IT'S INEVITABLE SOMEONE WILL GET SHOT!

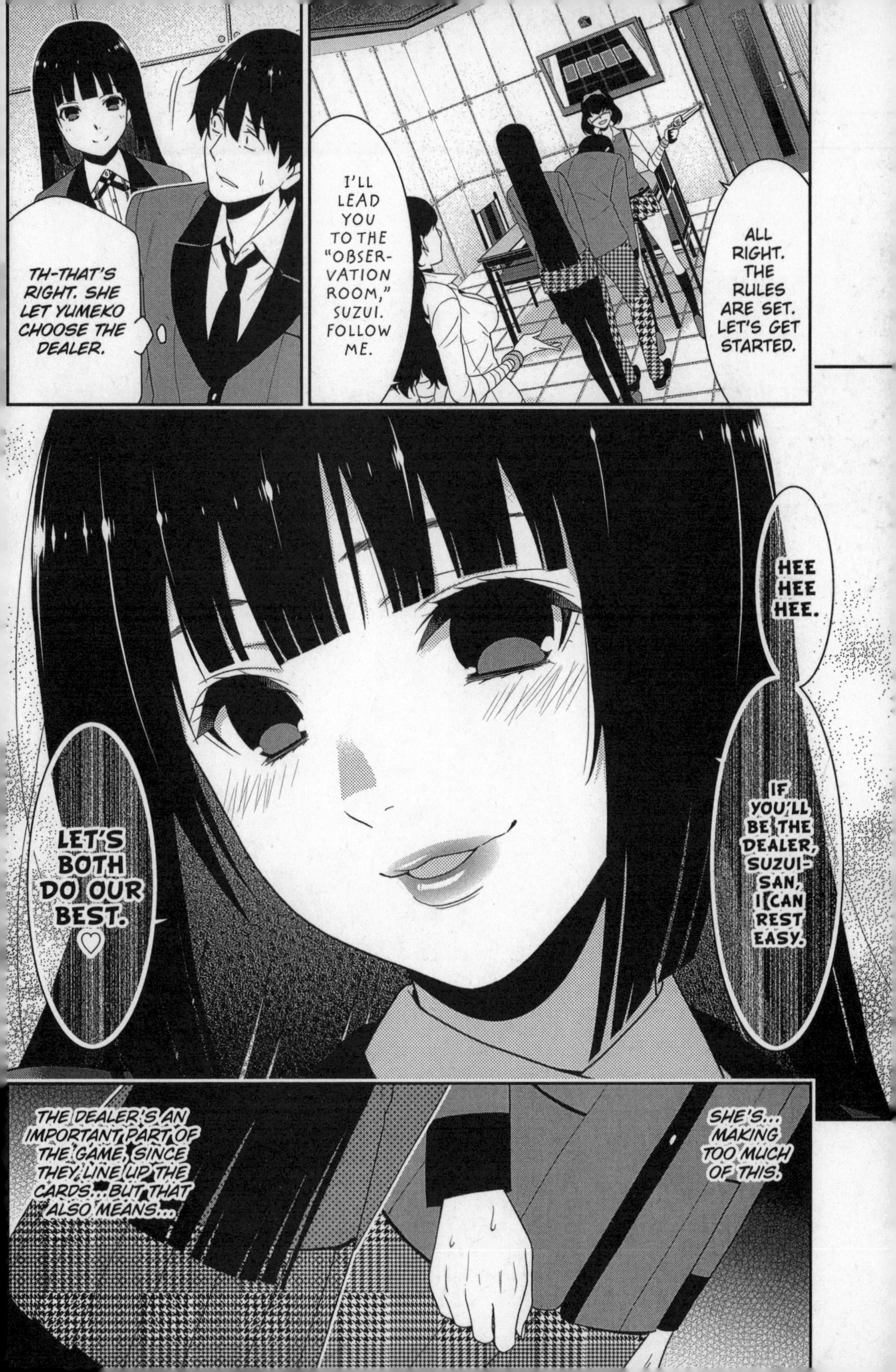
ALL RIGHT. THE RULES ARE SET. LET'S GET STARTED.
I'LL LEAD YOU TO THE "OBSERVATION ROOM," SUZUI. FOLLOW ME.
TH-THAT'S RIGHT. SHE LET YUMEKO CHOOSE THE DEALER.
HEE HEE HEE.
IF YOU'LL BE THE DEALER, SUZUI-SAN, I CAN REST EASY.
LET'S BOTH DO OUR BEST. ♡
SHE'S... MAKING TOO MUCH OF THIS.
THE DEALER'S AN IMPORTANT PART OF THE GAME, SINCE THEY LINE UP THE CARDS... BUT THAT ALSO MEANS...

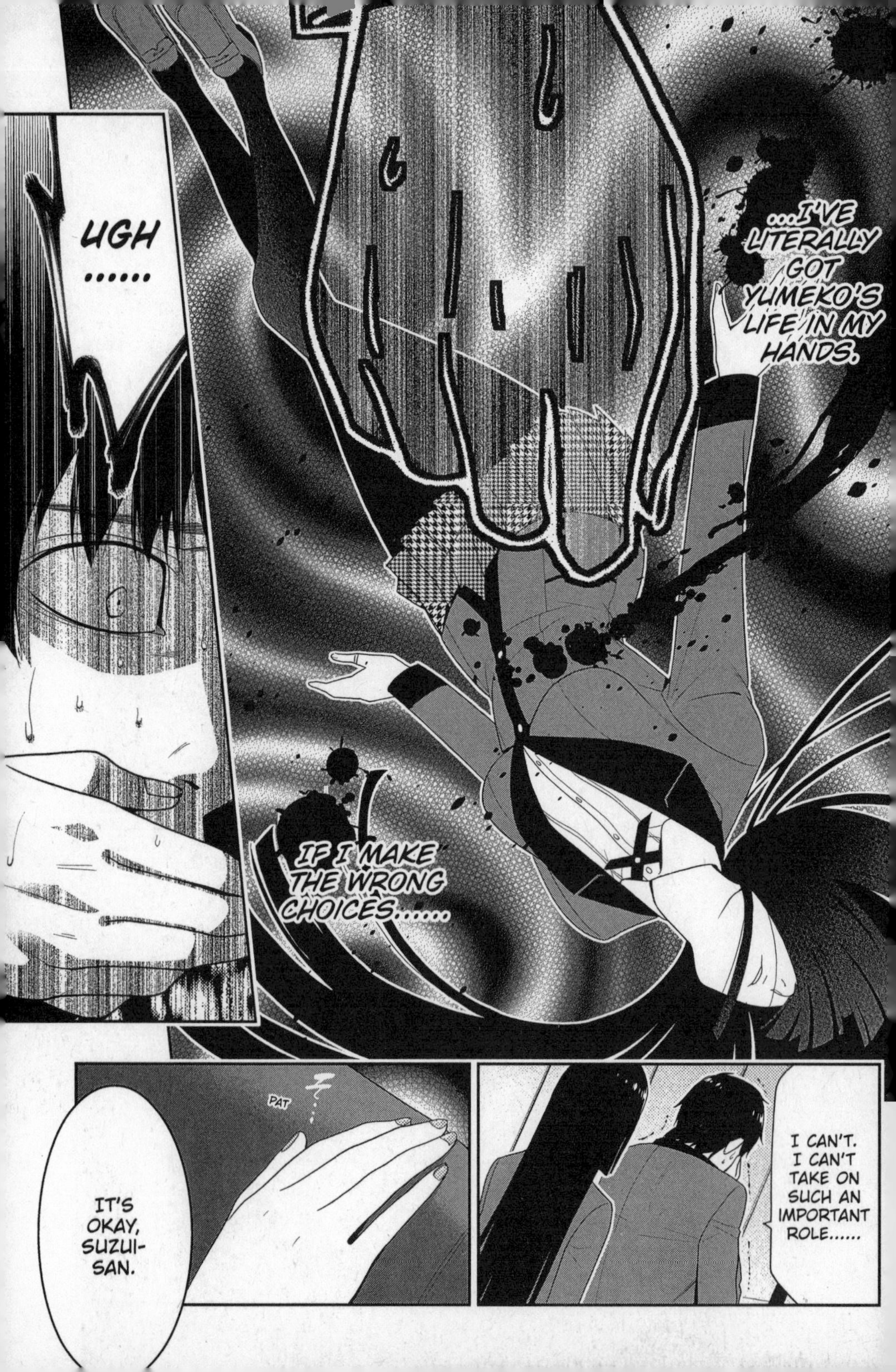
...I'VE LITERALLY GOT YUMEKO'S LIFE IN MY HANDS.
IF I MAKE THE WRONG CHOICES......
UGH ......
I CAN'T. I CAN'T TAKE ON SUCH AN IMPORTANT ROLE......
PAT
IT'S OKAY, SUZUI-SAN.

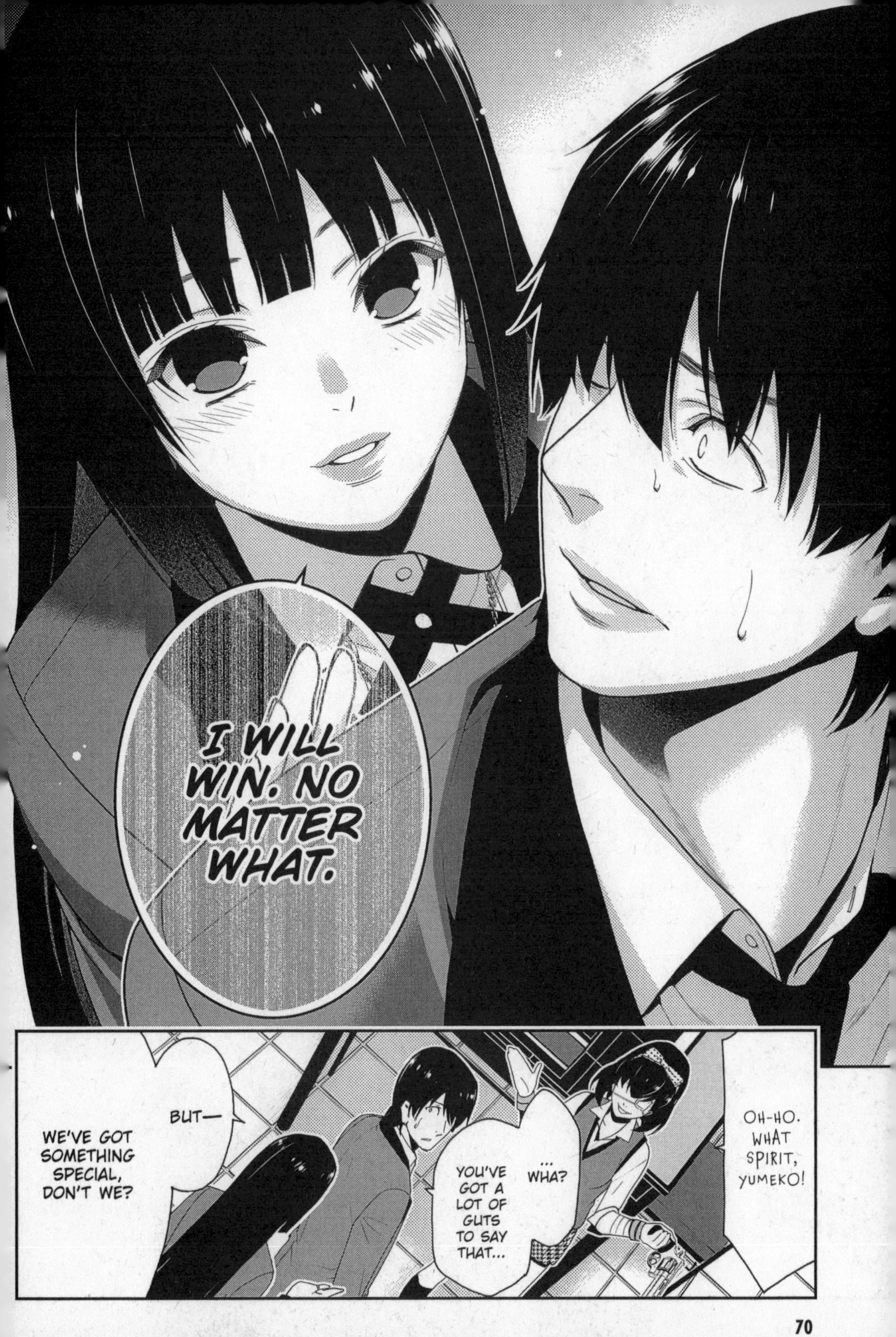
I WILL WIN. NO MATTER WHAT.
OH-HO. WHAT SPIRIT, YUMEKO!
... WHA?
YOU'VE GOT A LOT OF GUTS TO SAY THAT...
BUT—
WE'VE GOT SOMETHING SPECIAL, DON'T WE?

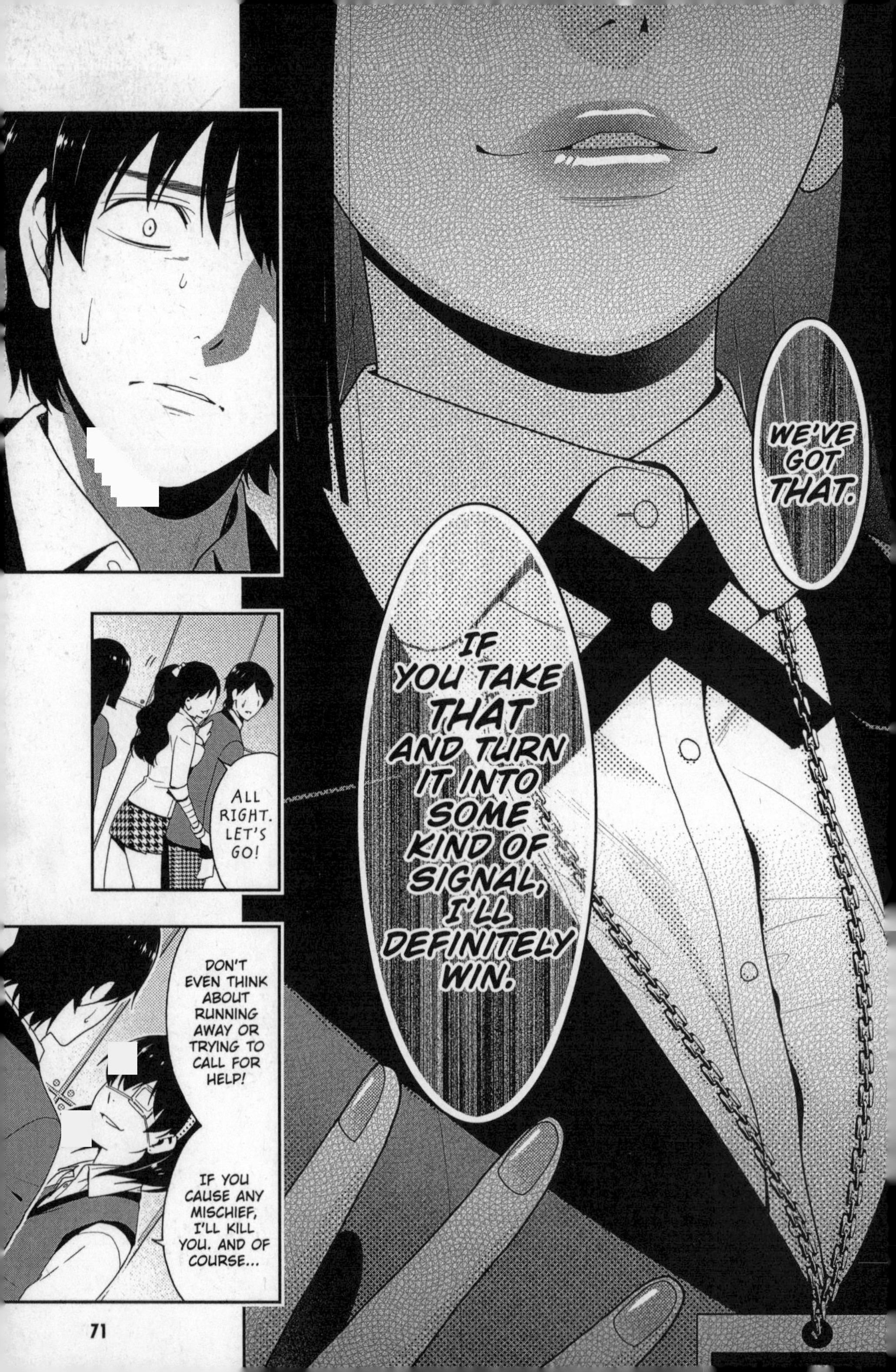
WE'VE GOT THAT.
IF YOU TAKE THAT AND TURN IT INTO SOME KIND OF SIGNAL, I'LL DEFINITELY WIN.
ALL RIGHT. LET'S GO!
DON'T EVEN THINK ABOUT RUNNING AWAY OR TRYING TO CALL FOR HELP!
IF YOU CAUSE ANY MISCHIEF, I'LL KILL YOU. AND OF COURSE...

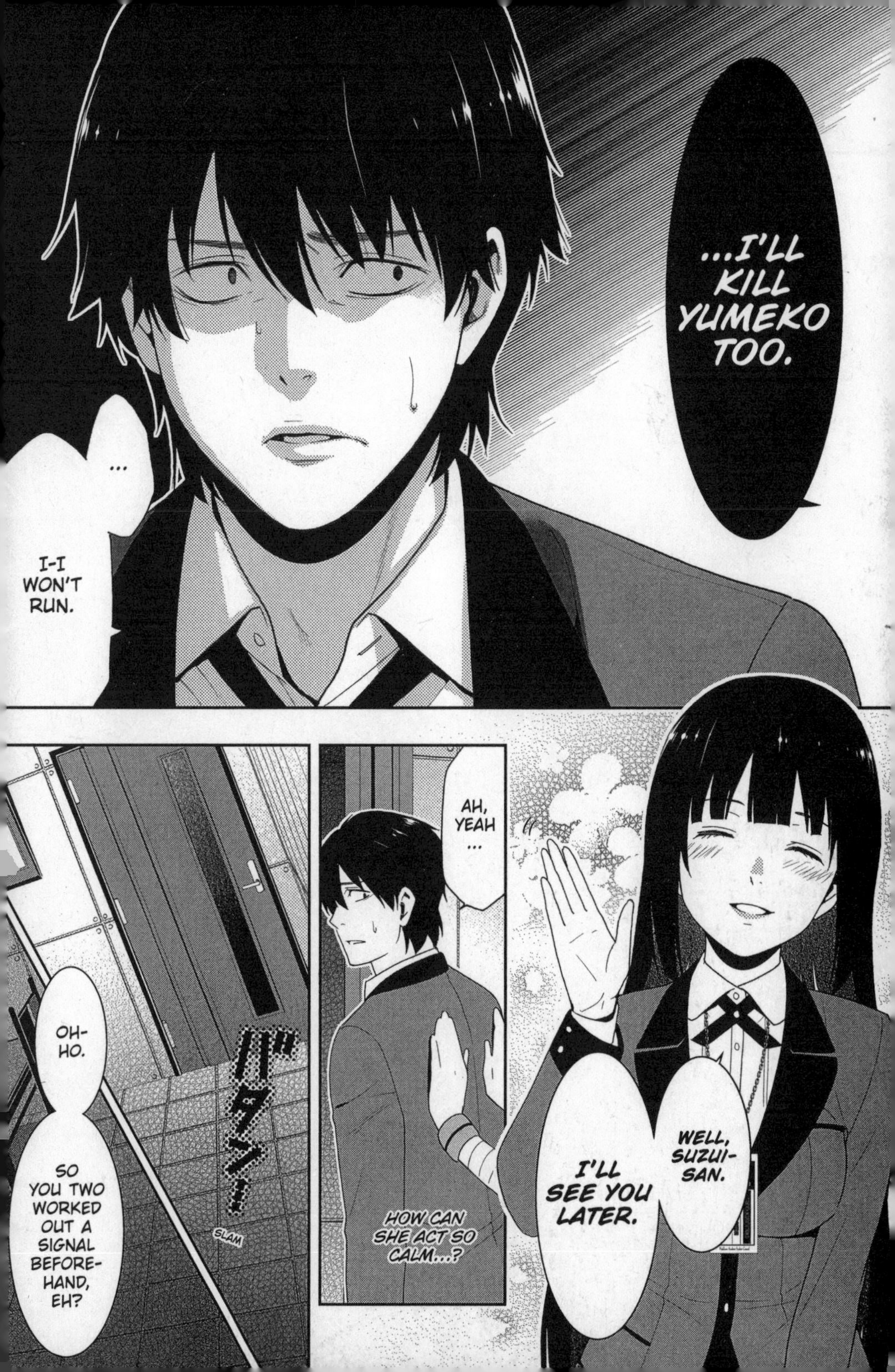
...I'LL KILL YUMEKO TOO.
...
I-I WON'T RUN.
WELL, SUZUI-SAN.
I'LL SEE YOU LATER.
AH, YEAH ...
HOW CAN SHE ACT SO CALM...?
SLAM
OH-HO.
SO YOU TWO WORKED OUT A SIGNAL BEFOREHAND, EH?

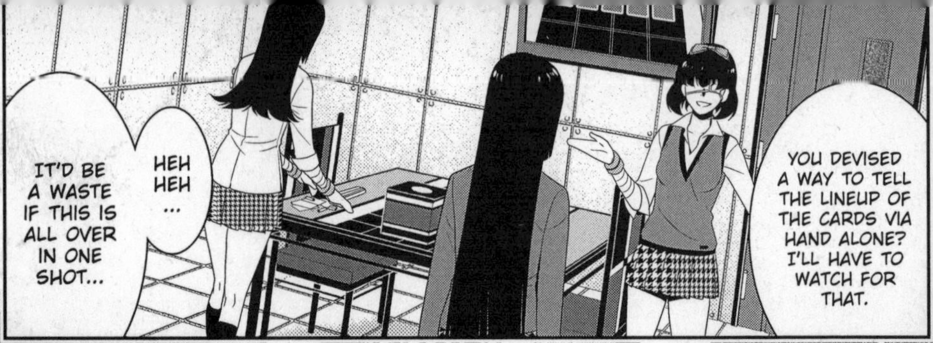
YOU DEVISED A WAY TO TELL THE LINEUP OF THE CARDS VIA HAND ALONE? I'LL HAVE TO WATCH FOR THAT.
HEH HEH ...
IT'D BE A WASTE IF THIS IS ALL OVER IN ONE SHOT...
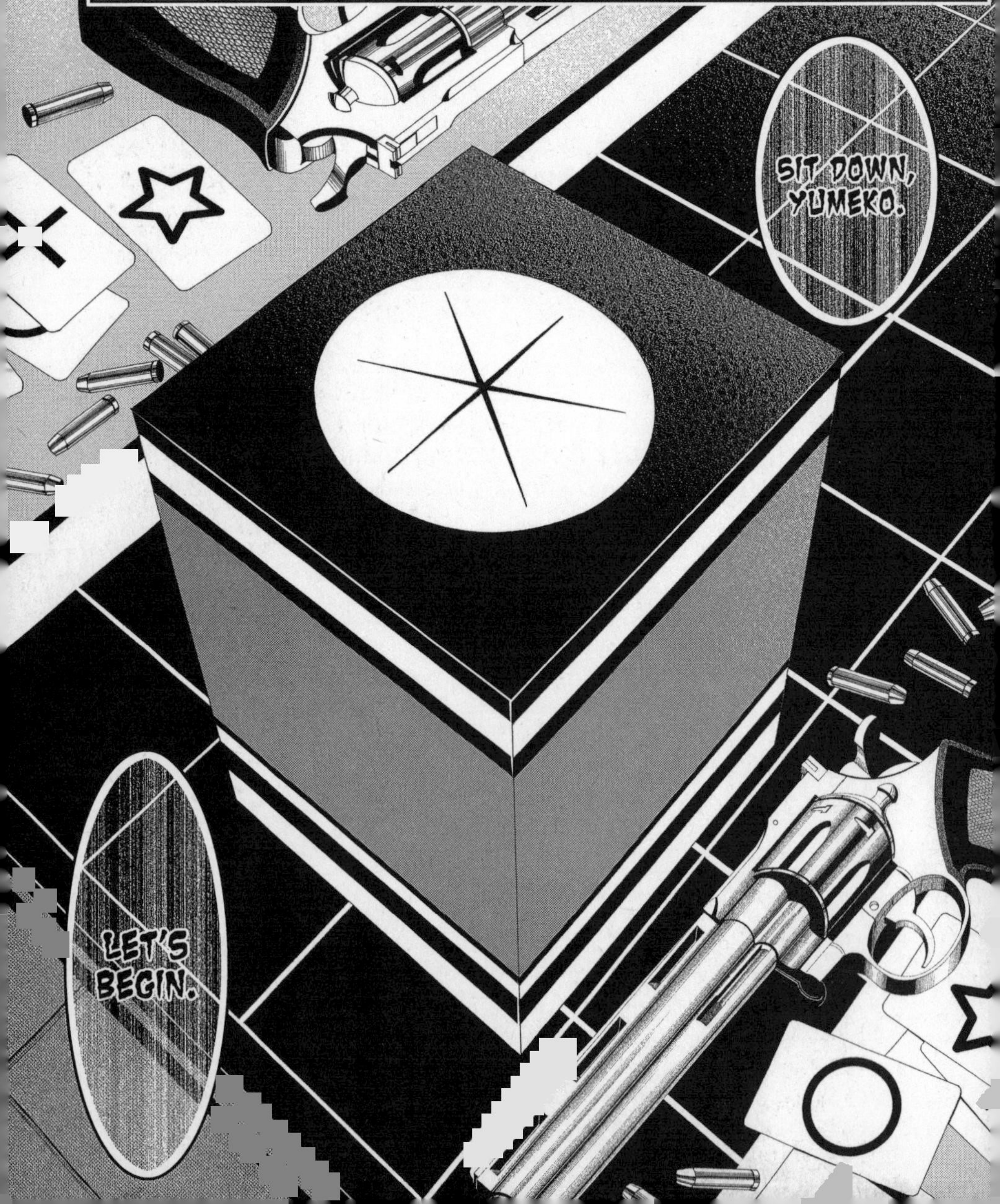
SIT DOWN, YUMEKO.
LET'S BEGIN.

KAKEGURUI
— Compulsive Gambler —

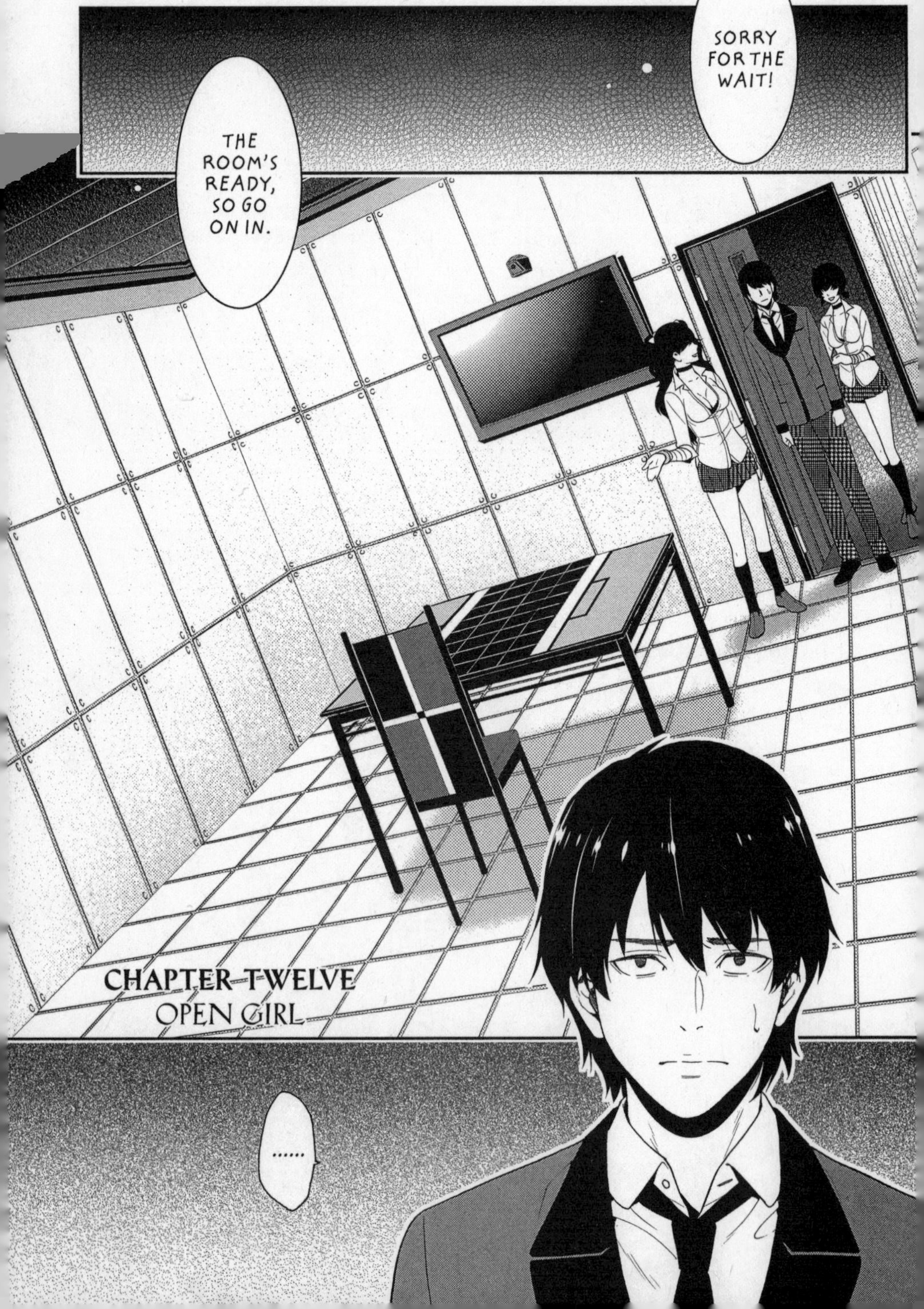
SORRY FOR THE WAIT!
THE ROOM'S READY, SO GO ON IN.
CHAPTER TWELVE
OPEN GIRL
……

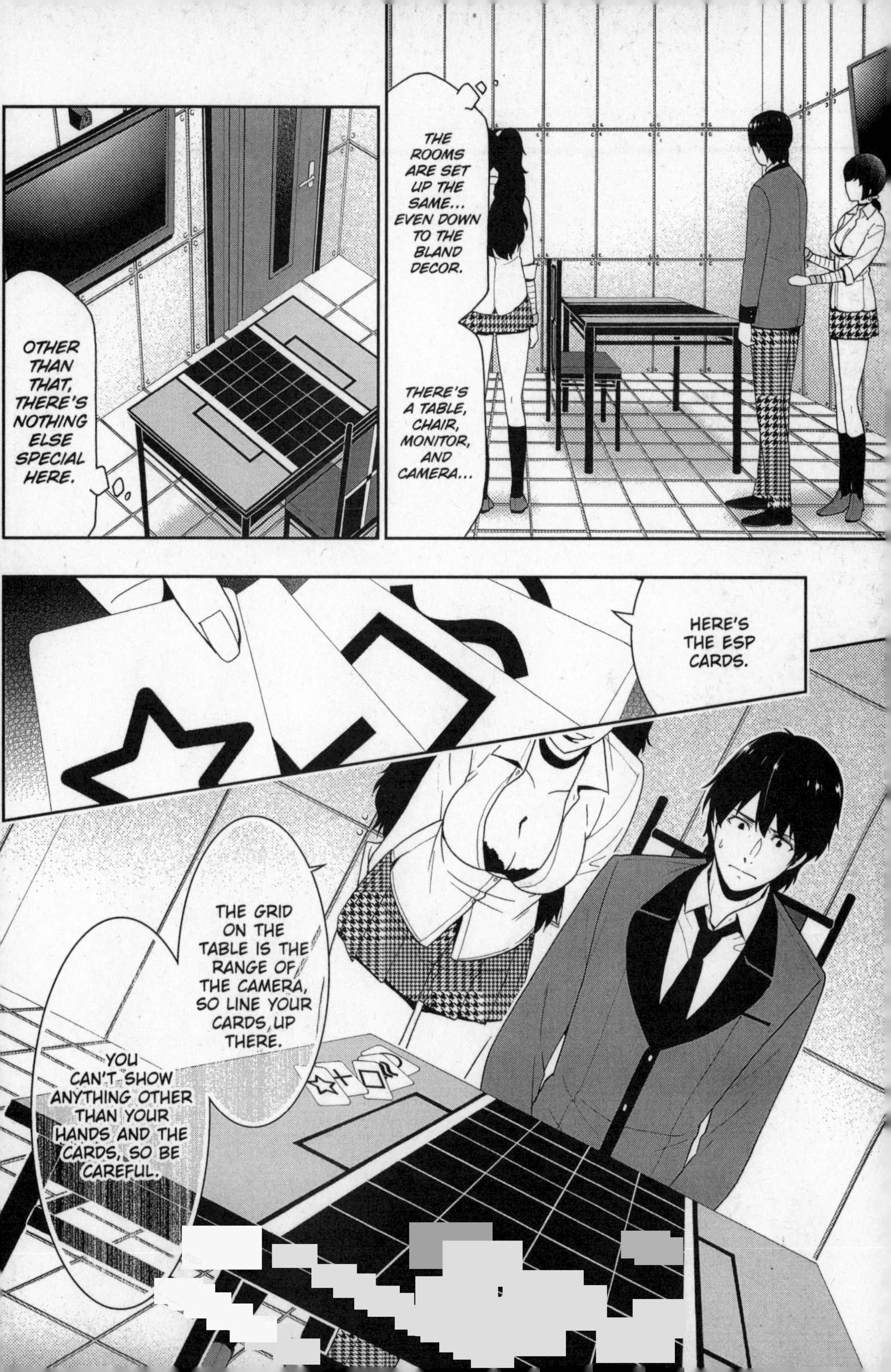
THE ROOMS ARE SET UP THE SAME... EVEN DOWN TO THE BLAND DECOR.
THERE'S A TABLE, CHAIR, MONITOR, AND CAMERA...
OTHER THAN THAT, THERE'S NOTHING ELSE SPECIAL HERE.
HERE'S THE ESP CARDS.
THE GRID ON THE TABLE IS THE RANGE OF THE CAMERA, SO LINE YOUR CARDS UP THERE.
YOU CAN'T SHOW ANYTHING OTHER THAN YOUR HANDS AND THE CARDS, SO BE CAREFUL.

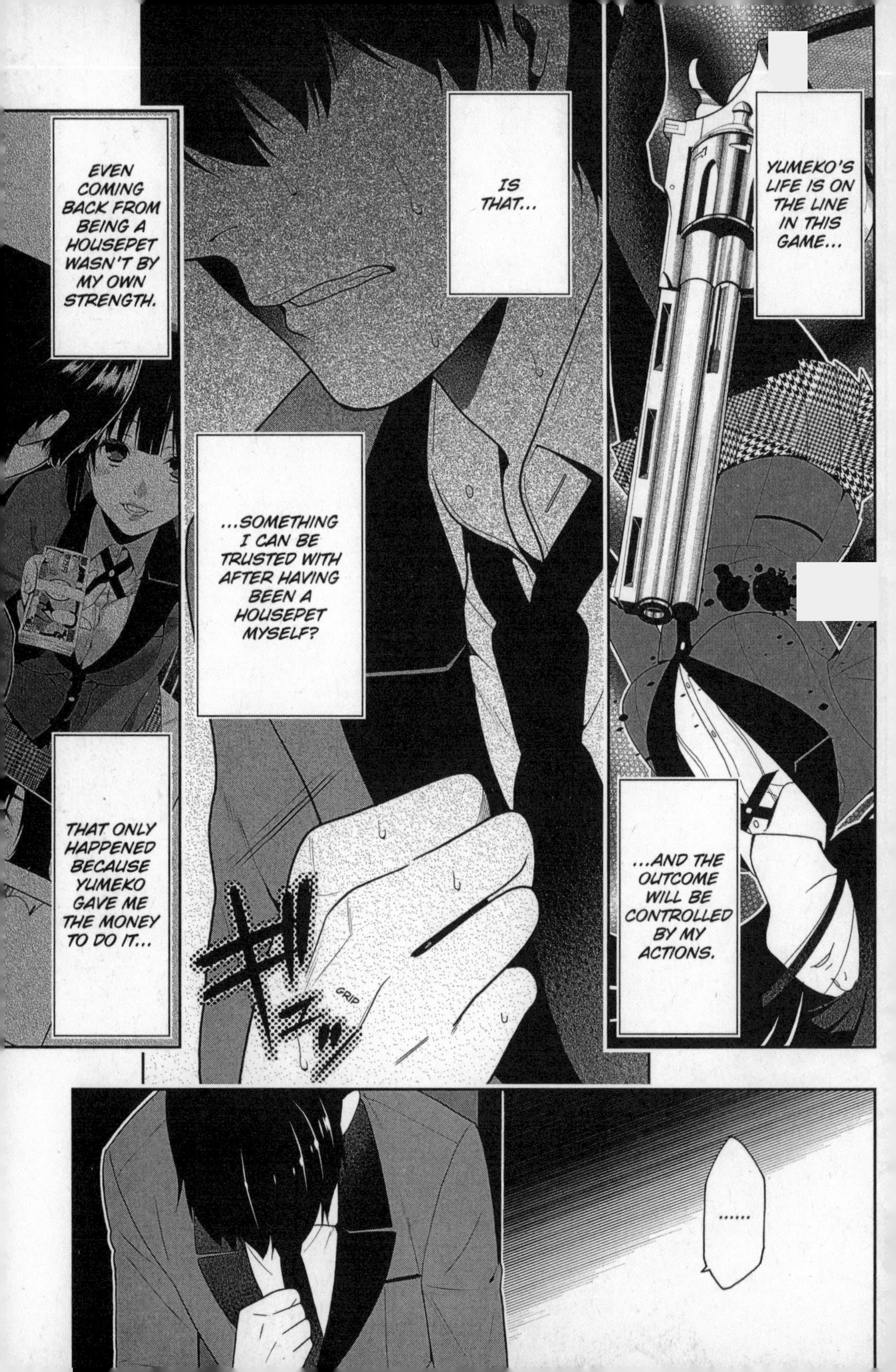
YUMEKO'S LIFE IS ON THE LINE IN THIS GAME...
...AND THE OUTCOME WILL BE CONTROLLED BY MY ACTIONS.
IS THAT...
...SOMETHING I CAN BE TRUSTED WITH AFTER HAVING BEEN A HOUSEPET MYSELF?
GRIP
EVEN COMING BACK FROM BEING A HOUSEPET WASN'T BY MY OWN STRENGTH.
THAT ONLY HAPPENED BECAUSE YUMEKO GAVE ME THE MONEY TO DO IT...
......

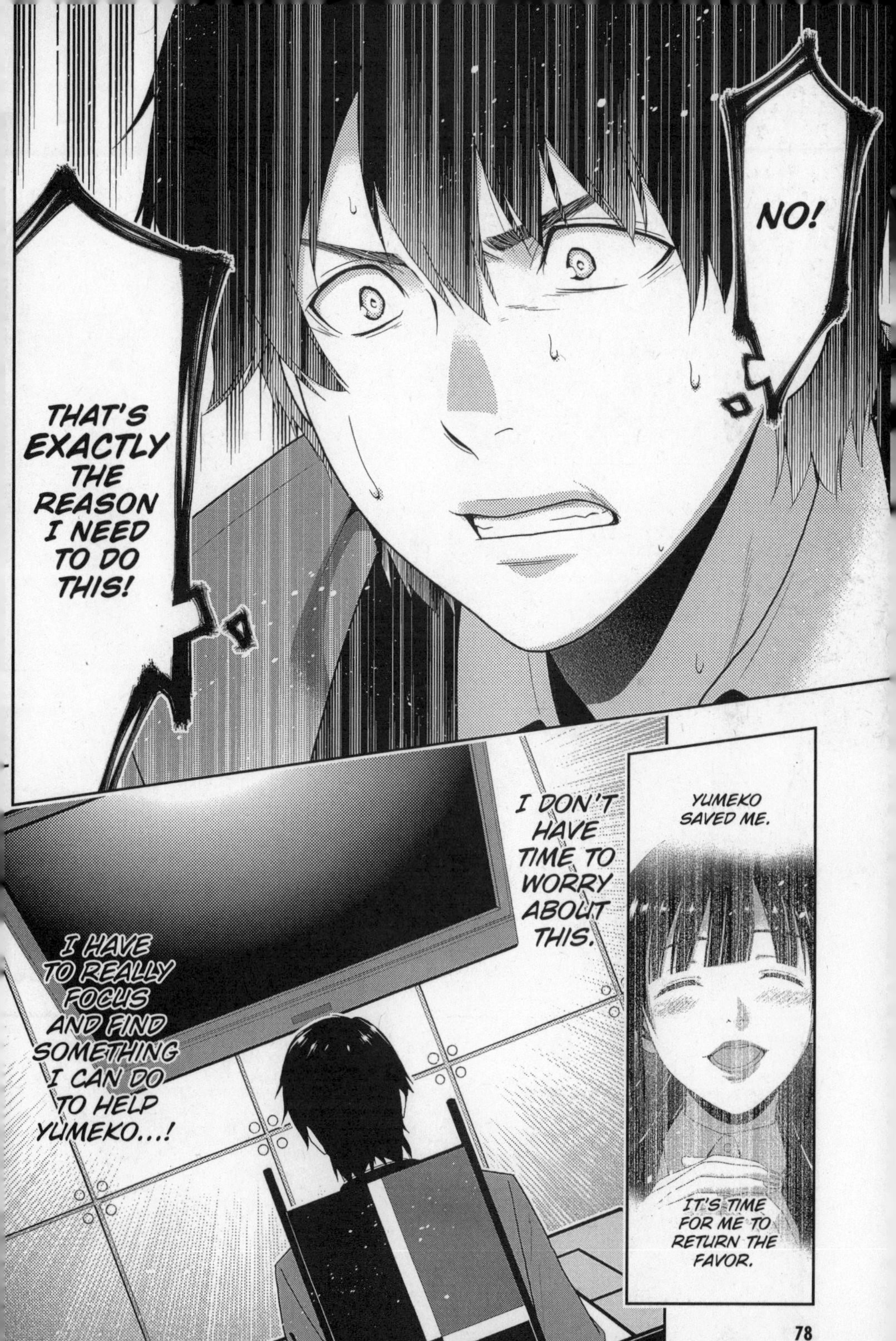
NO!
THAT'S EXACTLY THE REASON I NEED TO DO THIS!
YUMEKO SAVED ME.
IT'S TIME FOR ME TO RETURN THE FAVOR.
I DON'T HAVE TIME TO WORRY ABOUT THIS.
I HAVE TO REALLY FOCUS AND FIND SOMETHING I CAN DO TO HELP YUMEKO...!

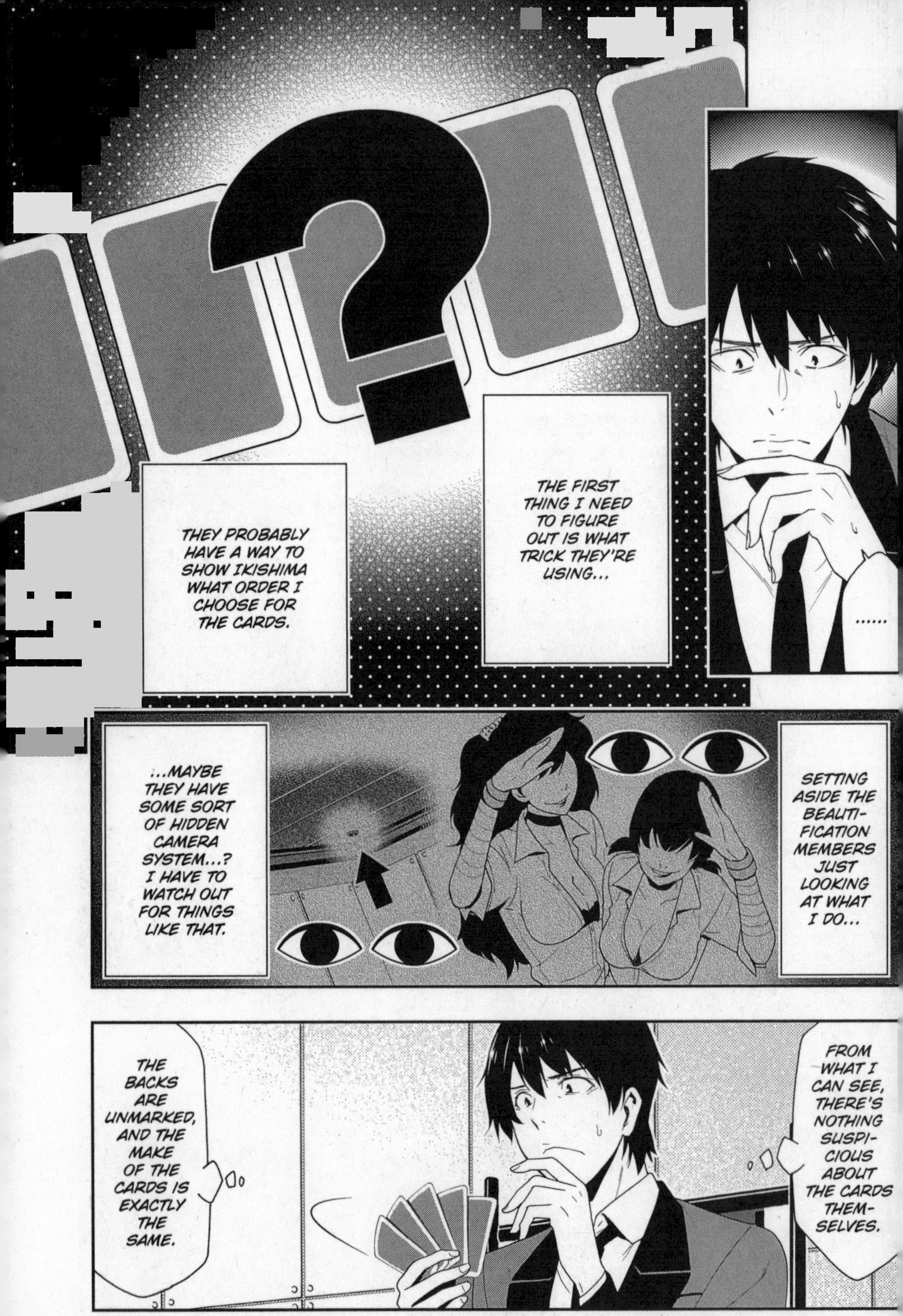
......
THE FIRST THING I NEED TO FIGURE OUT IS WHAT TRICK THEY'RE USING...
THEY PROBABLY HAVE A WAY TO SHOW IKISHIMA WHAT ORDER I CHOOSE FOR THE CARDS.
SETTING ASIDE THE BEAUTI-FICATION MEMBERS JUST LOOKING AT WHAT I DO...
...MAYBE THEY HAVE SOME SORT OF HIDDEN CAMERA SYSTEM...? I HAVE TO WATCH OUT FOR THINGS LIKE THAT.
FROM WHAT I CAN SEE, THERE'S NOTHING SUSPI-CIOUS ABOUT THE CARDS THEM-SELVES.
THE BACKS ARE UNMARKED, AND THE MAKE OF THE CARDS IS EXACTLY THE SAME.

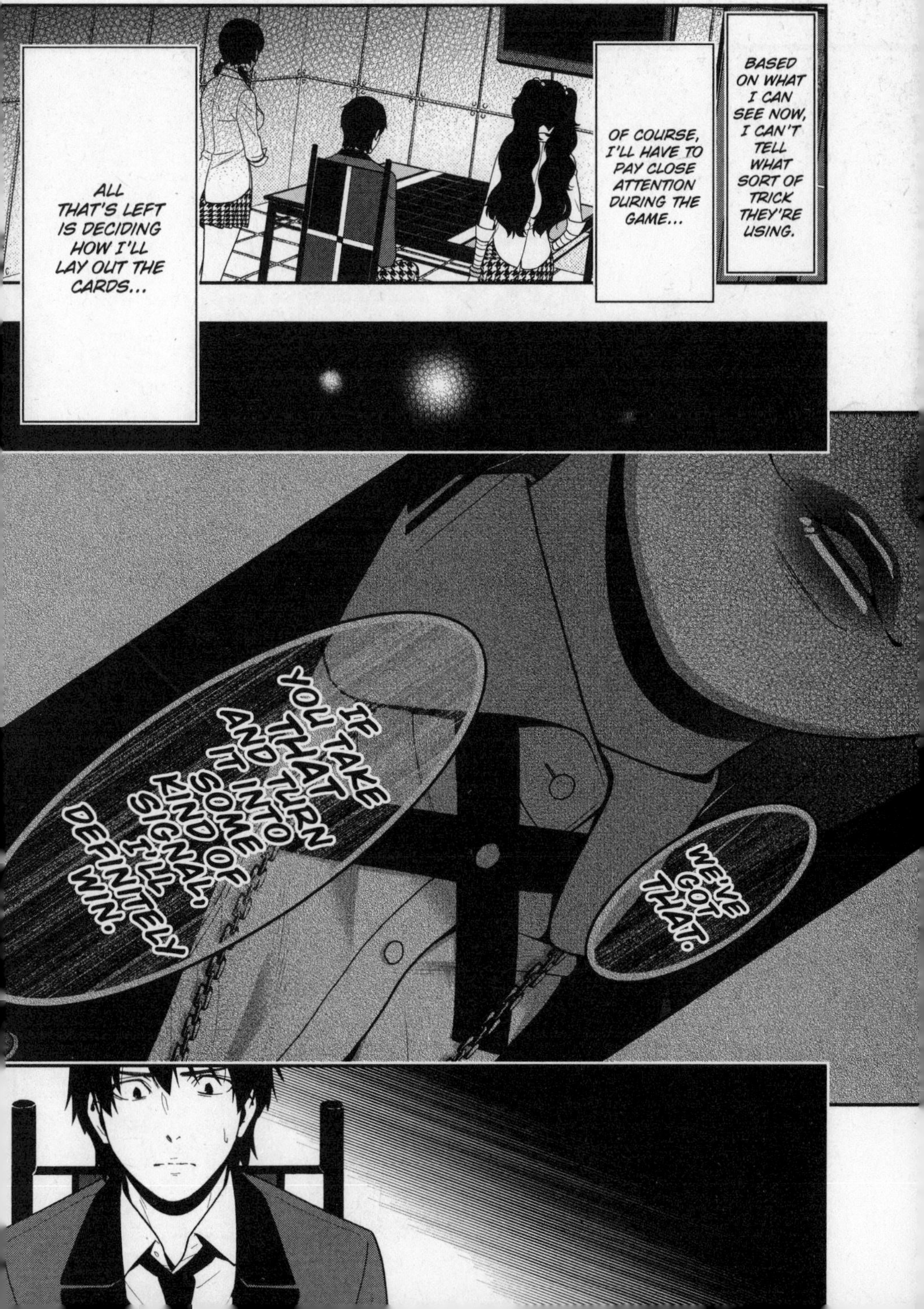
BASED ON WHAT I CAN SEE NOW, I CAN'T TELL WHAT SORT OF TRICK THEY'RE USING.
OF COURSE, I'LL HAVE TO PAY CLOSE ATTENTION DURING THE GAME...
ALL THAT'S LEFT IS DECIDING HOW I'LL LAY OUT THE CARDS...
IF YOU TAKE THAT AND TURN IT INTO SOME KIND OF SIGNAL, I'LL DEFINITELY WIN.
WE'VE GOT THAT.

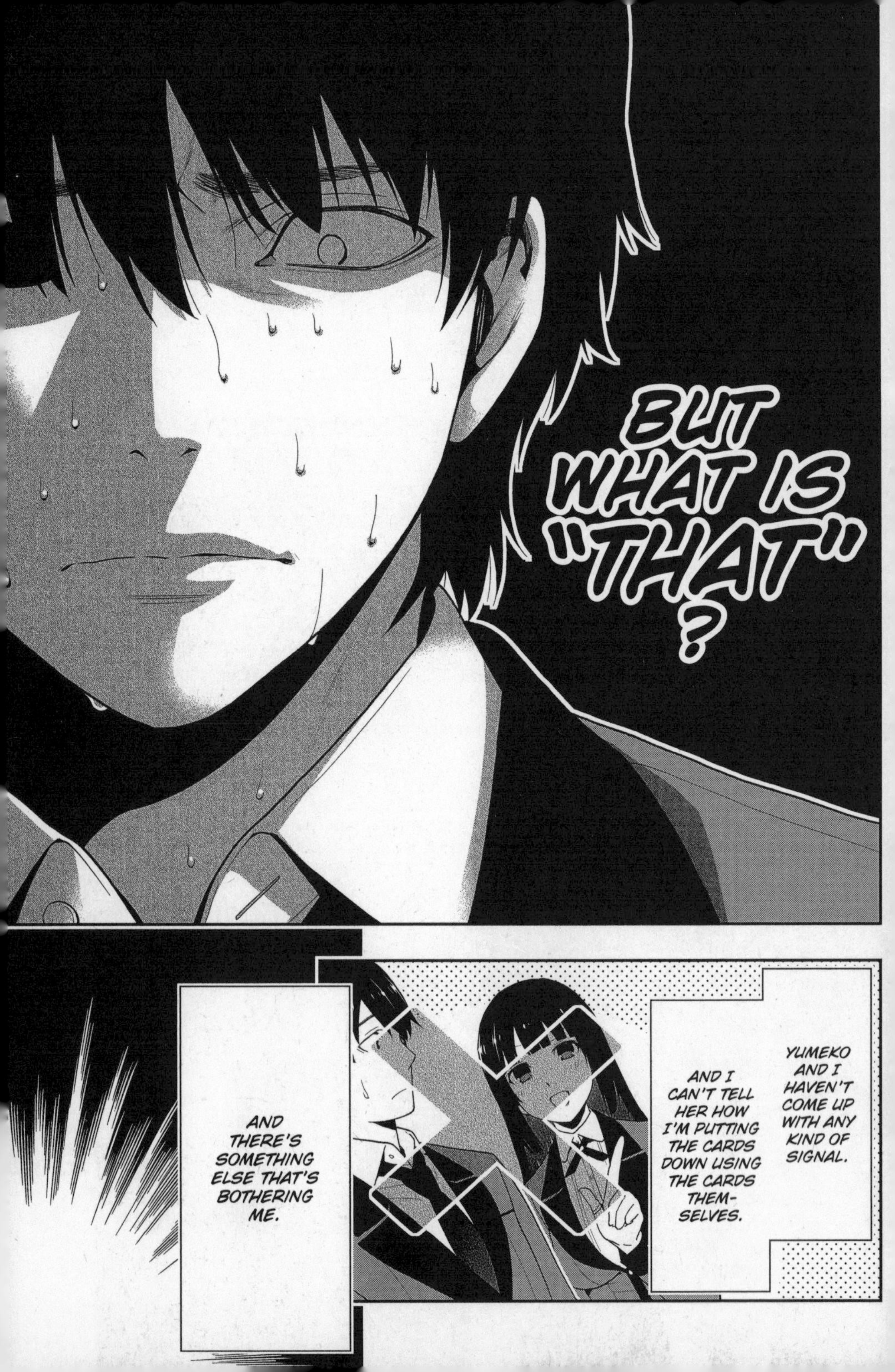
BUT WHAT IS "THAT"?
YUMEKO AND I HAVEN'T COME UP WITH ANY KIND OF SIGNAL.
AND I CAN'T TELL HER HOW I'M PUTTING THE CARDS DOWN USING THE CARDS THEM-SELVES.
AND THERE'S SOMETHING ELSE THAT'S BOTHERING ME.

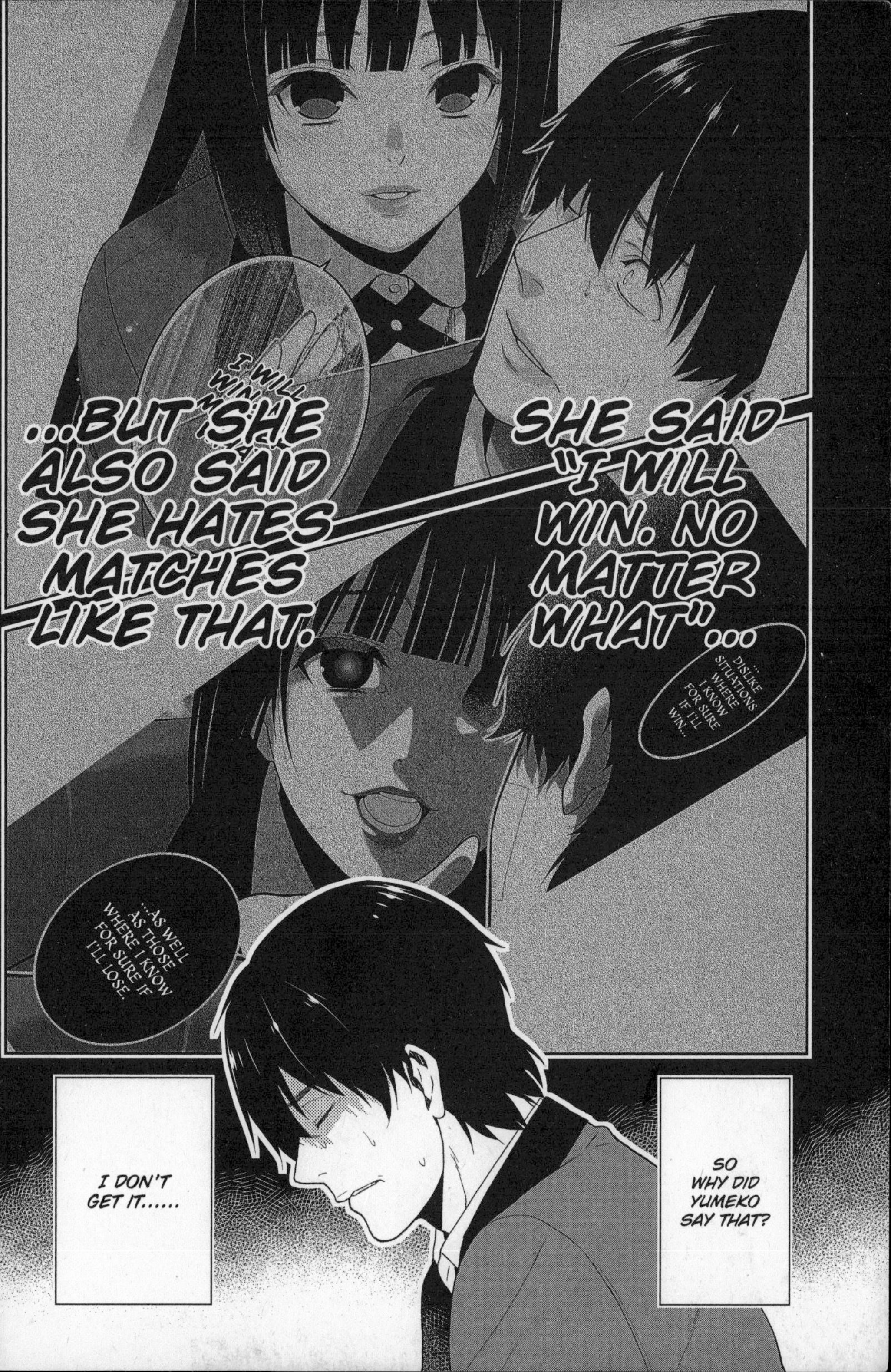

SHE SAID "I WILL WIN. NO MATTER WHAT"...
...BUT SHE ALSO SAID SHE HATES MATCHES LIKE THAT.
...DISLIKE SITUATIONS WHERE I KNOW FOR SURE IF I'LL WIN...
...AS WELL AS THOSE WHERE I KNOW FOR SURE IF I'LL LOSE.
SO WHY DID YUMEKO SAY THAT?
I DON'T GET IT......

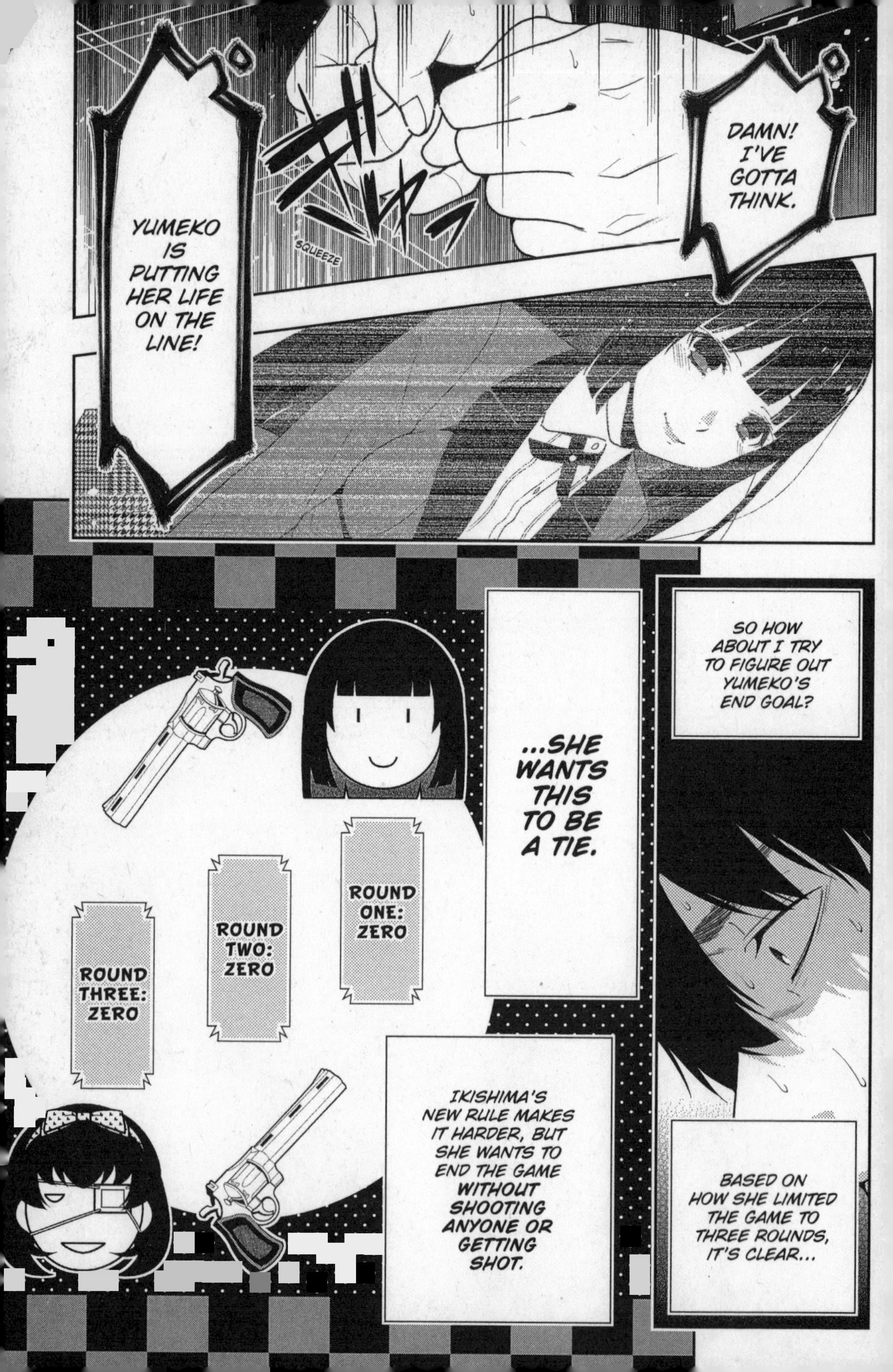
DAMN! I'VE GOTTA THINK.
SQUEEZE
YUMEKO IS PUTTING HER LIFE ON THE LINE!
SO HOW ABOUT I TRY TO FIGURE OUT YUMEKO'S END GOAL?
BASED ON HOW SHE LIMITED THE GAME TO THREE ROUNDS, IT'S CLEAR...
...SHE WANTS THIS TO BE A TIE.
IKISHIMA'S NEW RULE MAKES IT HARDER, BUT SHE WANTS TO END THE GAME WITHOUT SHOOTING ANYONE OR GETTING SHOT.
ROUND ONE: ZERO
ROUND TWO: ZERO
ROUND THREE: ZERO

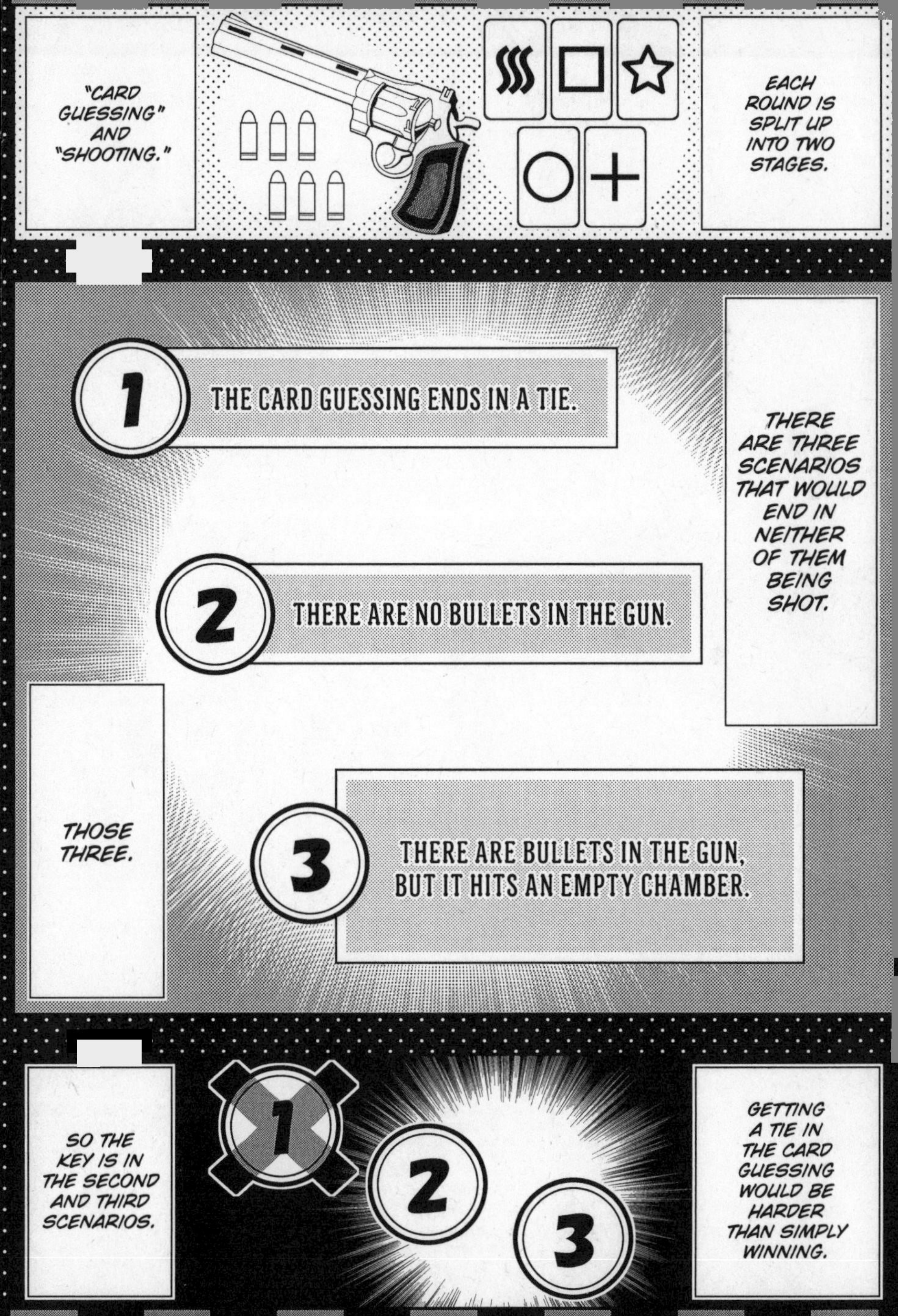
EACH ROUND IS SPLIT UP INTO TWO STAGES.
"CARD GUESSING" AND "SHOOTING."
THERE ARE THREE SCENARIOS THAT WOULD END IN NEITHER OF THEM BEING SHOT.
1
THE CARD GUESSING ENDS IN A TIE.
2
THERE ARE NO BULLETS IN THE GUN.
3
THERE ARE BULLETS IN THE GUN, BUT IT HITS AN EMPTY CHAMBER.
THOSE THREE.
GETTING A TIE IN THE CARD GUESSING WOULD BE HARDER THAN SIMPLY WINNING.
1
2
3
SO THE KEY IS IN THE SECOND AND THIRD SCENARIOS.

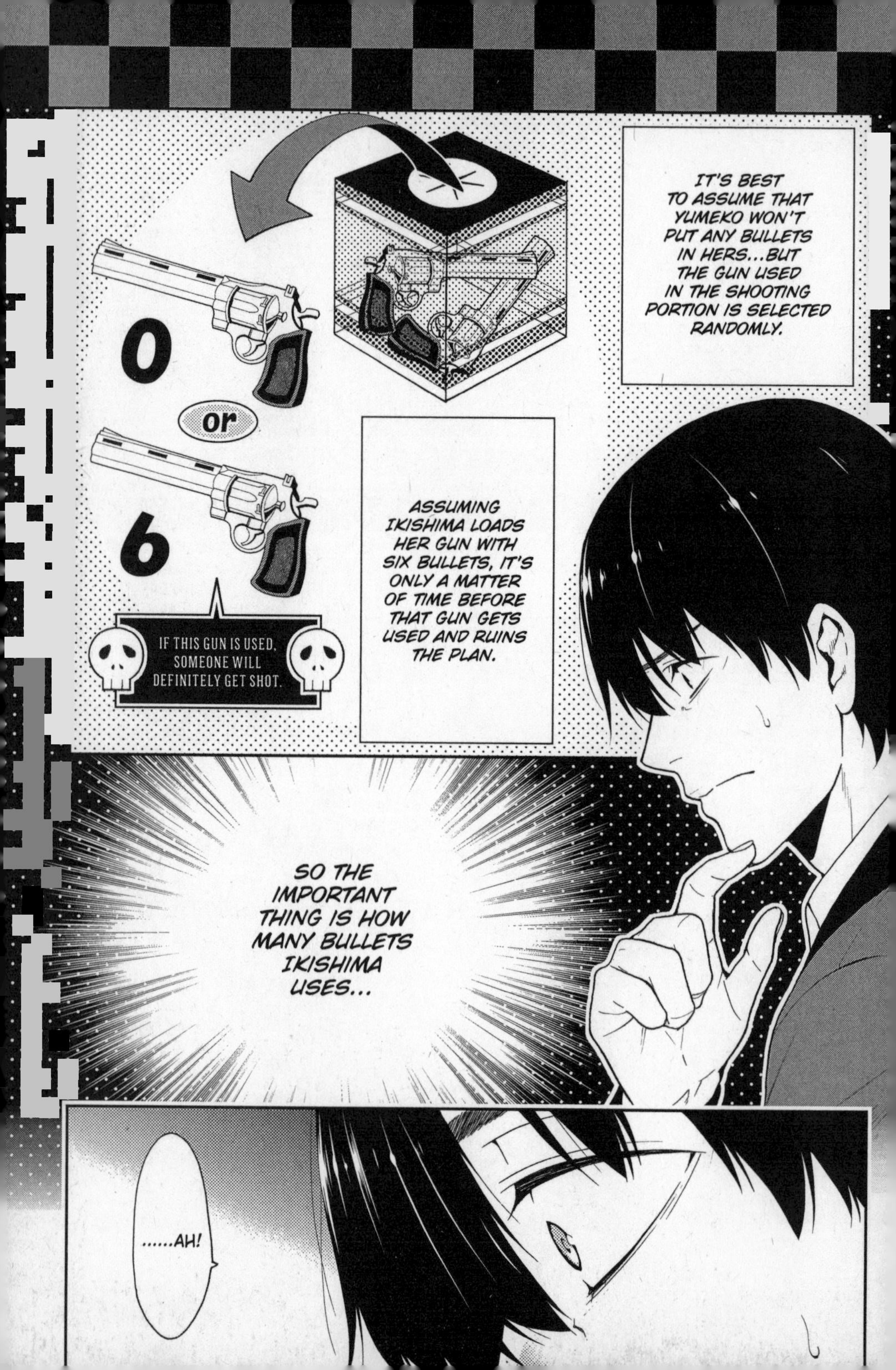
IT'S BEST TO ASSUME THAT YUMEKO WON'T PUT ANY BULLETS IN HERS...BUT THE GUN USED IN THE SHOOTING PORTION IS SELECTED RANDOMLY.
ASSUMING IKISHIMA LOADS HER GUN WITH SIX BULLETS, IT'S ONLY A MATTER OF TIME BEFORE THAT GUN GETS USED AND RUINS THE PLAN.
0
or
6
IF THIS GUN IS USED, SOMEONE WILL DEFINITELY GET SHOT.
SO THE IMPORTANT THING IS HOW MANY BULLETS IKISHIMA USES...
......AH!

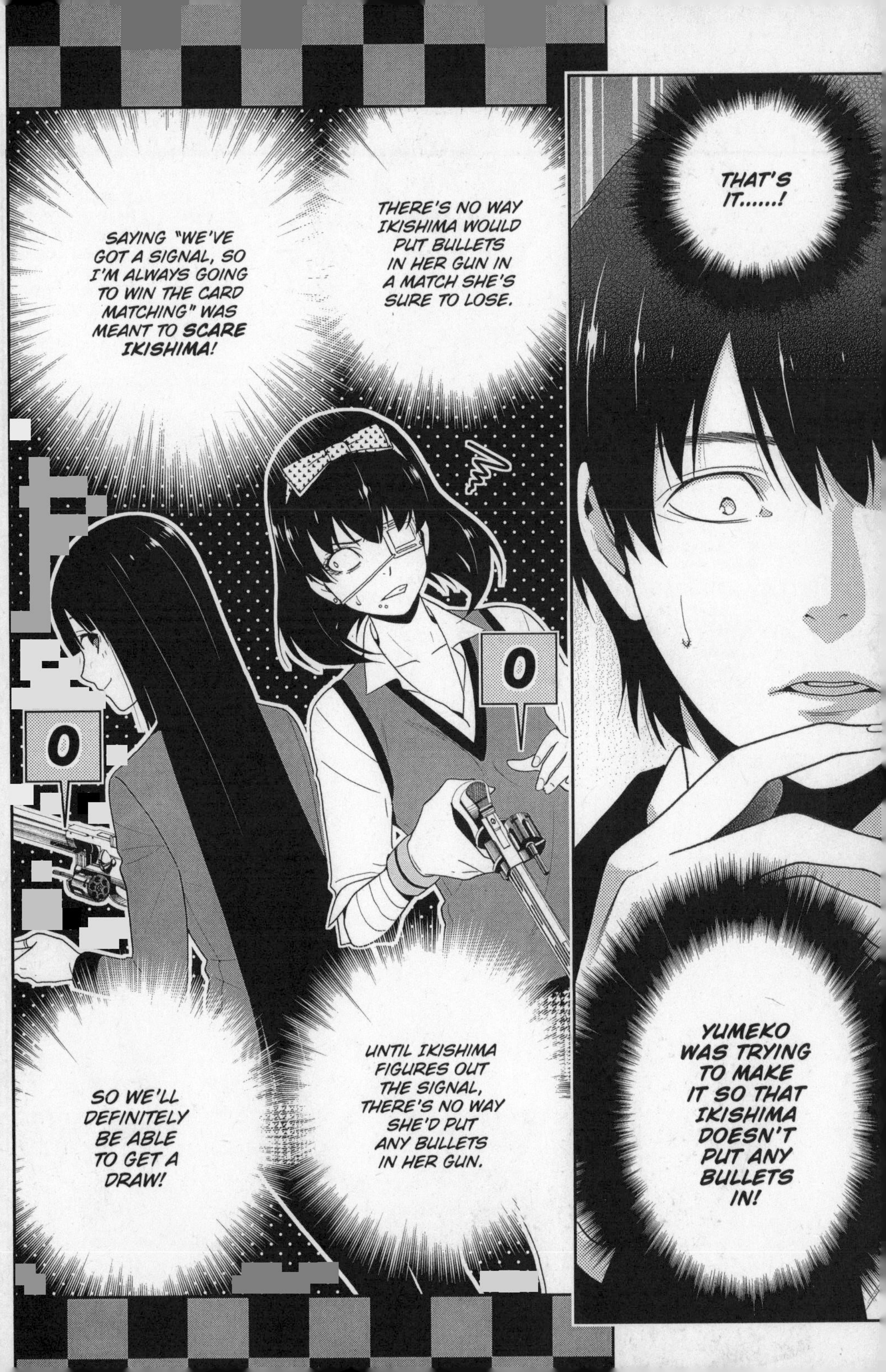
THAT'S IT......!
YUMEKO WAS TRYING TO MAKE IT SO THAT IKISHIMA DOESN'T PUT ANY BULLETS IN!
THERE'S NO WAY IKISHIMA WOULD PUT BULLETS IN HER GUN IN A MATCH SHE'S SURE TO LOSE.
SAYING "WE'VE GOT A SIGNAL, SO I'M ALWAYS GOING TO WIN THE CARD MATCHING" WAS MEANT TO SCARE IKISHIMA!
0
0
UNTIL IKISHIMA FIGURES OUT THE SIGNAL, THERE'S NO WAY SHE'D PUT ANY BULLETS IN HER GUN.
SO WE'LL DEFINITELY BE ABLE TO GET A DRAW!

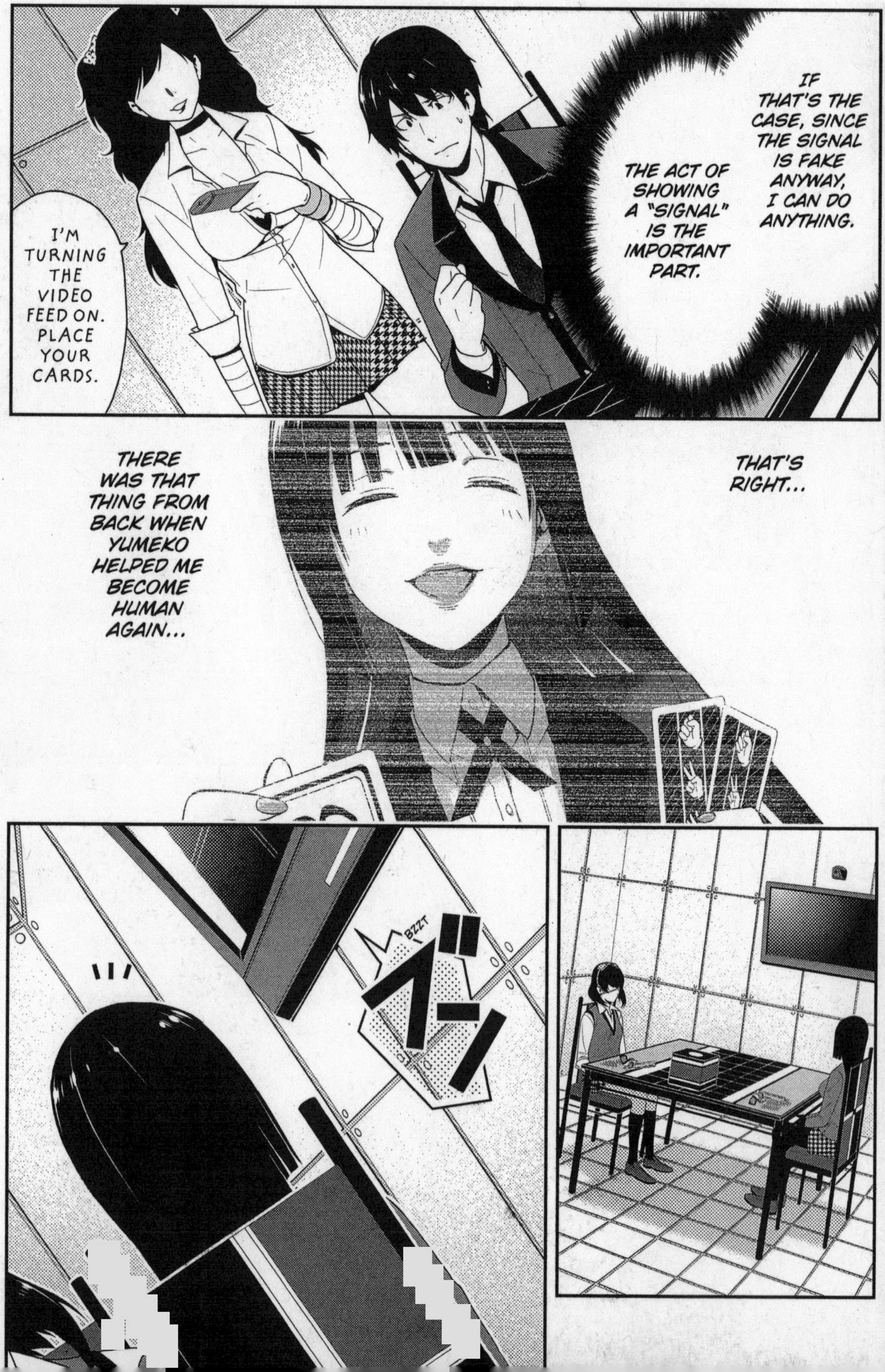
IF THAT'S THE CASE, SINCE THE SIGNAL IS FAKE ANYWAY, I CAN DO ANYTHING.
THE ACT OF SHOWING A "SIGNAL" IS THE IMPORTANT PART.
I'M TURNING THE VIDEO FEED ON. PLACE YOUR CARDS.
THAT'S RIGHT...
THERE WAS THAT THING FROM BACK WHEN YUMEKO HELPED ME BECOME HUMAN AGAIN...
BZZT

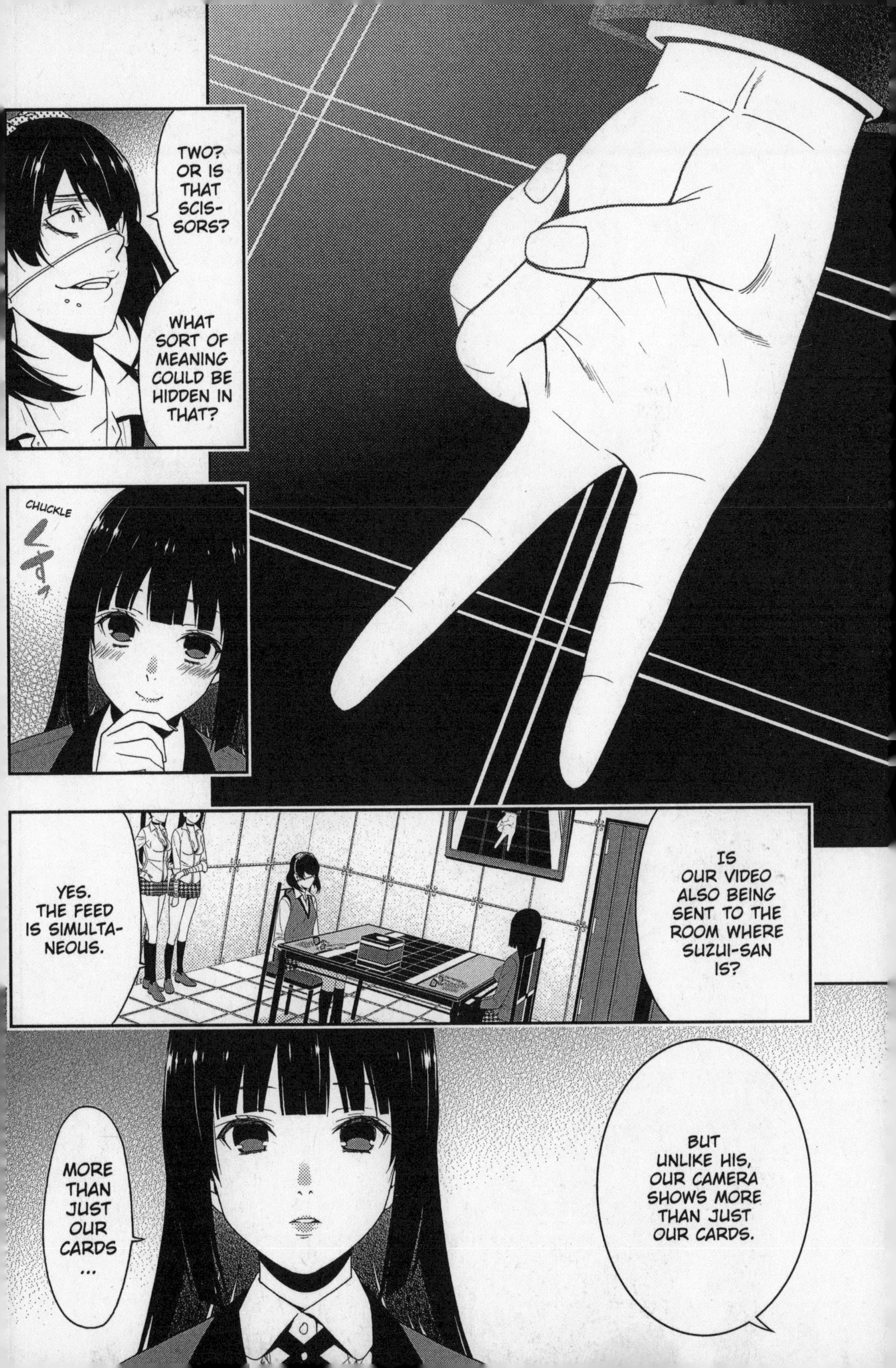
TWO? OR IS THAT SCISSORS?
WHAT SORT OF MEANING COULD BE HIDDEN IN THAT?
CHUCKLE
IS OUR VIDEO ALSO BEING SENT TO THE ROOM WHERE SUZUI-SAN IS?
YES. THE FEED IS SIMULTANEOUS.
BUT UNLIKE HIS, OUR CAMERA SHOWS MORE THAN JUST OUR CARDS.
MORE THAN JUST OUR CARDS ...

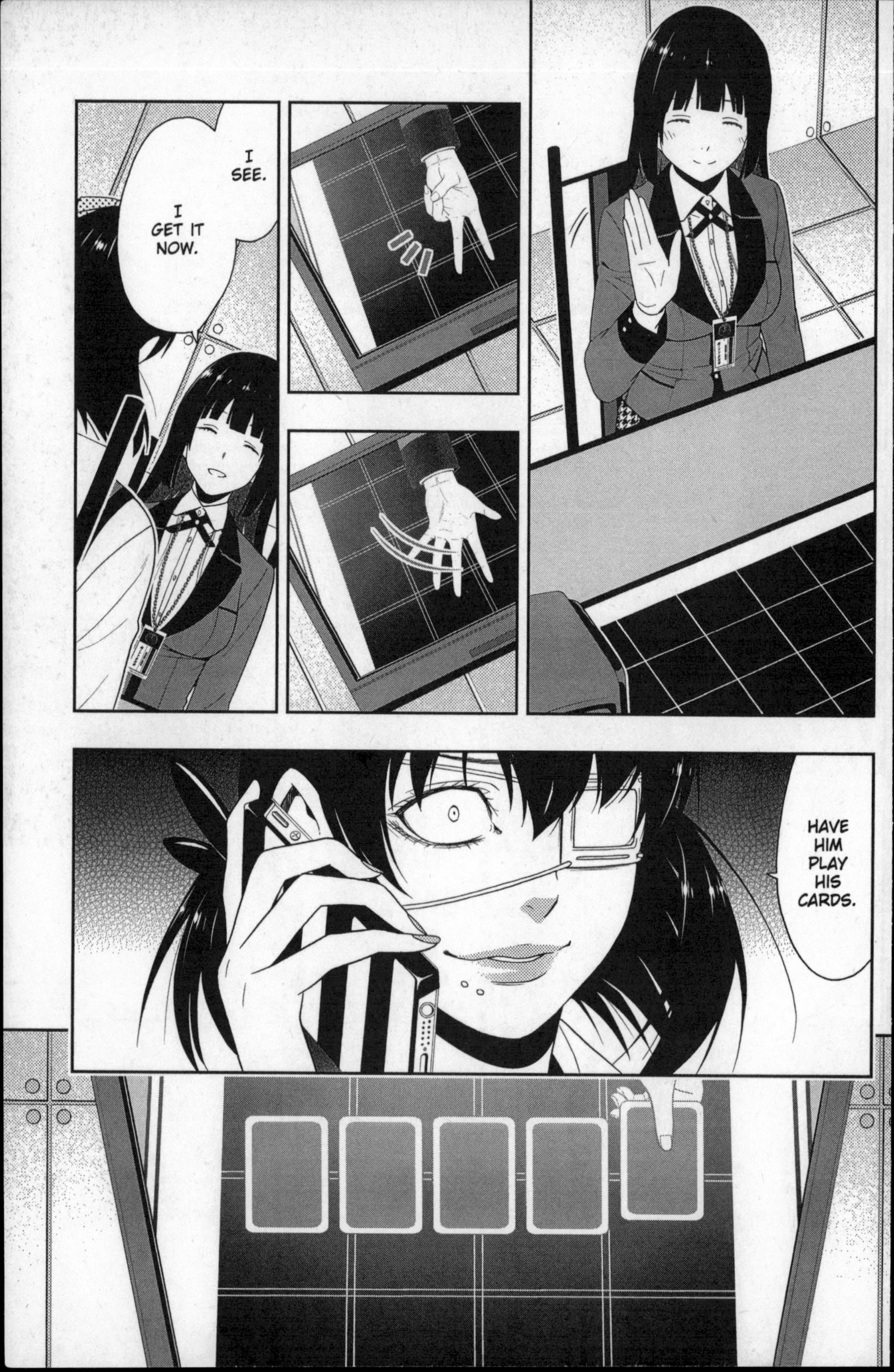
I SEE.
I GET IT NOW.
HAVE HIM PLAY HIS CARDS.

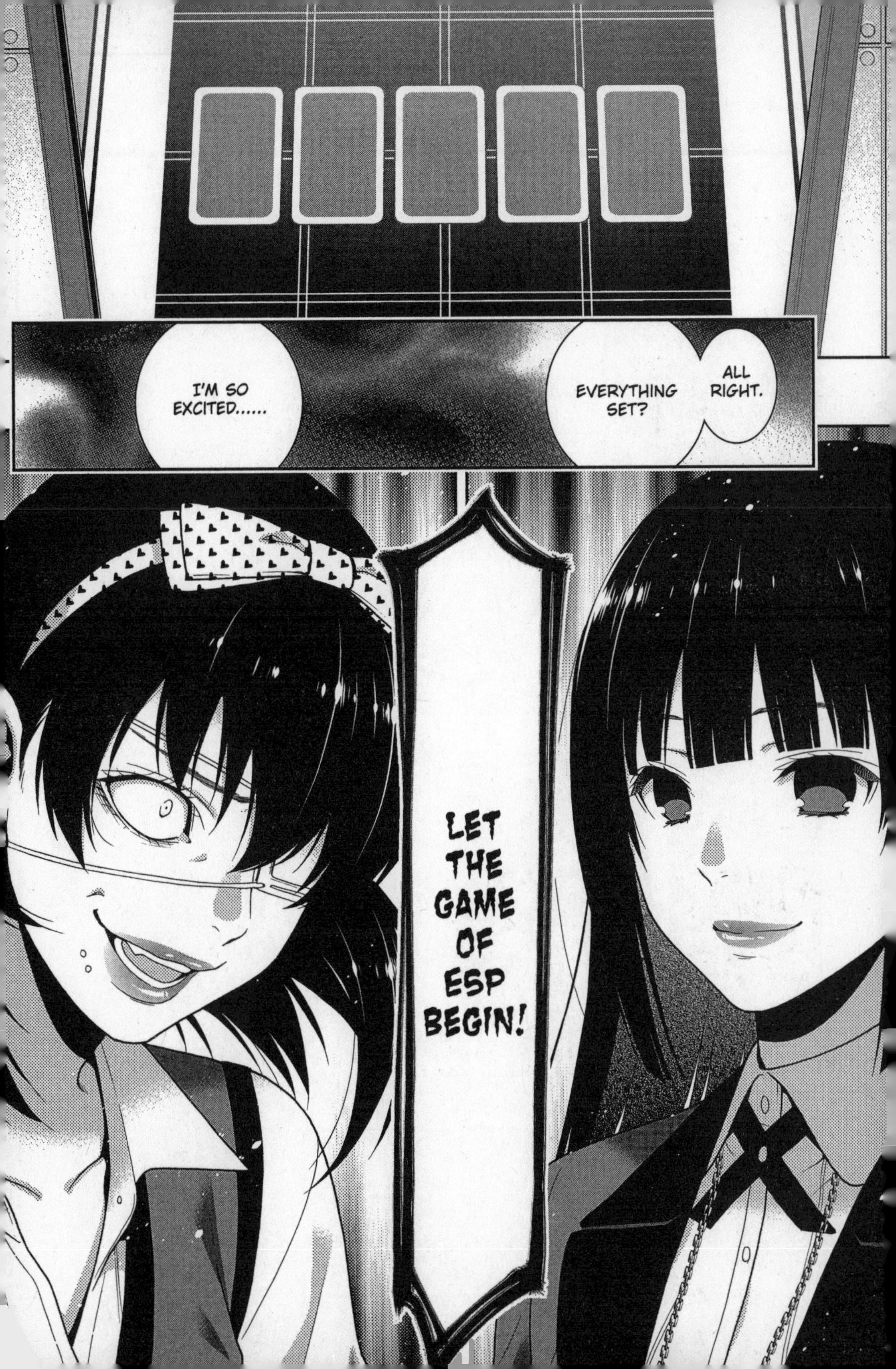
ALL RIGHT.
EVERYTHING SET?
I'M SO EXCITED......
LET THE GAME OF ESP BEGIN!

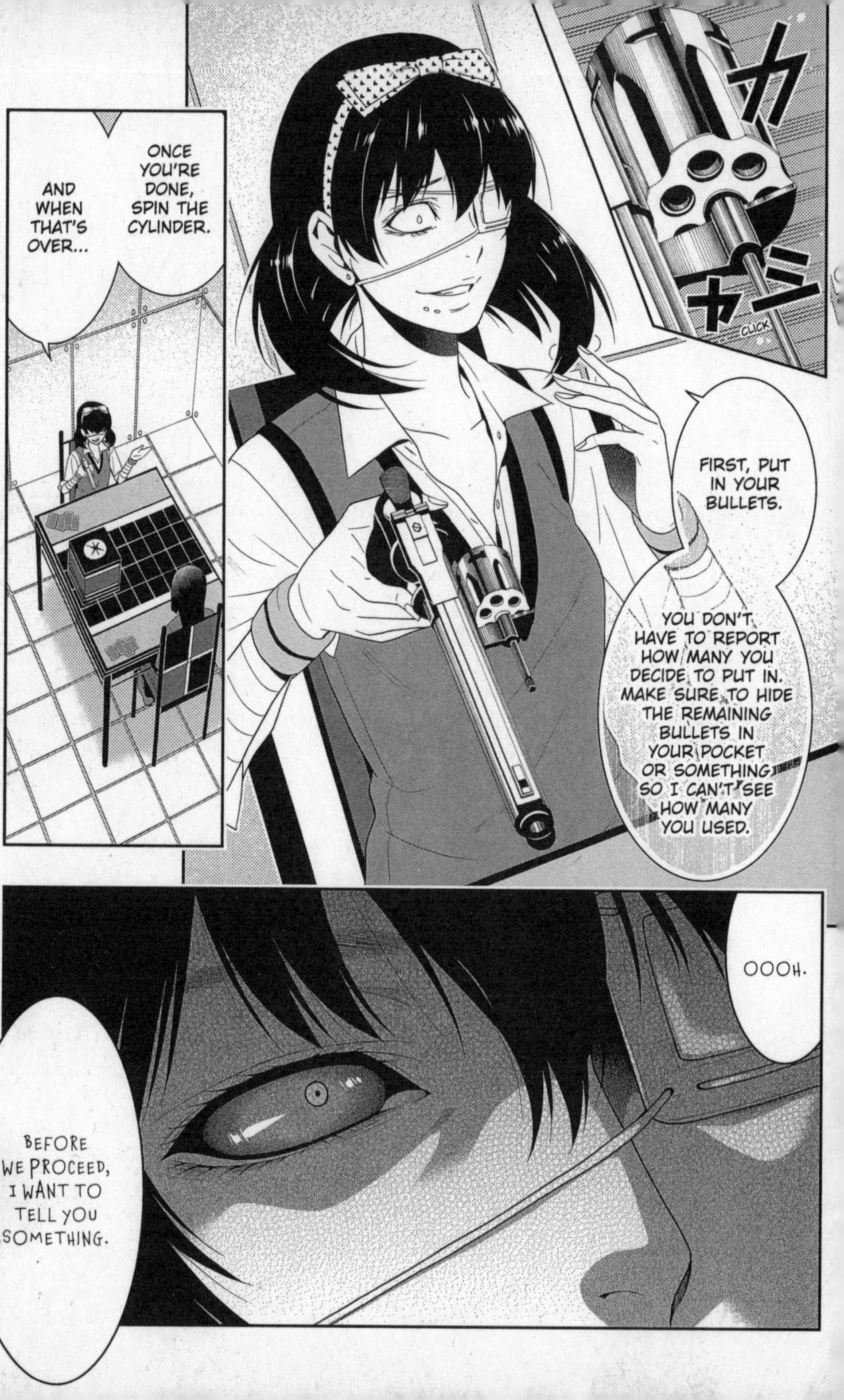

カシャ
CLICK
FIRST, PUT IN YOUR BULLETS.
YOU DON'T HAVE TO REPORT HOW MANY YOU DECIDE TO PUT IN. MAKE SURE TO HIDE THE REMAINING BULLETS IN YOUR POCKET OR SOMETHING SO I CAN'T SEE HOW MANY YOU USED.
ONCE YOU'RE DONE, SPIN THE CYLINDER.
AND WHEN THAT'S OVER...
OOOH.
BEFORE WE PROCEED, I WANT TO TELL YOU SOMETHING.

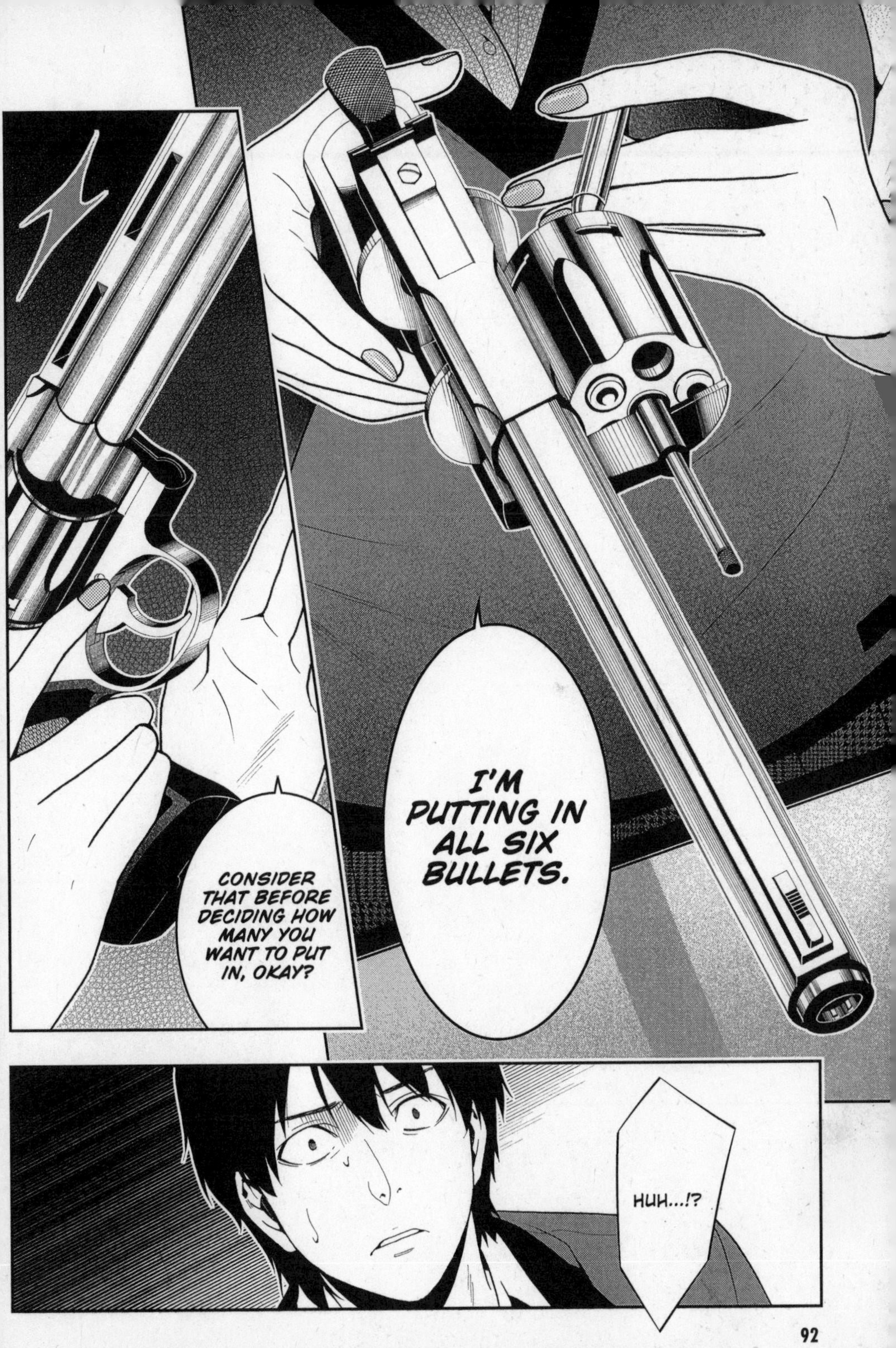
I'M PUTTING IN ALL SIX BULLETS.
CONSIDER THAT BEFORE DECIDING HOW MANY YOU WANT TO PUT IN, OKAY?
HUH...!?

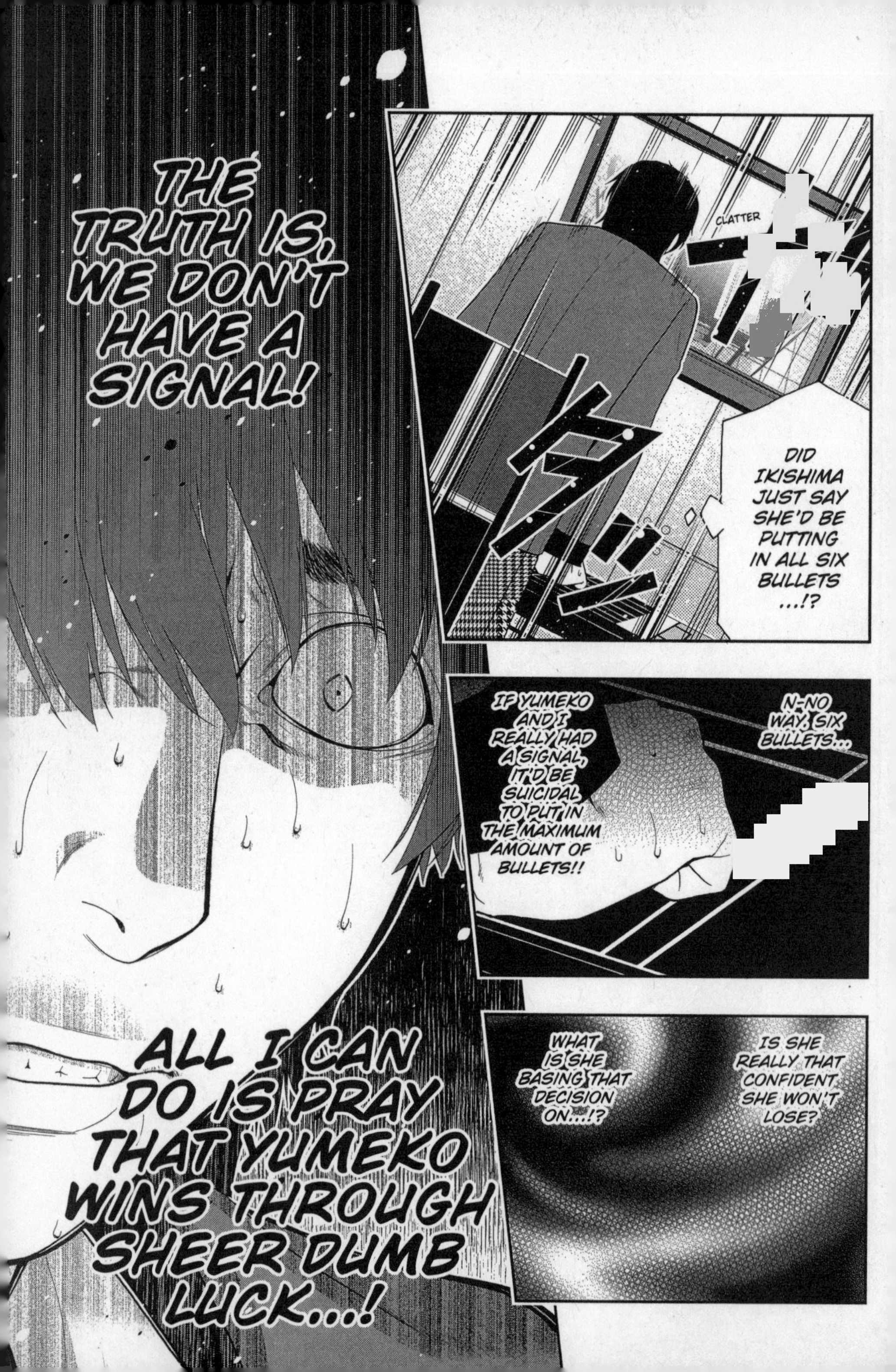
CLATTER
DID IKISHIMA JUST SAY SHE'D BE PUTTING IN ALL SIX BULLETS ...!?
N-NO WAY. SIX BULLETS...
IF YUMEKO AND I REALLY HAD A SIGNAL, IT'D BE SUICIDAL TO PUT IN THE MAXIMUM AMOUNT OF BULLETS!!
IS SHE REALLY THAT CONFIDENT SHE WON'T LOSE?
WHAT IS SHE BASING THAT DECISION ON...!?
THE TRUTH IS, WE DON'T HAVE A SIGNAL!
ALL I CAN DO IS PRAY THAT YUMEKO WINS THROUGH SHEER DUMB LUCK...!

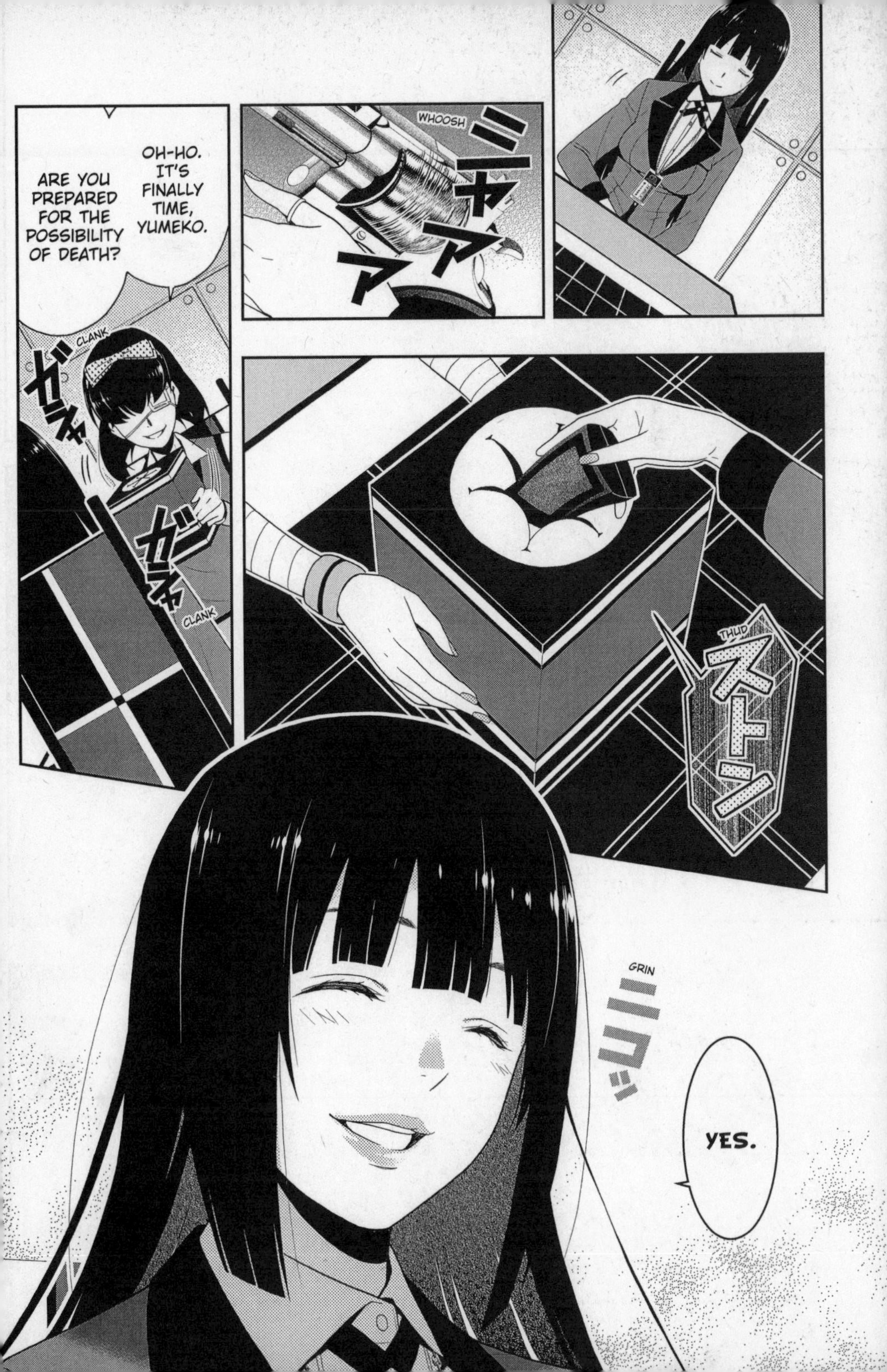
WHOOSH
OH-HO. IT'S FINALLY TIME, YUMEKO.
ARE YOU PREPARED FOR THE POSSIBILITY OF DEATH?
THUD
CLANK
CLANK
GRIN
YES.

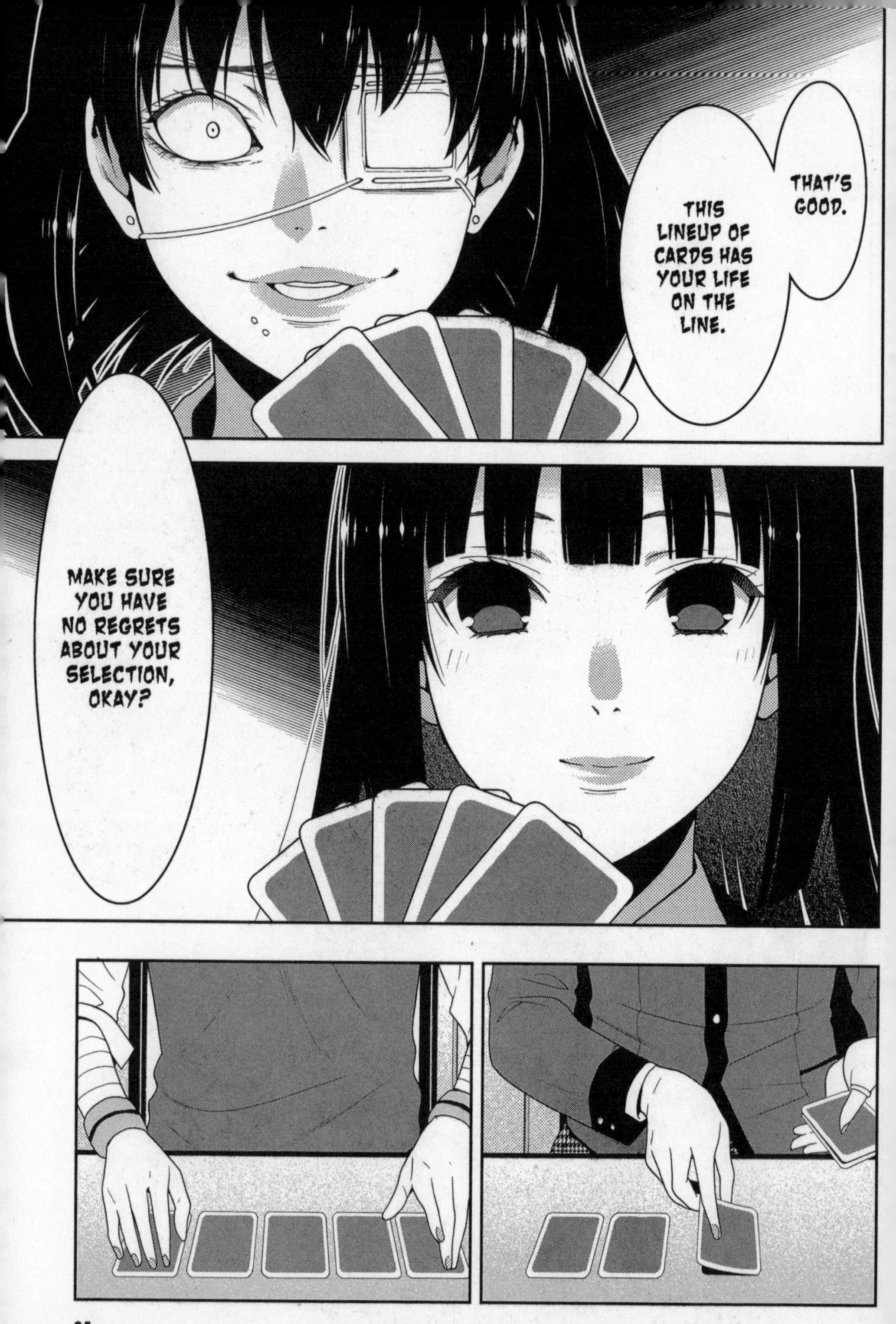
THAT'S GOOD.
THIS LINEUP OF CARDS HAS YOUR LIFE ON THE LINE.
MAKE SURE YOU HAVE NO REGRETS ABOUT YOUR SELECTION, OKAY?

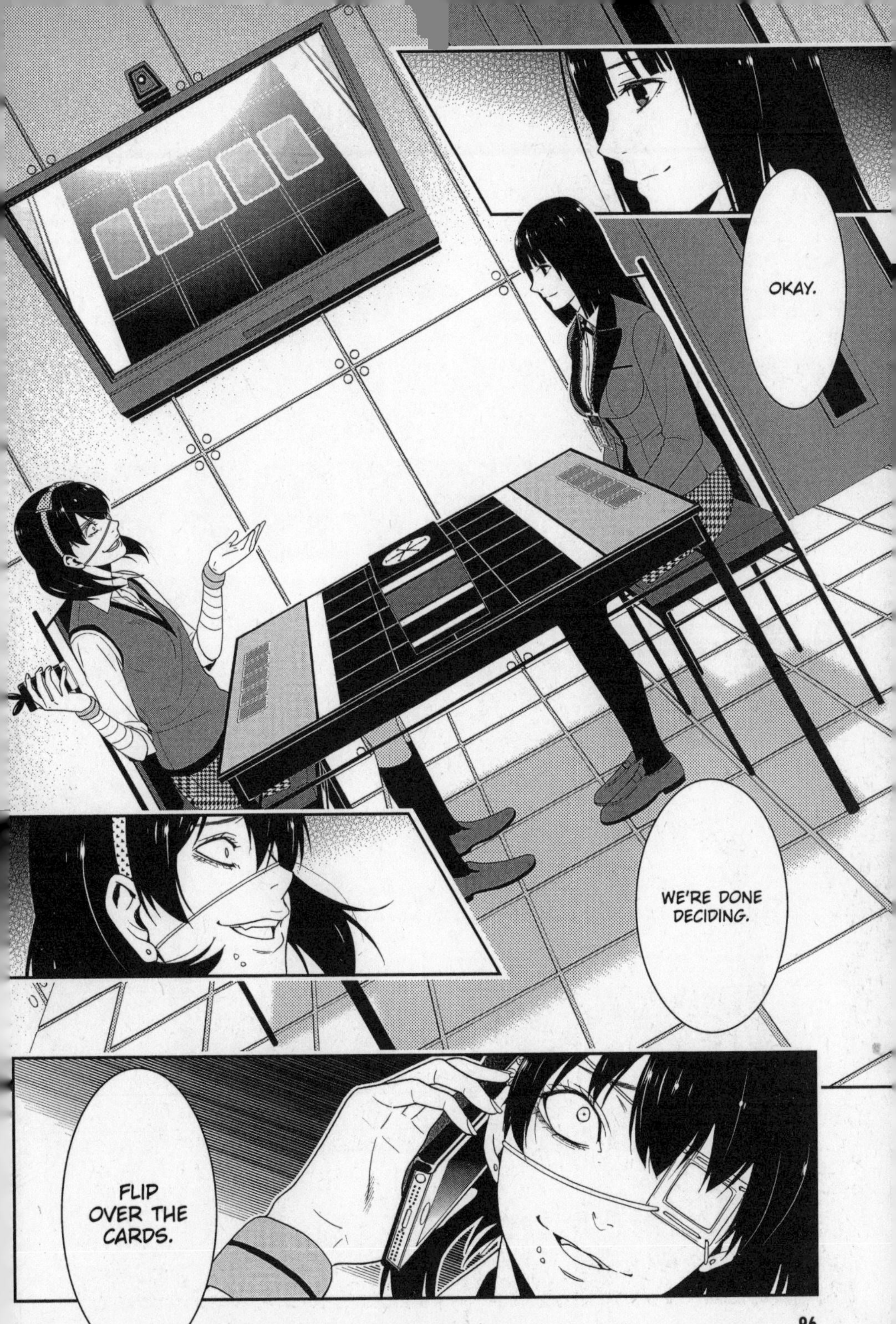
OKAY.
WE'RE DONE DECIDING.
FLIP OVER THE CARDS.

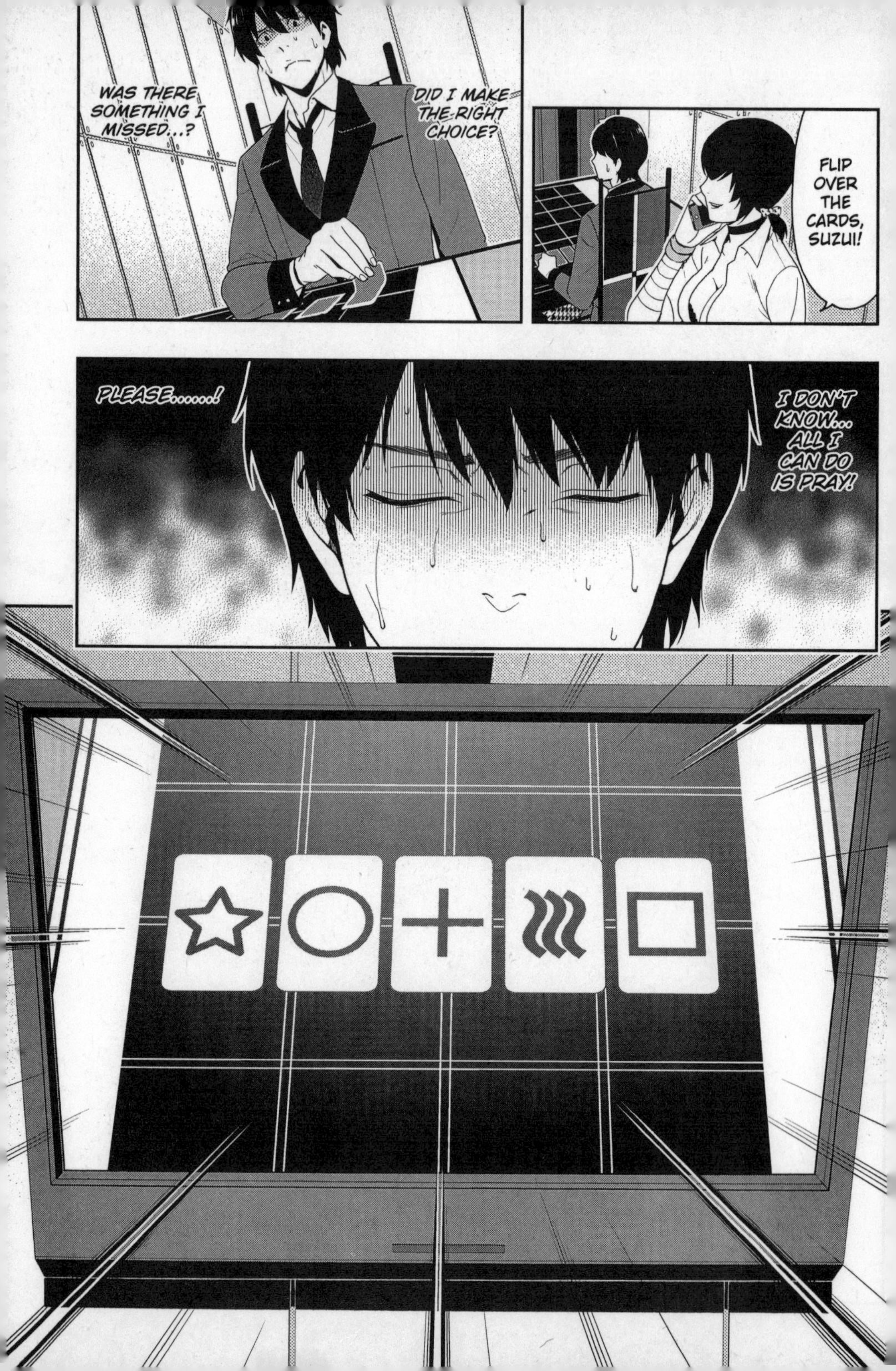
FLIP OVER THE CARDS, SUZUI!
DID I MAKE THE RIGHT CHOICE?
WAS THERE SOMETHING I MISSED...?
I DON'T KNOW... ALL I CAN DO IS PRAY!
PLEASE......!

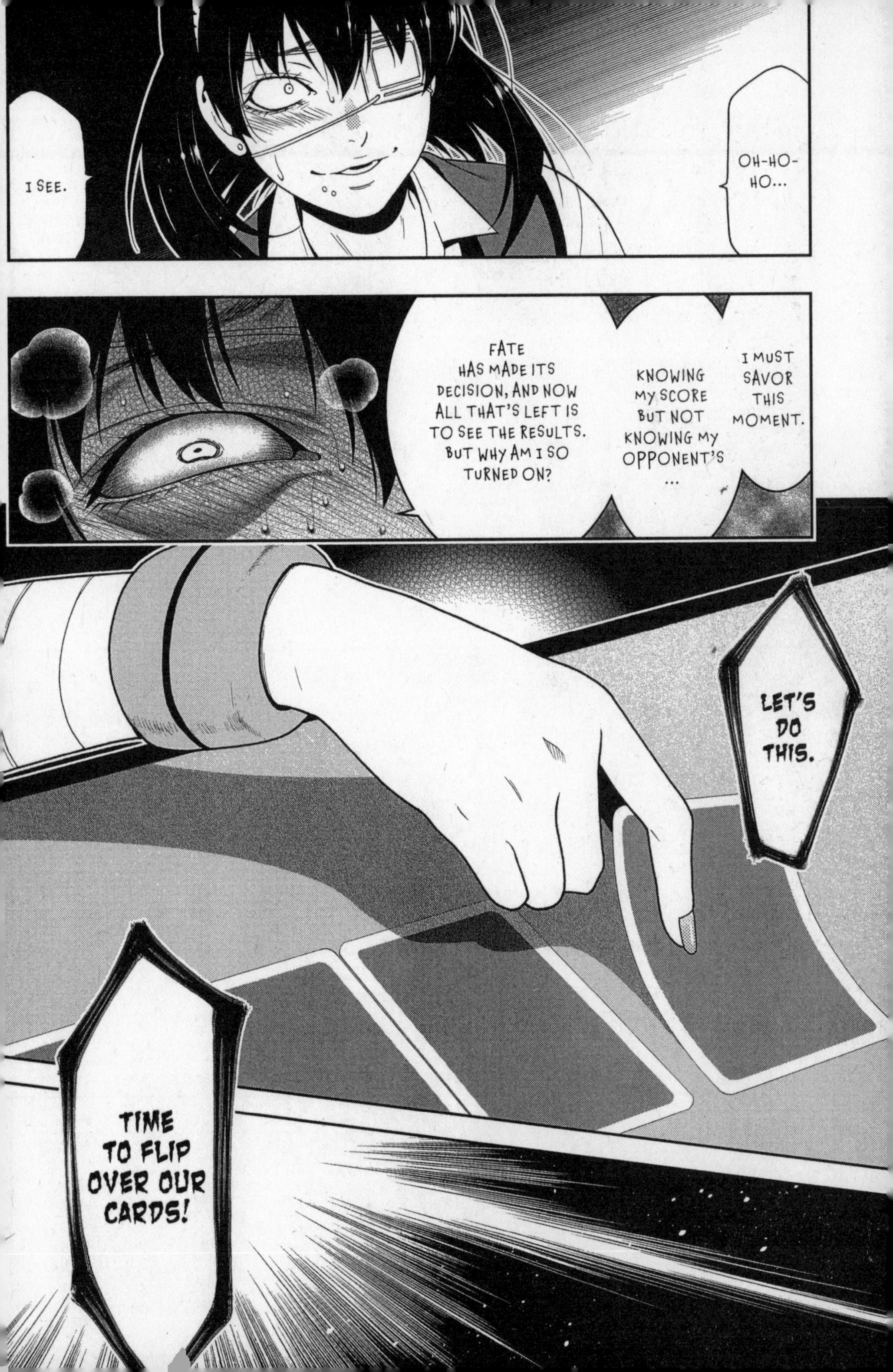
OH-HO-HO...
I SEE.
I MUST SAVOR THIS MOMENT.
KNOWING MY SCORE BUT NOT KNOWING MY OPPONENT'S...
FATE HAS MADE ITS DECISION, AND NOW ALL THAT'S LEFT IS TO SEE THE RESULTS. BUT WHY AM I SO TURNED ON?
LET'S DO THIS.
TIME TO FLIP OVER OUR CARDS!

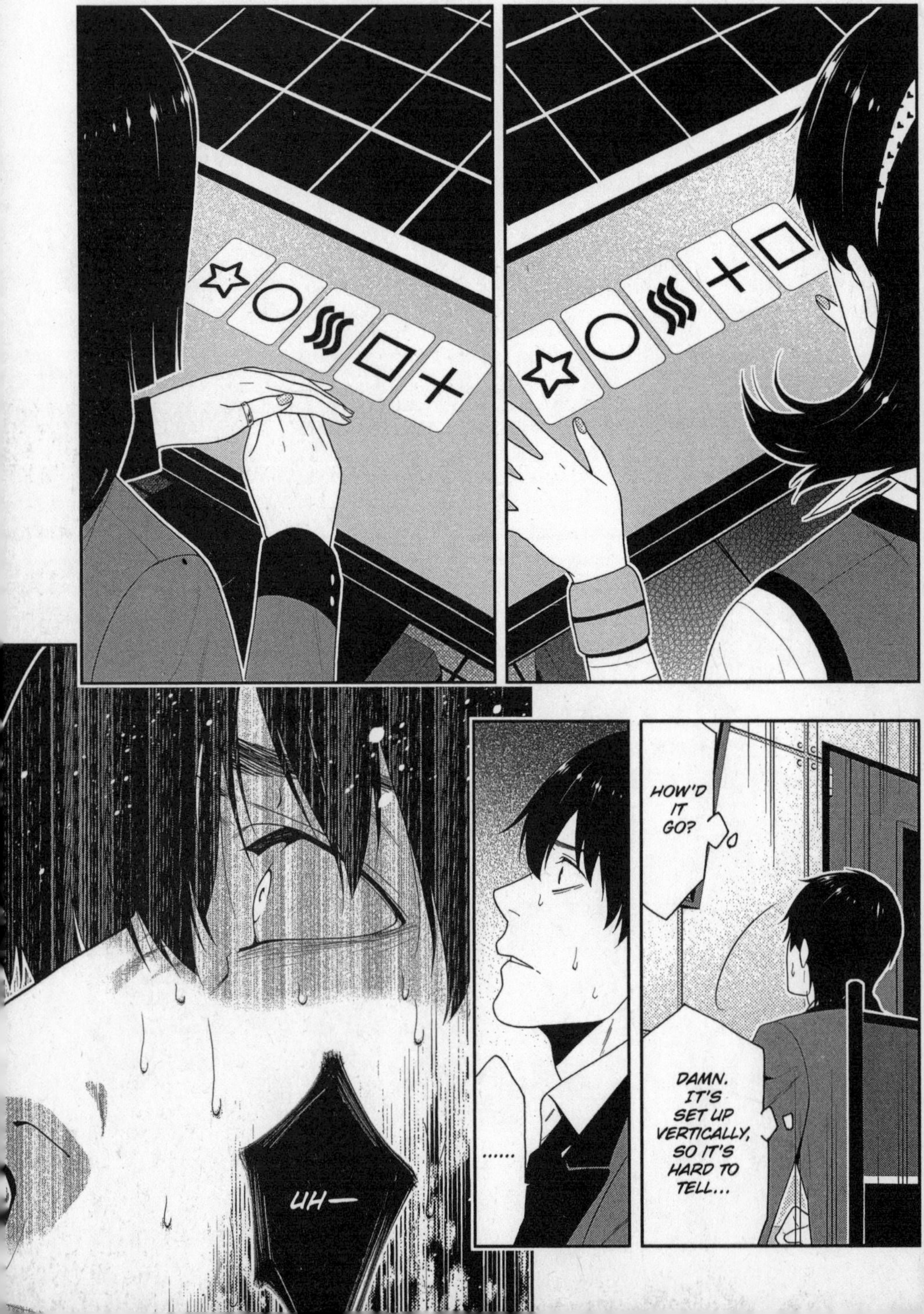
HOW'D IT GO?
DAMN. IT'S SET UP VERTICALLY, SO IT'S HARD TO TELL...
......
UH—

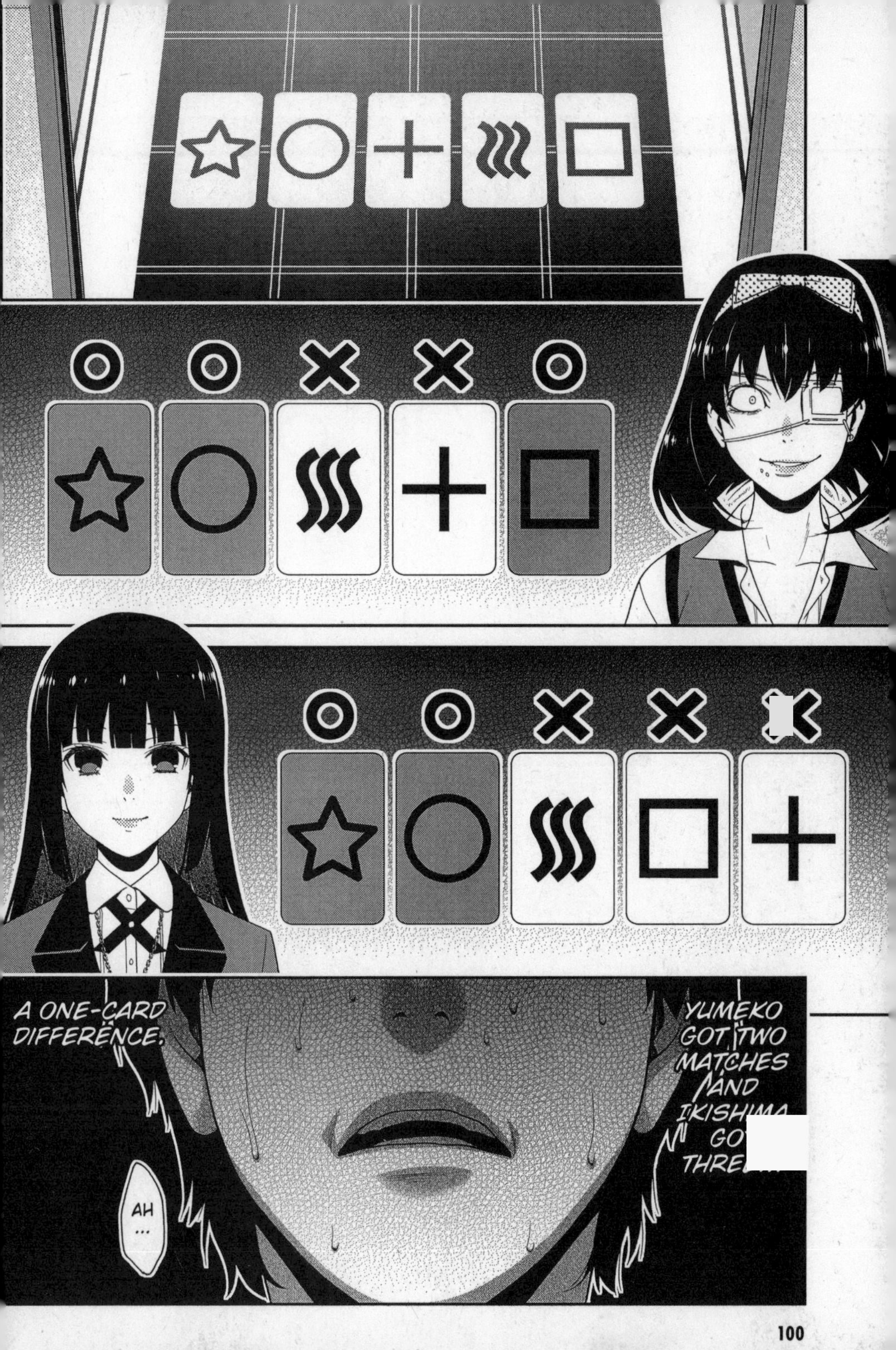
YUMEKO GOT TWO MATCHES AND IKISHIMA GO THRE
A ONE-CARD DIFFERENCE.
AH ...

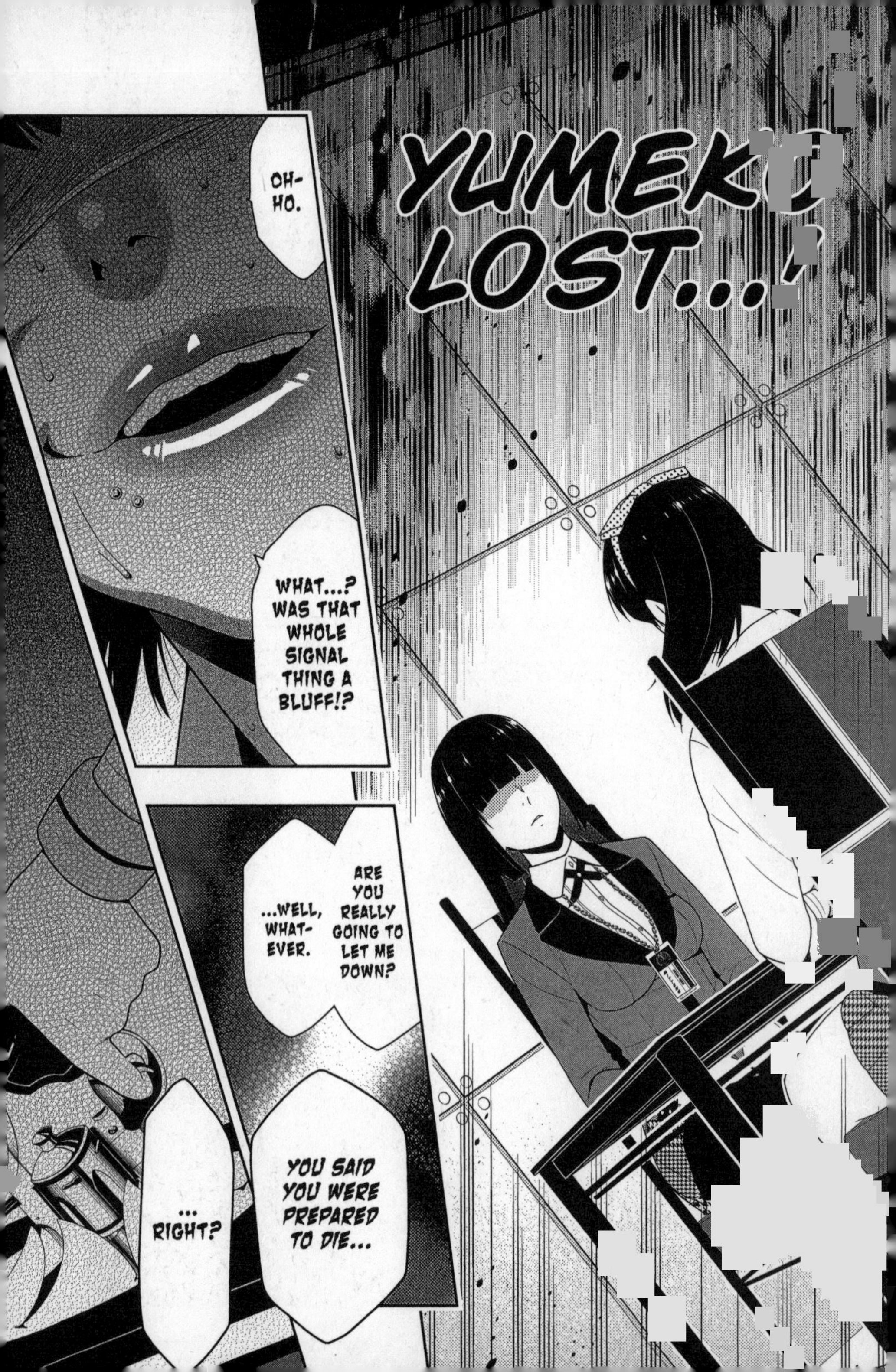
YUMEKO LOST...!?
OH-HO.
WHAT...? WAS THAT WHOLE SIGNAL THING A BLUFF!?
ARE YOU REALLY GOING TO LET ME DOWN?
...WELL, WHATEVER.
YOU SAID YOU WERE PREPARED TO DIE...
...RIGHT?

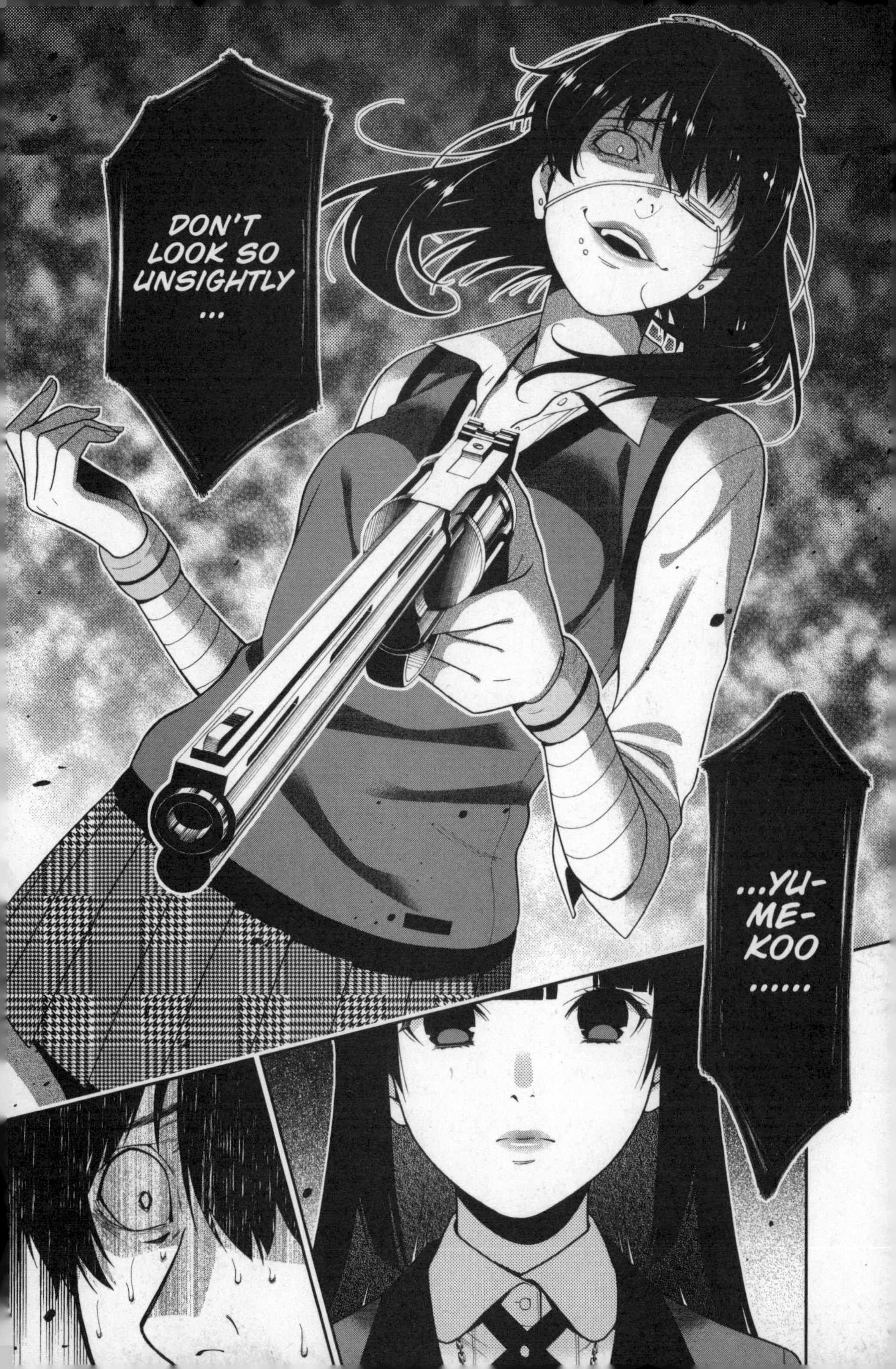
DON'T LOOK SO UNSIGHTLY ...
...YU-ME-KOO ......

CHAPTER THIRTEEN
DELIGHTED GIRL

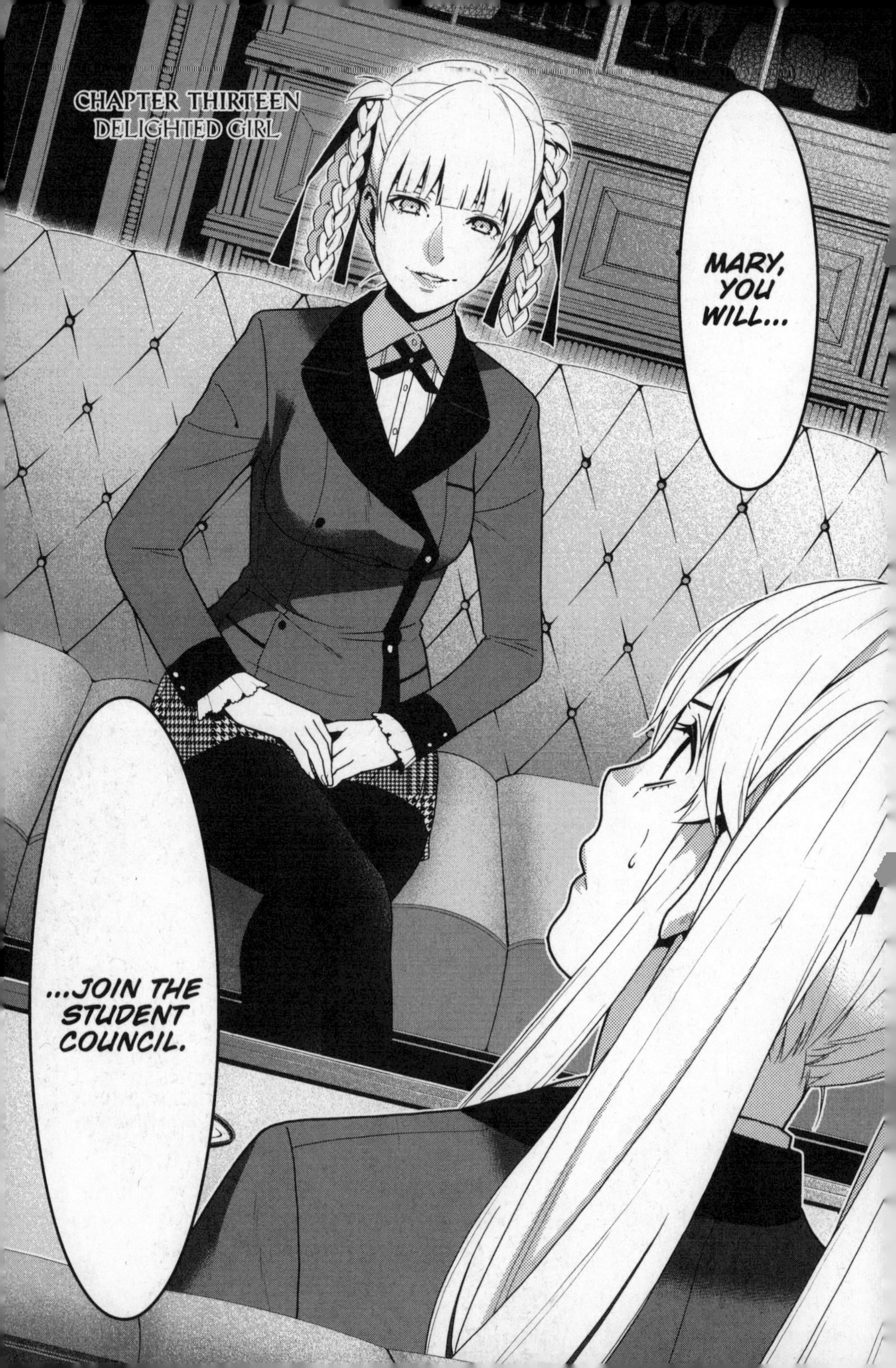
MARY, YOU WILL...
...JOIN THE STUDENT COUNCIL.

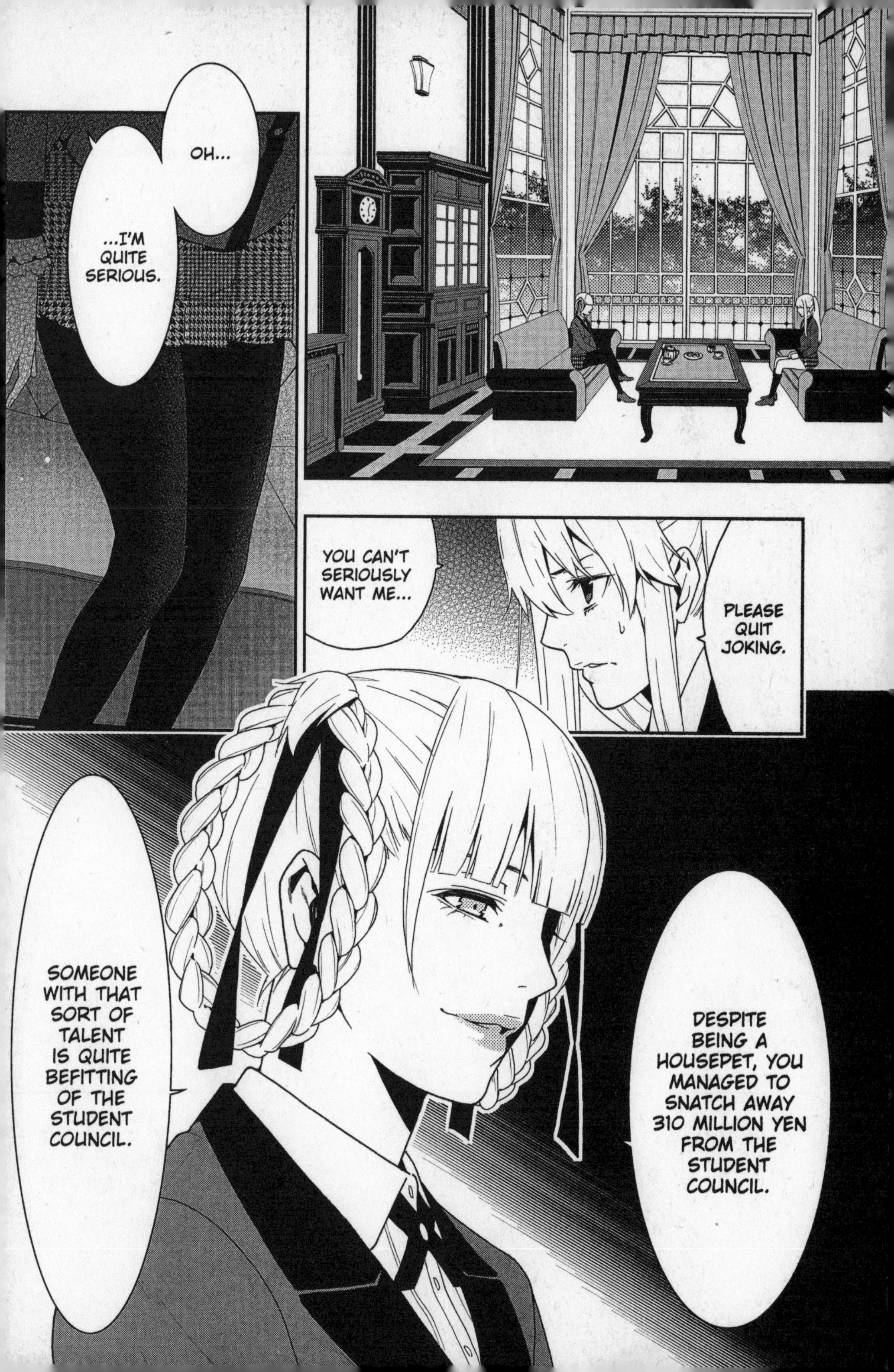
YOU CAN'T SERIOUSLY WANT ME...
PLEASE QUIT JOKING.
OH...
...I'M QUITE SERIOUS.
DESPITE BEING A HOUSEPET, YOU MANAGED TO SNATCH AWAY 310 MILLION YEN FROM THE STUDENT COUNCIL.
SOMEONE WITH THAT SORT OF TALENT IS QUITE BEFITTING OF THE STUDENT COUNCIL.

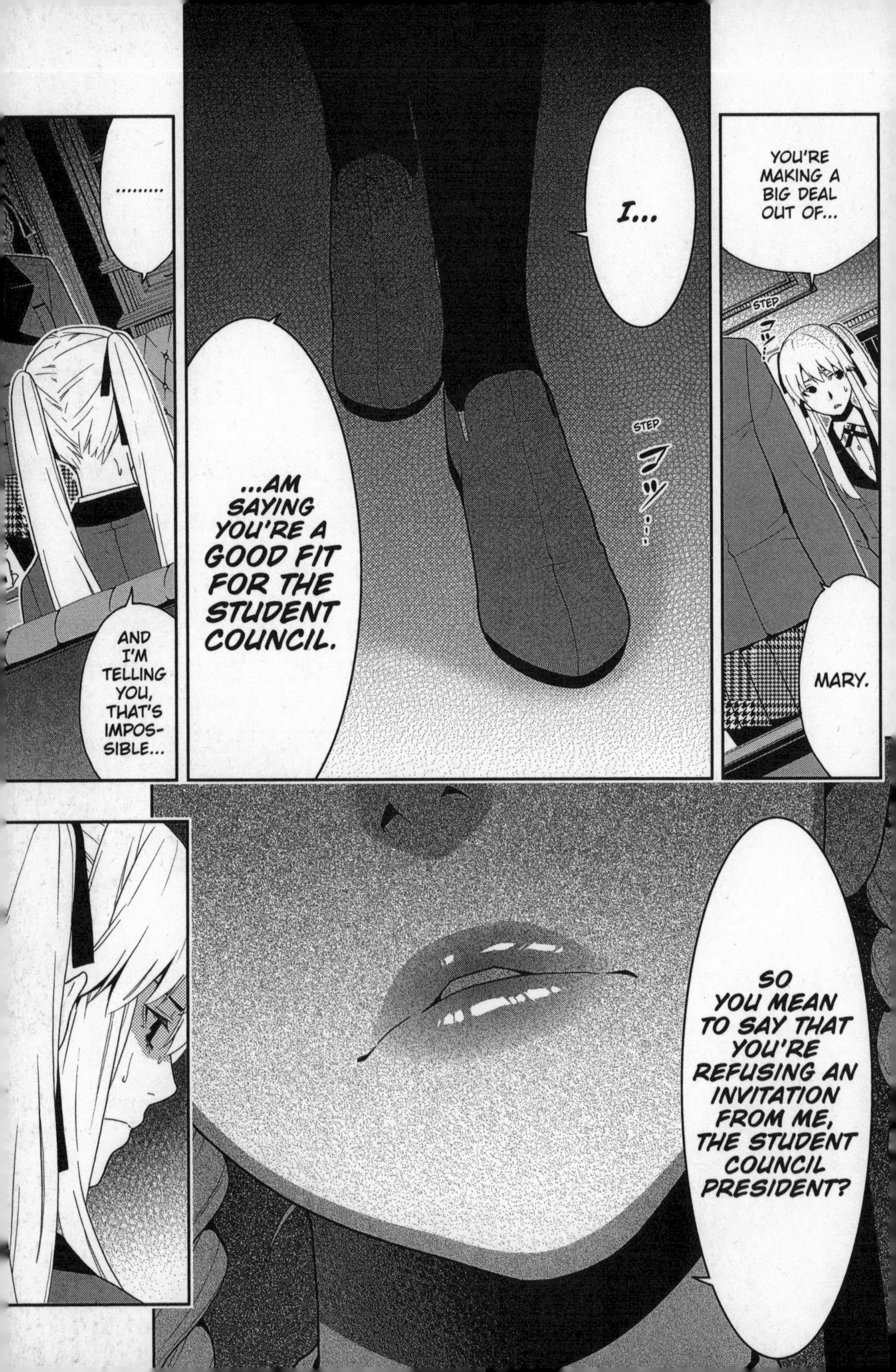
YOU'RE MAKING A BIG DEAL OUT OF...
STEP
フッ...
MARY.
I...
...AM SAYING YOU'RE A GOOD FIT FOR THE STUDENT COUNCIL.
STEP
フッ...
....
AND I'M TELLING YOU, THAT'S IMPOS-SIBLE...
SO YOU MEAN TO SAY THAT YOU'RE REFUSING AN INVITATION FROM ME, THE STUDENT COUNCIL PRESIDENT?

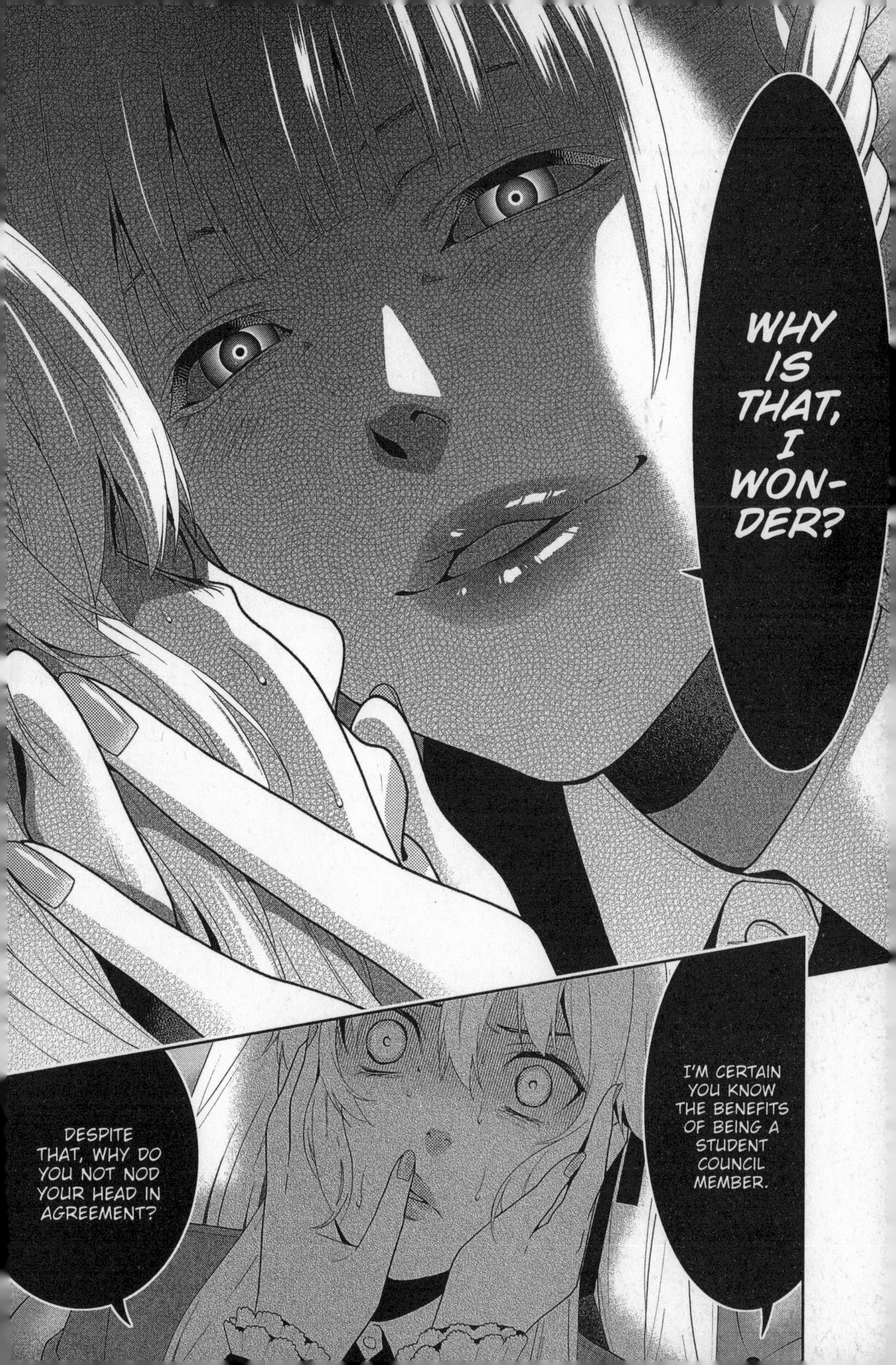
WHY IS THAT, I WONDER?
I'M CERTAIN YOU KNOW THE BENEFITS OF BEING A STUDENT COUNCIL MEMBER.
DESPITE THAT, WHY DO YOU NOT NOD YOUR HEAD IN AGREEMENT?

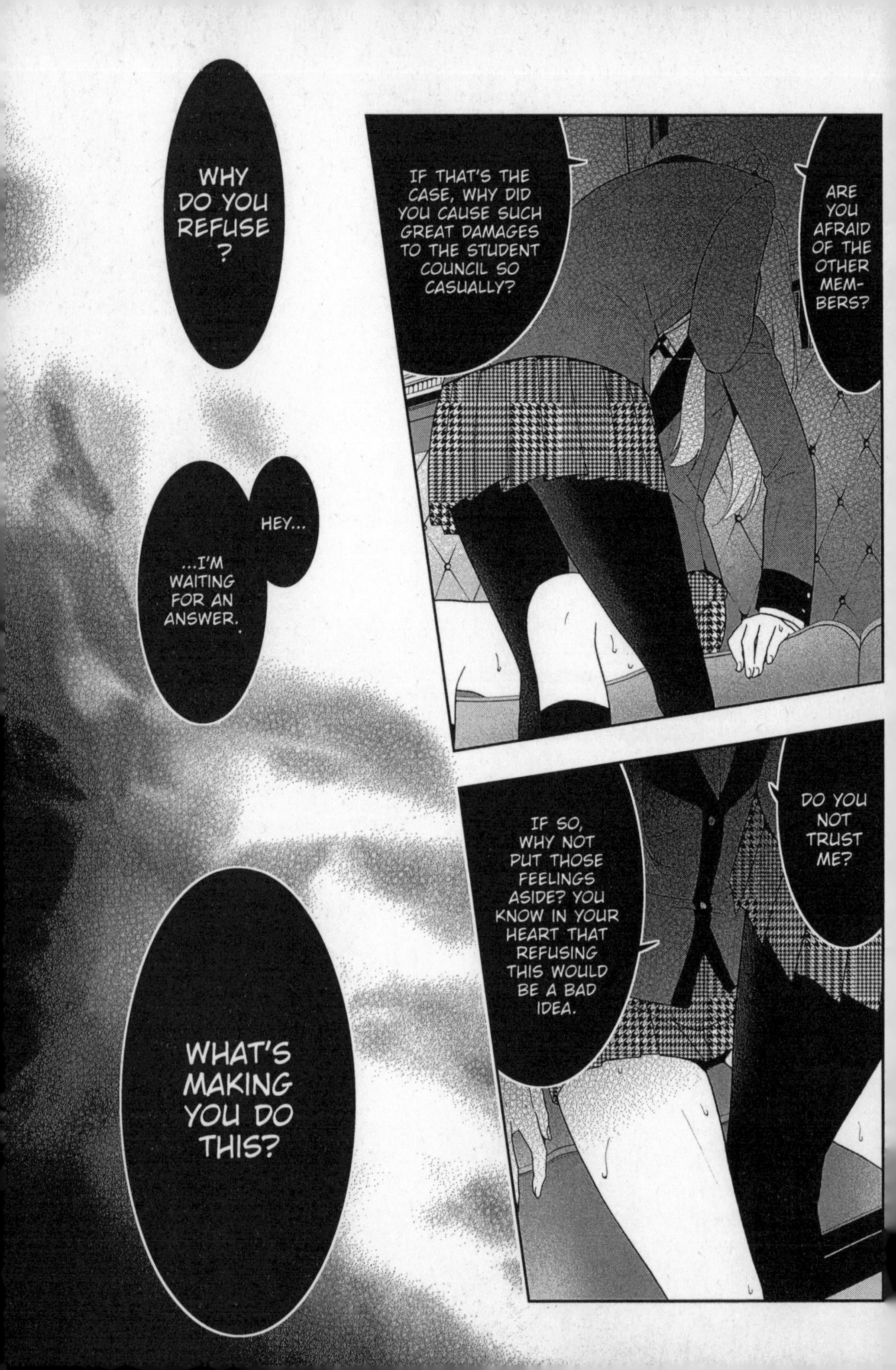
ARE YOU AFRAID OF THE OTHER MEM-BERS?
IF THAT'S THE CASE, WHY DID YOU CAUSE SUCH GREAT DAMAGES TO THE STUDENT COUNCIL SO CASUALLY?
WHY DO YOU REFUSE?
DO YOU NOT TRUST ME?
IF SO, WHY NOT PUT THOSE FEELINGS ASIDE? YOU KNOW IN YOUR HEART THAT REFUSING THIS WOULD BE A BAD IDEA.
HEY...
...I'M WAITING FOR AN ANSWER.
WHAT'S MAKING YOU DO THIS?

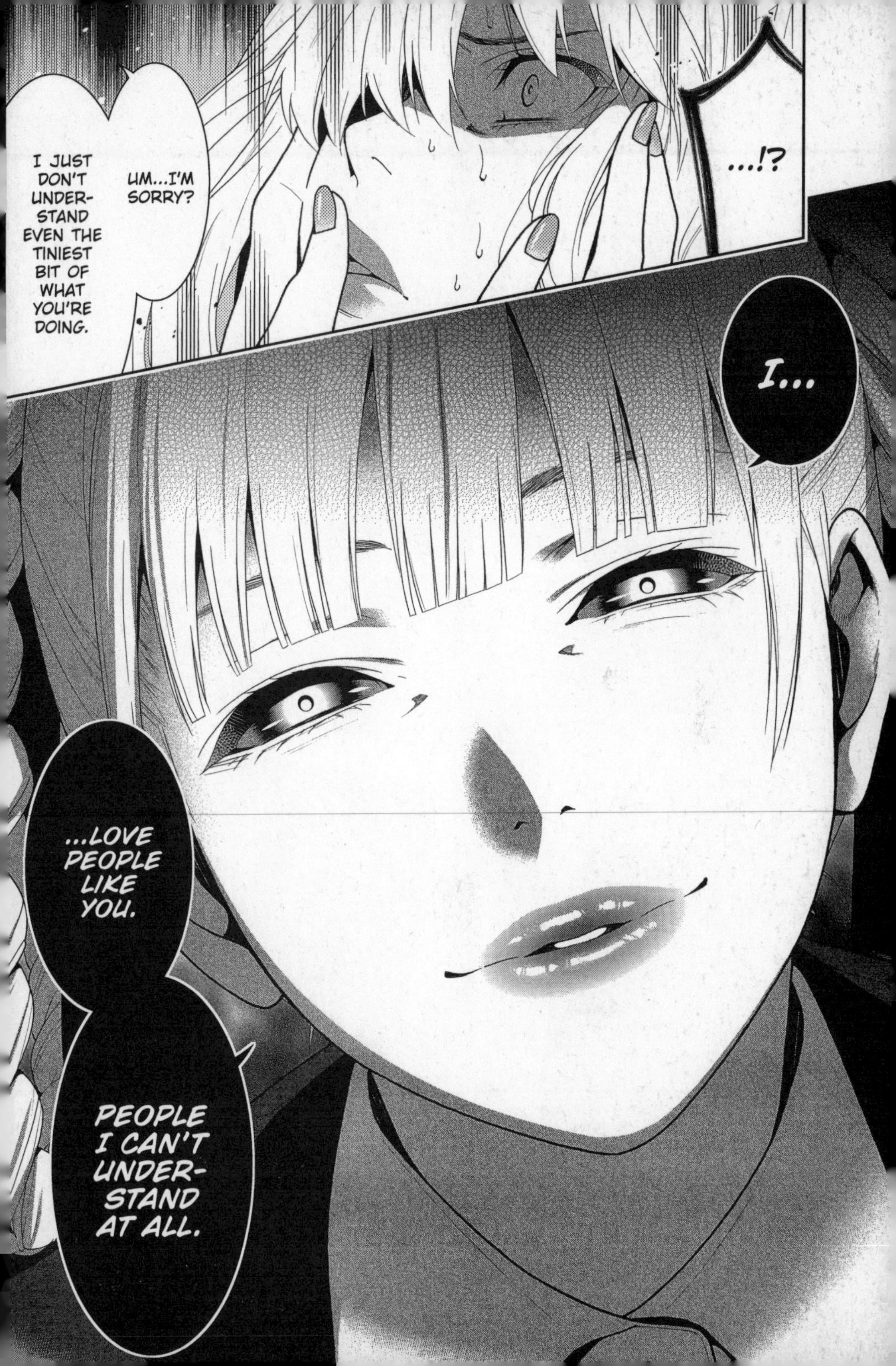
...!?
UM...I'M SORRY?
I JUST DON'T UNDERSTAND EVEN THE TINIEST BIT OF WHAT YOU'RE DOING.
I...
...LOVE PEOPLE LIKE YOU.
PEOPLE I CAN'T UNDERSTAND AT ALL.

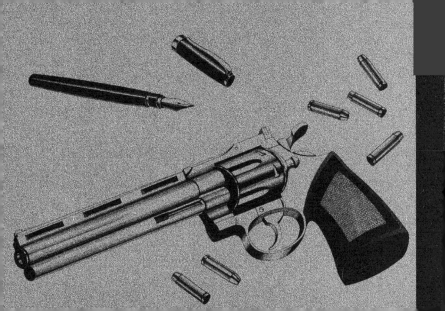

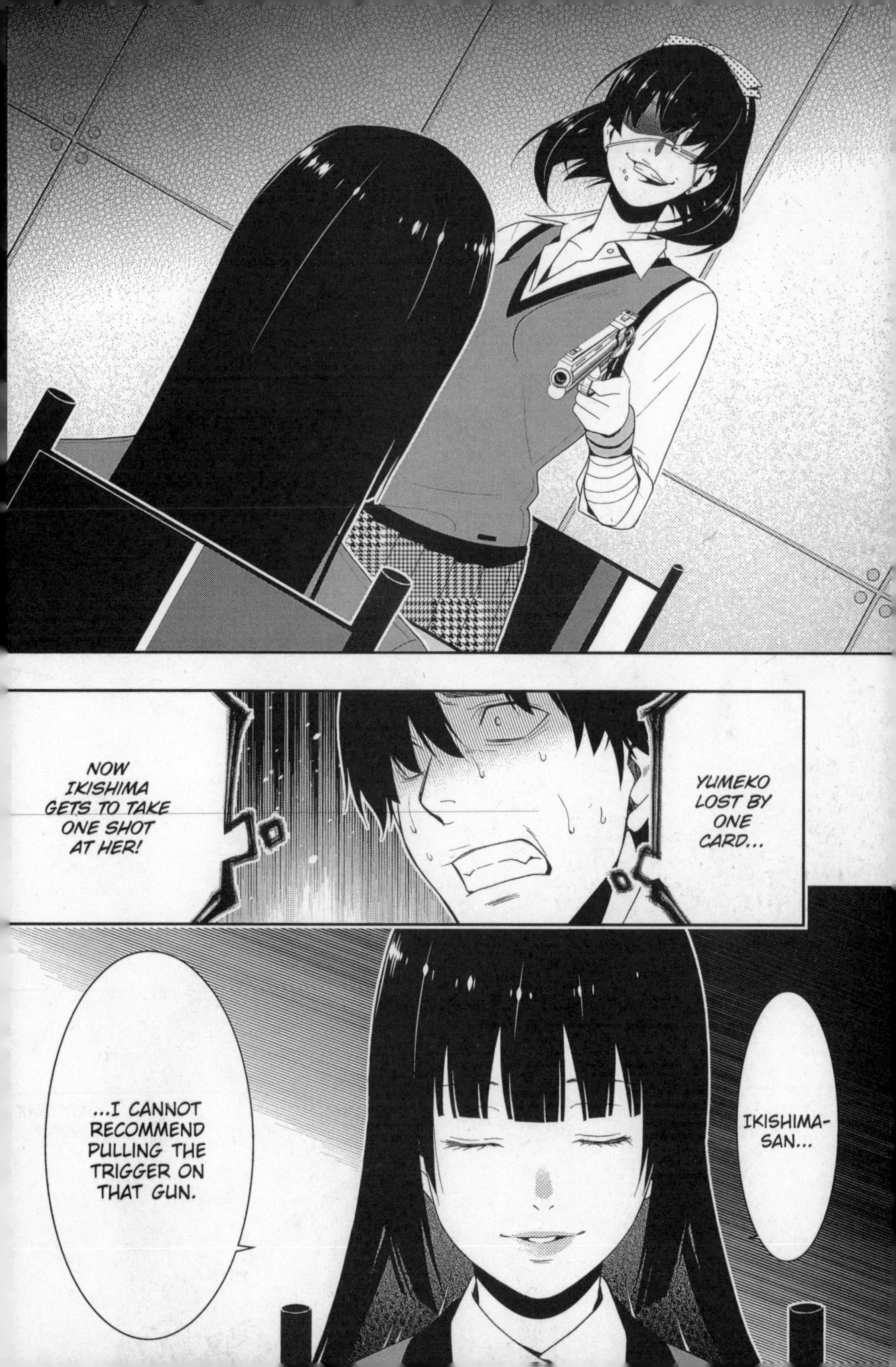
YUMEKO LOST BY ONE CARD...
NOW IKISHIMA GETS TO TAKE ONE SHOT AT HER!
IKISHIMA-SAN...
...I CANNOT RECOMMEND PULLING THE TRIGGER ON THAT GUN.

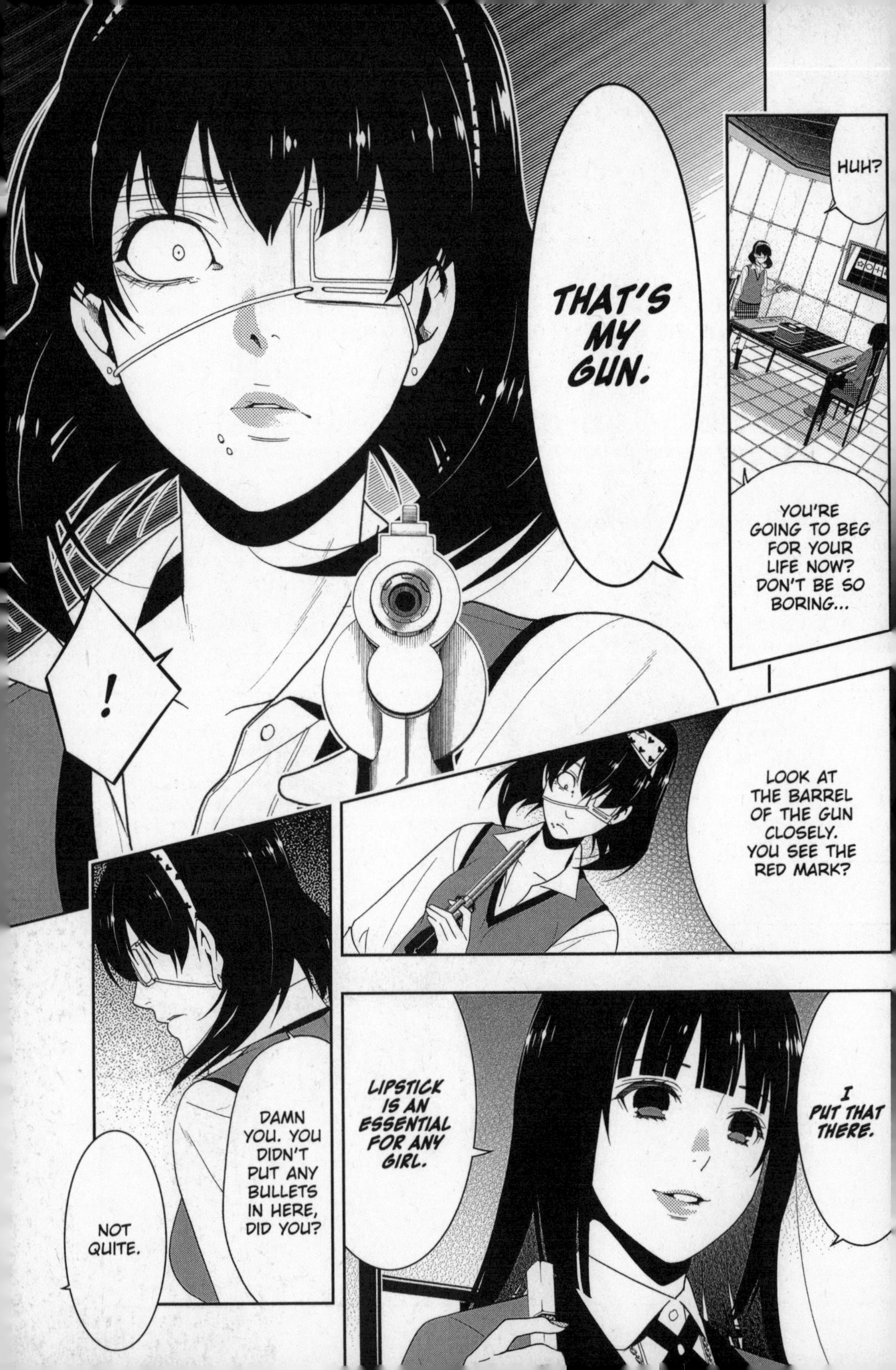
HUH?
YOU'RE GOING TO BEG FOR YOUR LIFE NOW? DON'T BE SO BORING...
THAT'S MY GUN.
!
LOOK AT THE BARREL OF THE GUN CLOSELY. YOU SEE THE RED MARK?
I PUT THAT THERE.
LIPSTICK IS AN ESSENTIAL FOR ANY GIRL.
DAMN YOU. YOU DIDN'T PUT ANY BULLETS IN HERE, DID YOU?
NOT QUITE.

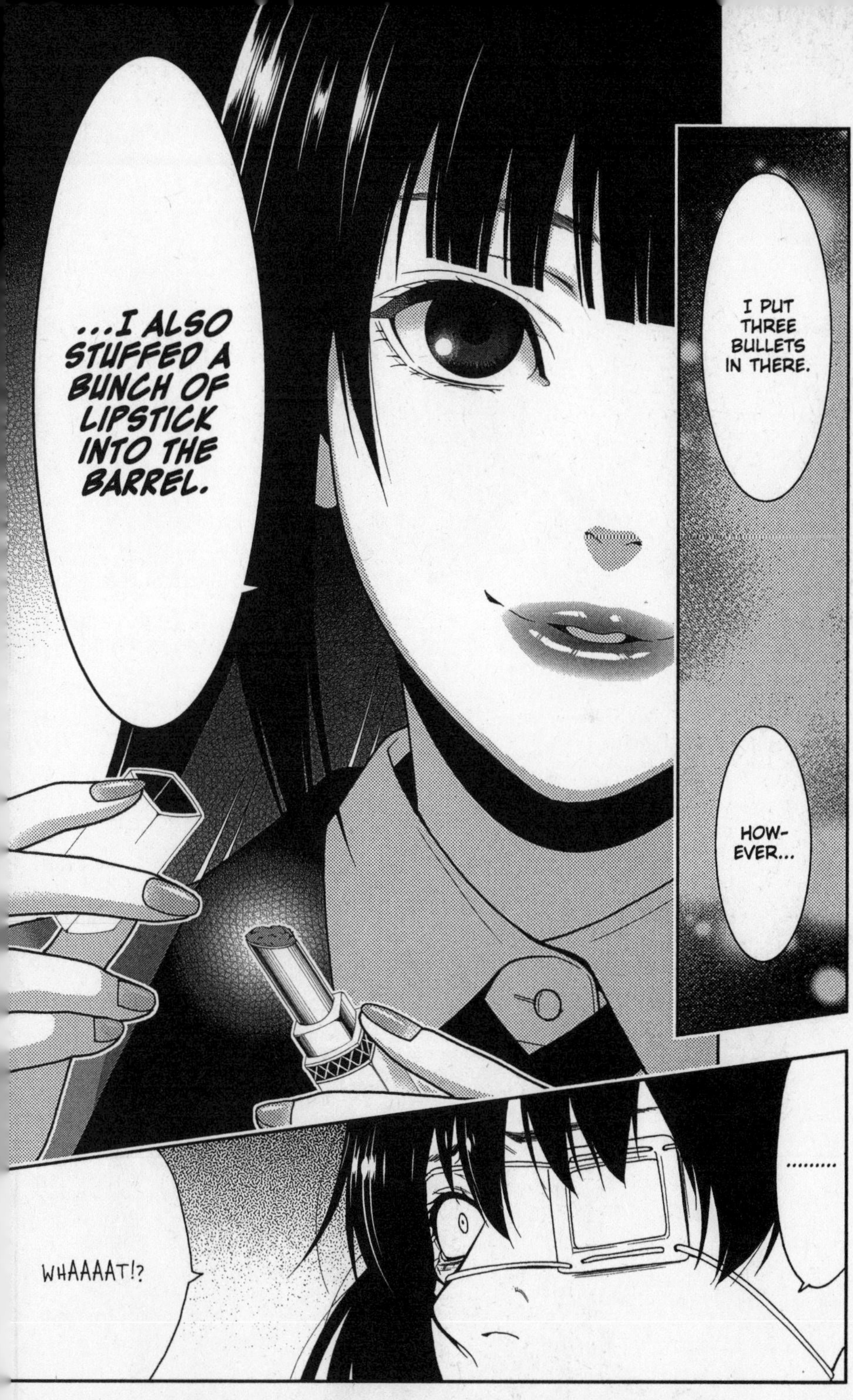
I PUT THREE BULLETS IN THERE.
HOW-EVER...
...I ALSO STUFFED A BUNCH OF LIPSTICK INTO THE BARREL.
....
WHAAAAT!?

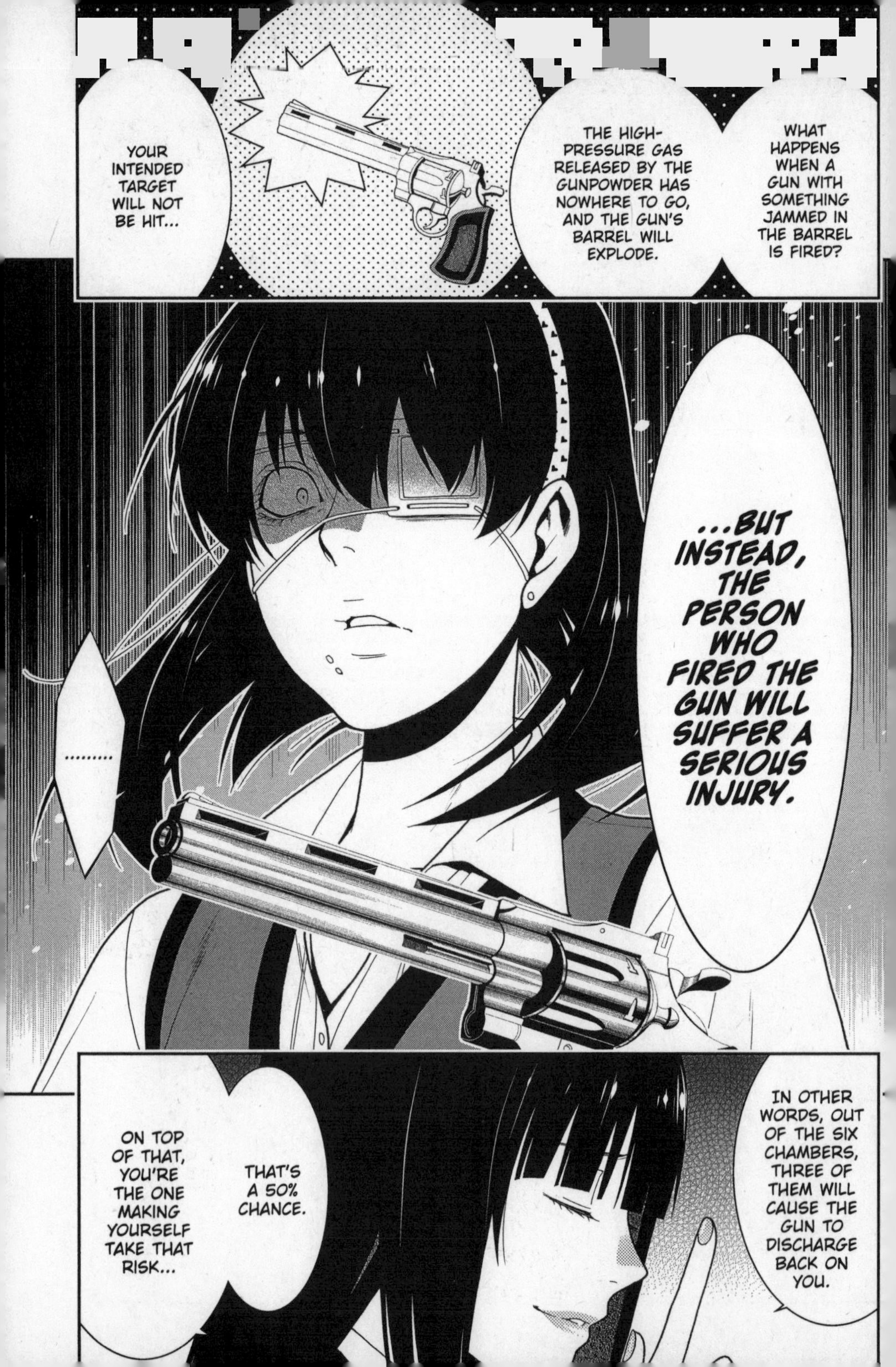
WHAT HAPPENS WHEN A GUN WITH SOMETHING JAMMED IN THE BARREL IS FIRED?
THE HIGH-PRESSURE GAS RELEASED BY THE GUNPOWDER HAS NOWHERE TO GO, AND THE GUN'S BARREL WILL EXPLODE.
YOUR INTENDED TARGET WILL NOT BE HIT...
...BUT INSTEAD, THE PERSON WHO FIRED THE GUN WILL SUFFER A SERIOUS INJURY.
....
IN OTHER WORDS, OUT OF THE SIX CHAMBERS, THREE OF THEM WILL CAUSE THE GUN TO DISCHARGE BACK ON YOU.
THAT'S A 50% CHANCE.
ON TOP OF THAT, YOU'RE THE ONE MAKING YOURSELF TAKE THAT RISK...

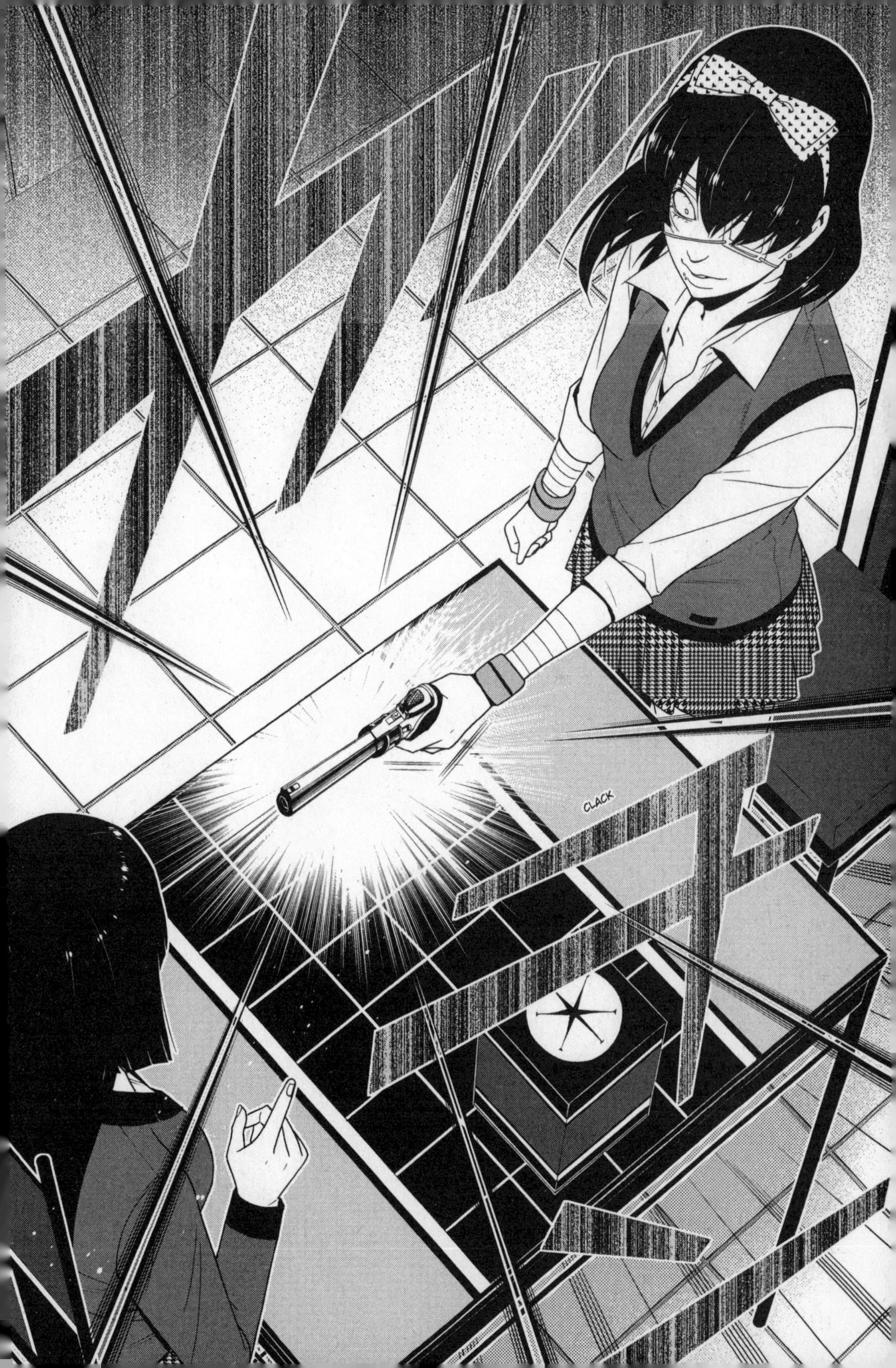
CLACK

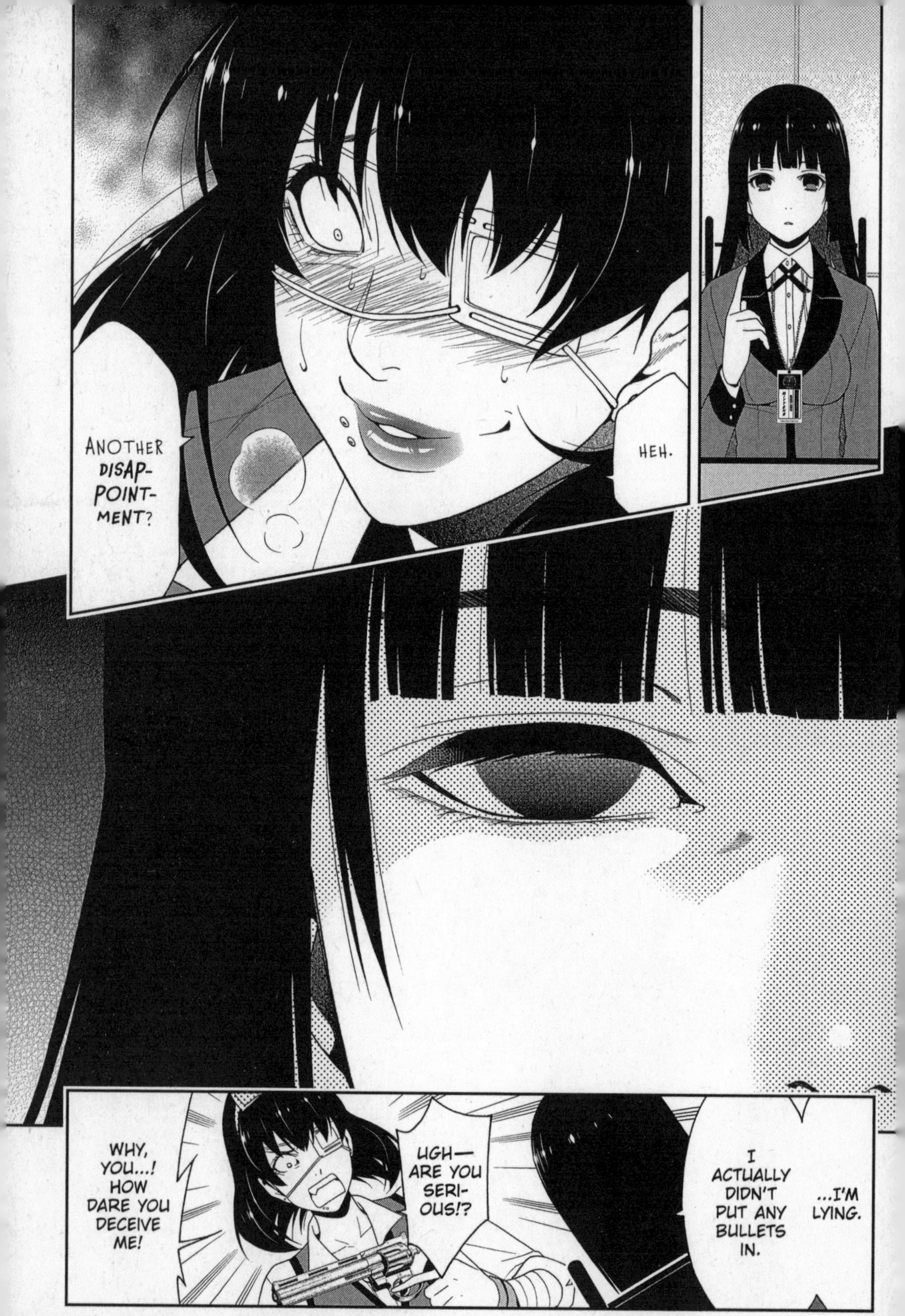
HEH.
ANOTHER DISAPPOINTMENT?
I ACTUALLY DIDN'T PUT ANY BULLETS IN.
...I'M LYING.
UGH— ARE YOU SERIOUS!?
WHY, YOU...! HOW DARE YOU DECEIVE ME!

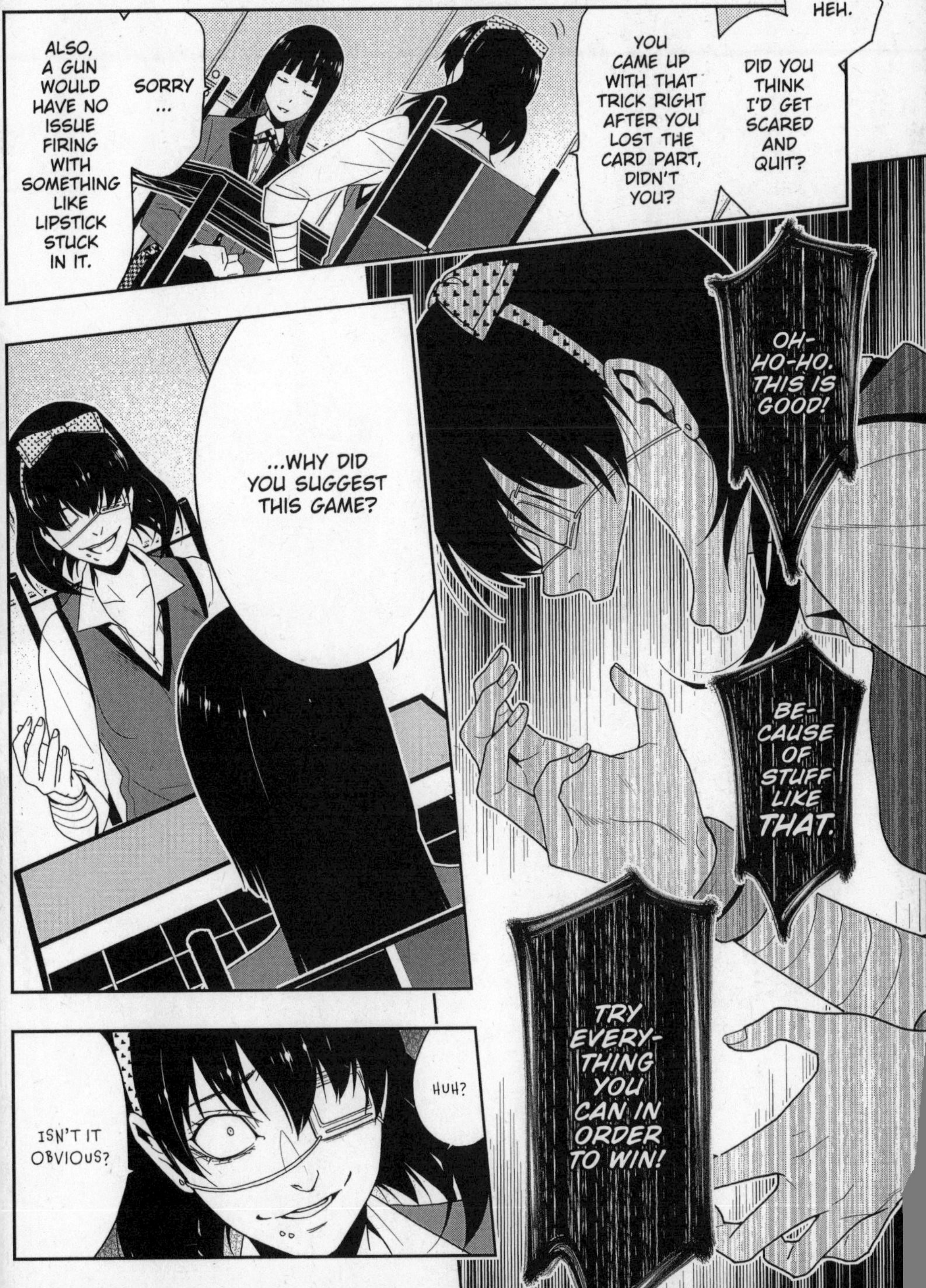
HEH.
DID YOU THINK I'D GET SCARED AND QUIT?
YOU CAME UP WITH THAT TRICK RIGHT AFTER YOU LOST THE CARD PART, DIDN'T YOU?
SORRY ...
ALSO, A GUN WOULD HAVE NO ISSUE FIRING WITH SOMETHING LIKE LIPSTICK STUCK IN IT.
OH-HO-HO. THIS IS GOOD!
BE-CAUSE OF STUFF LIKE THAT.
TRY EVERY-THING YOU CAN IN ORDER TO WIN!
...WHY DID YOU SUGGEST THIS GAME?
HUH?
ISN'T IT OBVIOUS?

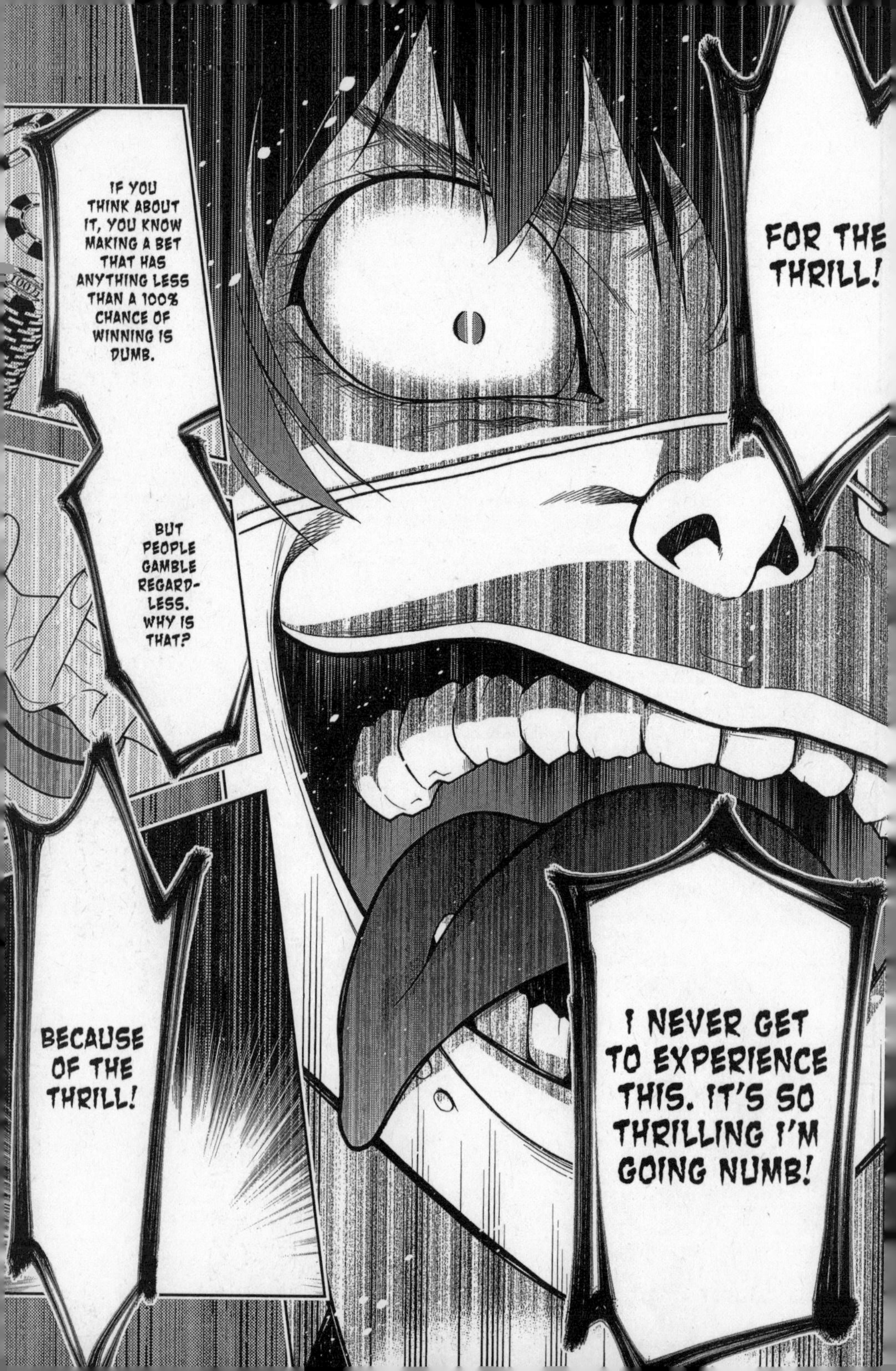
IF YOU THINK ABOUT IT, YOU KNOW MAKING A BET THAT HAS ANYTHING LESS THAN A 100% CHANCE OF WINNING IS DUMB.
BUT PEOPLE GAMBLE REGARD-LESS. WHY IS THAT?
BECAUSE OF THE THRILL!
FOR THE THRILL!
I NEVER GET TO EXPERIENCE THIS. IT'S SO THRILLING I'M GOING NUMB!

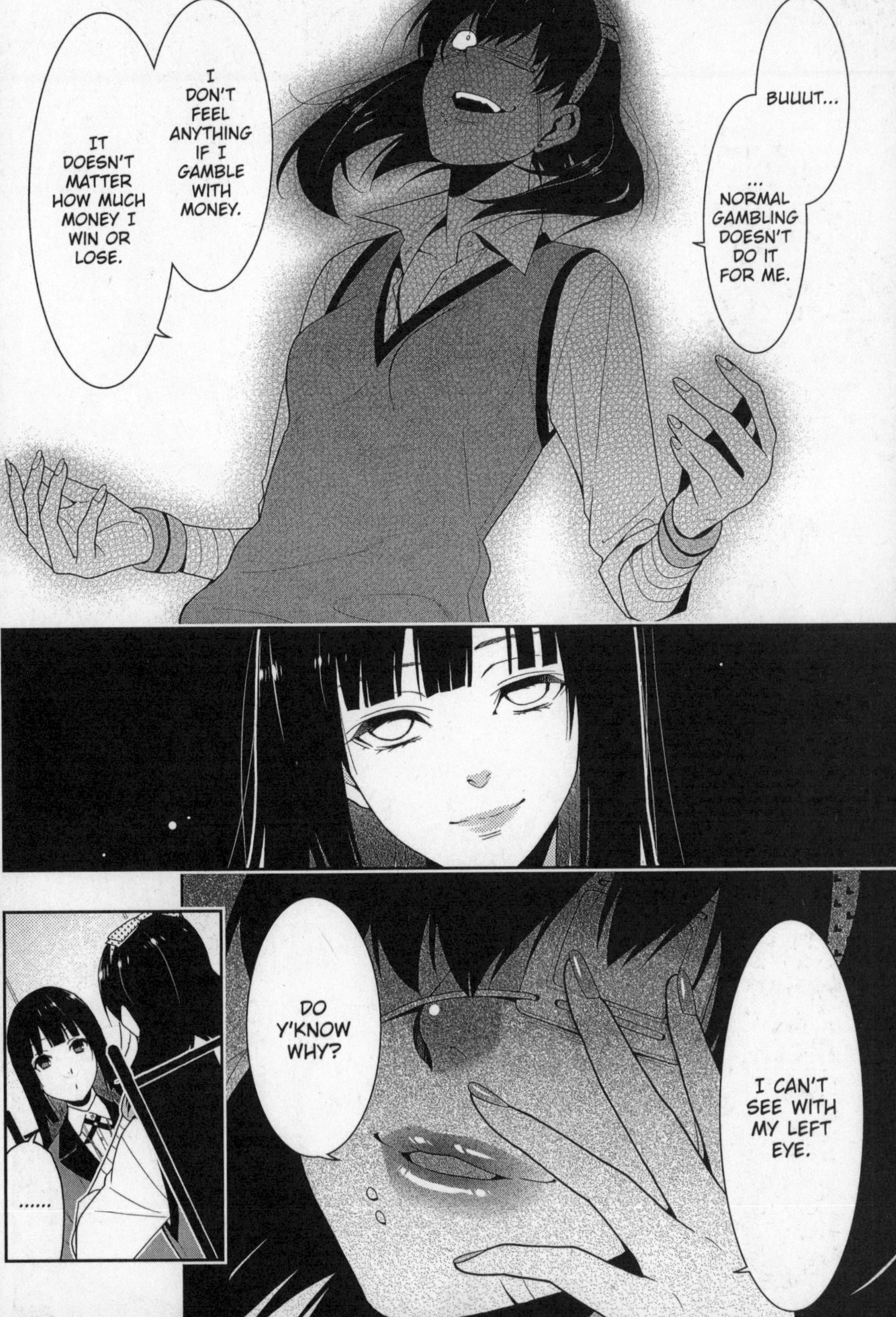
BUUUT...
... NORMAL GAMBLING DOESN'T DO IT FOR ME.
I DON'T FEEL ANYTHING IF I GAMBLE WITH MONEY.
IT DOESN'T MATTER HOW MUCH MONEY I WIN OR LOSE.
I CAN'T SEE WITH MY LEFT EYE.
DO Y'KNOW WHY?
......

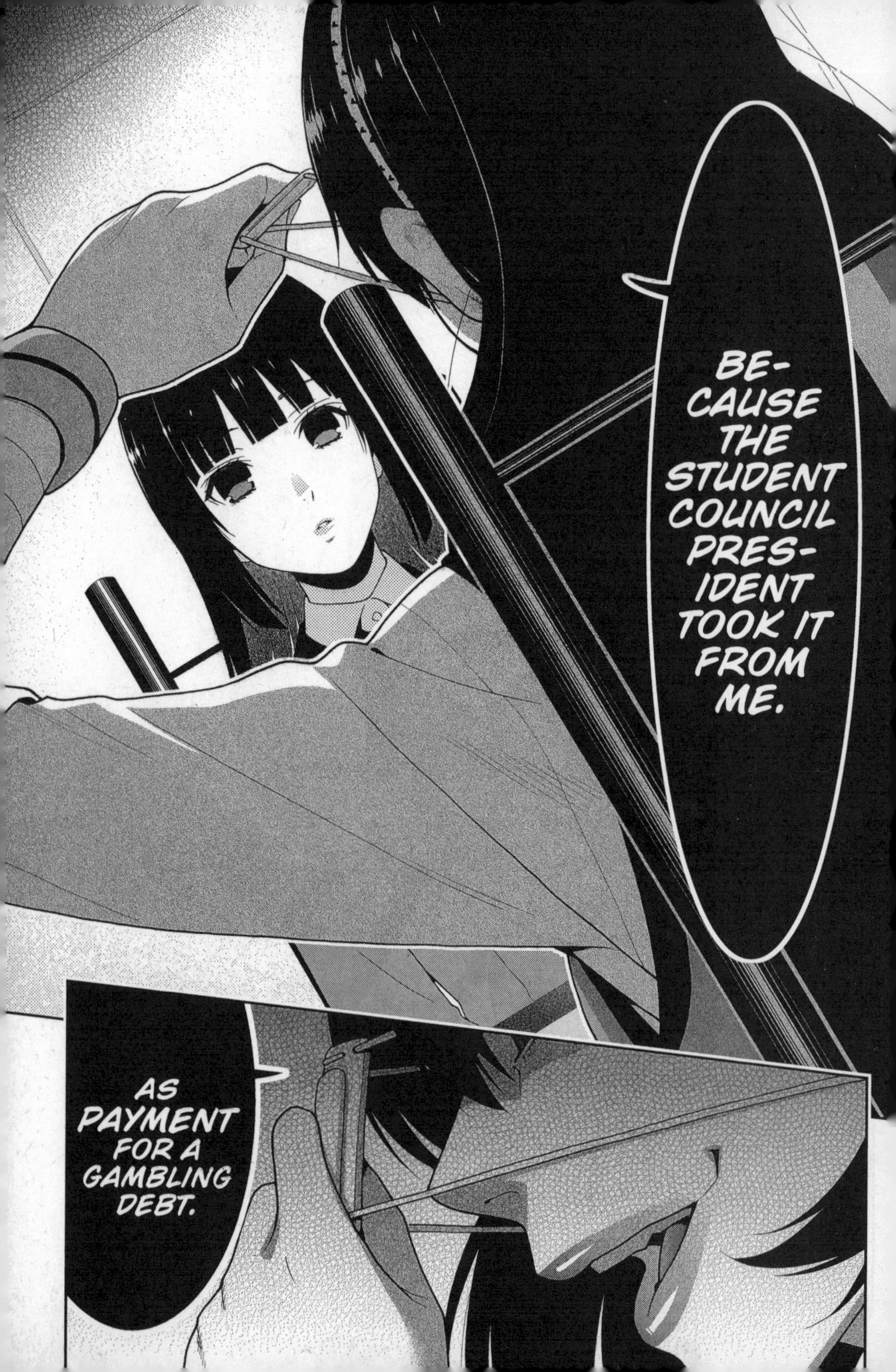
BE-CAUSE THE STUDENT COUNCIL PRES-IDENT TOOK IT FROM ME.
AS PAYMENT FOR A GAMBLING DEBT.

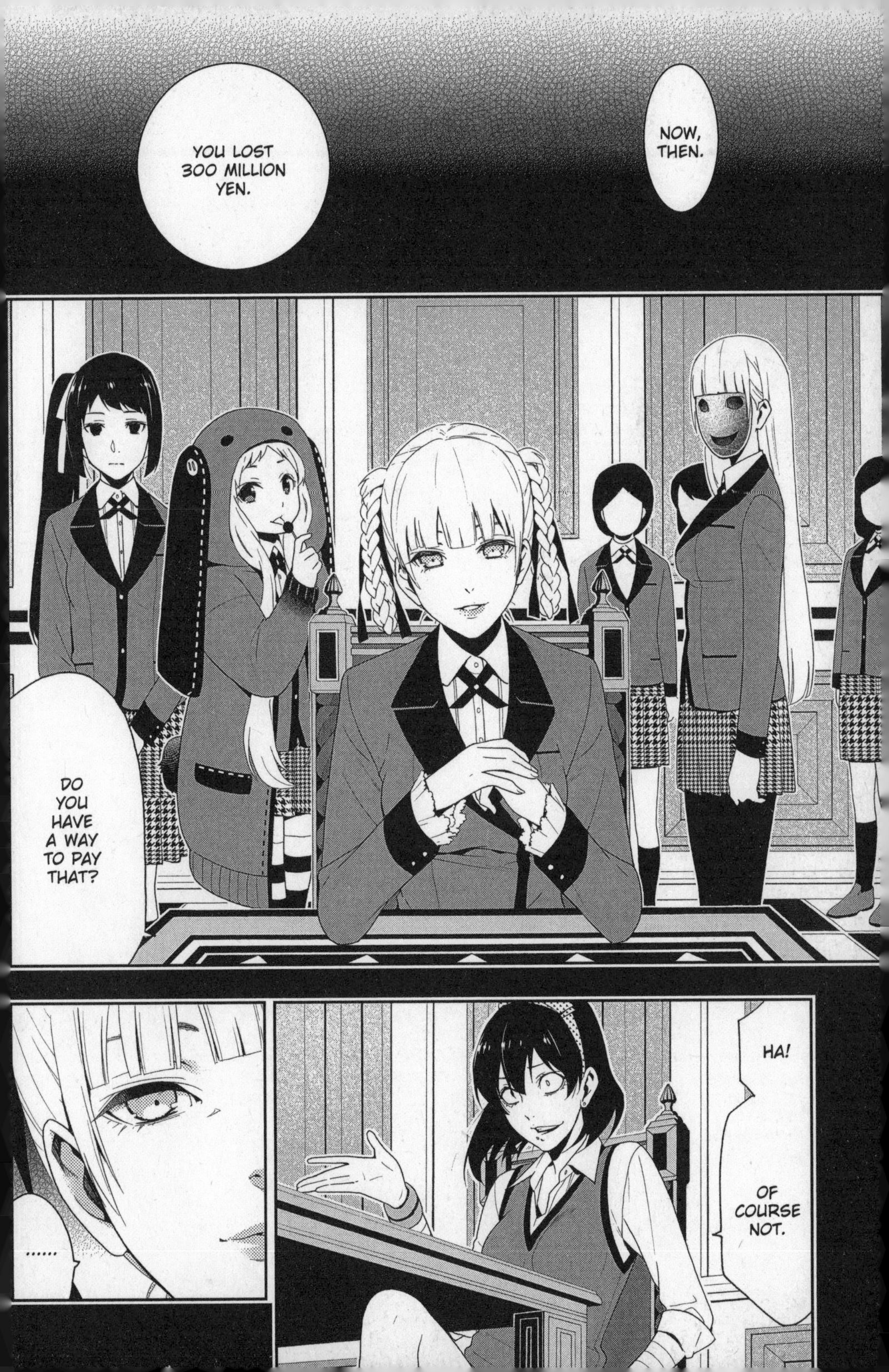
NOW, THEN.
YOU LOST 300 MILLION YEN.
DO YOU HAVE A WAY TO PAY THAT?
HA!
OF COURSE NOT.
......

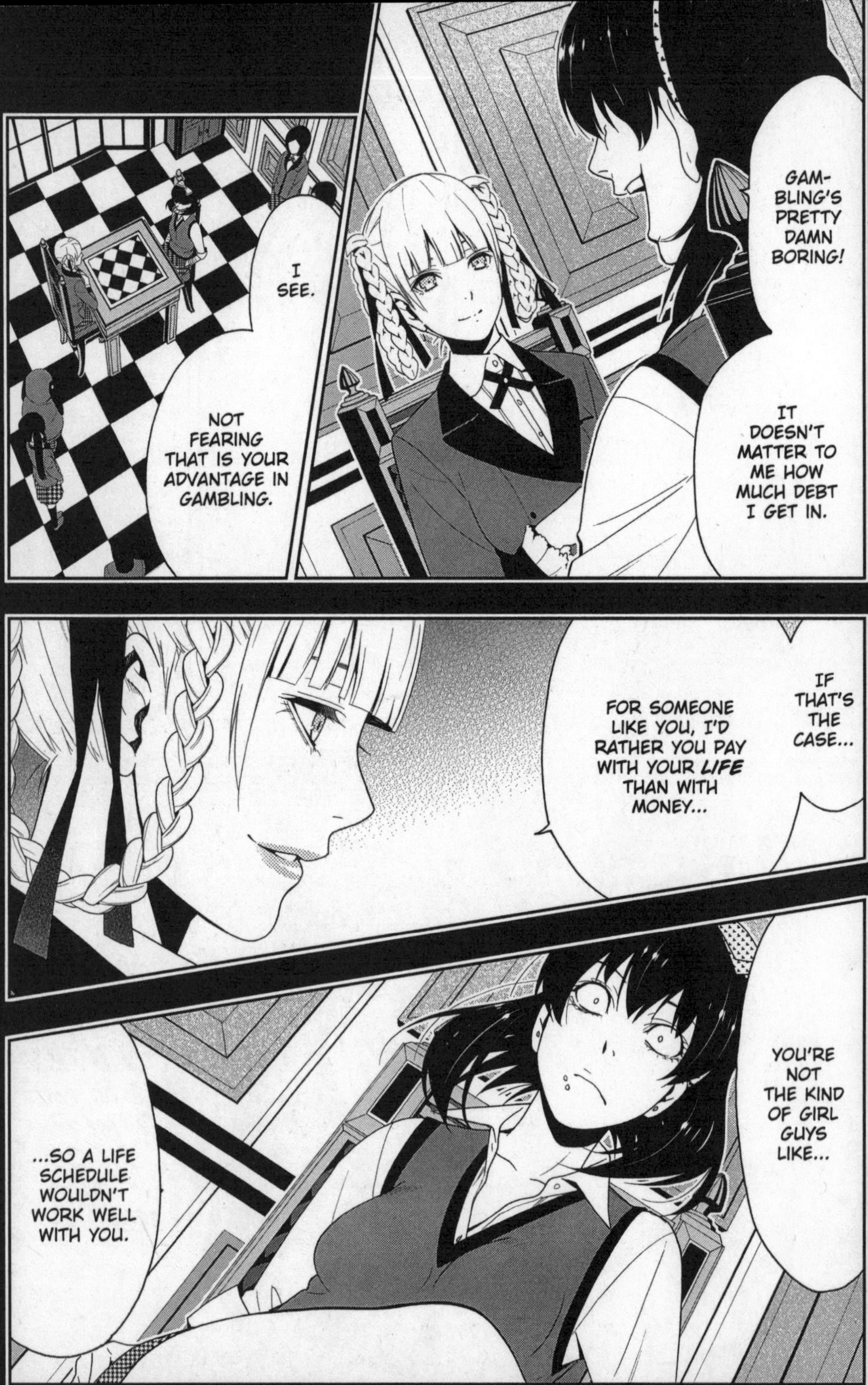
GAMBLING'S PRETTY DAMN BORING!
IT DOESN'T MATTER TO ME HOW MUCH DEBT I GET IN.
I SEE.
NOT FEARING THAT IS YOUR ADVANTAGE IN GAMBLING.
IF THAT'S THE CASE...
FOR SOMEONE LIKE YOU, I'D RATHER YOU PAY WITH YOUR *LIFE* THAN WITH MONEY...
YOU'RE NOT THE KIND OF GIRL GUYS LIKE...
...SO A LIFE SCHEDULE WOULDN'T WORK WELL WITH YOU.

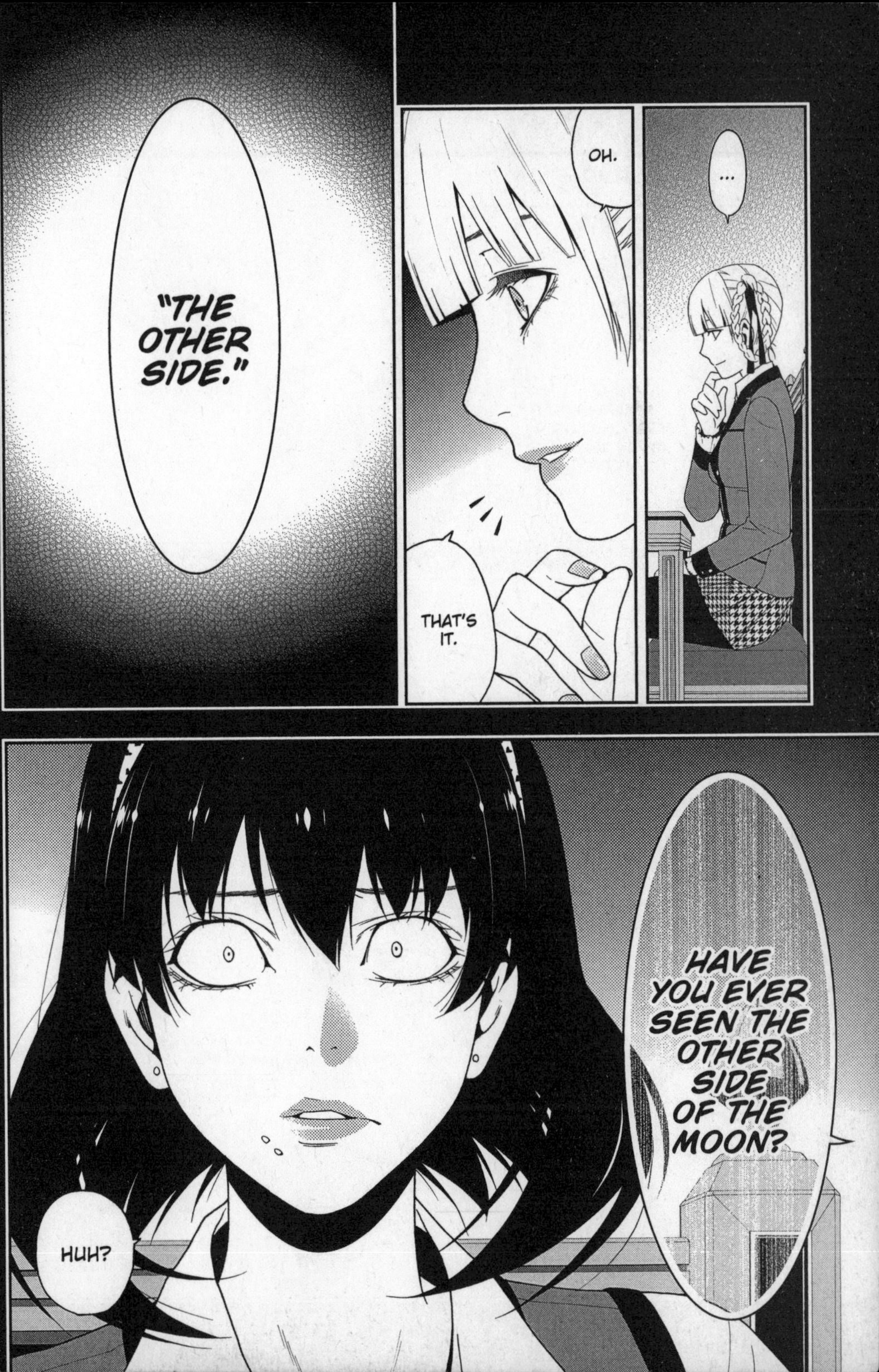
...
OH.
THAT'S IT.
"THE OTHER SIDE."
HAVE YOU EVER SEEN THE OTHER SIDE OF THE MOON?
HUH?

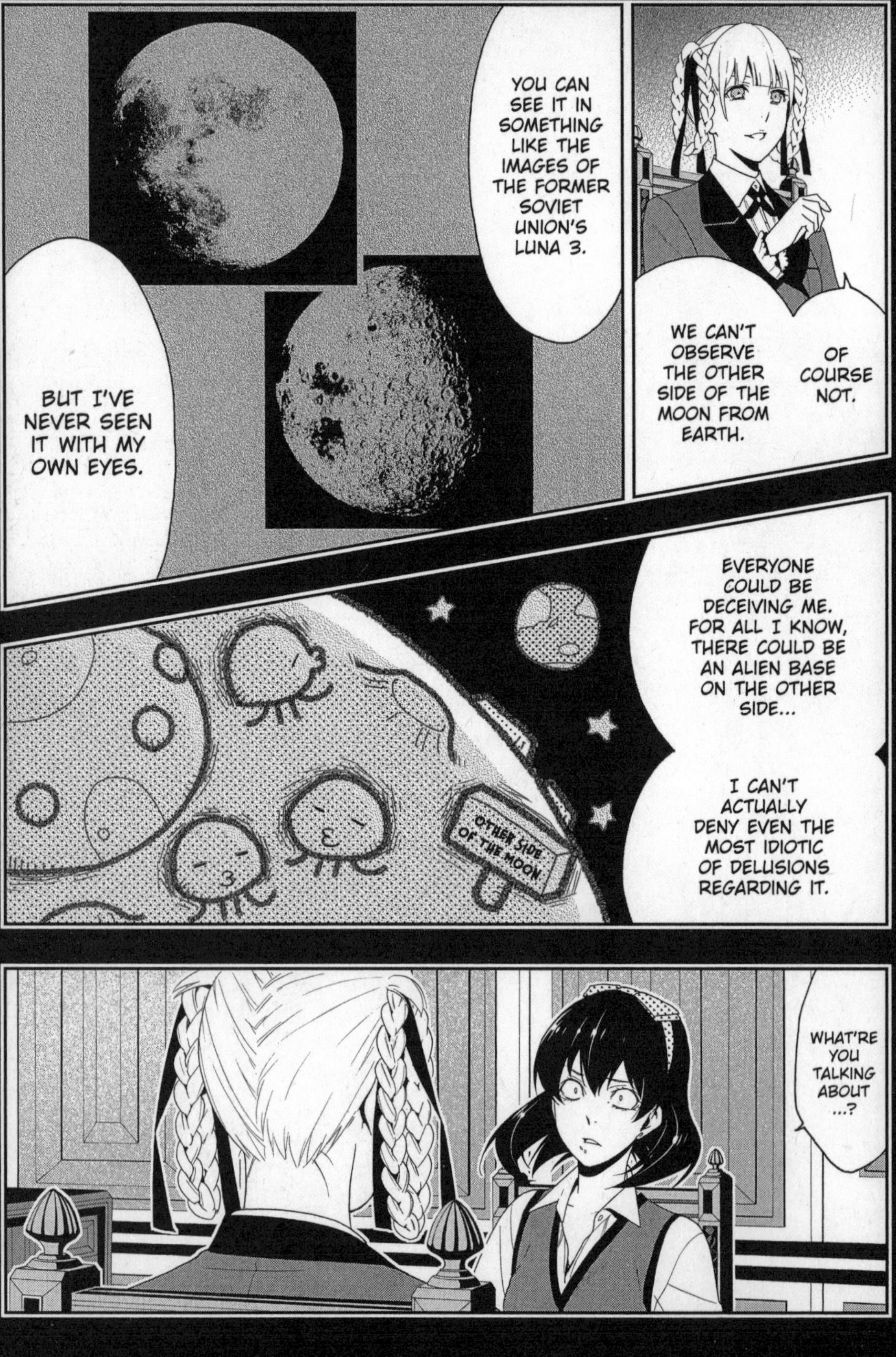
WE CAN'T OBSERVE THE OTHER SIDE OF THE MOON FROM EARTH.
OF COURSE NOT.
YOU CAN SEE IT IN SOMETHING LIKE THE IMAGES OF THE FORMER SOVIET UNION'S LUNA 3.
BUT I'VE NEVER SEEN IT WITH MY OWN EYES.
EVERYONE COULD BE DECEIVING ME. FOR ALL I KNOW, THERE COULD BE AN ALIEN BASE ON THE OTHER SIDE...
I CAN'T ACTUALLY DENY EVEN THE MOST IDIOTIC OF DELUSIONS REGARDING IT.
OTHER SIDE OF THE MOON
WHAT'RE YOU TALKING ABOUT ...?

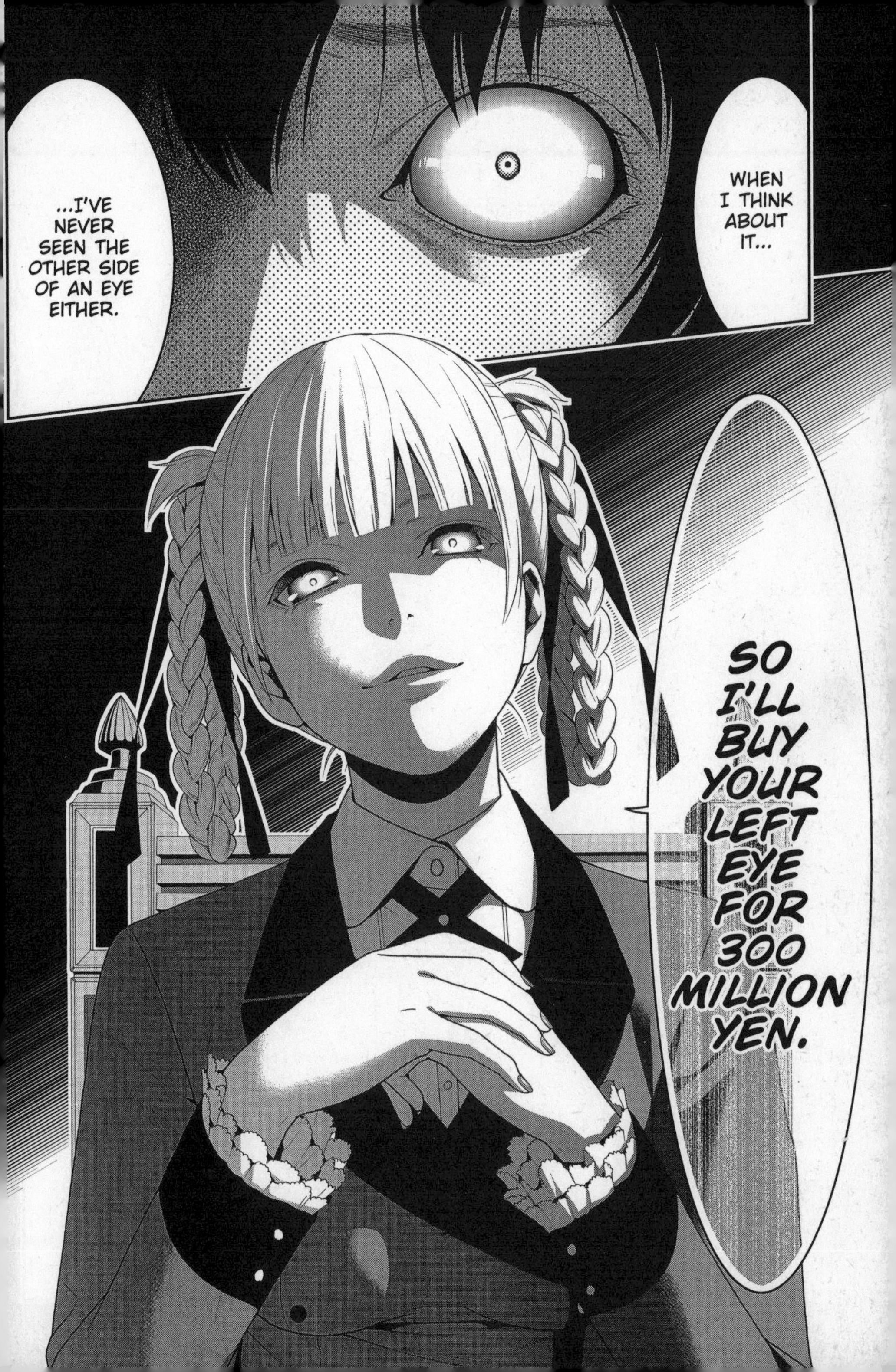
WHEN I THINK ABOUT IT...
...I'VE NEVER SEEN THE OTHER SIDE OF AN EYE EITHER.
SO I'LL BUY YOUR LEFT EYE FOR 300 MILLION YEN.

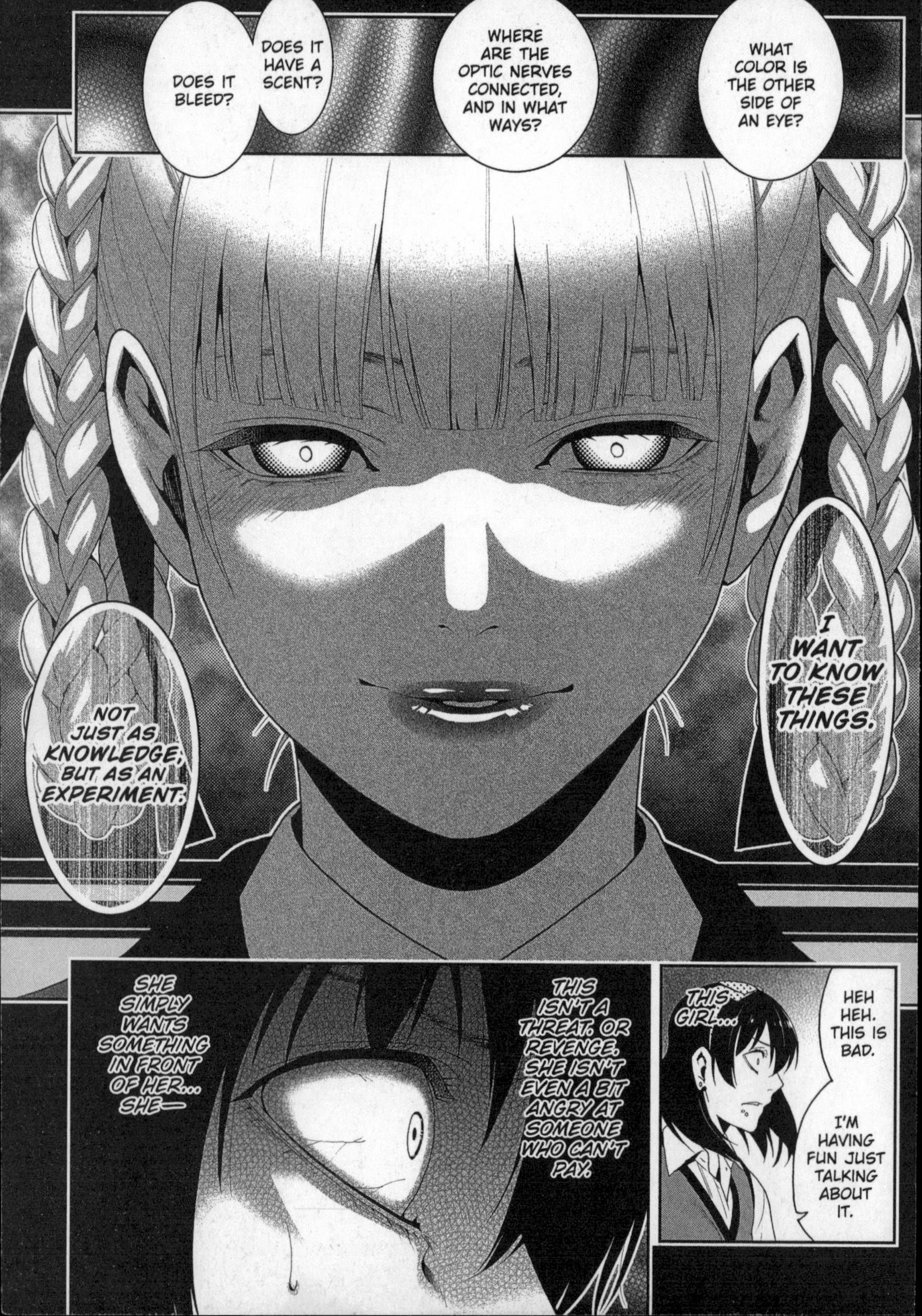
WHAT COLOR IS THE OTHER SIDE OF AN EYE?
WHERE ARE THE OPTIC NERVES CONNECTED, AND IN WHAT WAYS?
DOES IT HAVE A SCENT?
DOES IT BLEED?
I WANT TO KNOW THESE THINGS.
NOT JUST AS KNOWLEDGE, BUT AS AN EXPERIMENT.
HEH HEH. THIS IS BAD.
THIS GIRL...
I'M HAVING FUN JUST TALKING ABOUT IT.
THIS ISN'T A THREAT. OR REVENGE. SHE ISN'T EVEN A BIT ANGRY AT SOMEONE WHO CAN'T PAY.
SHE SIMPLY WANTS SOMETHING IN FRONT OF HER... SHE—

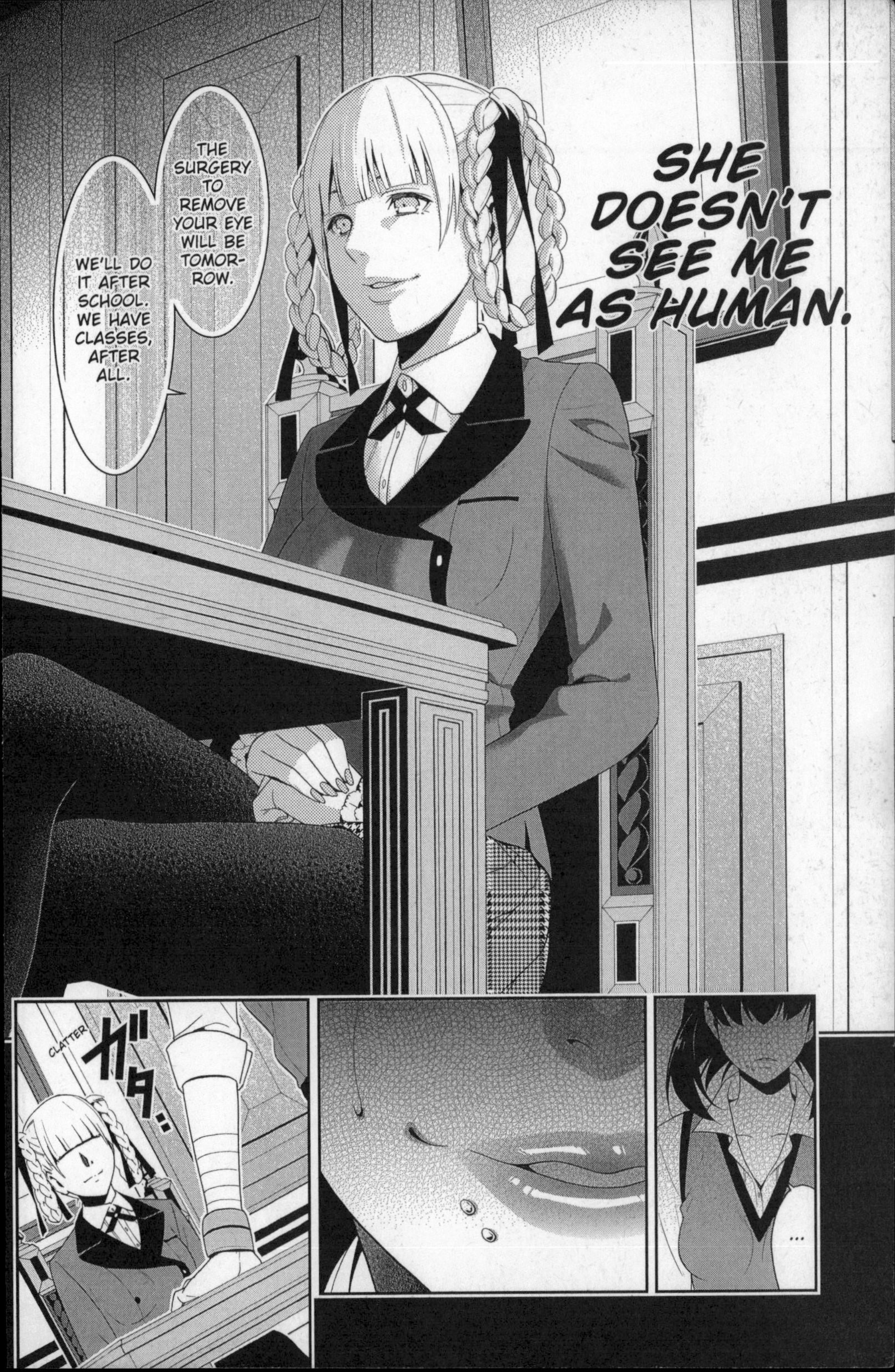
THE SURGERY TO REMOVE YOUR EYE WILL BE TOMORROW.
WE'LL DO IT AFTER SCHOOL. WE HAVE CLASSES, AFTER ALL.
SHE DOESN'T SEE ME AS HUMAN.
...
ガタ
CLATTER

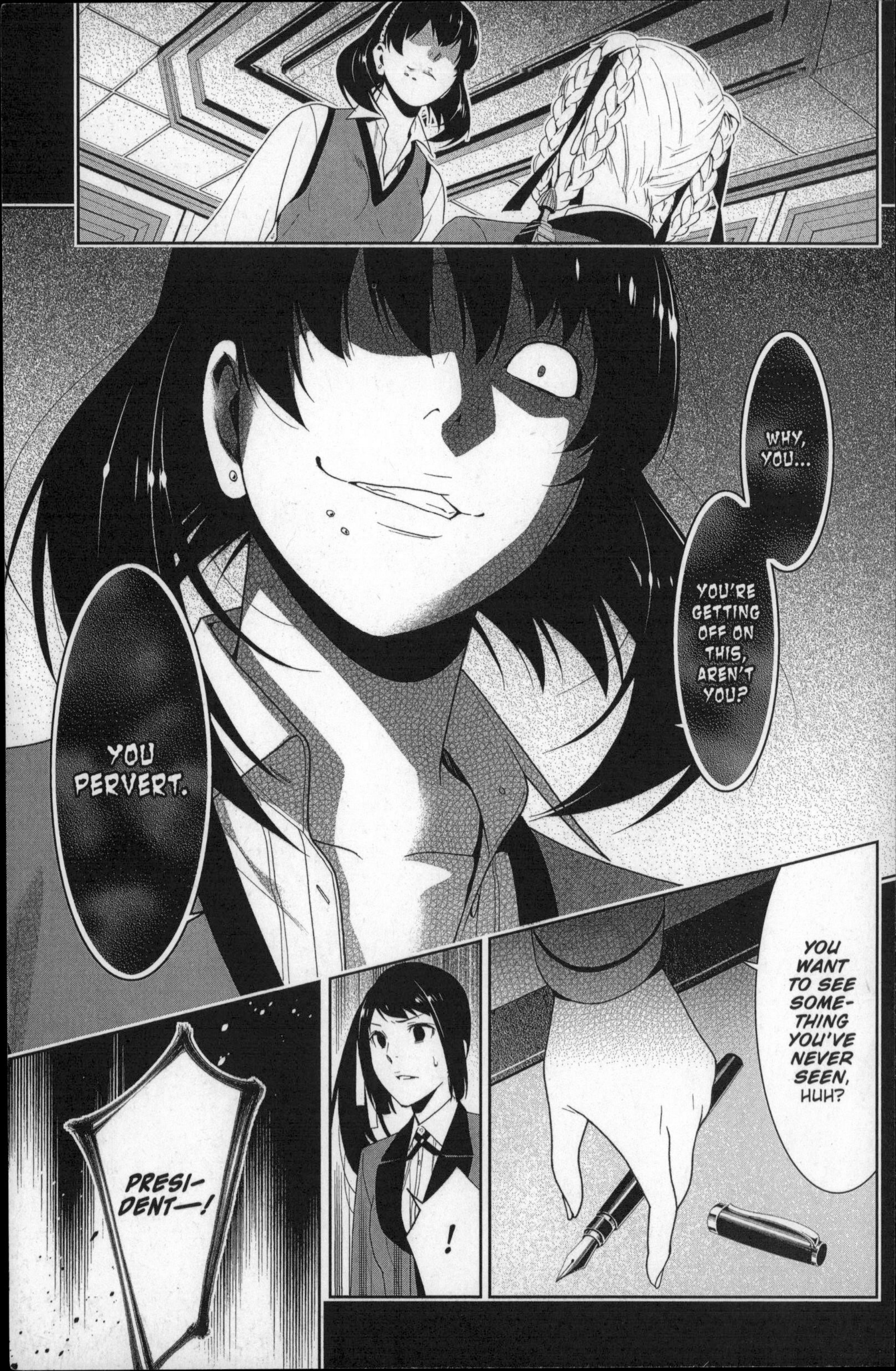
WHY, YOU...
YOU'RE GETTING OFF ON THIS, AREN'T YOU?
YOU PERVERT.
YOU WANT TO SEE SOMETHING YOU'VE NEVER SEEN, HUH?
!
PRESI-DENT—!

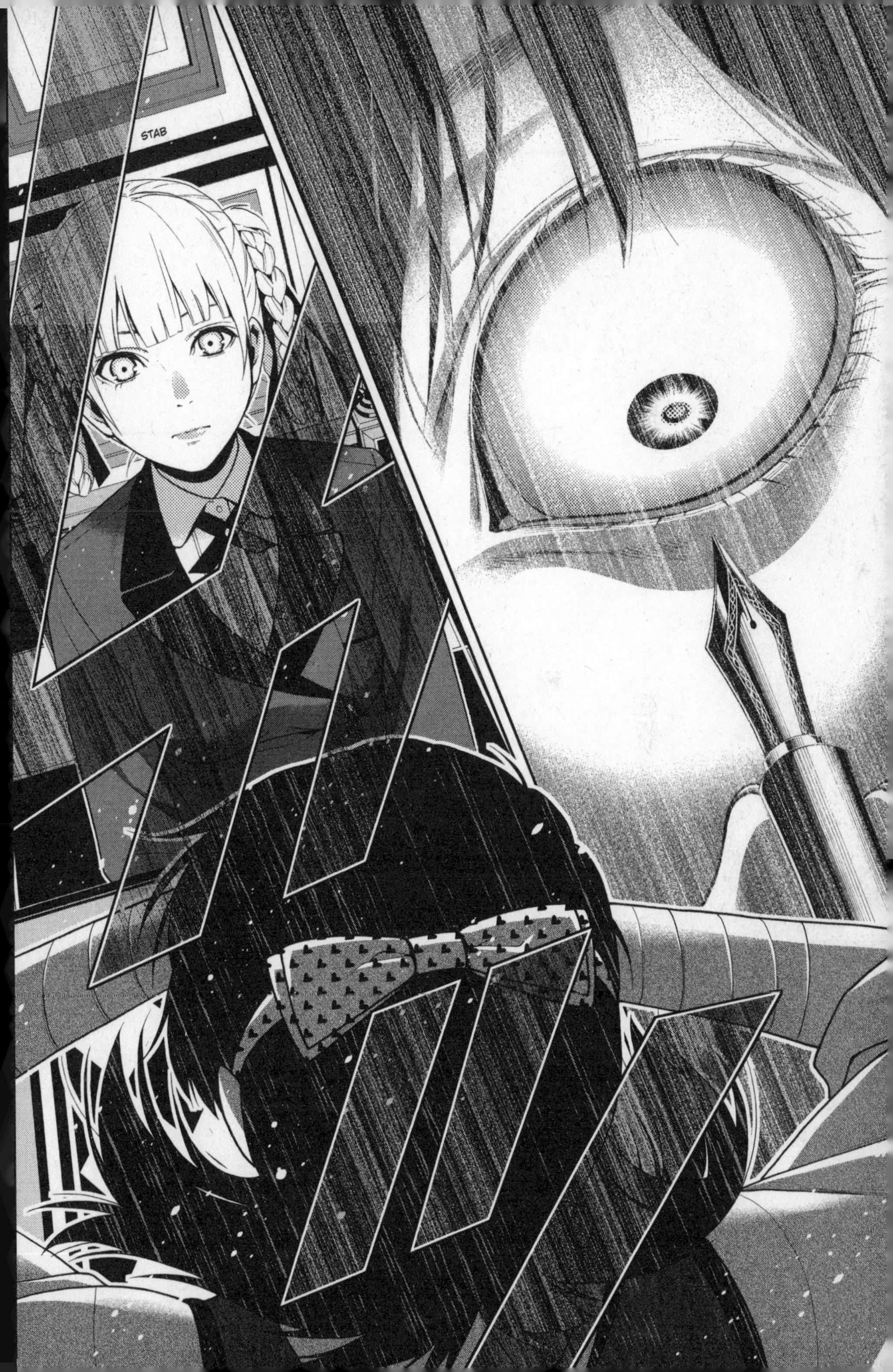
STAB

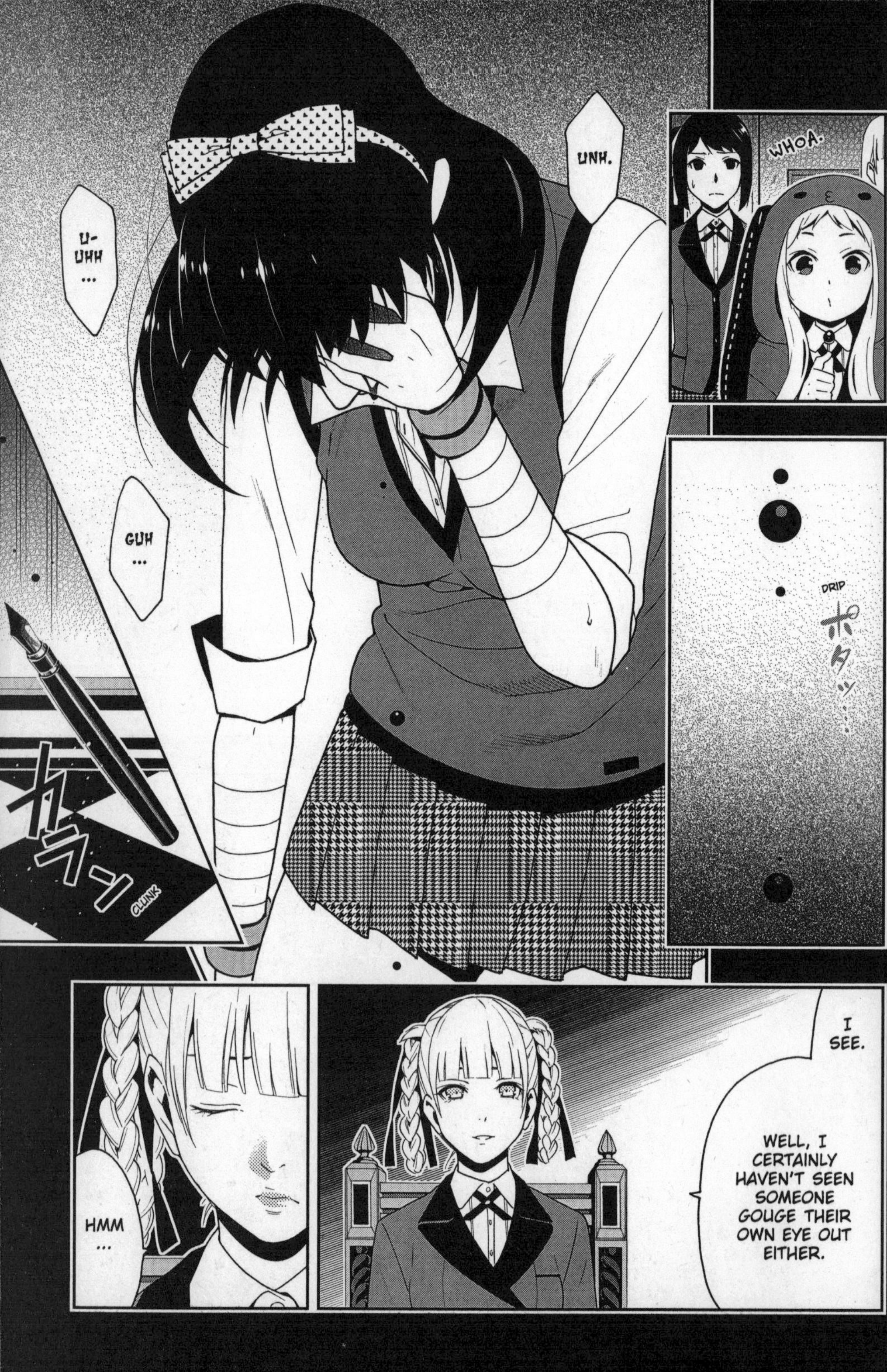
WHOA.
DRIP
ポタッ…
UNH.
U-UHH …
GUH …
カラーン
CLINK
I SEE.
WELL, I CERTAINLY HAVEN'T SEEN SOMEONE GOUGE THEIR OWN EYE OUT EITHER.
HMM …

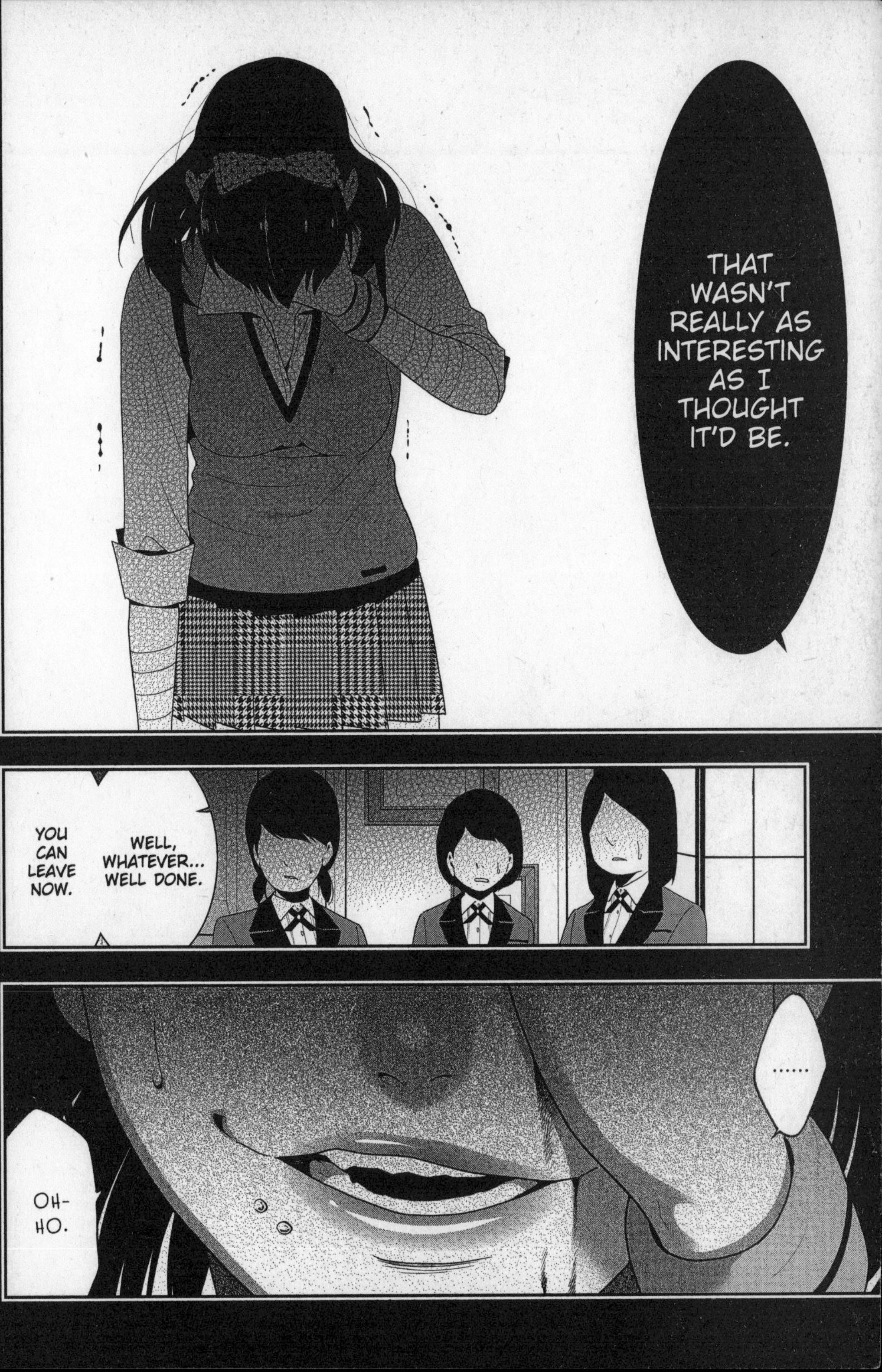
THAT WASN'T REALLY AS INTERESTING AS I THOUGHT IT'D BE.
WELL, WHATEVER... WELL DONE.
YOU CAN LEAVE NOW.
......
OH-HO.

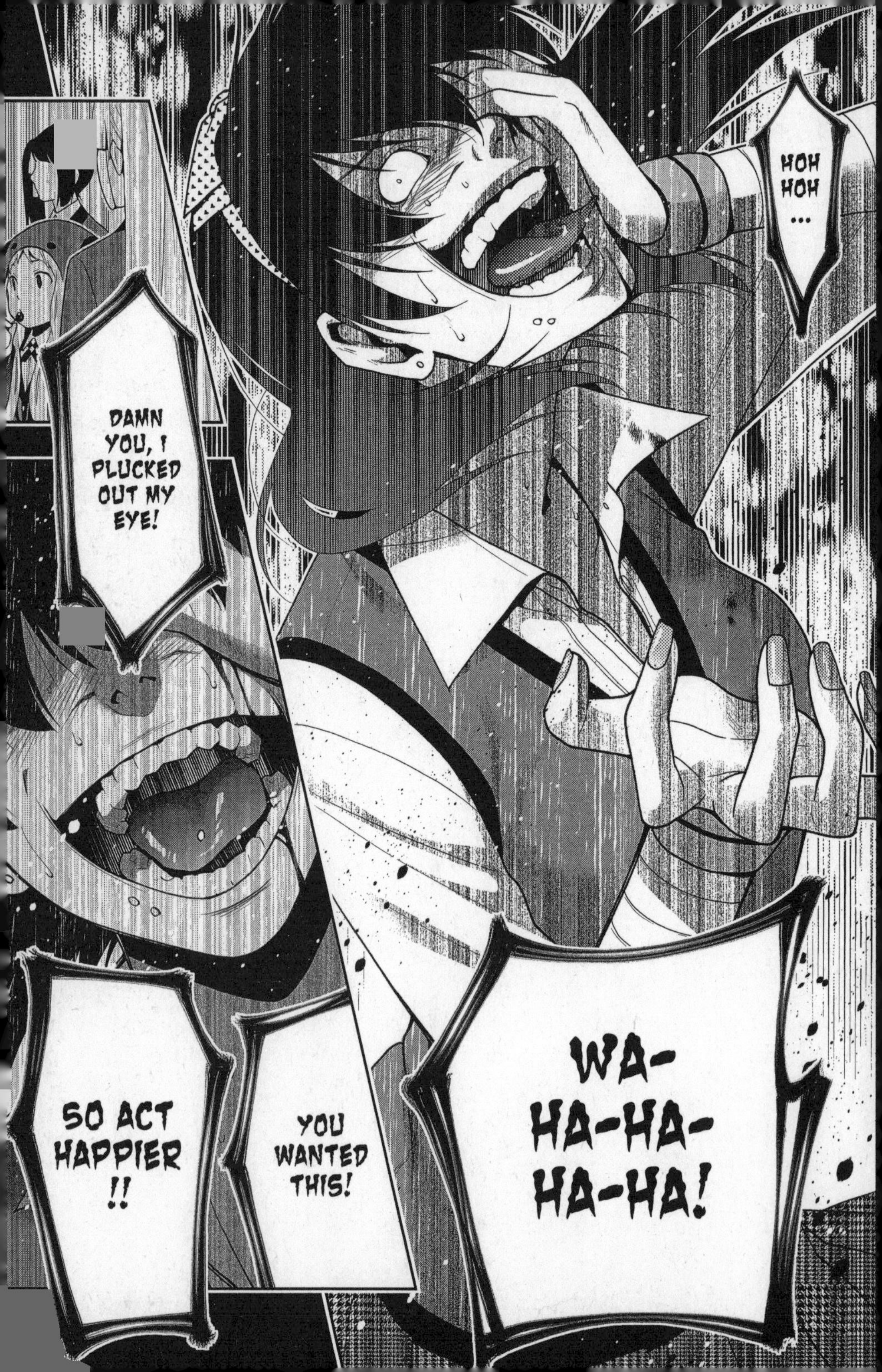
HOH HOH ...
DAMN YOU, I PLUCKED OUT MY EYE!
WA-HA-HA-HA-HA!
YOU WANTED THIS!
SO ACT HAPPIER !!

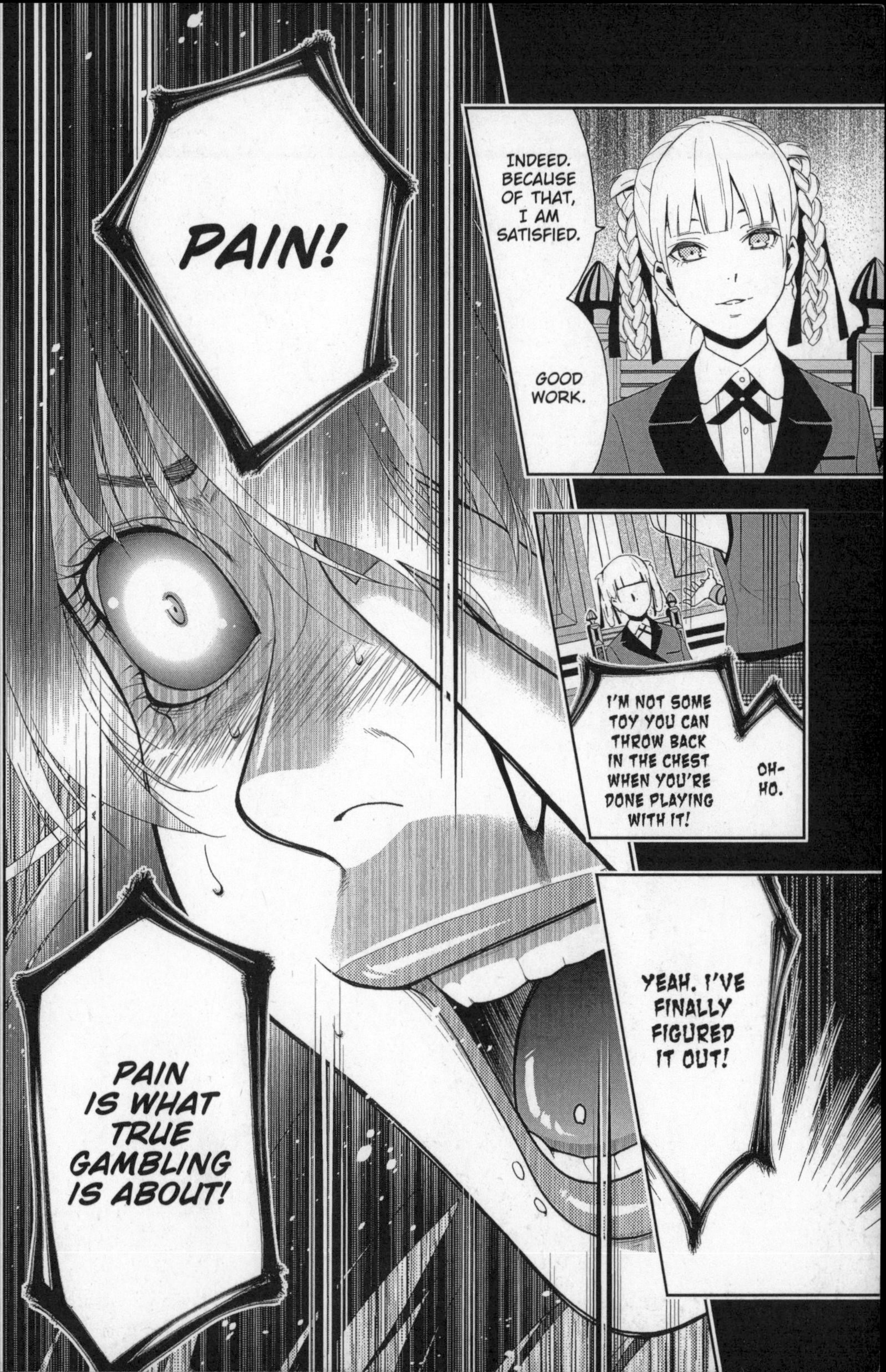
INDEED. BECAUSE OF THAT, I AM SATISFIED.
GOOD WORK.
I'M NOT SOME TOY YOU CAN THROW BACK IN THE CHEST WHEN YOU'RE DONE PLAYING WITH IT!
OH-HO.
YEAH. I'VE FINALLY FIGURED IT OUT!
PAIN!
PAIN IS WHAT TRUE GAMBLING IS ABOUT!

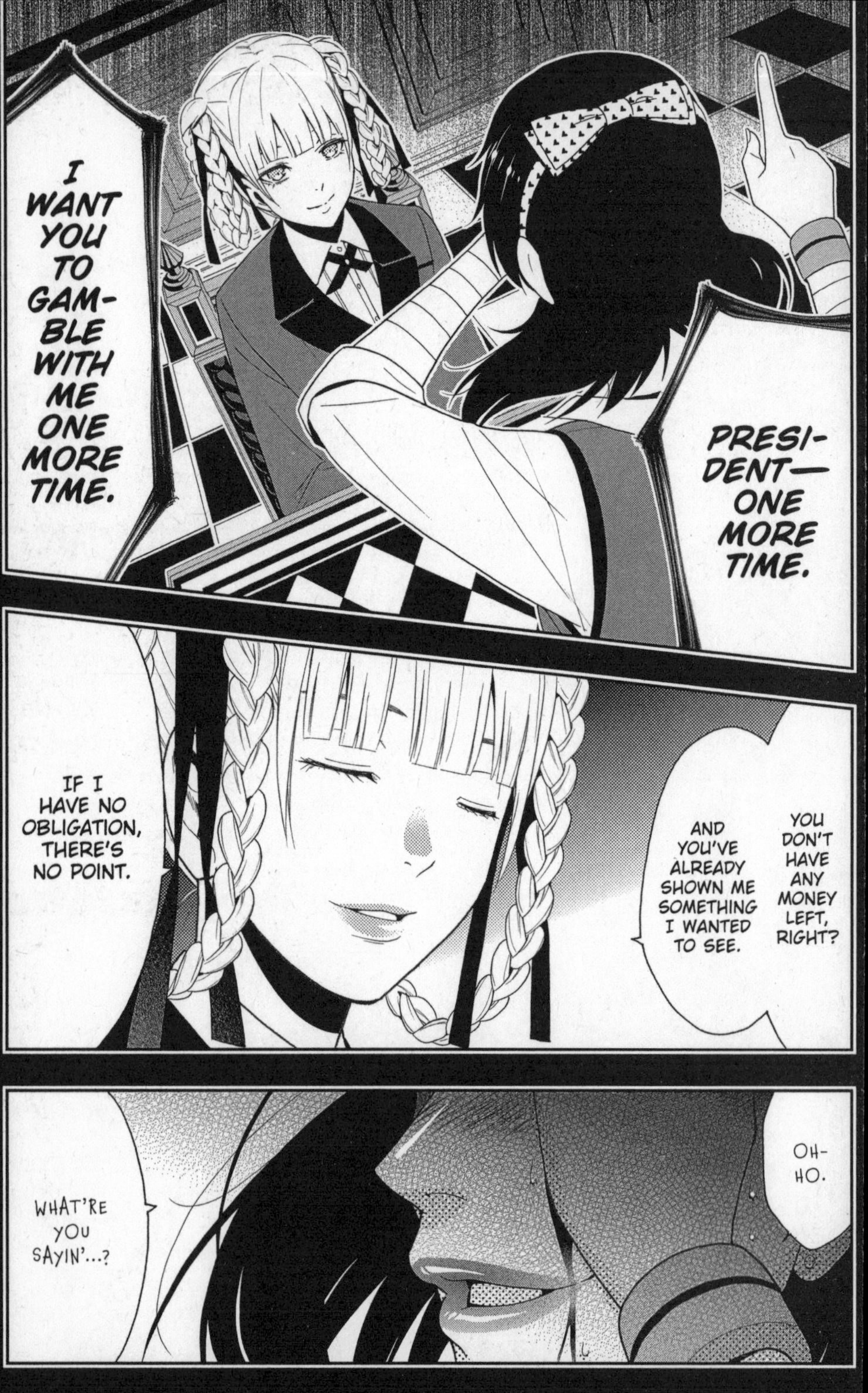
PRESI-DENT— ONE MORE TIME.
I WANT YOU TO GAM-BLE WITH ME ONE MORE TIME.
YOU DON'T HAVE ANY MONEY LEFT, RIGHT?
AND YOU'VE ALREADY SHOWN ME SOMETHING I WANTED TO SEE.
IF I HAVE NO OBLIGATION, THERE'S NO POINT.
OH-HO.
WHAT'RE YOU SAYIN'...?

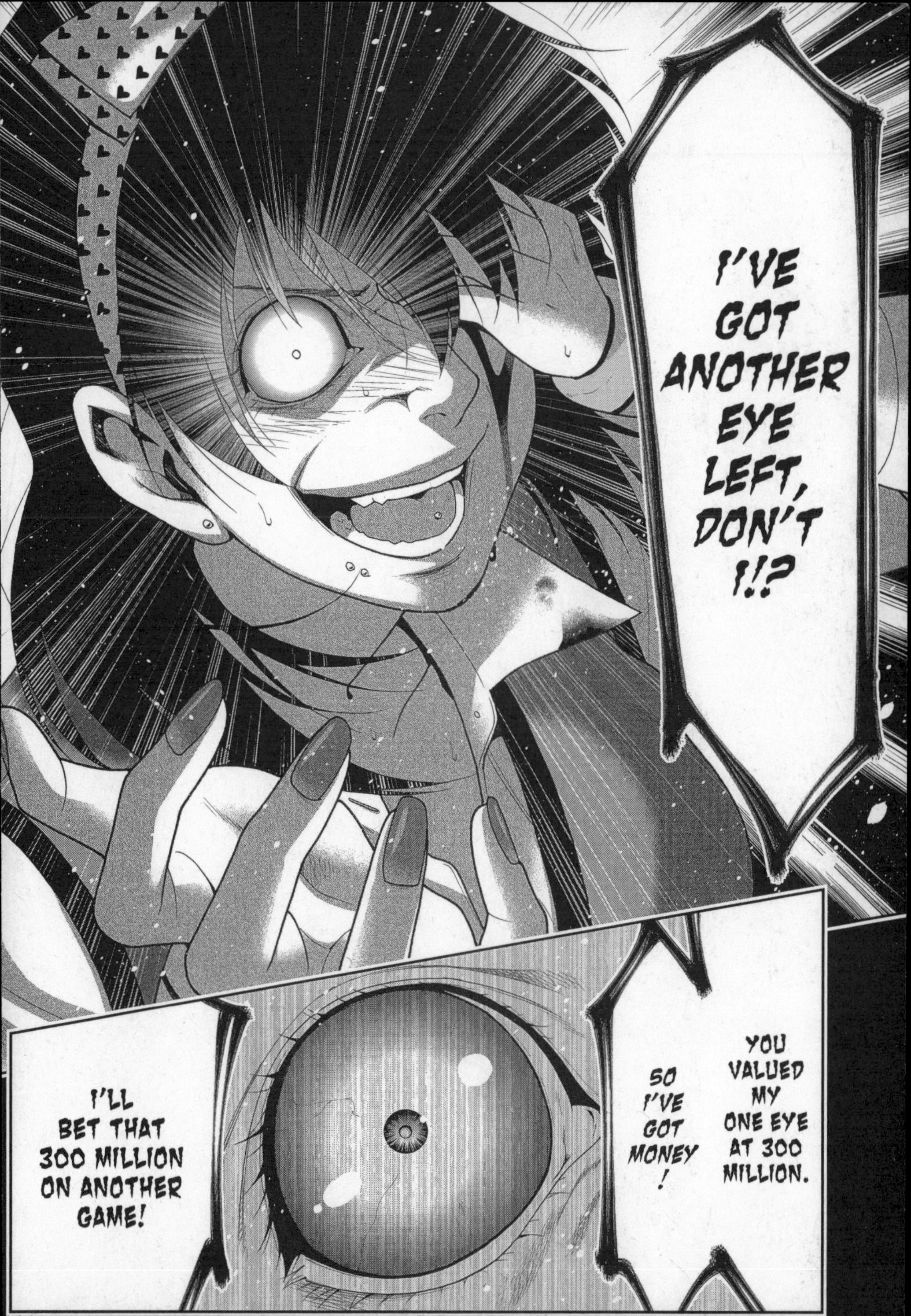
I'VE GOT ANOTHER EYE LEFT, DON'T I!?
YOU VALUED MY ONE EYE AT 300 MILLION.
SO I'VE GOT MONEY!
I'LL BET THAT 300 MILLION ON ANOTHER GAME!

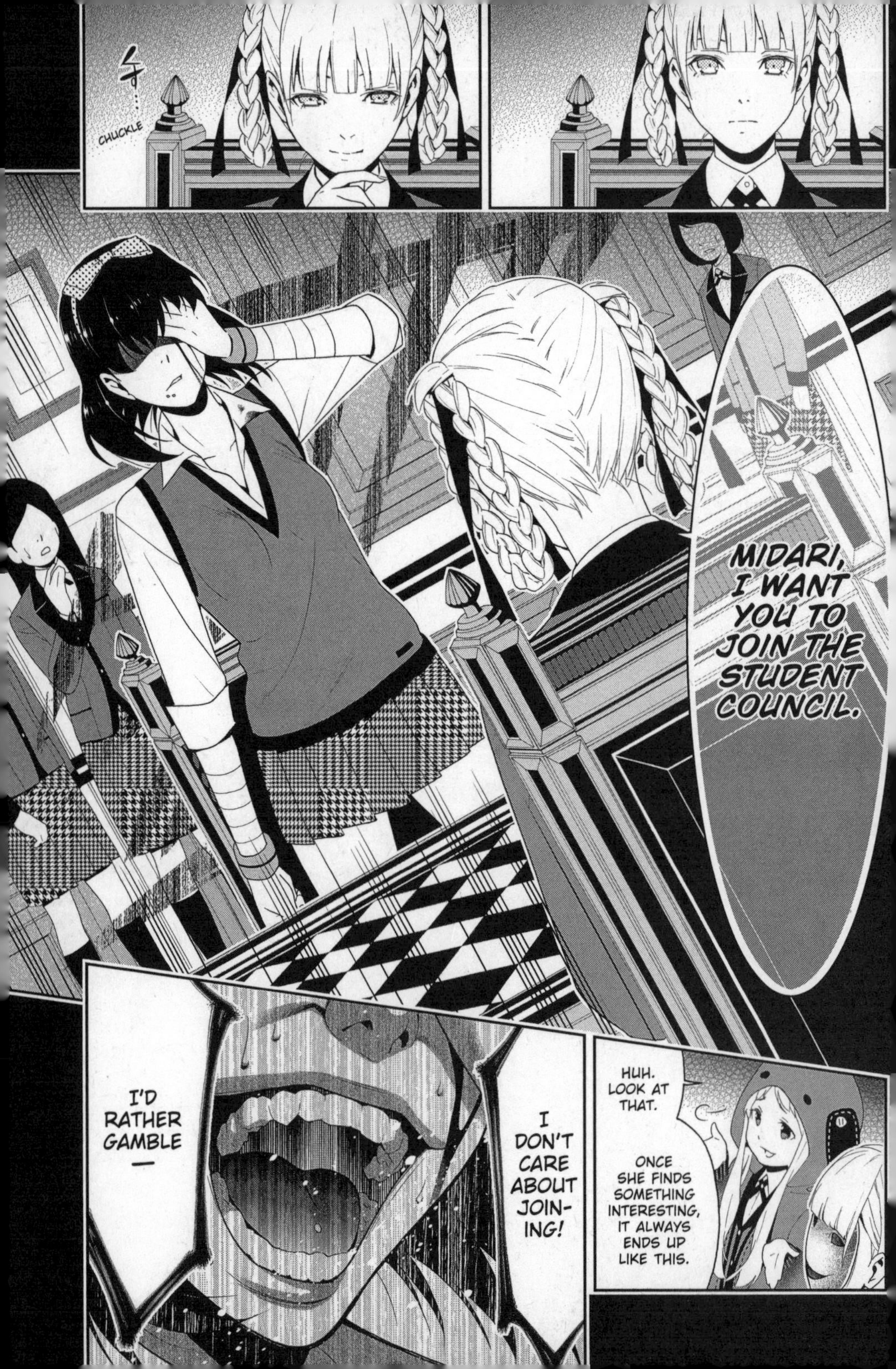
くす…
CHUCKLE
MIDARI, I WANT YOU TO JOIN THE STUDENT COUNCIL.
HUH. LOOK AT THAT.
ONCE SHE FINDS SOMETHING INTERESTING, IT ALWAYS ENDS UP LIKE THIS.
I DON'T CARE ABOUT JOIN-ING!
I'D RATHER GAMBLE —

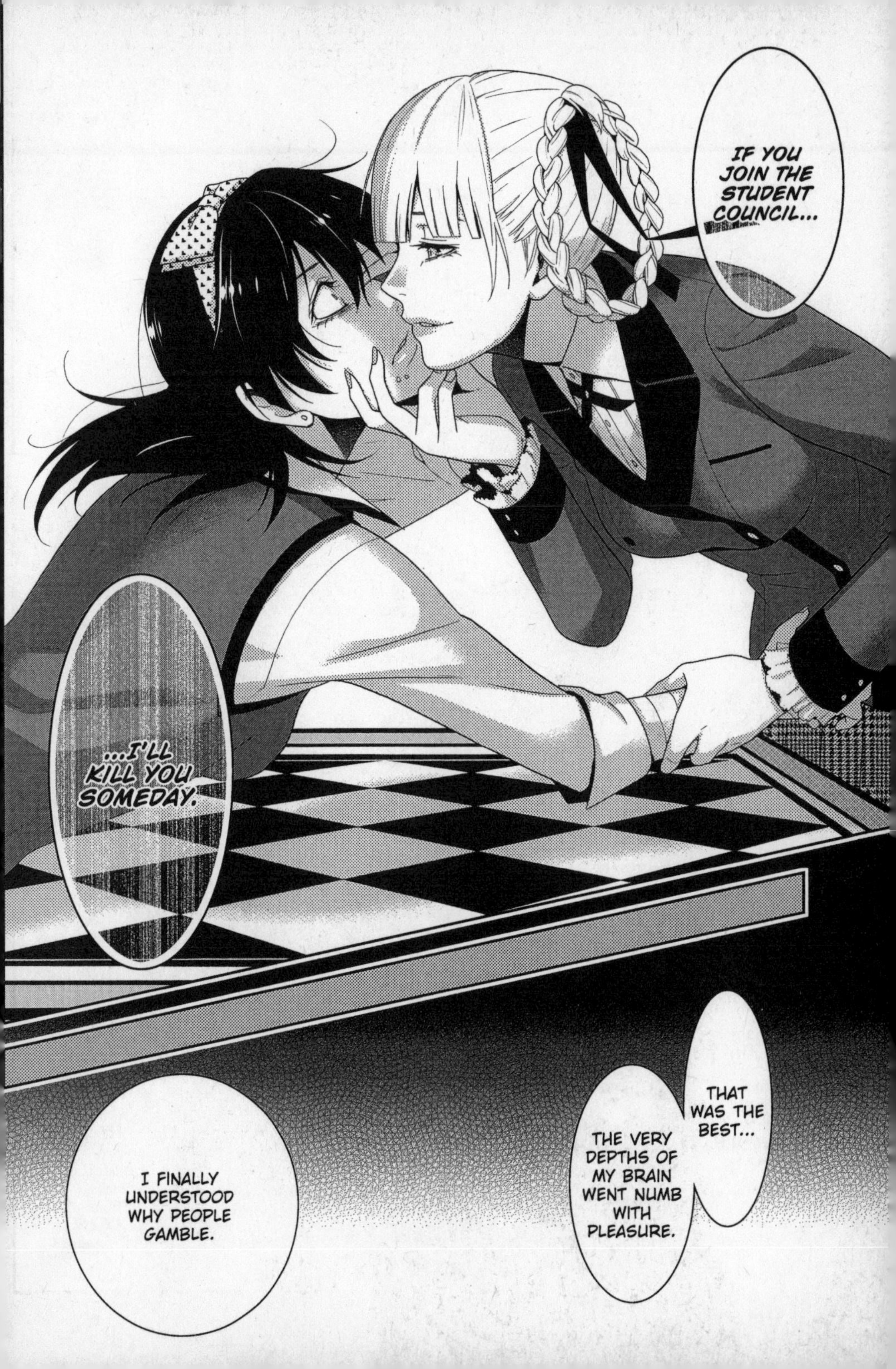
IF YOU JOIN THE STUDENT COUNCIL...
...I'LL KILL YOU SOMEDAY.
THAT WAS THE BEST...
THE VERY DEPTHS OF MY BRAIN WENT NUMB WITH PLEASURE.
I FINALLY UNDERSTOOD WHY PEOPLE GAMBLE.

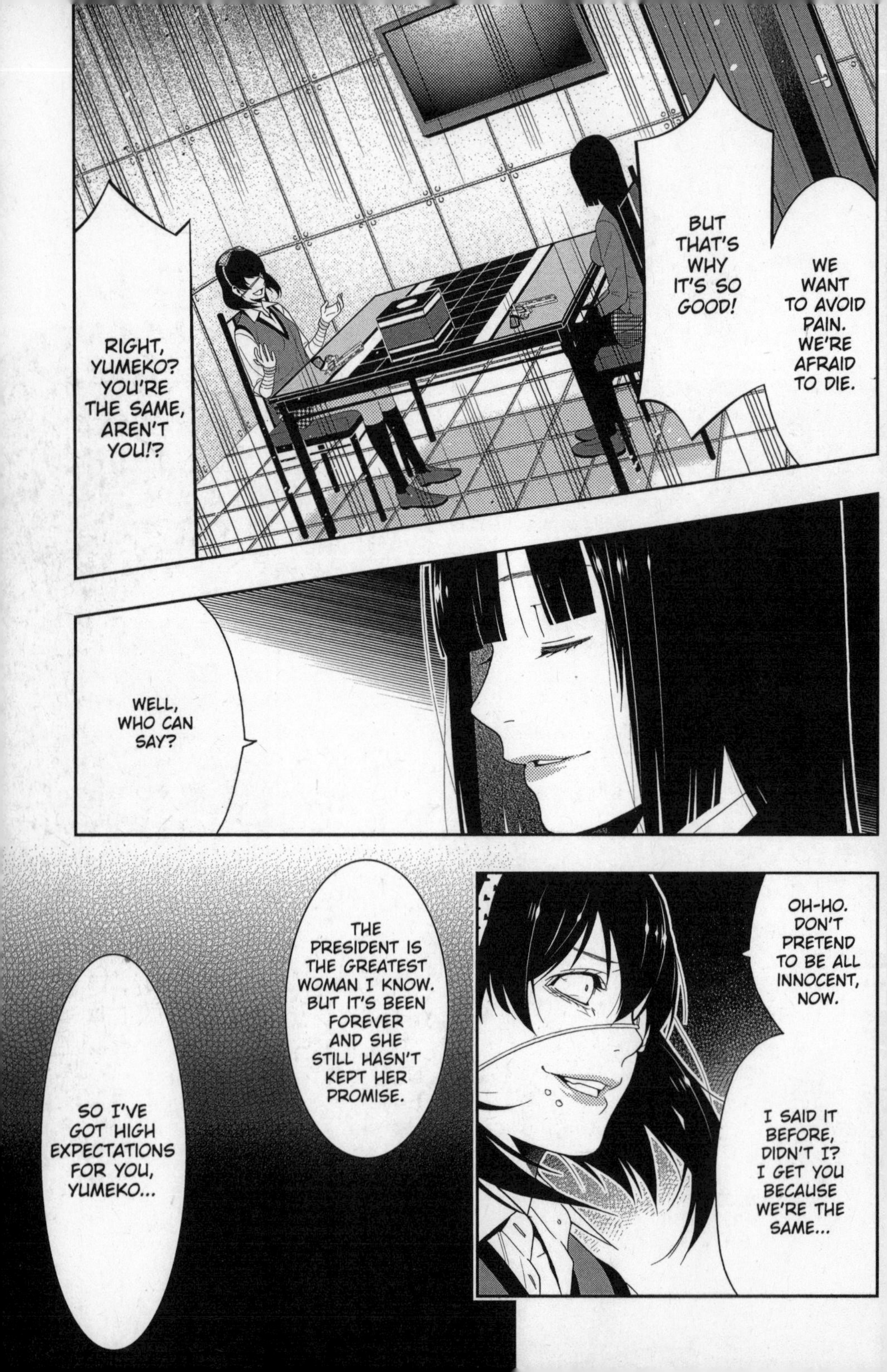
WE WANT TO AVOID PAIN. WE'RE AFRAID TO DIE.
BUT THAT'S WHY IT'S SO GOOD!
RIGHT, YUMEKO? YOU'RE THE SAME, AREN'T YOU!?
WELL, WHO CAN SAY?
OH-HO. DON'T PRETEND TO BE ALL INNOCENT, NOW.
I SAID IT BEFORE, DIDN'T I? I GET YOU BECAUSE WE'RE THE SAME...
THE PRESIDENT IS THE GREATEST WOMAN I KNOW. BUT IT'S BEEN FOREVER AND SHE STILL HASN'T KEPT HER PROMISE.
SO I'VE GOT HIGH EXPECTATIONS FOR YOU, YUMEKO...

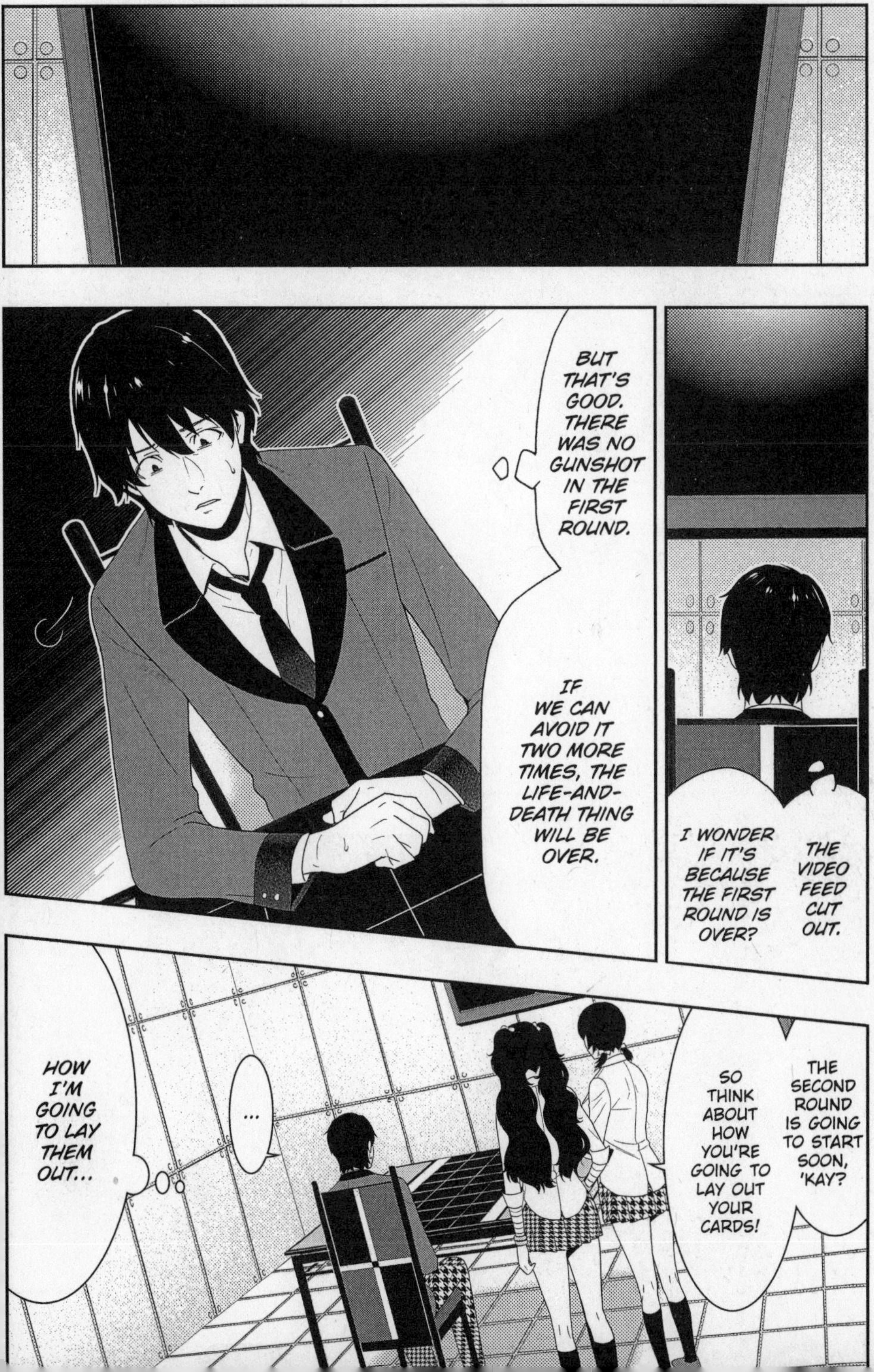
THE VIDEO FEED CUT OUT.
I WONDER IF IT'S BECAUSE THE FIRST ROUND IS OVER?
BUT THAT'S GOOD. THERE WAS NO GUNSHOT IN THE FIRST ROUND.
IF WE CAN AVOID IT TWO MORE TIMES, THE LIFE-AND-DEATH THING WILL BE OVER.
THE SECOND ROUND IS GOING TO START SOON, 'KAY?
SO THINK ABOUT HOW YOU'RE GOING TO LAY OUT YOUR CARDS!
...
HOW I'M GOING TO LAY THEM OUT...

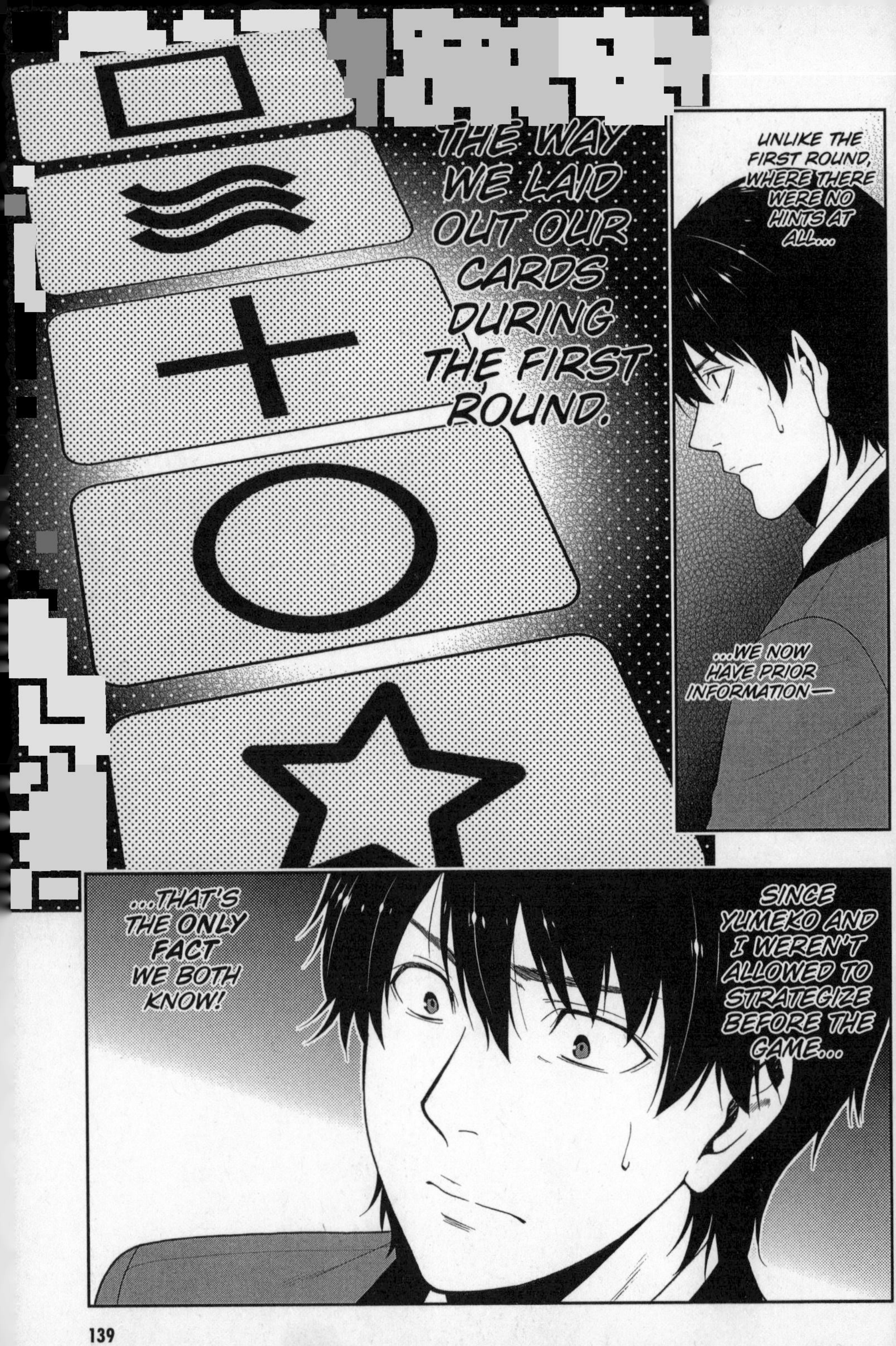
UNLIKE THE FIRST ROUND, WHERE THERE WERE NO HINTS AT ALL...
...WE NOW HAVE PRIOR INFORMATION—
THE WAY WE LAID OUT OUR CARDS DURING THE FIRST ROUND.
SINCE YUMEKO AND I WEREN'T ALLOWED TO STRATEGIZE BEFORE THE GAME...
...THAT'S THE ONLY FACT WE BOTH KNOW!

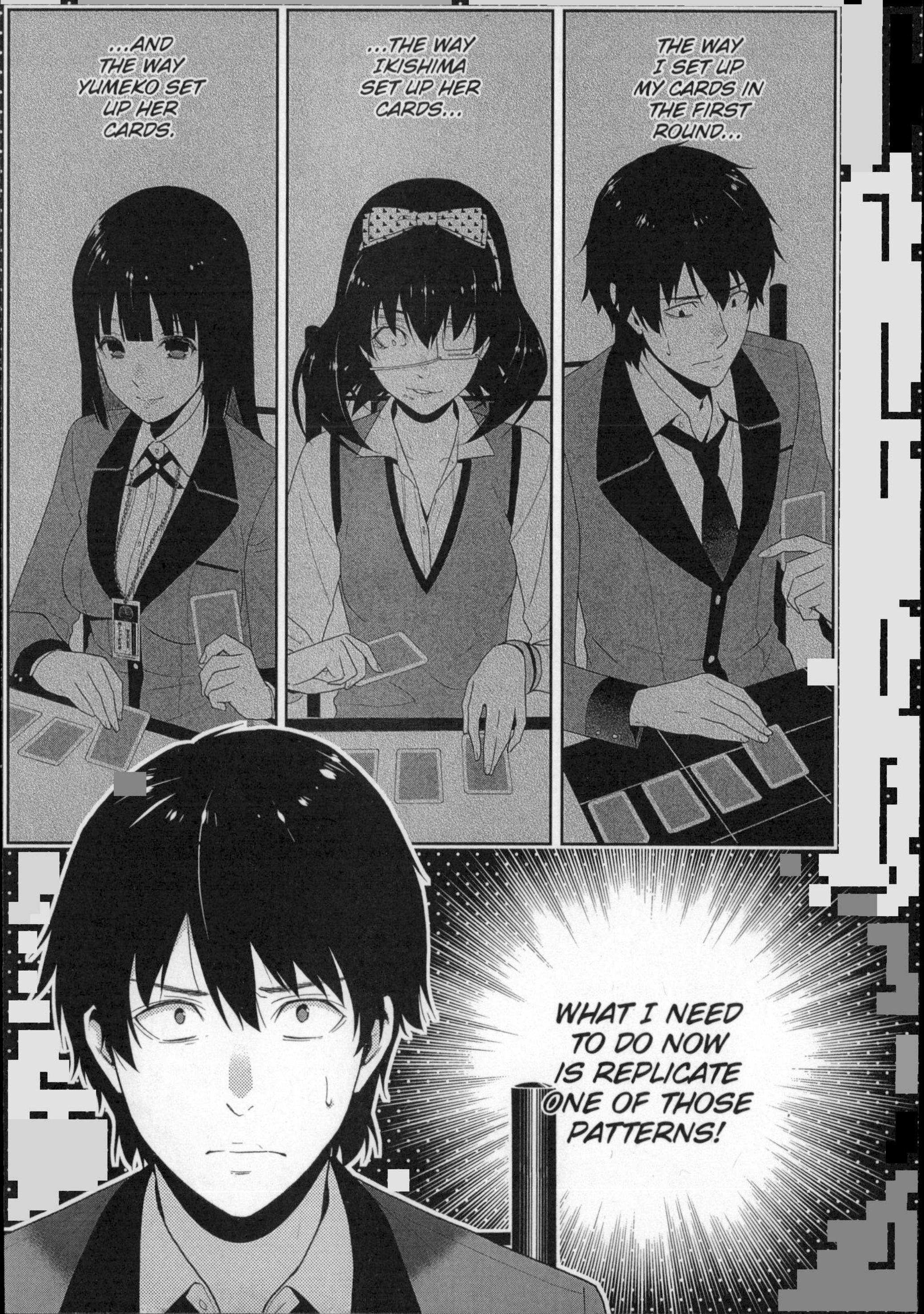
THE WAY I SET UP MY CARDS IN THE FIRST ROUND...
...THE WAY IKISHIMA SET UP HER CARDS...
...AND THE WAY YUMEKO SET UP HER CARDS.
WHAT I NEED TO DO NOW IS REPLICATE ONE OF THOSE PATTERNS!

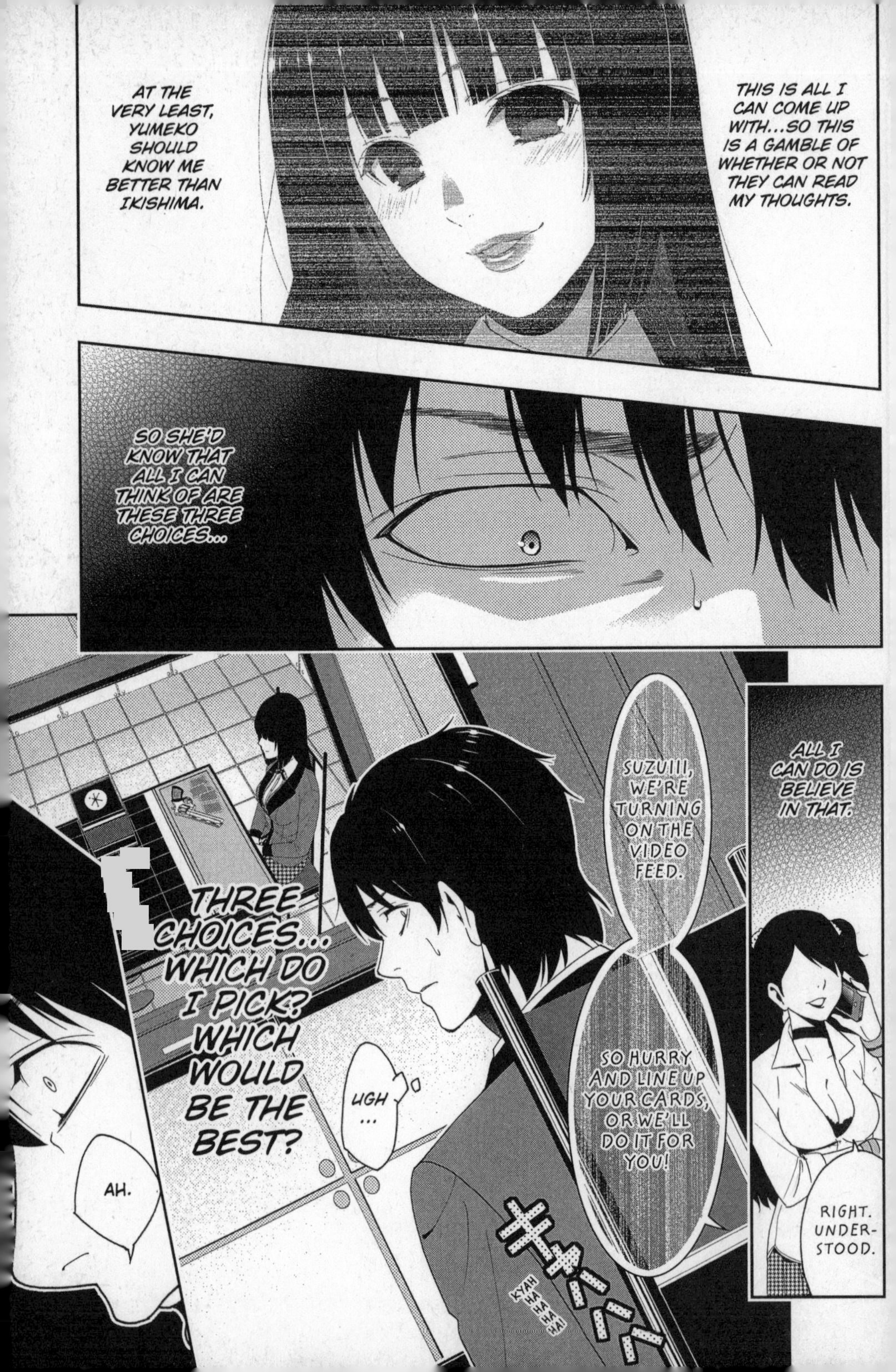
THIS IS ALL I CAN COME UP WITH...SO THIS IS A GAMBLE OF WHETHER OR NOT THEY CAN READ MY THOUGHTS.
AT THE VERY LEAST, YUMEKO SHOULD KNOW ME BETTER THAN IKISHIMA.
SO SHE'D KNOW THAT ALL I CAN THINK OF ARE THESE THREE CHOICES...
ALL I CAN DO IS BELIEVE IN THAT.
RIGHT. UNDER-STOOD.
SUZUIII, WE'RE TURNING ON THE VIDEO FEED.
SO HURRY AND LINE UP YOUR CARDS, OR WE'LL DO IT FOR YOU!
KYAH HA HA HA HA!
THREE CHOICES... WHICH DO I PICK? WHICH WOULD BE THE BEST?
UGH...
AH.

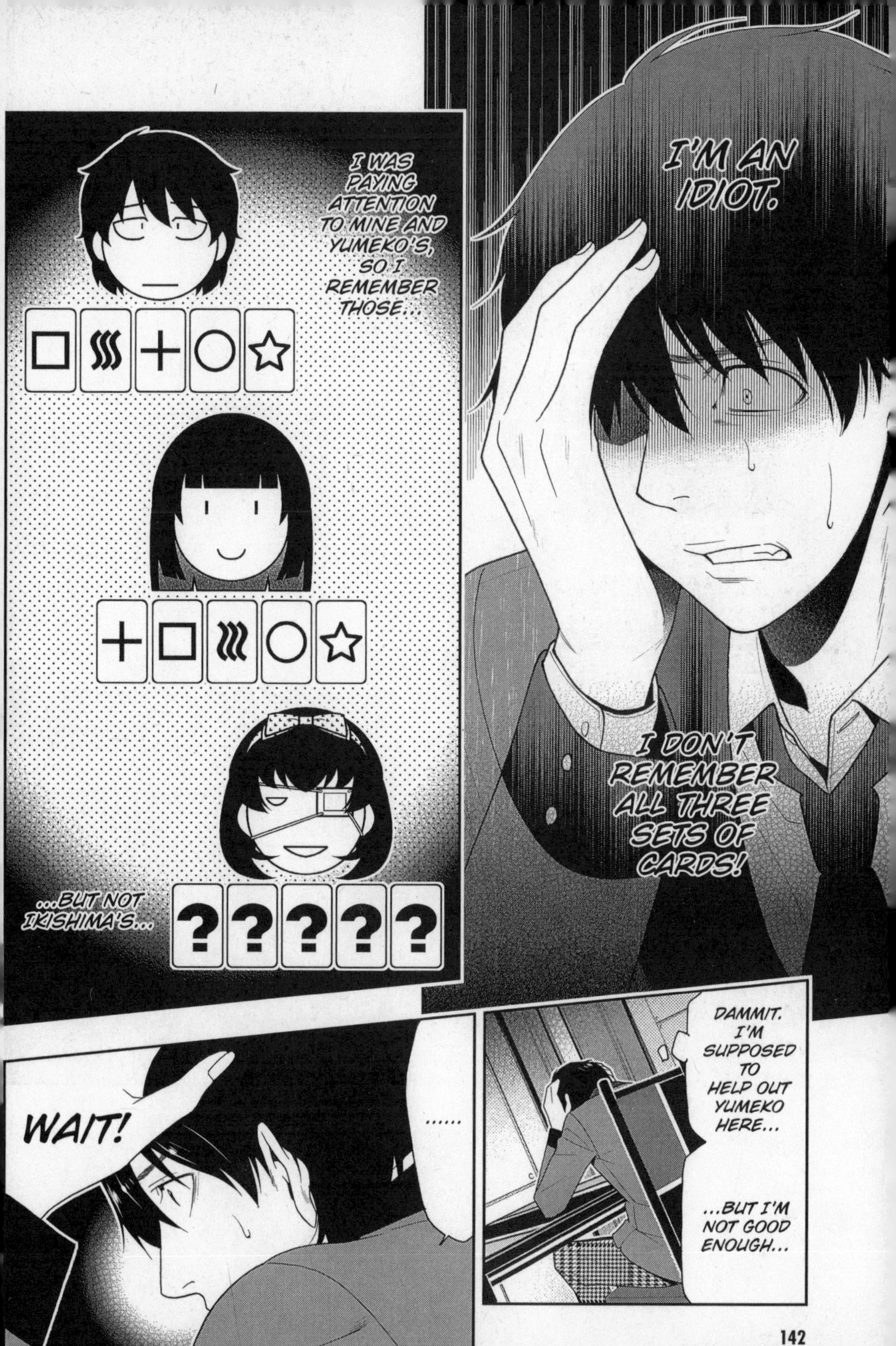
I'M AN IDIOT.
I DON'T REMEMBER ALL THREE SETS OF CARDS!
I WAS PAYING ATTENTION TO MINE AND YUMEKO'S, SO I REMEMBER THOSE...
...BUT NOT IKISHIMA'S...
DAMMIT. I'M SUPPOSED TO HELP OUT YUMEKO HERE...
...BUT I'M NOT GOOD ENOUGH...
......
WAIT!

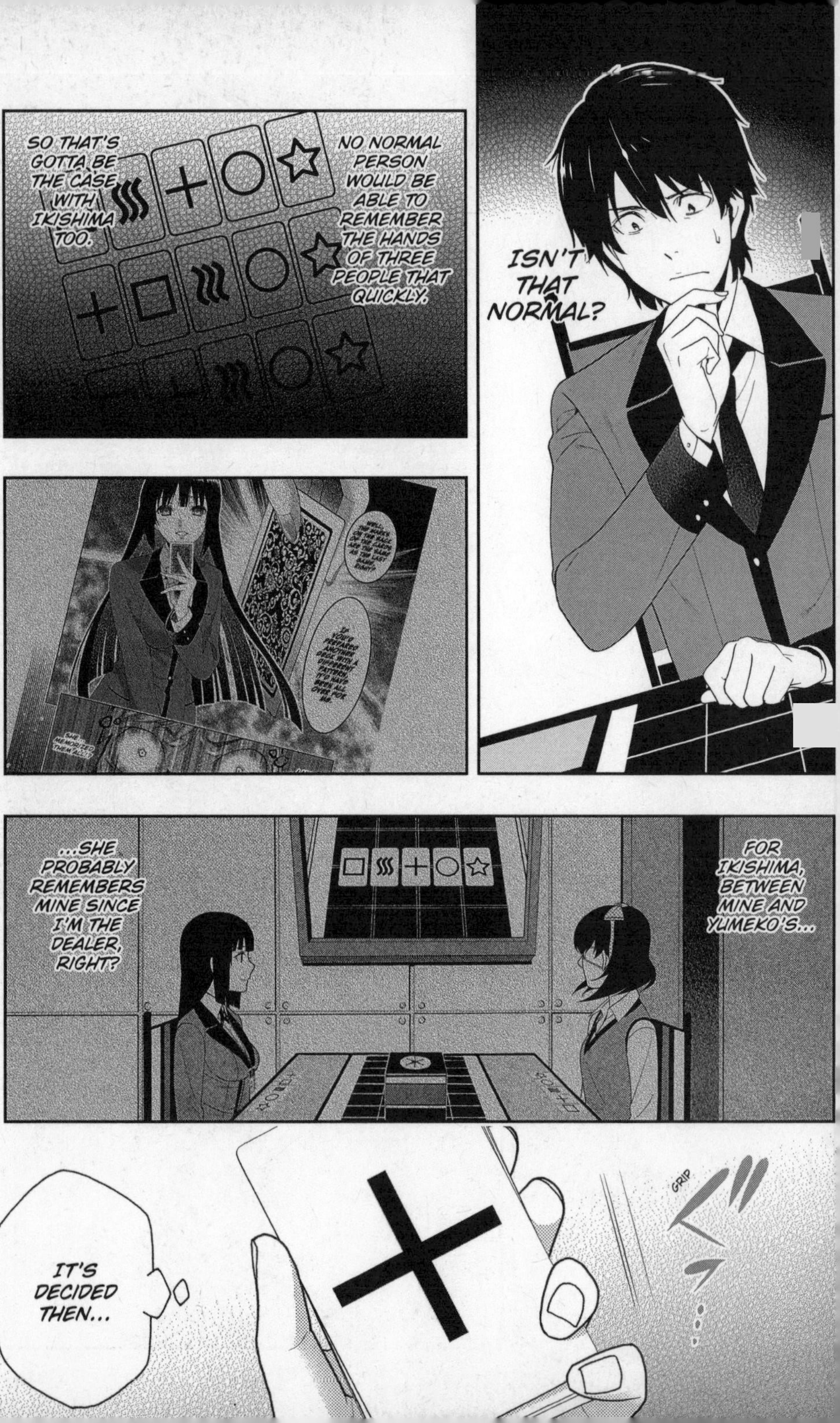
ISN'T THAT NORMAL?
NO NORMAL PERSON WOULD BE ABLE TO REMEMBER THE HANDS OF THREE PEOPLE THAT QUICKLY.
SO THAT'S GOTTA BE THE CASE WITH IKISHIMA TOO.
WELL... THE MARKS ON THE BACK OF THE CARDS ARE THE SAME AS THE LAST GAME, RIGHT?
IF YOU'D PREPARED ANOTHER DECK WITH A DIFFERENT PATTERN, IT'D HAVE BEEN ALL OVER FOR ME.
SHE... MEMORIZED THEM ALL!?
FOR IKISHIMA, BETWEEN MINE AND YUMEKO'S...
...SHE PROBABLY REMEMBERS MINE SINCE I'M THE DEALER, RIGHT?
GRIP
IT'S DECIDED THEN...

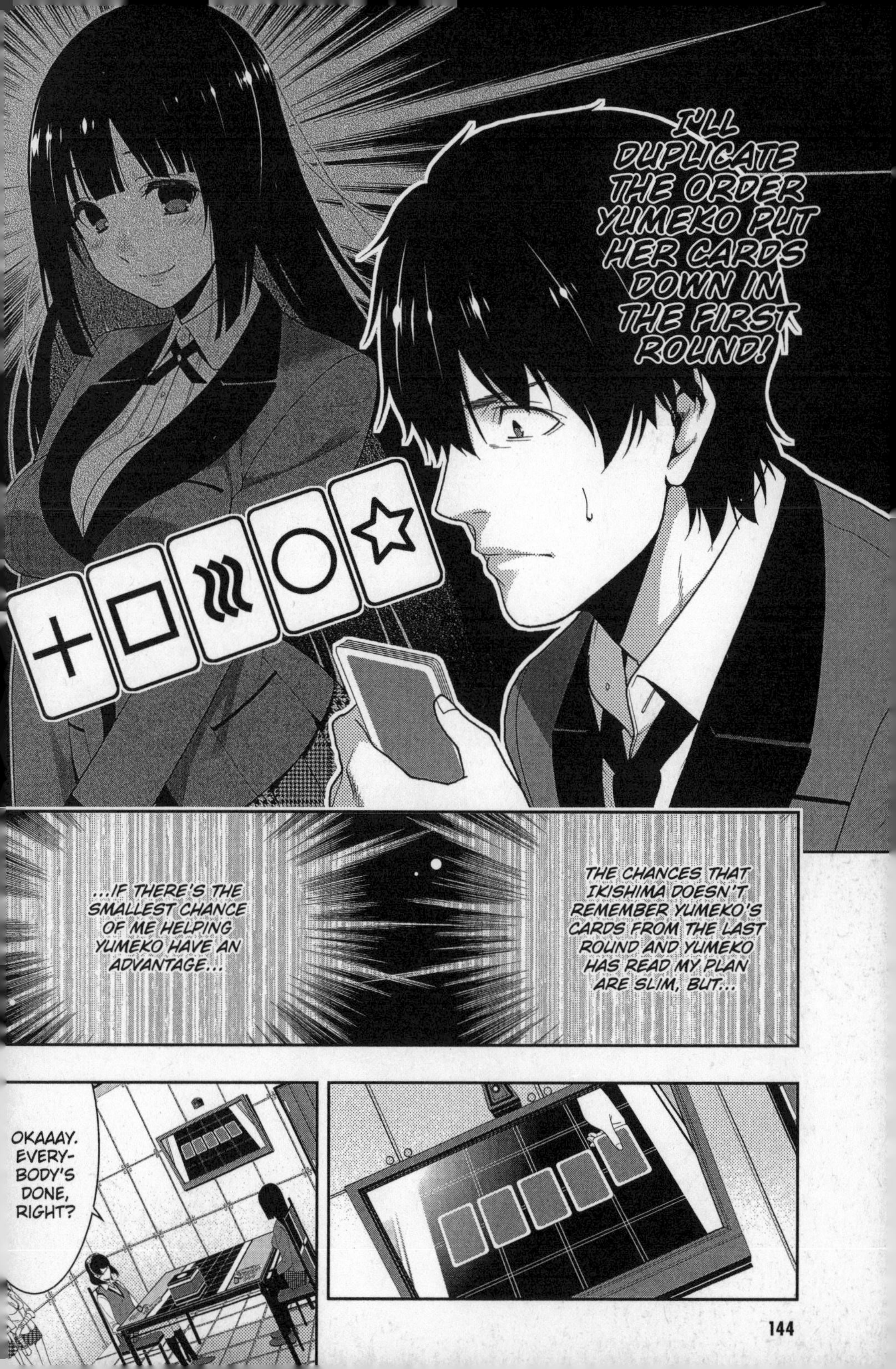
I'LL DUPLICATE THE ORDER YUMEKO PUT HER CARDS DOWN IN THE FIRST ROUND!
THE CHANCES THAT IKISHIMA DOESN'T REMEMBER YUMEKO'S CARDS FROM THE LAST ROUND AND YUMEKO HAS READ MY PLAN ARE SLIM, BUT...
...IF THERE'S THE SMALLEST CHANCE OF ME HELPING YUMEKO HAVE AN ADVANTAGE...
OKAAAY. EVERY-BODY'S DONE, RIGHT?

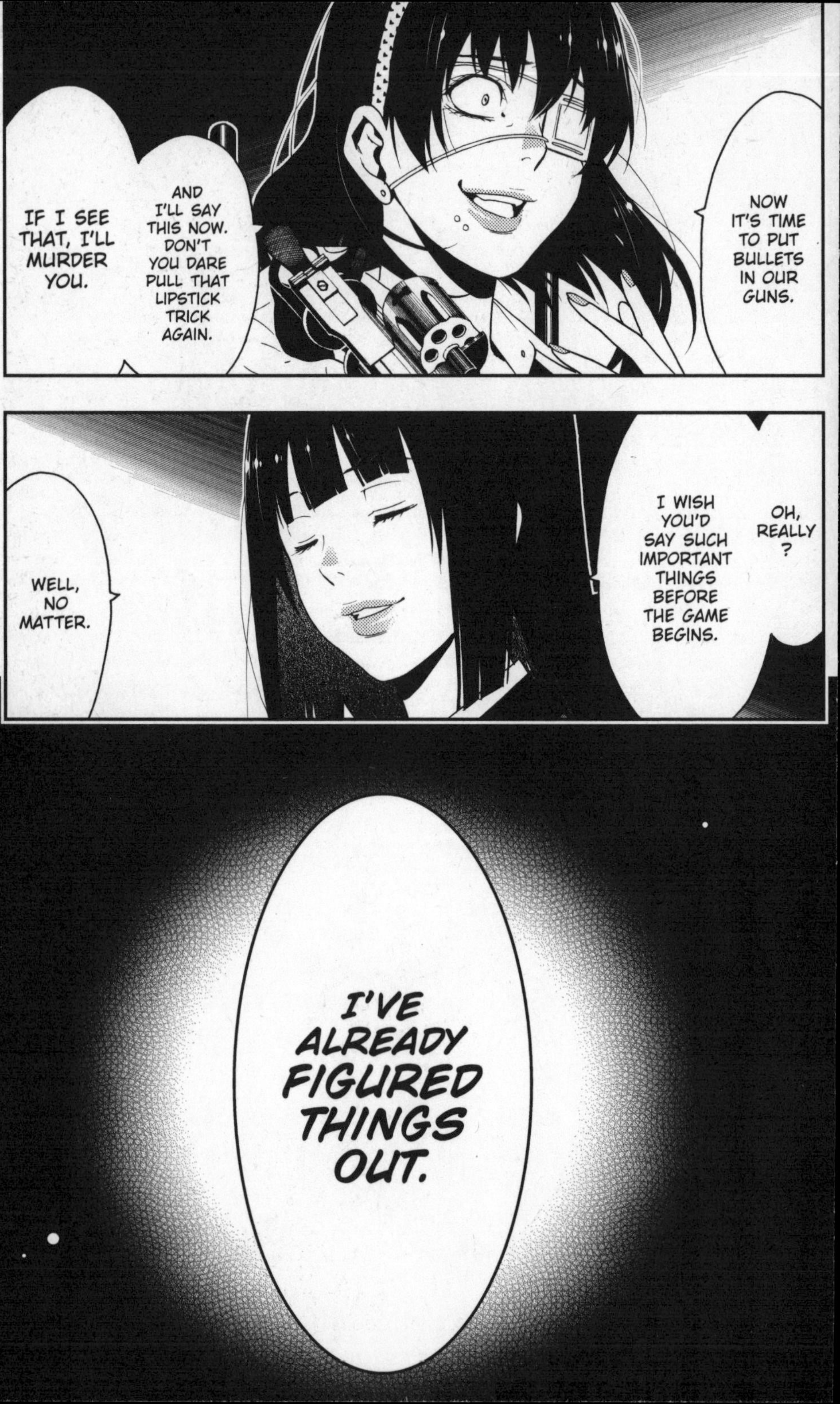
NOW IT'S TIME TO PUT BULLETS IN OUR GUNS.
AND I'LL SAY THIS NOW. DON'T YOU DARE PULL THAT LIPSTICK TRICK AGAIN.
IF I SEE THAT, I'LL MURDER YOU.
OH, REALLY?
I WISH YOU'D SAY SUCH IMPORTANT THINGS BEFORE THE GAME BEGINS.
WELL, NO MATTER.
I'VE ALREADY FIGURED THINGS OUT.

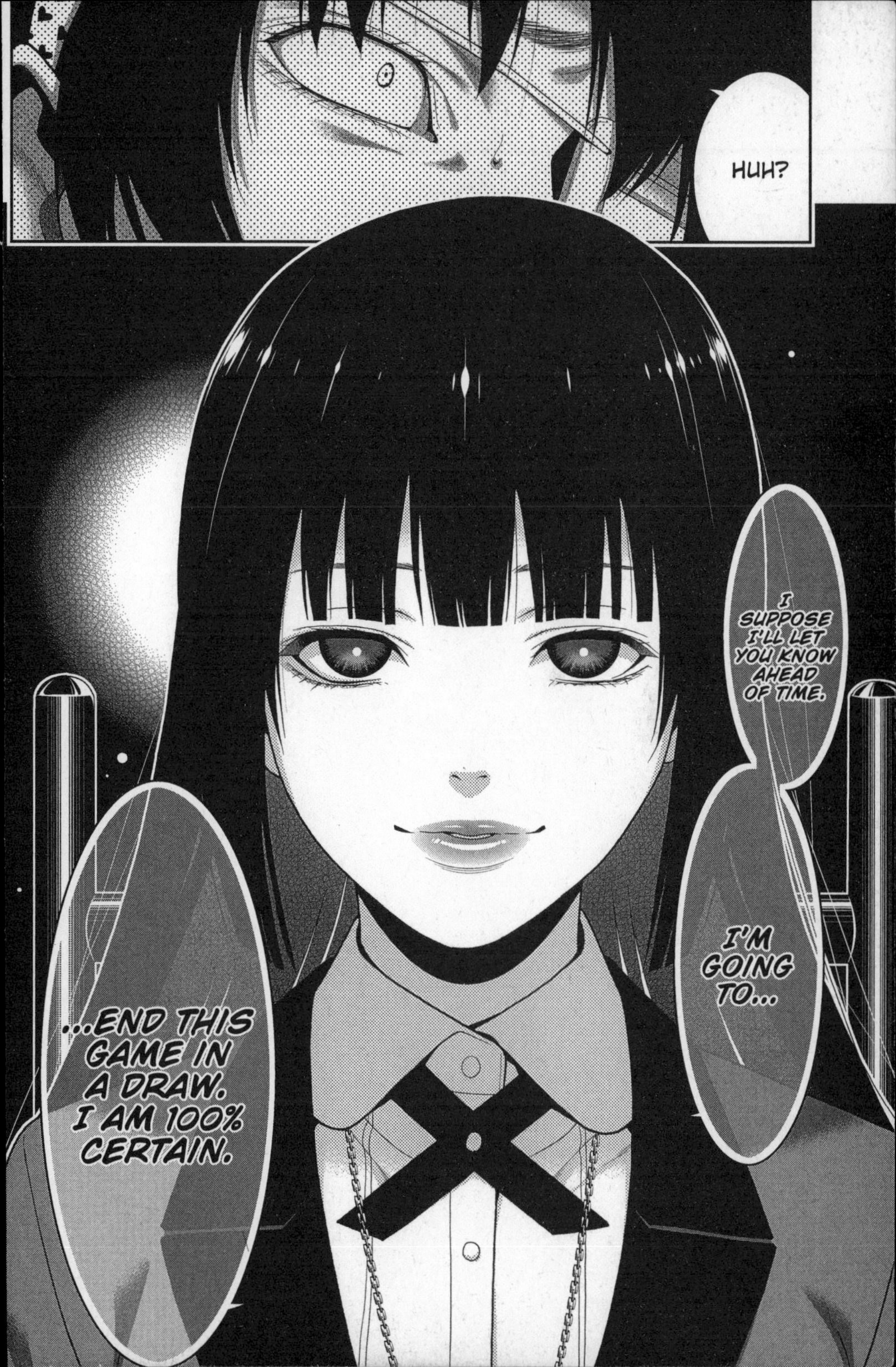
HUH?
I SUPPOSE I'LL LET YOU KNOW AHEAD OF TIME.
I'M GOING TO...
...END THIS GAME IN A DRAW. I AM 100% CERTAIN.

KAKEGURUI

— Compulsive Gambler —

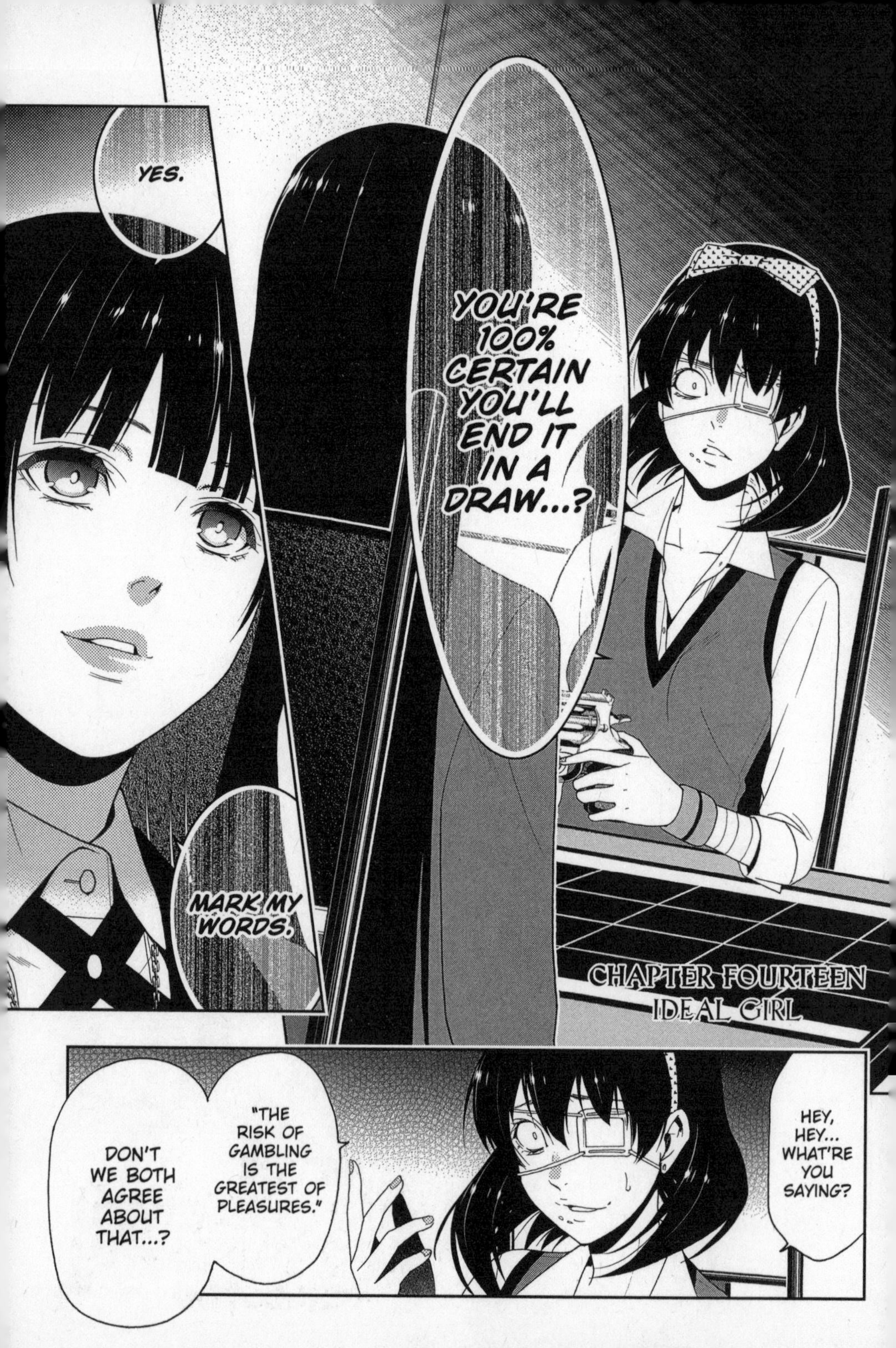
YOU'RE 100% CERTAIN YOU'LL END IT IN A DRAW...?
YES.
MARK MY WORDS.
CHAPTER FOURTEEN
IDEAL GIRL
HEY, HEY... WHAT'RE YOU SAYING?
"THE RISK OF GAMBLING IS THE GREATEST OF PLEASURES."
DON'T WE BOTH AGREE ABOUT THAT...?

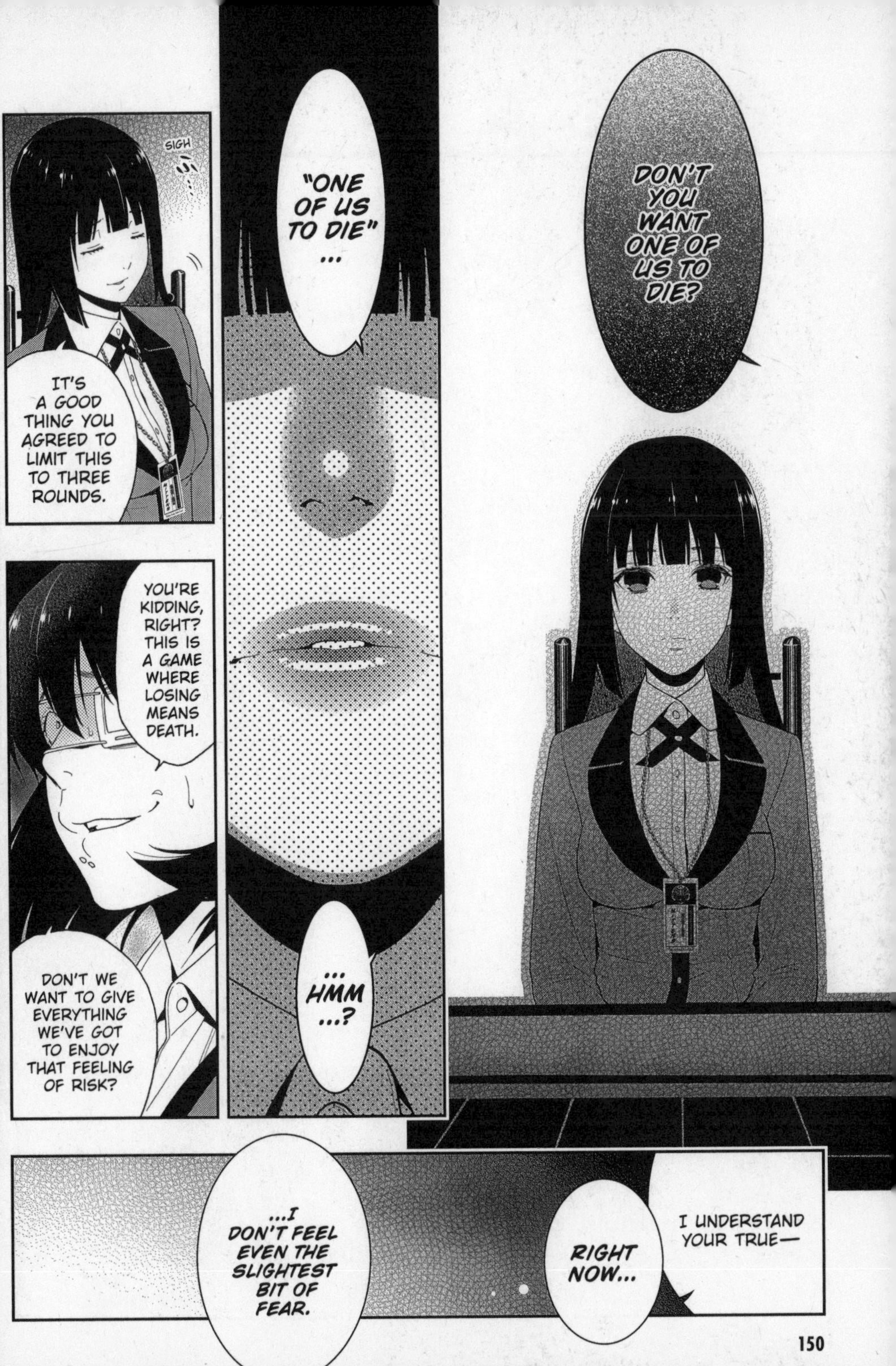
DON'T YOU WANT ONE OF US TO DIE?
"ONE OF US TO DIE" ...
... HMM ...?
SIGH
IT'S A GOOD THING YOU AGREED TO LIMIT THIS TO THREE ROUNDS.
YOU'RE KIDDING, RIGHT? THIS IS A GAME WHERE LOSING MEANS DEATH.
DON'T WE WANT TO GIVE EVERYTHING WE'VE GOT TO ENJOY THAT FEELING OF RISK?
I UNDERSTAND YOUR TRUE—
RIGHT NOW...
...I DON'T FEEL EVEN THE SLIGHTEST BIT OF FEAR.

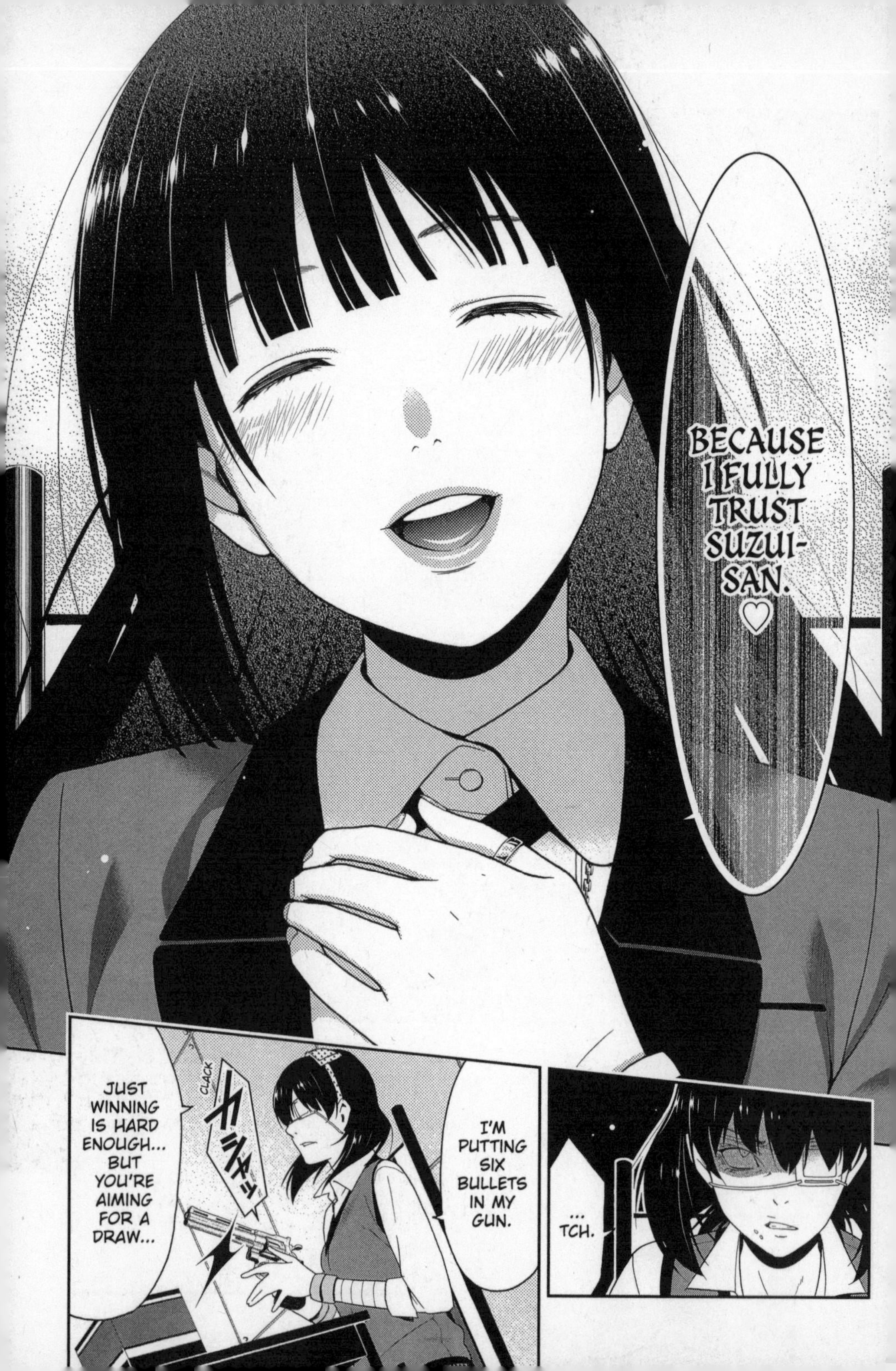
BECAUSE I FULLY TRUST SUZUI-SAN. ♡
...TCH.
I'M PUTTING SIX BULLETS IN MY GUN.
CLACK
JUST WINNING IS HARD ENOUGH... BUT YOU'RE AIMING FOR A DRAW...

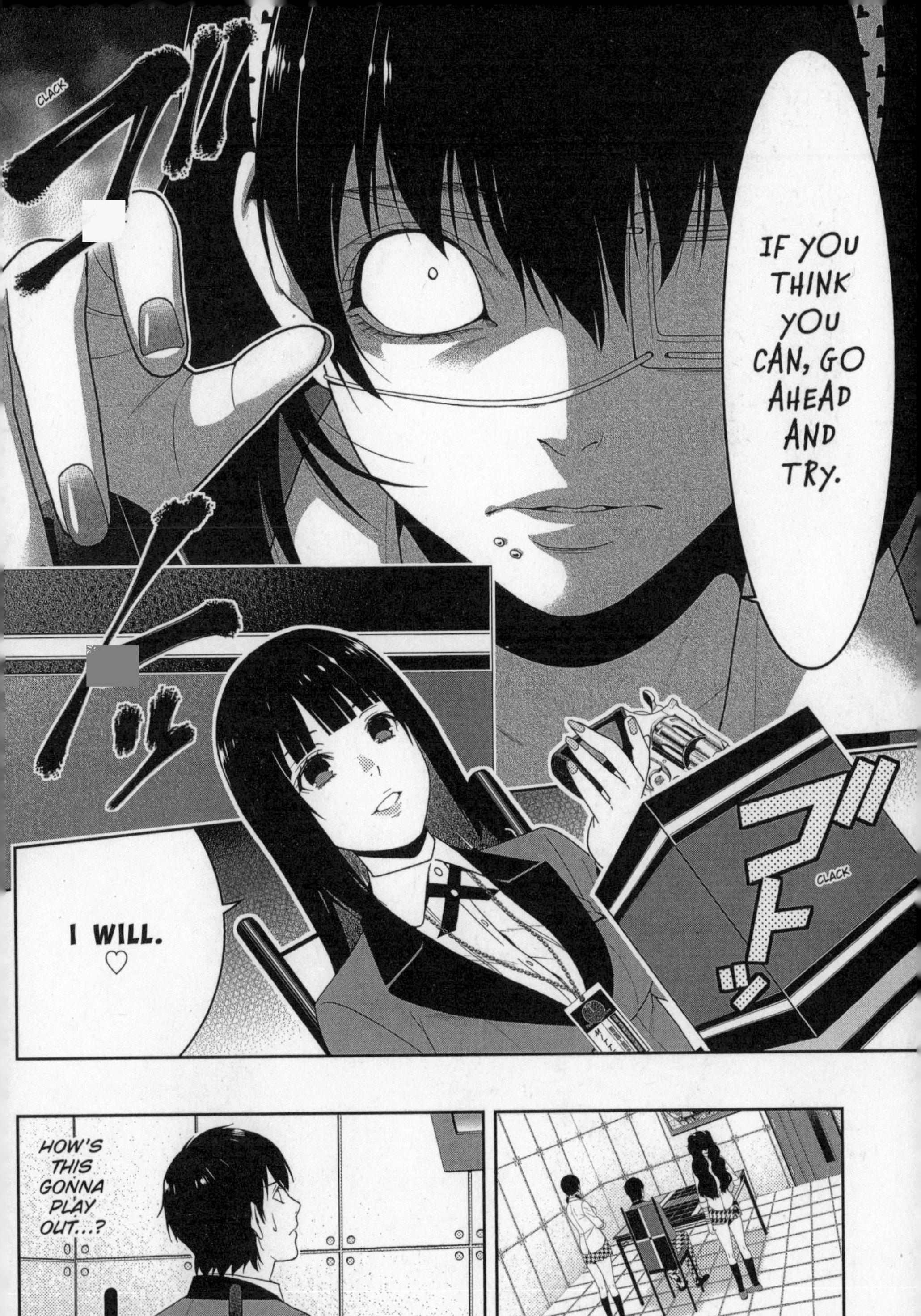
IF YOU THINK YOU CAN, GO AHEAD AND TRY.
CLACK
CLACK
I WILL. ♡
HOW'S THIS GONNA PLAY OUT...?

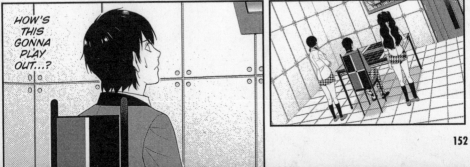

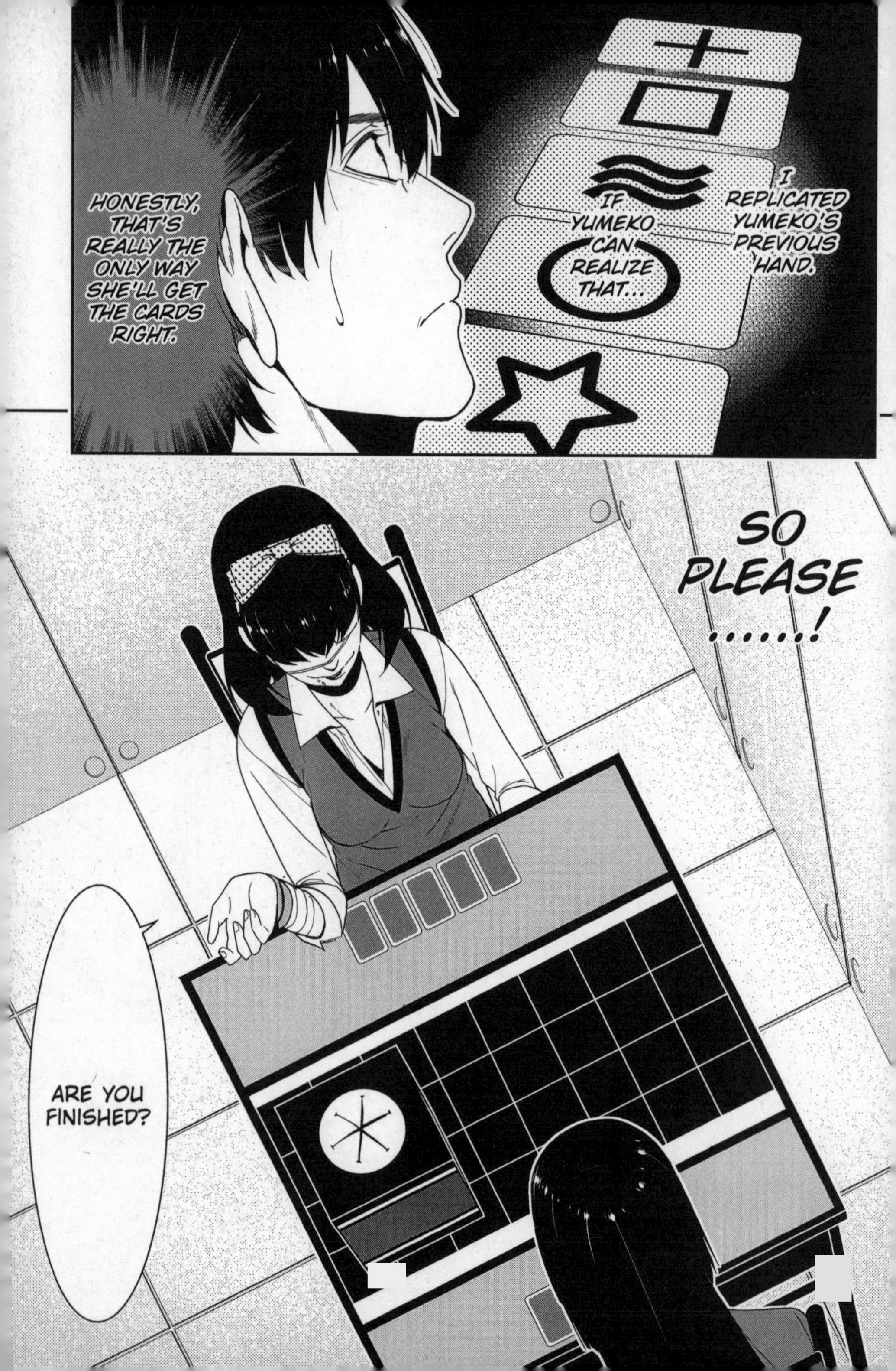
I REPLICATED YUMEKO'S PREVIOUS HAND.
IF YUMEKO CAN REALIZE THAT...
HONESTLY, THAT'S REALLY THE ONLY WAY SHE'LL GET THE CARDS RIGHT.
SO PLEASE ......!
ARE YOU FINISHED?

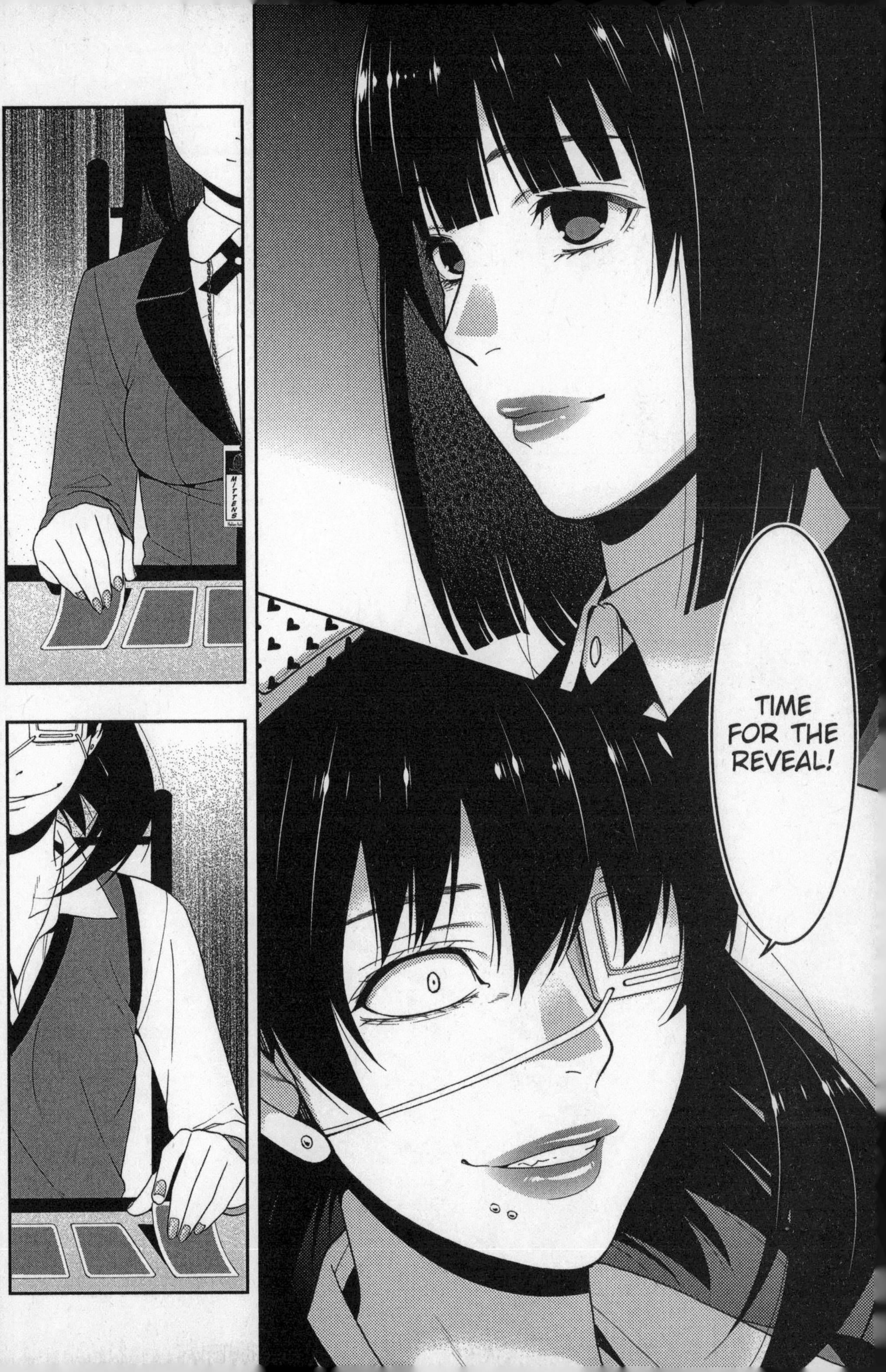
TIME FOR THE REVEAL!
MITTENS

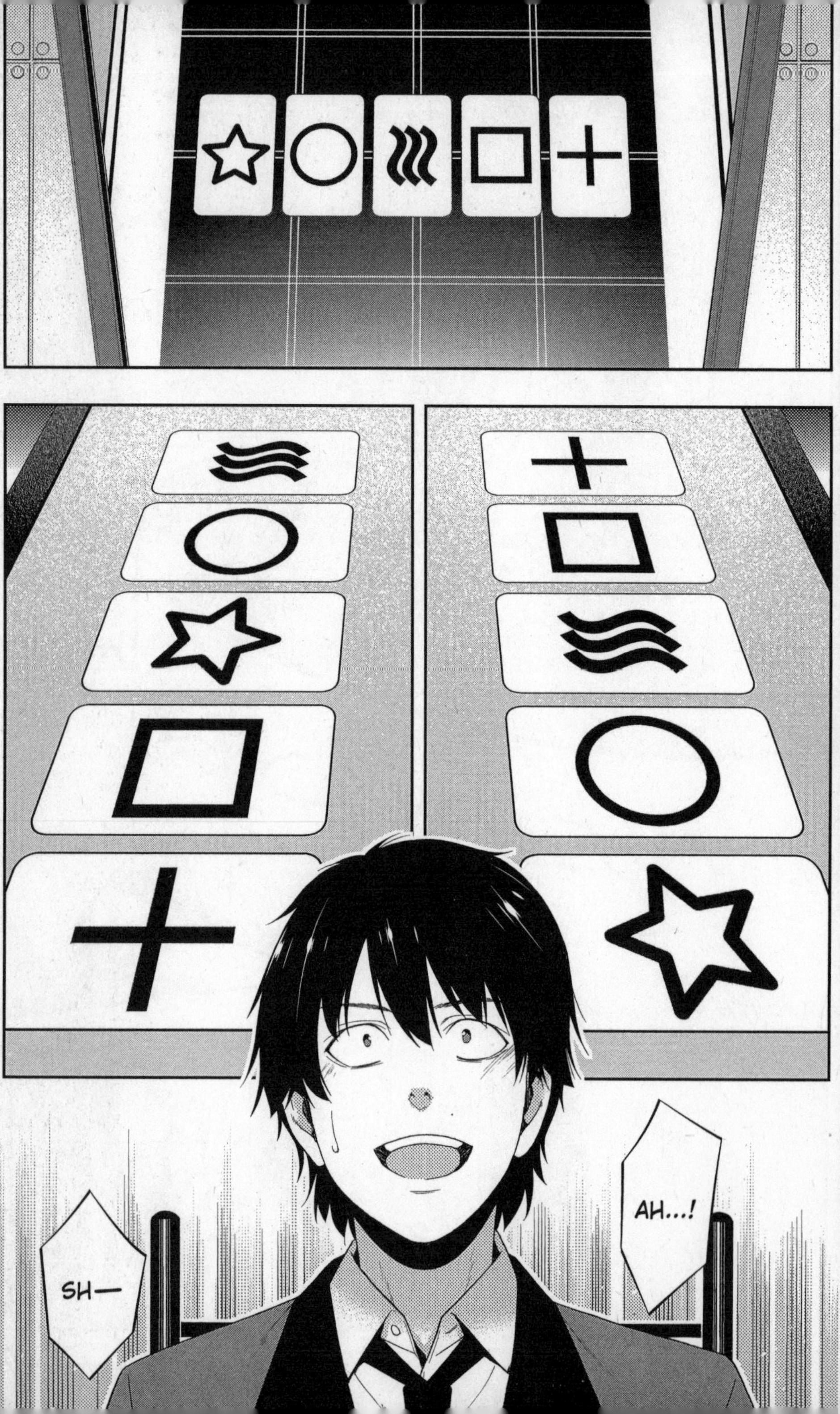
AH...!
SH—

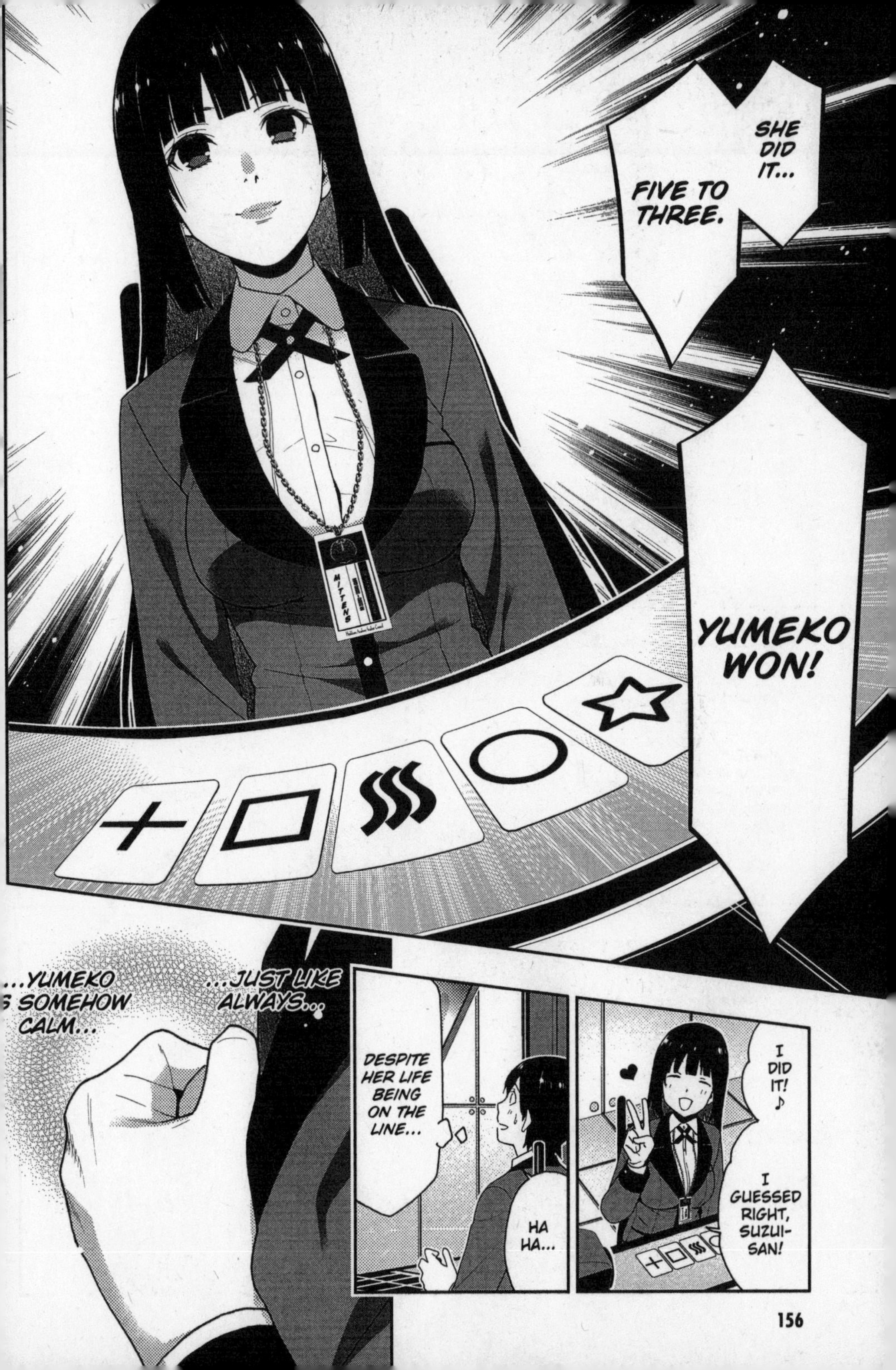
SHE DID IT...
FIVE TO THREE.
YUMEKO WON!
I DID IT! ♪
I GUESSED RIGHT, SUZUI-SAN!
DESPITE HER LIFE BEING ON THE LINE...
HA HA...
...JUST LIKE ALWAYS...
...YUMEKO S SOMEHOW CALM...

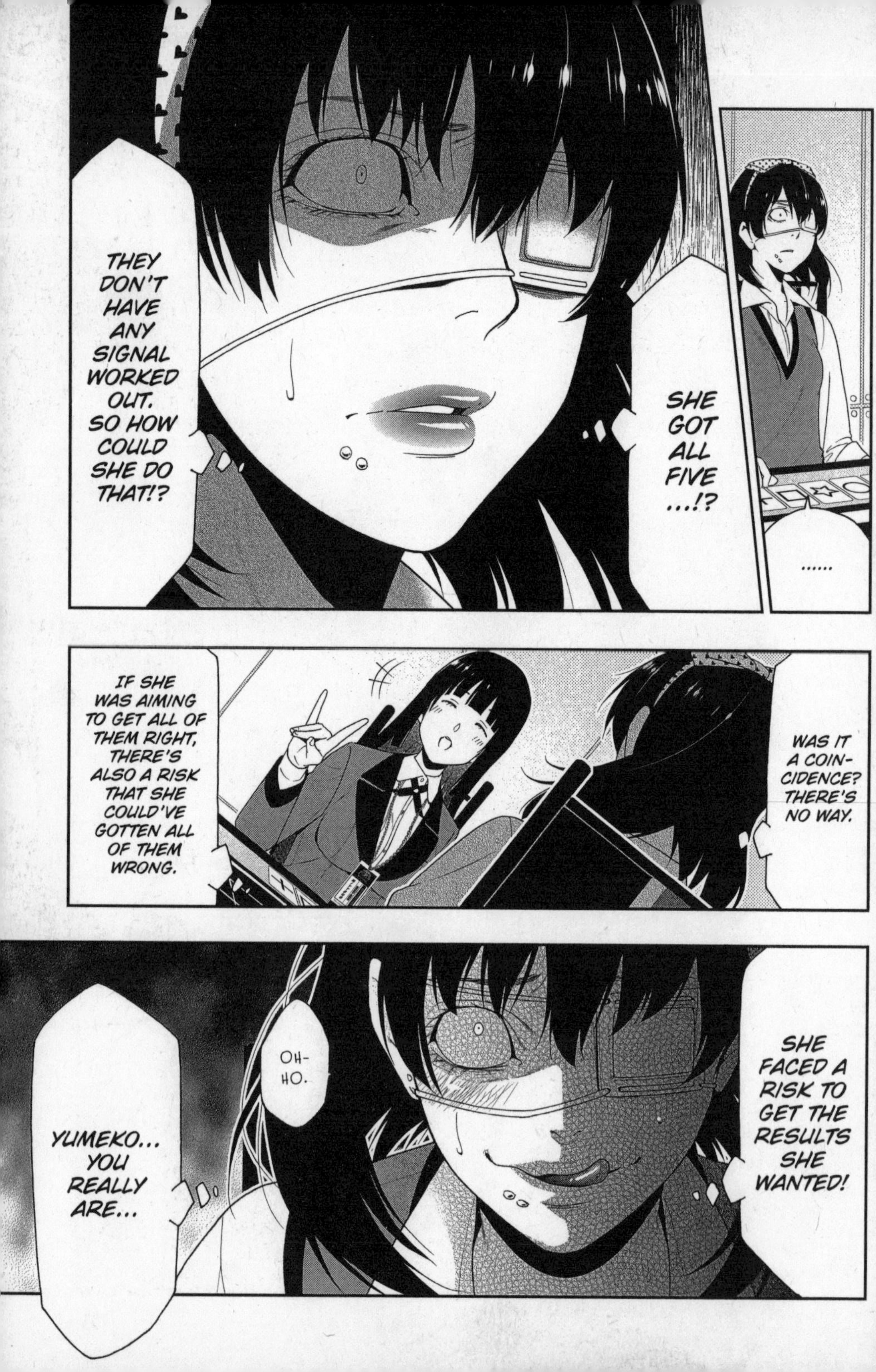
......
SHE GOT ALL FIVE ...!?
THEY DON'T HAVE ANY SIGNAL WORKED OUT. SO HOW COULD SHE DO THAT!?
WAS IT A COINCIDENCE? THERE'S NO WAY.
IF SHE WAS AIMING TO GET ALL OF THEM RIGHT, THERE'S ALSO A RISK THAT SHE COULD'VE GOTTEN ALL OF THEM WRONG.
SHE FACED A RISK TO GET THE RESULTS SHE WANTED!
OH-HO.
YUMEKO... YOU REALLY ARE...

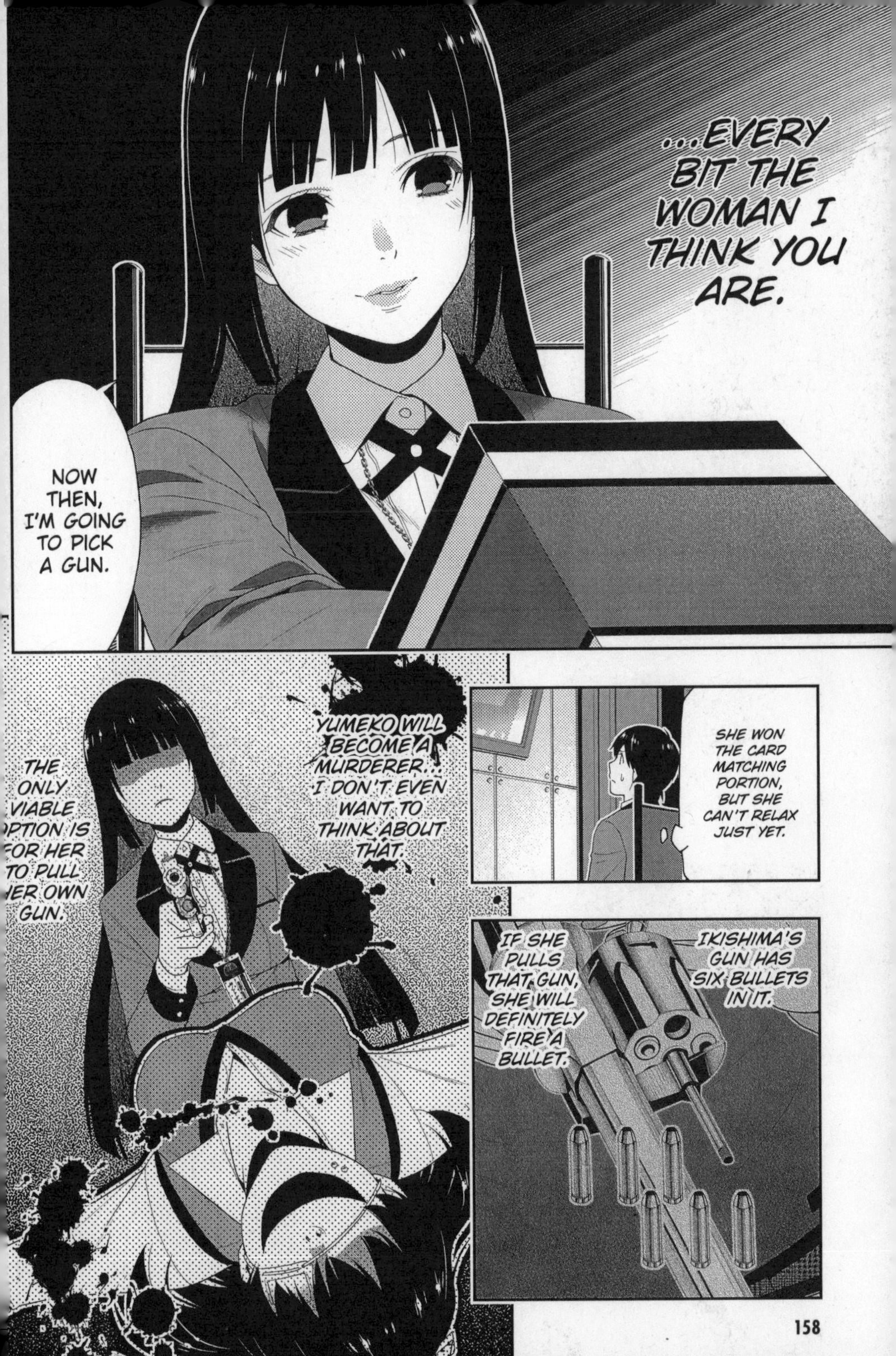
...EVERY BIT THE WOMAN I THINK YOU ARE.
NOW THEN, I'M GOING TO PICK A GUN.
SHE WON THE CARD MATCHING PORTION, BUT SHE CAN'T RELAX JUST YET.
IKISHIMA'S GUN HAS SIX BULLETS IN IT.
IF SHE PULLS THAT GUN, SHE WILL DEFINITELY FIRE A BULLET.
YUMEKO WILL BECOME A MURDERER... I DON'T EVEN WANT TO THINK ABOUT THAT.
THE ONLY VIABLE OPTION IS FOR HER TO PULL HER OWN GUN.

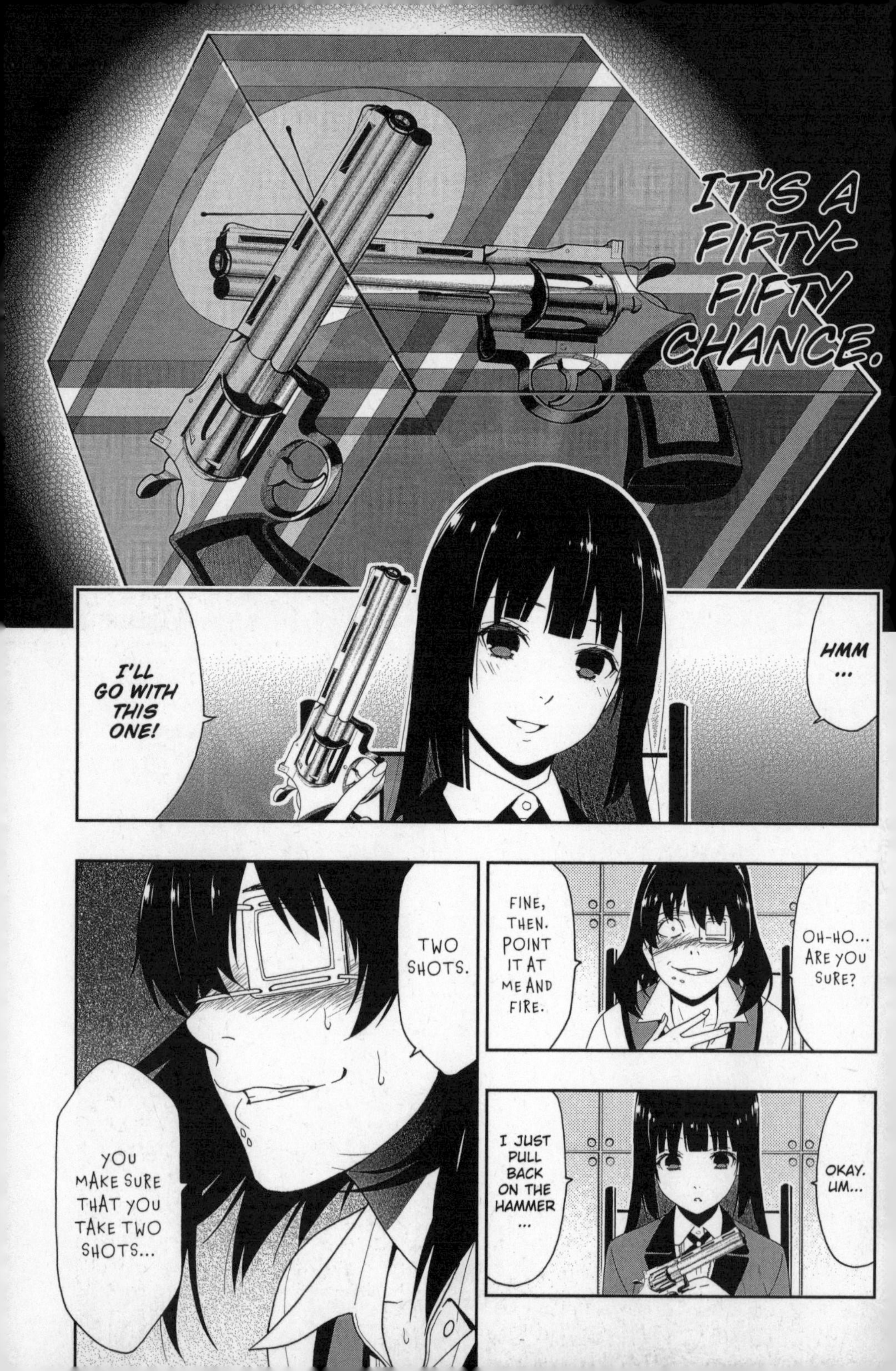
IT'S A FIFTY-FIFTY CHANCE.
HMM...
I'LL GO WITH THIS ONE!
OH-HO... ARE YOU SURE?
FINE, THEN. POINT IT AT ME AND FIRE.
OKAY. UM...
I JUST PULL BACK ON THE HAMMER...
TWO SHOTS.
YOU MAKE SURE THAT YOU TAKE TWO SHOTS...

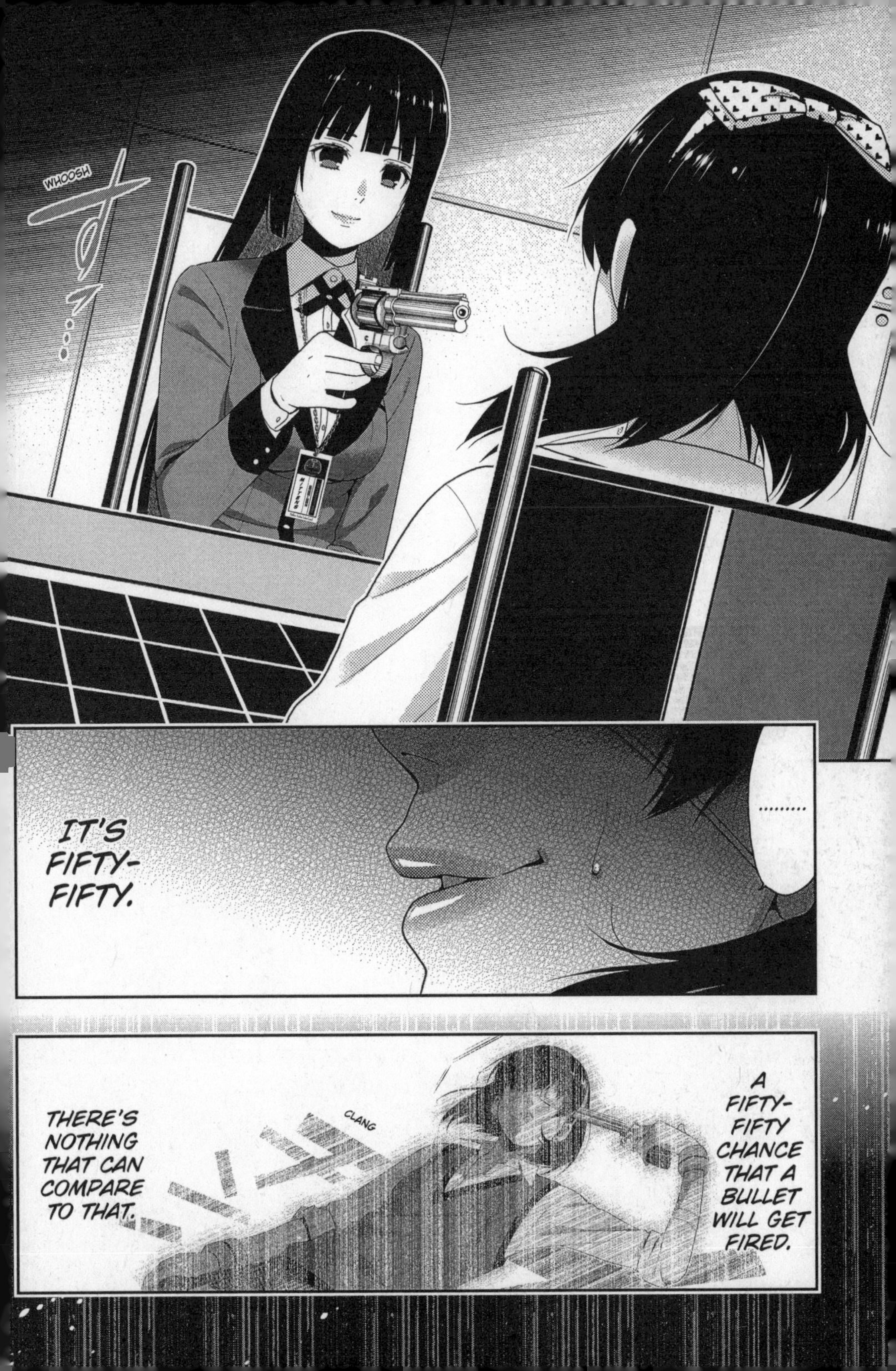
WHOOSH
....
IT'S FIFTY-FIFTY.
A FIFTY-FIFTY CHANCE THAT A BULLET WILL GET FIRED.
CLANG
THERE'S NOTHING THAT CAN COMPARE TO THAT.

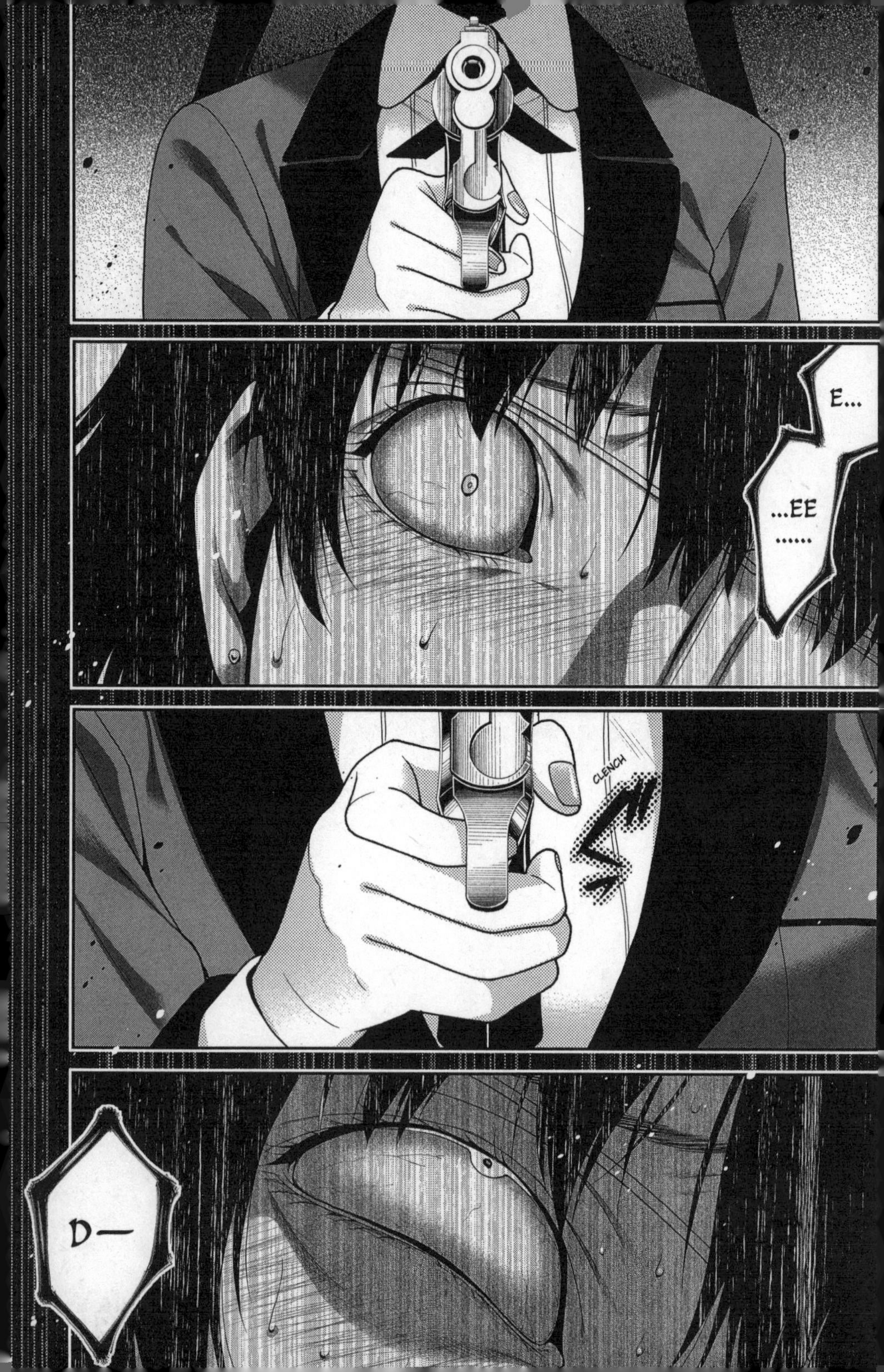
E...
...EE
......
CLENCH
D—

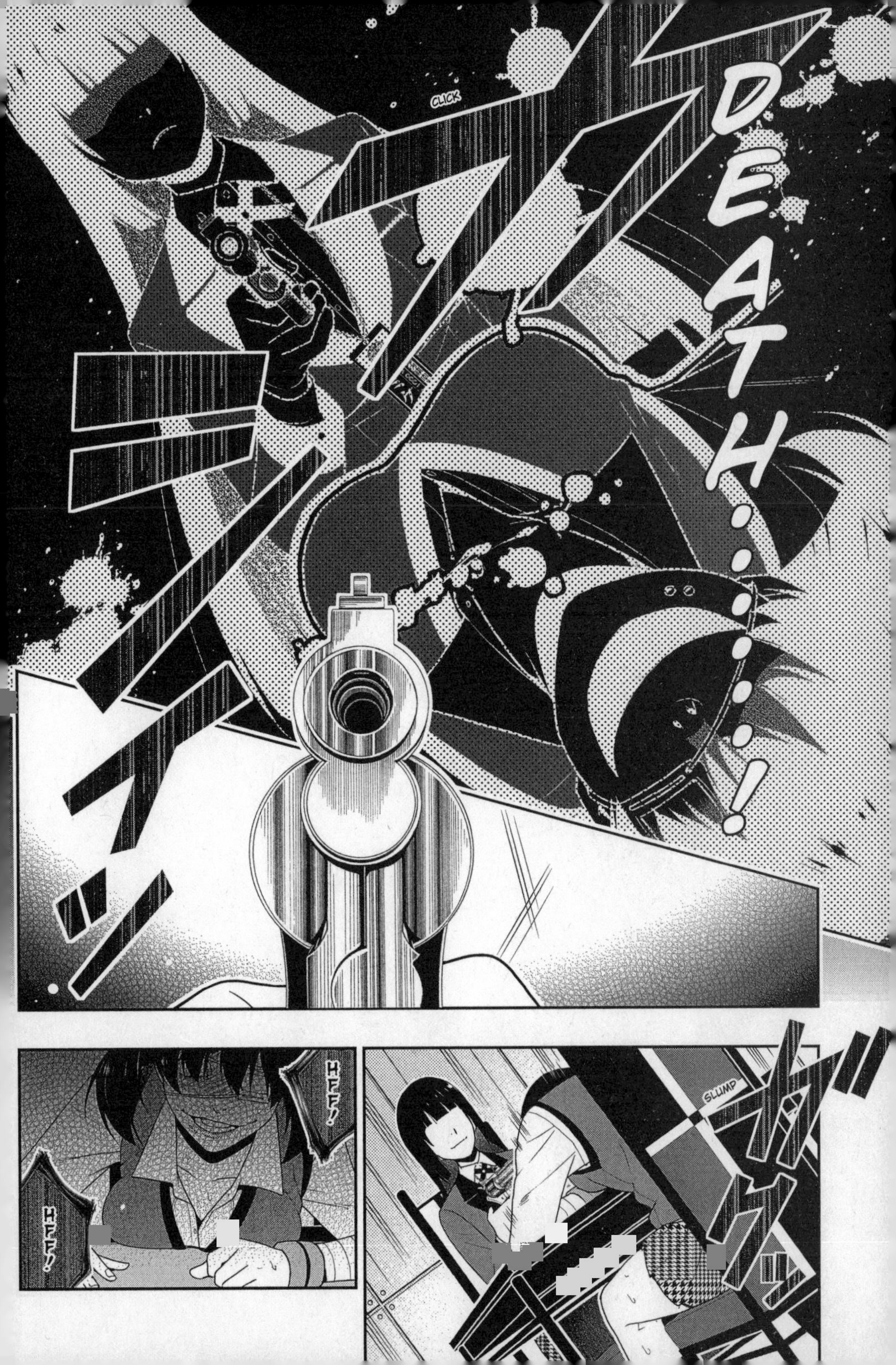
CLICK
DEATH......!
SLUMP
HFF!
HFF!

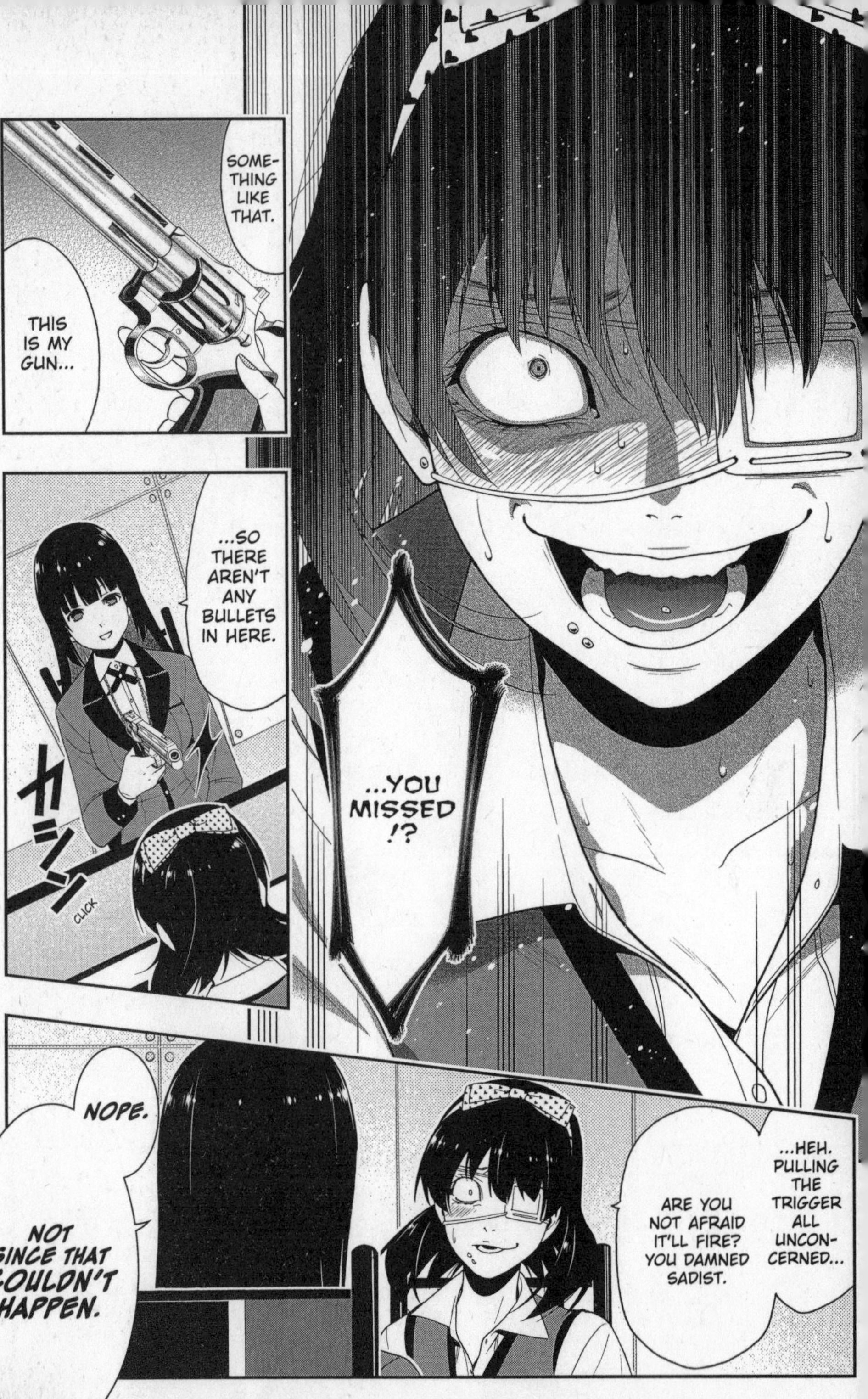
...YOU MISSED !?
SOME-THING LIKE THAT.
THIS IS MY GUN...
...SO THERE AREN'T ANY BULLETS IN HERE.
CLICK
...HEH. PULLING THE TRIGGER ALL UNCON-CERNED...
ARE YOU NOT AFRAID IT'LL FIRE? YOU DAMNED SADIST.
NOPE.
NOT SINCE THAT COULDN'T HAPPEN.

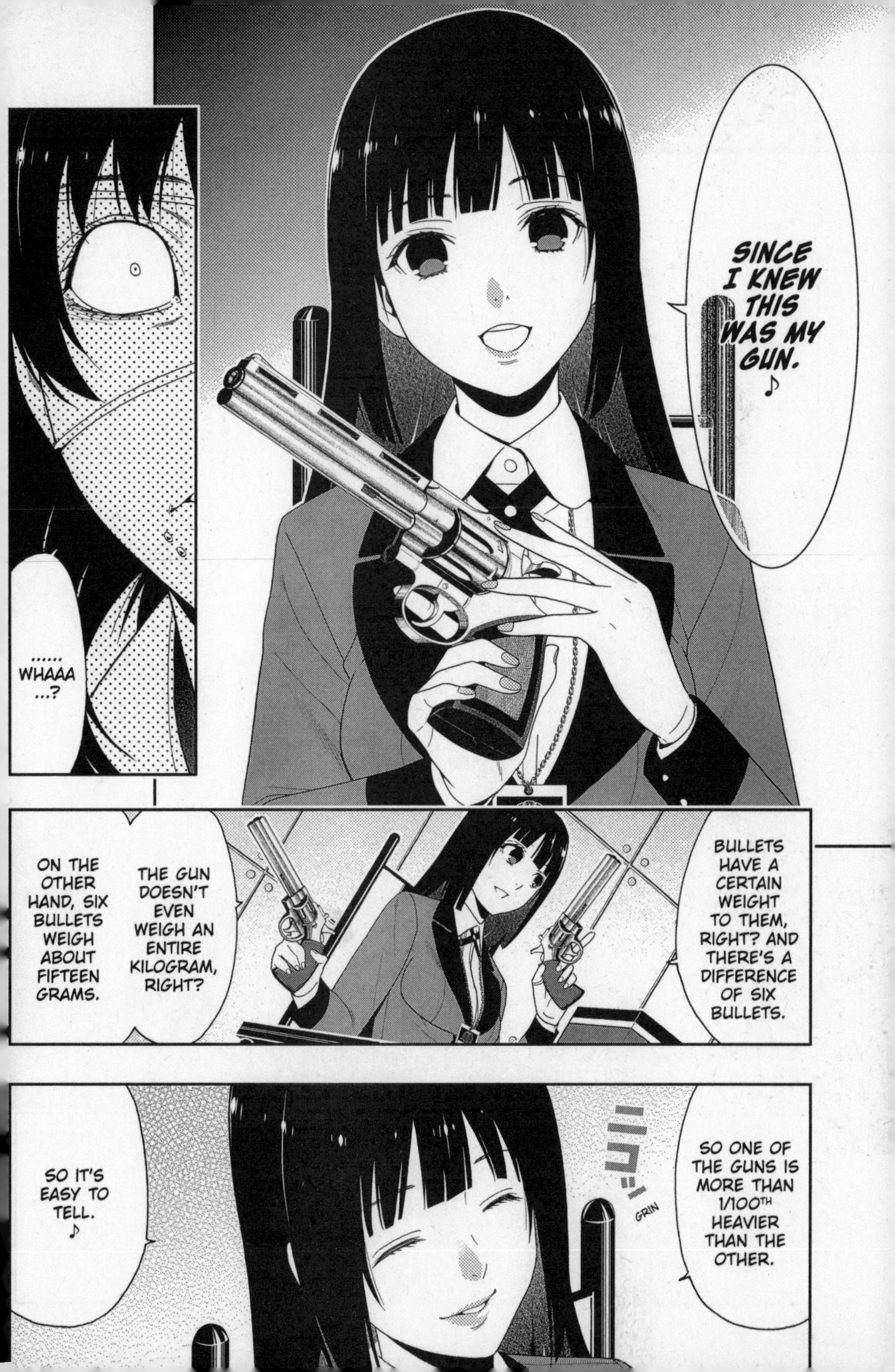
SINCE I KNEW THIS WAS MY GUN. ♪
...... WHAAA ...?
BULLETS HAVE A CERTAIN WEIGHT TO THEM, RIGHT? AND THERE'S A DIFFERENCE OF SIX BULLETS.
THE GUN DOESN'T EVEN WEIGH AN ENTIRE KILOGRAM, RIGHT?
ON THE OTHER HAND, SIX BULLETS WEIGH ABOUT FIFTEEN GRAMS.
SO ONE OF THE GUNS IS MORE THAN 1/100TH HEAVIER THAN THE OTHER.
ニコッ
GRIN
SO IT'S EASY TO TELL. ♪

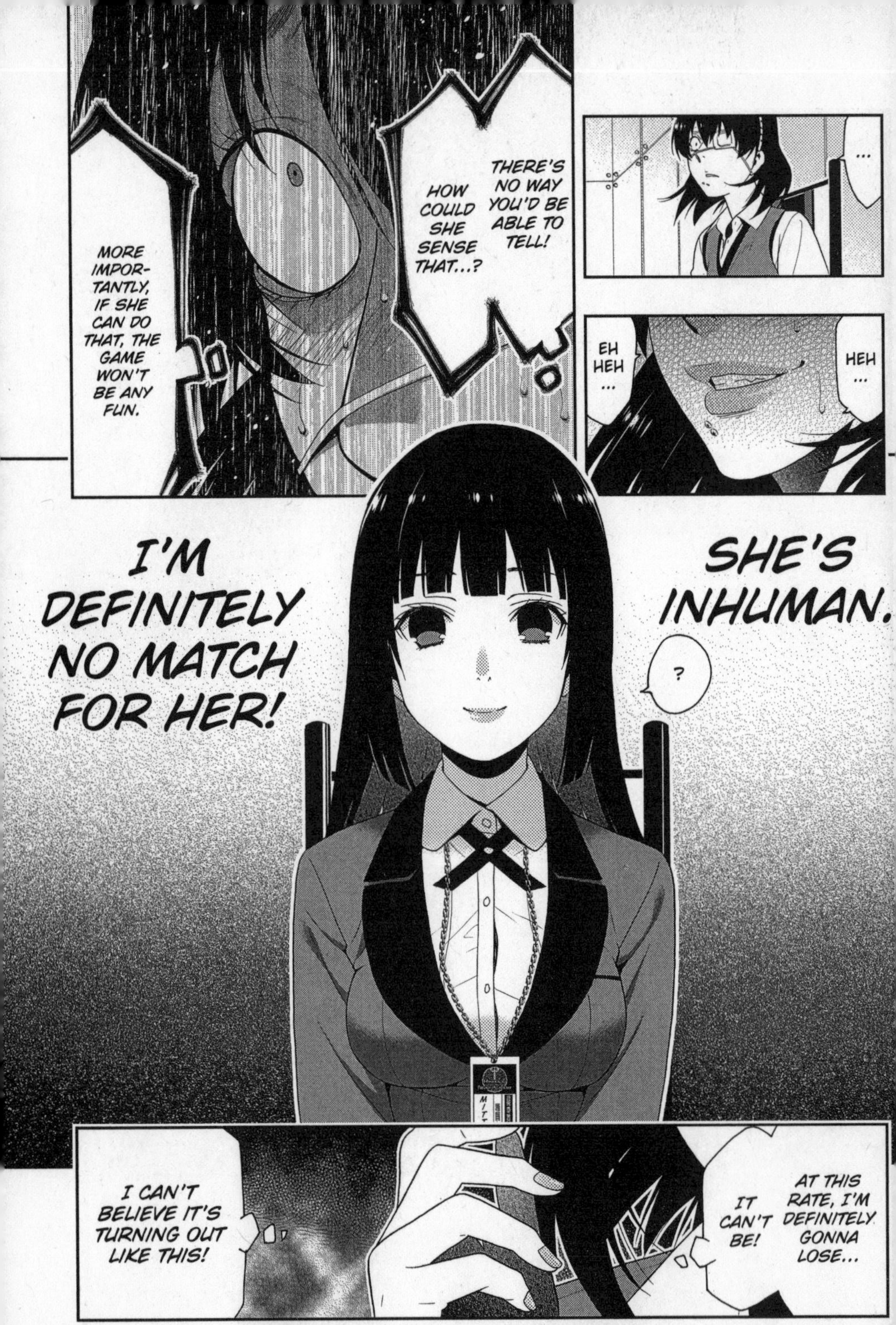
...
HEH ...
EH HEH ...
THERE'S NO WAY YOU'D BE ABLE TO TELL!
HOW COULD SHE SENSE THAT...?
MORE IMPORTANTLY, IF SHE CAN DO THAT, THE GAME WON'T BE ANY FUN.
SHE'S INHUMAN.
?
I'M DEFINITELY NO MATCH FOR HER!
AT THIS RATE, I'M DEFINITELY GONNA LOSE...
IT CAN'T BE!
I CAN'T BELIEVE IT'S TURNING OUT LIKE THIS!

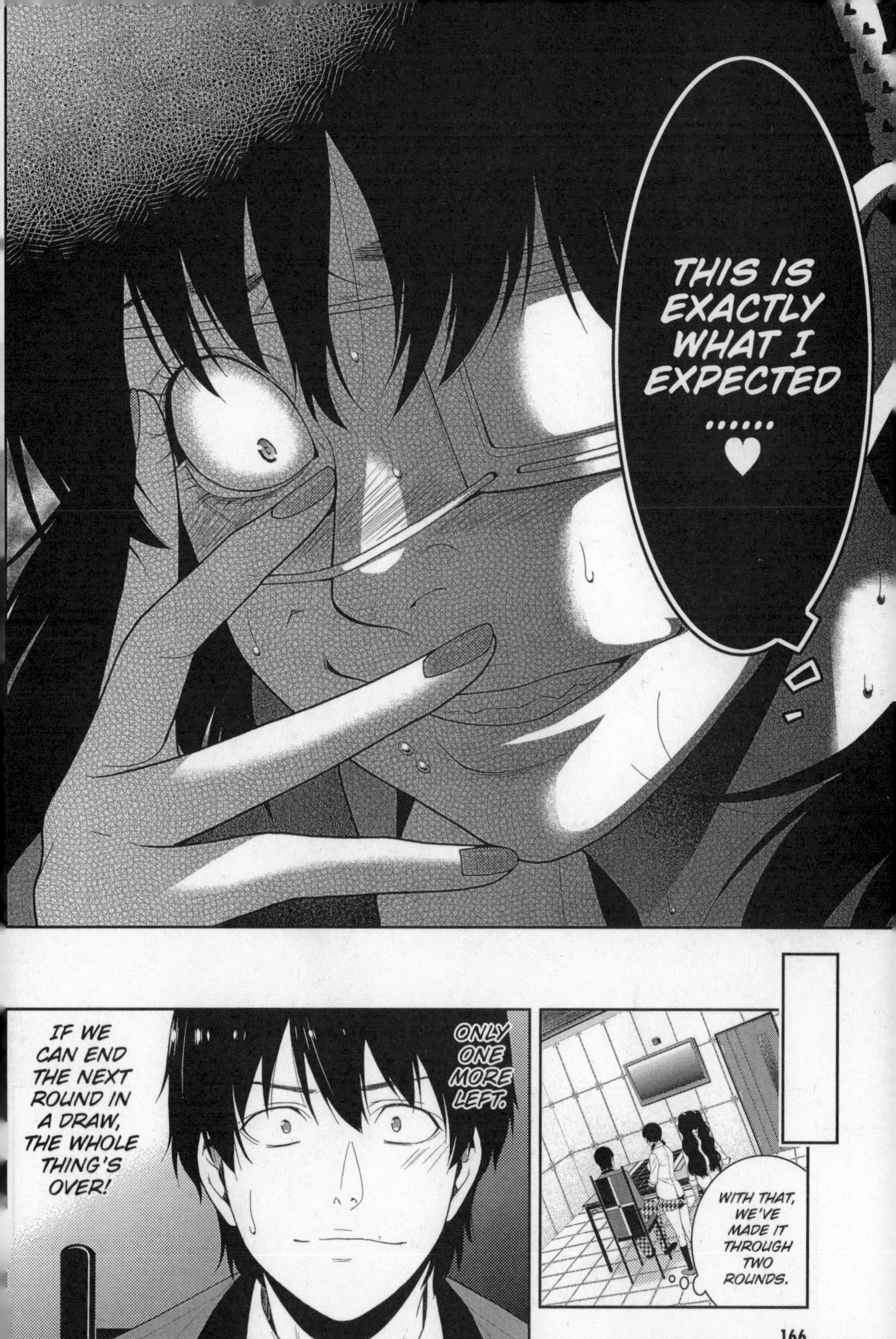
THIS IS EXACTLY WHAT I EXPECTED ......♥
WITH THAT, WE'VE MADE IT THROUGH TWO ROUNDS.
ONLY ONE MORE LEFT.
IF WE CAN END THE NEXT ROUND IN A DRAW, THE WHOLE THING'S OVER!

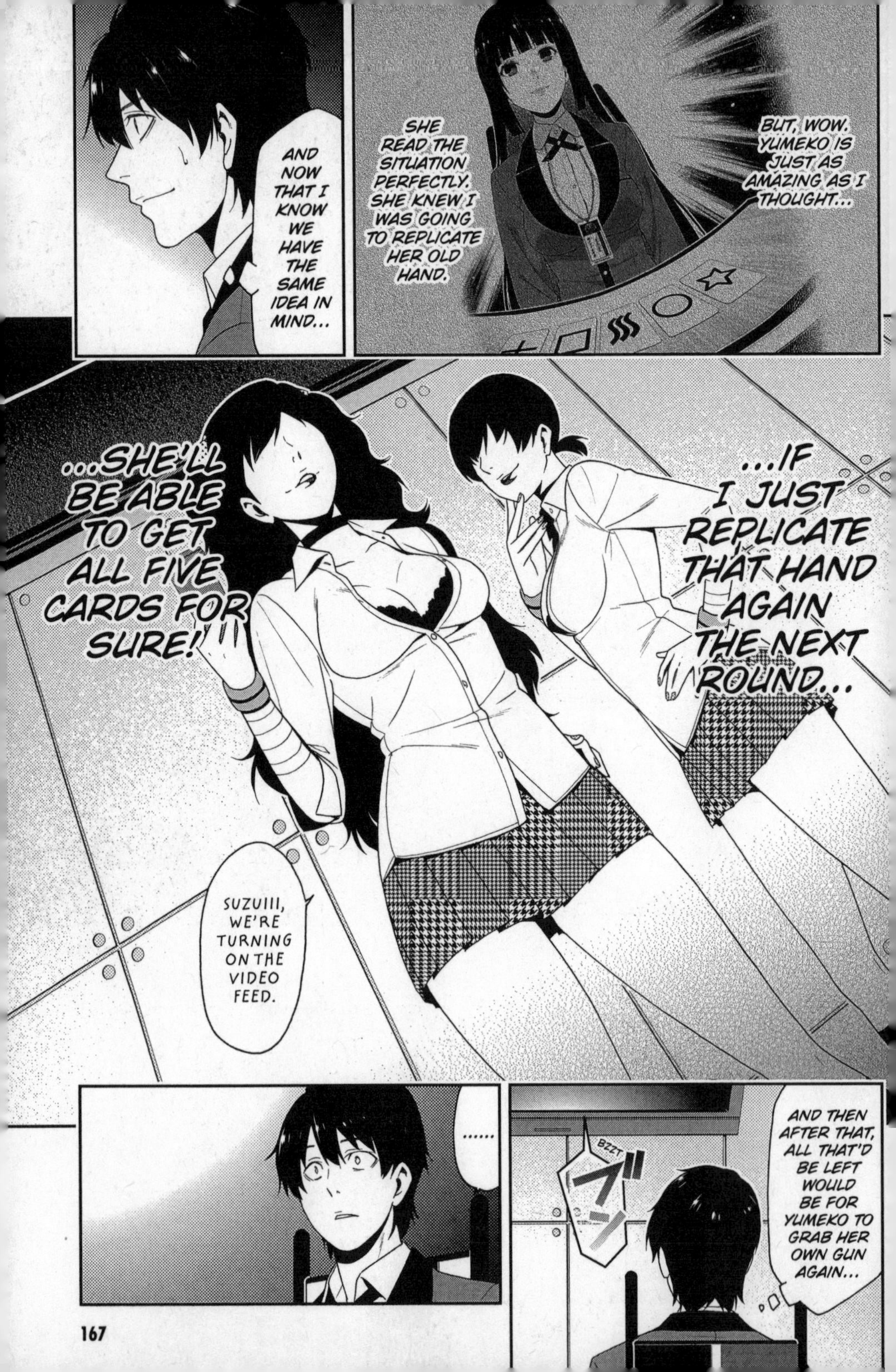
BUT, WOW. YUMEKO IS JUST AS AMAZING AS I THOUGHT...
SHE READ THE SITUATION PERFECTLY. SHE KNEW I WAS GOING TO REPLICATE HER OLD HAND.
AND NOW THAT I KNOW WE HAVE THE SAME IDEA IN MIND...
...IF I JUST REPLICATE THAT HAND AGAIN THE NEXT ROUND...
...SHE'LL BE ABLE TO GET ALL FIVE CARDS FOR SURE!
SUZUIII, WE'RE TURNING ON THE VIDEO FEED.
AND THEN AFTER THAT, ALL THAT'D BE LEFT WOULD BE FOR YUMEKO TO GRAB HER OWN GUN AGAIN...
BZZT
......

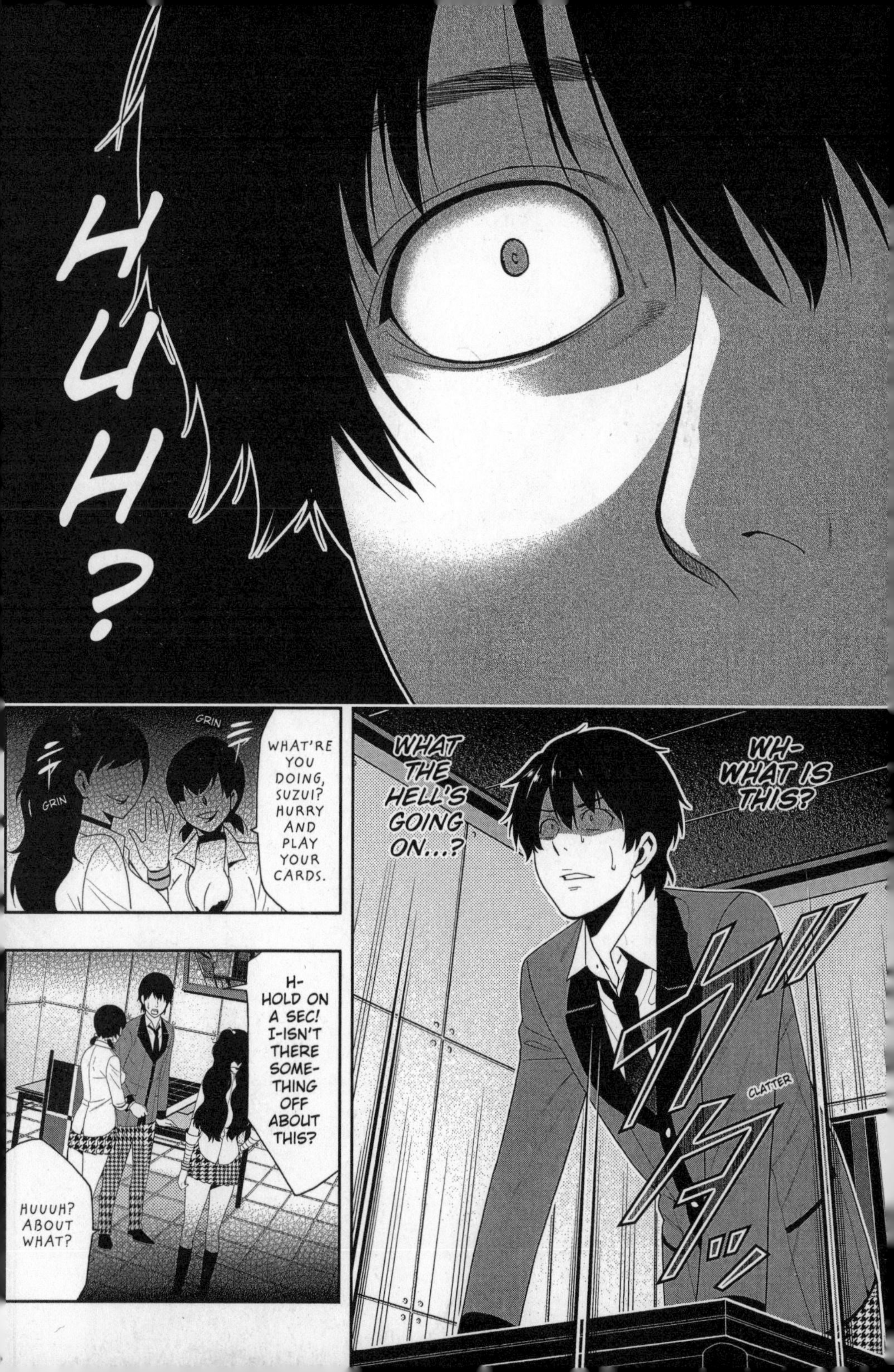
HUH?
WH-WHAT IS THIS?
WHAT THE HELL'S GOING ON...?
CLATTER
GRIN
GRIN
WHAT'RE YOU DOING, SUZUI? HURRY AND PLAY YOUR CARDS.
H-HOLD ON A SEC! I-ISN'T THERE SOMETHING OFF ABOUT THIS?
HUUUH? ABOUT WHAT?

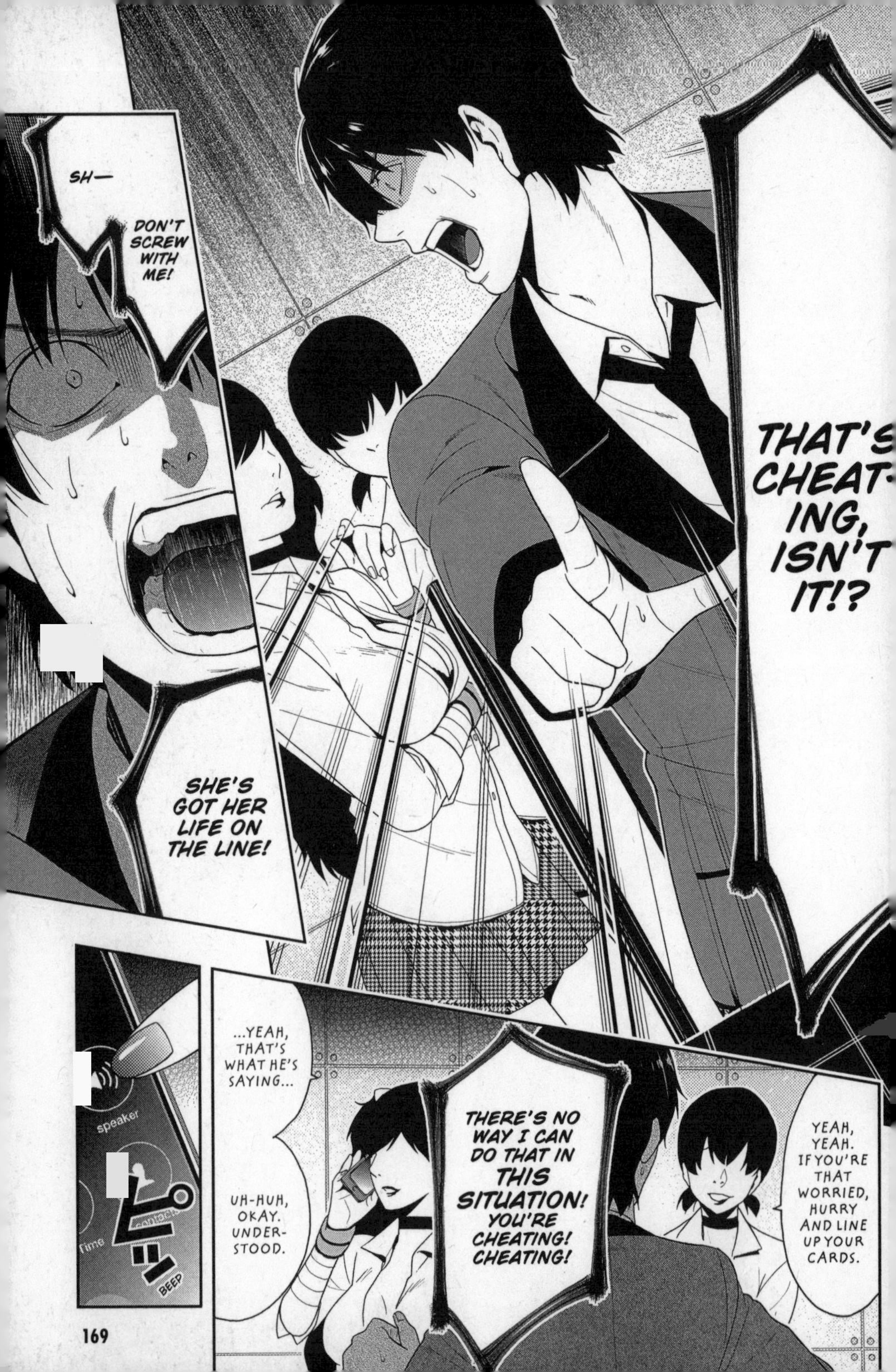
THAT'S CHEAT-ING, ISN'T IT!?
SH—
DON'T SCREW WITH ME!
SHE'S GOT HER LIFE ON THE LINE!
YEAH, YEAH. IF YOU'RE THAT WORRIED, HURRY AND LINE UP YOUR CARDS.
THERE'S NO WAY I CAN DO THAT IN THIS SITUATION! YOU'RE CHEATING! CHEATING!
...YEAH, THAT'S WHAT HE'S SAYING...
UH-HUH, OKAY. UNDERSTOOD.
speaker
time
BEEP

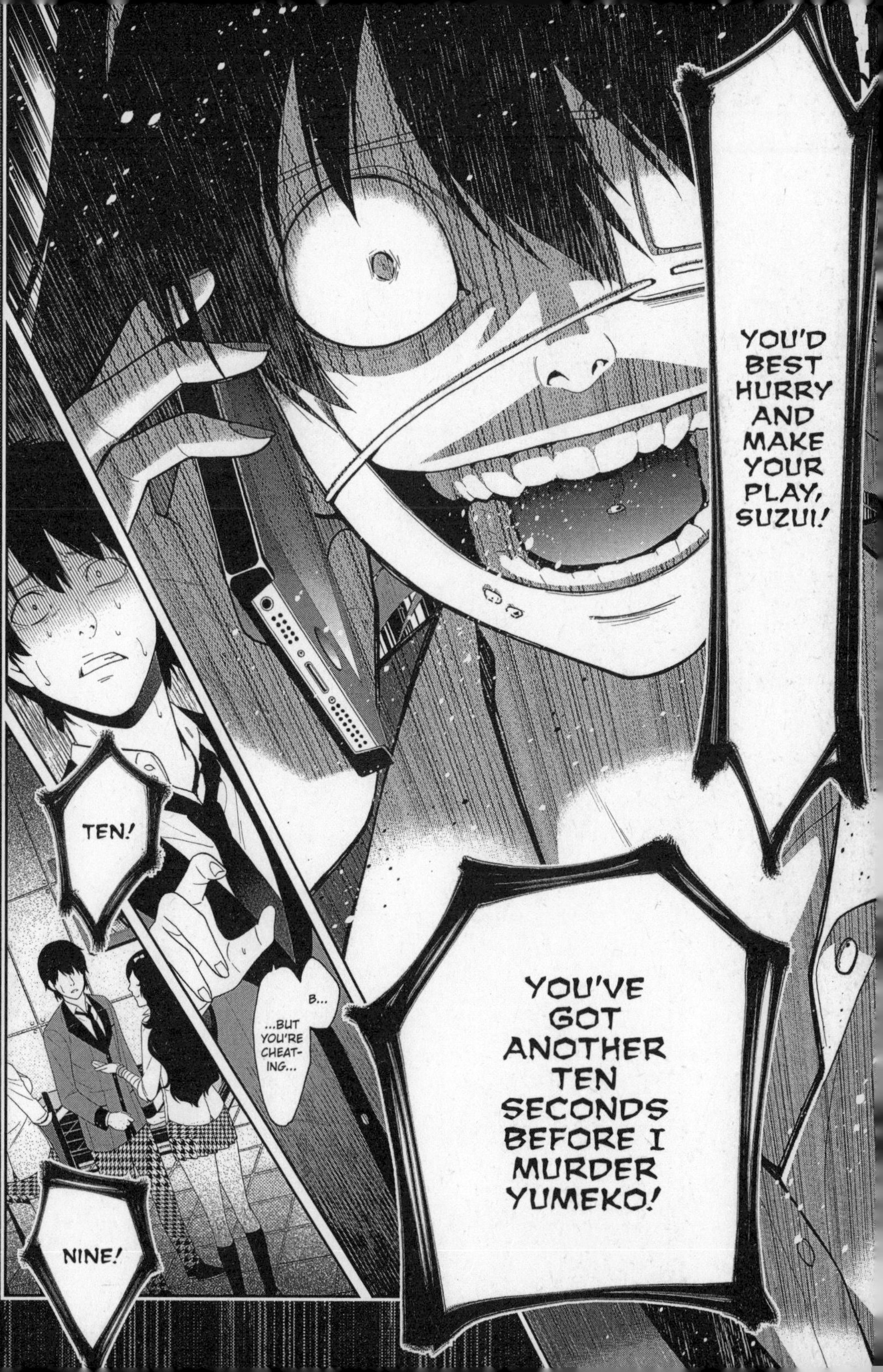
YOU'D BEST HURRY AND MAKE YOUR PLAY, SUZUI!
YOU'VE GOT ANOTHER TEN SECONDS BEFORE I MURDER YUMEKO!
TEN!
B...
...BUT YOU'RE CHEAT-ING...
NINE!

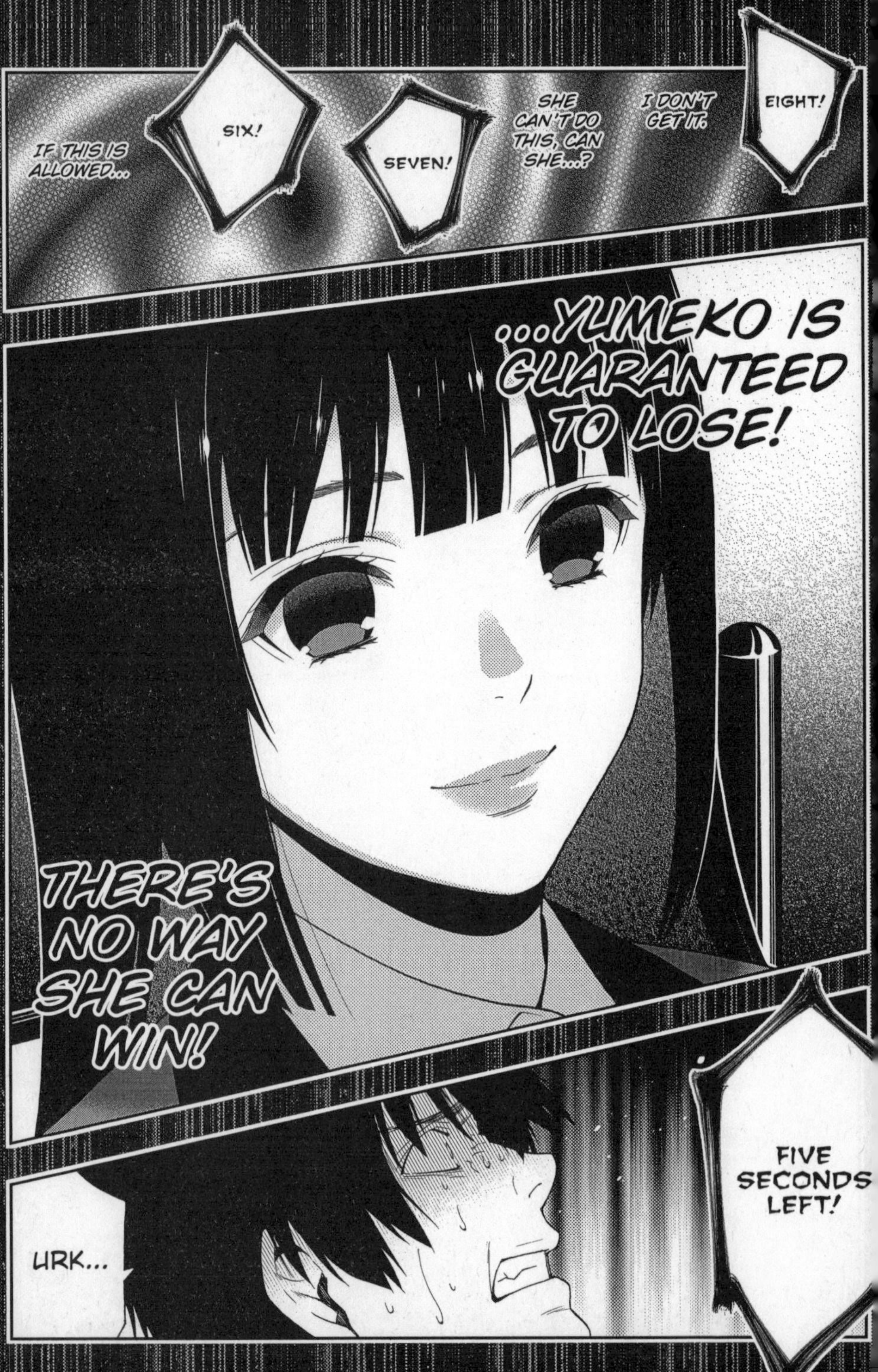
EIGHT!
I DON'T GET IT.
SHE CAN'T DO THIS, CAN SHE...?
SEVEN!
SIX!
IF THIS IS ALLOWED...
...YUMEKO IS GUARANTEED TO LOSE!
THERE'S NO WAY SHE CAN WIN!
FIVE SECONDS LEFT!
URK...

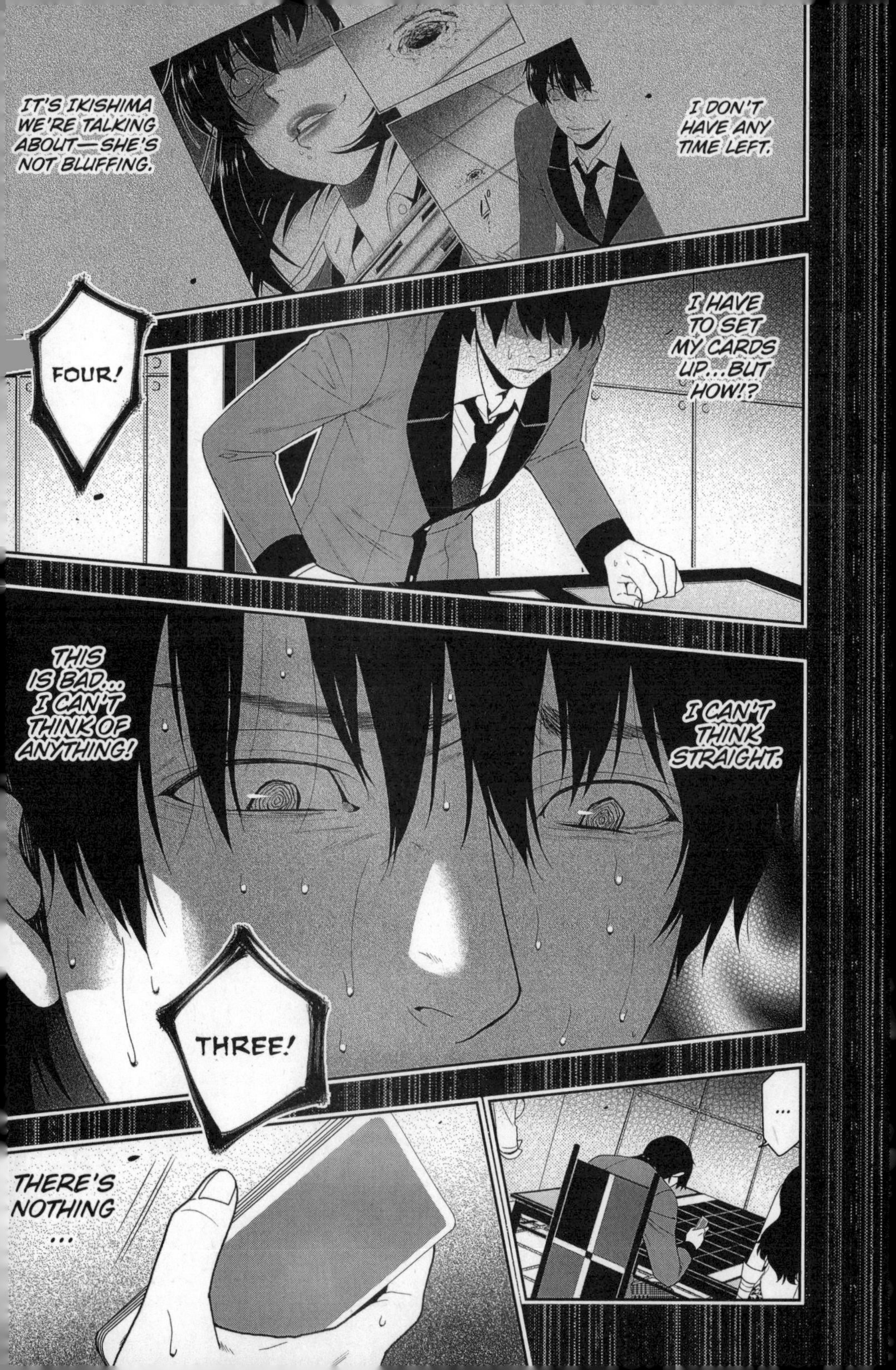
I DON'T HAVE ANY TIME LEFT.
IT'S IKISHIMA WE'RE TALKING ABOUT—SHE'S NOT BLUFFING.
I HAVE TO SET MY CARDS UP...BUT HOW!?
FOUR!
I CAN'T THINK STRAIGHT.
THIS IS BAD... I CAN'T THINK OF ANYTHING!
THREE!
...
THERE'S NOTHING ...

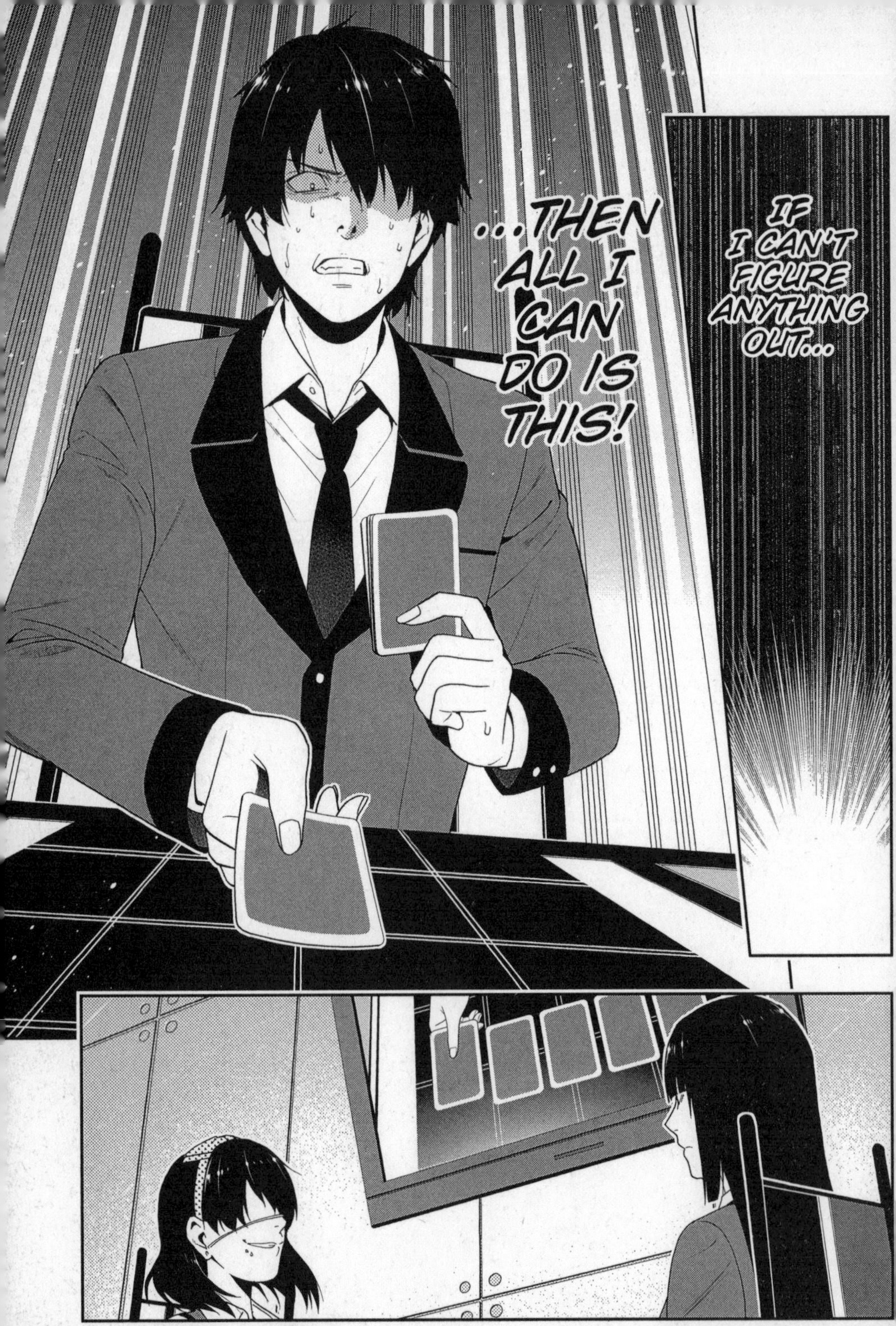
IF I CAN'T FIGURE ANYTHING OUT...
...THEN ALL I CAN DO IS THIS!

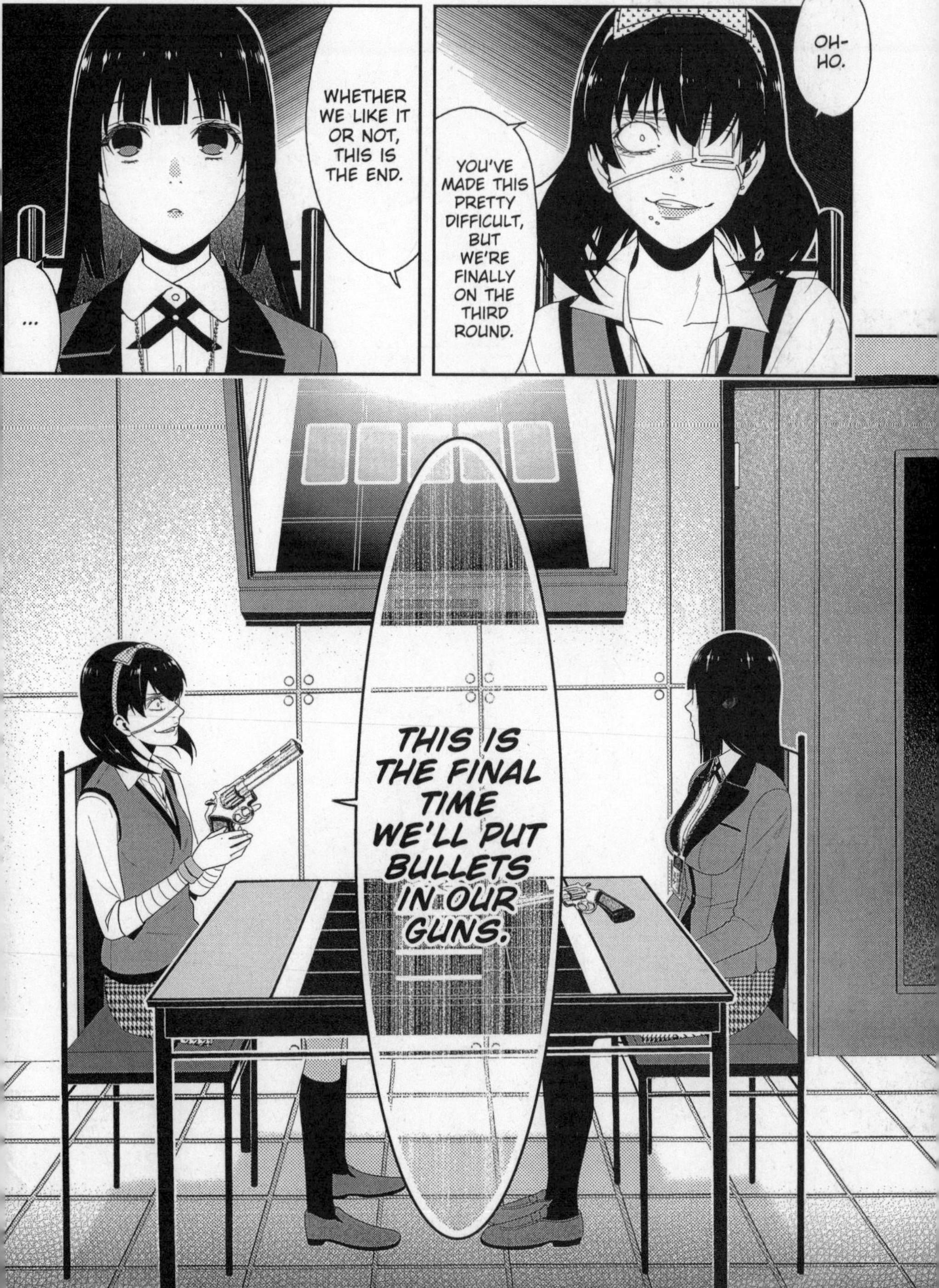
OH-HO.
YOU'VE MADE THIS PRETTY DIFFICULT, BUT WE'RE FINALLY ON THE THIRD ROUND.
WHETHER WE LIKE IT OR NOT, THIS IS THE END.
...
THIS IS THE FINAL TIME WE'LL PUT BULLETS IN OUR GUNS.

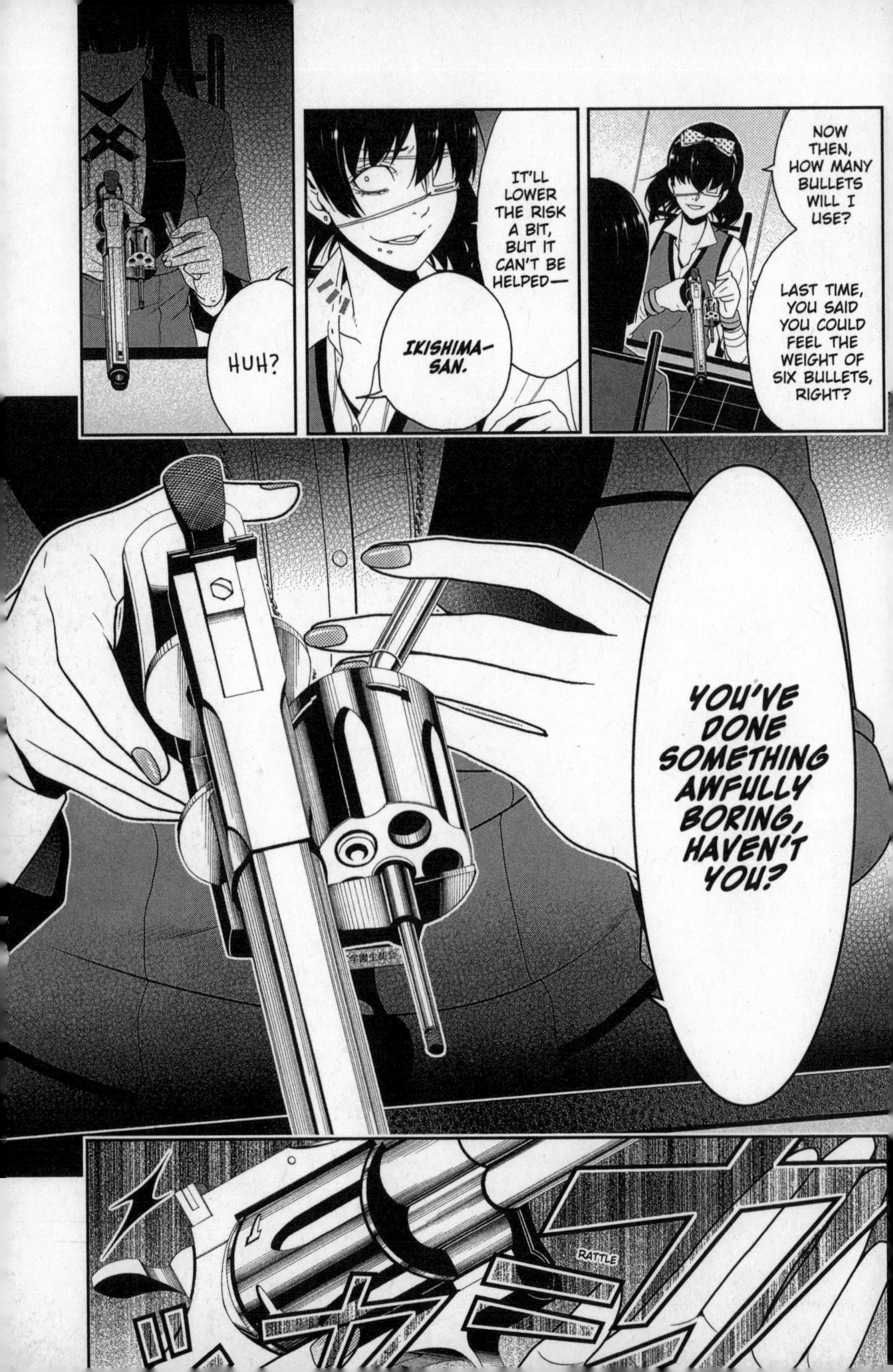
NOW THEN, HOW MANY BULLETS WILL I USE?
LAST TIME, YOU SAID YOU COULD FEEL THE WEIGHT OF SIX BULLETS, RIGHT?
IT'LL LOWER THE RISK A BIT, BUT IT CAN'T BE HELPED—
IKISHIMA-SAN.
HUH?
YOU'VE DONE SOMETHING AWFULLY BORING, HAVEN'T YOU?
RATTLE

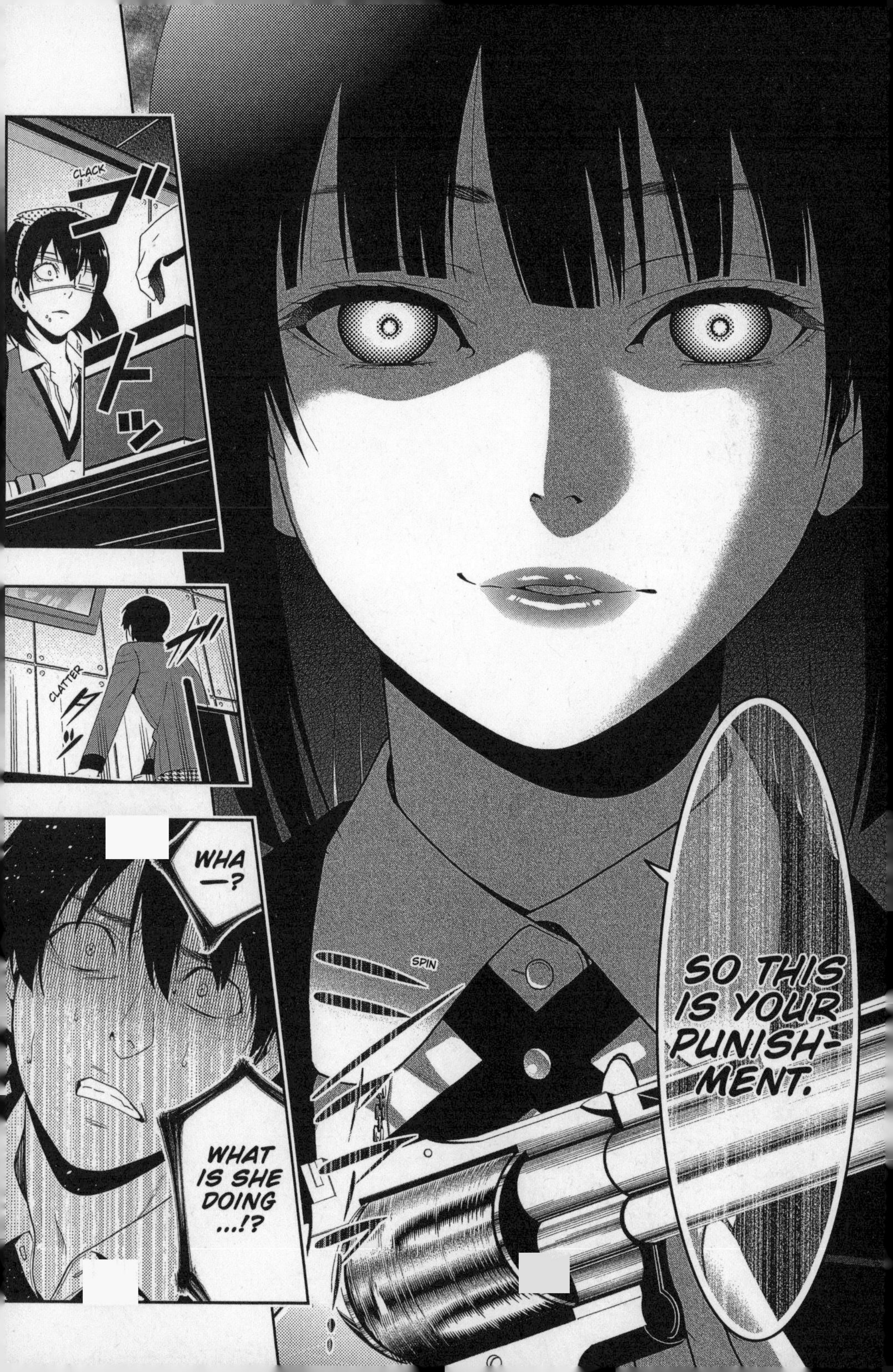
SPIN
SO THIS IS YOUR PUNISH-MENT.
CLACK
CLATTER
WHA—?
WHAT IS SHE DOING ...!?

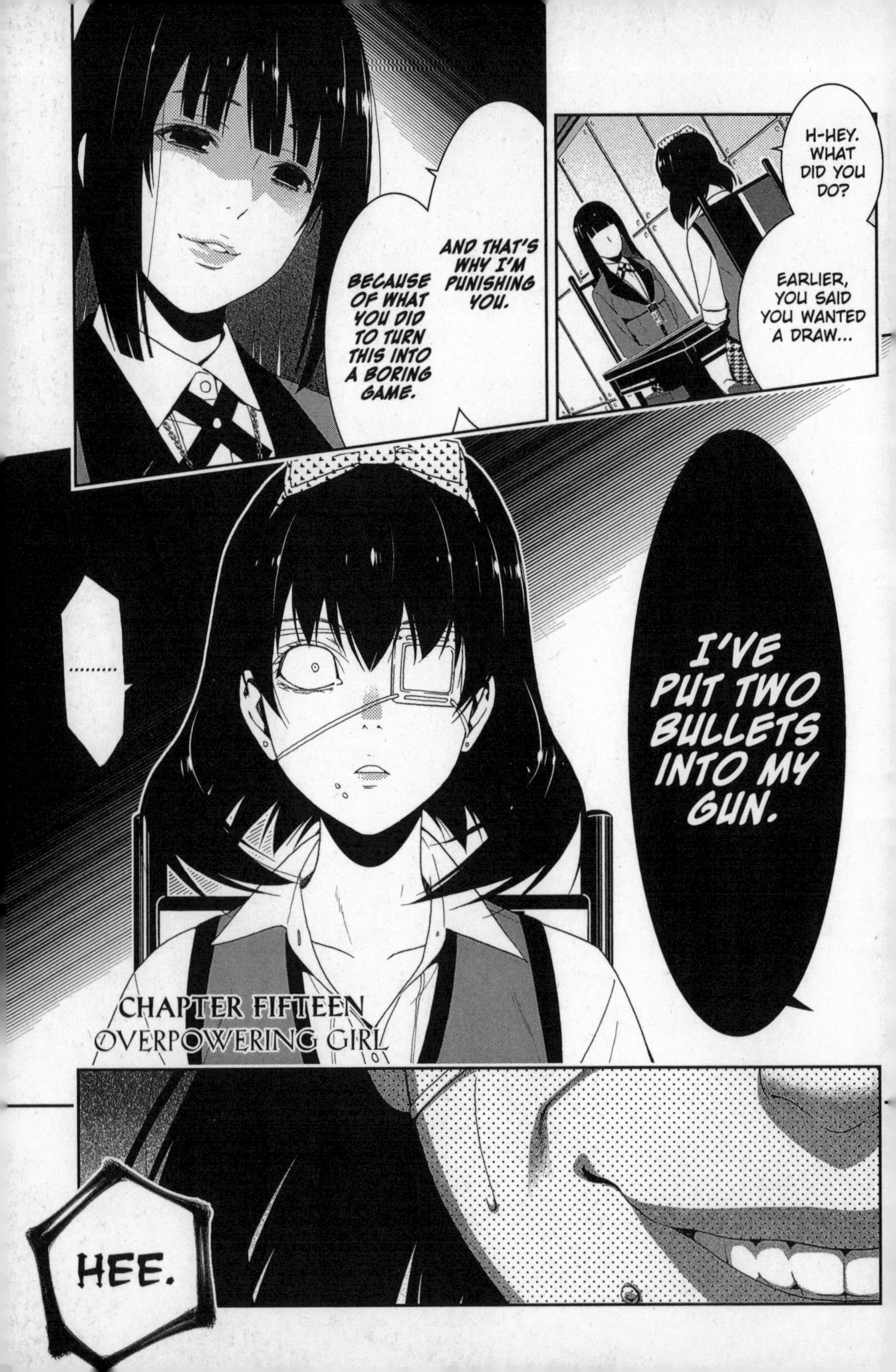
H-HEY. WHAT DID YOU DO?
EARLIER, YOU SAID YOU WANTED A DRAW...
AND THAT'S WHY I'M PUNISHING YOU.
BECAUSE OF WHAT YOU DID TO TURN THIS INTO A BORING GAME.
I'VE PUT TWO BULLETS INTO MY GUN.
....
CHAPTER FIFTEEN
OVERPOWERING GIRL
HEE.

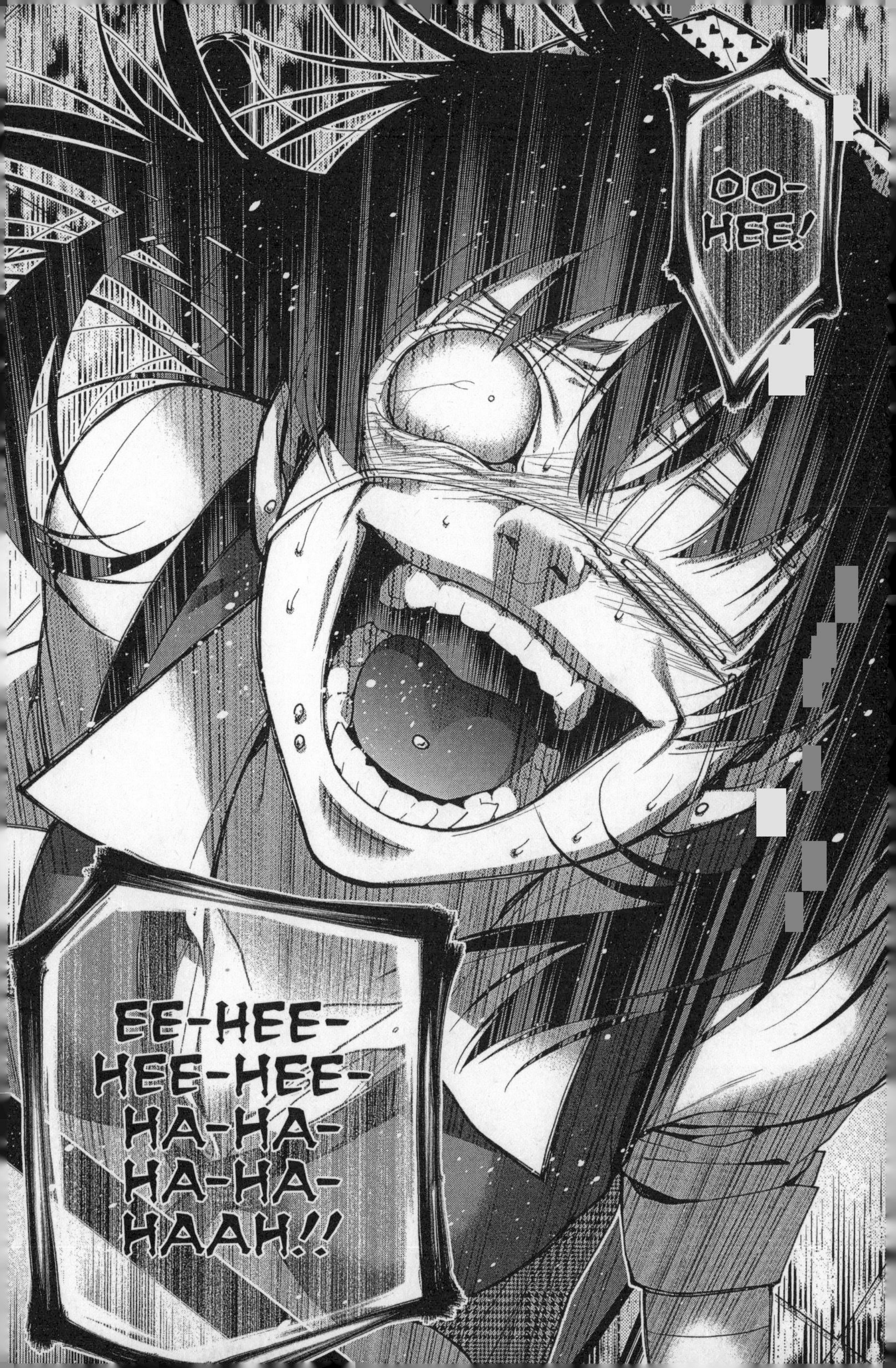
OO-HEE!
EE-HEE-HEE-HEE-HA-HA-HA-HA-HAAAH!!

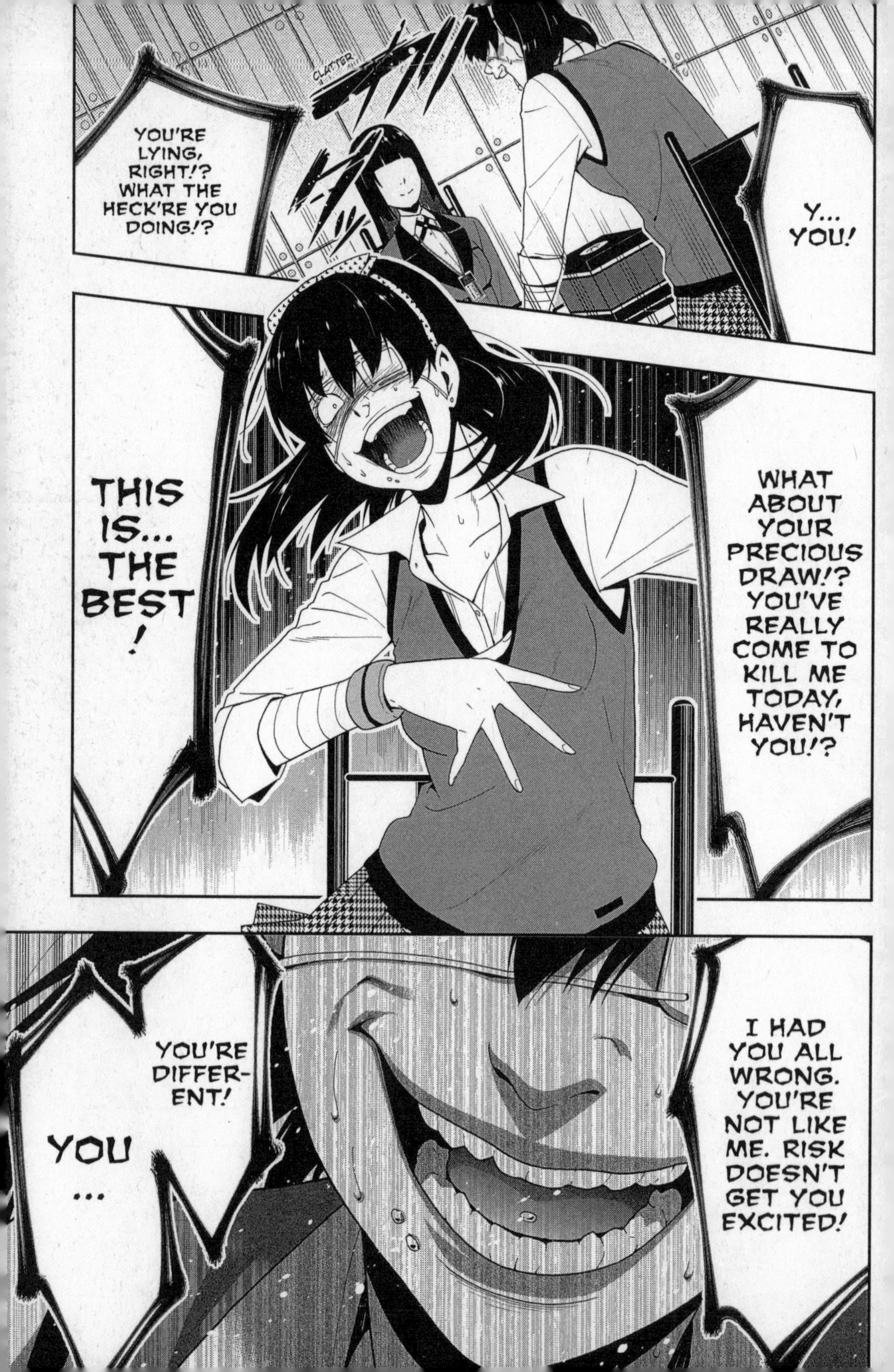
Y... YOU!
CLUTTER
YOU'RE LYING, RIGHT!? WHAT THE HECK'RE YOU DOING!?
WHAT ABOUT YOUR PRECIOUS DRAW!? YOU'VE REALLY COME TO KILL ME TODAY, HAVEN'T YOU!?
THIS IS... THE BEST!
I HAD YOU ALL WRONG. YOU'RE NOT LIKE ME. RISK DOESN'T GET YOU EXCITED!
YOU'RE DIFFER-ENT!
YOU ...

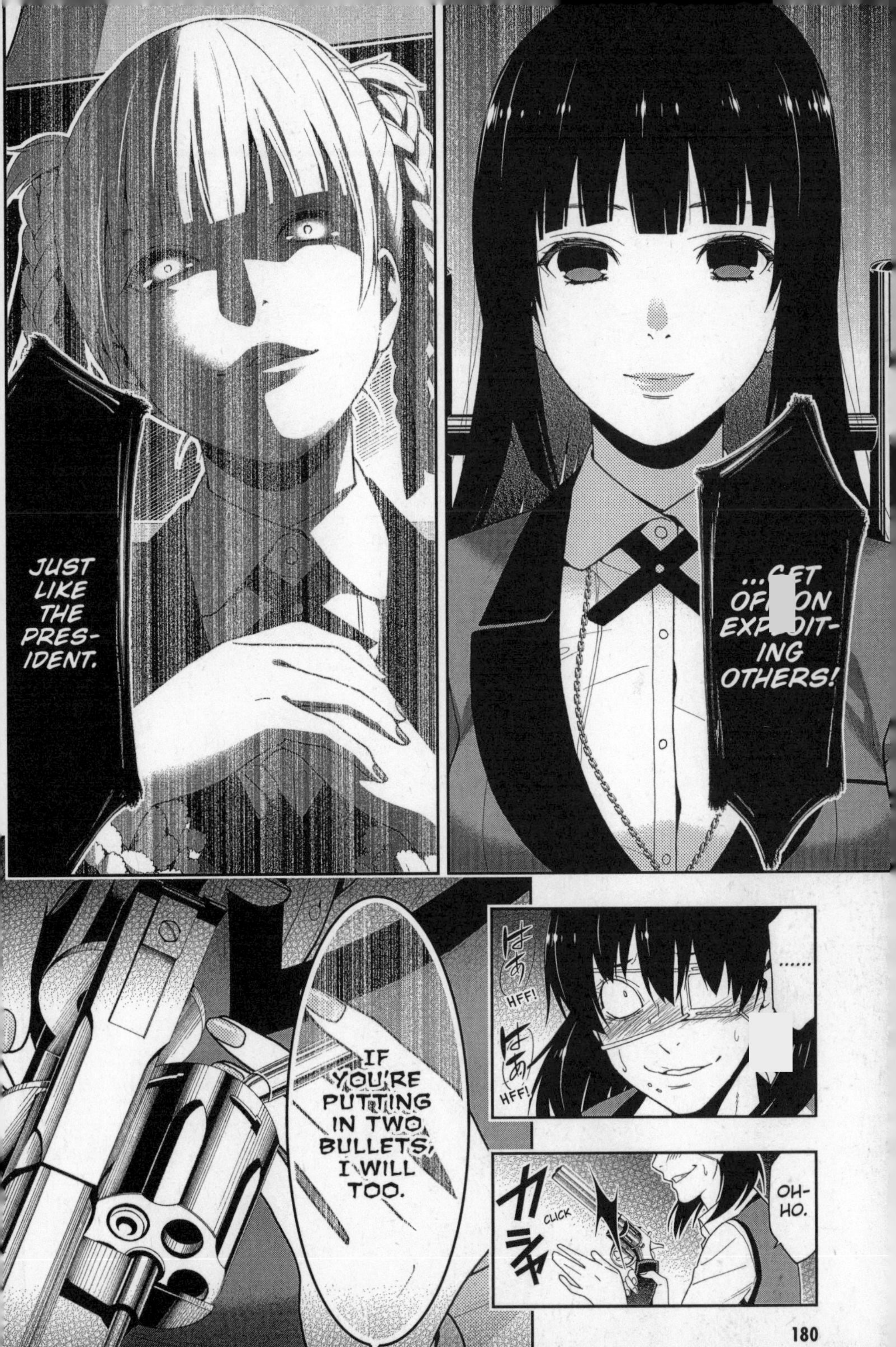
...GET OFF ON EXPLOITING OTHERS!
JUST LIKE THE PRESIDENT.
......
はあ HFF!
はあ HFF!
OH-HO.
カチャ CLICK
IF YOU'RE PUTTING IN TWO BULLETS, I WILL TOO.

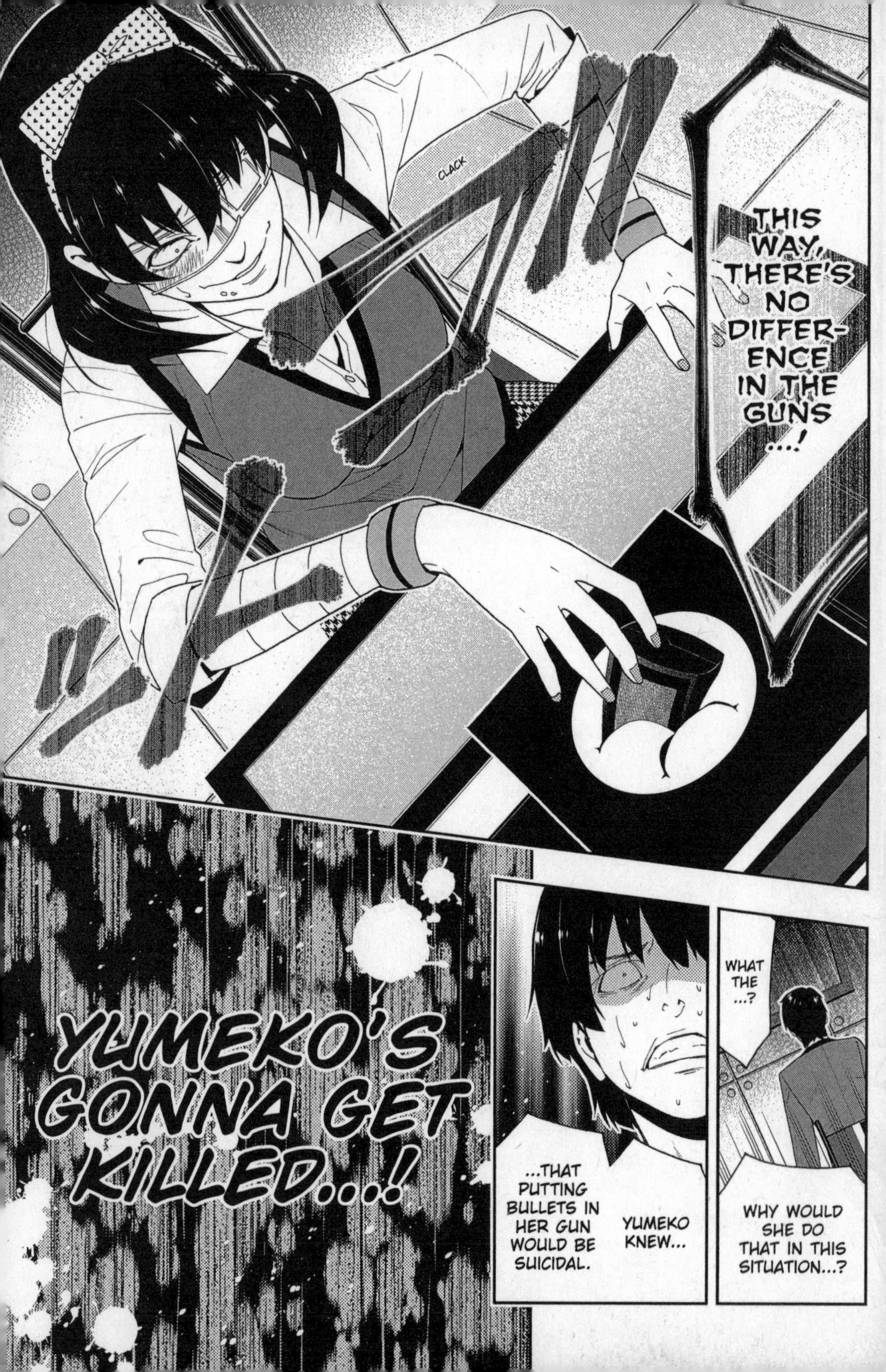
THIS WAY, THERE'S NO DIFFERENCE IN THE GUNS...!
CLACK
WHAT THE ...?
WHY WOULD SHE DO THAT IN THIS SITUATION...?
YUMEKO KNEW...
...THAT PUTTING BULLETS IN HER GUN WOULD BE SUICIDAL.
YUMEKO'S GONNA GET KILLED...!

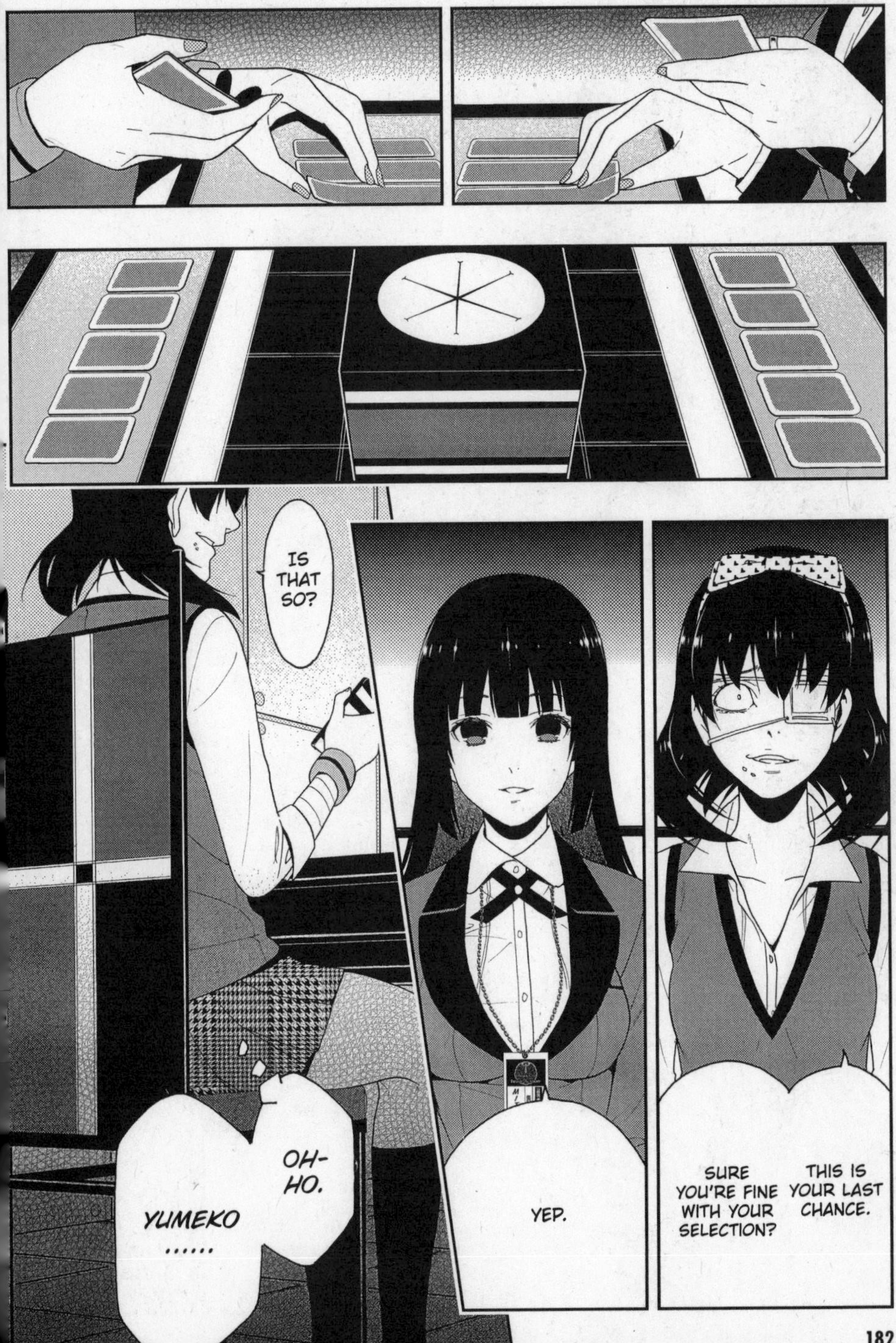

THIS IS YOUR LAST CHANCE.
SURE YOU'RE FINE WITH YOUR SELECTION?
YEP.
IS THAT SO?
OH-HO.
YUMEKO ......

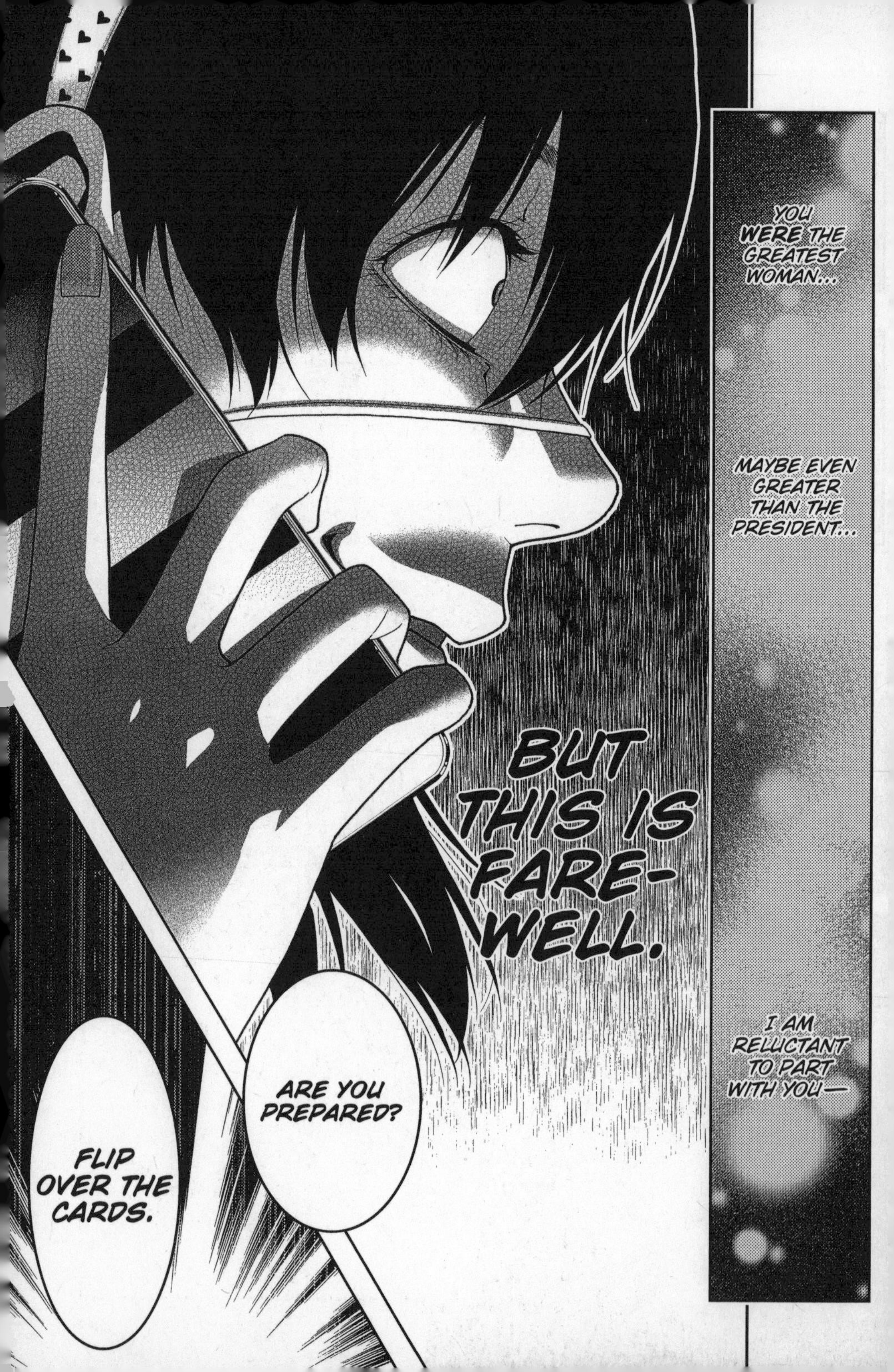
YOU WERE THE GREATEST WOMAN...
MAYBE EVEN GREATER THAN THE PRESIDENT...
I AM RELUCTANT TO PART WITH YOU—
BUT THIS IS FARE-WELL.
ARE YOU PREPARED?
FLIP OVER THE CARDS.

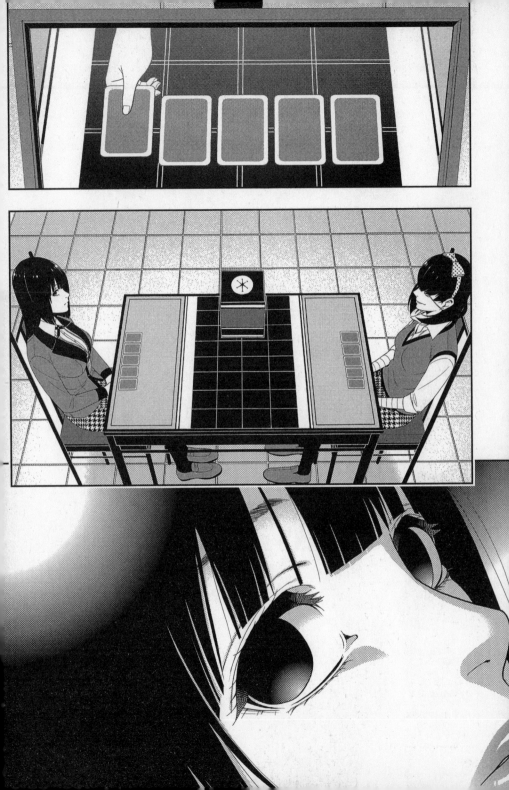

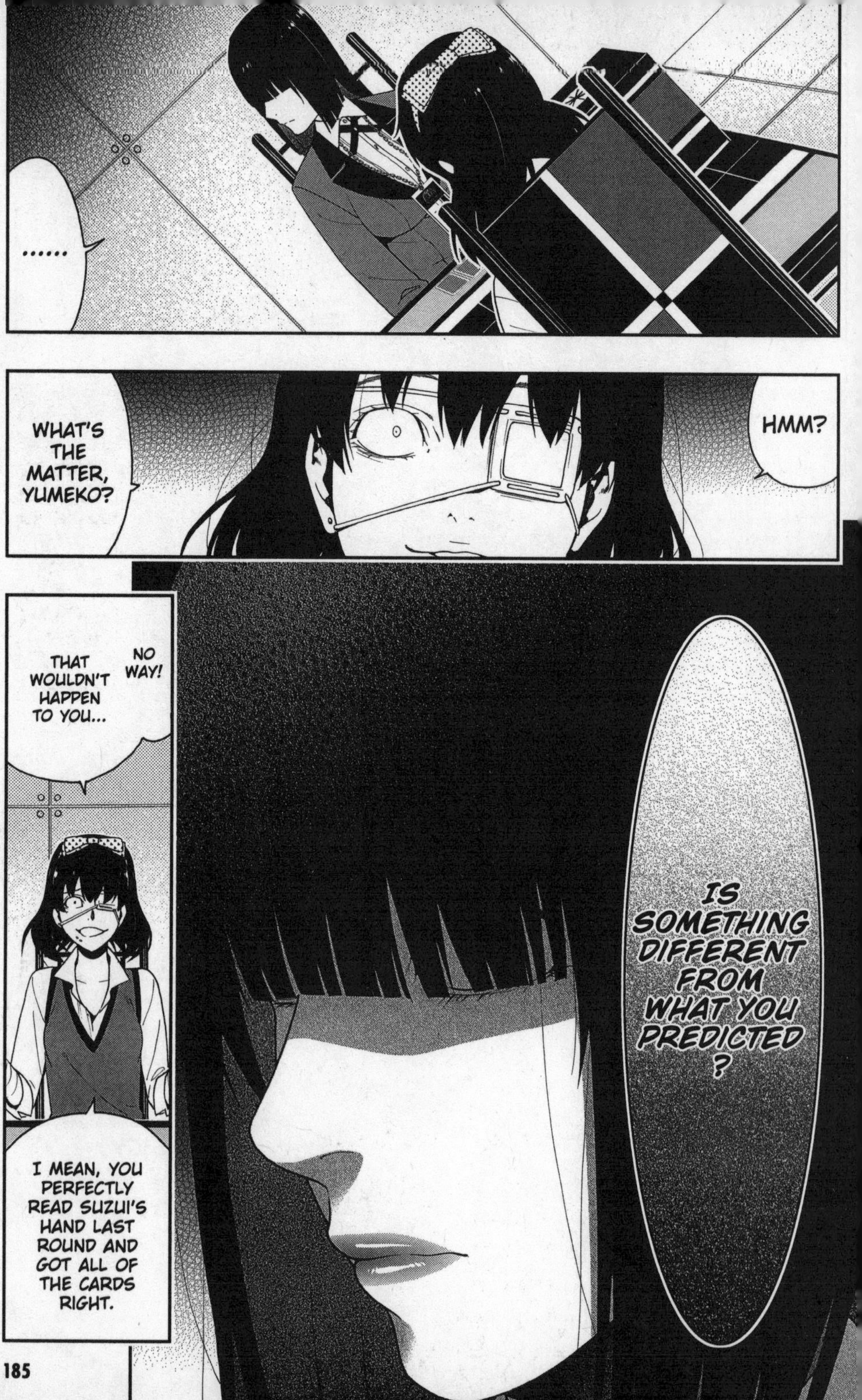

......
HMM?
WHAT'S THE MATTER, YUMEKO?
IS SOMETHING DIFFERENT FROM WHAT YOU PREDICTED?
NO WAY!
THAT WOULDN'T HAPPEN TO YOU...
I MEAN, YOU PERFECTLY READ SUZUI'S HAND LAST ROUND AND GOT ALL OF THE CARDS RIGHT.

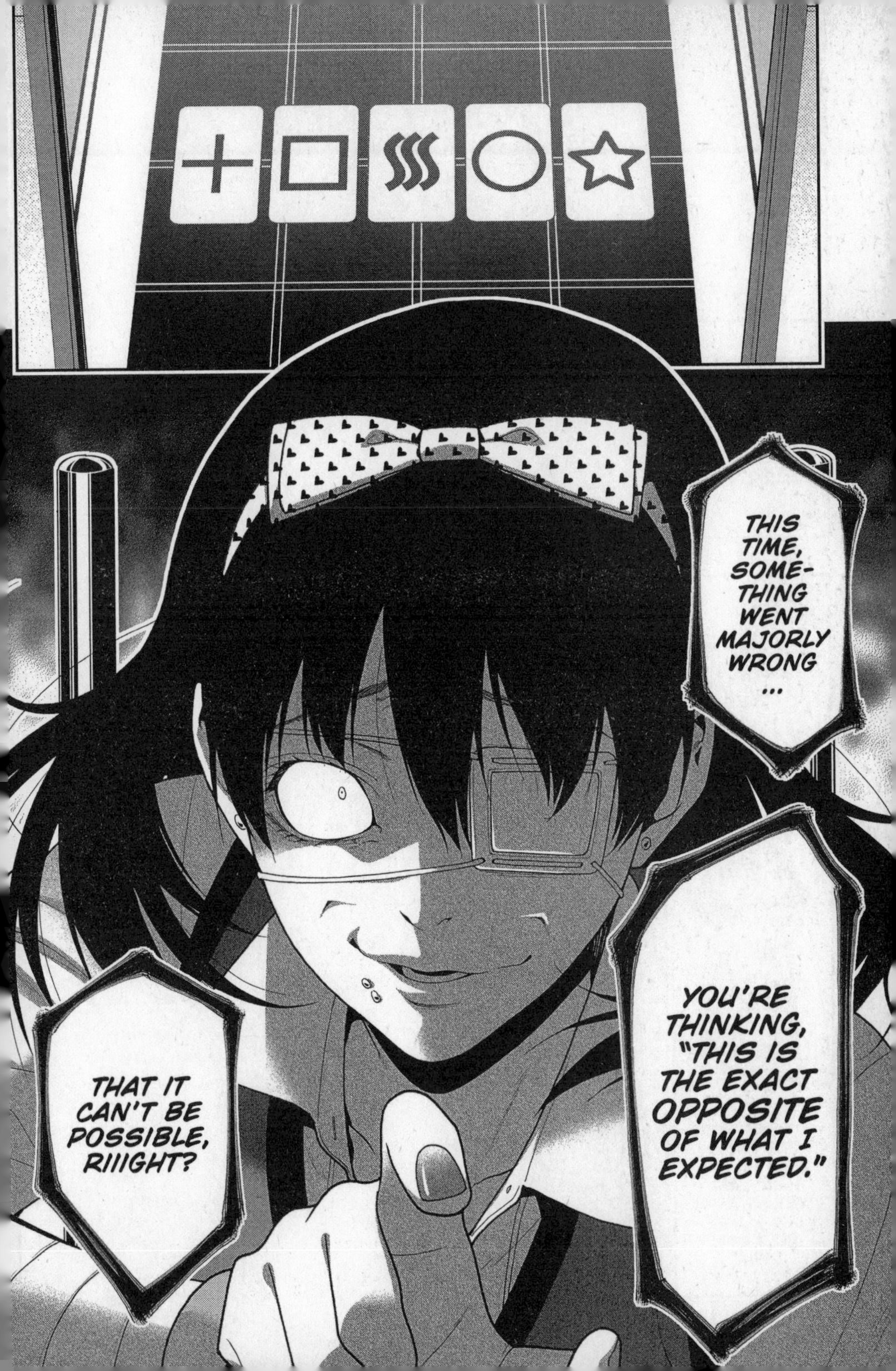
THIS TIME, SOME-THING WENT MAJORLY WRONG ...
YOU'RE THINKING, "THIS IS THE EXACT OPPOSITE OF WHAT I EXPECTED."
THAT IT CAN'T BE POSSIBLE, RIIIGHT?

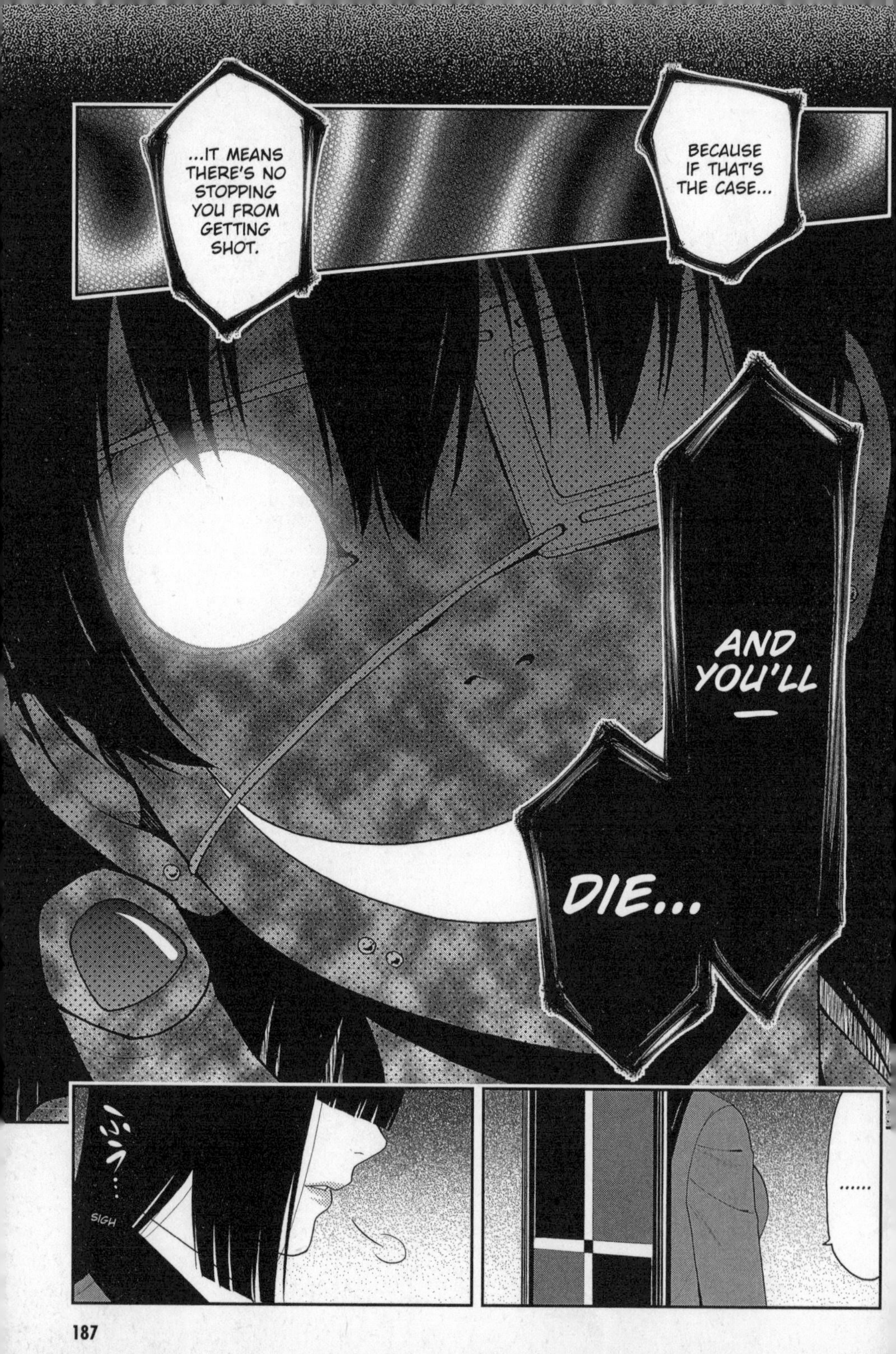
BECAUSE IF THAT'S THE CASE...
...IT MEANS THERE'S NO STOPPING YOU FROM GETTING SHOT.
AND YOU'LL —
DIE...
......
SIGH

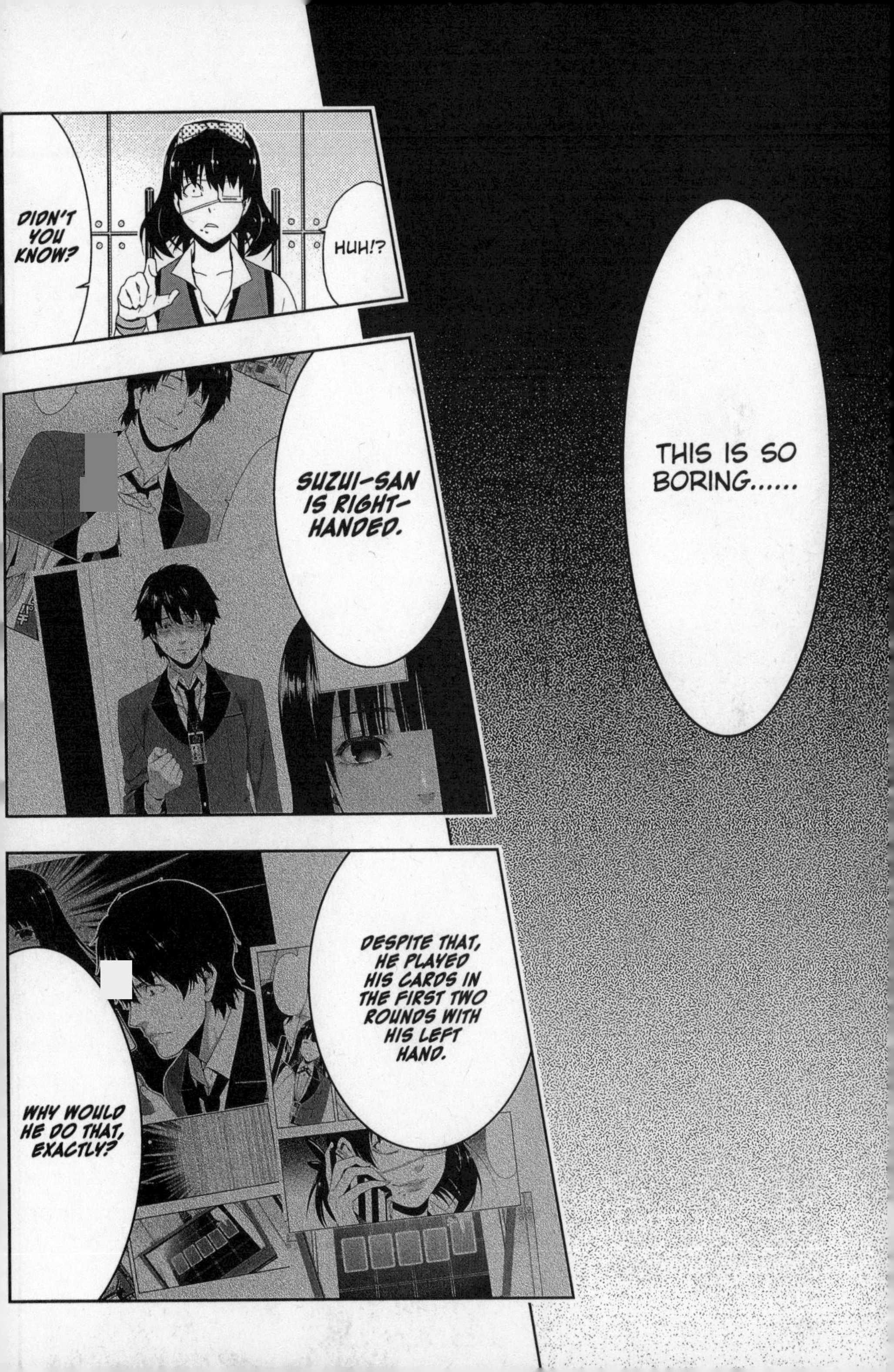
THIS IS SO BORING......
HUH!?
DIDN'T YOU KNOW?
SUZUI-SAN IS RIGHT-HANDED.
DESPITE THAT, HE PLAYED HIS CARDS IN THE FIRST TWO ROUNDS WITH HIS LEFT HAND.
WHY WOULD HE DO THAT, EXACTLY?

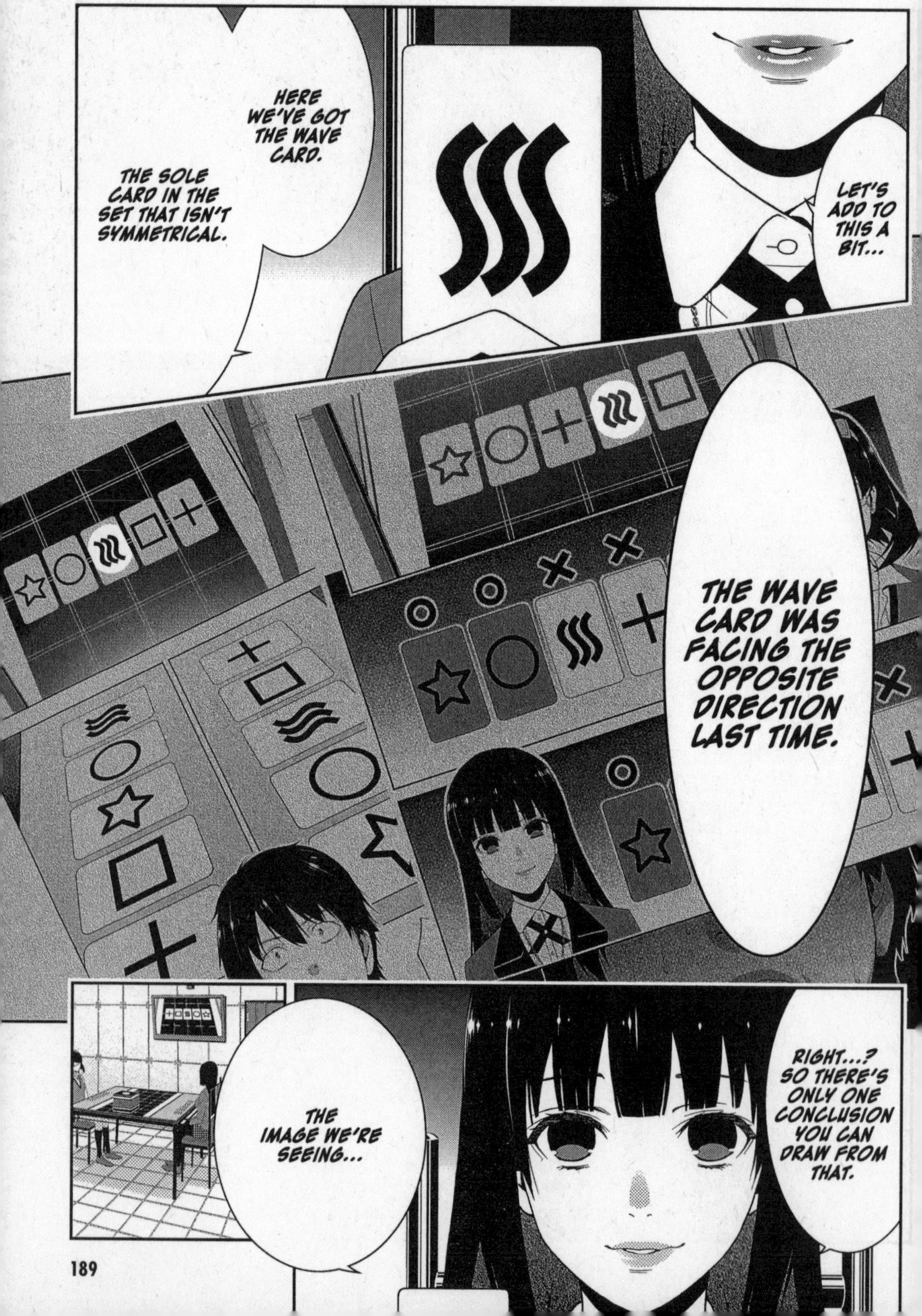
HERE WE'VE GOT THE WAVE CARD.
THE SOLE CARD IN THE SET THAT ISN'T SYMMETRICAL.
LET'S ADD TO THIS A BIT...
THE WAVE CARD WAS FACING THE OPPOSITE DIRECTION LAST TIME.
RIGHT...? SO THERE'S ONLY ONE CONCLUSION YOU CAN DRAW FROM THAT.
THE IMAGE WE'RE SEEING...

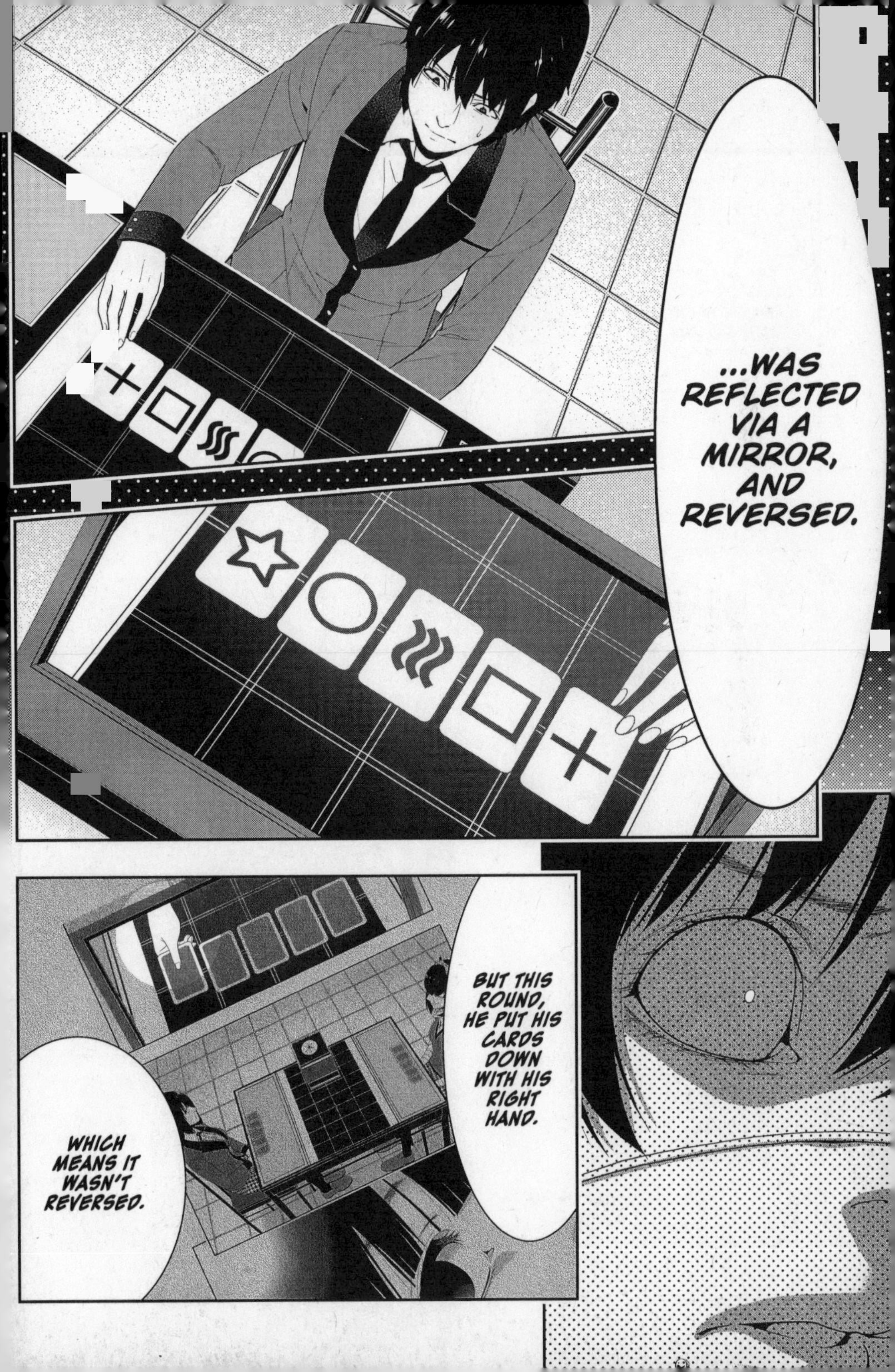
...WAS REFLECTED VIA A MIRROR, AND REVERSED.
BUT THIS ROUND, HE PUT HIS CARDS DOWN WITH HIS RIGHT HAND.
WHICH MEANS IT WASN'T REVERSED.

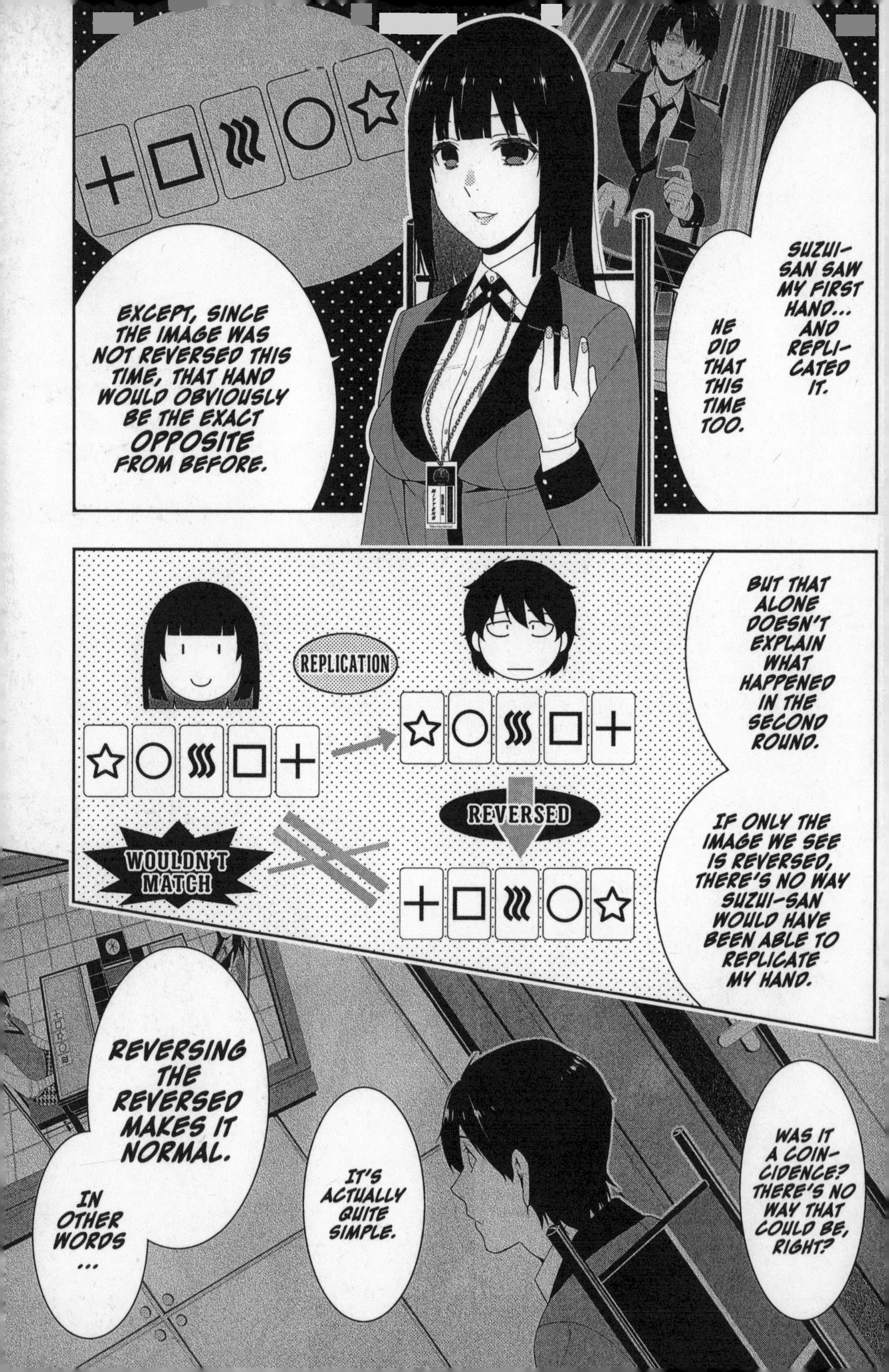

SUZUI-SAN SAW MY FIRST HAND... AND REPLICATED IT.
HE DID THAT THIS TIME TOO.
EXCEPT, SINCE THE IMAGE WAS NOT REVERSED THIS TIME, THAT HAND WOULD OBVIOUSLY BE THE EXACT OPPOSITE FROM BEFORE.
BUT THAT ALONE DOESN'T EXPLAIN WHAT HAPPENED IN THE SECOND ROUND.
IF ONLY THE IMAGE WE SEE IS REVERSED, THERE'S NO WAY SUZUI-SAN WOULD HAVE BEEN ABLE TO REPLICATE MY HAND.
REPLICATION
REVERSED
WOULDN'T MATCH
WAS IT A COINCIDENCE? THERE'S NO WAY THAT COULD BE, RIGHT?
IT'S ACTUALLY QUITE SIMPLE.
IN OTHER WORDS...
REVERSING THE REVERSED MAKES IT NORMAL.

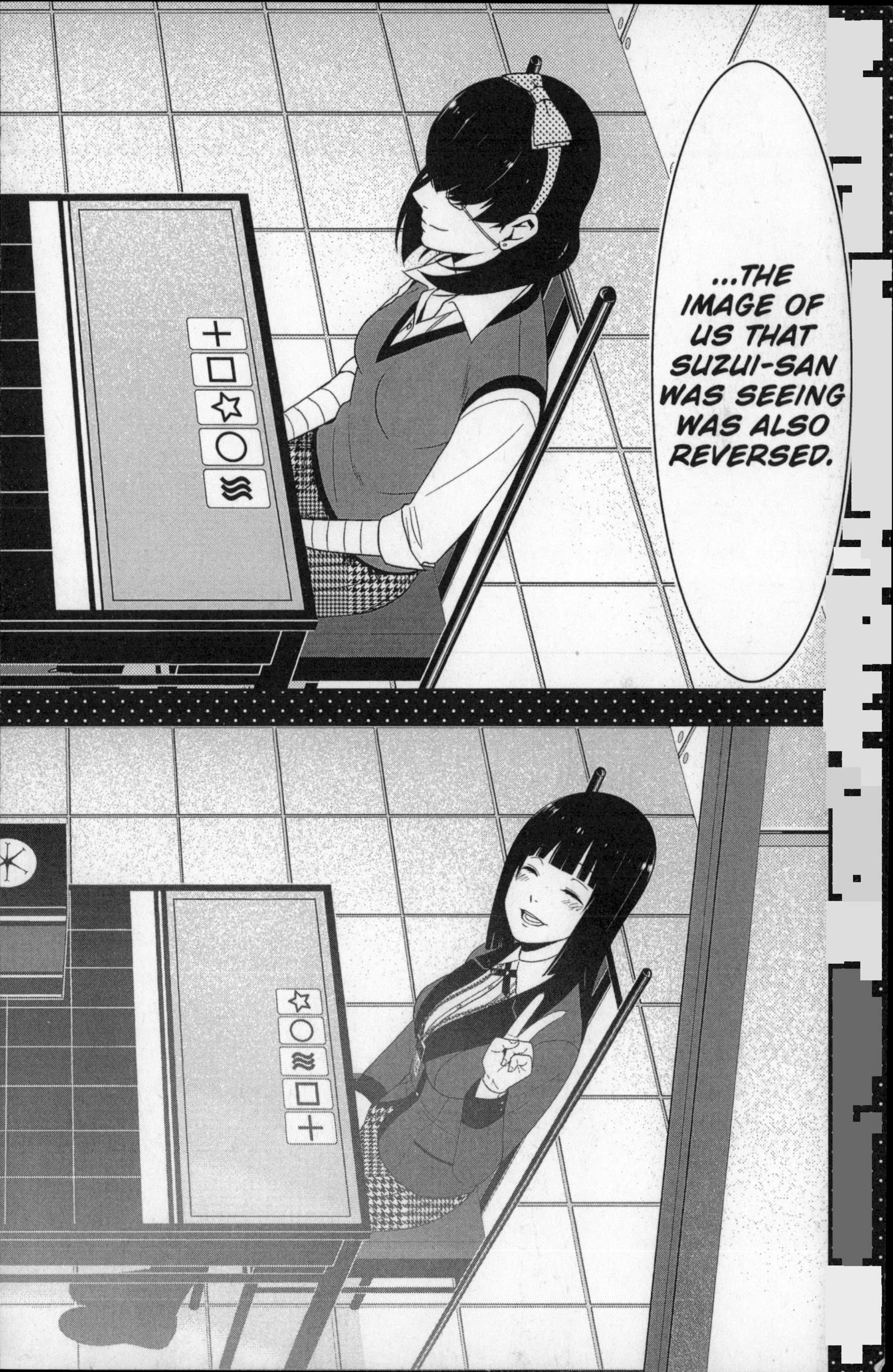
...THE IMAGE OF US THAT SUZUI-SAN WAS SEEING WAS ALSO REVERSED.

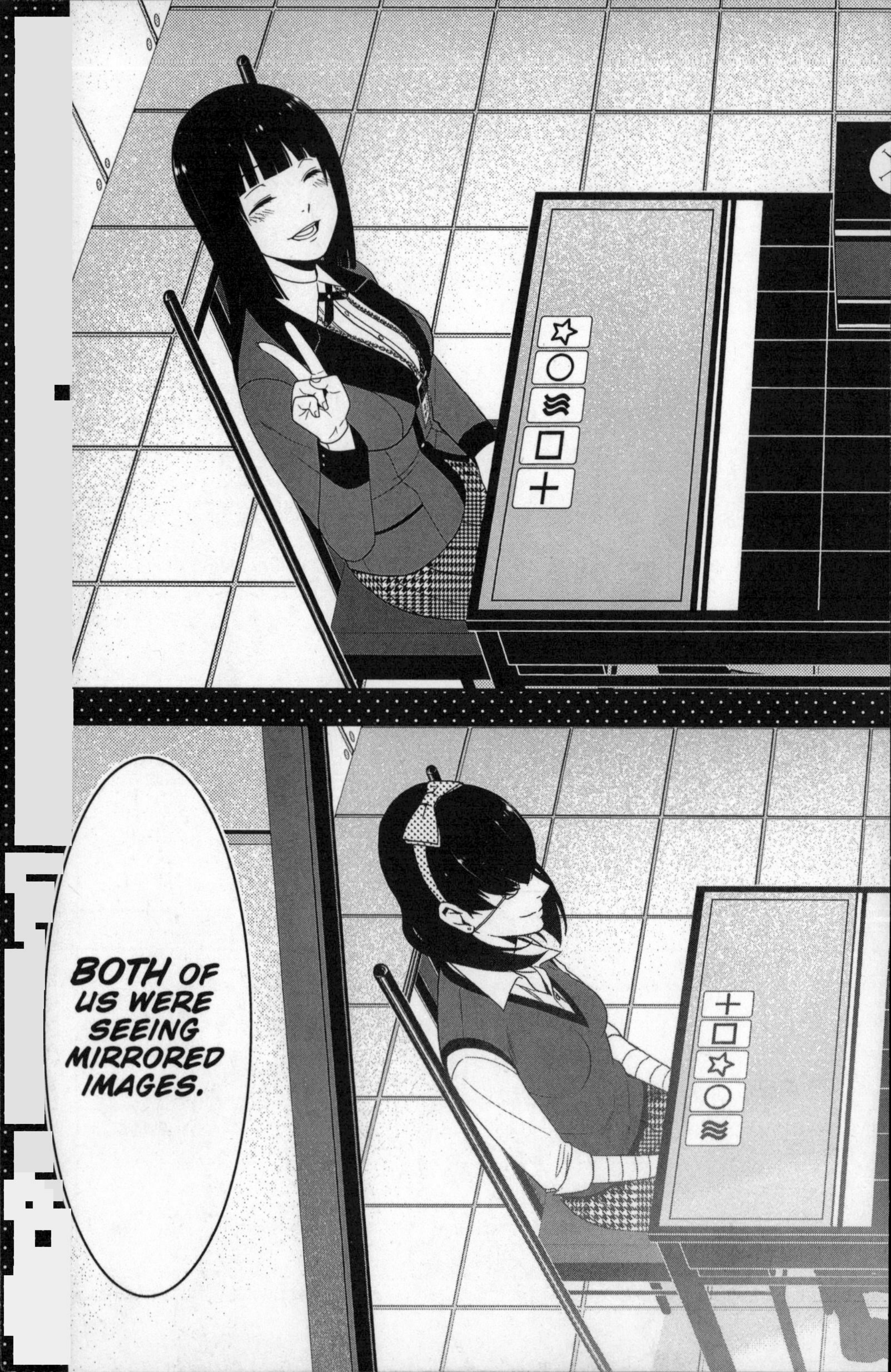
BOTH OF US WERE SEEING MIRRORED IMAGES.

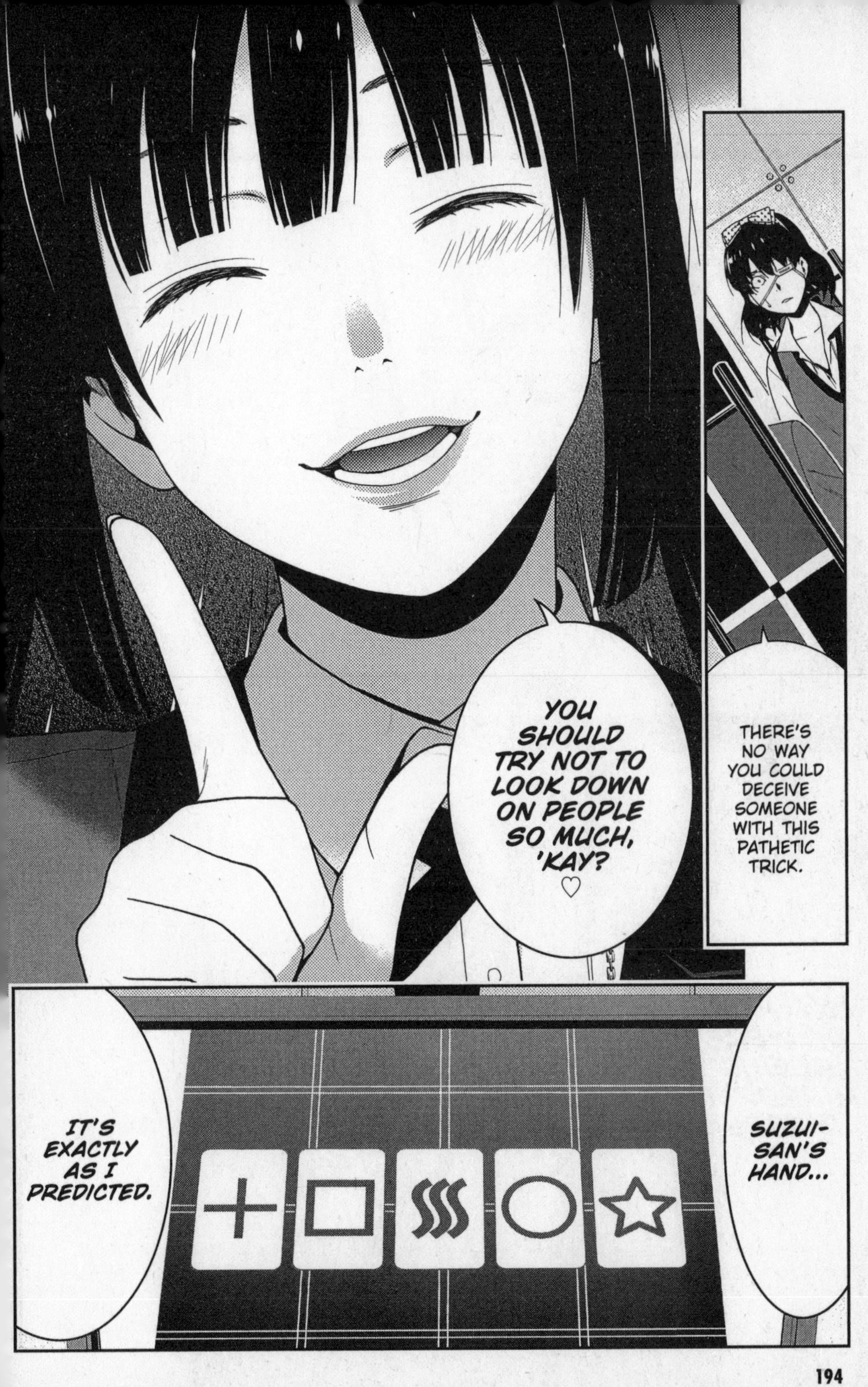
THERE'S NO WAY YOU COULD DECEIVE SOMEONE WITH THIS PATHETIC TRICK.
YOU SHOULD TRY NOT TO LOOK DOWN ON PEOPLE SO MUCH, 'KAY? ♡
SUZUI-SAN'S HAND...
IT'S EXACTLY AS I PREDICTED.

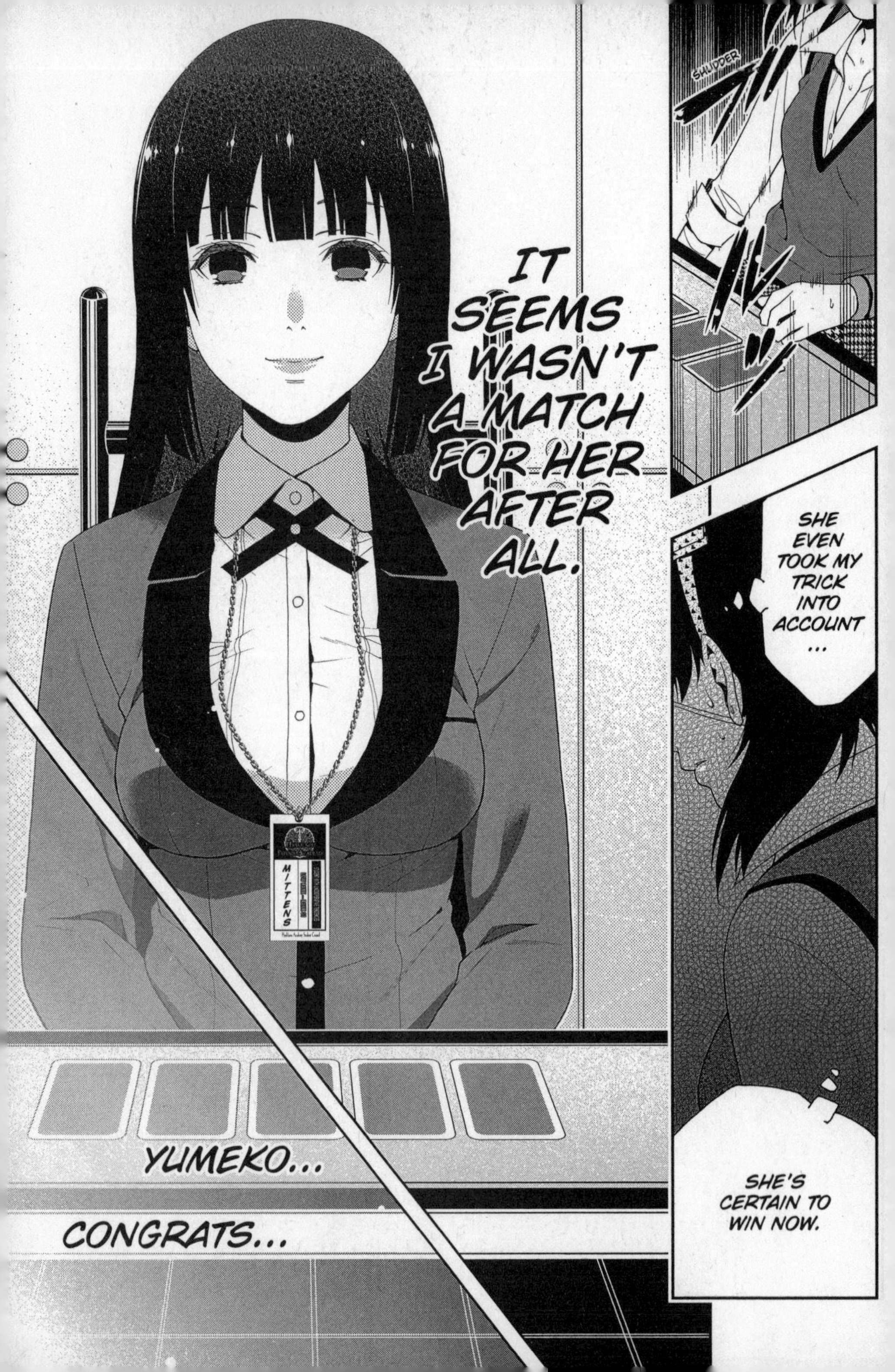
SHUDDER
SHE EVEN TOOK MY TRICK INTO ACCOUNT...
SHE'S CERTAIN TO WIN NOW.
IT SEEMS I WASN'T A MATCH FOR HER AFTER ALL.
MITTENS
YUMEKO...
CONGRATS...

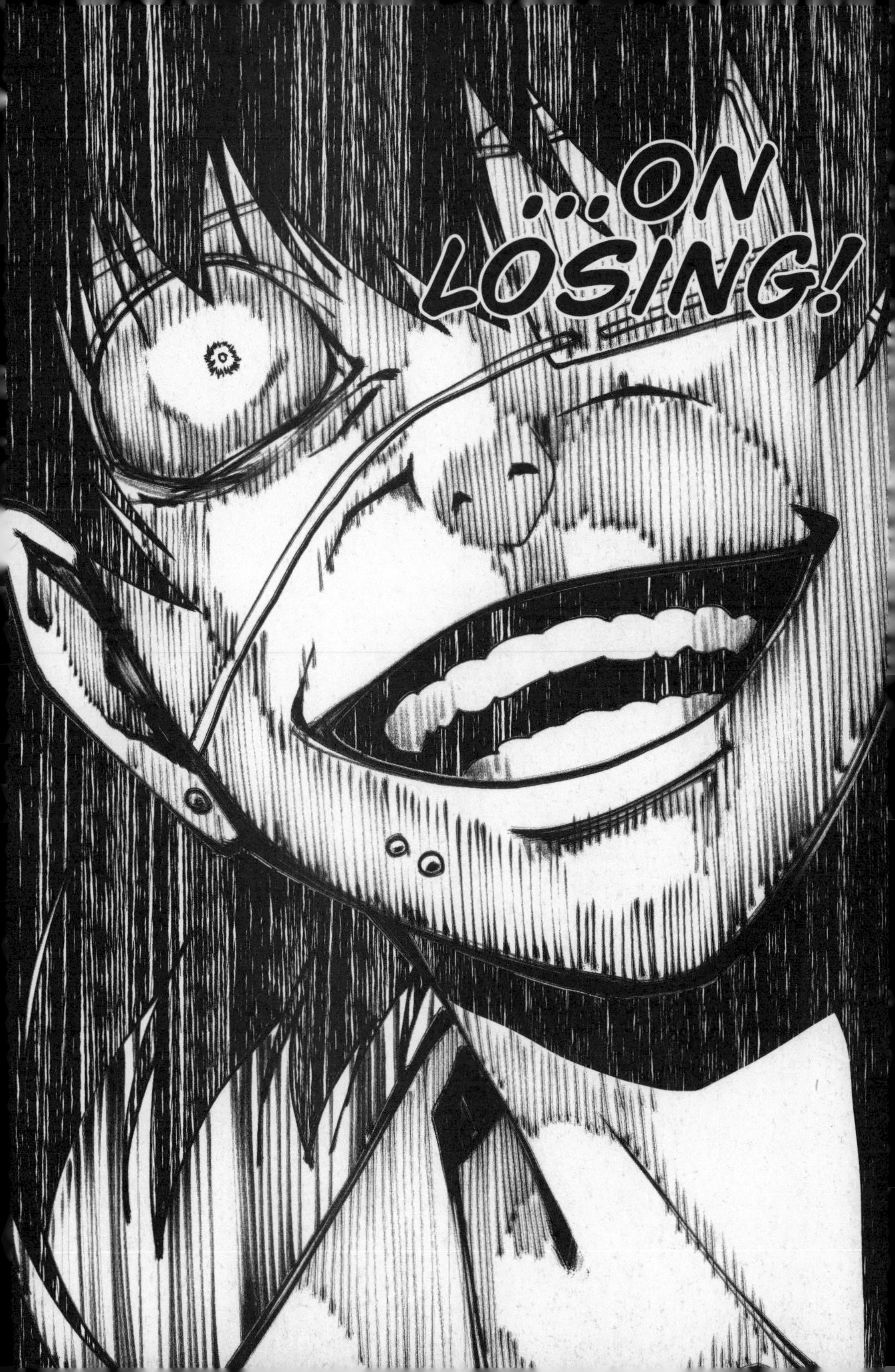
...ON LOSING!

KAKEGURUI

— Compulsive Gambler —

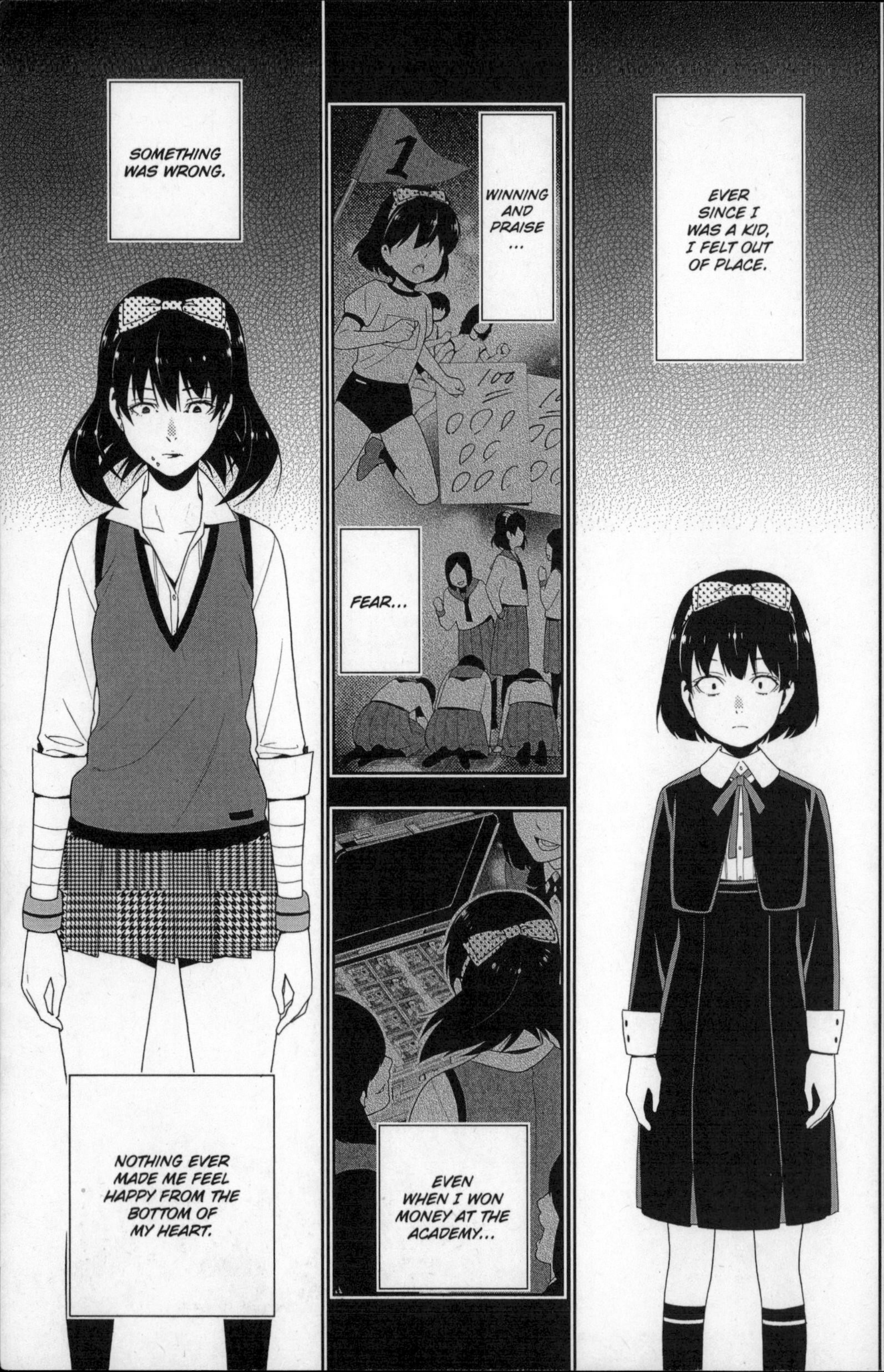
EVER SINCE I WAS A KID, I FELT OUT OF PLACE.
WINNING AND PRAISE ...
FEAR...
EVEN WHEN I WON MONEY AT THE ACADEMY...
SOMETHING WAS WRONG.
NOTHING EVER MADE ME FEEL HAPPY FROM THE BOTTOM OF MY HEART.

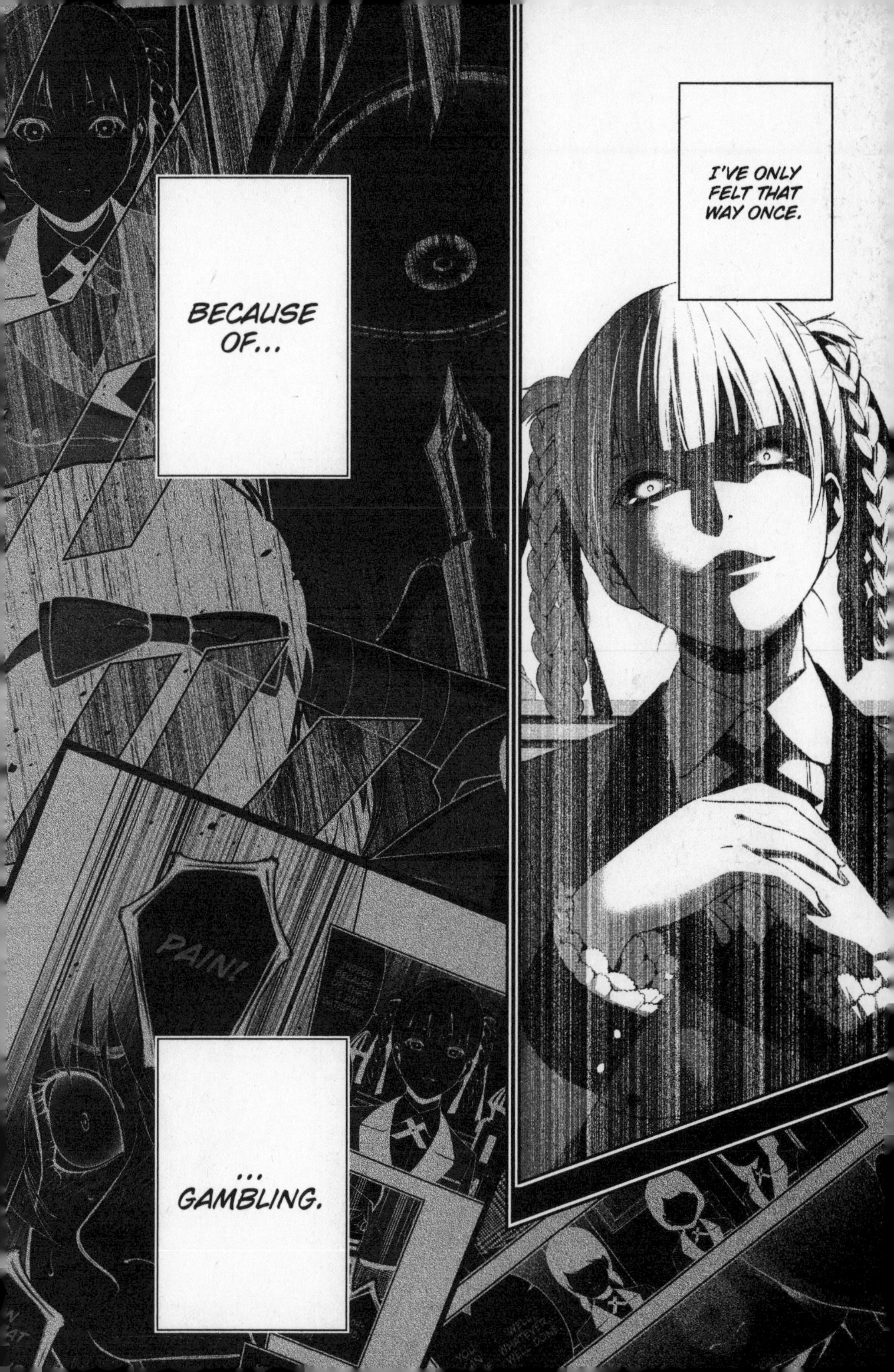
I'VE ONLY FELT THAT WAY ONCE.
BECAUSE OF...
PAIN!
...GAMBLING.

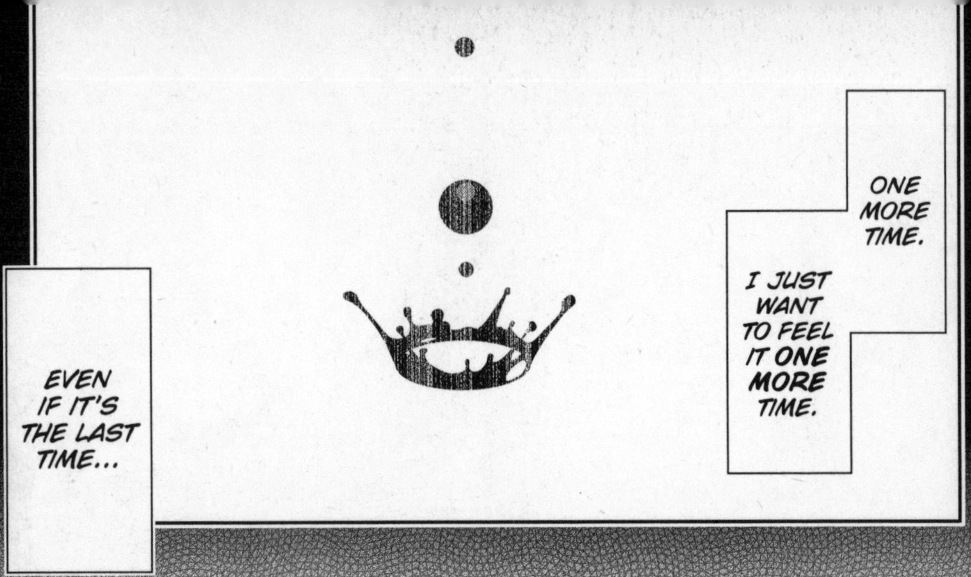
ONE MORE TIME.
I JUST WANT TO FEEL IT ONE MORE TIME.
EVEN IF IT'S THE LAST TIME...

CHAPTER SIXTEEN
REFUSING GIRLS

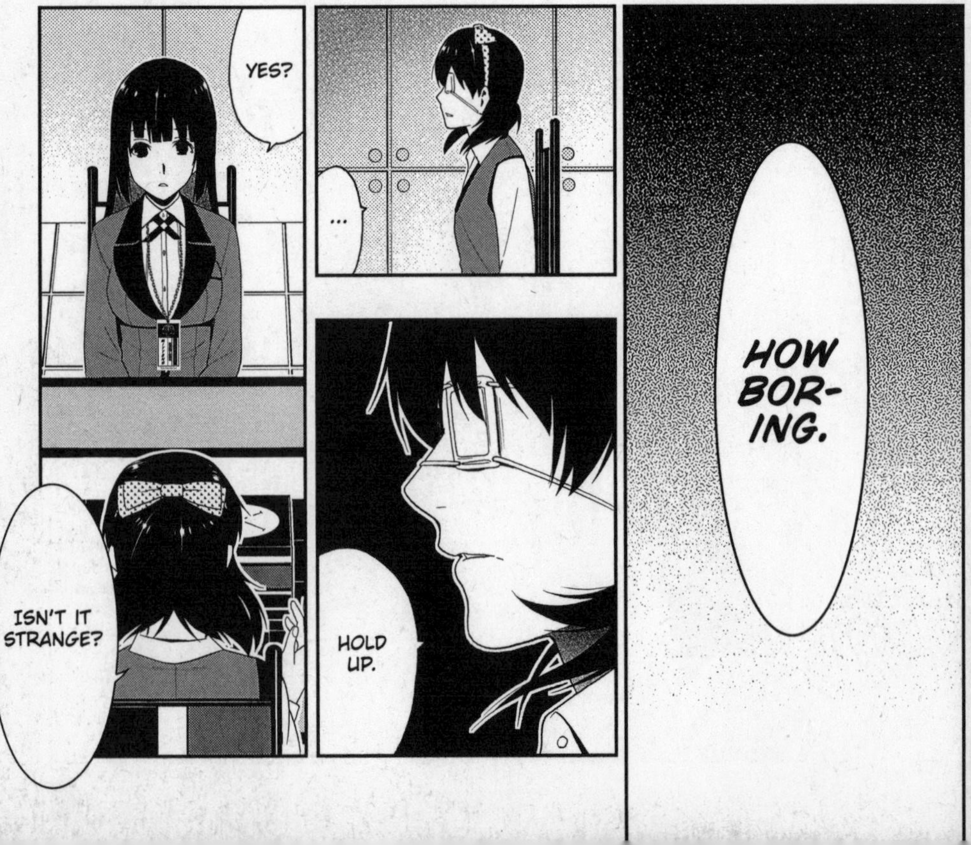
HOW BOR-ING.
...
YES?
HOLD UP.
ISN'T IT STRANGE?

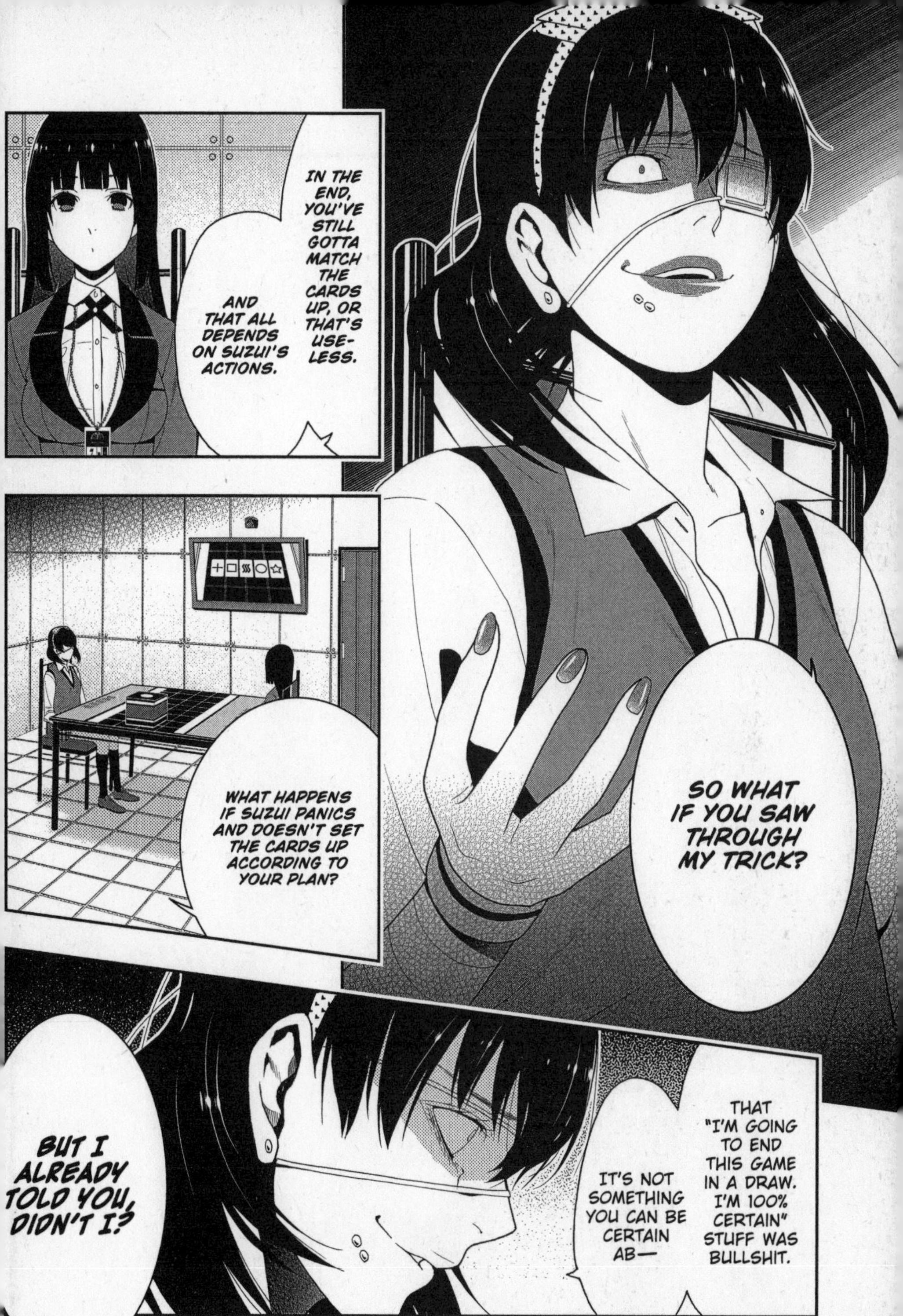
SO WHAT IF YOU SAW THROUGH MY TRICK?
IN THE END, YOU'VE STILL GOTTA MATCH THE CARDS UP, OR THAT'S USELESS.
AND THAT ALL DEPENDS ON SUZUI'S ACTIONS.
WHAT HAPPENS IF SUZUI PANICS AND DOESN'T SET THE CARDS UP ACCORDING TO YOUR PLAN?
THAT "I'M GOING TO END THIS GAME IN A DRAW. I'M 100% CERTAIN" STUFF WAS BULLSHIT.
IT'S NOT SOMETHING YOU CAN BE CERTAIN AB—
BUT I ALREADY TOLD YOU, DIDN'T I?

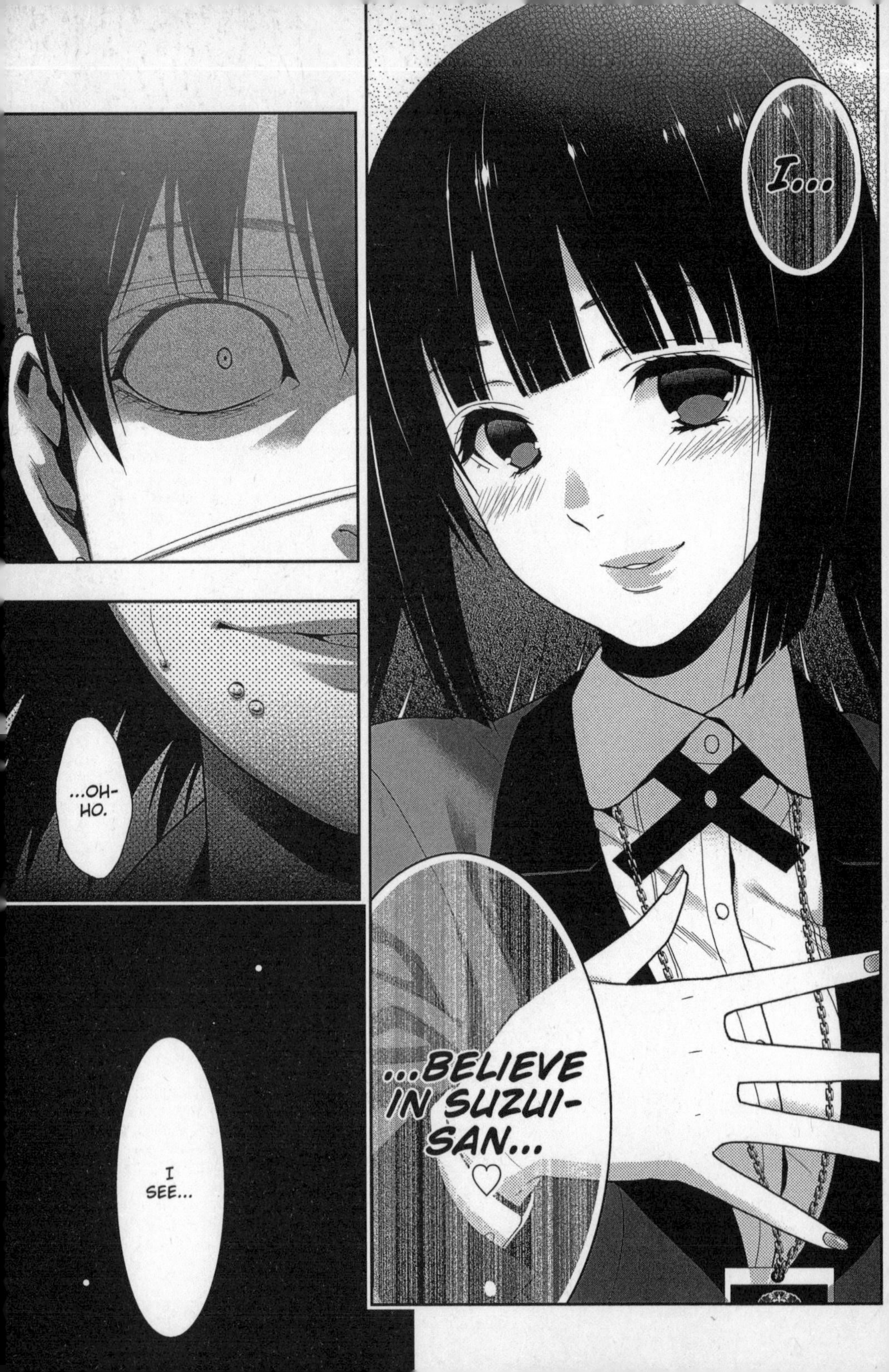
I...
...BELIEVE IN SUZUI-SAN... ♡
...OH-HO.
I SEE...

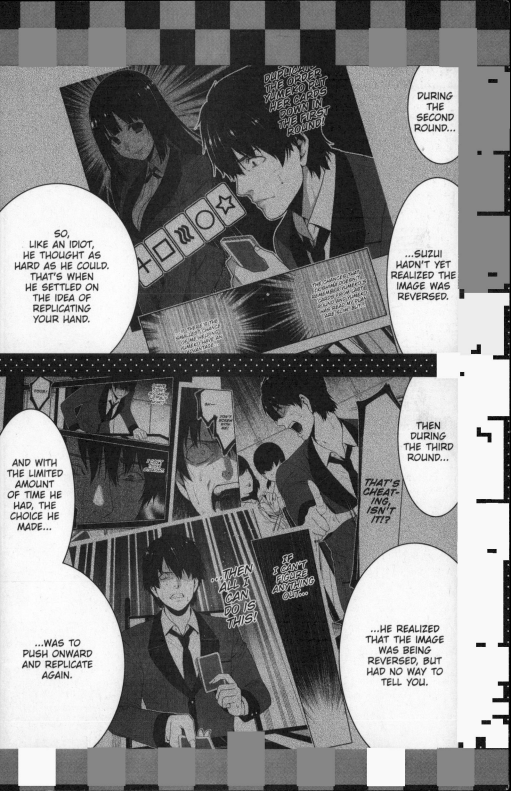

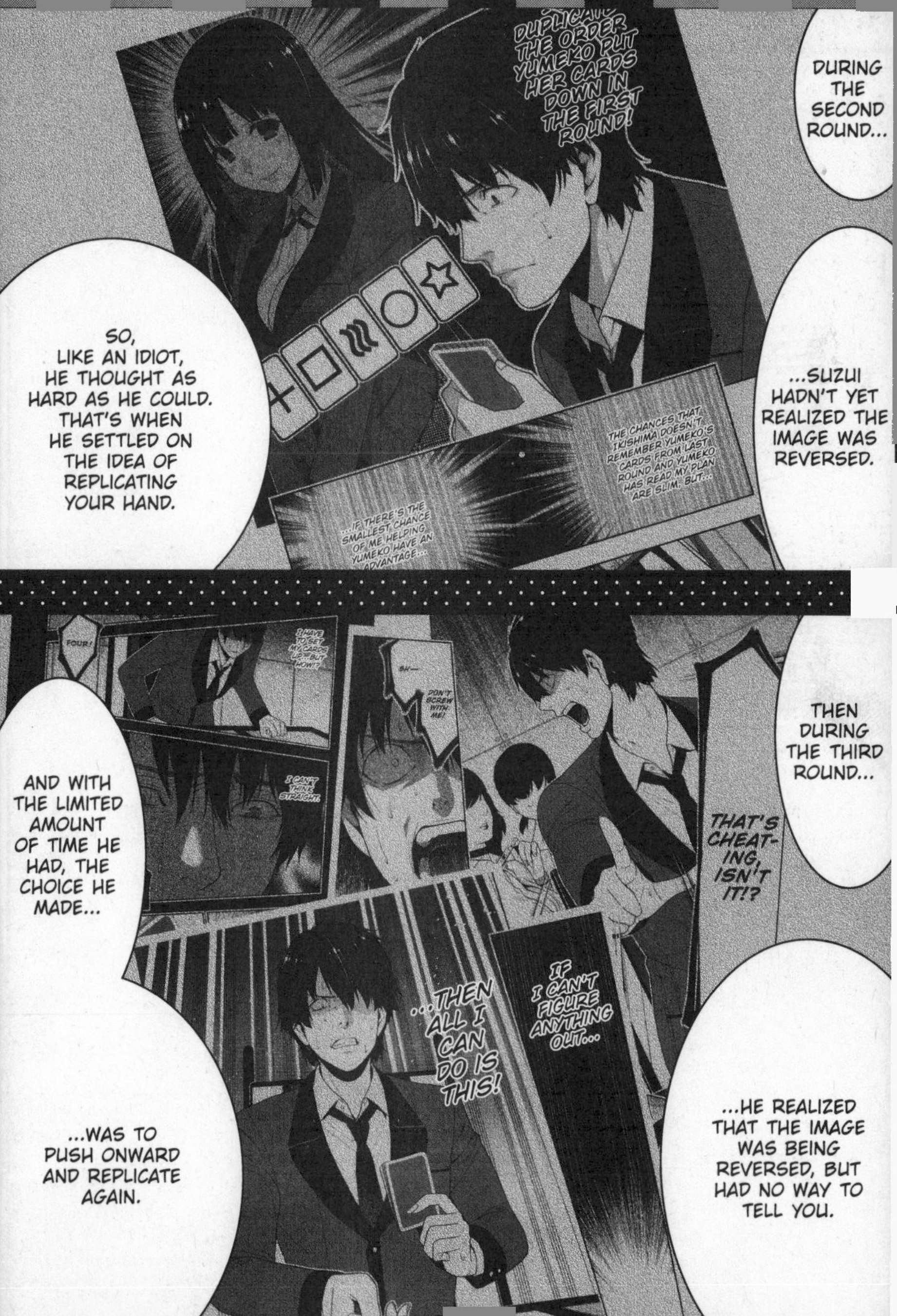
DURING THE SECOND ROUND...
DUPLICATE THE ORDER YUMEKO PUT HER CARDS DOWN IN THE FIRST ROUND!
...SUZUI HADN'T YET REALIZED THE IMAGE WAS REVERSED.
THE CHANCES THAT IKISHIMA DOESN'T REMEMBER YUMEKO'S CARDS FROM LAST ROUND AND YUMEKO HAS READ MY PLAN ARE SLIM. BUT...
...IF THERE'S THE SMALLEST CHANCE OF ME HELPING YUMEKO HAVE AN ADVANTAGE...
SO, LIKE AN IDIOT, HE THOUGHT AS HARD AS HE COULD. THAT'S WHEN HE SETTLED ON THE IDEA OF REPLICATING YOUR HAND.
THEN DURING THE THIRD ROUND...
THAT'S CHEATING, ISN'T IT!?
SH—
DON'T SCREW WITH ME!
FOUR!
I HAVE TO SET MY CARDS UP... BUT HOW!?
I CAN'T THINK STRAIGHT.
AND WITH THE LIMITED AMOUNT OF TIME HE HAD, THE CHOICE HE MADE...
...HE REALIZED THAT THE IMAGE WAS BEING REVERSED, BUT HAD NO WAY TO TELL YOU.
IF I CAN'T FIGURE ANYTHING OUT...
...THEN ALL I CAN DO IS THIS!
...WAS TO PUSH ONWARD AND REPLICATE AGAIN.

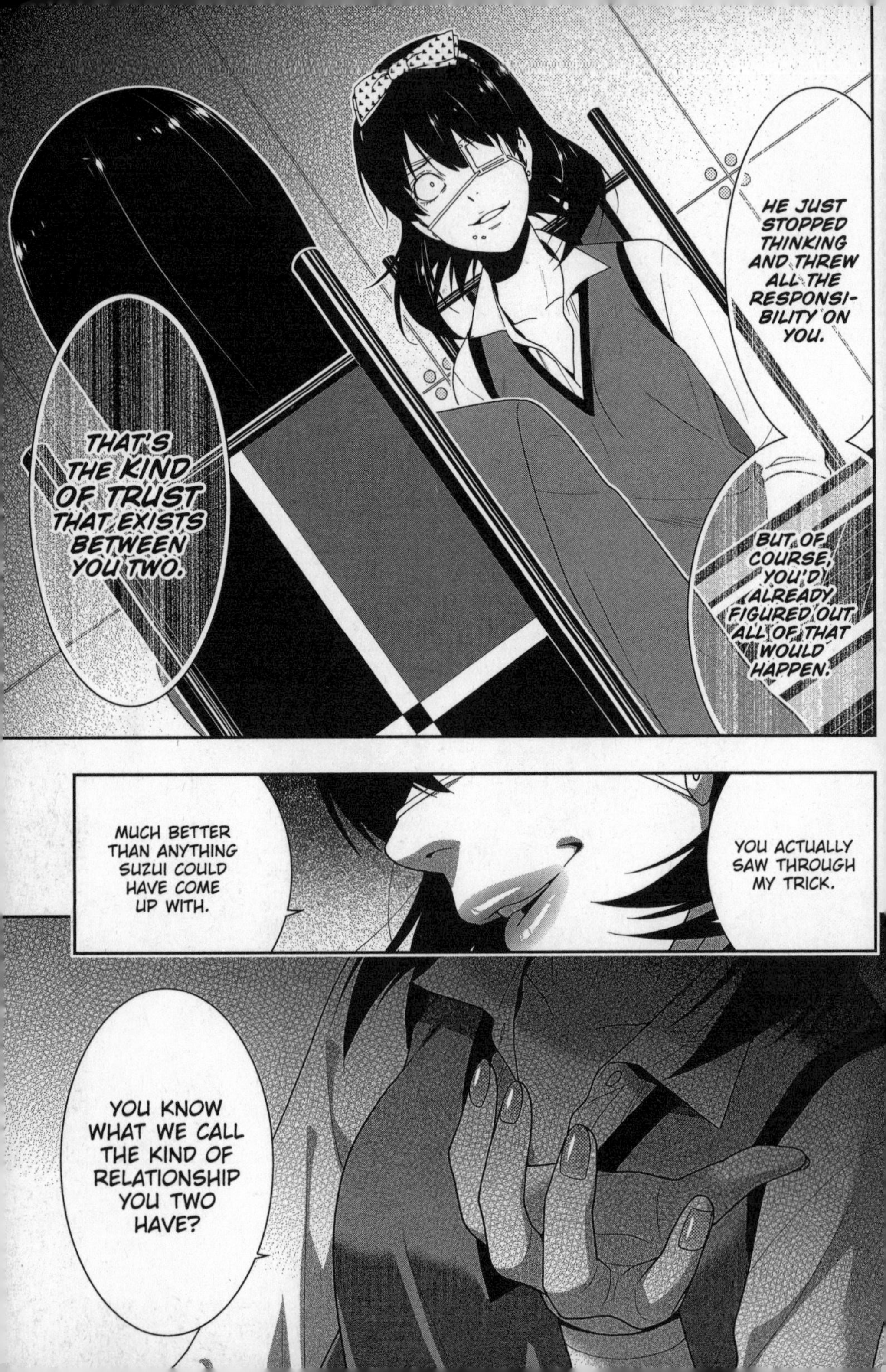
HE JUST STOPPED THINKING AND THREW ALL THE RESPONSIBILITY ON YOU.
BUT OF COURSE, YOU'D ALREADY FIGURED OUT ALL OF THAT WOULD HAPPEN.
THAT'S THE KIND OF TRUST THAT EXISTS BETWEEN YOU TWO.
YOU ACTUALLY SAW THROUGH MY TRICK.
MUCH BETTER THAN ANYTHING SUZUI COULD HAVE COME UP WITH.
YOU KNOW WHAT WE CALL THE KIND OF RELATIONSHIP YOU TWO HAVE?

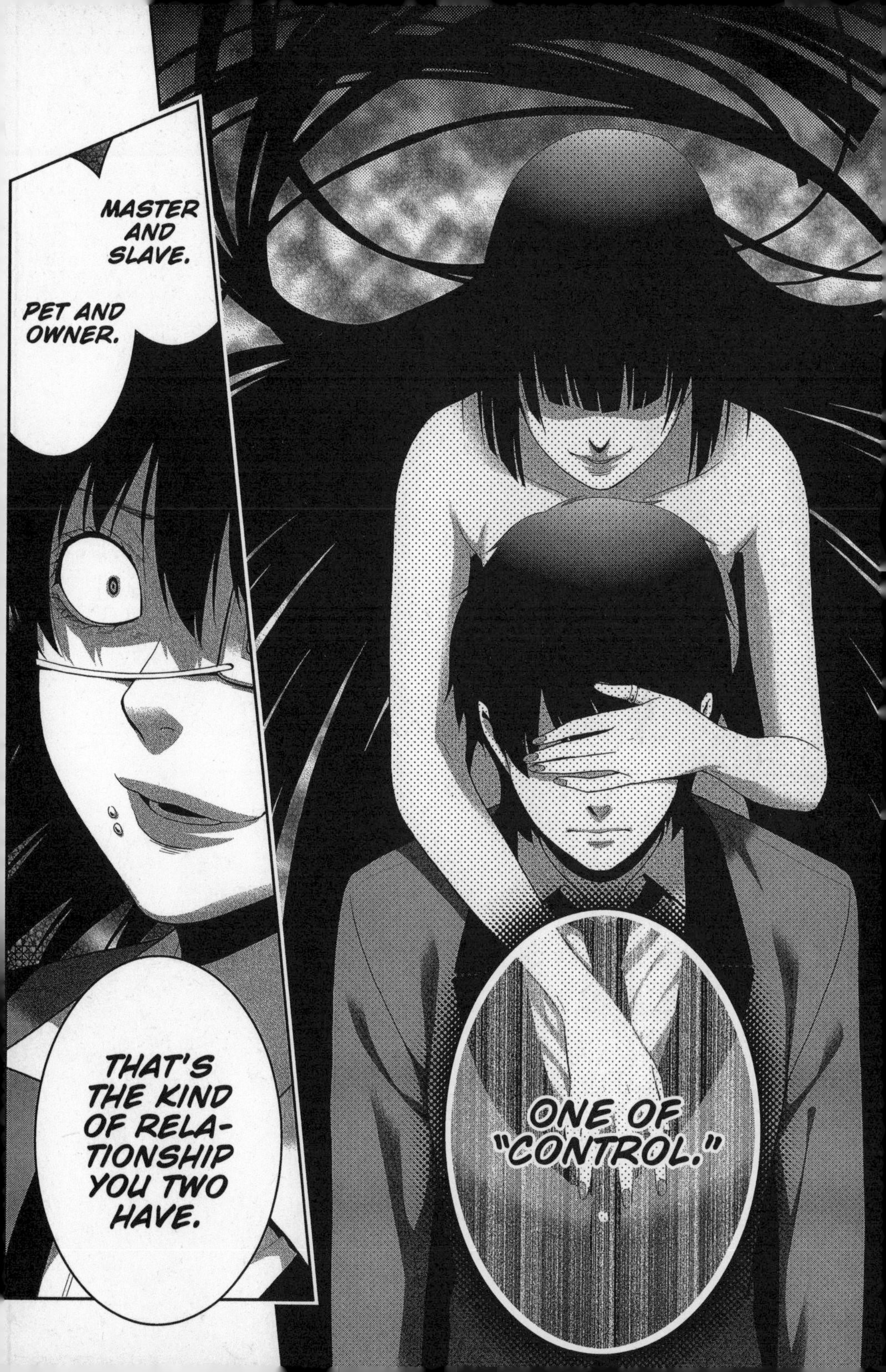
MASTER AND SLAVE.
PET AND OWNER.
THAT'S THE KIND OF RELA-TIONSHIP YOU TWO HAVE.
ONE OF "CONTROL."

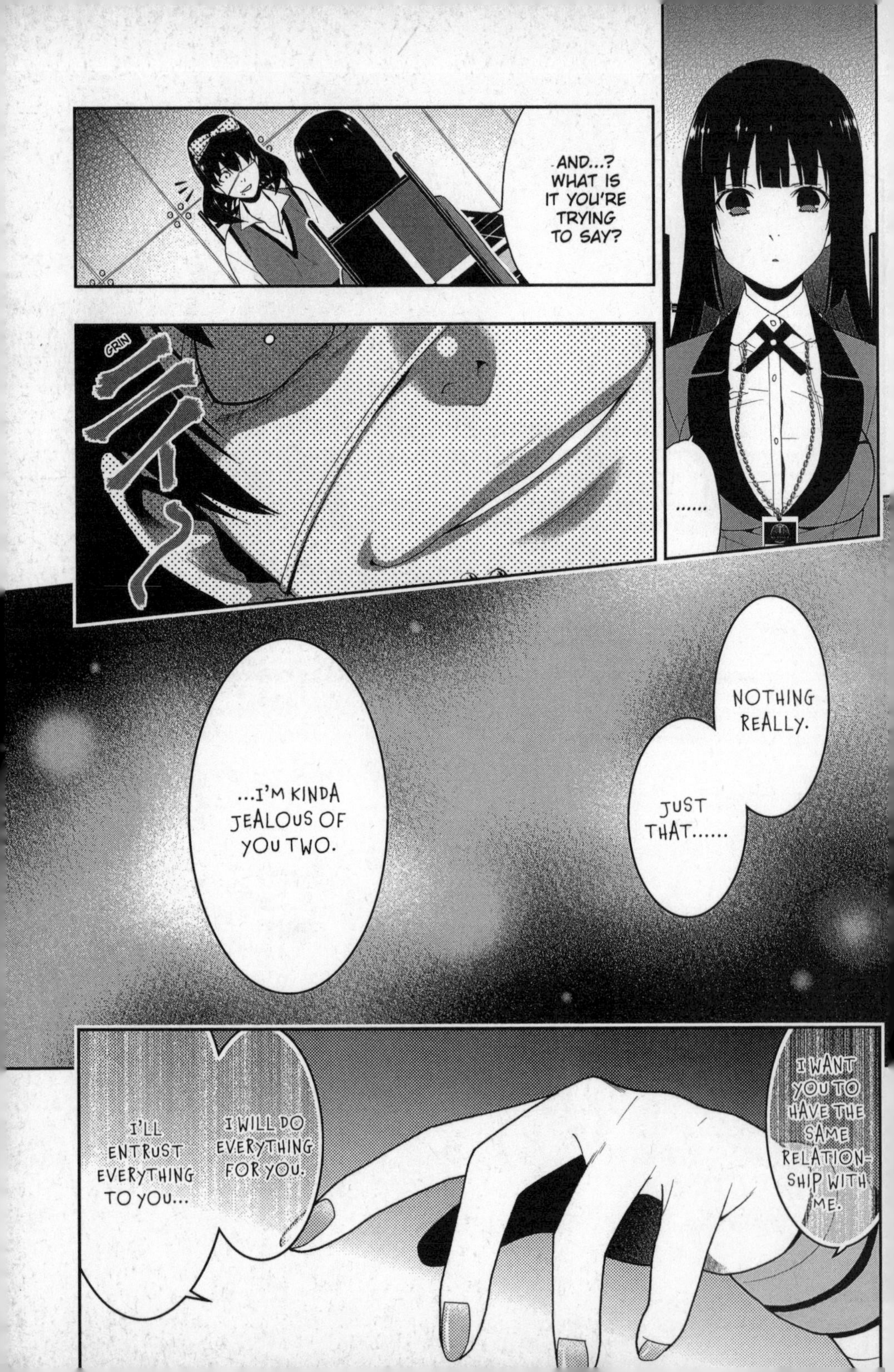
......
AND...? WHAT IS IT YOU'RE TRYING TO SAY?
GRIN
NOTHING REALLY.
JUST THAT......
...I'M KINDA JEALOUS OF YOU TWO.
I WANT YOU TO HAVE THE SAME RELATIONSHIP WITH ME.
I WILL DO EVERYTHING FOR YOU.
I'LL ENTRUST EVERYTHING TO YOU...

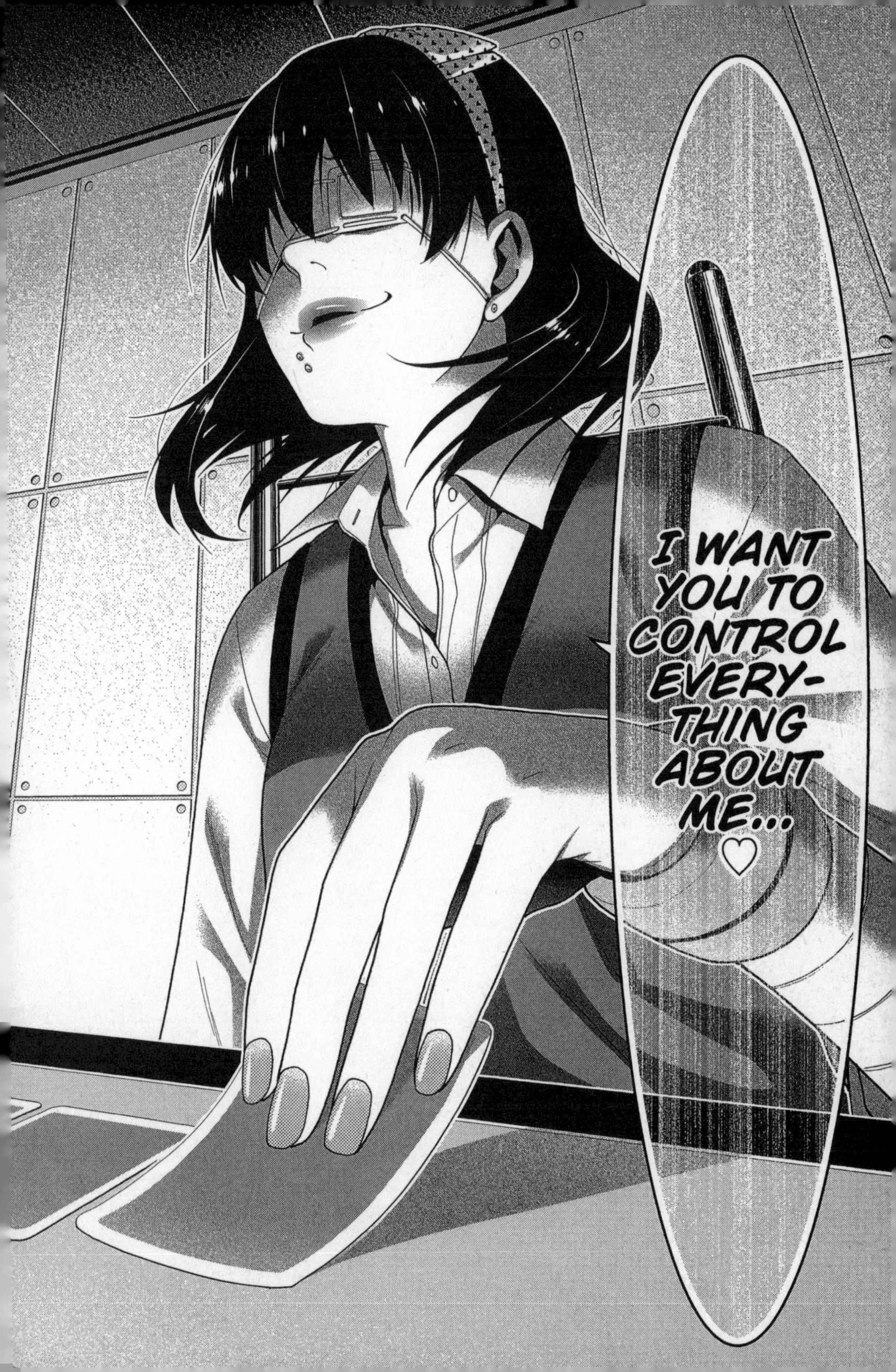
I WANT YOU TO CONTROL EVERY-THING ABOUT ME...♡

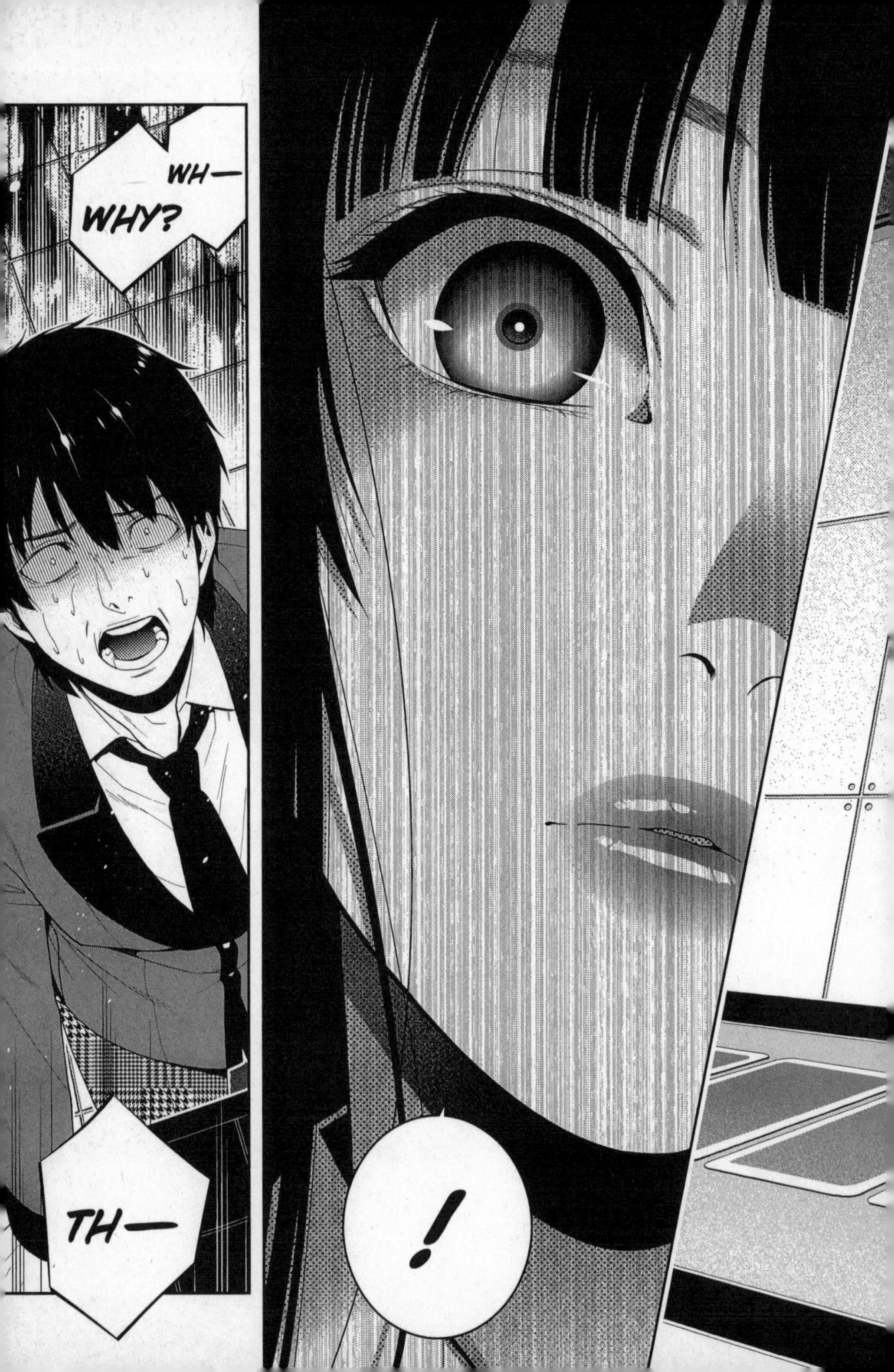
!
WH— WHY?
TH—

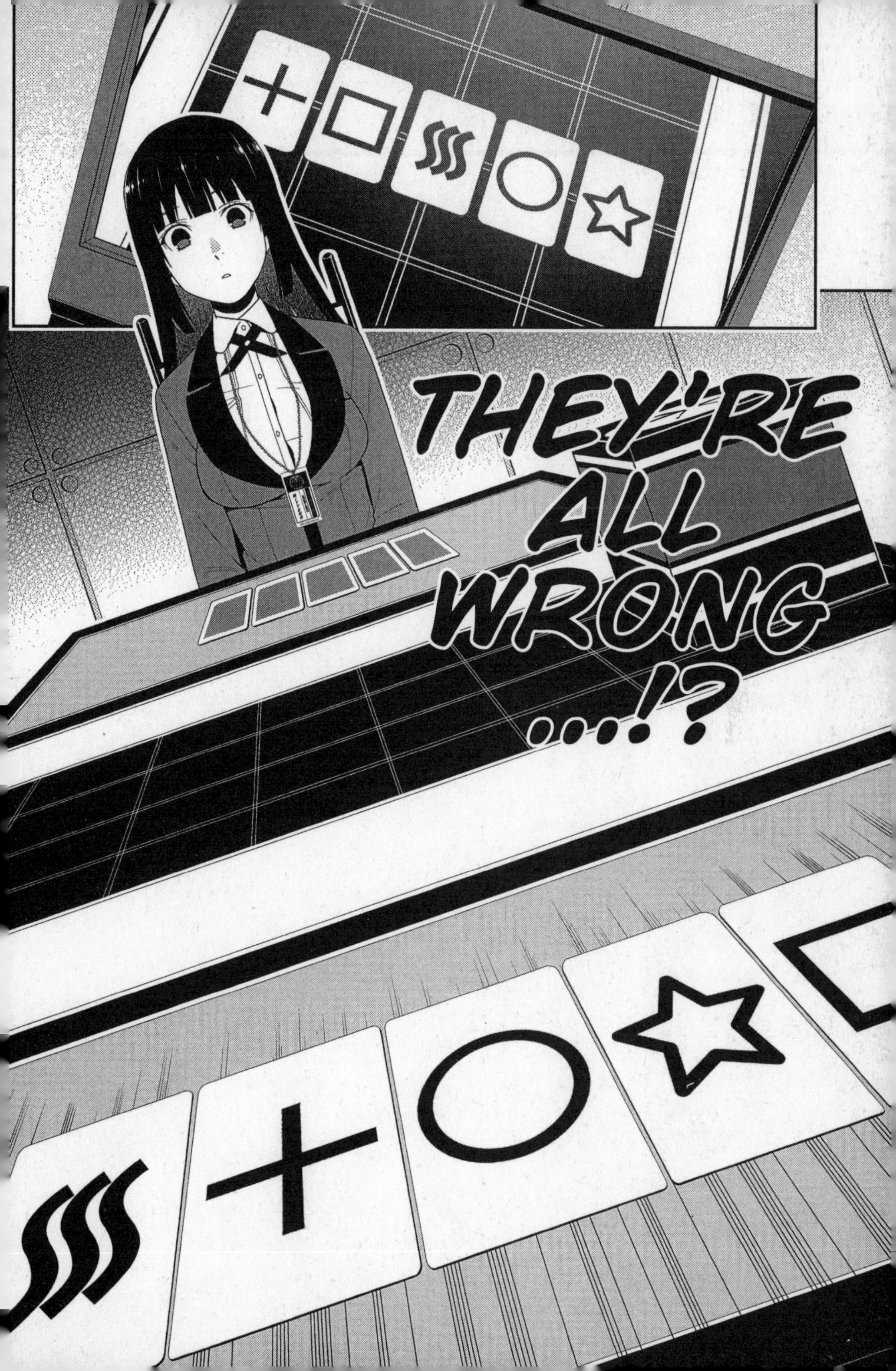
THEY'RE ALL WRONG ...!?

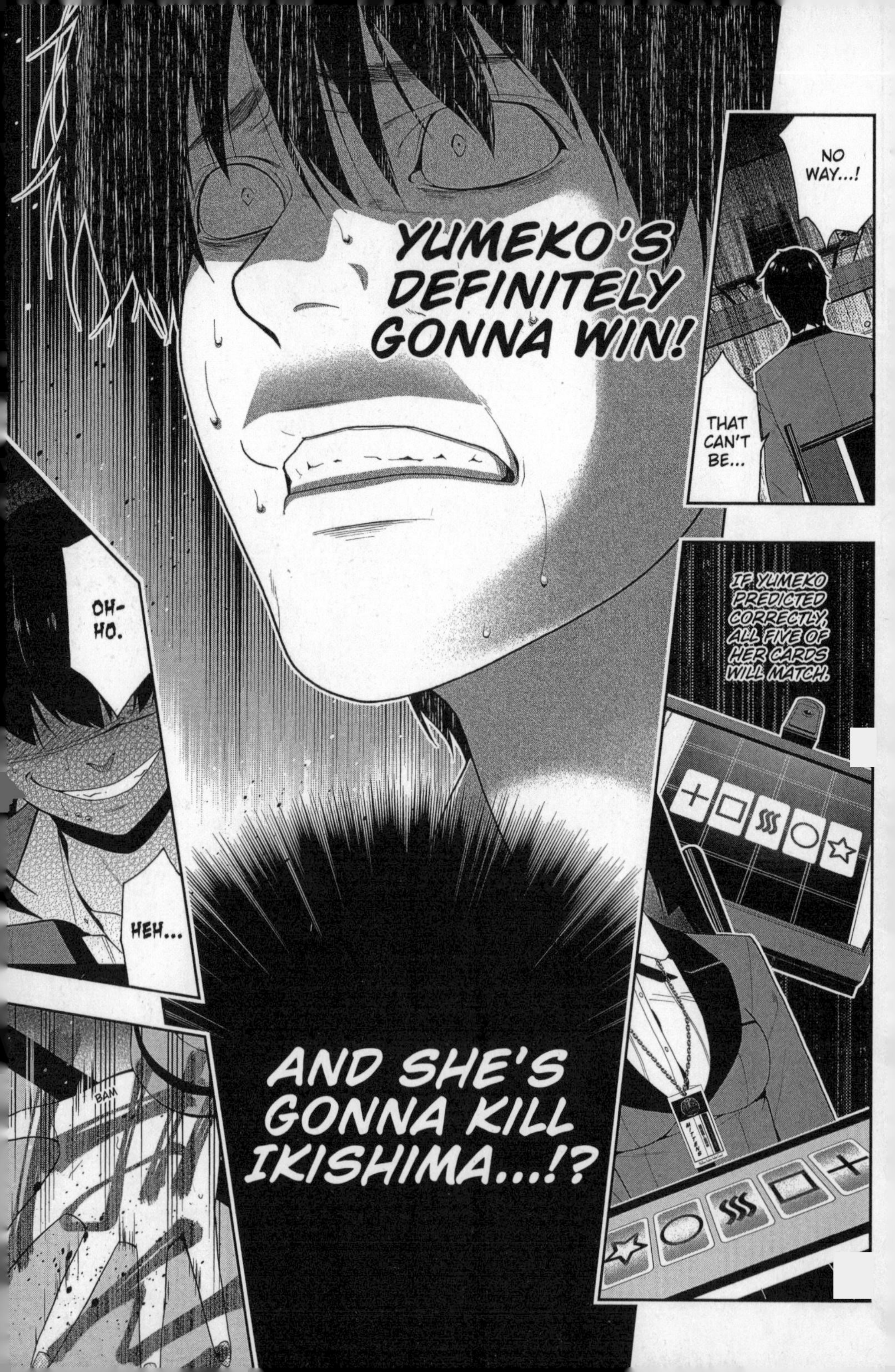
NO WAY...!
THAT CAN'T BE...
YUMEKO'S DEFINITELY GONNA WIN!
IF YUMEKO PREDICTED CORRECTLY, ALL FIVE OF HER CARDS WILL MATCH.
OH-HO.
HEH...
AND SHE'S GONNA KILL IKISHIMA...!?
BAM

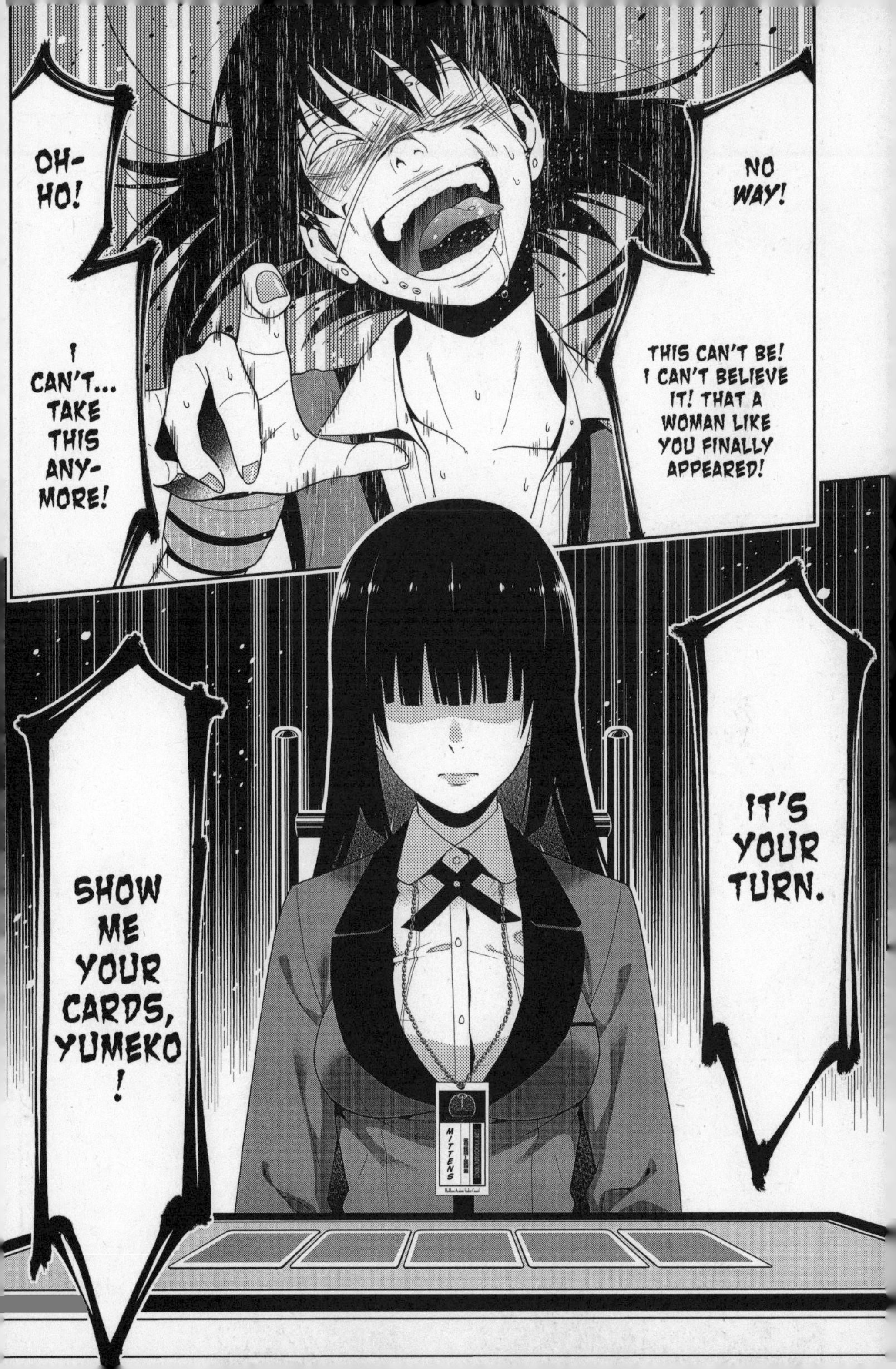
NO WAY!
OH-HO!
THIS CAN'T BE! I CAN'T BELIEVE IT! THAT A WOMAN LIKE YOU FINALLY APPEARED!
I CAN'T... TAKE THIS ANYMORE!
IT'S YOUR TURN.
SHOW ME YOUR CARDS, YUMEKO!
MITTENS

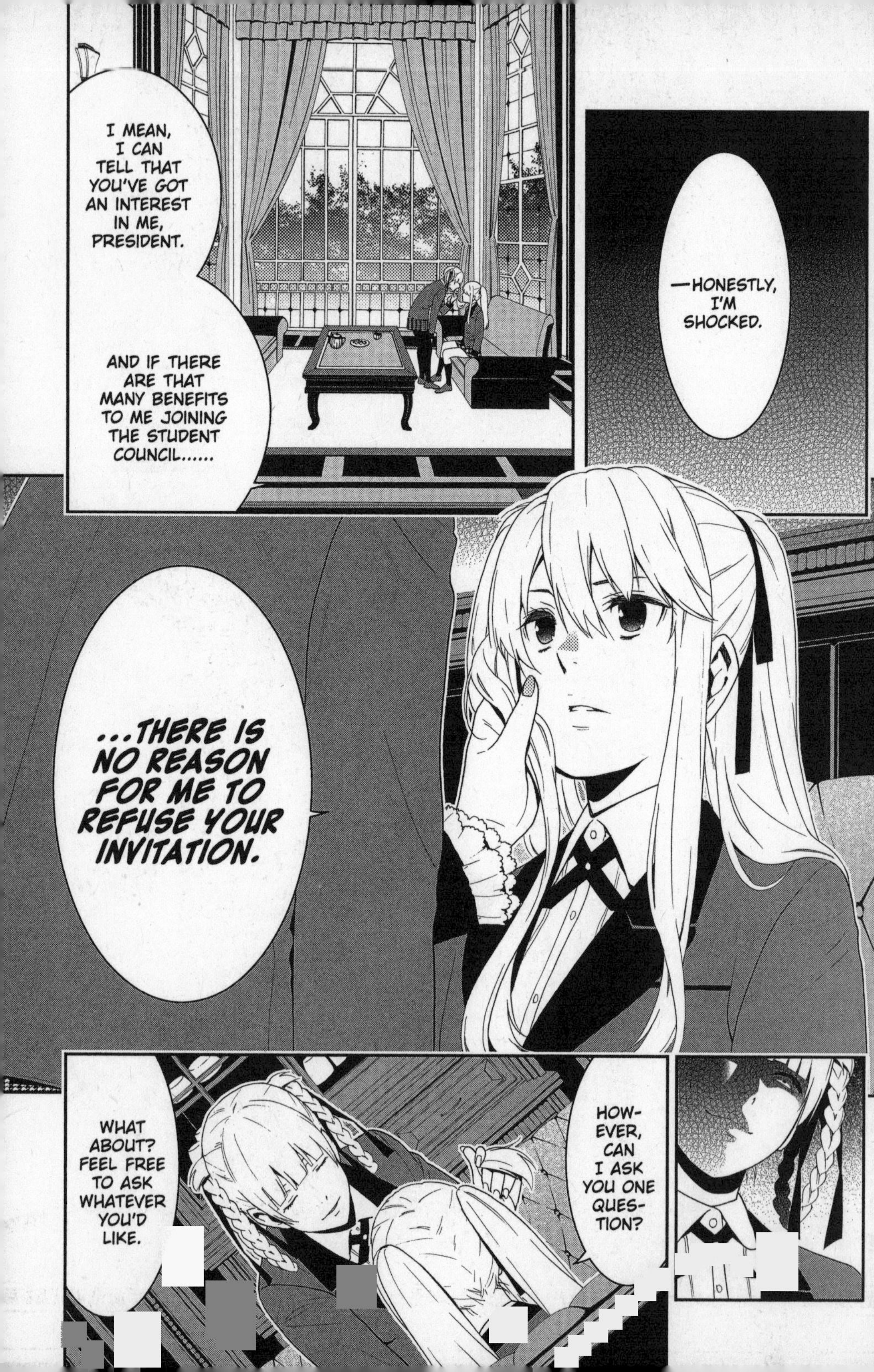
—HONESTLY, I'M SHOCKED.
I MEAN, I CAN TELL THAT YOU'VE GOT AN INTEREST IN ME, PRESIDENT.
AND IF THERE ARE THAT MANY BENEFITS TO ME JOINING THE STUDENT COUNCIL......
...THERE IS NO REASON FOR ME TO REFUSE YOUR INVITATION.
HOW-EVER, CAN I ASK YOU ONE QUES-TION?
WHAT ABOUT? FEEL FREE TO ASK WHATEVER YOU'D LIKE.

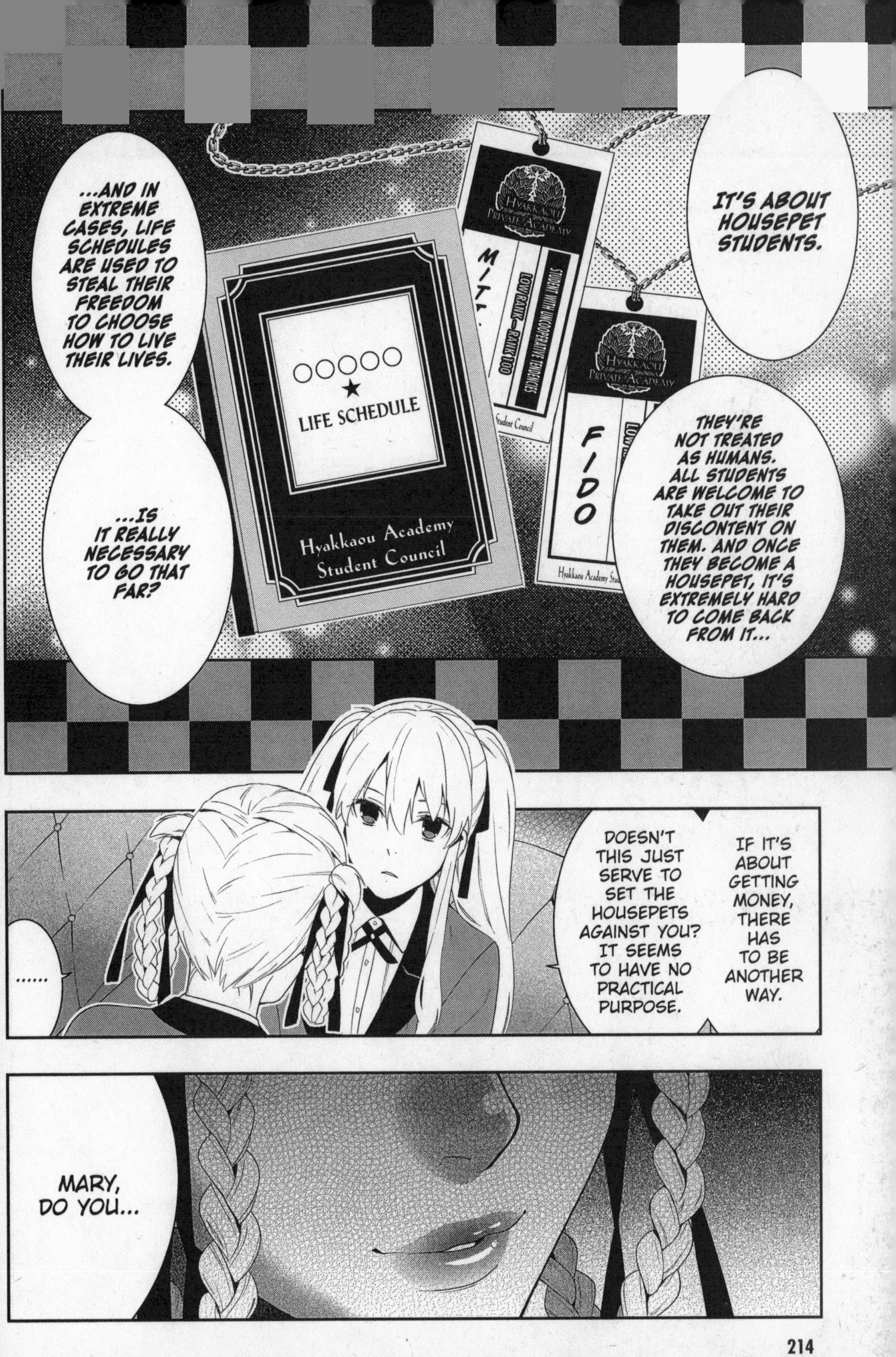
IT'S ABOUT HOUSEPET STUDENTS.
THEY'RE NOT TREATED AS HUMANS. ALL STUDENTS ARE WELCOME TO TAKE OUT THEIR DISCONTENT ON THEM. AND ONCE THEY BECOME A HOUSEPET, IT'S EXTREMELY HARD TO COME BACK FROM IT...
HYAKKAOU PRIVATE ACADEMY
STUDENT WITH UNCOOPERATIVE TENDENCIES
LOW RANK—RANK 100
Student Council
FIDO
LIFE SCHEDULE
Hyakkaou Academy Student Council
...AND IN EXTREME CASES, LIFE SCHEDULES ARE USED TO STEAL THEIR FREEDOM TO CHOOSE HOW TO LIVE THEIR LIVES.
...IS IT REALLY NECESSARY TO GO THAT FAR?
IF IT'S ABOUT GETTING MONEY, THERE HAS TO BE ANOTHER WAY.
DOESN'T THIS JUST SERVE TO SET THE HOUSEPETS AGAINST YOU? IT SEEMS TO HAVE NO PRACTICAL PURPOSE.
......
MARY, DO YOU...

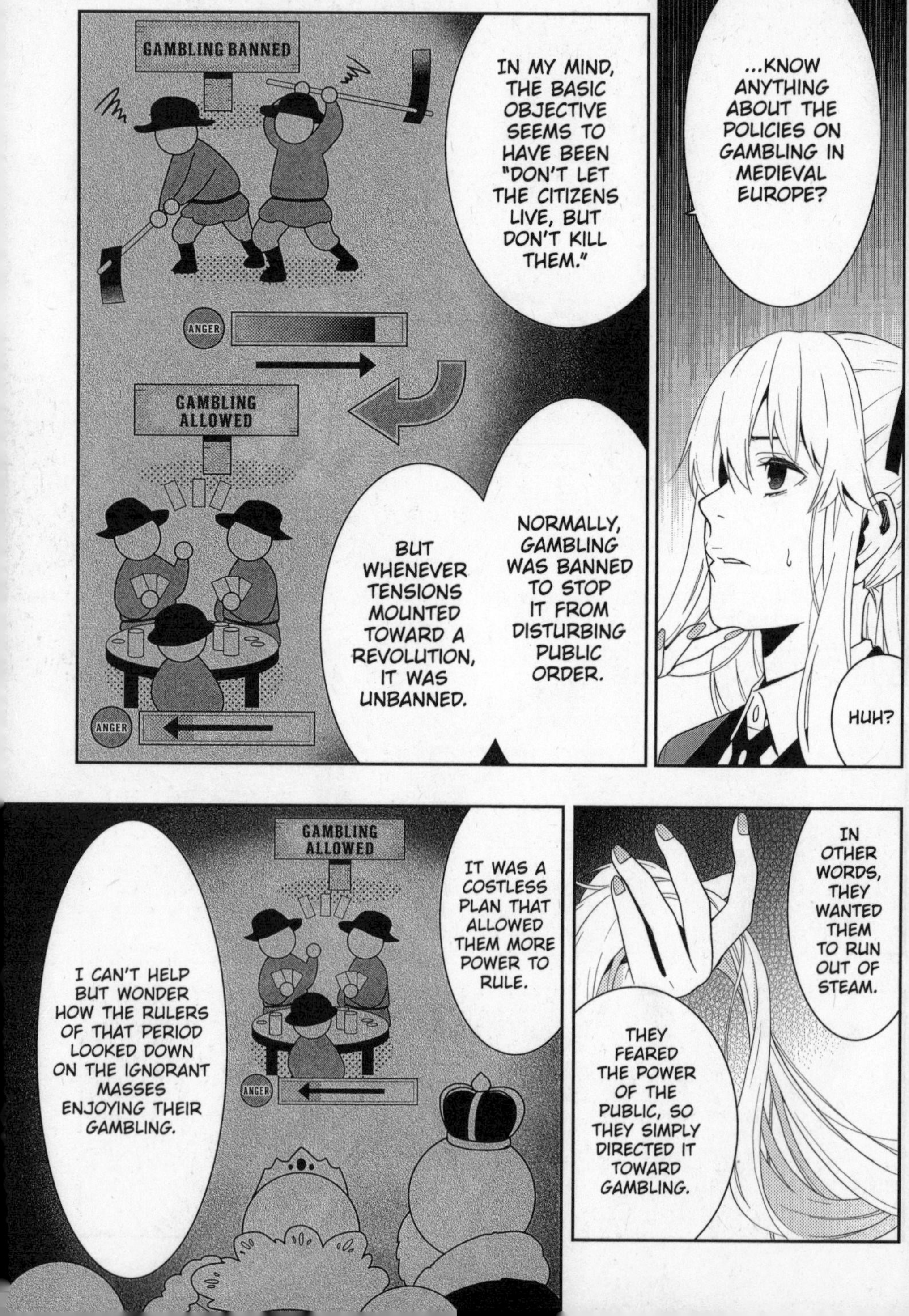
...KNOW ANYTHING ABOUT THE POLICIES ON GAMBLING IN MEDIEVAL EUROPE?
HUH?
IN MY MIND, THE BASIC OBJECTIVE SEEMS TO HAVE BEEN "DON'T LET THE CITIZENS LIVE, BUT DON'T KILL THEM."
GAMBLING BANNED
ANGER
GAMBLING ALLOWED
ANGER
NORMALLY, GAMBLING WAS BANNED TO STOP IT FROM DISTURBING PUBLIC ORDER.
BUT WHENEVER TENSIONS MOUNTED TOWARD A REVOLUTION, IT WAS UNBANNED.
IN OTHER WORDS, THEY WANTED THEM TO RUN OUT OF STEAM.
THEY FEARED THE POWER OF THE PUBLIC, SO THEY SIMPLY DIRECTED IT TOWARD GAMBLING.
IT WAS A COSTLESS PLAN THAT ALLOWED THEM MORE POWER TO RULE.
GAMBLING ALLOWED
ANGER
I CAN'T HELP BUT WONDER HOW THE RULERS OF THAT PERIOD LOOKED DOWN ON THE IGNORANT MASSES ENJOYING THEIR GAMBLING.

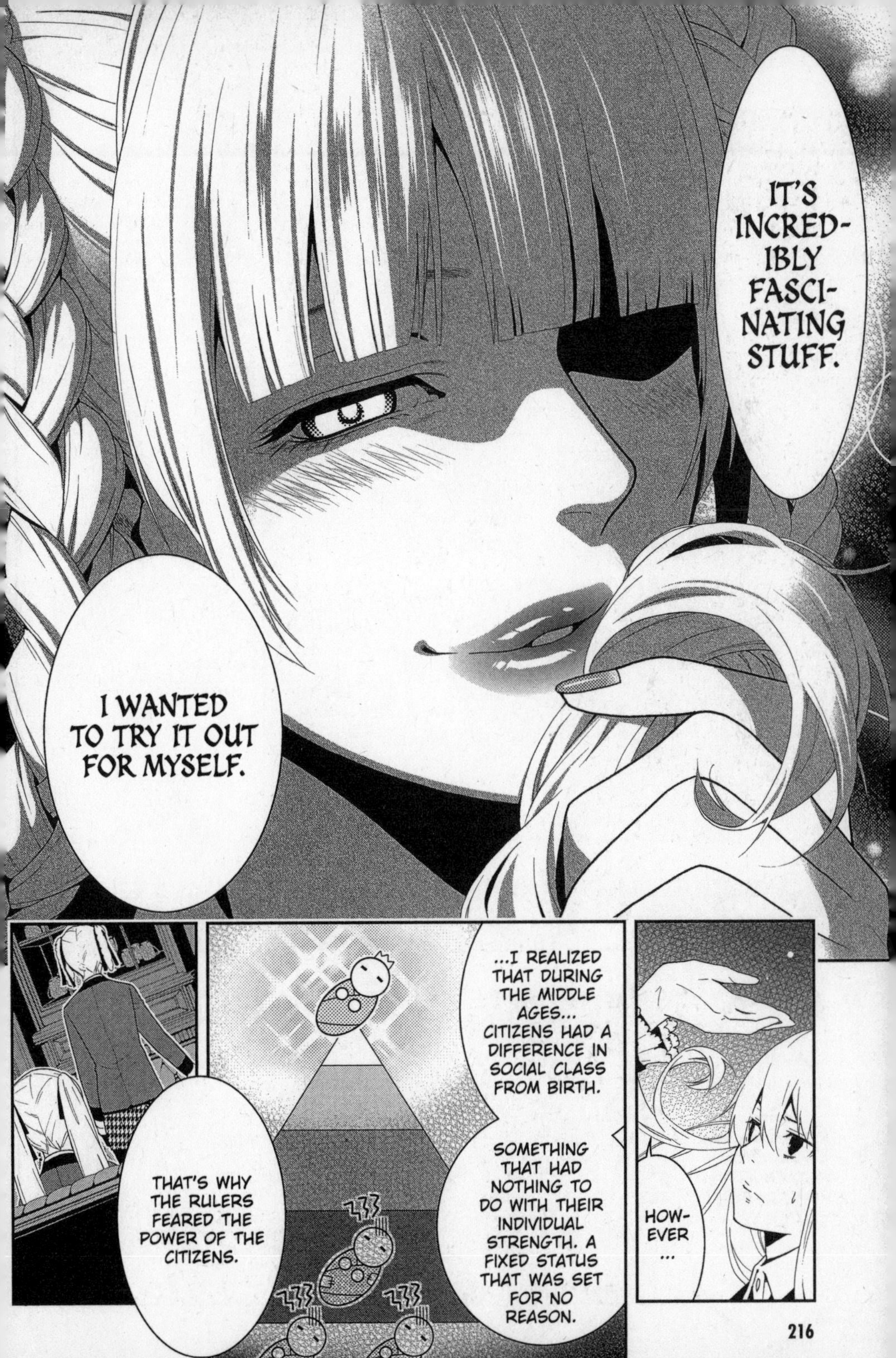
IT'S INCRED-IBLY FASCI-NATING STUFF.
I WANTED TO TRY IT OUT FOR MYSELF.
HOW-EVER ...
...I REALIZED THAT DURING THE MIDDLE AGES... CITIZENS HAD A DIFFERENCE IN SOCIAL CLASS FROM BIRTH.
SOMETHING THAT HAD NOTHING TO DO WITH THEIR INDIVIDUAL STRENGTH. A FIXED STATUS THAT WAS SET FOR NO REASON.
THAT'S WHY THE RULERS FEARED THE POWER OF THE CITIZENS.

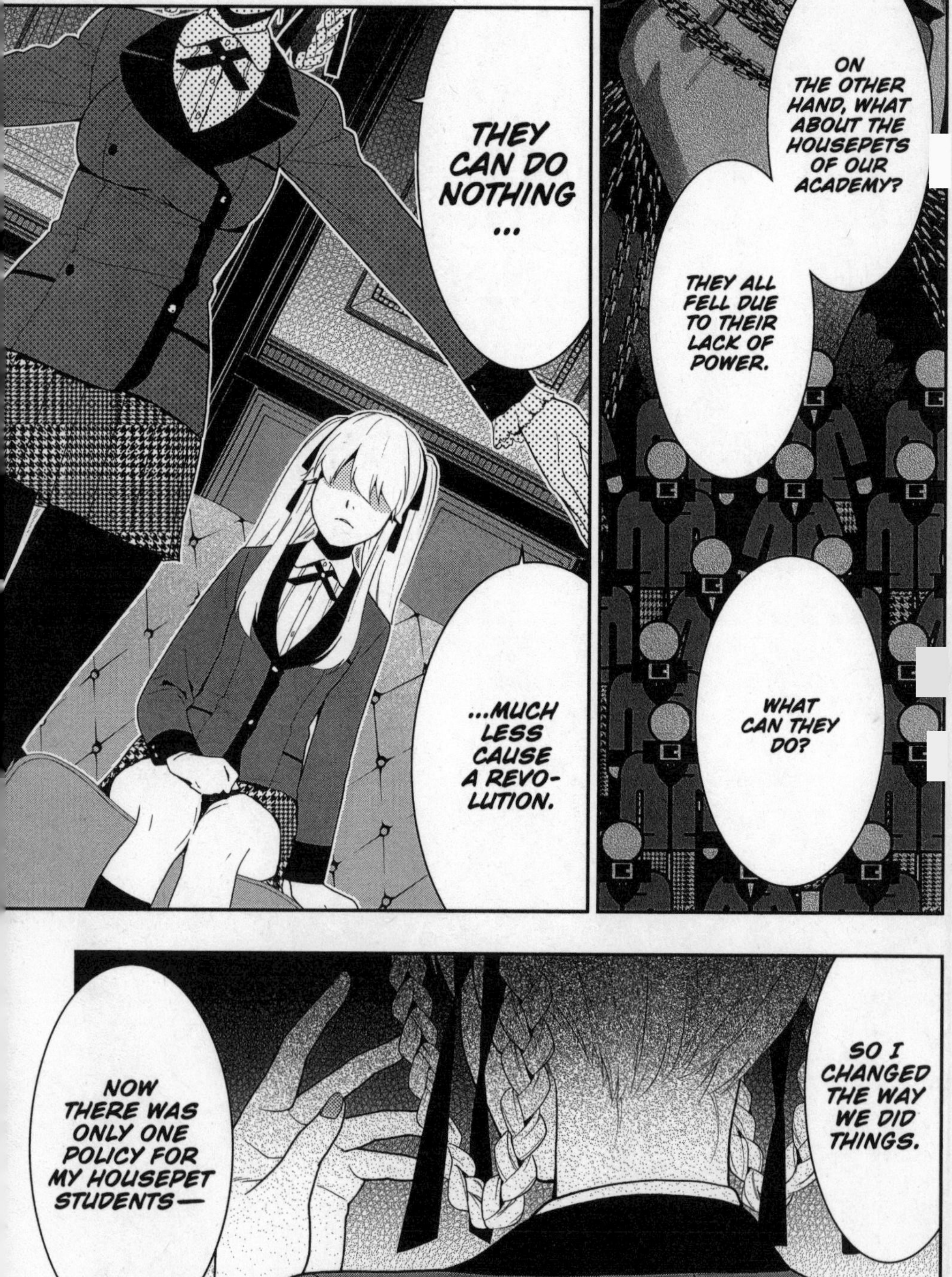
ON THE OTHER HAND, WHAT ABOUT THE HOUSEPETS OF OUR ACADEMY?
THEY ALL FELL DUE TO THEIR LACK OF POWER.
WHAT CAN THEY DO?
THEY CAN DO NOTHING ...
...MUCH LESS CAUSE A REVO-LUTION.
SO I CHANGED THE WAY WE DID THINGS.
NOW THERE WAS ONLY ONE POLICY FOR MY HOUSEPET STUDENTS—

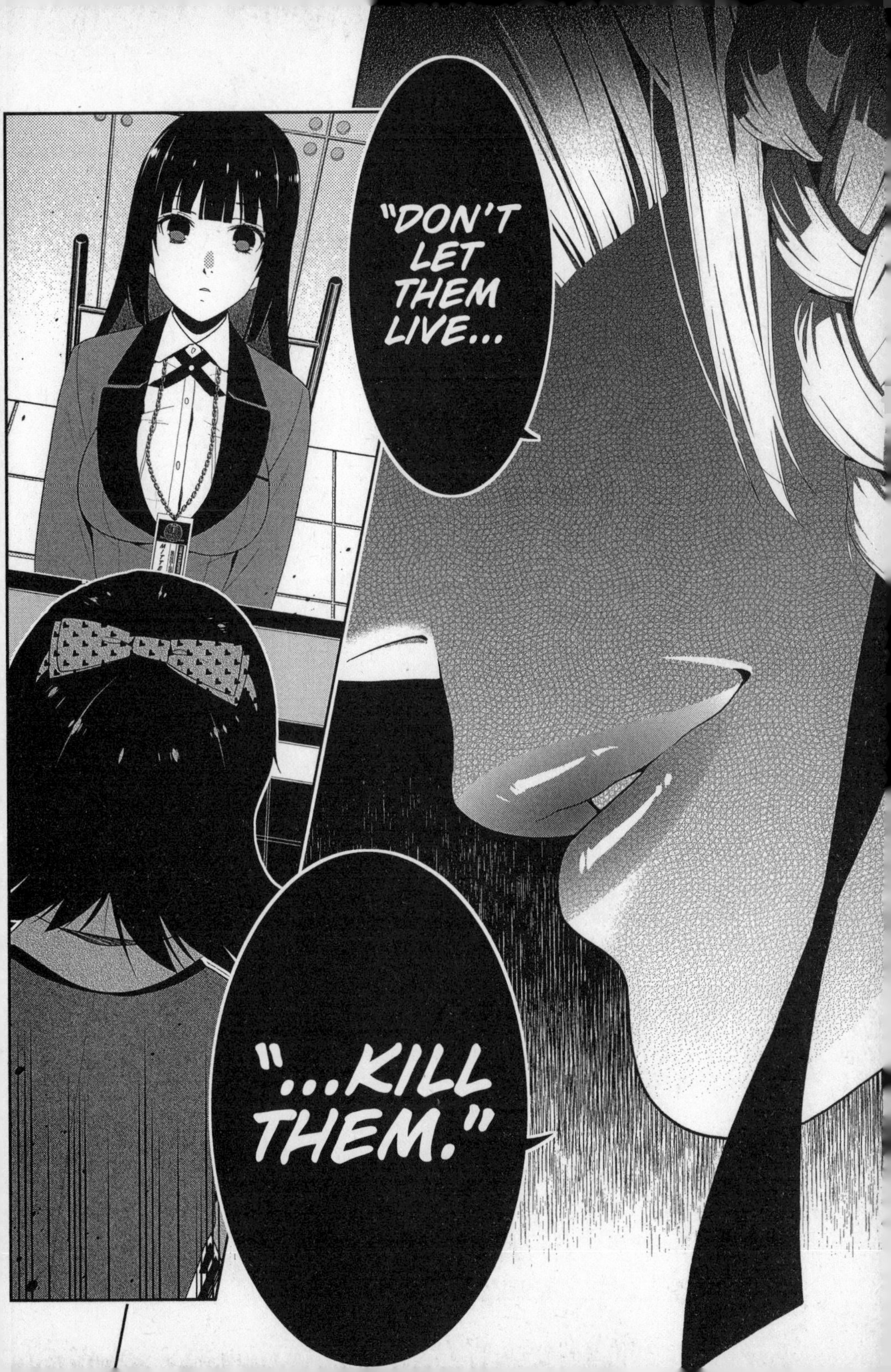
"DON'T LET THEM LIVE...
"...KILL THEM."

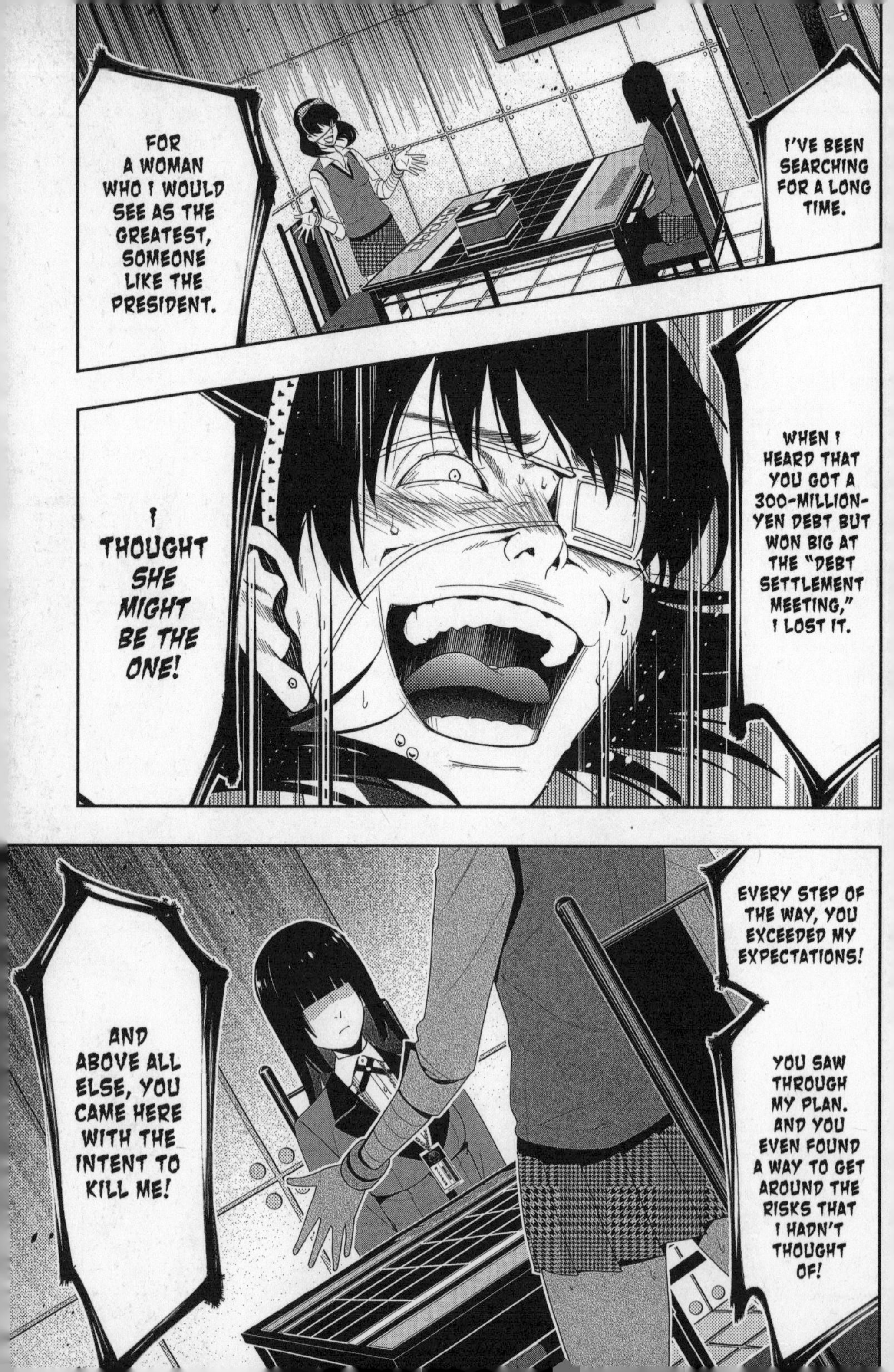
I'VE BEEN SEARCHING FOR A LONG TIME.
FOR A WOMAN WHO I WOULD SEE AS THE GREATEST, SOMEONE LIKE THE PRESIDENT.
WHEN I HEARD THAT YOU GOT A 300-MILLION-YEN DEBT BUT WON BIG AT THE "DEBT SETTLEMENT MEETING," I LOST IT.
I THOUGHT *SHE MIGHT* BE THE ONE!
EVERY STEP OF THE WAY, YOU EXCEEDED MY EXPECTATIONS!
YOU SAW THROUGH MY PLAN. AND YOU EVEN FOUND A WAY TO GET AROUND THE RISKS THAT I HADN'T THOUGHT OF!
AND ABOVE ALL ELSE, YOU CAME HERE WITH THE INTENT TO KILL ME!

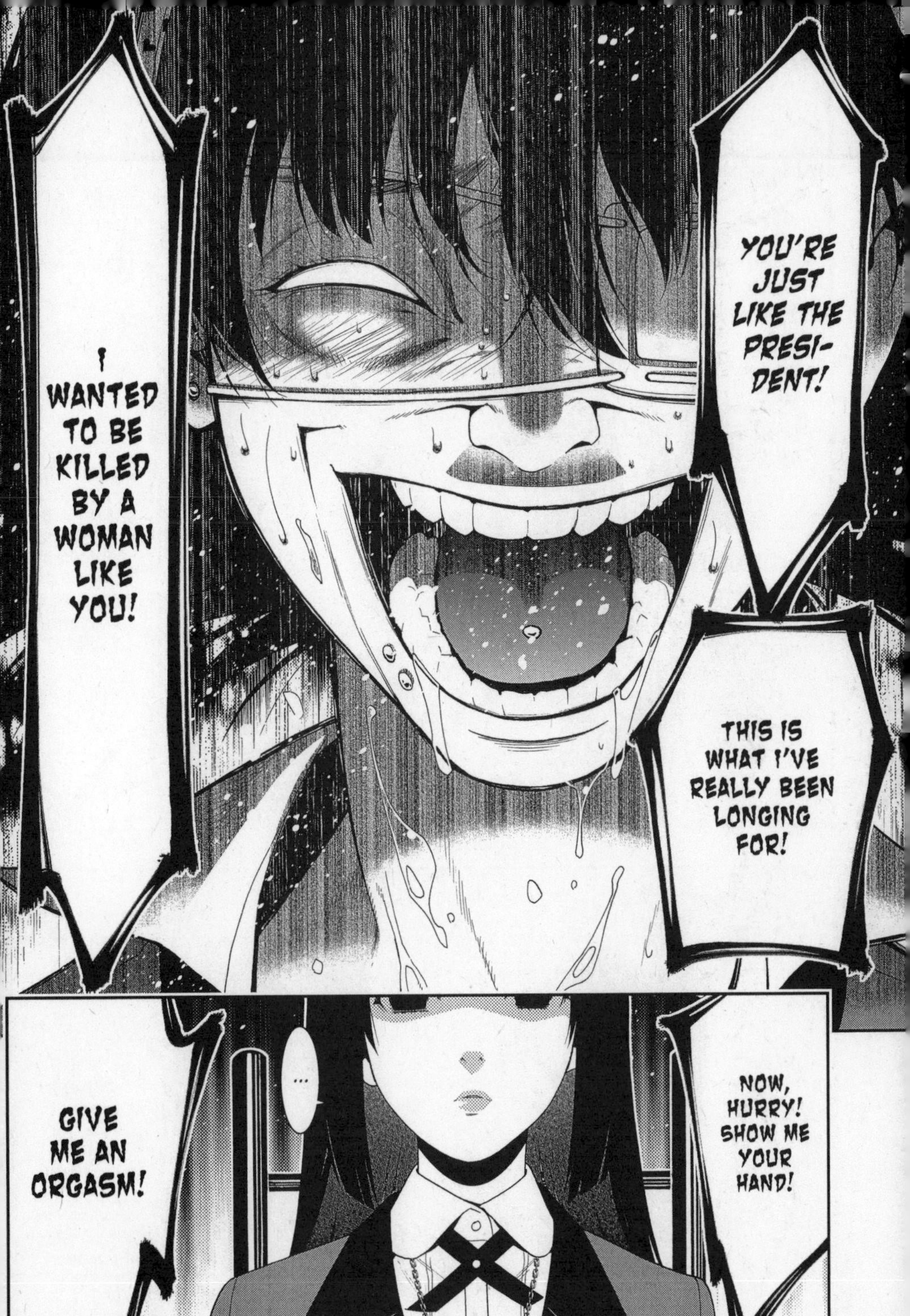
YOU'RE JUST LIKE THE PRESIDENT!
THIS IS WHAT I'VE REALLY BEEN LONGING FOR!
I WANTED TO BE KILLED BY A WOMAN LIKE YOU!
NOW, HURRY! SHOW ME YOUR HAND!
...
GIVE ME AN ORGASM!

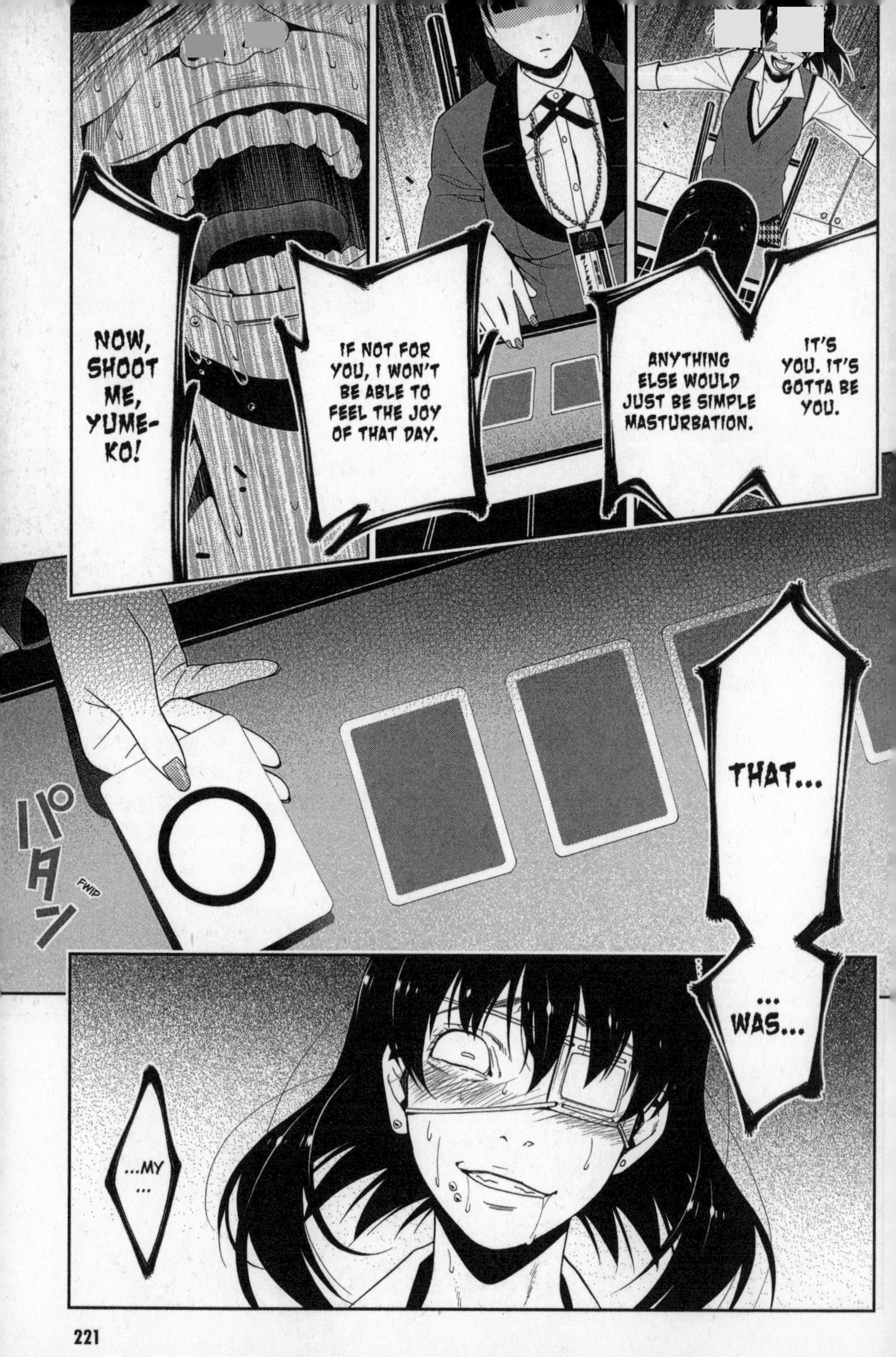
IT'S YOU. IT'S GOTTA BE YOU.
ANYTHING ELSE WOULD JUST BE SIMPLE MASTURBATION.
IF NOT FOR YOU, I WON'T BE ABLE TO FEEL THE JOY OF THAT DAY.
NOW, SHOOT ME, YUME-KO!
THAT...
...WAS...
パタン
FWIP
...MY
...

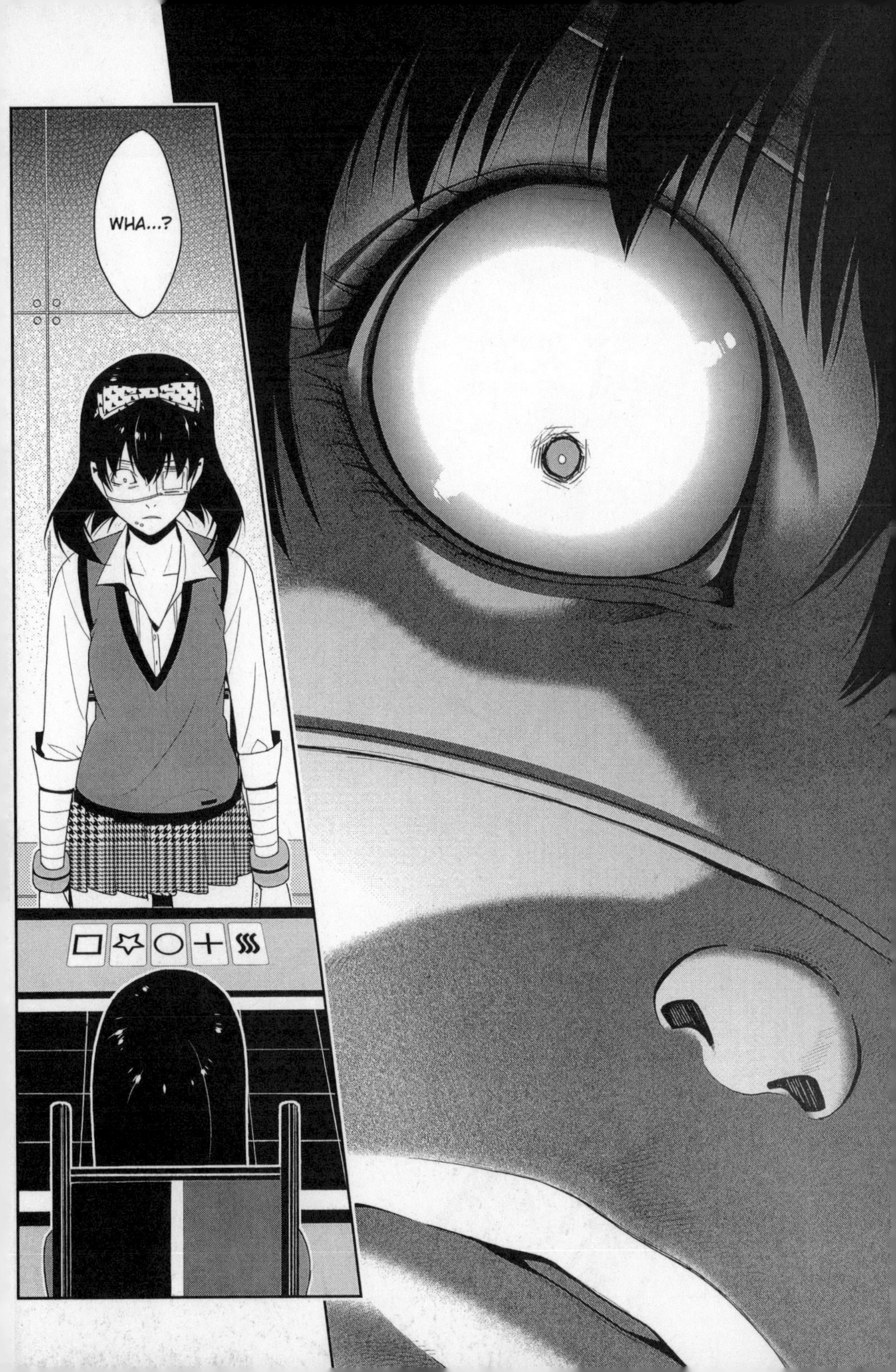
WHA...?

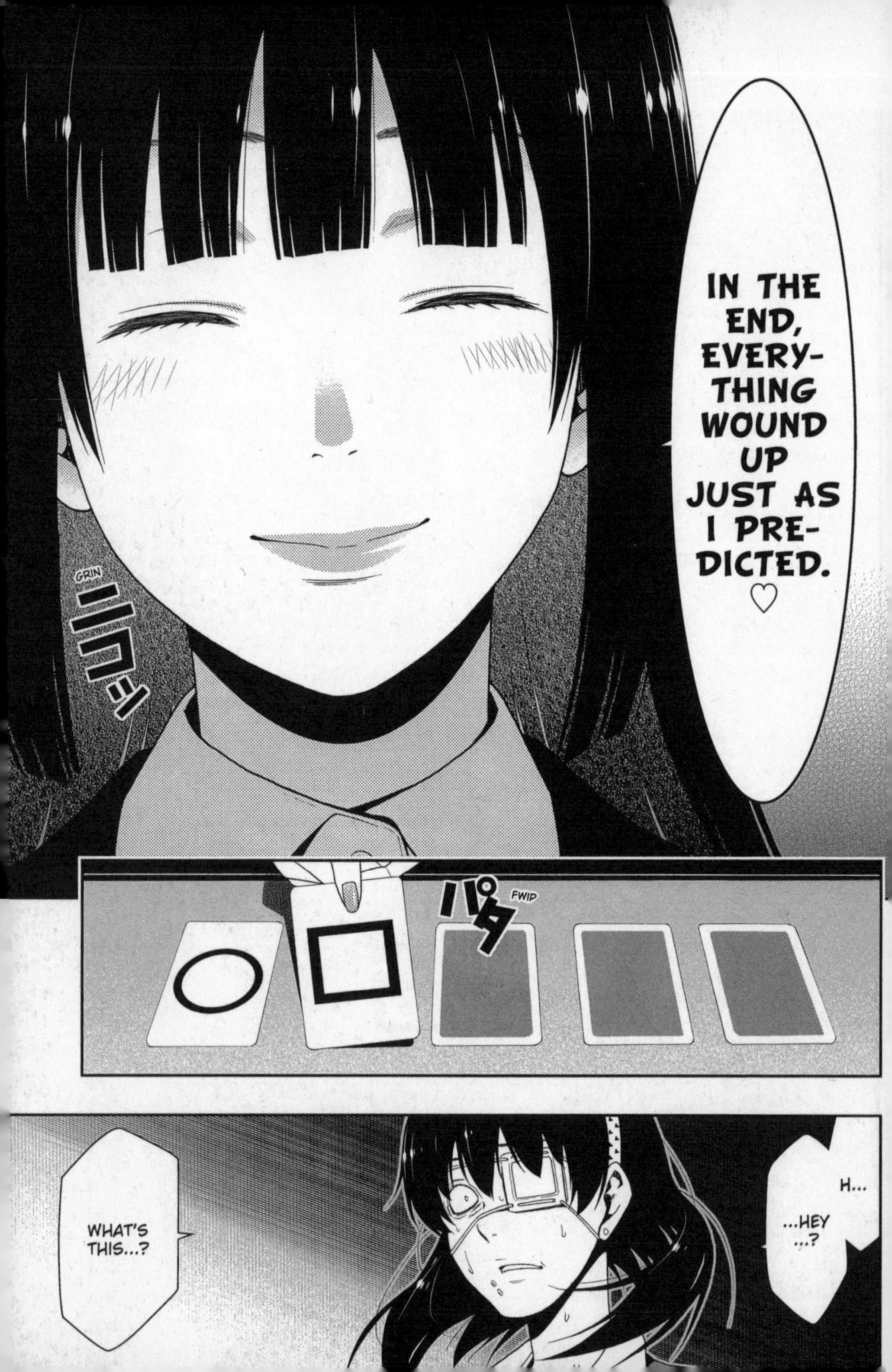
IN THE END, EVERYTHING WOUND UP JUST AS I PREDICTED. ♡
GRIN
ニコッ
パタ
FWIP
H...
...HEY ...?
WHAT'S THIS...?

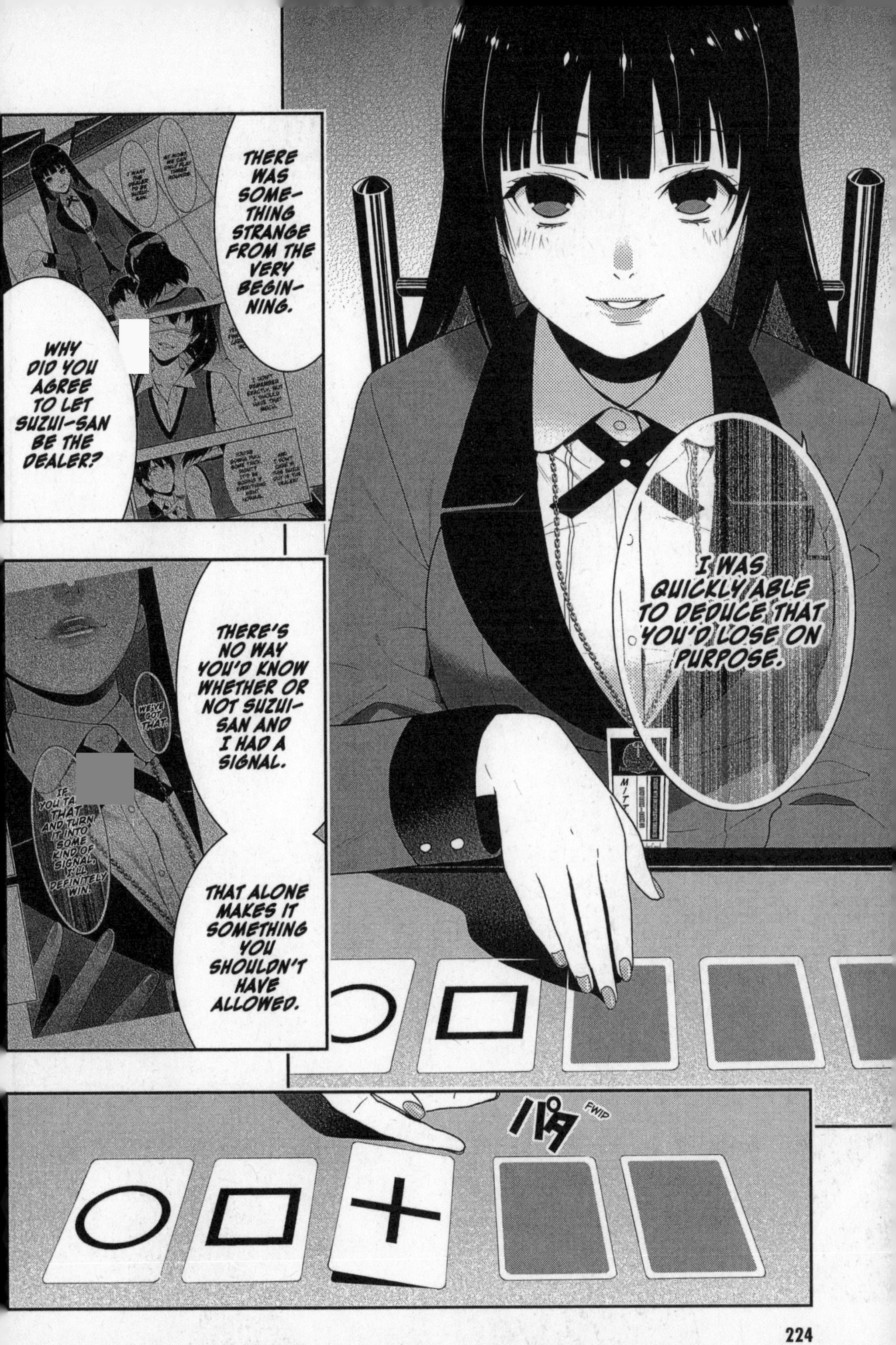

I WAS QUICKLY ABLE TO DEDUCE THAT YOU'D LOSE ON PURPOSE.
THERE WAS SOMETHING STRANGE FROM THE VERY BEGINNING.
WHY DID YOU AGREE TO LET SUZUI-SAN BE THE DEALER?
THERE'S NO WAY YOU'D KNOW WHETHER OR NOT SUZUI-SAN AND I HAD A SIGNAL.
THAT ALONE MAKES IT SOMETHING YOU SHOULDN'T HAVE ALLOWED.
WE'VE GOT THAT.
IF YOU TA THAT AND TURN IT INTO SOME KIND OF SIGNAL, I'LL DEFINITELY WIN.
パタ
FWIP

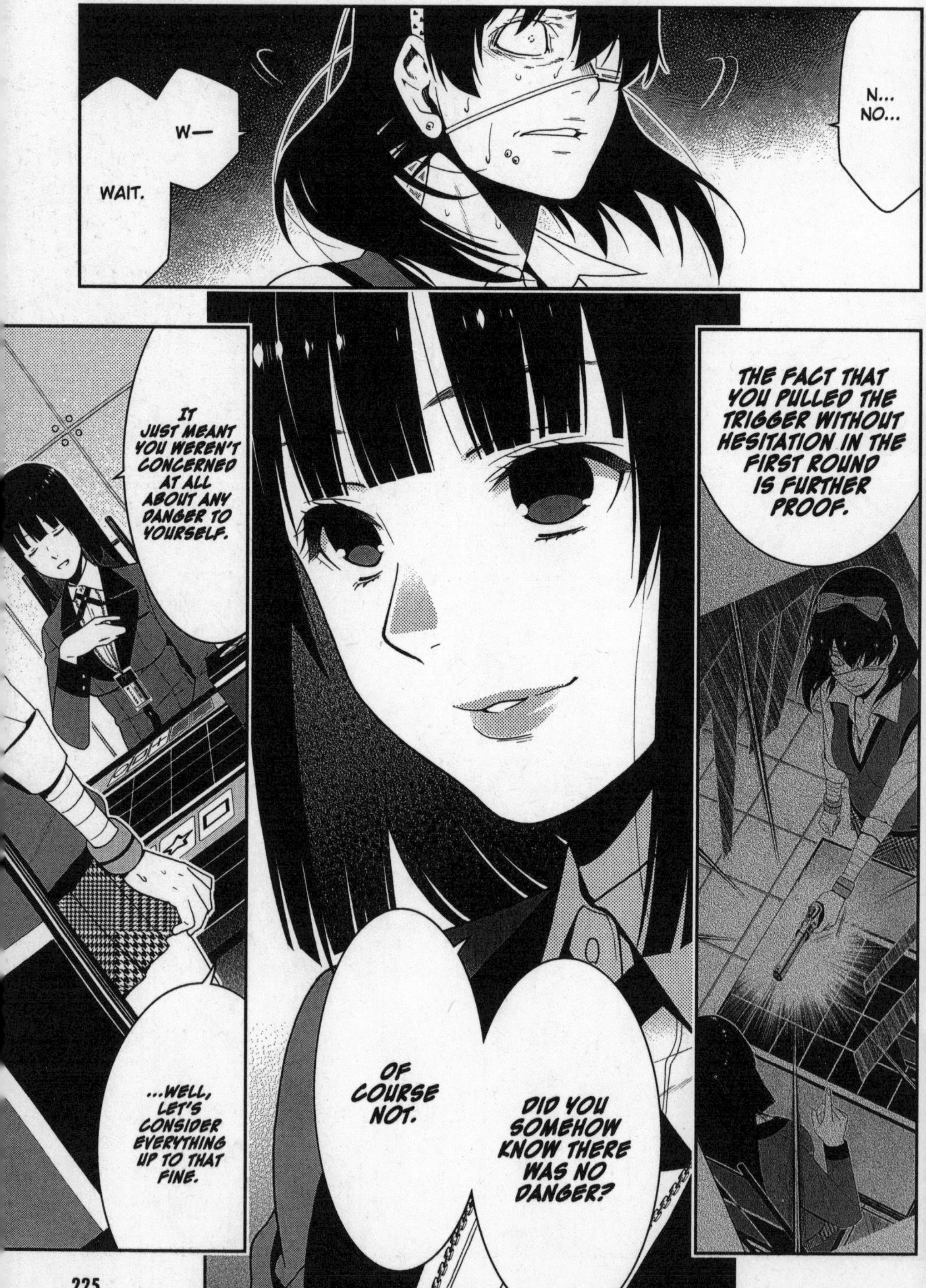
N... NO...
W—
WAIT.
THE FACT THAT YOU PULLED THE TRIGGER WITHOUT HESITATION IN THE FIRST ROUND IS FURTHER PROOF.
DID YOU SOMEHOW KNOW THERE WAS NO DANGER?
OF COURSE NOT.
IT JUST MEANT YOU WEREN'T CONCERNED AT ALL ABOUT ANY DANGER TO YOURSELF.
...WELL, LET'S CONSIDER EVERYTHING UP TO THAT FINE.

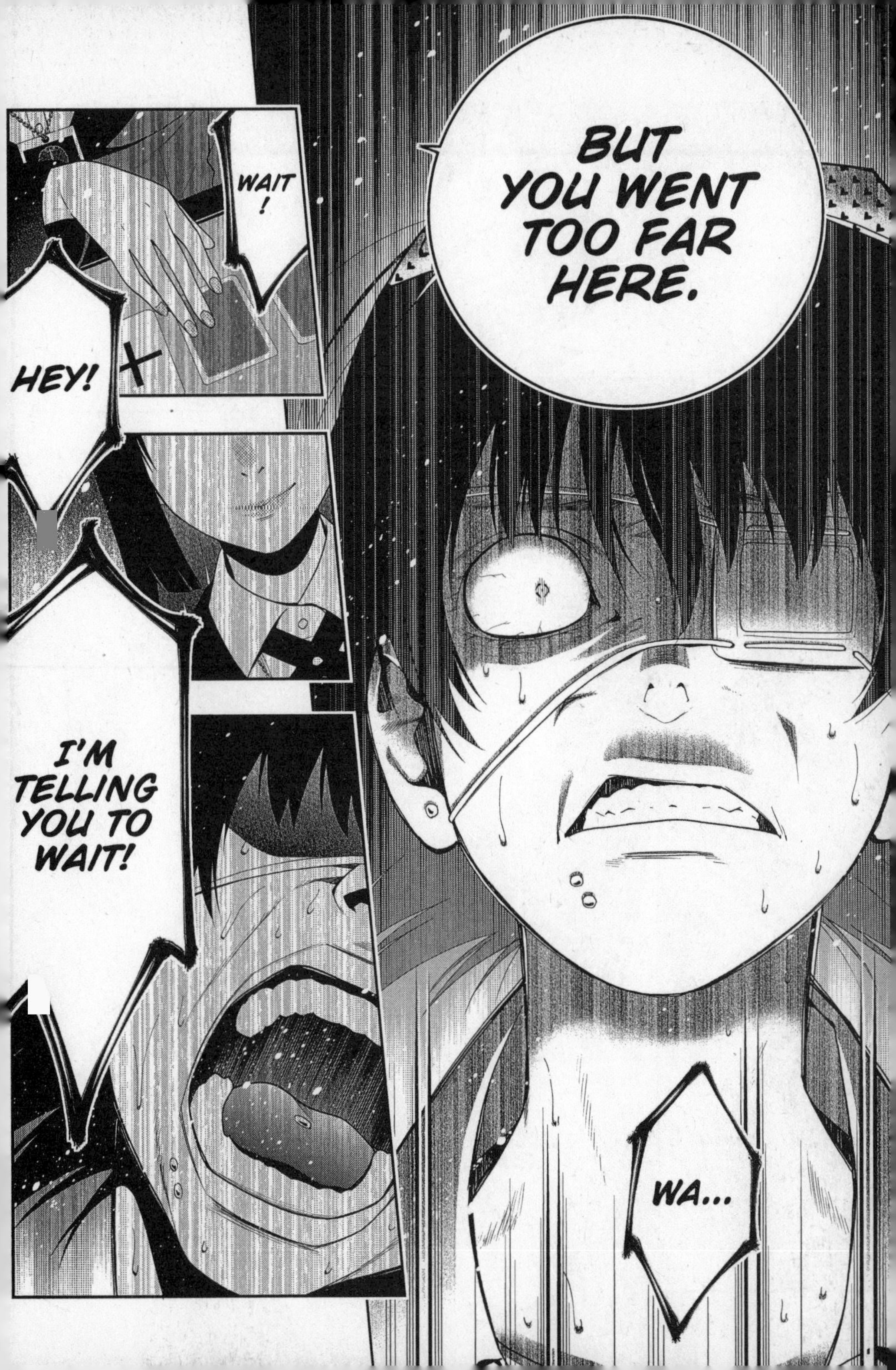
BUT YOU WENT TOO FAR HERE.
WA...
WAIT!
HEY!
I'M TELLING YOU TO WAIT!

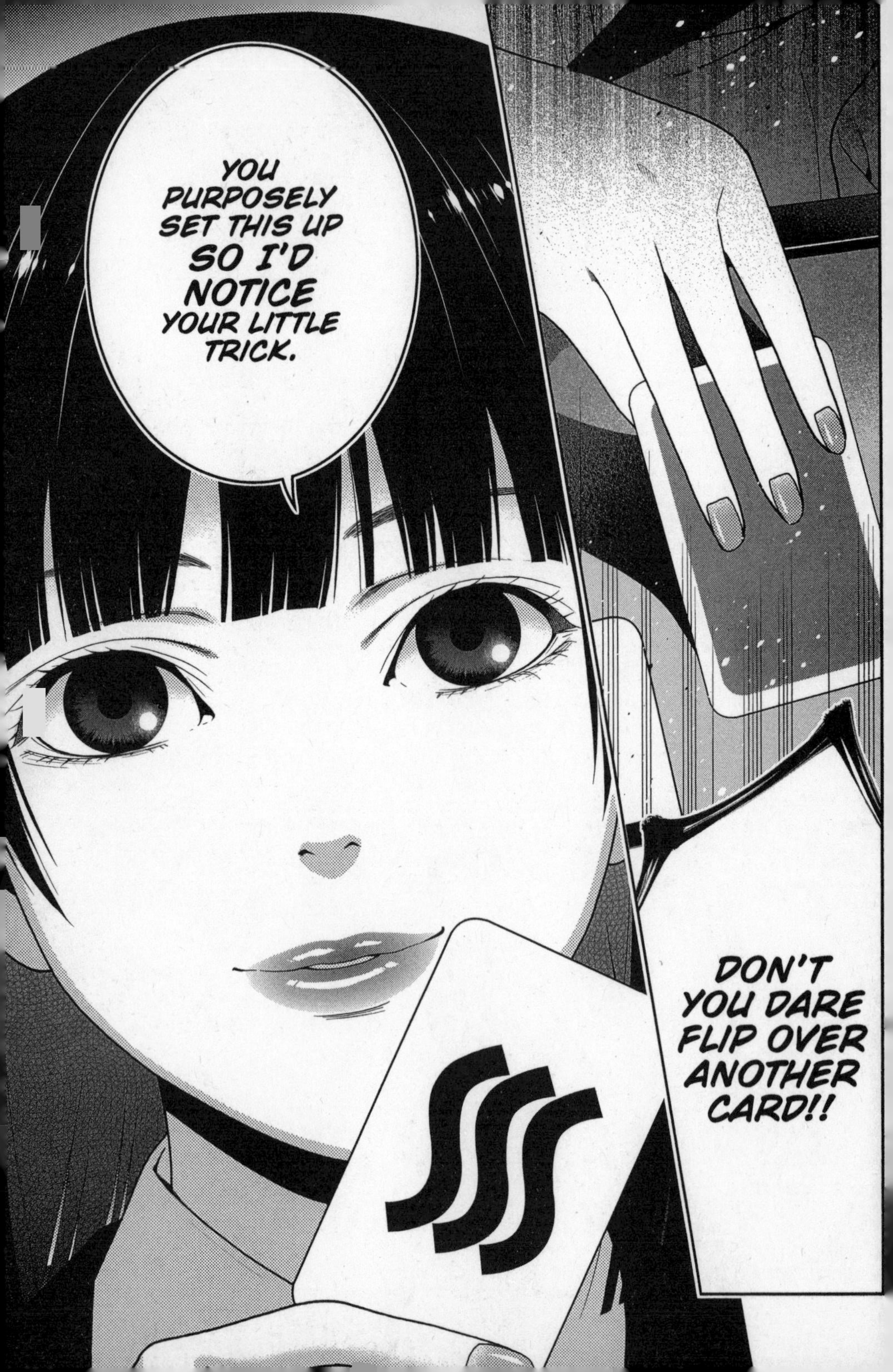
DON'T YOU DARE FLIP OVER ANOTHER CARD!!
YOU PURPOSELY SET THIS UP SO I'D NOTICE YOUR LITTLE TRICK.

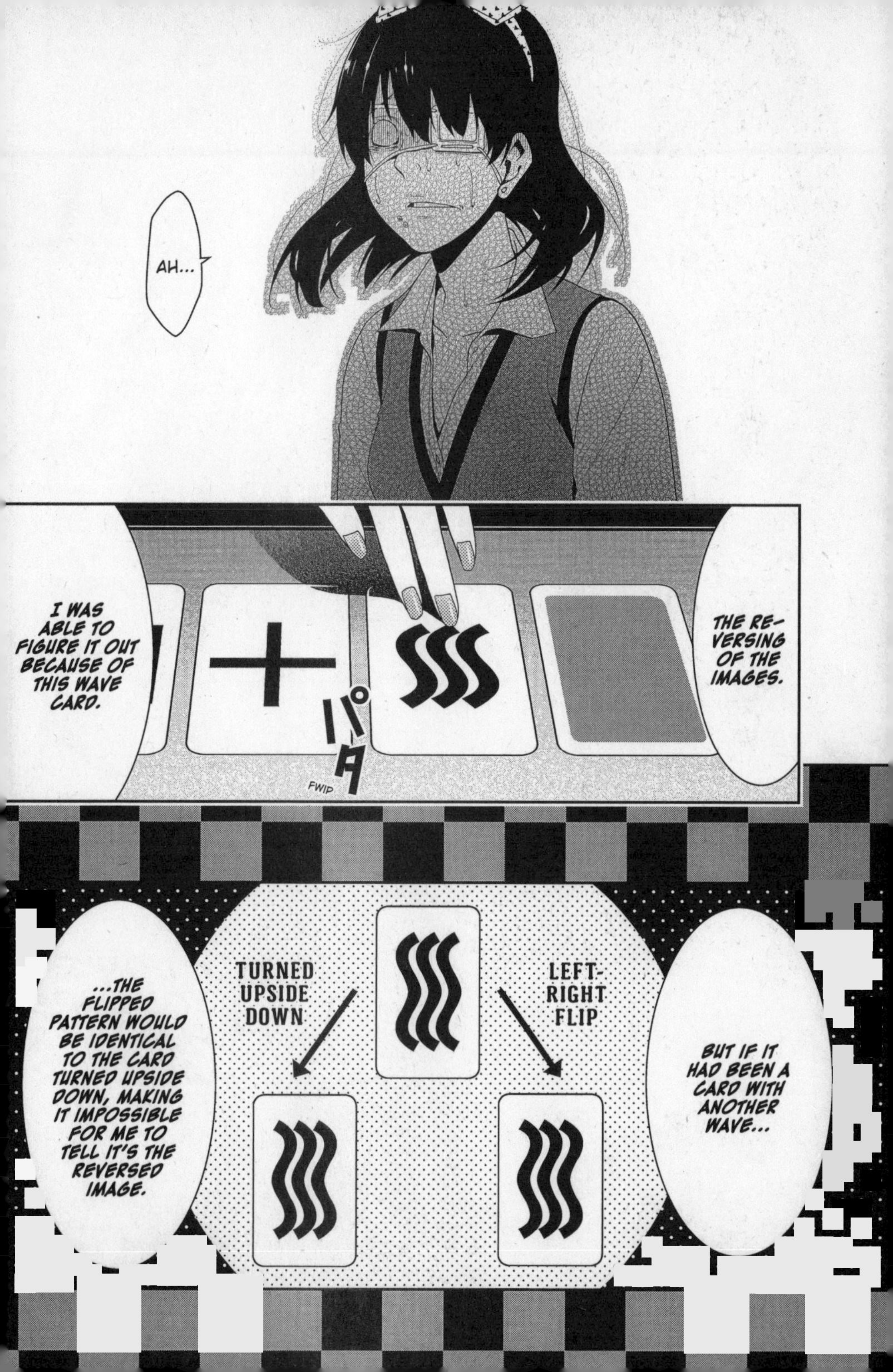
AH...
THE REVERSING OF THE IMAGES.
I WAS ABLE TO FIGURE IT OUT BECAUSE OF THIS WAVE CARD.
パタ
FWIP
BUT IF IT HAD BEEN A CARD WITH ANOTHER WAVE...
LEFT-RIGHT FLIP
TURNED UPSIDE DOWN
...THE FLIPPED PATTERN WOULD BE IDENTICAL TO THE CARD TURNED UPSIDE DOWN, MAKING IT IMPOSSIBLE FOR ME TO TELL IT'S THE REVERSED IMAGE.

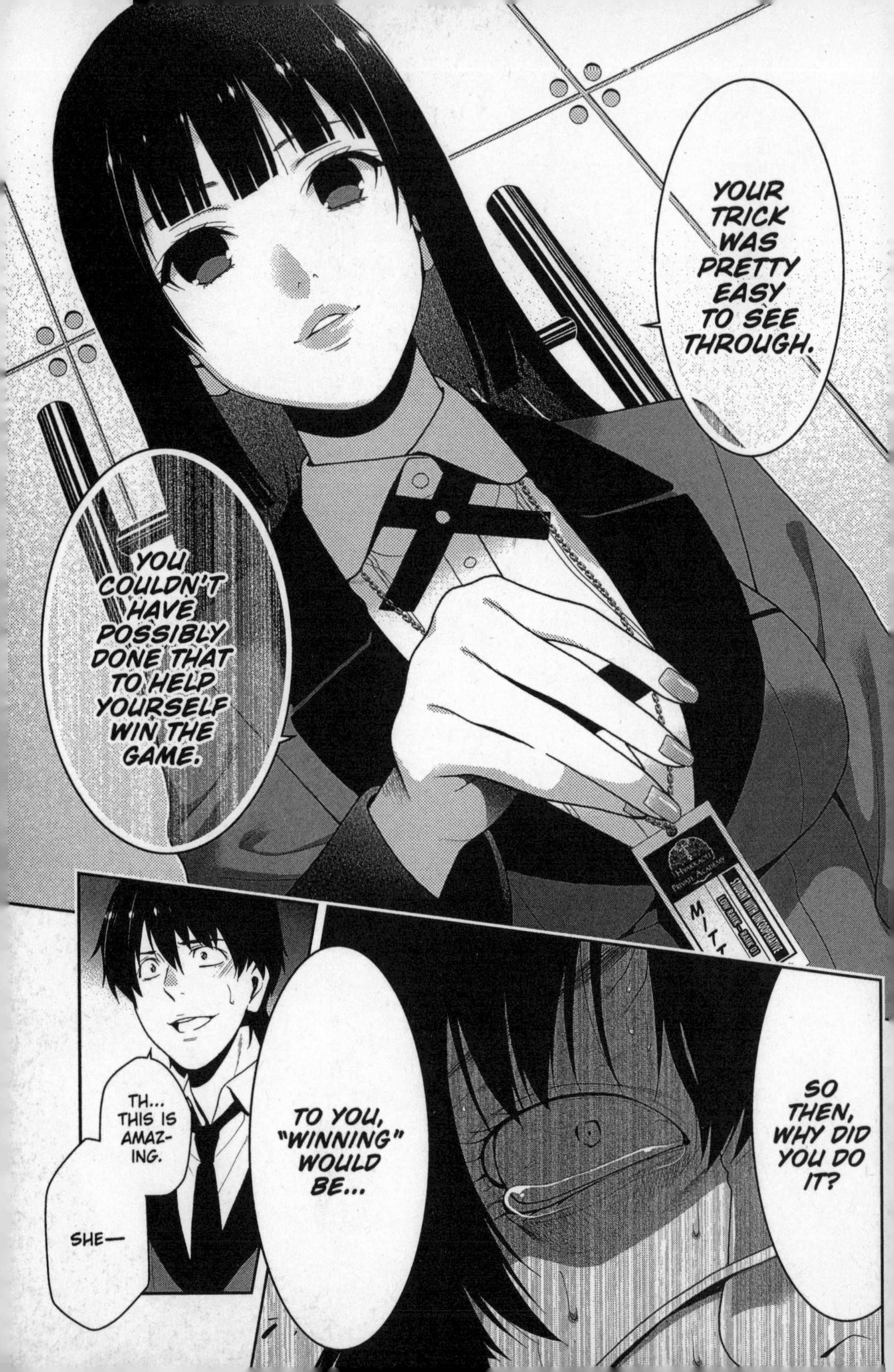
YOUR TRICK WAS PRETTY EASY TO SEE THROUGH.
YOU COULDN'T HAVE POSSIBLY DONE THAT TO HELP YOURSELF WIN THE GAME.
SO THEN, WHY DID YOU DO IT?
TO YOU, "WINNING" WOULD BE...
TH... THIS IS AMAZ-ING.
SHE—

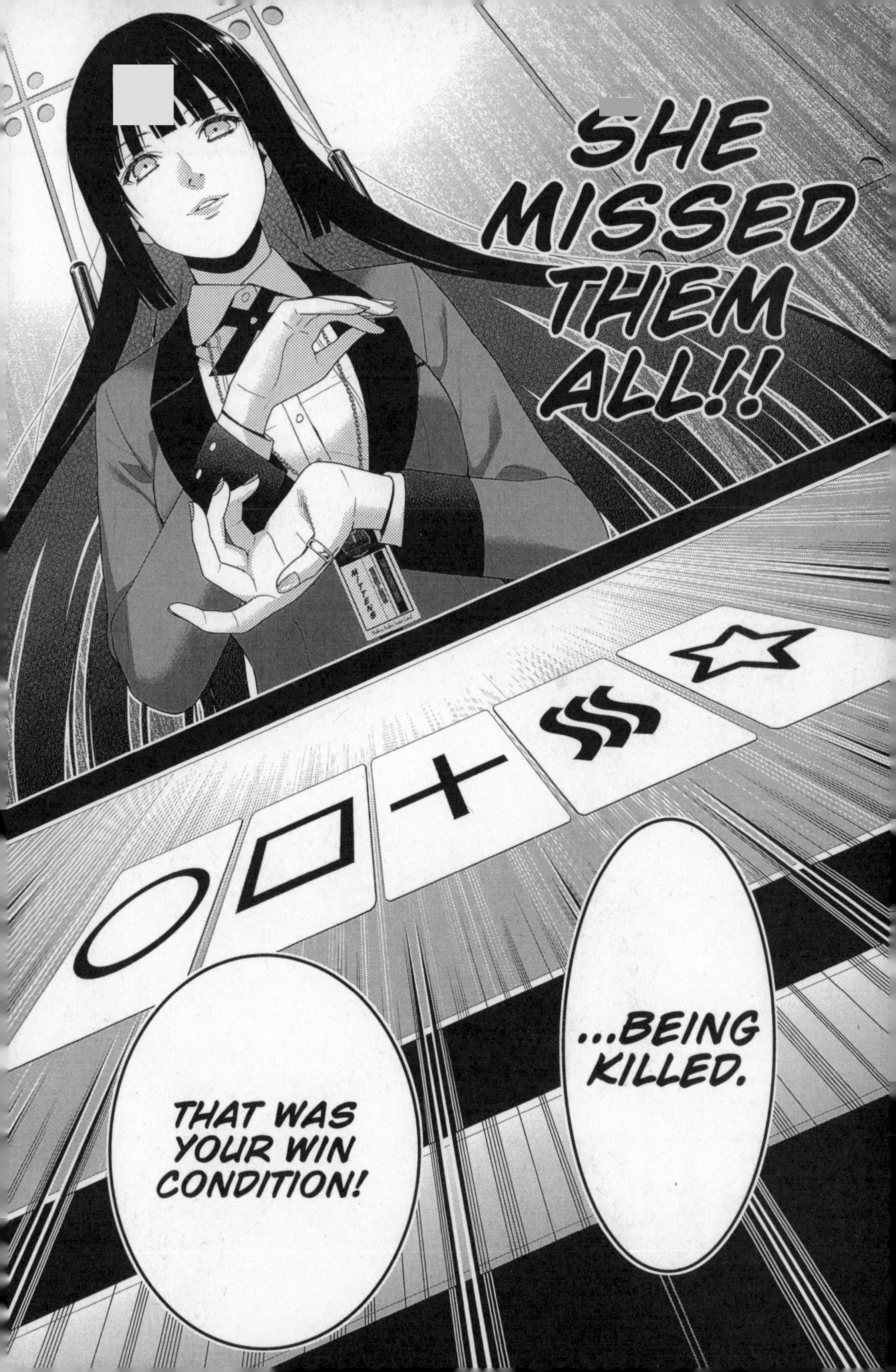
SHE MISSED THEM ALL!!
...BEING KILLED.
THAT WAS YOUR WIN CONDITION!

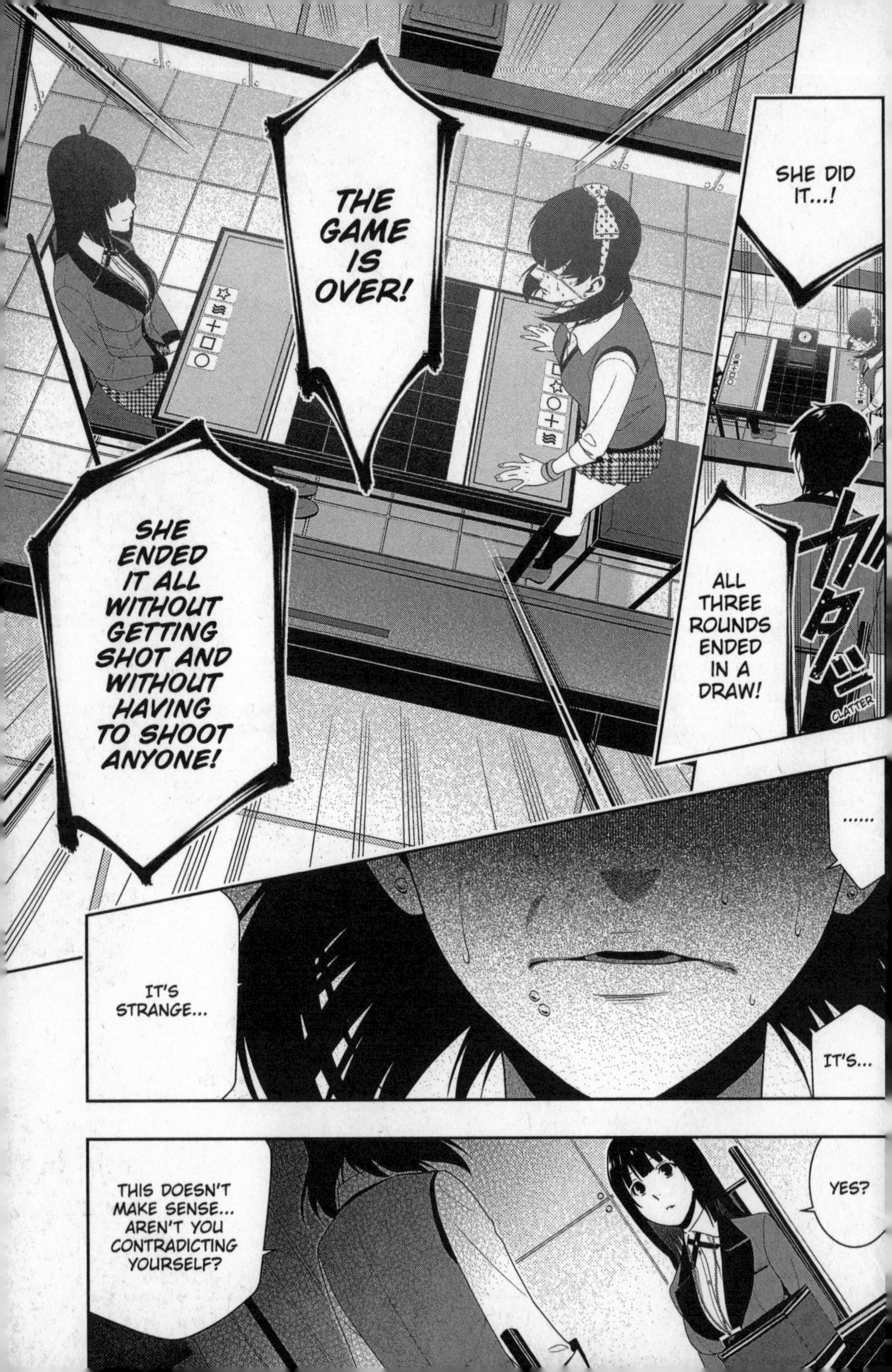
SHE DID IT...!
ALL THREE ROUNDS ENDED IN A DRAW!
CLATTER
THE GAME IS OVER!
SHE ENDED IT ALL WITHOUT GETTING SHOT AND WITHOUT HAVING TO SHOOT ANYONE!
......
IT'S...
IT'S STRANGE...
YES?
THIS DOESN'T MAKE SENSE... AREN'T YOU CONTRADICTING YOURSELF?

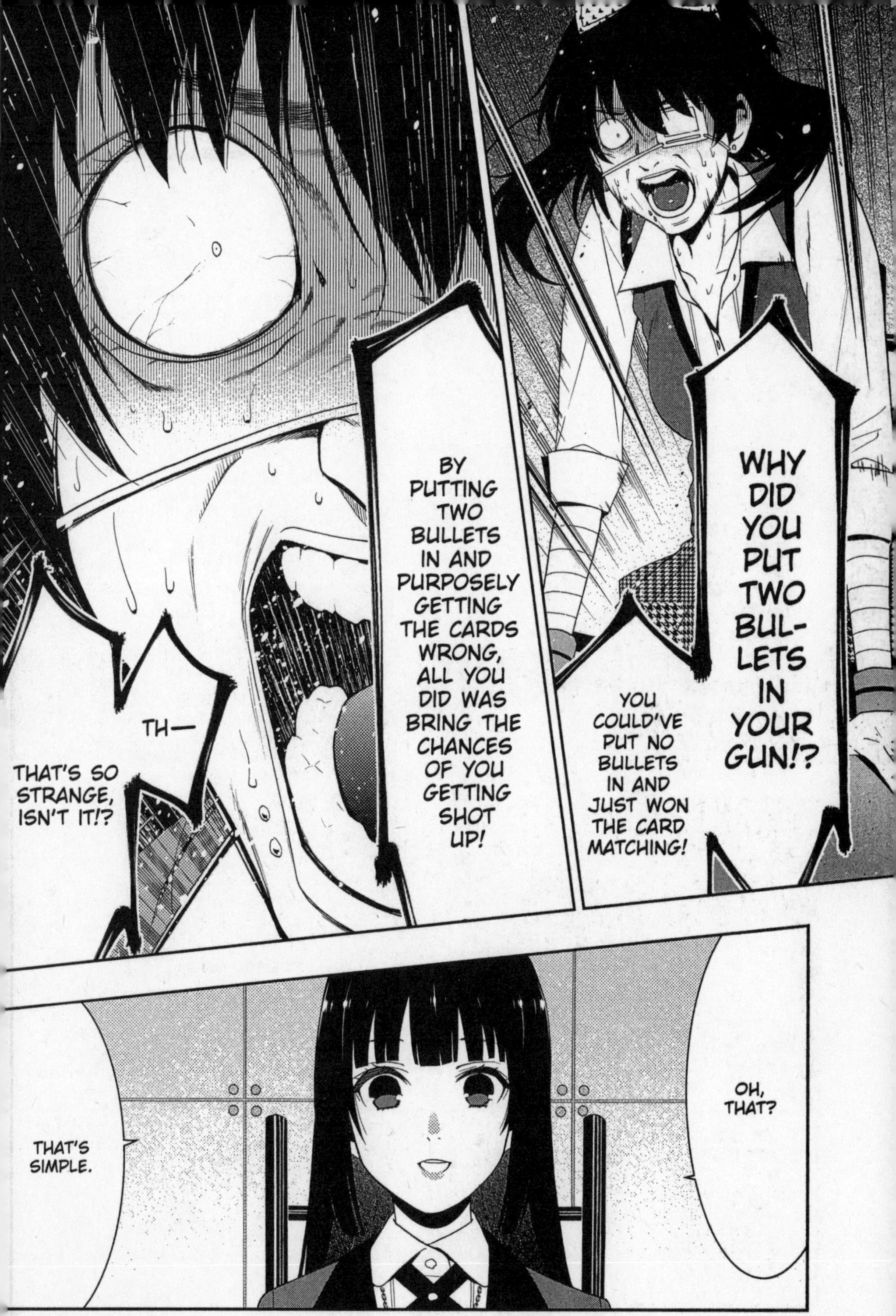
WHY DID YOU PUT TWO BUL-LETS IN YOUR GUN!?
YOU COULD'VE PUT NO BULLETS IN AND JUST WON THE CARD MATCHING!
BY PUTTING TWO BULLETS IN AND PURPOSELY GETTING THE CARDS WRONG, ALL YOU DID WAS BRING THE CHANCES OF YOU GETTING SHOT UP!
TH—
THAT'S SO STRANGE, ISN'T IT!?
OH, THAT?
THAT'S SIMPLE.

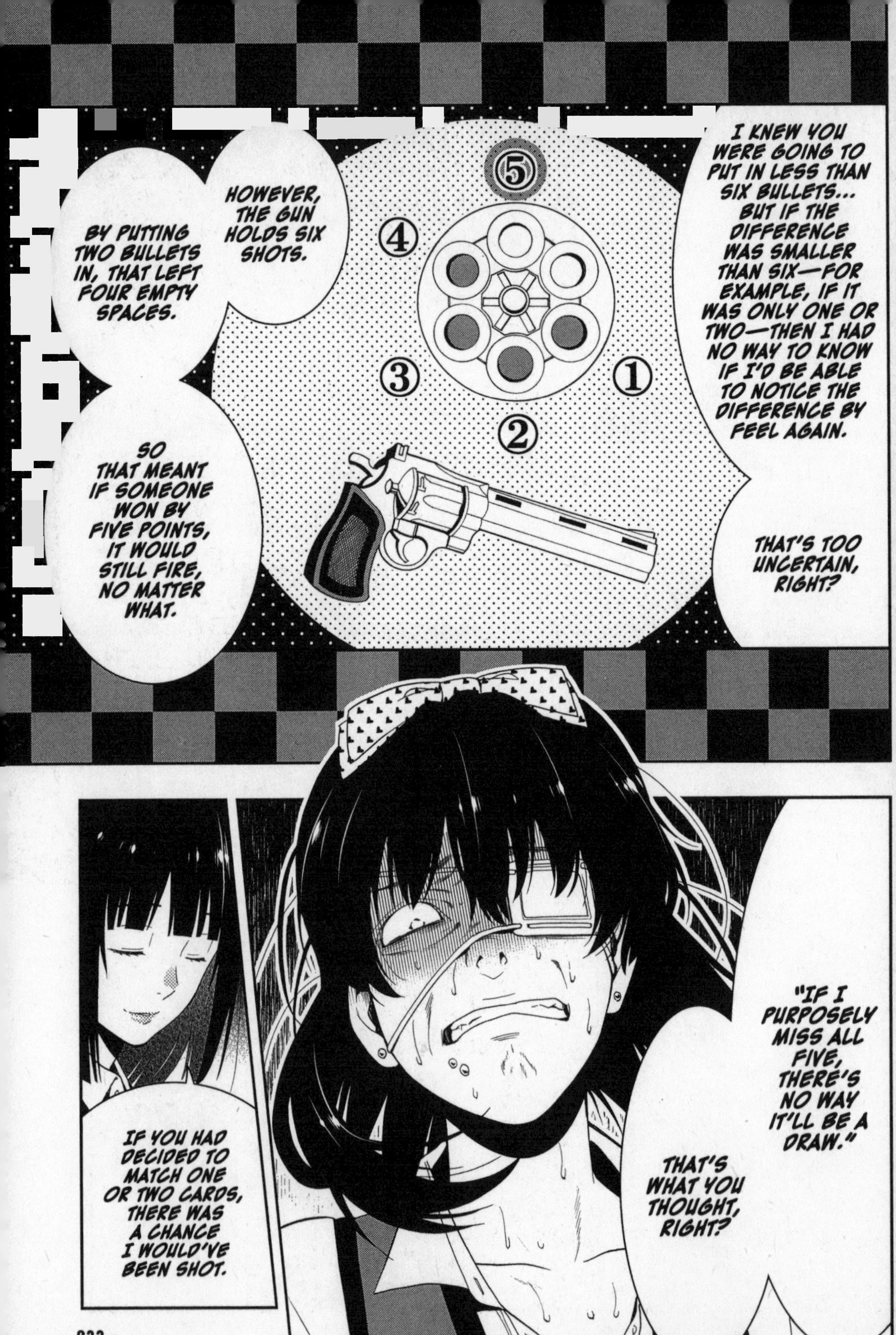
I KNEW YOU WERE GOING TO PUT IN LESS THAN SIX BULLETS... BUT IF THE DIFFERENCE WAS SMALLER THAN SIX—FOR EXAMPLE, IF IT WAS ONLY ONE OR TWO—THEN I HAD NO WAY TO KNOW IF I'D BE ABLE TO NOTICE THE DIFFERENCE BY FEEL AGAIN.
THAT'S TOO UNCERTAIN, RIGHT?
⑤
④
③
②
①
HOWEVER, THE GUN HOLDS SIX SHOTS.
BY PUTTING TWO BULLETS IN, THAT LEFT FOUR EMPTY SPACES.
SO THAT MEANT IF SOMEONE WON BY FIVE POINTS, IT WOULD STILL FIRE, NO MATTER WHAT.
"IF I PURPOSELY MISS ALL FIVE, THERE'S NO WAY IT'LL BE A DRAW."
THAT'S WHAT YOU THOUGHT, RIGHT?
IF YOU HAD DECIDED TO MATCH ONE OR TWO CARDS, THERE WAS A CHANCE I WOULD'VE BEEN SHOT.

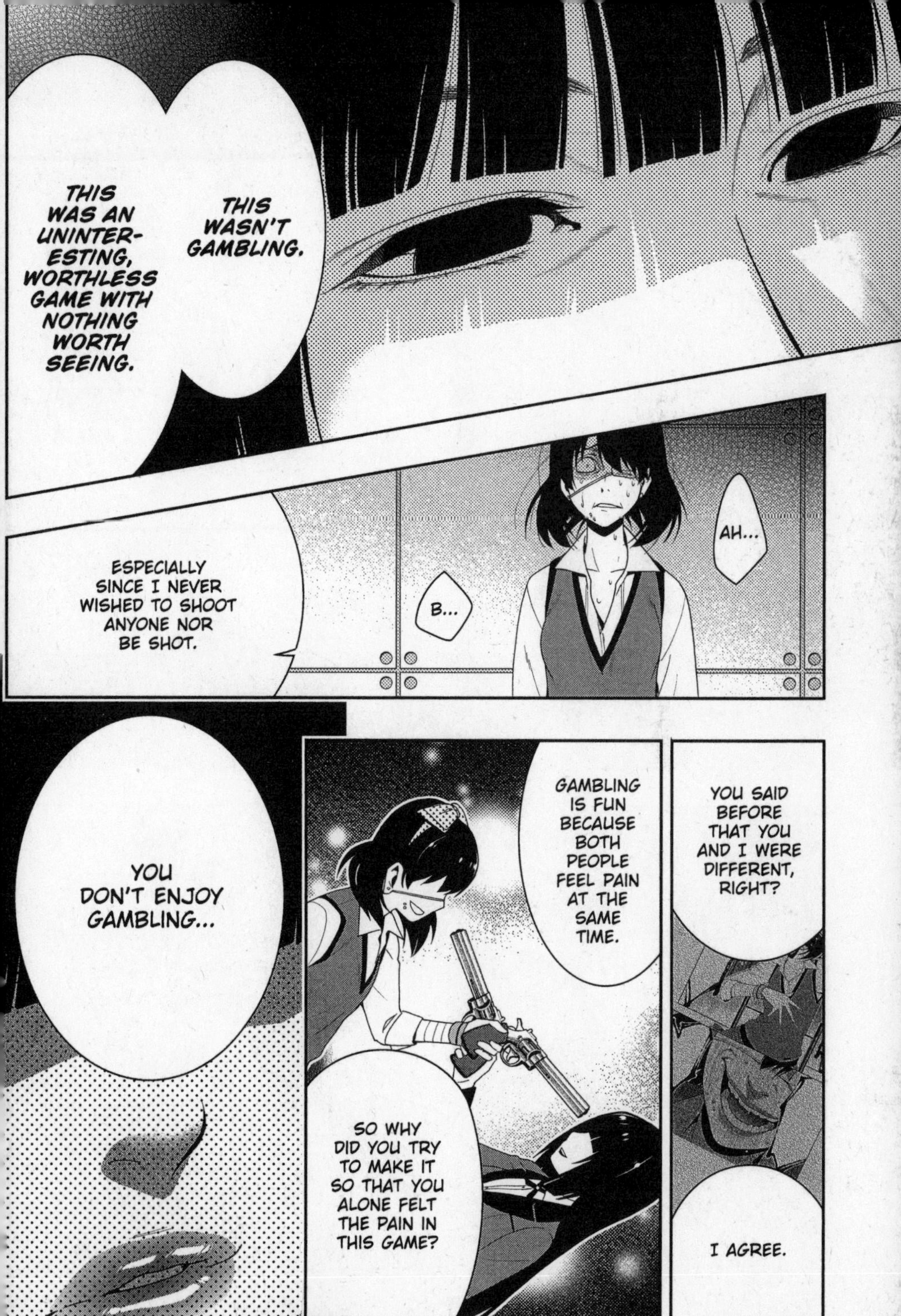
THIS WASN'T GAMBLING.
THIS WAS AN UNINTER-ESTING, WORTHLESS GAME WITH NOTHING WORTH SEEING.
AH...
B...
ESPECIALLY SINCE I NEVER WISHED TO SHOOT ANYONE NOR BE SHOT.
YOU SAID BEFORE THAT YOU AND I WERE DIFFERENT, RIGHT?
I AGREE.
GAMBLING IS FUN BECAUSE BOTH PEOPLE FEEL PAIN AT THE SAME TIME.
SO WHY DID YOU TRY TO MAKE IT SO THAT YOU ALONE FELT THE PAIN IN THIS GAME?
YOU DON'T ENJOY GAMBLING...

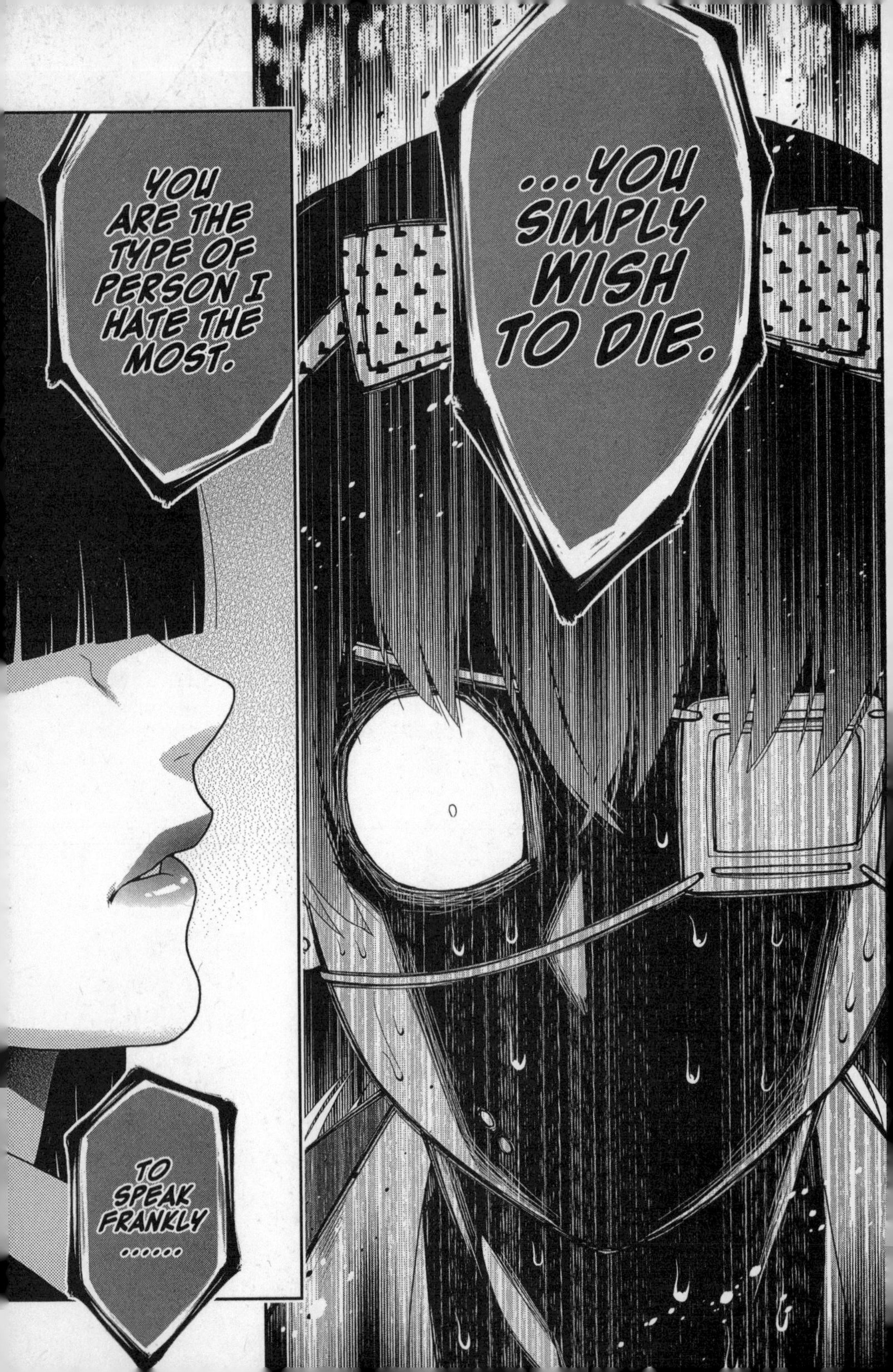
...YOU SIMPLY WISH TO DIE.
YOU ARE THE TYPE OF PERSON I HATE THE MOST.
TO SPEAK FRANKLY ......

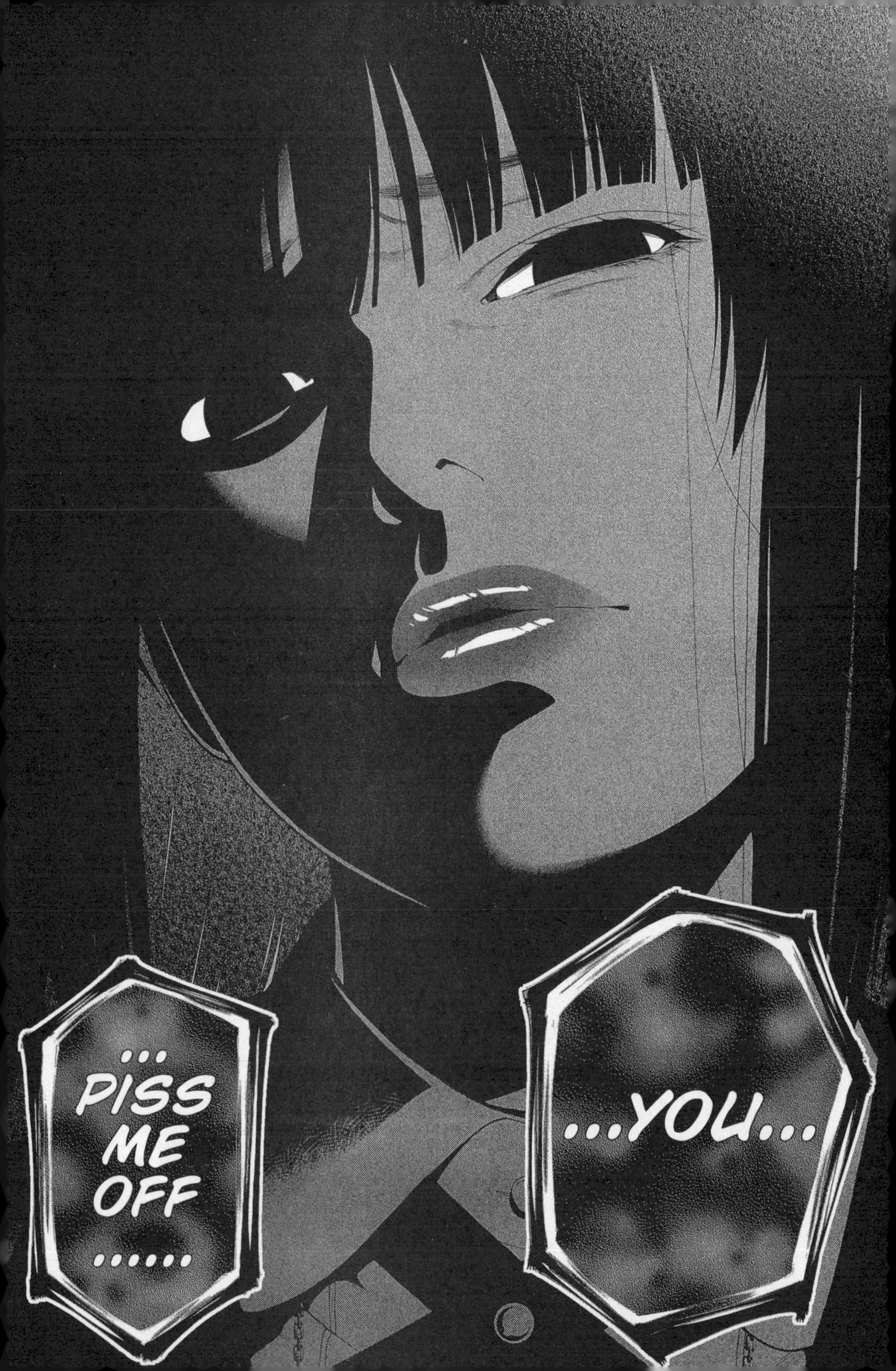
...YOU...
... PISS ME OFF ......

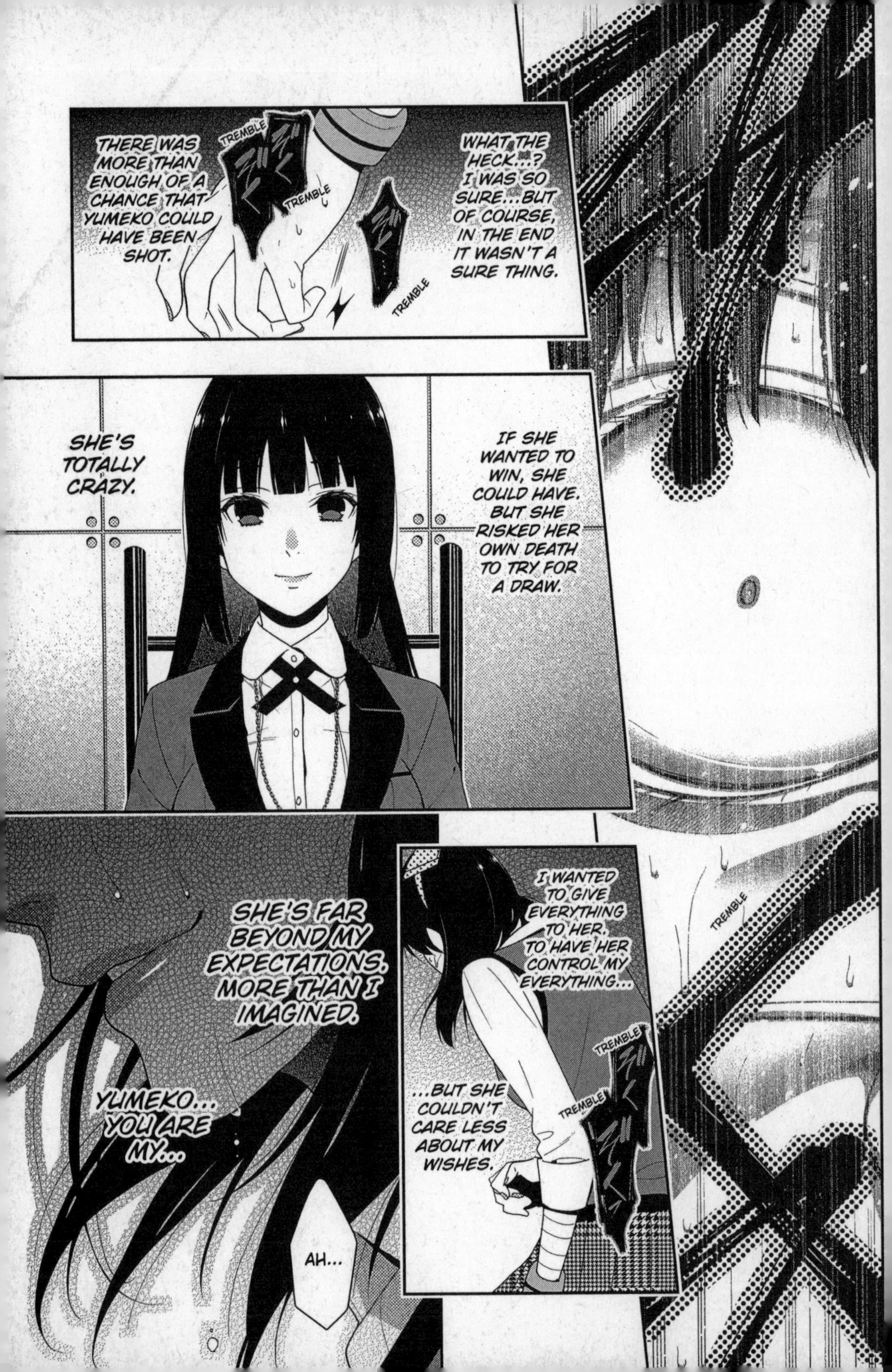
TREMBLE
WHAT THE HECK...? I WAS SO SURE...BUT OF COURSE, IN THE END IT WASN'T A SURE THING.
THERE WAS MORE THAN ENOUGH OF A CHANCE THAT YUMEKO COULD HAVE BEEN SHOT.
TREMBLE
TREMBLE
TREMBLE
IF SHE WANTED TO WIN, SHE COULD HAVE. BUT SHE RISKED HER OWN DEATH TO TRY FOR A DRAW.
SHE'S TOTALLY CRAZY.
I WANTED TO GIVE EVERYTHING TO HER. TO HAVE HER CONTROL MY EVERYTHING...
TREMBLE
TREMBLE
...BUT SHE COULDN'T CARE LESS ABOUT MY WISHES.
SHE'S FAR BEYOND MY EXPECTATIONS. MORE THAN I IMAGINED.
YUMEKO... YOU ARE MY...
AH...

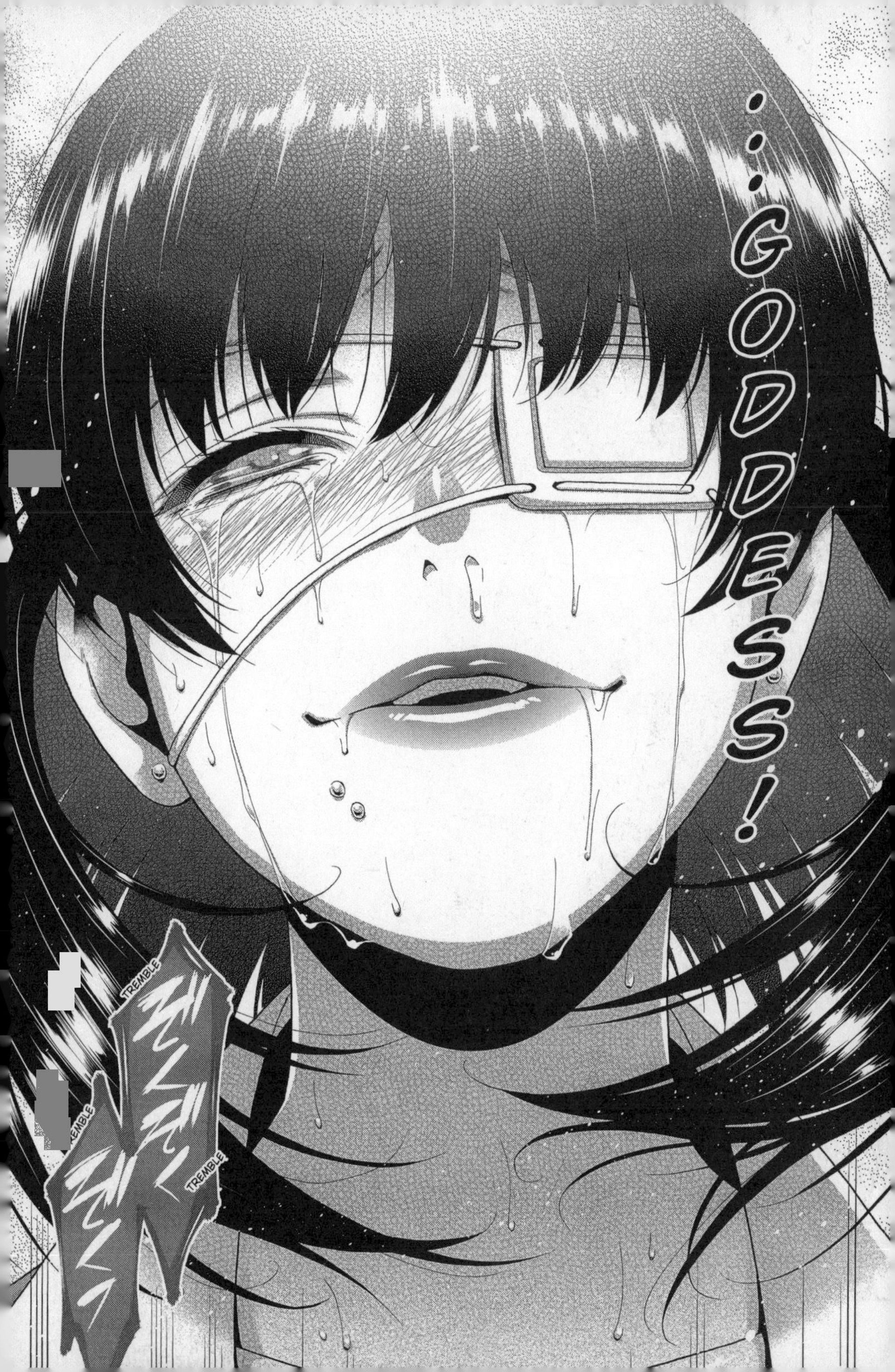
...GODDESS!
TREMBLE
TREMBLE
TREMBLE

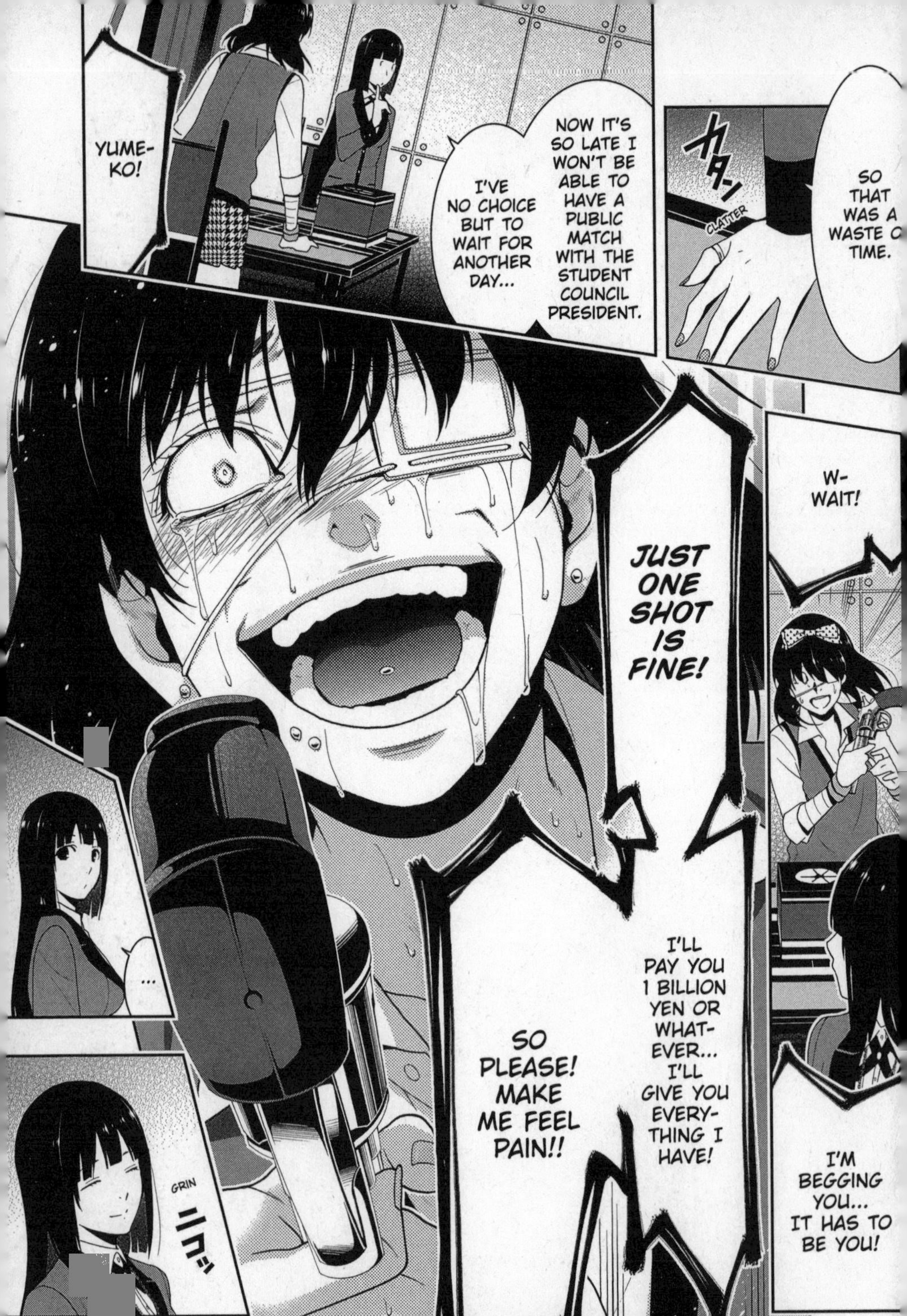
カタン
CLATTER
SO THAT WAS A WASTE O TIME.
NOW IT'S SO LATE I WON'T BE ABLE TO HAVE A PUBLIC MATCH WITH THE STUDENT COUNCIL PRESIDENT.
I'VE NO CHOICE BUT TO WAIT FOR ANOTHER DAY...
YUME-KO!
W-WAIT!
I'M BEGGING YOU... IT HAS TO BE YOU!
JUST ONE SHOT IS FINE!
I'LL PAY YOU 1 BILLION YEN OR WHAT-EVER... I'LL GIVE YOU EVERY-THING I HAVE!
SO PLEASE! MAKE ME FEEL PAIN!!
...
ニコッ
GRIN

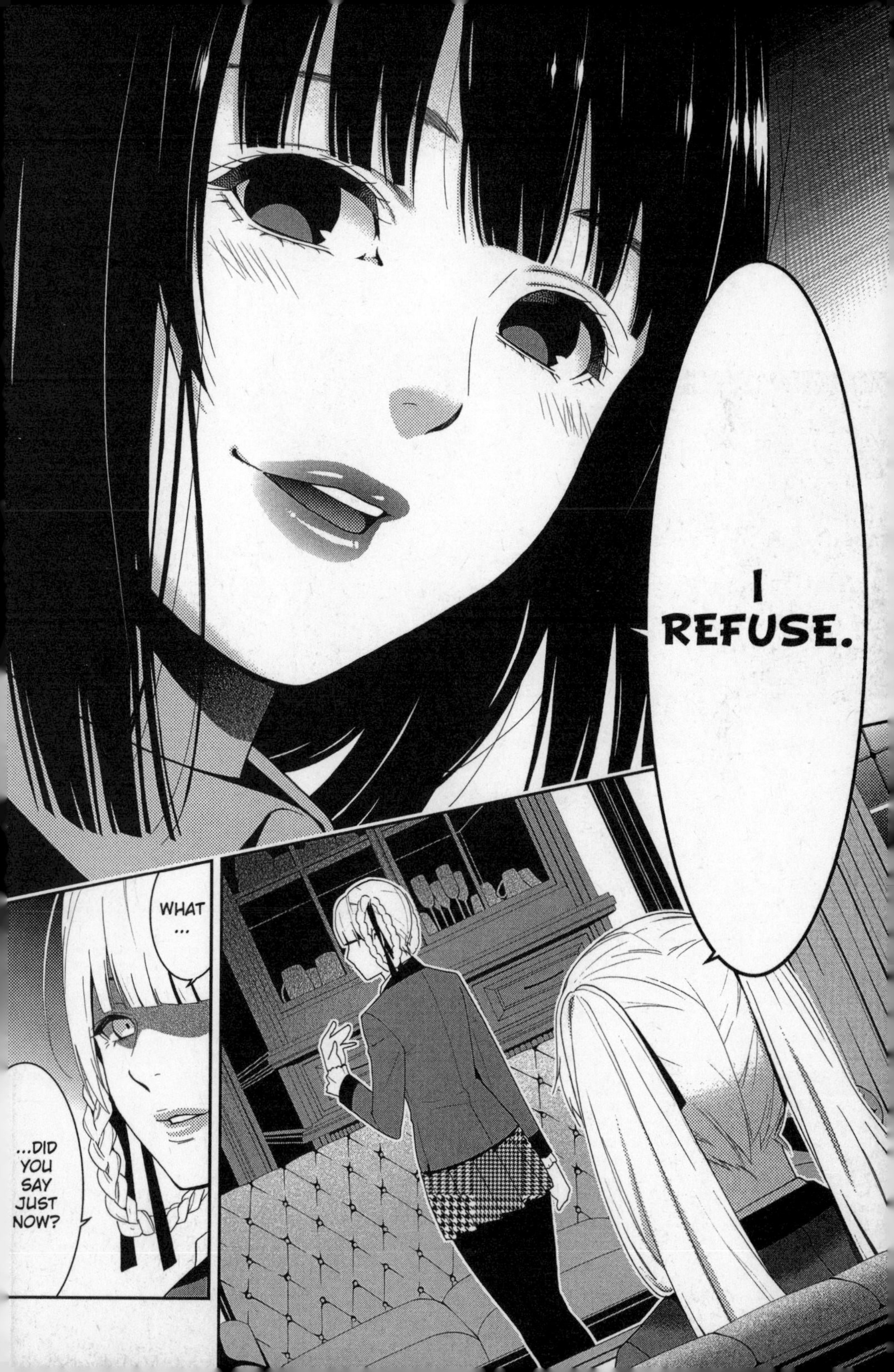
I REFUSE.
WHAT ...
...DID YOU SAY JUST NOW?

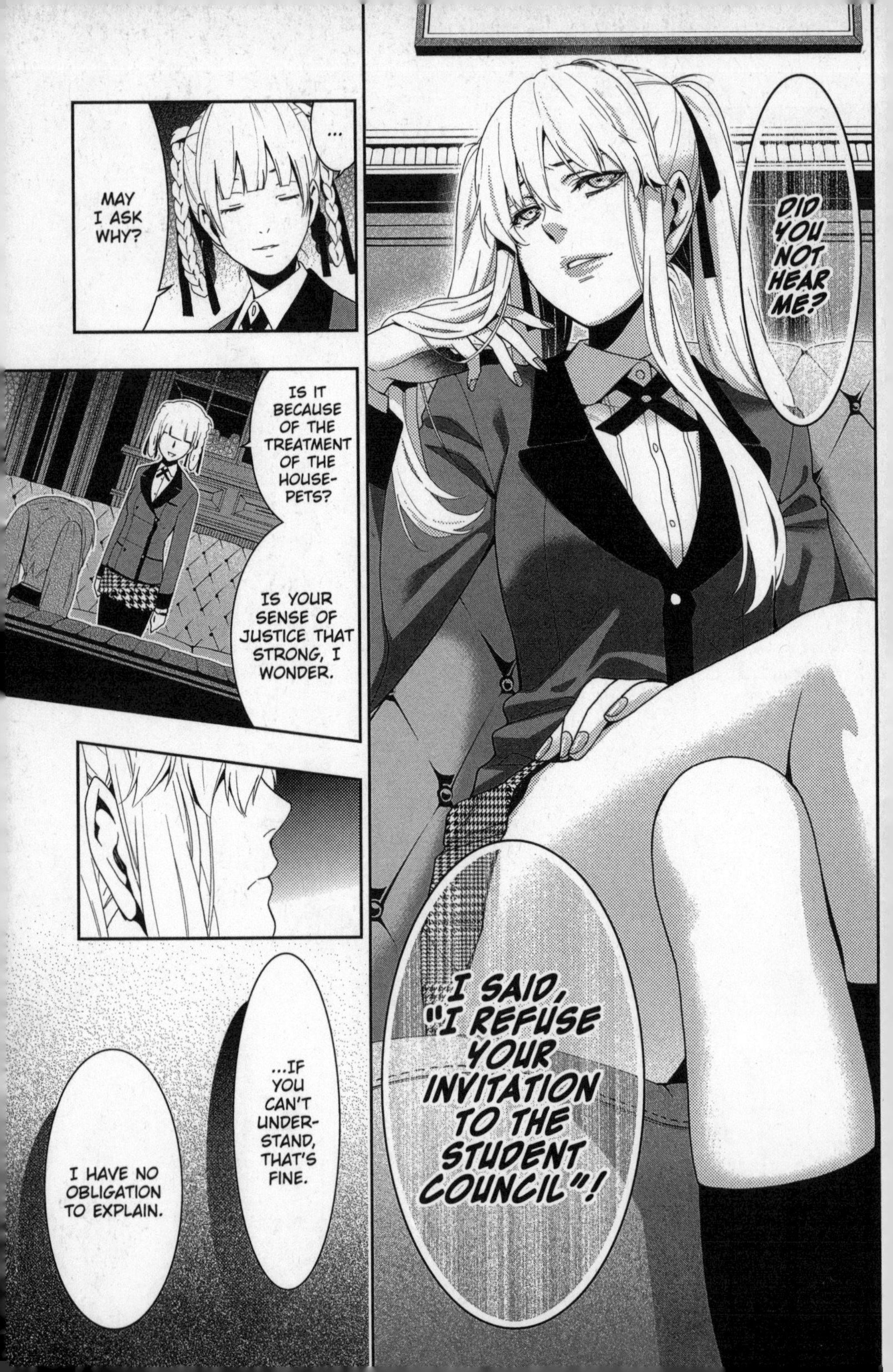
DID YOU NOT HEAR ME?
I SAID, "I REFUSE YOUR INVITATION TO THE STUDENT COUNCIL"!
...
MAY I ASK WHY?
IS IT BECAUSE OF THE TREATMENT OF THE HOUSE-PETS?
IS YOUR SENSE OF JUSTICE THAT STRONG, I WONDER.
...IF YOU CAN'T UNDER-STAND, THAT'S FINE.
I HAVE NO OBLIGATION TO EXPLAIN.

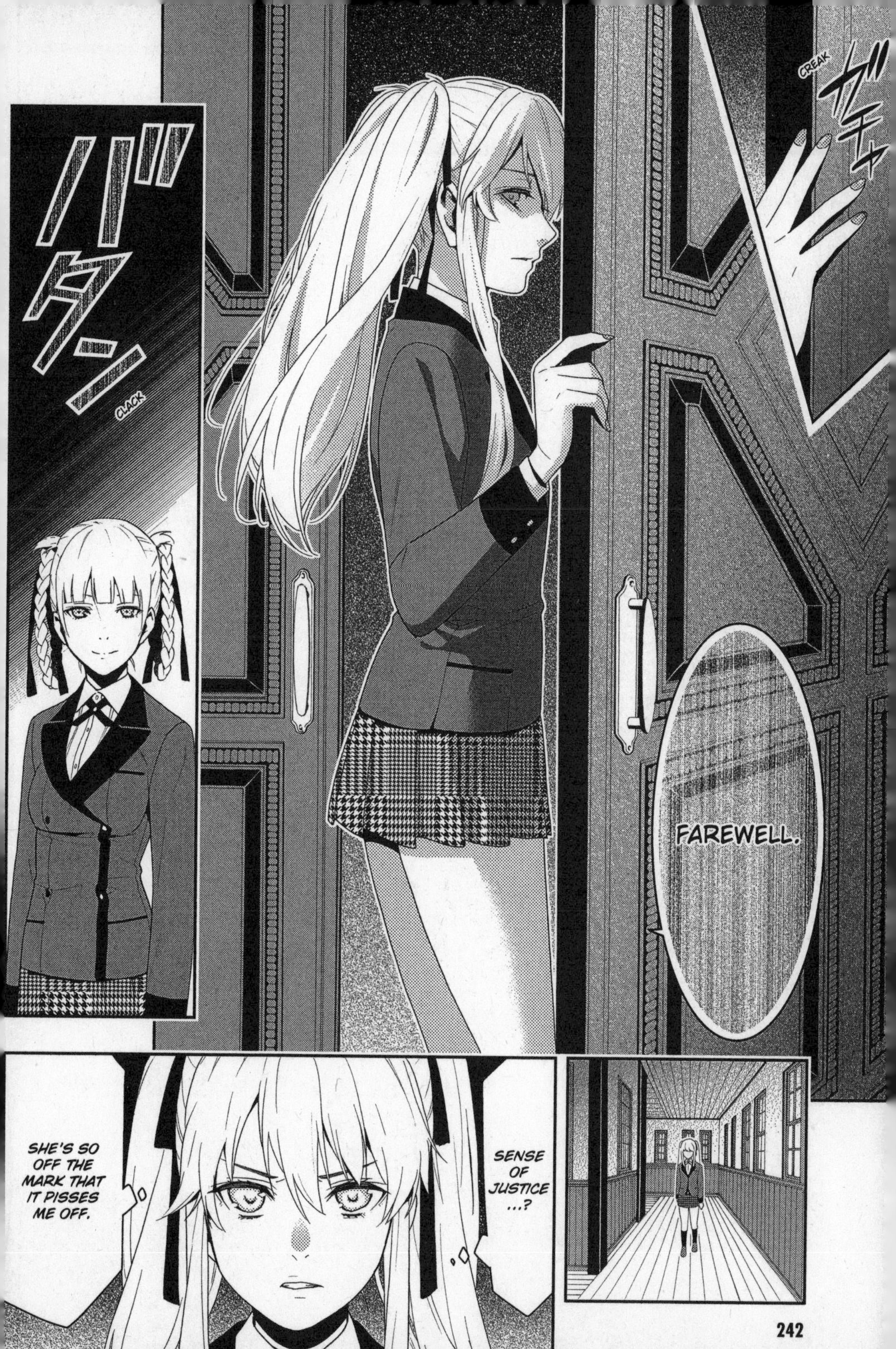
ガチャ
CREAK
FAREWELL.
バタン
CLACK
SENSE OF JUSTICE ...?
SHE'S SO OFF THE MARK THAT IT PISSES ME OFF.

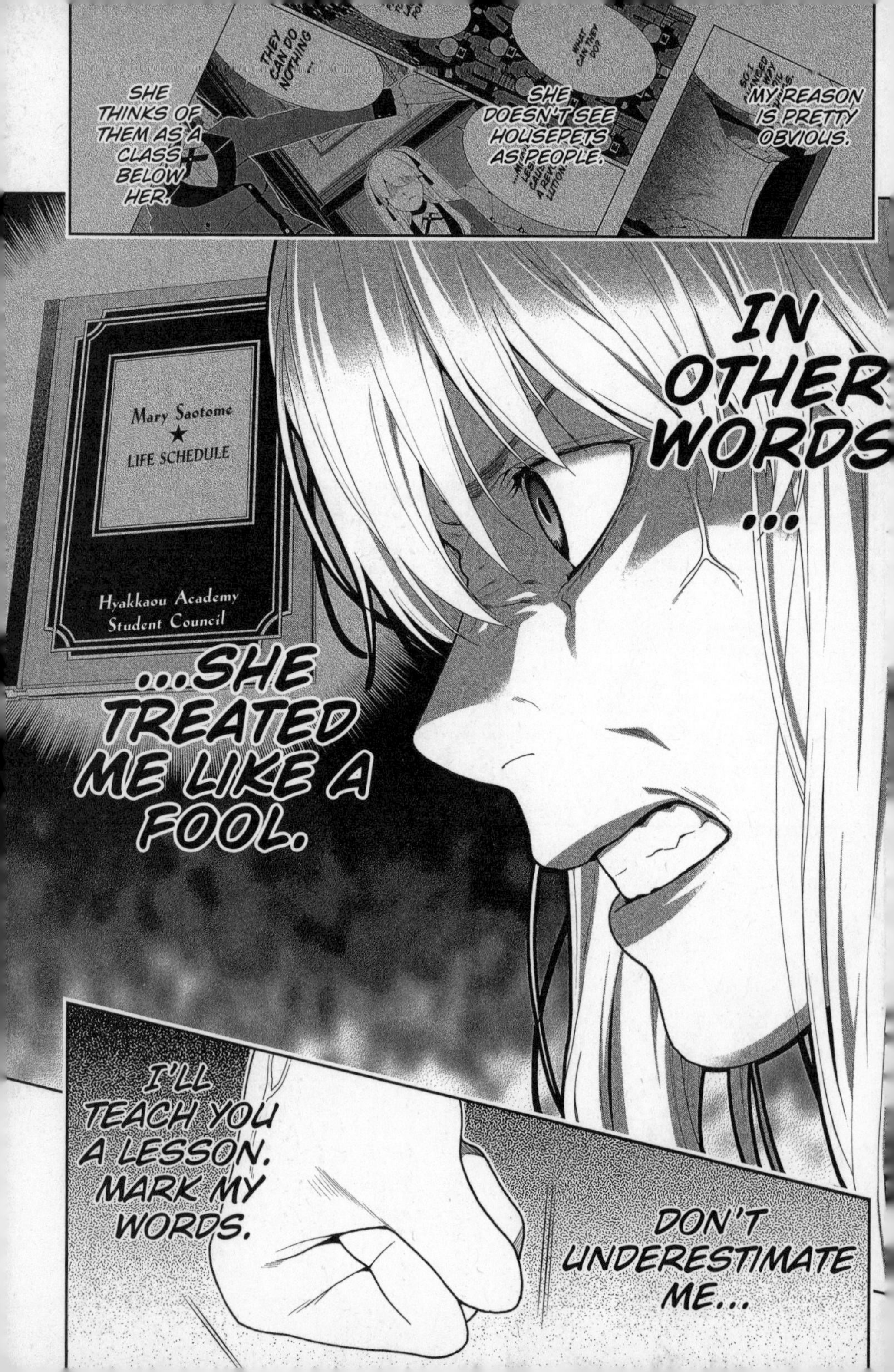
MY REASON IS PRETTY OBVIOUS.
WHAT CAN THEY DO?
SHE DOESN'T SEE HOUSEPETS AS PEOPLE.
THEY CAN DO NOTHING...
SHE THINKS OF THEM AS A CLASS BELOW HER.
IN OTHER WORDS...
Mary Saotome ★ LIFE SCHEDULE
Hyakkaou Academy Student Council
...SHE TREATED ME LIKE A FOOL.
DON'T UNDERESTIMATE ME...
I'LL TEACH YOU A LESSON. MARK MY WORDS.

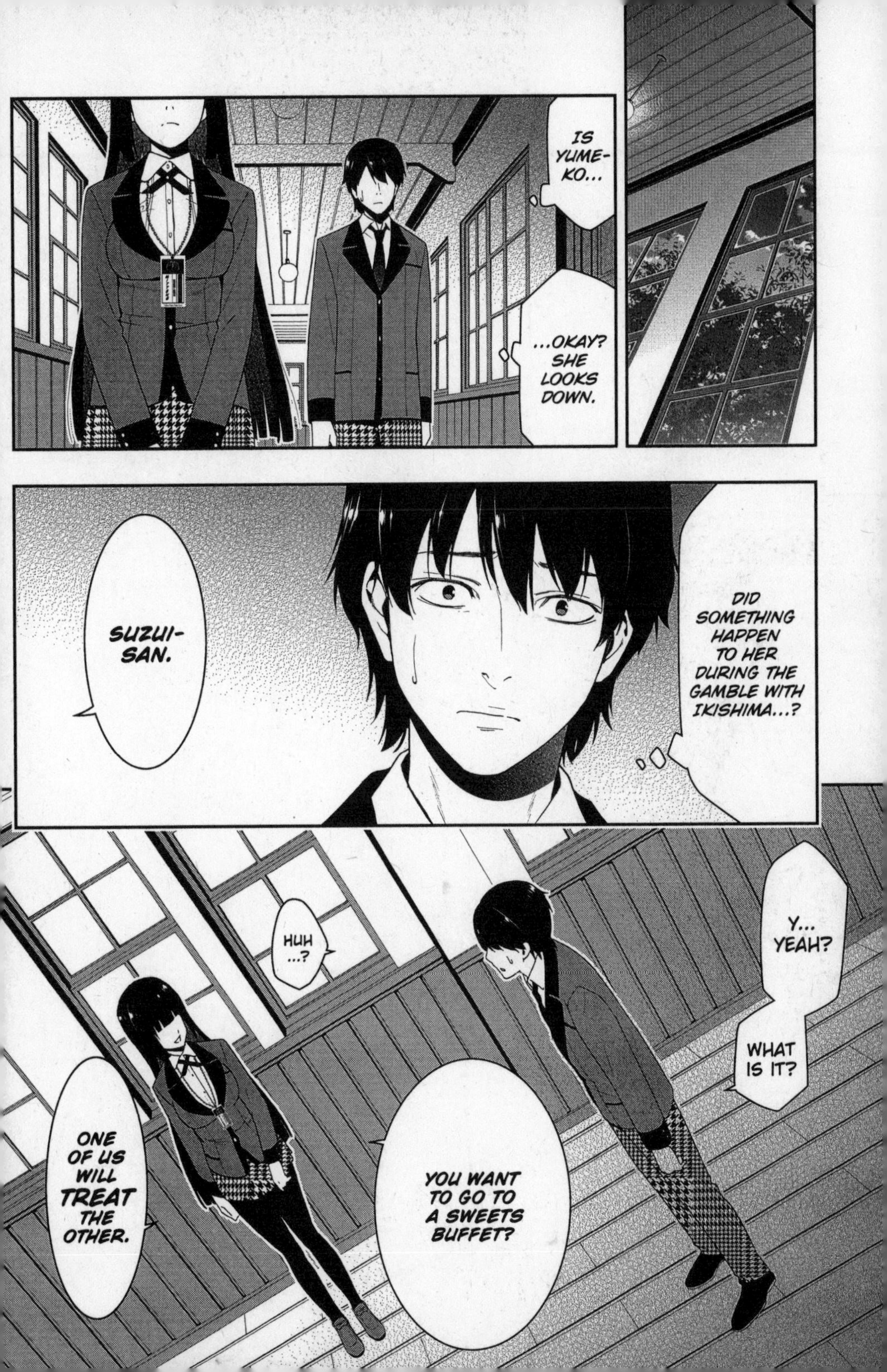
IS YUME-KO...
...OKAY? SHE LOOKS DOWN.
DID SOMETHING HAPPEN TO HER DURING THE GAMBLE WITH IKISHIMA...?
SUZUI-SAN.
Y... YEAH?
WHAT IS IT?
HUH ...?
YOU WANT TO GO TO A SWEETS BUFFET?
ONE OF US WILL TREAT THE OTHER.

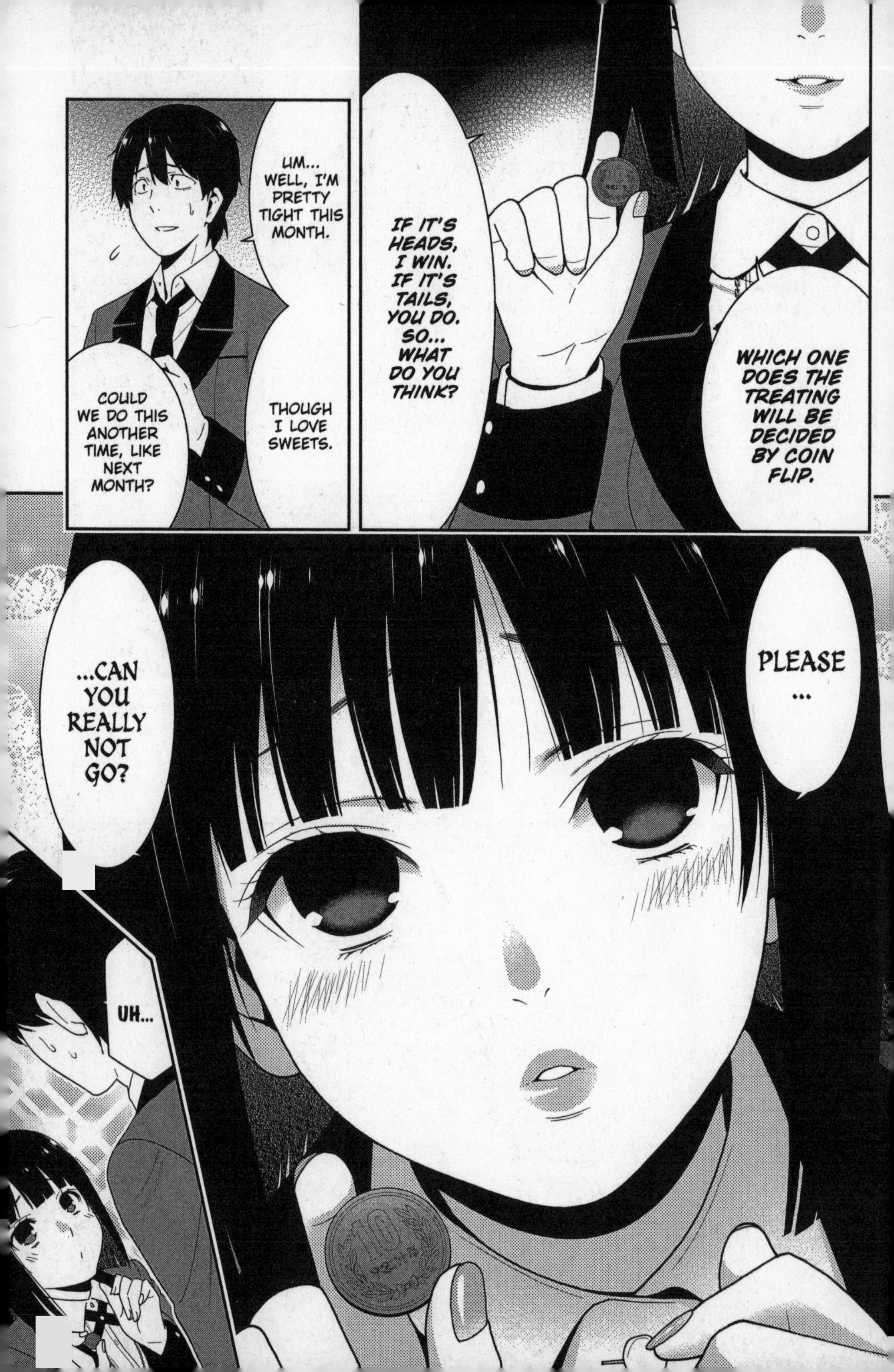
WHICH ONE DOES THE TREATING WILL BE DECIDED BY COIN FLIP.
IF IT'S HEADS, I WIN. IF IT'S TAILS, YOU DO. SO... WHAT DO YOU THINK?
UM... WELL, I'M PRETTY TIGHT THIS MONTH.
THOUGH I LOVE SWEETS.
COULD WE DO THIS ANOTHER TIME, LIKE NEXT MONTH?
PLEASE ...
...CAN YOU REALLY NOT GO?
UH...

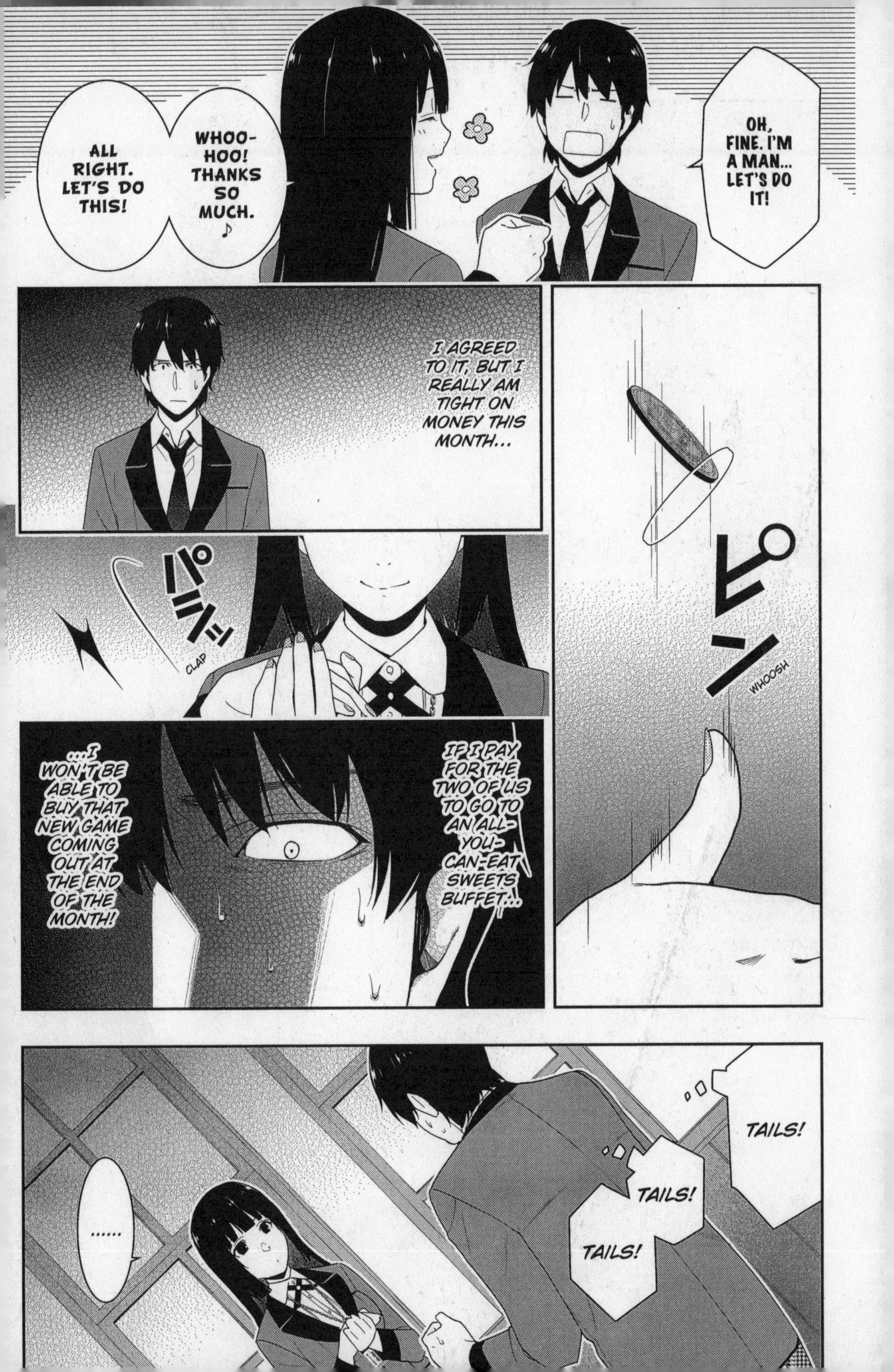
OH, FINE. I'M A MAN... LET'S DO IT!
WHOO-HOO! THANKS SO MUCH. ♪
ALL RIGHT. LET'S DO THIS!
WHOOSH
I AGREED TO IT, BUT I REALLY AM TIGHT ON MONEY THIS MONTH...
CLAP
IF I PAY FOR THE TWO OF US TO GO TO AN ALL-YOU-CAN-EAT SWEETS BUFFET...
...I WON'T BE ABLE TO BUY THAT NEW GAME COMING OUT AT THE END OF THE MONTH!
TAILS!
TAILS!
TAILS!
......

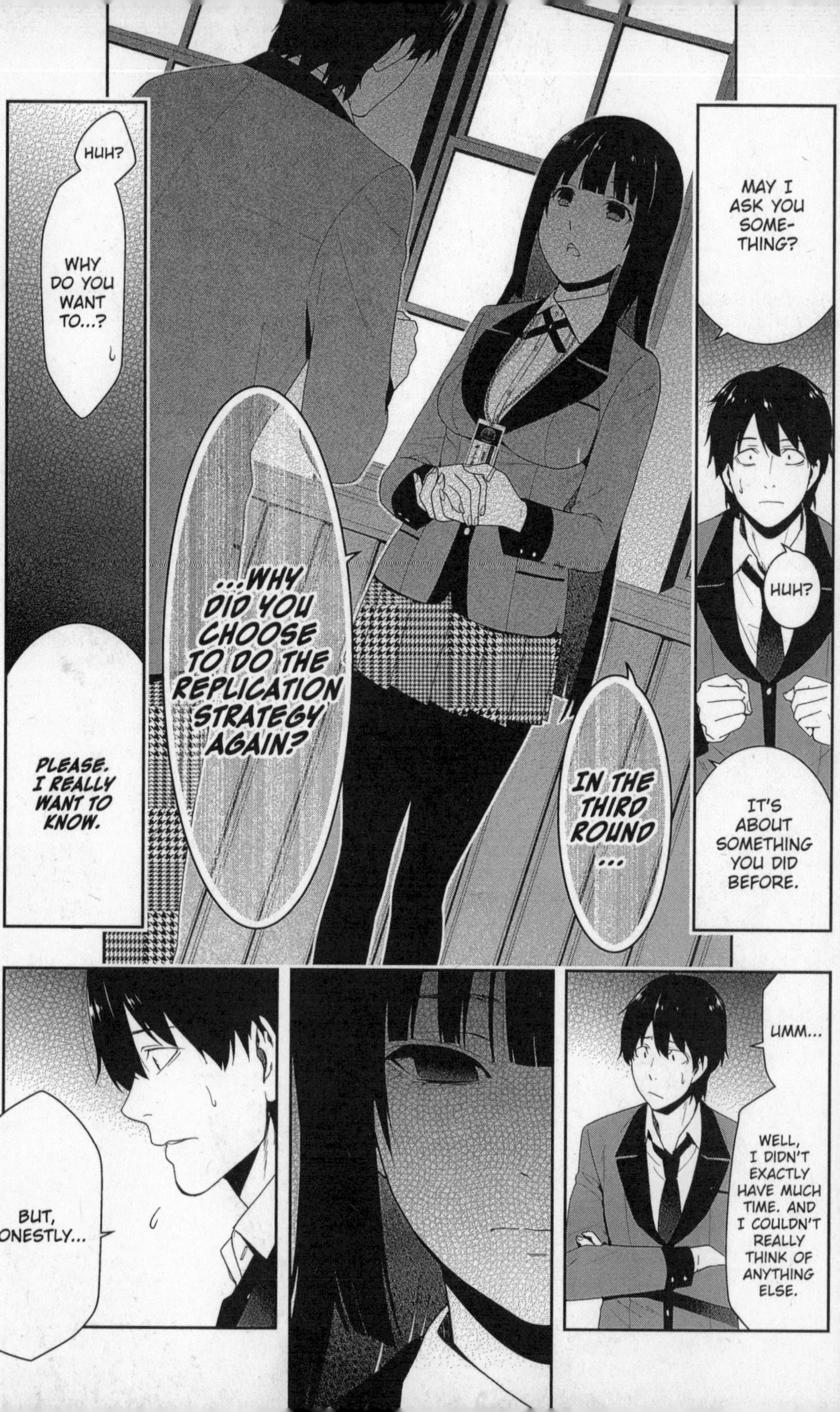
MAY I ASK YOU SOMETHING?
HUH?
IT'S ABOUT SOMETHING YOU DID BEFORE.
IN THE THIRD ROUND...
...WHY DID YOU CHOOSE TO DO THE REPLICATION STRATEGY AGAIN?
HUH? WHY DO YOU WANT TO...?
PLEASE. I REALLY WANT TO KNOW.
UMM...
WELL, I DIDN'T EXACTLY HAVE MUCH TIME. AND I COULDN'T REALLY THINK OF ANYTHING ELSE.
BUT, HONESTLY...

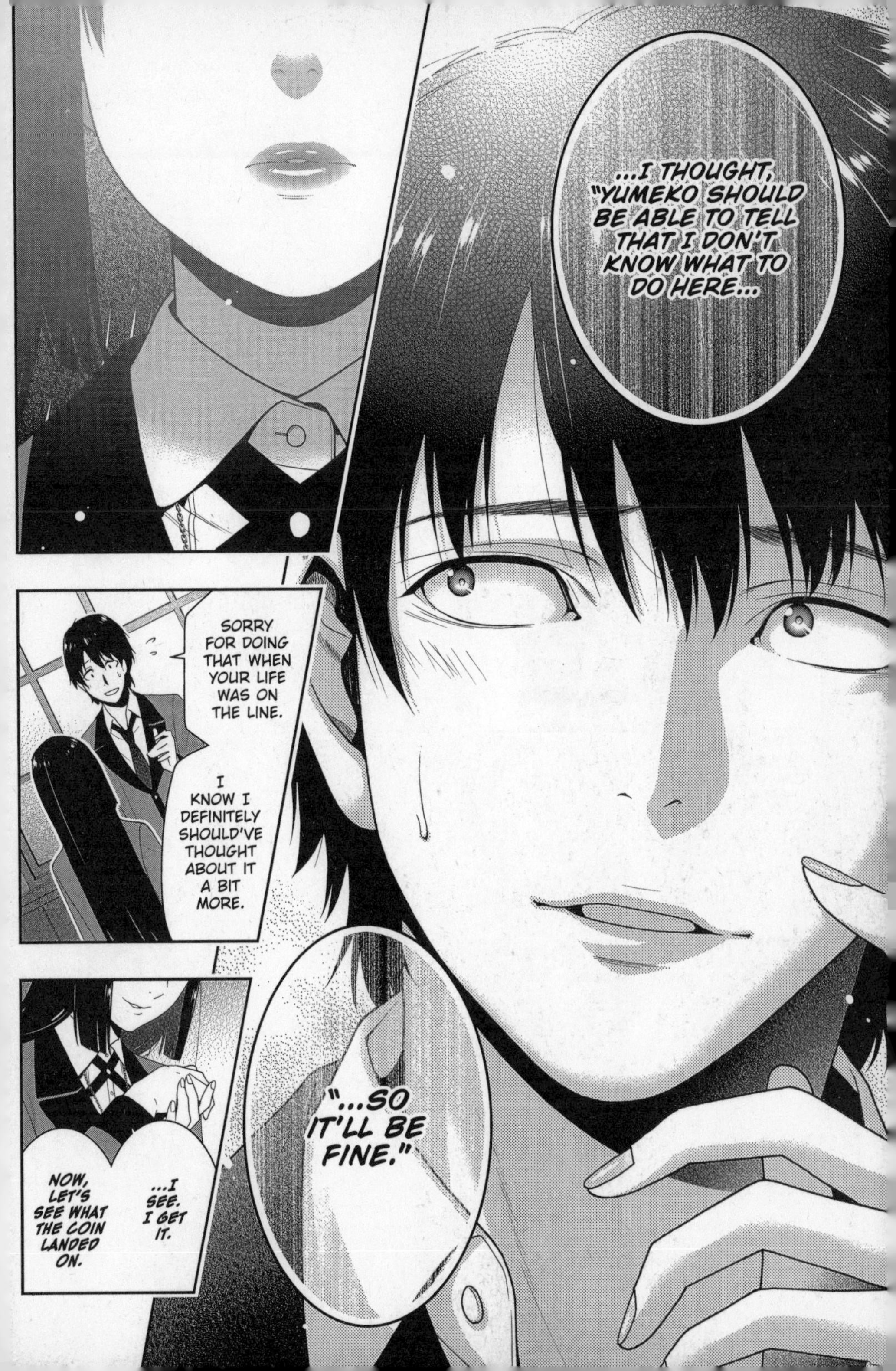
...I THOUGHT, "YUMEKO SHOULD BE ABLE TO TELL THAT I DON'T KNOW WHAT TO DO HERE...
"...SO IT'LL BE FINE."
SORRY FOR DOING THAT WHEN YOUR LIFE WAS ON THE LINE.
I KNOW I DEFINITELY SHOULD'VE THOUGHT ABOUT IT A BIT MORE.
...I SEE. I GET IT.
NOW, LET'S SEE WHAT THE COIN LANDED ON.

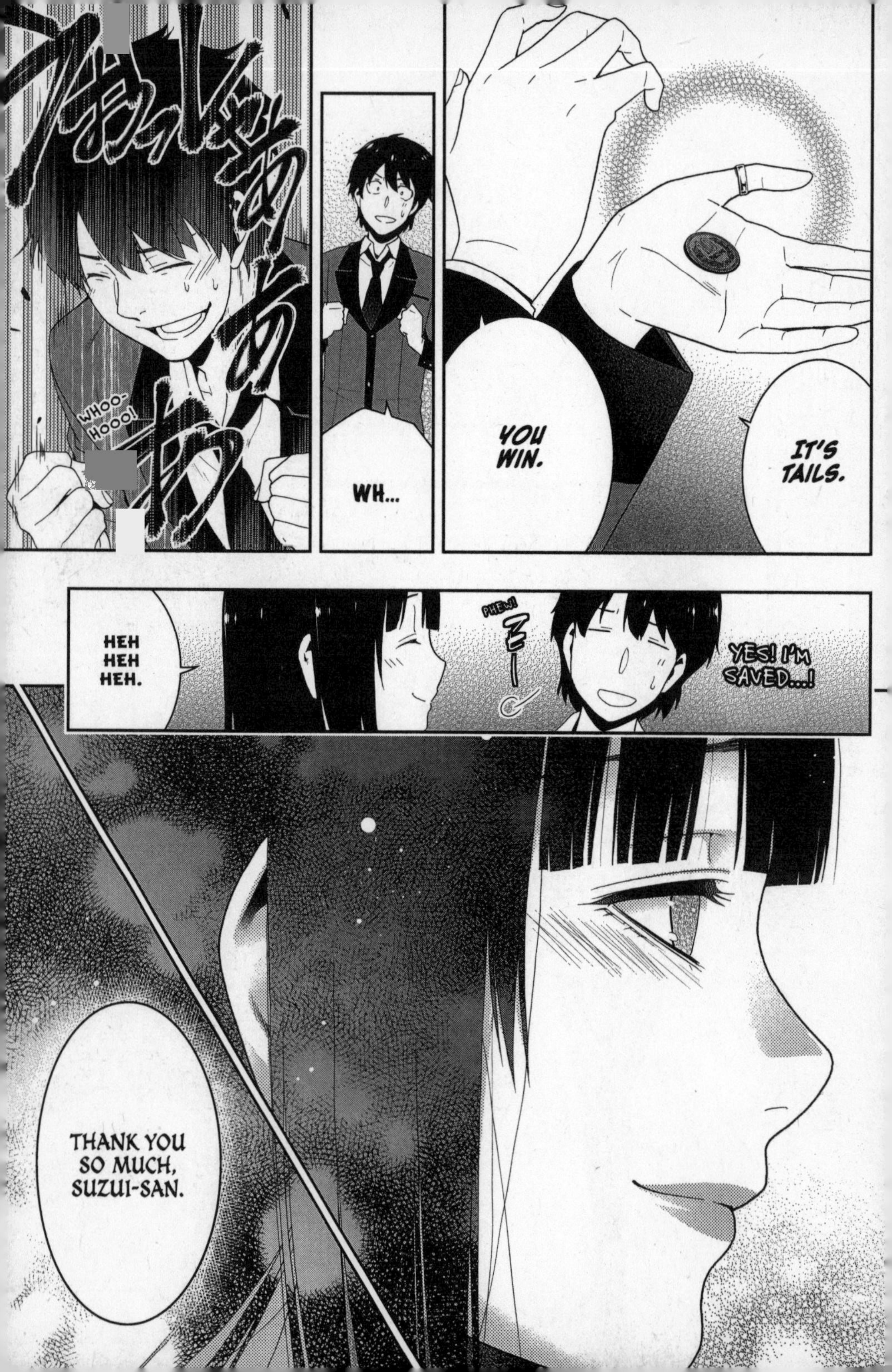
IT'S TAILS.
YOU WIN.
WH...
WHOO-HOOO!
YES! I'M SAVED...!
PHEW!
HEH HEH HEH.
THANK YOU SO MUCH, SUZUI-SAN.

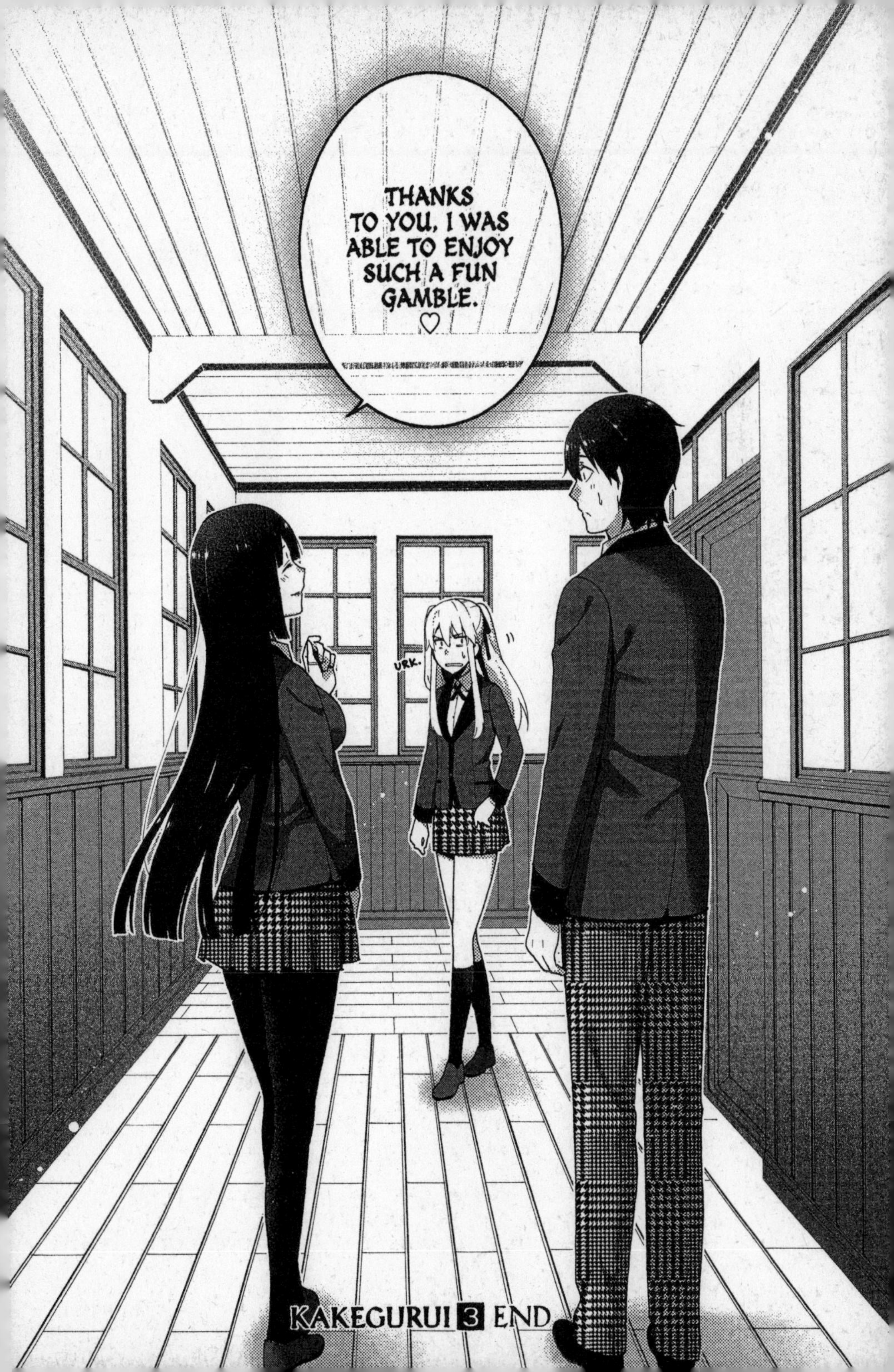
THANKS TO YOU, I WAS ABLE TO ENJOY SUCH A FUN GAMBLE. ♡
URK.
KAKEGURUI 3 END

TIME FOR SOME END-OF-THE-VOLUME BONUS COMICS!

YOU CAN DO IT, MIDARI-CHAN!

※THIS HAS NO RELATION TO THE ACTUAL STORY.

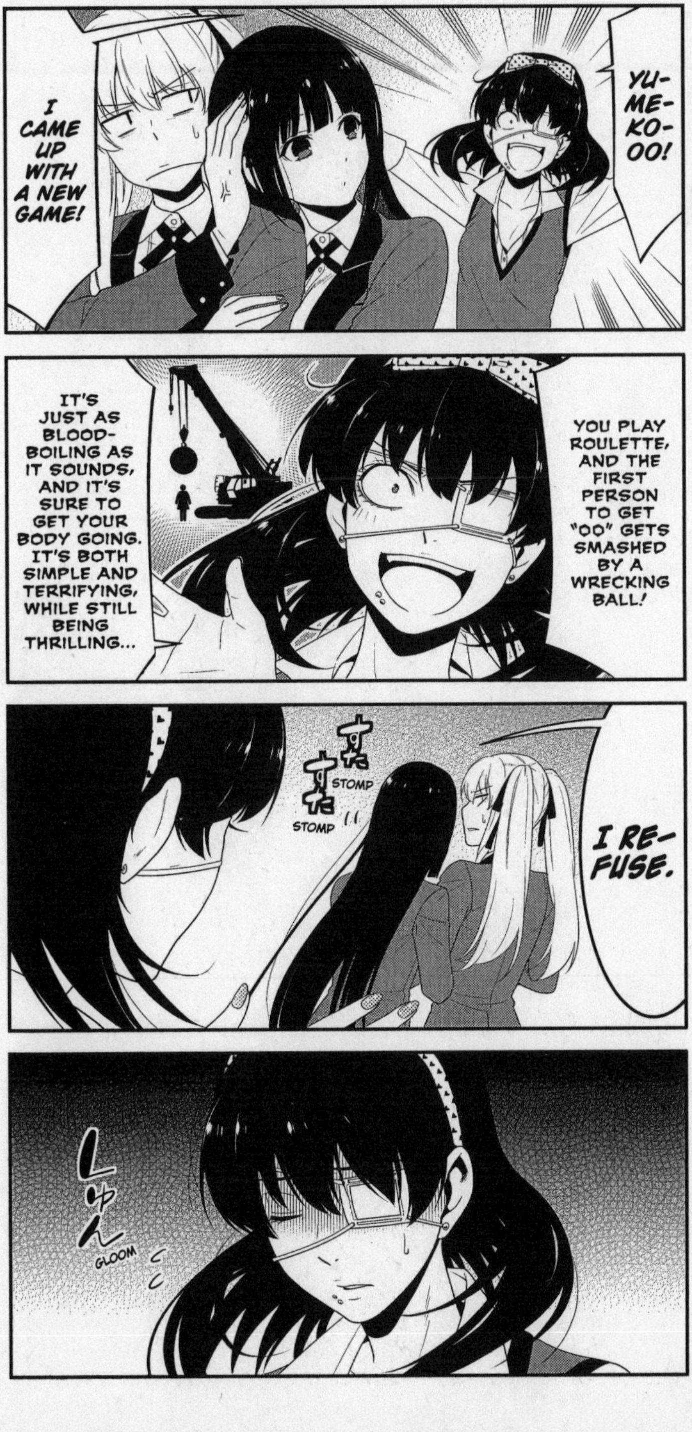
YU-ME-KO-OO!
I CAME UP WITH A NEW GAME!
YOU PLAY ROULETTE, AND THE FIRST PERSON TO GET "OO" GETS SMASHED BY A WRECKING BALL!
IT'S JUST AS BLOOD-BOILING AS IT SOUNDS, AND IT'S SURE TO GET YOUR BODY GOING. IT'S BOTH SIMPLE AND TERRIFYING, WHILE STILL BEING THRILLING...
I RE-FUSE.
すた すた
STOMP STOMP
しゅん
GLOOM

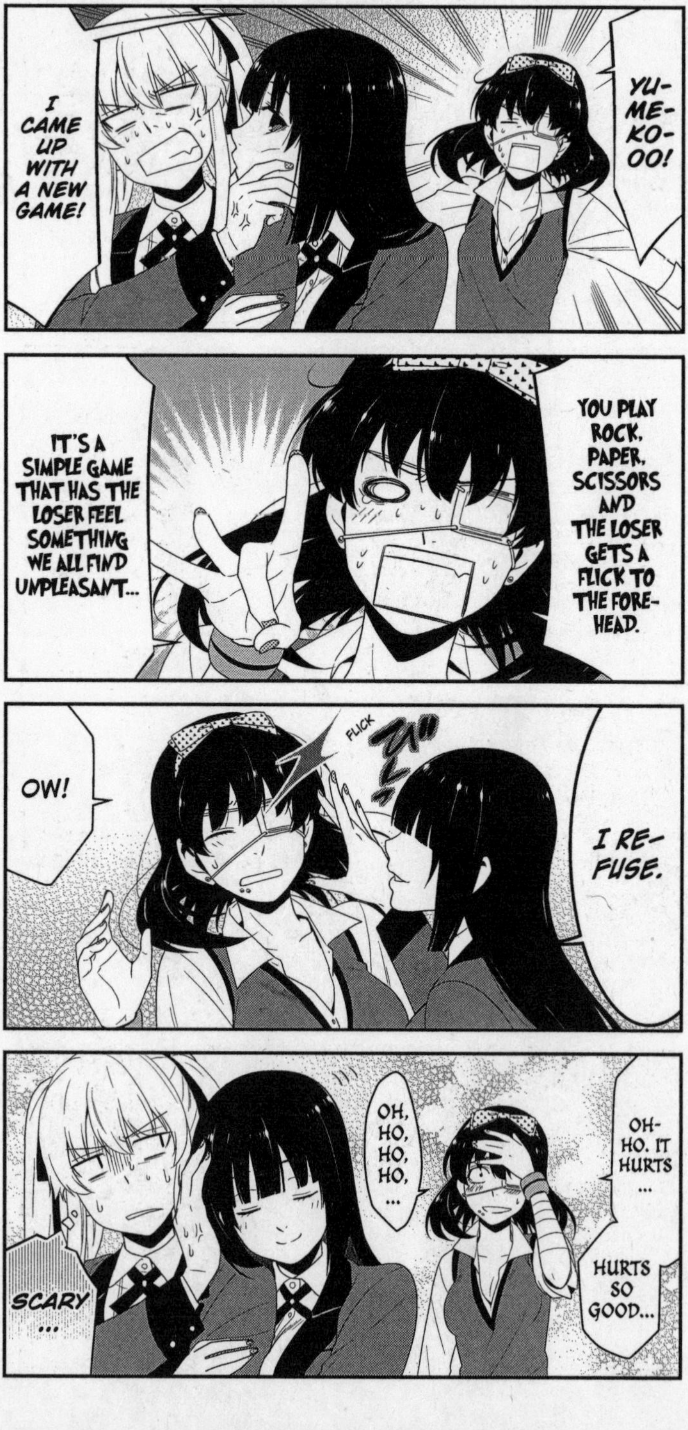
YU-ME-KO-OO!
I CAME UP WITH A NEW GAME!
YOU PLAY ROCK, PAPER, SCISSORS AND THE LOSER GETS A FLICK TO THE FORE-HEAD.
IT'S A SIMPLE GAME THAT HAS THE LOSER FEEL SOMETHING WE ALL FIND UNPLEASANT...
I RE-FUSE.
FLICK
OW!
OH-HO. IT HURTS...
HURTS SO GOOD...
OH, HO, HO, HO, ...
SCARY...

GAMBLING, THAT IS MY RAISON D'ÊTRE.

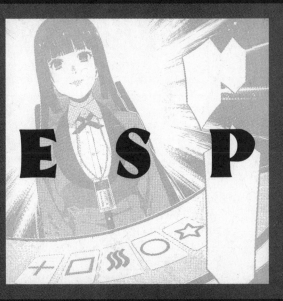

The cards used in ESP are called "Zener cards" or "ESP cards," said to be designed to conduct experiments about ESP (extrasensory perception). I believe ESP would be an incredibly difficult game to play. However, in the story, since Suzui-kun and Yumeko trust each other so much, they somehow make it through all right. But when actually playing the game, there's a high chance you'll find yourself in a situation where, no matter how much you try to analyze what's going on, you'll never match the cards of whoever's in the other room. Of course, it would be quite another story if you actually had ESP.

Thank you very much for reading *Kakegurui* Volume 3. Midari is a character packed with all the things I like, so it made me very happy that I was able to use her a lot in this volume. Anyone who liked her insanity someone I'd be glad to call a sworn friend. And as with every volume, I'd like to say, "I can't thank everyone at Gangan JOKER enough......for letting me make this!" Now then, being that this is Volume 3, I've got a lot of people to thank. First, Naomura-sensei and his assistants, who do the amazing art for the series. He's far too good for me, and every volume I keep thinking he can't get any better, but he always does. He clears every hurdle with a seemingly endless amount of stamina. My editors, Sasagi-sama and Yumoto-sama, who guide me with their never-ending patience despite me never learning anything ever. And finally, all of you readers. I've got so much to write, but I wouldn't be able to do it alone, so I cannot thank you guys enough. In Volume 4, I plan on filling it with even more of my interests, so it would please me greatly if you kept reading.

I wish for Tanaka to have a bright future.　　　　Homura Kawamoto

Afterword

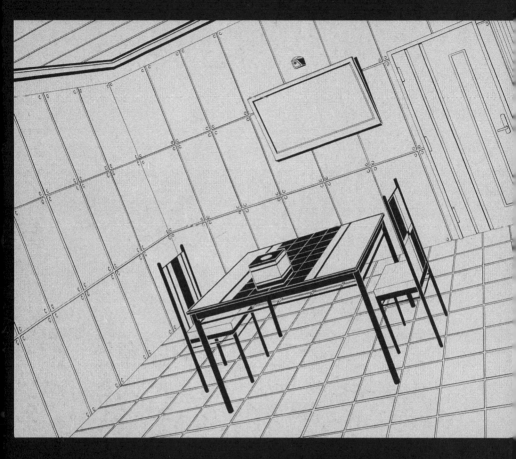

Thank you for picking up Volume 3 of *Kakegurui*.
While drawing the Midari chapters, I met many new people and said
farewell to others. To have no regrets, I will do my best not to forget to
communicate my feelings of thanks to those around me every day.
Thank you so very much...! Please enjoy our work...!!

SPECIAL THANKS:

My editors • Kawamoto-sama • Imoutoko • H1-sama • H2-sama •
AO-sama • U-sama • M-sama • T-sama • A-sama

Toru Naomura (artist), June 2015

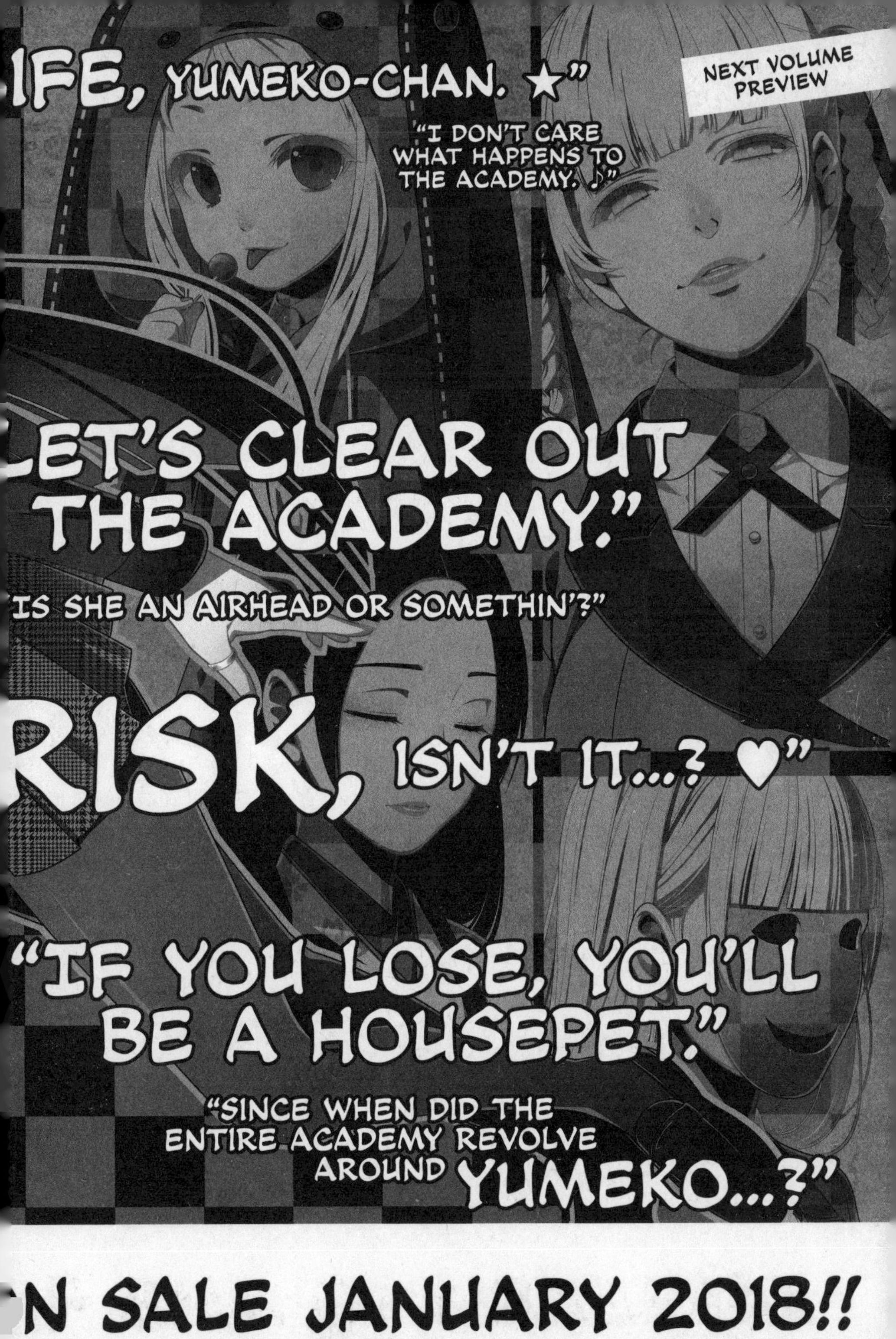
NEXT VOLUME PREVIEW
IFE, YUMEKO-CHAN. ★"
"I DON'T CARE WHAT HAPPENS TO THE ACADEMY. ♪"
LET'S CLEAR OUT THE ACADEMY."
"IS SHE AN AIRHEAD OR SOMETHIN'?"
RISK, ISN'T IT...? ♥"
"IF YOU LOSE, YOU'LL BE A HOUSEPET."
"SINCE WHEN DID THE ENTIRE ACADEMY REVOLVE AROUND YUMEKO...?"

N SALE JANUARY 2018!!

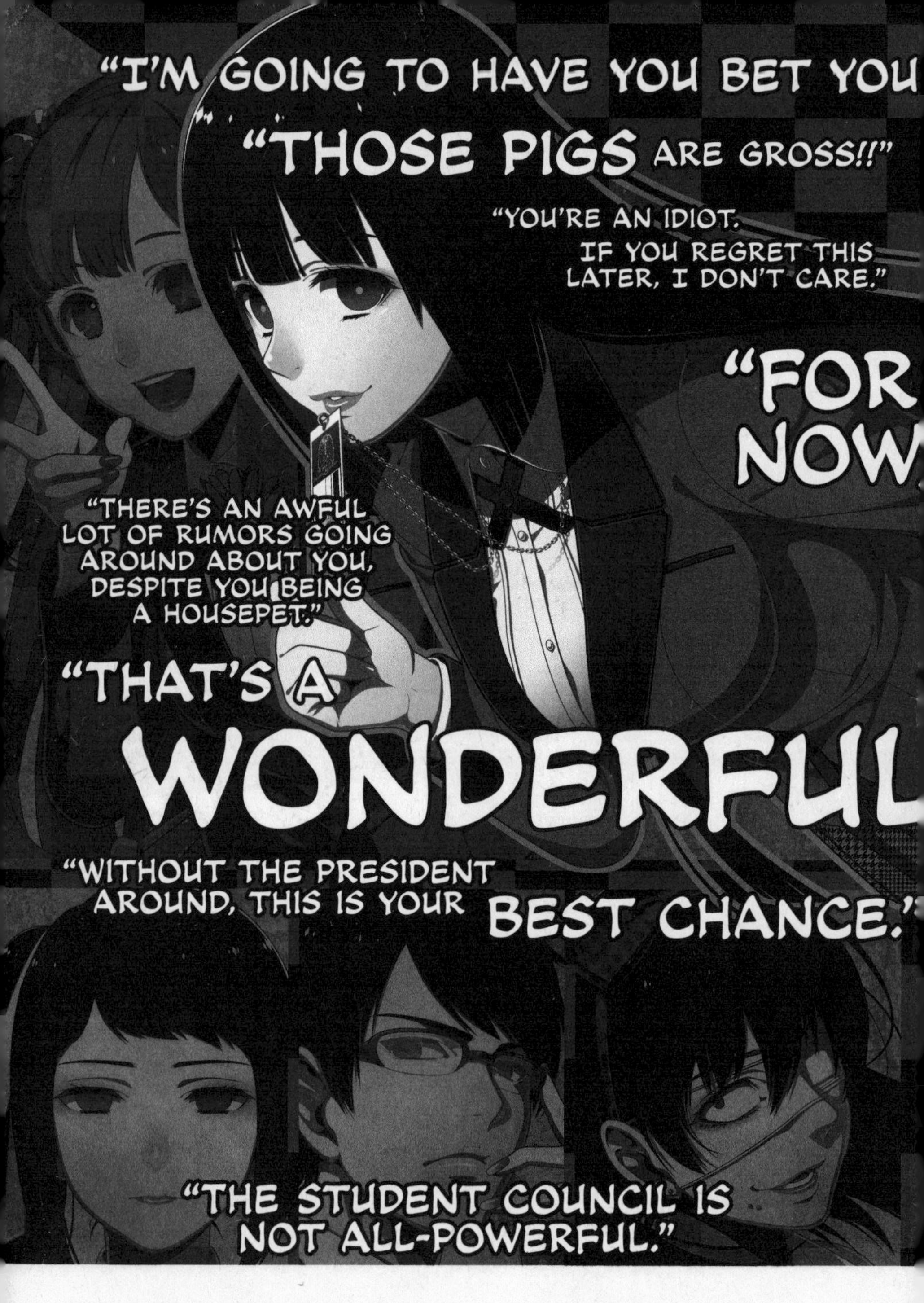
"I'M GOING TO HAVE YOU BET YOU
"THOSE PIGS ARE GROSS!!"
"YOU'RE AN IDIOT. IF YOU REGRET THIS LATER, I DON'T CARE."
"FOR NOW,
"THERE'S AN AWFUL LOT OF RUMORS GOING AROUND ABOUT YOU, DESPITE YOU BEING A HOUSEPET."
"THAT'S A WONDERFUL
"WITHOUT THE PRESIDENT AROUND, THIS IS YOUR BEST CHANCE."
"THE STUDENT COUNCIL IS NOT ALL-POWERFUL."

KAKEGURUI VOLUME 4,

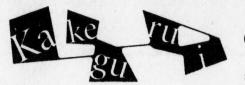 ③

STORY: **Homura Kawamoto**
ART: **Toru Naomura**

Translation: Matthew Alberts
Lettering: Anthony Quintessenza

Kakegurui Vol. 3 ©2015 Homura Kawamoto, Toru Naomura/SQUARE ENIX CO., LTD. First published in Japan in 2015 by SQUARE ENIX CO., LTD. English translation rights arranged with SQUARE ENIX CO., LTD. and Yen Press, LLC through Tuttle-Mori Agency, Inc.

English translation ©2015 by SQUARE ENIX CO., LTD.

Yen Press
1290 Avenue of the Americas
New York, NY 10104

Visit us at yenpress.com
facebook.com/yenpress
twitter.com/yenpress
yenpress.tumblr.com
instagram.com/yenpress

D0103534

First Yen Press Print Edition: November 2017
Originally published as an eBook in September 2015 by Yen Press.

Yen Press is an imprint of Yen Press, LLC.
The Yen Press name and logo are trademarks of Yen Press, LLC.

The publisher is not responsible for websites (or their content) that are not owned by the publisher.

Library of Congress Control Number: 2017939211

ISBN: 978-0-316-41280-3 (paperback)

10 9 8 7 6 5 4 3 2

BVG

Printed in the United States of America